Adolescence in Context

To my favorite former adolescents, FHM and JRM

Sara Miller McCune founded SAGE Publishing in 1965 to support the dissemination of usable knowledge and educate a global community. SAGE publishes more than 1000 journals and over 600 new books each year, spanning a wide range of subject areas. Our growing selection of library products includes archives, data, case studies and video. SAGE remains majority owned by our founder and after her lifetime will become owned by a charitable trust that secures the company's continued independence.

Los Angeles | London | New Delhi | Singapore | Washington DC | Melbourne

Adolescence in Context

Tara L. Kuther

Western Connecticut State University

Los Angeles | London | New Delhi
Singapore | Washington DC | Melbourne

FOR INFORMATION:

SAGE Publications, Inc.
2455 Teller Road
Thousand Oaks, California 91320
E-mail: order@sagepub.com

SAGE Publications Ltd.
1 Oliver's Yard
55 City Road
London EC1Y 1SP
United Kingdom

SAGE Publications India Pvt. Ltd.
B 1/I 1 Mohan Cooperative Industrial Area
Mathura Road, New Delhi 110 044
India

SAGE Publications Asia-Pacific Pte. Ltd.
18 Cross Street #10-10/11/12
China Square Central
Singapore 048423

Acquisitions Editor: Lara Parra
Editorial Assistant: Natalie Elliott
Content Development Editor: Emma Newsom
Production Editor: Tracy Buyan
Copy Editor: Christina West
Typesetter: C&M Digitals (P) Ltd.
Proofreader: Sally Jaskold
Indexer: Sheila Hill
Cover Designer: Gail Buschman
Marketing Manager: Katherine Hepburn

Medical illustrations created by Body Scientific International.

Printed in Canada

Library of Congress Cataloging-in-Publication Data

Names: Kuther, Tara L., author.

Title: Adolescence in context / Tara L. Kuther, Western Connecticut State University.

Description: Thousand Oaks : SAGE Publishing, 2020. | Includes bibliographical references and index.

Identifiers: LCCN 2020010453 | ISBN 9781506376097 (paperback) | ISBN 9781071812495 (loose-leaf) | ISBN 9781506376073 (epub) | ISBN 9781506376080 (epub) | ISBN 9781506376103 (pdf)

Subjects: LCSH: Adolescent psychology. | Developmental psychology.

Classification: LCC BF724 .K88 2020 | DDC 155.5—dc23

LC record available at https://lccn.loc.gov/2020010453

MIX
Paper from
responsible sources
FSC® C011825

20 21 22 23 24 10 9 8 7 6 5 4 3 2 1

BRIEF CONTENTS

DETAILED CONTENTS

iStock.com/skynesher

iStock.com/LuckyBusiness

iStock.com/South_agency

Jan H Andersen/Shutterstock.com

AP Photo/Kat Lopez

iStock.com/Martin Dimitrov

iStock.com/YinYang

iStock.com/FG Trade

iStock.com/SolStock

Michael L. Abramson/Contributor/Getty Images

iStock.com/cerro_photography

iStock.com/pixelfit

iStock.com/rez-art

PART 4. PROBLEMS IN DEVELOPMENT

Chapter 12. Socioemotional and Behavioral Problems During Adolescence   245

PREFACE

Adolescence is perhaps the most fascinating and stereotyped period in the life span. Over the past two and a half decades, I have taught adolescent development to undergraduate students at a small regional comprehensive state university. I have found that teaching adolescent development poses unique opportunities and challenges because all undergraduate students have been—or are currently—adolescents. Students have experiences in most or all of the topics we discuss and sharing personal experiences engages students. However, sometimes students are puzzled when their experiences do not match the theoretical and research conclusions we discuss. How do we make sense of the differences? In class, as well as in this text, I adopt a contextual perspective to help students understand variability in development and to make sense of the growing body of findings in adolescent development.

CONTEXTUAL PERSPECTIVE

A key theme of *Adolescence in Context* is that development occurs in context. We are all embedded in many interacting layers of context, including tangible and intangible circumstances that influence and are influenced by us, including family, ethnicity, culture, neighborhood, community, norms, values, and historical events. At all points in life, human development is the result of dynamic transactions among individuals, their physical, cognitive, and socioemotional capacities, and the web of contexts in which they are immersed. *Adolescence in Context* discusses these processes, emphasizing how individual factors combine with the places, sociocultural environments, and ways in which we are raised to influence development.

A contextual approach can address one of the greatest challenges adolescent development instructors face: helping students understand the complex influences on development, that outcomes do not vary randomly or simply "depend on the person." With enough information, we can predict and understand development. A contextual approach can provide the backstory to development and help us understand why adolescents vary. In addition, the emerging body of research on intersectionality in development offers opportunities to shed light on these complex processes and their role in development. My goal in writing this text is to explain the sophisticated interactions that constitute development in a way that is comprehensive yet concise.

PEDAGOGY

Research in the scholarship of teaching and learning has shown that students learn best when they manipulate information and consider it at multiple levels. Students often experience difficulty with metacognition and are often unaware of what they don't know. This is particularly true for students of adolescent development. Everyone has some experience as an adolescent, which can make it difficult to objectively assess their knowledge. Several types of questions, designed to target different levels of analysis, appear at the end of each section, in each chapter.

Review items assess the lower levels of Bloom's taxonomy (recalling and explaining concepts). *Thinking in Context* items ask students to consider the role of context in the topic as well as reflect on their experience. For example, readers might identify examples of Bronfenbrenner's bioecological systems and apply the perspective to a problem, consider how findings might vary with socioeconomic status or other demographic factors, or discuss the role of intersectionality in development. *Thinking in Context* items are organized to assess the higher levels of Bloom's taxonomy (e.g., apply, analyze, and evaluate). These items also provide students opportunities to reflect on how the content compares with their own experience. Students find reflection items engaging (e.g., "To what extent was your adolescence stormy and stressful?") and such items offer powerful opportunities for students to engage with the material. Finally, *Apply* items typically provide a short scenario involving adolescents and ask readers to provide insight and solve a problem.

In addition, learning objectives at the beginning of each chapter provide clear goals for readers. The end-of-chapter summary returns to each learning objective, recapping the key concepts presented in the chapter related to that objective.

CURRENT RESEARCH

Developmental science instructors face the challenge of covering the growing mass of research findings within the confines of a single semester. *Adolescence in Context* integrates recently published and classic findings. Rather than present an exhaustive review of current work simply for the sake of including recent references, I carefully select the most relevant findings. I integrate cutting-edge and classic research to present a unified story of what is currently known about adolescent development.

ACCESSIBLE WRITING STYLE

Having taught at a regional public university since 1996, I write in a style intended to engage diverse undergraduate readers like my own students. This text is intended to help them understand challenging concepts in language that will not overwhelm. I avoid jargon but maintain the use of research terms that students need to know in order to digest classic and current findings in the field of adolescent development. I attempt to write in the same voice as I teach, carefully structuring sections to build explanations and integrating content with examples that are relevant to students. I regularly use my own texts in class, students work with me in preparing elements of each text, and my students' responses and learning guide my writing.

ORGANIZATION

Adolescence in Context is organized into 12 topical chapters covered in four parts that examine the biological, cognitive, and socioemotional changes that occur during adolescence and the contexts in which adolescents are embedded. Part 1 covers biological and cognitive foundations of development with an introduction to adolescent development (Chapter 1), biological development (Chapter 2), and cognitive development (Chapter 3). Part 2 examines psychosocial and socioemotional development with chapters on identity (Chapter 4), gender (Chapter 5), sexuality (Chapter 6), and morality, religion, and values (Chapter 7). Part 3 explores contexts of development: family (Chapter 8), peer (Chapter 9), school and work (Chapter 10), and media and online (Chapter 11) contexts. Finally, Part 4, problems in development, contains one chapter covering the range of common socioemotional and behavioral problems during adolescence (Chapter 12).

ACKNOWLEDGMENTS

This book has benefitted from the input of many bright, enthusiastic, and generous people. I am fortunate to work with a talented team at SAGE and I am grateful for their support. I thank Lara Parra, Jen Thomas, Reid Hester, and Katherine Hepburn. Thank you to Tracy Buyan for overseeing production and Emma Newsom for stepping in to steer this book through its final content development phase. Michele Sordi convinced me to write my first text and I am forever grateful for her confidence. Christina West, copyeditor extraordinaire, has shared her sharp eyes and keen input.

I thank my students for surprising me with new questions, sharing their experiences, and teaching me about what it means to be young in this millennium. I am especially appreciative of those who have shared their feedback and helped me to improve this book. Lauren Schwarz provided invaluable brainstorming assistance in crafting much of the pedagogy in this book. I appreciate Ed Lindblom's input throughout. Thank you to the many instructors who have reviewed and provided feedback on these chapters.

Finally, I thank my family, especially my parents, Phil and Irene. Freddy and Julia provided a crash course in adolescence and emerging adulthood—I hope I passed. Most of all, I am thankful for the support of my husband, Fred, for his input on this project. His unwavering support and optimism encourage me to see the good in all and to be a better person. Thank you, babe.

SAGE wishes to thank the following reviewers for their valuable contributions to the development of this manuscript:

Susan L. O'Donnell, George Fox University

Michele C. Wolfson, PhD, Cape Cod Community College

Christina S. Sinisi, Charleston Southern University

Dale Fryxell, Chaminade University

Mary E. Shuttlesworth, La Roche University

Nicolette Salerno, EdD, Caldwell University

Kelly A. Minor, PhD, Winston-Salem State University

Professor L. Michael Guillory, Brandman University

Claire Ford, C.A.G.S., N.C.S.P., Bridgewater State University

Melinda A. Gonzales-Backen, PhD, Florida State University

Celeste Uthe-Burow, EdD, Augustana University

Melanie Evans Keyes, Eastern Connecticut State University

Meeta Banerjee, California State University, Northridge

Jean M. Gerard, Bowling Green State University

Casey Knifsend, CSU Sacramento

Nathan Avani, San Francisco State University

Karlyn Adams-Wiggins, Portland State University

Kathryn E. Frazier, Worcester State University

Robert S. Weisskirch, MSW, PhD, Professor of Human Development, California State University, Monterey Bay, Seaside, California

Victoria M. Ferrara, Adjunct Professor, Marist College

Kristi Moore, Angelo State University

Amanda Harmon, Charleston Southern University

Kaite Yang, Stockton University

Deanna Edens, Florida State College at Jacksonville

Theresa J. Canada, Western Connecticut State University

Dinah F. Meyer, Muskingum University

Carla Bluhm, PhD, College of Coastal Georgia

Alan Reifman, Texas Tech University

Dr. Shinder Gill, California State University, Sacramento

ABOUT THE AUTHOR

Tara L. Kuther is professor of psychology at Western Connecticut State University where she has taught courses in child, adolescent, and adult development since 1996. She earned her BA in psychology from Western Connecticut State University and her MA and PhD in developmental psychology from Fordham University. Dr. Kuther is the author of the award-winning title *Lifespan Development: Lives in Context*, as well as *Child and Adolescent Development in Context, The Psychology Major's Handbook*, and *Careers in Psychology: Opportunities in a Changing World*. She is fellow of the Society for the Teaching of Psychology (American Psychological Association, Division 2), has served in various capacities in the Society for the Teaching of Psychology and the Society for Research on Adolescence, and is the former chair of the Teaching Committee for the Society for Research in Child Development. Her research interests include social cognition and risky activity in adolescence and adulthood. She is also interested in promoting undergraduate and graduate students' professional development and helping them navigate the challenges of pursuing undergraduate and graduate degrees in psychology.

PART 1

Biological and Cognitive Foundations of Development

Introduction to Adolescent Development

Learning Objectives

1.1 Discuss the historical origins of adolescence and evidence for popular stereotypes about adolescents.

1.2 Analyze the developmental processes, contexts, and timing of adolescence and emerging adulthood.

1.3 Summarize theoretical approaches to studying adolescent development.

1.4 Describe methods and designs used to study adolescent development.

1.5 Explain the scope of applied developmental science and some of the challenges that arise in this field.

Chapter Contents

Imagine a rapid period of change, in which you grow taller and heavier and take on new body proportions that feel strange and uncomfortable. Your brain changes radically, influencing how you view the world around yourself and sometimes making you respond to others in ways that you don't expect and perhaps may regret. You become better able to think and reason but may find yourself focusing on your self-consciousness, worrying about your appearance, replaying what you should have said in response to a friend or teacher, and fearing that others will notice your faults. Suddenly your friends become life rafts that keep you from drowning in the tumultuous surroundings and are essential to your very survival. Sound familiar? If you're like most people, you'll probably answer, "In some ways, yes, and some ways, no." These changes occur during a period of life known as **adolescence**, the transition from childhood to adulthood. Although all young people undergo a myriad of physical, cognitive, and social changes as they progress through adolescence, not everyone experiences the changes as chaotic. Instead, some young people undergo relatively smooth transitions. In this book we will examine the developmental changes that occur during adolescence as well as variations in young people's experiences.

HISTORY OF ADOLESCENCE

The transition from childhood to adulthood is gradual, occurring over many years. Most people take that idea for granted. However, adolescence as we know it today is a new concept (Baxter, 2008). Although philosophers speculated about development beyond childhood, it was not until the late 19th century that adolescence became recognized as a distinct period in life.

Early History of Adolescence

In ancient Greece in the fourth century, Plato proposed several stages in the lifespan, including a period between childhood and adulthood. Plato argued that childhood education should emphasize sports and music because children's minds are undeveloped. Adolescents become capable of reasoning and therefore should study science and mathematics. Aristotle, a student of Plato, described three 7-year periods of maturation that correspond to current views of development. The period Aristotle referred to as *infancy* spanned from birth to age 7 years. *Boyhood* comprised ages 7 to 14 and *young manhood*, ages 14 to 21. Specifically, Aristotle proposed that reasoning may first emerge in boyhood and develops through young manhood, at age 21. Similar to current views of adolescence, Aristotle viewed independent

decision-making and the ability to carry out one's choices as a marker of maturity (Lerner & Steinberg, 2009). Of course, the labels Aristotle chose for his developmental periods are sexist in today's world, but at the time Aristotle wrote, virtually all theory and research were based on male models. As we will discuss, gender—and race as well as other characteristics—influence people's experiences and development (Ghavami, Katsiaficas, & Rogers, 2016). For example, theories created solely from examinations of boys and men often cannot adequately account for girls' and women's development.

Although philosophers Plato and Aristotle theorized about the unique nature of childhood and adolescence, for centuries children were viewed and treated as miniature adults and expected to work alongside adults (Aries & van den Berg, 1978). About 1,500 years passed before the term *adolescence* was first used. A derivative of the Latin word *adolescere*, meaning to grow into maturity, was used in the 15th century (Lerner & Steinberg, 2009). In the 18th century, Jean-Jacques Rousseau defined three stages in maturation. The first stage is birth to age 12, in which children are guided by their impulses. Reasoning develops in the second stage (age 12 to 16) and individuals mature cognitively and emotionally in the third stage (age 16 and to about 20). Rousseau explained that during the adolescent years, reasoning begins to override and inhibit impulses and young people mature. However, it was about a hundred years later, in the late 19th century, that the term *adolescence* became commonly used (Kett, 2003). It was a shift in societal conditions that led adolescence to be defined as it is today—a distinct period in life.

The Age of Adolescence

Between 1890 and 1920, a number of social changes came together to create the concept of adolescence that we have today. At the end of the 19th century, the Industrial Revolution influenced the nature of work and family life in the United States as many people moved from working on farms to urban factories. As the demand for labor rose, children and adolescents began to work in factories and coal mines. Often preferred because they were less expensive than adults, children and adolescents routinely worked long hours and few U.S. states regulated children's work.

As the Industrial Revolution progressed and more jobs became mechanized, the need for unskilled labor fell. Adults replaced children and adolescents as unskilled labor positions declined. In addition, the demand for skilled labor, which required schooling, rose. At the same time, a growing body of youth workers, educators, and professionals argued that children did not belong in the adult workplace and must be protected from the hazards of the adult workplace.

Greek philosopher Plato (left), disciple of Socrates, and classic philosopher and developmental theorist, Aristotle.
Chronicle / Alamy Stock Photo
Science History Images / Alamy Stock Photo

Soon many U.S. states created laws prohibiting child employment and limiting the hours that young adolescents can work (Kett, 2003).

Likewise, before 1890, few U.S. states required children to attend school. Between 1890 and 1920, all U.S. states passed laws requiring students to attend both primary and secondary school. In 1890, only about 5% of adolescents age 14 to 17 attended school; this number rose to 30% by 1920 and to 51% by 1930 (see Figure 1.1) (National Center for Education Statistics, 2017). As adolescents were separated from adults and grouped with other adolescents, it became increasingly clear that they are different from adults—and current conceptions of adolescence emerged.

Adolescence as a Period of Storm and Stress

While the creation of labor and compulsory education laws marked adolescence as distinct from adulthood (Lapsley, Enright, & Serlin, 1985), the invention of adolescence, as we know it, is attributed to G. Stanley Hall (1844–1924). Often referred to as the father of adolescence, Hall is credited with beginning the scientific study of adolescence. In 1904, he wrote a two-volume

set, titled *Adolescence: Its Psychology and Its Relations to Physiology, Anthropology, Sociology, Sex, Crime, Religion, and Education*, in which he defined adolescence as a period of "storm and stress." Hall (1904) believed that storm and stress were inevitable and extreme upheaval was triggered by puberty, the biological transition to reproductive maturity, and therefore universal.

Hall based his theory on then-popular recapitulation theory, based on Lamarckian evolutionary theory. He held that memories and acquired characteristics can be inherited from generation to generation and that the development of the individual recapitulates or reenacts the development of the human species as a whole (Buchanan & Bruton, 2016). Hall explained that adolescents' extreme volatility is inherited and reflects a time in human history characterized by upheaval and disorder that corresponded to the birth of civilization. Therefore, intense turmoil, such as serious depression, severe troubles with parents, and extreme delinquent activity, was to be expected and was a sign of normal healthy development, triggered by puberty. Lamarckian evolution and recapitulation theory have both been discredited in favor of Darwinian evolution and many scholars reject Hall's

FIGURE 1.1

High School Enrollment Trends, 1890–2017

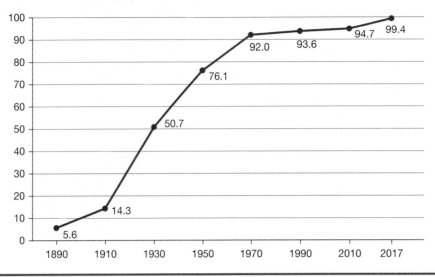

Source: National Center for Education Statistics, Digest of Education Statistics (2017).

extreme views on adolescence (Youniss, 2006). Yet Hall's premise that adolescence is a period of storm and stress, rooted in biology, remains a popular view (Arnett, 2006).

Research suggests that, contrary to Hall's view, turmoil is not universal or healthy (Buchanan & Bruton, 2016). For example, emotional volatility or moodiness may become more common during adolescence, particularly early adolescence, but, as we will discuss throughout this book, most young people function well and maintain close relationships with their parents. In one classic study, adolescents from 10 countries (Australia, Bangladesh, Germany, Hungary, Israel, Italy, Japan, Taiwan, Turkey, and the United States) reported that they were usually happy, felt that they got along with their parents, and felt good about their progress toward adulthood (Offer, Ostrov, Howard, & Atkinson, 1988). Most adolescents engage in some risk behaviors, such as extreme sports and experimentation with alcohol, and some problems, such as substance abuse, may emerge during adolescence. However, for the majority of adolescents, risk behaviors are mild and temporary, and most adolescents do not experience serious problems (Boyer & Byrnes, 2016; Lerner et al., 2015a). Instead, many researchers who study adolescence adopt a modified storm-and-stress view in which problems are viewed as more likely to emerge during adolescence but are not inevitable (Arnett, 1999).

Although puberty and biological changes undoubtedly influence adolescents' experiences, environmental influences also play a role. Moreover, the theory of recapitulation, which underlay Hall's explanation for development, has long been debunked in favor of Darwinian evolution. Hall's view of adolescence as a universal, biologically based, period of extreme storm and stress is not supported by research, yet his view of the nature of adolescence has influenced popular culture (Hollenstein & Lougheed, 2013).

Stereotypes About Adolescence

Most adults agree with statements such as "Adolescence is a difficult time of life" and adolescents "will be more difficult to get along with" (Hines & Paulson, 2006). For example, one recent study followed adolescents and their parents during adolescence,

Most adolescents sometimes feel sad, but adolescence is not the period of turmoil G. Stanley Hall envisioned.
iStock.com/recep-bg

from fifth grade through eighth grade (Göllner et al., 2017). Over the 3-year period, parents viewed their adolescents as becoming less agreeable and conscientious (i.e., less "nice"), whereas the adolescents perceived no change. However, like parents, young people often endorse storm and stress notions, and such beliefs can create self-fulfilling prophecies, whereby adolescents' expectations influence their behavior (Buchanan & Bruton, 2016). Adolescents' conceptions of adolescence influence their behavior. Specifically, one study of boys followed from seventh to ninth grade found that those who expected adolescence to be a period of declining relationships with parents experienced increases in risk-taking over the transition from middle to high school (Qu, Pomerantz, McCormick, & Telzer, 2018). The more they saw adolescence as a time of ignoring family, the more their risk-taking increased.

However, conceptions of adolescence and expectations for adolescent behavior are culture bound. For example, U.S. adolescents were more likely than Chinese adolescents to report that adolescence is a time of decreased family responsibility and heightened school disengagement and peer orientation; these beliefs predicted a rise in disengagement from school in U.S. youth over the seventh and eighth grades (Qu, Pomerantz, Wang, Cheung, & Cimpian, 2016). Cultural values in North American and other Western countries tend to emphasize individuality and view development as a process of becoming independent, whereas Asian and non-Western cultures tend to emphasize collectivism, in which individuals develop close supportive ties with their family and community (Markus & Kitayama, 2010). Cultural values shape adolescents' experiences and their expectations for development.

Conceptions of adolescence are culture bound.
iStock.com/TAGSTOCK1

THINKING IN CONTEXT 1.1

1. To what extent was your adolescence stormy and stressful? Explain. How well does your experience match Hall's perspective?

2. How might cultural values, such as individualism or collectivism, influence how young people experience adolescence? What kinds of activities and experiences might boys and girls have growing up in a culture that values independence as compared with community? What similarities and differences might you expect?

· ·

APPLY 1.1

As a child, Megan was easygoing, well liked, and kind to everyone. Now, at age 14, it's a different story. Megan says she hates her parents, gets into fistfights at school, and has started smoking marijuana with her 18-year-old boyfriend. Megan's parents are desperate to know: "Is this normal? Do all adolescents go through this?" How do you respond?

· ·

REVIEW 1.1

1. What are the origins of the term *adolescence*?

2. Why is 1890–1920 called the Age of Adolescence?

3. How did Hall describe adolescence?

4. What evidence is there for adolescent storm and stress?

5. What are some of the ways that adolescents are stereotyped?

· ·

ADOLESCENT DEVELOPMENT

A central tenet of development is that we grow and change throughout our lives, from conception to death, as shown in Figure 1.2 (Sawyer, Azzopardi, Wickremarathne, & Patton, 2018). Adolescence is a distinct period of the lifespan, but its boundaries have been a source of debate. For example, Hall (1904) defined adolescence as a period ranging from age 14 to 24 years. More than 50 years ago, the World Health Organization proposed that adolescence spanned from 10 to 20 years of age, noting that although it commenced with puberty, the endpoint was less well defined (World Health Organization, 1977). The United Nations has defined adolescence as the period between 10 and 19 years of age (Kuruvilla et al., 2016). The U.S. Census Bureau specifies 12 to 19 years in their definition and the Centers for Disease Control and Prevention generally marks adolescence as high school age (ninth to twelfth grade, or about age 14 to 18) (Centers for Disease Control and Prevention, 2018; U.S. Bureau of the Census, 2018). Researchers have recently proposed age 10 as the beginning and age 24 (Sawyer et al., 2018) or 25 (Curtis, 2015) as the end of adolescence. These varying ages illustrate the concept that the boundaries of adolescence are a social construction (Linders, 2017). That is, the beginning and the end of adolescence are not set in stone; rather, they vary depending on the characteristics ascribed to the period.

Early, Middle, and Late Adolescence

Adolescence is characterized by biological and social transitions. The onset of puberty, the transition to biological maturity, often marks the beginning of adolescence. The end of adolescence is often marked by role transitions and the adoption of adult roles, such as, historically, marriage. Today, the end of adolescence is more vague and influenced by individuals' surroundings and experiences, occurring at different times for different people.

As we have discussed, there is a lack of consensus on the beginning and end of adolescence. For our purposes, we will define the phases of adolescence as follows:

- **Early adolescence** (age 10 to 14), corresponding roughly to the middle or junior high school years in the U.S. school system.

- **Middle adolescence** (age 14 to 16), corresponding to the first half of high school in the United States.

- **Late adolescence** (age 16 to 18), corresponding to the later high school years.

- **Emerging adulthood** (age 18 to 25), not a period of adolescence, but a period between adolescence and adulthood, corresponding to postsecondary education (discussed next).

The phases of adolescence overlap because this period is characterized by variability. Adolescents

---

FIGURE 1.2

Ages in Life

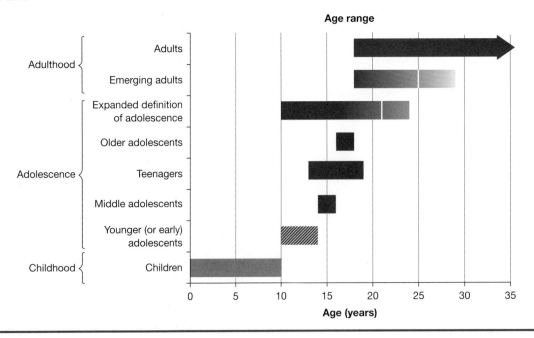

Source: Sawyer et al. (2018).

vary in the timing of their biological transitions and their social transitions and behaviors. For example, one 14-year-old may be an eighth grader in middle school and another might be enrolled in high school. Academic and social expectations and opportunities vary dramatically from middle to high school, with high school students typically experiencing more stringent academic expectations as well as more social opportunities to engage in risk behaviors. Historically, the end of adolescence was marked by the adoption of adult roles, such as marriage, which until about 50 years ago occurred typically at about age 20 for females and 22 for males (U.S. Bureau of the Census, 2017). Social changes have changed the boundaries of both adolescence and adulthood.

Emerging adulthood, ages 18 to 25, is marked by diversity in lifestyle, including friendships, residence, and more.
iStock.com/South_agency

Emerging Adulthood

We have seen that social changes such as the Industrial Revolution played a role in marking adolescence as a distinct period of life. In a similar way, recent social changes, such as the dramatic increase in college attendance and later onset of marriage and parenthood, have prolonged the transition to adulthood, creating a new period in life known as emerging adulthood (Arnett, 2015). Emerging adulthood begins upon leaving secondary school, at about age 18, ends at about age 25 (or as late as 29) when most young people begin to live independently and adopt adult roles such as worker, spouse, and parent. In the interim, young people in emerging adulthood occupy an "in-between" status in which they are no longer adolescents but have not yet assumed the roles that comprise adulthood.

Emerging adulthood is marked by instability and diversity in lifestyles (Arnett, Žukauskienė, & Sugimura, 2014). People aged 18 to 25 have the highest rates of residential change of any age group, shifting among residences and living situations, such as from living with parents to roommates to romantic partners. Changes in romantic relationships are also frequent. As we will discuss in Chapter 4, emerging adulthood is an important time for **identity development**, coming to a sense of self. Perhaps most strikingly, emerging adults tend to report a sense of being in between, neither adolescents nor adults. As young people make progress toward resolving their identity, they are more likely to perceive themselves as adults (Schwartz, Zamboanga, Luyckx, Meca, & Ritchie, 2013). Finally, although emerging adults experience many transitions, instability, and mixed emotions,

most have a sense of optimism. For example, in one study of more than a thousand 18- to 29-year-olds in the United States, 89% agreed with the statement, "I am confident that eventually I will get what I want out of life," and over 75% agreed with the statement, "I believe that, overall, my life will be better than my parents' lives have been" (Arnett & Schwab, 2012).

How young people traverse this stage, and how long it takes, is a result of the interaction of the individual's capacities and the environment in which he or she lives—family, social, economic, and community resources (Wood et al., 2018). Transitions do not occur at the same pace or in the same order for everyone. Emerging adults adopt adult roles at different times. Young people vary with regard to when they enter careers, when they marry, and when they become parents (Eisenberg, Spry, & Patton, 2015). Most research on emerging adulthood has sampled college students, potentially yielding a narrow view of this period in life (Hendry & Kloep, 2010; Mitchell & Syed, 2015). College enrollment often delays residential and financial independence, as most college students tend to depend on their parents for financial and often residential support. In contrast to college students, young people who are employed are more likely to be financially self-supporting and to live in a residence independent of their parents, markers of adulthood. Young people who drop out of high school, experience early parenthood, begin working at a job immediately after high school, or live in low socioeconomic status homes and communities may experience only a limited period of emerging adulthood or may not experience emerging adulthood at all (du Bois-Reymond, 2015; Maggs, Jager, Patrick, & Schulenberg, 2012). Thus, emerging adulthood may be interwoven with socioeconomic status (du Bois-Reymond, 2015).

Emerging adulthood may be extended into the late 20s for young people who obtain advanced training, such as attending medical school or law school, which delays entry into a career, other adult roles, and financial independence. Some theorists therefore argue that emerging adulthood is not a life stage—it does not exist everywhere and for everyone—but is simply an indicator of medium to high socioeconomic status and the educational and career opportunities that accompany such status (Côté, 2014; Syed, 2015). Given that ethnicity is often interwoven with socioeconomic status, people of color may be less likely to experience emerging adulthood (du Bois-Reymond, 2015; Syed & Mitchell, 2014).

Although emerging adulthood is not universal, it has been observed among young people in many cultures, including many countries in North and South America, Northern and Eastern Europe, Israel, China, and Japan (Arnett & Padilla-Walker, 2015; Arnett et al., 2014; Nelson, 2009; Sirsch, Dreher, Mayr, & Willinger, 2009; Swanson, 2016). However, the theory of emerging adulthood is based on samples of youth from Western countries, especially the United States. For example, one recent analysis found that three-quarters of research on emerging adulthood published between 2013 and 2015 examined U.S. samples (Ravert, Stoddard, & Donnellan, 2018). Findings obtained with Western samples cannot necessarily be generalized to people in other parts of the world. In fact, most published research examines people from the English-speaking world and Western Europe, with little representation from Latin America, Asia, Africa, or the Middle East. Henrich, Heine, and Norenzayan (2010) refer to the majority of research samples published in international journals as "Western, Educated, Industrialized, Rich, and Democratic" or WEIRD. Worldwide, few people are categorized as WEIRD, yet findings from WEIRD samples are treated as applicable to the rest of the world.

The majority of studies of emerging adulthood are conducted in Western nations without attention to whether the features that mark emerging adulthood generalize to non-Western contexts. In non-Western cultures, entry to adulthood is often marked by rituals and is similar for everyone. For example, isolated hunter-gatherer communities tend to have scripted roles, responsibilities, and trajectories. Young people in these communities likely do not take time to decide what to do with their lives, engage in social experimentation, and find themselves (Schwartz, 2016). Instead, they adopt the roles ascribed to them and aid their communities. Emerging adulthood likely does not exist in these communities.

Developmental Processes of Adolescence

The developmental changes that we experience throughout life are *multidimensional* and include changes in physical, cognitive, and socioemotional development (Baltes, Lindenberger, & Staudinger, 2006). **Physical development** refers to body maturation and growth. Physical development in adolescence is driven by puberty, the attainment of reproductive maturity, and includes changes in body size and shape, including the growth of breasts in girls and facial hair in boys.

Cognitive development refers to the maturation of thought processes and the tools that we use to obtain knowledge, become aware of the world around us, and solve problems. Adolescents become faster, more efficient, and more sophisticated thinkers than children. Most notably, adolescents develop the ability to think abstractly. They become able to solve hypothetical problems, often in similar ways as adults.

Socioemotional development includes changes in emotions, views of oneself, interactions with others and understanding of relationships, and social competence. They become driven to understand themselves and find their place in the world. **Emotion regulation**, the ability to control emotions, improves throughout adolescence. Adolescents also get better at taking other people's perspectives, improving relationships with others.

These domains of development interact in complex ways to influence adolescent functioning. For example, brain maturation, a physical development, underlies advances in abstract reasoning, a cognitive development, which might enable adolescents to become better at understanding their best friend's point of view (Braams & Crone, 2017). In turn, they might become more empathetic and sensitive to their friends' needs and develop more mature friendships, influencing their socioemotional development.

Developmental Tasks of Adolescence

Adolescents' physical, cognitive, and socioemotional development influences their progression on several interacting developmental tasks unique to the adolescent period. We are faced with developmental tasks throughout our lives, each specific to particular ages (Havighurst, 1972). Our progression on each task is influenced by physical, cognitive, and socioemotional development and the social resources and supports available to us.

Identity

Often depicted in movies and other media, the task of **identity** refers to forming a sense of self. Advances in cognition permit adolescents to think about themselves, their families, and their peers in more sophisticated ways. Adolescents begin to recognize their uniqueness and for the first time in life wonder,

"Who am I?" Identity development entails developing a sense of individuality in multiple realms, such as gender, physical attributes, sexuality, and career, while retaining a sense of connection to others. Social interactions with parents and peers help adolescents determine their sense of identity.

Autonomy

Generally speaking, **autonomy** refers to self-governance or independence. The developmental task for adolescents is to become capable of governing their emotions, values, and behavior. As adolescents develop emotional autonomy, they become more self-reliant and less emotionally dependent on their parents while retaining emotional closeness with them. Cognitive autonomy develops as adolescents adjust to their emerging cognitive skills and apply them to reason about the social world. Adolescents develop a multifaceted understanding of moral behavior and an internalized sense of right and wrong—a personal value system. A third component of autonomy, behavioral autonomy, refers to the ability to control impulses, resist pressure from others, and make and carry out decisions. Autonomy is related to identity, as adolescents with a more developed sense of self may be more prepared to demonstrate autonomy. In turn, the capacity for self-governance may facilitate identity development.

Intimacy

Adolescents' abilities to understand other people's perspectives influence their interactions and relationships. Cognitive and socioemotional development are critical contributors to developing a sense of **intimacy**, the ability to form and sustain close relationships. The task for adolescence is to develop the capacity for close, genuine relationships characterized by honesty, trust, and mutual respect. Intimacy is linked with emotional autonomy, as adolescents who are emotionally independent from their parents yet retain a connection to them are better prepared to establish intimate relationships with peers and romantic partners. Likewise, a sense of identity may contribute to intimacy because adolescents who understand themselves may be better able to focus on others' needs and make intimate connections.

Sexuality

With puberty, adolescents' bodies transform, often quickly. Adolescents must become comfortable with their bodies and the reactions of others. Developing a positive body image and comfort with one's body influences **sexuality**, the understanding and expression of sexual feelings and behaviors. Adolescents must become aware of and manage sexual feelings and engage in healthy sexual behaviors. Sexuality is linked with identity, as adolescents' grasp of their sexual identity may help them interpret their sexual feelings and behavior. Intimacy is also relevant to sexuality, as it is through close relationships that adolescents may experiment and come to understand their sexuality. Autonomy also influences sexuality, as self-reliance, personal values, and behavioral control contribute to adolescents' sexual behavior.

Contexts of Adolescence

All adolescents experience biological, cognitive, and socioemotional changes. However, the meaning ascribed to these changes, and their effects on adolescents' behavior and relationships, varies. The physical changes of puberty are accompanied by excitement in some adolescents and heightened self-consciousness in others. The advances in abstract thinking and hypothetical reasoning enable some adolescents to excel in school. Others may engage in intense introspection that can influence depression. With advances in socioemotional development, adolescents are driven to understand themselves. Some adolescents learn about themselves by exploring new activities and hobbies, others read philosophy and consider different values, and others engage in risk-taking activities such as antisocial activities and substance use. Why are these universal physical, cognitive, and socioemotional changes experienced so differently?

Development is shaped by the environments in which we live. All adolescents undergo the same physical, cognitive, and socioemotional transitions, but the effects of these changes are influenced by their unique physical and social worlds. More specifically, adolescent development is influenced by its **context**. Most simply, context refers to where and when a person develops. Context encompasses many aspects of the physical and social environment, such as family, neighborhood, country, and historical time period. It includes intangible factors, characteristics that are not visible to the naked eye, such as values, customs, ideals, and culture. In order to understand a given individual's development, we must look to his or her context. Adolescents are immersed in several contexts.

Home context. The home context includes family; interactions with parents, siblings, and other household members; and family demographics, such as ethnicity, race, socioeconomic status, and composition (single parent, divorced, two parents, same-sex parents).

School context. The school context includes interactions with teachers, coaches, administrators, and classmates. The school's location, size, resources, and quality influence adolescents' development.

The school context includes classmates, teachers, classrooms, and school resources.
iStock.com/monkeybusinessimages

Sociohistorical context. The sociohistorical context refers to the unique influence of societal and historical forces that shape development, such as politics, wars, epidemics, natural disasters, economic booms, and recessions.

Contexts interact dynamically. For example, the peer and school contexts often overlap as peer relationships influence interactions at school. Adolescents are not only influenced by their contexts, but they influence their contexts. Adolescents interact with family members and peers, thereby influencing the home and peer contexts and, in turn, influencing their own development.

Peer context. The peer context includes friendships, social relationships, and romantic relationships. Peer groups differ in interests, activities, and orientation toward academics, risk-taking, and peer culture.

Neighborhood context. The neighborhood context includes its location, demographics, socioeconomic status, resources, and opportunities and challenges.

Online context. Historically speaking, the online context is new, having emerged over the past 2 decades. It includes interactions with people, activities and games played alone or with others, and access to resources and information.

Cultural context. The cultural context refers to the culture in which we are immersed and includes culturally relevant values, ideals, and beliefs.

Adolescents interact with others online, through social media and gaming, making the online context an important influence on development.
iStock.com/MStudioImages

REVIEW 1.2

1. What are markers of the three phases of adolescence?

2. What characteristics comprise emerging adulthood?

3. Provide examples of the three types of developmental processes of adolescence.

4. What are the major developmental tasks of adolescence?

5. Identify the contexts in which adolescents are embedded.

• •

THINKING IN CONTEXT 1.2

1. How do you define the boundaries of adolescence? What indicators of its beginning and end are important to you? Why?

2. What are some of the contextual factors that might influence the experience of emerging adulthood? Do you think that young people from high and low socioeconomic backgrounds experience emerging adulthood in similar ways? Why or why not?

3. Do gender, race, and ethnicity influence the experience of emerging adulthood? Why or why not?

• •

APPLY 1.2

Micah, a college student, is confused. He lives away from home, on campus, and is experiencing more freedom than ever. He can stay up all night, go out whenever he wants, and decide whether or not to go to class. Sometimes Micah feels all grown up, but other times he feels like a kid, such as when he has to ask his parents to replenish his meal card and put some cash in his account. Micah still hasn't chosen a career path or even a major.

How would you characterize Micah's development? Consider his progress in the domains and tasks of development. What phase of adolescence do you think Micah is experiencing, if any? Why?

• •

THEORIES OF ADOLESCENT DEVELOPMENT

Why do adolescents behave as they do? The study of adolescence is part of a larger field of study known as **developmental science**, the scientific study of lifespan development. Over the past century, scientists have learned much about lifespan development, how individuals grow from infants, to children, to adolescents, and to adults, as well as how they change throughout adulthood. Developmental scientists explain their observations by constructing theories of human development. A **theory** is a way of organizing a set of observations or facts into a comprehensive explanation of how something works. Theories are important tools for compiling and interpreting the growing body of research in human development as well as determining gaps in our knowledge and making predictions about what is not yet known. Most theories about adolescent development are embedded within developmental theories that encompass the entire lifespan, as discussed in the following sections.

Psychoanalytic Theories

Are there powerful forces within us that make us behave as we do? Are we pushed by inner drives? **Psychoanalytic theories** describe development and behavior as a result of the interplay of inner drives, memories, and conflicts we are unaware of and cannot control. These inner forces influence our behavior throughout our lives. Freud and Erikson are two key psychoanalytic theorists whose theories remain influential today.

Freud's Psychosexual Theory

Sigmund Freud (1856–1939), a Viennese physician, is credited as the father of the psychoanalytic perspective. Freud believed that much of our behavior is driven by unconscious impulses that are outside of our awareness. Freud believed we progress through a series of *psychosexual stages*, periods in which unconscious drives are focused on different parts of

the body, making stimulation to those parts a source of pleasure. Freud explained that the task for parents is to strike a balance between overgratifying and undergratifying a child's desires at each stage in order to help the child develop a healthy personality with the capacity for mature relationships throughout life. During adolescence, Freud posed that young people enter the genital stage and basic unconscious drives focus on the genitals. Adolescents become concerned with sexuality and developing mature and satisfying sexual relationships. Note that the genital stage is the final stage in Freud's scheme, suggesting that he viewed adolescents as similar to adults.

Notably, Freud's theory grew from his work with female psychotherapy patients; he did not study children (Crain, 2016). In part because of its heavy emphasis on childhood sexuality, Freud's psychosexual stage framework is not widely accepted (Westen, 1998). Yet some of Freud's ideas have stood up well to the test of time and have permeated popular culture, such as the notion of unconscious processes of which we are unaware, the importance of early family experience, and the role of emotions in development (Bargh, 2013). Another reason why Freud's theory tends to be unpopular with developmental scientists is that it cannot be directly tested and is therefore not supported by research (Miller, 2016). How are we to study unconscious drives, for instance, when we are not aware of them?

Erikson's Psychosocial Theory of Development

Erik Erikson (1902–1994) was influenced by Freud, but he placed less emphasis on unconscious motivators of development and instead focused on the role of the social world, society, and culture. Erikson posed a lifespan theory of development in which individuals progress through eight *psychosocial stages* that include changes in how they understand and interact with others, as well as changes in how they understand themselves and their roles as members of society (Erikson, 1950). Each age presents a unique developmental task, which Erikson referred to as a crisis or conflict that must be resolved. How well individuals address the crisis determines their ability to deal with the demands made by the next stage of development.

Erikson posited that adolescents face the crisis of identity verses role confusion, a time in which they must come to a sense of self by exploring various possibilities and committing to those that fit. Identity verses role confusion is perhaps the most well-known stage in Erikson's scheme and although his theory is criticized as difficult to test, a great deal of research has examined identity development in adolescence and emerging adulthood. We will examine Erikson's ideas about identity in Chapter 4. Erikson's psychosocial theory is one of the first theories of adolescent development and of lifespan development (Crain, 2016).

Behaviorist and Social Learning Theories

Behavior and development are influenced by the physical and social environment. Theorists who study **behaviorism** examine environmental influences on behavior—specifically, only those that can be observed (rather than unobservable unconscious impulses, for example). Operant conditioning is an example of a behaviorist theory.

Operant Conditioning

Perhaps it is human nature to notice that the consequences of our behavior influence our future behavior. A teenager who arrives home after curfew and is greeted with a severe scolding may be less likely to return home late in the future. A teacher who distributes cupcakes to students in an early morning class and notices that students arrive to class on time and in good spirits may be more likely to bring cupcakes in the future. These two examples illustrate the basic tenet of B. F. Skinner's (1905–1990) theory of **operant conditioning**, which holds that behavior becomes more or less probable depending on its consequences. According to Skinner, a behavior followed by a rewarding or pleasant outcome, called **reinforcement**, will be more likely to recur, but one followed by an aversive or unpleasant outcome, called **punishment**, will be less likely to recur.

All people and animals—even insects—can learn though operant conditioning. Although reinforcement and punishment can explain and influence

adolescent behavior, behaviorism does not offer a theory of adolescent development itself. Moreover, developmental scientists tend to disagree with operant conditioning's emphasis on external events (reinforcing and punishing consequences) over internal events (thoughts and emotions) as influences on behavior (Crain, 2016). That is, controlling an adolescent's environment can influence his or her development, but change can also arise from an adolescent's own thoughts and actions, as described by social learning theory.

Social Learning Theory

Like behaviorists, Albert Bandura (born 1925) pointed to the role of the environment, but he also advocated for the role of thought and emotion as contributors to development. According to Bandura's **social learning theory**, people actively process information—they think and they feel emotion—and their thoughts and feelings influence their behavior. Adolescents who are tempted to break curfew, for example, might anticipate their parents' worry and decide to return home on time. Our thoughts and emotions about the consequences of our behavior influence our future behavior. We do not need to experience punishment or reinforcement in order to change our behavior (Bandura, 2012). We can learn by thinking about the potential consequences of our actions. One of Bandura's most enduring ideas about development is that people learn through observing and imitating others, which he referred to as **observational learning** (Bandura, 2010). This finding suggests that people learn by observing the consequences of others' actions. Our observations influence our beliefs about a given behavior. Observational learning is one of the most powerful ways in which we learn.

FIGURE 1.3

Bandura's Model of Reciprocal Determinism

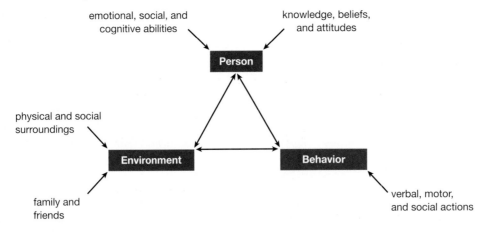

Bandura did not theorize specifically about adolescent development; however, his ideas, especially the concept of reciprocal determinism, have implications for understanding adolescent development. **Reciprocal determinism** refers to the concept that individuals and the environment interact and influence each other over time (Bandura, 2011). Specifically, development is a result of interactions between the individual's characteristics, his or her behavior, and the physical and social environment (see Figure 1.3).

As an example, consider how adolescents' characteristics might influence their behavior and the surrounding social environment. Suppose Isaac is naturally quick to debate with others. This behavior stimulates those around him to engage in debate. Isaac's behavior (e.g., being quick to debate) is influenced by his personal characteristics (e.g., being bright and talkative). Isaac's behavior is also influenced by the environment (e.g., being surrounded by smart people who enjoy debating) and his behavior influences the environment (e.g., people who enjoy debating are more likely to talk to Isaac, while people who avoid debating are less likely to talk to him). This is an example of the complex interplay among the person, behavior, and physical and social environment that underlies much of what we will discuss throughout this book.

Cognitive Theories

Cognitive theorists view cognition, thought, as essential to understanding people's functioning throughout life. In this section, we look at some of the ideas offered by cognitive-developmental theory and information processing theory.

Piaget's Cognitive-Developmental Theory

Swiss scholar Jean Piaget (1896–1980) was the first scientist to systematically examine infants' and children's thinking. Piaget's **cognitive-developmental perspective** on child development views individuals as active explorers of their world, driven to learn by interacting with the world around them and organizing what they learn into **cognitive schemas**, or concepts, ideas, and ways of interacting with the world. Through these interactions, they construct and refine their own cognitive schemas, thereby contributing to their own cognitive development. Piaget proposed that children's drive to explore and understand the world—to construct more sophisticated cognitive schemas—propels them through four stages of cognitive development, from infancy through adolescence. Throughout much of childhood, we are incapable of logic. Piaget posed that logic emerges in late childhood but it is simplistic, referring only to clear concrete examples.

It is not until adolescence that we reach the pinnacle of development—**formal operational reasoning**, or abstract thought. Adolescents become capable of abstract reasoning, can devise hypotheses about real and imagined phenomena, and can apply the scientific method to solve problems. Now adolescents can understand that a statement can be interpreted in more than one way—that a comment such as "great" can be interpreted positively and also as a sarcastic retort, for example. The ability to consider multiple perspectives influences adolescents' relationships because they can imagine and act on other peoples' feelings. We will consider Piaget's ideas about adolescent development in Chapter 3.

Piaget's cognitive-developmental theory transformed the field of developmental psychology and remains one of the most widely cited developmental theories. It was the first to consider *how* children and adolescents think and to view people as active contributors to their development. In addition, Piaget's concept of cognitive stages and the suggestion that individuals' reasoning is limited by their stage has implications for education—specifically, the idea that effective instruction must match children and adolescents' developmental level. Critics of cognitive-developmental theory argue that Piaget focused too heavily on cognition and ignored emotional and social factors in development (Crain, 2016). Others believe that Piaget neglected the influence of contextual factors by assuming that cognitive-developmental stages are universal—that all individuals everywhere progress through the stages in a sequence that does not vary. Other theorists, like Vygotsky, discussed next, emphasize the role of context in cognitive development.

Vygotsky's Sociocultural Theory

We are immersed in a culture that influences how we think and approach the world. Russian scholar Lev Vygotsky (1896–1934) emphasized the importance of **culture** in development. Culture refers to the beliefs, values, customs, and skills of a group; it is a product of people's interactions in everyday settings (Markus & Kitayama, 2010). Vygotsky's **sociocultural theory** examines how culture is transmitted from one generation to the next through social interaction (Vygotsky, 1978). This process begins in infancy but continues throughout childhood, adolescence, and beyond. Children and adolescents interact with adults and more experienced peers as they talk, play, and work alongside them. It is through these formal and informal social contacts that individuals learn about their culture and what it means to belong to it. By participating in cooperative dialogues and receiving guidance from adults and more expert peers, children and adolescents adopt their culture's perspectives and practices, learning to think and behave as members

Lev Vygotsky (1896–1934) emphasized the importance of culture and social interaction in development.
SPUTNIK / Alamy Stock Photo

of their group (Rogoff, 2016). Over time, they become able to apply these ways of thinking to guide their own actions, thus requiring less assistance from adults and peers (Rogoff, Moore, Correa-Chavez, & Dexter, 2014).

Like Piaget, Vygotsky emphasized that children and adolescents actively participate in their development by engaging with the world around them. However, Vygotsky also viewed development as a social process that relies on interactions with adults, more mature peers, and other members of their culture. Vygotsky's sociocultural theory is an important addition to the field of human development because it is the first theory to emphasize the role of the cultural context in influencing people's development throughout life. Critics of sociocultural theory argue that it overemphasizes the role of context, minimizes the role of individuals in their own development, and neglects the influence of genetic and biological factors (Crain, 2016). Some cognitive theorists focus on the process of thinking itself, positing that cognitive development is a continuous process of growth and skill development (Birney & Sternberg, 2011), as described in the following section.

Information Processing Theory

A popular way of considering cognition emphasizes that the mind works in ways similar to a computer, in that information enters and then is manipulated, stored, recalled, and used to solve problems (Halford & Andrews, 2011). Unlike the theories we have discussed thus far, **information processing theory** is not one theory that is attributed to an individual theorist.

Instead, there are many information processing theories and each emphasizes a different aspect of thinking (Callaghan & Corbit, 2015; Müller, Kerns, Müller, & Kerns, 2015; Ristic & Enns, 2015). Some theories focus on how people perceive, focus on, and take in information. Others examine how people store memories and retrieve them. Still others examine problem-solving—how people approach and solve problems in academic settings and in everyday life.

According to information processing theorists, our mental processes of noticing, taking in, manipulating, storing, and retrieving information do not show the radical changes associated with stage theories. Instead, we are born with these abilities and development largely entails changes in the efficiency and speed with which we think (Luna, Marek, Larsen, Tervo-Clemmens, & Chahal, 2015). Information processing theory examines cognition throughout the lifespan, not simply in adolescence, because cognition changes throughout life occur alongside changes in brain functioning, experience, and social interactions. Information processing abilities mature over adolescence, enabling young people to consider and solve complex problems in their everyday world. Neurological development plays a critical role in the development of information processing abilities in adolescence.

Information processing theory offers a detailed explanation of thinking that permits scientists to make and test specific predictions about behavior and performance. Indeed, information processing theory has generated a great many research studies and has garnered much empirical support (Halford & Andrews, 2011). Critics of the information processing perspective argue that a computer model cannot capture the complexity of the human mind and people's unique cognitive abilities. In addition, findings from laboratory research may not extend to everyday contexts in which adolescents must adapt to changing circumstances and challenges to attention (Miller, 2016).

Contextual Theories

As we have discussed, adolescents are immersed in a variety of interacting social contexts that influence their development, such as family, peer group, school, neighborhood, and culture. Contextual theories emphasize the role of the sociocultural context in development. Specifically, Urie Bronfenbrenner proposed that the individual-in-context is the smallest unit of study because development occurs through social interaction and can only be understood as a function of interactions within multiple settings.

Bronfenbrenner's Bioecological Systems Theory

Similar to Vygotsky's sociocultural theory, Urie Bronfenbrenner (1917–2005) emphasized the interplay between the individual and context in development. Specifically, Bronfenbrenner's **bioecological systems theory** poses that development is a result of the ongoing interactions among biological, cognitive, and socioemotional changes within the person and his or her changing context, including home, school, neighborhood, culture, and society, as shown in Figure 1.4 (Bronfenbrenner & Morris, 2006). The bioecological systems theory offers a comprehensive perspective on the role of context as an influence on development. As shown in Figure 1.4, contexts are organized into a series of systems in which individuals are embedded and that interact with one another and the person to influence development.

Ontogenetic development refers to the changes that take place in the individual, the center of the bioecological model. Ontogenetic development comprises the developing adolescent's interacting biological, cognitive, and socioemotional traits.

Genetic, psychological, emotional, and personality traits interact, for example, influencing each other. Physical development, such as brain maturation, may influence cognitive development, such as the ability to consider other people's perspectives, which in turn may influence social development, the ability to have more complex and intimate friendships. In turn, social development may influence cognitive development, as adolescents learn from each other. In this way, the various forms of development interact. Ontogenetic development is influenced by, but also influences, the many contexts in which we are embedded (Bronfenbrenner & Morris, 2006).

Perhaps the most visible context is the **microsystem**, the innermost level of the bioecological system, which includes interactions with the immediate physical and social environment surrounding the person, such as family, peers, and school. Because the microsystem contains the developing person, it has

FIGURE 1.4

Bronfenbrenner's Bioecological Theory

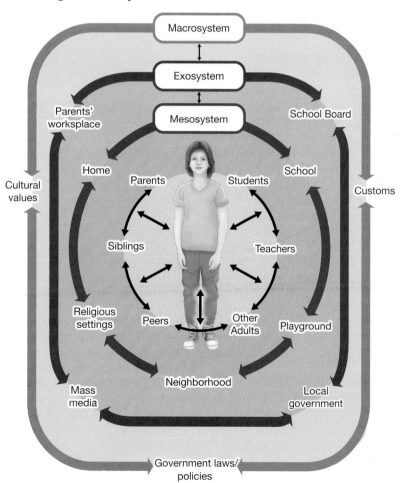

Source: Carolina Hrejsa/Body Scientific Intl.

an immediate and direct influence on his or her development. For example, peer relationships can influence an adolescent's sense of self-esteem, social skills, and emotional development.

Microsystems naturally interact. For example, experiences in the home influence those at school, or peer interactions occur across multiple settings, such as home, school, and neighborhood. These interactions comprise the **mesosystem**, which refers to the relations among microsystems or connections among contexts. Like the microsystem, the mesosystem has a direct influence on the individual because he or she is a participant in it.

The **exosystem** consists of settings in which the individual is not a participant but that nevertheless influence him or her. For example, the availability of funding for schools indirectly affects adolescents by influencing the availability of classroom resources. Funding for after-school community centers, exposure to public service announcements (such as anti-drug messages), and the availability of part-time employment are all exosystem factors that influence adolescents. The exosystem is an important contribution to our understanding of development because it shows us how the effects of outside factors trickle down and indirectly affect individuals.

The **macrosystem** is the greater sociocultural context in which the microsystem, mesosystem, and exosystem are embedded. It includes cultural values of the society at large. The macrosystem indirectly influences the individual because it affects each of the other contextual levels. For example, cultural beliefs about the value of education (macrosystem) influence funding decisions made at national and local levels (exosystem), as well as what happens in the classroom and in the home (mesosystem and microsystem).

By its very nature, the bioecological model is always shifting because individuals and their contexts interact dynamically and perpetually, resulting in a constant state of change. The final element of the bioecological system is the **chronosystem**, which refers to the element of time. The bioecological system changes over time and the time in which we live influences our development. Large-scale social changes, such as those that accompany war, natural disasters, and epidemics, can influence each level of the bioecological system. For example, neighborhood resources may change over time with changes in local policies and funding. Our relationships with parents, friends, and teachers change over time.

Recently, the bioecological model has been criticized for its vague explanation of development, especially the role of culture (Vélez-Agosto, Soto-Crespo, Vizcarrondo-Oppenheimer, Vega-Molina, & García Coll, 2017). Situated in the macrosystem, culture is said to influence development through the interdependence of the systems. Yet current conceptualizations

of culture view it all encompassing and occurring at all ecological levels because culture refers to the processes used by people as they make meaning or think through interactions with group members (Mistry et al., 2016; Yoshikawa, Mistry, & Wang, 2016). Critics therefore argue that since culture is manifested in our daily activities, it is inherent in each bioecological level (Vélez-Agosto et al., 2017). A second criticism arises from the sheer complexity of the bioecological model and its attention to patterns and dynamic interactions. We can never measure and account for all of the potential individual and contextual influences on development at once, making it difficult to devise research studies to test the validity of the model. Proponents, however, argue that it is not necessary to test all of the model's components at once. Instead, smaller studies can examine each component over time (Jaeger, 2016; Tudge et al., 2016). The bioecological model can be a source of hypotheses that can be tested through scientific research.

REVIEW 1.3

1. What are the major developments during adolescence according to Freud and Erikson?

2. How do behaviorists account for adolescent development and behavior?

3. What is social learning and how might it help us understand adolescents?

4. Contrast Piagetian and information processing approaches to cognitive development.

5. What is Vygotsky's sociocultural theory?

6. Identify the six parts of Bronfenbrenner's bioecological model.

• •

THINKING IN CONTEXT 1.3

Apply Bronfenbrenner's bioecological model to your context.

1. Describe your microsystem and mesosystem. Identify at least three examples of each.

2. What are some ways in which your exosystem has influenced your development?

3. Finally, identify at least two examples that illustrate the effect of the macrosystem on your development.

• •

APPLY 1.3

Twelve-year-old Crystal sits in the store manager's office after being caught shoplifting. Given Crystal's age and her show of remorse, the store manager decides to contact Crystal's mother rather than press charges. Crystal's mother is shocked to hear of her daughter's activities.

Apply developmental theories to explain Crystal's behavior and suggest ways of helping Crystal. Specifically, describe four theories that might account for Crystal's shoplifting behavior and how each might be applied to help Crystal.

• •

THE SCIENCE OF ADOLESCENT DEVELOPMENT

Theories are the result of scientists' attempts to organize observations. Developmental scientists who study adolescents conduct research to gather information and answer questions about how they grow and change over time. They devise theories to organize research findings and conduct new studies whose findings are applied to modify theories. By conducting multiple studies over time, developmental scientists refine their theories about human development.

Methods of Collecting Data

The basic challenge that scientists face in conducting research is determining what information is important and how to gather it. Scientists use the term **data** to refer to the information they collect. How can we gather data about adolescents? Should we simply talk with them, watch them as they progress through their days, or hook them up to machines that measure physiological activity such as heart rate or brain waves? Developmental scientists use a variety of different measures to collect information.

Observational Measures

Researchers who use observational measures collect information by watching and monitoring adolescents' behavior. Researchers who use **naturalistic observation** observe and record behavior in natural, real-world settings. For example, in one study, researchers examined peer interaction patterns over the transition to adolescence by observing 9- to 12-year-old children in the schoolyard during recess and lunch (Coplan, Ooi, & Nocita, 2015). They recorded the early adolescents' activity and interaction with peers and found that those who were consistently unengaged with peers tended to show high levels of problems such as anxiety, depression, and loneliness, as reported by both the adolescents and their mothers.

A challenge of using naturalistic observation is that sometimes the presence of an observer causes those being observed to behave unnaturally. This is known as *participant reactivity*. One way of reducing the effect of participant reactivity is to conduct multiple observations so that the participants get used to the observer and return to their normal behavior. Another promising method of minimizing participant reactivity is to use an *electronically activated voice recorder* (EAR) (Mehl, 2017). Participants carry the EAR as they go about their daily life. The EAR captures segments of audio information over time: hours, days, or even weeks. It yields a log of people's activities as they naturally unfold. The EAR minimizes participant reactivity because the participant is unaware of exactly when the EAR is recording. For example, in one study, adolescents with asthma carried the EAR for a 4-day period and reported on their experience of parent-adolescent conflict and asthma symptoms (Tobin et al., 2015). This study found that daily conflict (recorded by the EAR) predicted adolescents' self-reported asthma symptoms, suggesting that family relationships can influence health.

Naturalistic observation permits researchers to observe patterns of behavior in everyday settings. However, sometimes a participant may seldom show the behavior under study, requiring a researcher to observe for very long periods of time to obtain data. For this reason, many researchers make **structured observations**, in a controlled environment, a situation constructed by the experimenter. For example, adolescents might be observed in a laboratory setting as they complete a puzzle-solving task or interact with peers they have just met. The laboratory environment permits researchers to exert more control over the situation than is possible in natural settings, making it more likely that they will observe the behavior of interest. One challenge to conducting structured observations is that people do not always behave in laboratory settings as they do in real life.

Self-Report Measures

Interviews and questionnaires are known as self-report measures because the person under study answers questions to "report" about his or her experiences, beliefs, and behavior. Interviews can take place in person, over the phone, or over the Internet.

In an **open-ended interview**, a trained interviewer uses a conversational style that encourages the adolescent to expand his or her responses. The scientist begins with a question and then follows up with additional questions to obtain a better understanding of the adolescent's response. However, when questions are phrased differently for each person, responses may not capture real differences in how adolescents think about a given topic and instead may reflect differences in how the questions were posed and followed up by the interviewer. In contrast, a **structured interview** poses the same set of questions

Interviews are commonly used to gather data from adolescents.
iStock.com/Sladic

to each participant in the same way. Because all adolescents receive the same set of questions, differences in responses are more likely to reflect true differences among adolescents and not merely differences in the manner of interviewing.

Questionnaires, also called surveys, are composed of sets of questions, typically multiple choice, and can be administered in person, online, or by telephone, e-mail, or postal mail. Questionnaires are popular data collection methods because they enable scientists to collect information from many people quickly and inexpensively. Questionnaires are also popular because they can easily be administered anonymously, protecting participants' privacy. For example, the Monitoring the Future Study is an annual survey of 50,000 eighth-, tenth-, and twelfth-grade students that collects information about their behaviors, attitudes, and values concerning drug and alcohol use (Miech et al., 2017). The survey permits scientists to gather an enormous amount of data, yet its anonymity protects the adolescents from the consequences of sharing personal information that they might not otherwise reveal.

A challenge of self-report measures is that sometimes people give socially desirable answers: They respond in ways they would like themselves to be perceived or believe researchers desire. A middle school student completing a survey about cheating, for example, might respond that she never cheats, despite sometimes looking at nearby students' papers during examinations. The student's answers might instead match the person she aspires to be or the behaviors she believes the world values—that is, someone who does not cheat on exams. Self-report data may not always reflect people's true attitudes and behavior.

Physiological Measures

Our bodies are an important source of information that can be used to understand psychological phenomena. Physiological measures offer important information increasingly used in developmental research because cognition, emotion, and behavior have physiological indicators. For example, do you feel your heart beat more rapidly or your palms grow sweaty when you give a class presentation? Increases in heart rate and perspiration are physiological measures of anxiety. Other researchers might measure cortisol, a hormone triggered by the experience of stress (Simons, Cillessen, & de Weerth, 2017).

Eye movements and pupil dilation can indicate attention and interest. For example, researchers who tracked participants' eye movements as they viewed Facebook feeds learned that people are naturally attracted to social media and news posts that are rich with pictures and links, yet most people are unable to report what they have viewed, even immediately after viewing it (Vraga, Bode, & Troller-Renfree, 2016). A researcher might measure pupil dilation as an indicator of physiological arousal (Feurer, Burkhouse, Siegle, & Gibb, 2017). Physiological measures do not rely on verbal reports and they generally cannot be faked. However, physiological responses may be difficult to interpret. For example, excitement and anger may both cause an increase in heart rate.

Physiological measures of brain activity are a particularly promising source of data. Several tools are used to study the brain. **Electroencephalography (EEG)** measures electrical activity patterns produced by the brain via electrodes placed on the scalp. Researchers study fluctuations in activity that occur when participants are presented with stimuli or when they sleep. EEG recordings measure electrical activity in the brain, but they do not provide information about the location of activity or the brain structures that are the source of brain activity.

Computerized tomography (CT) compiles multiple X-ray images to create a three-dimensional picture of a person's brain, providing images of brain structures, bone, brain vasculature, and tissue (Cierniak, 2011). CT scans can provide researchers with information about the density of brain structures to illustrate, for example, how the thickness of the cortex changes with development.

Positron emission tomography (PET) involves injecting a small dose of radioactive material into the participant's bloodstream to monitor the flow of blood

(Portnow, Vaillancourt, & Okun, 2013). Blood flows more readily to active areas of the brain and the resulting images can illustrate what parts of the brain are active as participants view stimuli and solve problems.

Functional magnetic resonance imaging (fMRI) measures brain activity with a powerful magnet that uses radio waves and to measure blood oxygen level (Bandettini, 2012). Active areas of the brain require more oxygen-rich blood; fMRI enables researchers to determine what parts of the brain are active as individuals complete cognitive tasks. fMRI images are much more detailed than PET scans and do not rely on radioactive molecules, which can only be administered a few times before becoming unsafe.

Diffusion tensor imaging (DTI) uses an MRI machine to track how water molecules move in and around the fibers connecting different parts of the brain (Soares, Marques, Alves, & Sousa, 2013). DTI gauges the thickness and density of the brain's connections, permitting researchers to measure the brain's white matter and determine changes that occur with development.

Research Designs

Just as there are many ways to collect information, scientists have many options for conducting their studies. In addition to determining the research question and deciding what information to collect, scientists must choose a research design—a technique for conducting the research study.

Case Study

A **case study** is an in-depth examination of a single individual or small group of individuals. In conducting a case study, a researcher gathers information from many sources, such as through observations, interviews, and conversations with the adolescent's family, teachers, friends, and others who know him or her. A case study may include samples or interpretations of an adolescent's writing, such as poetry or journal entries, artwork, and other creations. A case study results in a rich description of an adolescent and is useful for documenting individuals who have unique and unusual experiences, abilities, or disorders. However, conclusions drawn from a case study may not be generalized or applied to others because they are based on extensive study of a single person. Case studies can be a source of hypotheses to examine in large-scale research.

Correlational Research

Are adolescents with high self-esteem more likely to excel at school? Are college students who work part-time less likely to graduate? Both of these questions can be studied with **correlational research**, which permits researchers to examine relations among measured characteristics, behaviors, and events. For example, in one study of the relationship between physical fitness and academic performance in middle school students, the adolescents with higher aerobic capacity scored higher on achievement tests than did those with poorer aerobic capacity (Bass, Brown, Laurson, & Coleman, 2013). However, note that this correlation does not tell us *why* aerobic capacity was associated with academic achievement. Correlational research cannot answer this question because it simply describes relationships that exist among variables; it does not enable us to reach conclusions about the causes of those relationships. It is likely that other variables influence both an adolescent's aerobic ability and achievement (e.g., health), but correlation does not enable us to determine the causes for behavior—for that we need an experiment.

Experimental Research

Scientists who seek to test hypotheses about *causal* relationships, such as whether media exposure influences behavior or whether hearing particular types of music influences mood, employ **experimental research**. An experiment is a procedure that uses control to determine causal relationships among variables. Specifically, one or more variables thought to influence a behavior of interest are changed, or manipulated, while other variables are held constant. Researchers can then examine how the changing variable influences the behavior under study. If the behavior changes as the variable changes, this suggests that the variable caused the change in the behavior.

For example, Gentile, Bender, and Anderson (2017) examined the effect of playing violent video games on early adolescents' physiological stress and aggressive thoughts. Participants were randomly assigned to play a violent video game (*Superman*) or a nonviolent video game (*Finding Nemo*) for 25 minutes in the researchers' lab. The researchers measured physiological stress as indicated by heart rate and cortisol levels before and after the adolescents played the video game. The participants also completed a word completion task that the researchers used to measure the frequency of aggressive thoughts. The researchers found that adolescents who played violent video games showed higher levels of physiological stress and aggressive thoughts than did those who played nonviolent video games. They concluded that the type of video game influenced adolescents' stress reactions and aggressive thoughts.

Let's take a closer look at the components of this experiment. Conducting an experiment requires choosing at least one **dependent variable**, the behavior under study (e.g., physiological stress—heart rate and cortisol—and aggressive thoughts) and at least one **independent variable**, factors proposed to change the behavior under study (e.g., type of video game). The independent variable is manipulated or varied systematically by the researcher during the experiment (e.g., a child plays with a violent or a nonviolent video game). The dependent variable is expected to change as a result of varying the independent variable, and how it changes is thought to depend on how the independent variable is manipulated (e.g., physiological stress and aggressive thoughts vary in response to the type of video game). After the independent variable is manipulated, if the experimental and control groups differ on the dependent variable, it is concluded that the independent variable *caused* the change in the dependent variable. That is, a cause-and-effect relationship has been demonstrated.

Developmental scientists conduct studies that use both correlational and experimental research. Studying development, however, requires that scientists pay close attention to age and how young people change over time, which requires the use of specialized research designs, as described in the following sections.

Developmental Research Designs

Do shy children become shy adolescents? Do relationships with parents in early adolescence influence romantic relationships in emerging adulthood? These questions require that developmental scientists examine relationships among variables over time. The following sections discuss the designs that researchers use to learn about human development. As you learn about each design, consider how we might employ it to answer a question about development. For example, how does alcohol use among adolescents change from sixth grade through twelfth grade?

Cross-Sectional Research Design

A **cross-sectional research study** compares groups of people of different ages at a single point in time. For example, to examine how alcohol use varies from sixth through twelfth grade, a scientist might visit a school system in 2022 and administer a survey about alcohol use to students ages 12, 14, 16, and 18. By analyzing the survey, the scientist can describe *age differences* in alcohol use and identify how 12-year-olds differ from 18-year-olds. However, the results do not tell us whether the observed age differences in alcohol use reflect age-related or developmental change. In other words, we don't know whether the 12-year-olds will show the same patterns of alcohol use as the current 18-year-olds when they are 18, 6 years from now.

Cross-sectional research permits age comparisons, but participants differ not only in age but in cohort. A **cohort** is a group of people of the same age who are exposed to similar historical events and cultural and societal influences. Cohorts refer to generations; however, we can also speak of smaller cohorts based on factors such as the year of entry to school, for example. In this example, the 12-year-olds and the 18-year-olds are different ages, but they are also in different cohorts, so the two groups may differ in reported alcohol use because of development (age-related changes) or cohort (group-related changes). For example, perhaps the 12-year-olds received a new early prevention program at school that was not available to the 18-year-olds when they were 12. The difference in alcohol use between 12-year-olds and 18-year-olds might then be related to the prevention program, a cohort factor, and not to age. Cross-sectional research is an important source of information about age differences, but it cannot provide information about age-related changes because participants are assessed only once.

Longitudinal Research Design

A **longitudinal research study** follows the same group of participants over many points in time. Returning to the previous example, to examine how alcohol use changes from 12 to 18 years of age, a developmental scientist using longitudinal research might administer a survey on alcohol use to 12-year-olds and then follow up 2 years later when they are 14, again when they are 16, and finally when they are 18. If a researcher began this study in 2022, the last round of data collection would not occur until 2028.

Longitudinal research provides information about age-related change because it follows individuals over time, enabling scientists to describe how the 12-year-olds' alcohol use changed as they progressed through adolescence. However, longitudinal research studies only one cohort, calling into question whether findings indicate developmental change or whether they are an artifact of the cohort under study. Was the group of 12-year-olds that the scientist chose to follow for 6 years somehow different from the cohorts or groups of students who came before or after? Because only one cohort is assessed, it is not possible to determine whether the observed changes are age-related changes or changes that are unique to the cohort examined.

Sequential Research Designs

A **sequential research design** combines the best features of cross-sectional and longitudinal research by assessing multiple cohorts over time, enabling scientists to make comparisons that disentangle the effects of cohort and age (see Figure 1.5). Consider the alcohol use study once more. A sequential design would begin in 2022 with a survey to students ages 12, 14, 16, and 18. Two years later, in 2024, the initial sample is surveyed again; the 12-year-olds are now

TABLE 1.1

Comparing Research Designs

DESIGN	STRENGTHS	LIMITATIONS
Research Designs		
Case study	Provides a rich description of an individual.	Conclusions may not be generalized to other individuals.
Correlational	Permits the analysis of relationships among variables as they exist in the real world.	Cannot determine cause-and-effect relations.
Experimental	Permits a determination of cause-and-effect relations.	Data collected in artificial environments may not represent behavior in real-world environments.
Developmental Research Designs		
Longitudinal	Permits the determination of age-related changes in a sample of participants assessed for a period of time.	Requires a great deal of time, resources, and expense. Participant attrition may limit conclusions. Cohort-related changes may limit the generalizability of conclusions.
Cross-sectional	More efficient and less costly than the longitudinal design. Permits the determination of age differences.	Does not permit inferences regarding age change. Confounds age and cohort.
Sequential	More efficient and less costly than the longitudinal model. Allows for both longitudinal and cross-sectional comparisons, which reveal age differences and age change, as well as cohort effects.	Time-consuming, expensive, and complicated in data collection and analysis.

Source: Sawyer et al. (2018).

FIGURE 1.5

Sequential Design

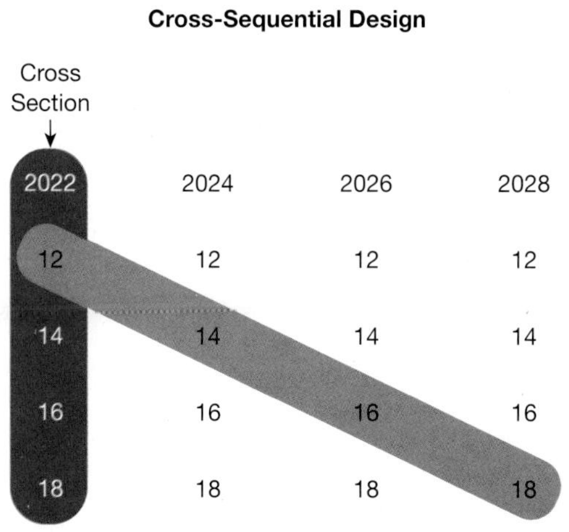

Cross-Sequential Design

14, the 14-year-olds are now 16, and the 16-year-olds are now 18. The 18-year-olds are now 20 and are not assessed, because they have aged out of the study. Now a new group of 12-year-olds is surveyed. Two years later, in 2026, the participants are surveyed again, and so on.

The sequential design provides information about age, cohort, and age-related change. The cross-sectional data (comparisons of 12-, 14-, 16-, and 18-year-olds from a given year) provide information about age differences, how the age groups differ from one another. The longitudinal data (annual follow-up of participants ages 12 through 18) captures age-related change because participants are followed up over time. The sequential component helps scientists separate cohort effects from age-related change. Because several cohorts are examined at once, the effect of cohort can be studied. The sequential design is complex, but it permits human development researchers to disentangle the effects of age and cohort and answer questions about developmental change. See Table 1.1 for a comparison of research designs.

REVIEW 1.4

1. Compare observational, self-report, and physiological measures.

2. Differentiate among the case study method, correlational research, and experimental research.

3. Contrast cross-sectional, longitudinal, and sequential research designs.

THINKING IN CONTEXT 1.4

1. Did you ever complete a survey in middle school or high school? Do you remember the topic?

2. How do you think adolescents view surveys distributed in school? What are some of the challenges for researchers who collect survey data from adolescents?

3. Suppose you conducted a research study and found that ninth graders who spent more time on social media, like Instagram and Snapchat, scored lower on a math achievement test. How would you describe these findings to a friend? Identify other variables that might influence this finding.

• •

APPLY 1.4

1. Suppose you wanted to study influences on academic achievement in high school. What are some factors that might influence adolescents' achievement? Identify at least four.

2. Choose one factor to study. How might you measure it? Would you choose an observational, self-report, or physiological measure? Describe your choice.

3. What type of research design would you use? Why?

4. Suppose you wanted to understand how academic achievement changes from middle school to high school. Describe how you might study this question.

• •

THE PROMISE AND CHALLENGE OF APPLIED DEVELOPMENTAL SCIENCE

In its early years, the study of human development was based on laboratory research devoted to uncovering universal aspects of development by stripping away contextual influences. This basic research was designed to examine how development unfolds, with the assumption that development is a universal process with all people changing in similar ways and in similar timeframes. In the early 1980s, influenced by contextual theories (such as Bronfenbrenner's bioecological approach) and the growing assumption that people are active in their development (a cornerstone of lifespan developmental theory), developmental scientists began to examine developmental processes outside of the laboratory (Lerner, Johnson, & Buckingham, 2015b). It quickly became apparent that there are a great many individual differences in development that vary with a myriad of contextual influences. The field of **applied developmental science**

emerged, studying individuals within the contexts in which they live and applying research findings to improve people's lives.

By its very nature, research in applied developmental science is multidisciplinary because real-world problems are complex and require the expertise of scientists from many fields, such as human development, psychology, medicine, biology, anthropology, and more. Applied developmental scientists examine and contribute to policies on a wide range of issues that affect individuals and families, such as health and health care delivery, violence, and school failure. For example, they might study contextual influences such as the impact of environmental contaminants, poor access to clean water, or exposure to poverty on physical, cognitive, and socioemotional development (Aizer, 2017; Gauvain, 2018; Golinkoff, Hirsh-Pasek, Grob, & Schlesinger, 2017; Huston, 2018). It is through applied research that scientists have come to appreciate the full range of contextual influences on development and how factors such as sex, ethnicity, and socioeconomic status influence development.

Intersectionality and Development

Adolescents interact with family, peers, teachers, and other individuals, influencing and being influenced by them. In our discussion of Bronfenbrenner's bioecological model, we have seen that adolescents are immersed in many interacting contexts, such as home, school, and neighborhood. Adolescents' experiences in these settings and the sense they make of these experiences varies dramatically with demographic variables, such as gender, race and ethnicity, sexual orientation, and socioeconomic status, for example. There is a growing awareness among developmental scientists that the effects of demographic variables are not universal (Ghavami, Katsiaficas, & Rogers, 2016; Godfrey & Burson, 2018). Instead, individuals' unique experiences and perspectives are influenced by **intersectionality**, the dynamic interrelations of demographic factors, such as gender, race and ethnicity, and sexual orientation, and social factors, such as socioeconomic status and disabilities (Crenshaw, 1989).

We are all members of multiple intertwined social categories, such as gender, race, and sexual orientation. Our understanding of each category is influenced by our membership in other categories. For example, adolescents' understanding of gender may be filtered through the lens of their membership in another social category, such as ethnicity. In turn, their experiences as members of an ethnic group are intertwined with their gender. For example, Latina girls' views of themselves and their worlds may be quite different from those of Latinx boys as well as girls of other ethnicities, such as Black or Asian American girls. In this example, the intersection of ethnicity and gender combine to influence girls' self-understanding. Most people are members of multiple social categories, in addition to ethnicity and gender, that interact to influence their perception. The importance of social categories and the meaning ascribed to them vary with context, such that social categories such as gender, race, and sexual orientation may be more salient and meaningful in some contexts and at some times than others.

Intersectionality emphasizes a contextual approach toward understanding how perceptions, stereotypes, and discrimination about gender, ethnicity and race, sexual orientation, and socioeconomic status, for example, overlap and interlock, creating distinct experiences for subgroup members with implications for development (Crenshaw, 1989; Syed & Ajayi, 2018). For instance, intersecting expectations about race and gender may uniquely shape the experience of Black boys in classroom settings, how they are perceived and treated, that is unique from those experienced by boys of other races and ethnicities and the experiences of Black girls—with implications for their academic performance, development, and long-term outcomes (Roy, 2018). Until recently, people of color have been largely excluded from research studies or research participants of all ethnicities and races have been grouped, masking differences and contributing to a sense of invisibility among people of color (Syed, Santos, Yoo, & Juang, 2018). For example, one analysis of articles published between 2006 and 2010 in leading developmental science journals (*Developmental Psychology*, *Child Development*, and *Developmental Science*) found that only 14% included samples that were predominantly people of color and a surprisingly high 28% did not mention the racial/ethnic composition at all (Nielsen, Haun, Kärtner, & Legare, 2017).

The study of intersectionality sheds light on how discrimination, marginalization, oppression, and privilege combine to influence adolescents' experiences in unique ways (Crenshaw, 1989). Intersectionality is an emerging approach in developmental science with a small but rapidly growing body of research that recognizes the many ways that gender, ethnicity and race, sexual orientation, socioeconomic status, and disability interact to influence development (Godfrey & Burson, 2018). Throughout this book, we will examine adolescent development through an intersectional lens whenever possible.

Research Ethics and Applied Developmental Science

Researchers have responsibilities to conduct research that is scientifically sound. They are also obligated to adhere to standards of ethical conduct in research. Research with adolescents can pose tricky ethical questions. For example, suppose a researcher wanted to determine the effects of an illegal drug on adolescent brain development or the effects of bullying on emotional development. Would it be possible to design a study in which some adolescents were assigned to ingest the illegal drug or a study in which adolescents are exposed to bullying? Of course not. These studies violate the basic ethical principles that guide developmental scientists' work: (1) beneficence and nonmaleficence, (2) responsibility, (3) integrity, (4) justice, and (5) respect for autonomy (American Psychological Association, 2010).

Beneficence and nonmaleficence are the dual responsibilities to do good and to avoid doing harm. Researchers must protect and help the individuals, families, and communities with which they work by maximizing the benefits and minimizing the potential harms of their work. Above all, participating in research must never pose threats to adolescents beyond those they might encounter in everyday life. Researchers also have the responsibility to help participants, for example, by directing a distressed adolescent toward help-seeking resources.

The ethical principle of **responsibility** requires that researchers act responsibly by adhering to professional standards of conduct and clarifying their obligations and roles to others. For example, a researcher conducting interviews with adolescents and parents must clarify her role as scientist and not counselor and help her participants understand that she is simply gathering information from them rather than conducting therapy. Researchers' responsibility extends beyond their participants to society at large. Sometimes researchers' findings have social and political implications that they may not expect. For example, one highly publicized study compiled the results of many research studies examining college students who had become sexually involved with an adult prior to reaching the legal age of consent (Rind, Tromovitch, & Bauserman, 1998). The scientists concluded that the young people's adjustment and development varied widely and depended on a number of factors within the individual, situation, and broader context. The participants who were older when the relationship began, such as in late adolescence, just prior to reaching the age of consent, showed fewer negative effects and appeared to be well adjusted. These findings were misinterpreted by some organizations, media outlets, and politicians as suggesting that sexual involvement with minors was acceptable or even beneficial, which was clearly not the researchers' conclusion (Garrison & Kobor, 2002). Although it is not always easy to anticipate how research findings might be portrayed in the media and understood by the public, the principle of responsibility means that researchers must attempt to foresee ways in which their results may be misinterpreted and correct any misinterpretations that occur (Lilienfeld, 2002; Society for Research in Child Development, 2007).

The principle of **integrity** requires that scientists be accurate, honest, and truthful in their work by being mindful of the promises they make to participants and making every effort to keep their promises. According to the principle of **justice**, the risks and benefits of research participation must be spread equitably across individuals and groups. Every participant should have access to the contributions and benefits of research. For example, when an intervention is found to be successful, all participants must be given the opportunity to benefit from it.

Perhaps the most important principle of research ethics is **respect for autonomy**. Scientists have a special obligation to respect participants' autonomy, their ability to make and implement decisions. Ethical codes of conduct require that researchers protect participants' autonomy by obtaining **informed consent**—participants' informed, rational, and voluntary agreement to participate. Soliciting informed consent requires providing the individuals under study information about the research study, answering questions, and ensuring that they understand that they are free to decide not to participate in the research study and that they will not be penalized if they refuse. Respecting people's autonomy also means protecting those who are not capable of making judgments and asserting themselves. Parents provide parental permission for their minor children to participate because researchers (and lawmakers) assume that minors are not able to meet the rational criteria of informed consent. Although adolescents are minors, their growing capacities for decision-making require researchers to seek their agreement to participate in ways that are appropriate to their age and developmental capacities. Adolescents must provide their **assent** to participate (Tait & Geisser, 2017). For example, a researcher about to administer early adolescents a questionnaire about their experiences with parental divorce might explain the kinds of questions the adolescents will encounter; explain that, in some cases, a question might feel personal and might bring up memories; remind the adolescents that they are free to stop or skip any questions they choose; and, finally, remind the adolescents that if they feel uncomfortable or would like to talk to someone about their feelings about the issues examined in the study, a counselor is available or the researcher can help them find someone who can help them. Seeking assent from adolescents has the benefit of helping them learn how to make decisions and participate in decision-making within safe contexts (Oulton et al., 2016).

Ethical Issues in Studying Adolescents

Studying adolescents often raises unique ethical questions. For example, adolescent research participants are often very concerned about how their information and samples will be used and, in particular, whether information would be shared with their parents (Crane & Broome, 2017). Adolescents and parents tend to have different opinions about research disclosures; parents often want to receive their children's research information, but adolescents tend to report wanting to withhold private and sensitive findings (Brawner, Volpe, Stewart, & Gomes, 2013).

Sometimes seeking consent from parents may interfere with researchers' goals or may pose risks to minor participants. In one study, lesbian, gay, bisexual, and transgender (LGBT) adolescents believed that participating in research on sexuality and health is important for advancing science, yet they indicated that they would not participate if guardian permission were required, citing negative parental attitudes or not being "out" about their LGBT identity (Macapagal, Coventry, Arbeit, Fisher, & Mustanski, 2017). As one 15-year-old bisexual participant explained,

> I believe it could harm some [teens] because the risk of being let out of the closet. I know some people whose family would not approve of any other sexuality [other than heterosexuality]. Such as my own, my mother would turn on me for not being her perfect image.

In response to these ethical challenges, researchers frequently obtain **passive consent** for conducting research on sensitive topics with adolescents. Passive consent procedures typically involve notifying parents about the research and requiring them to reply if they do *not* want their child to participate.

Another issue developmental scientists face in studying adolescents is that the researchers' desire to learn about development and solve problems may conflict with the need to protect adolescents in research studies. For example, researchers generally promise participants, including adolescents, **confidentiality**, that their responses will remain confidential and will not be disclosed to others. Suppose a researcher studying adolescents learns that a participant is in jeopardy, whether engaging in health-compromising behaviors (e.g., cigarette smoking, unsafe driving, or unhealthy behavior), contemplating suicide, or engaging in illegal or harmful activities (e.g., drug addiction, stealing, or violence). Does the researcher have a duty to disclose the risk to an outside party that can help the adolescent, such as parents? Does the researcher's promise of confidentiality outweigh the duty to disclose?

Researchers who study risky and health-compromising behaviors *expect* to encounter participants who are engaged in potentially dangerous activities. Helping the adolescent might involve removing him or her from the study and may potentially compromise the study. In addition, adolescents generally expect that researchers will maintain confidentiality

(Fisher et al., 1996); violating their confidentiality may be harmful. Is there ever an instance in which a researcher should break confidentiality and disclose information about an at-risk adolescent? Ethical guidelines published by research and medical associations address researchers' obligations to help and not harm and to protect participants' confidentiality, but they generally fail to offer specific recommendations about how researchers can manage the conflicting duties to maintain confidentiality and disclose participant problems (Hiriscau, Stingelin-Giles, Stadler, Schmeck, & Reiter-Theil, 2014; Sharkey, Reed, & Felix, 2017). Instead, researchers must decide for themselves how to balance their sometimes conflicting obligations to their adolescent participants. ●

REVIEW 1.5

1. What is intersectionality?

2. Describe ethical principles that apply to researchers' work.

3. What are some ethical issues that may arise when studying adolescents?

· ·

THINKING IN CONTEXT 1.5

1. Consider the social categories of which you are a member (perhaps gender, race or ethnicity, socioeconomic status, or religion). Which are most important to you? How might these social categories interact to influence your experiences? What are some of the challenges of studying development through an intersectional lens?

2. Researchers may commonly encounter adolescents with problems, big and small. What kinds of problems do you think merit a researcher taking action? In those cases, what action should a researcher take? Is it ever permissible to do nothing? To tell a parent? What guidelines would you use in making these decisions?

· ·

APPLY 1.5

As an adolescent development researcher, you are planning to conduct a study on risky behavior with high school students.

1. Imagine your participants. Describe their characteristics. Provide examples of intersectionality and anticipate how intersections of ethnicity and race, socioeconomic status, and gender might affect participants' responses.

2. In your view, what ethical principle is the most important for you to uphold? Why?

3. What are the pros and cons of parental consent and passive consent? Which would you choose?

· ·

CHAPTER SUMMARY

1.1 Discuss the historical origins of adolescence and evidence for popular stereotypes about adolescents.

The transition from childhood to adulthood, known as adolescence, occurs over many years. Although philosophers described the period of adolescence, adolescents were treated much like adults until the 19th century. Several social changes occurred from 1890 to 1920, making this time the Age of Adolescence. G. Stanley Hall is credited with beginning the scientific study of adolescence. Hall believed that adolescence was characterized by universal upheaval, storm, and stress. However, current research suggests that turmoil is not universal or healthy. Instead, most researchers propose a modified storm-and-stress view, in which problems are more likely to emerge during adolescence but are not inevitable. Despite this, stereotypes about adolescence abound.

1.2 Analyze the developmental processes, contexts, and timing of adolescence and emerging adulthood.

Adolescence is characterized by biological and social transitions. Although its boundaries are a source of debate, adolescence can be defined in three phases: early adolescence (age 10 to 14), middle adolescence (age 14 to 16), and late adolescence (age 16 to 18). Emerging adulthood (roughly age 18 to 25) is a period distinct from adolescence and adulthood in which young people have diverse experiences, experience instability, engage in identity development, and feel somewhat in between, neither adolescent nor adult. Adolescents experience interacting changes in physical, cognitive, and socioemotional development and they undertake several developmental tasks: establishing a sense of identity, autonomy, sexuality, and intimacy. All of these changes take place in several contexts in which adolescents are immersed, such as home, school, peer, neighborhood, and culture.

1.3 Summarize theoretical approaches to studying adolescent development.

Developmental scientists explain their observations by constructing theories of human development. Psychoanalytic theories describe development and behavior as a result of the interplay of inner drives, memories, and conflicts we are unaware of and cannot control. Whereas Freud emphasized sexuality, Erikson described identity development as the task of adolescence. Behaviorist and social learning theory emphasize environmental influences on behavior, such as operant conditioning and observational learning. Cognitive theorists view cognition as essential to understanding people's functioning. Piaget's cognitive-developmental theory describes cognitive development as an active process; adolescents achieve the final stage of his scheme, formal operations. Vygotsky emphasized the importance of context and culture in influencing development. Information processing theorists study the steps involved in cognition: perceiving and attending, representing, encoding, retrieving, and problem-solving. Bronfenbrenner's bioecological model explains development as a function of the ongoing reciprocal interaction among biological and psychological changes in the person and his or her changing context.

1.4 Describe methods and designs used to study adolescent development.

A case study is an in-depth examination of an individual. Observational measures are methods that scientists use to collect and organize information based on watching and monitoring people's behavior. Interviews and questionnaires are called self-report measures because they ask the persons under study questions about their own experiences, attitudes, opinions, beliefs, and behavior. Physiological measures gather the body's physiological responses as data. Scientists use correlational research to describe relations among measured characteristics, behaviors, and events. To test hypotheses about causal relationships among variables, scientists employ experimental research. Developmental designs include cross-sectional research, which compares groups of people at different ages simultaneously, and longitudinal research, which studies one group of participants at many points in time. Cross-sequential research combines the best features of cross-sectional and longitudinal designs by assessing multiple cohorts over time.

1.5 Explain the scope of applied developmental science and some of the challenges that arise in this field.

Applied developmental science refers to the study of developmental processes outside of the laboratory, studying individuals within the contexts in which they live and applying research findings to improve people's lives. Recently, applied developmental scientists have begun to study development through an intersectional lens, recognizing that individuals' experiences and perceptions vary with their membership in intersecting social categories, such as gender, race, and sexual orientation. Several ethical principles guide applied developmental scientists' work: beneficence and nonmaleficence, responsibility, integrity, justice, and respect for autonomy. Studying adolescents raises ethical issues such as the use of confidentiality and passive consent.

KEY TERMS

adolescence, 4

applied developmental science, 24

assent, 26

autonomy, 11

behaviorism, 14

beneficence and nonmaleficence, 25

bioecological systems theory, 17

case study, 21

chronosystem, 18

cognitive development, 10

cognitive-developmental perspective, 15

cognitive schema, 15

cohort, 22

computerized tomography (CT), 20

confidentiality, 26

context, 11

correlational research, 21

cross-sectional research study, 22

culture, 15

data, 19

dependent variable, 21

developmental science, 13

diffusion tensor imaging (DTI), 21

early adolescence, 8

electroencephalography (EEG), 20

emerging adulthood, 8

emotion regulation, 10

exosystem, 18

experimental research, 21

formal operational reasoning, 15

functional magnetic resonance imaging (fMRI), 21

identity, 10

identity development, 9

independent variable, 22

information processing theory, 16

informed consent, 26

integrity, 26

intersectionality, 24

intimacy, 11

Biological Development

Learning Objectives

2.1 Summarize the physical changes that accompany puberty in boys and girls.

2.2 Describe adolescents' experience of puberty and its influence on their relationships with parents.

2.3 Examine the effects of pubertal timing on adolescents.

2.4 Analyze influences on pubertal timing.

2.5 Discuss common health problems in adolescence and ways of promoting health.

Chapter Contents

Adolescents experience dramatic changes during puberty. They may grow several inches taller over a summer or experience unexpected shifts in weight, size, and strength. Boys' shoulders tend to broaden, and girls' hips do the same. **Puberty** is the biological transition to adulthood, in which adolescents mature physically and become capable of reproduction.

Puberty is often considered the hallmark of adolescence. The physical changes of puberty are also accompanied by social changes. As adolescents appear more mature, they are treated more like adults. The physical changes serve as a signal to others of entry into a new life stage and convey personal and social meaning about new roles, expectations, and status.

PUBERTY

Although many people view puberty as an event, it is a process that includes many physical changes that occur over about 4 years but can vary dramatically from 1 to 7 years (Mendle, 2014). Puberty entails the development of reproductive capacity, but that is not the whole story. Puberty influences a great variety of physical changes—not simply those typically associated with sexual maturity—such as changes in body size, shape, and function. The brain triggers the onset of puberty through its influence on the endocrine system.

The Endocrine System

In late childhood, by about age 8 or 9 in girls and roughly 2 years later in boys, the brain signals the endocrine system to gradually increase the release of hormones that trigger the onset of puberty (Berenbaum, Beltz, & Corley, 2015). The **endocrine system** produces and regulates levels of **hormones**, chemical substances that are released into the bloodstream to influence body processes. Hormones drive puberty as well as many other functions, including growth, appetite, stress responses, and sexual responses.

Hormone levels in the body are regulated by a feedback loop that can be likened to a thermostat. Levels of a particular hormone are set to a certain point. When the levels drop below the set point, the endocrine system releases hormones into the bloodstream. This process is similar to setting a thermostat to maintain a room temperature at 70 degrees, for example. When the temperature drops below 70 degrees, the heat turns on, warms the room, and stops when the room temperature reaches 70 degrees. Hormone levels are regulated by a similar feedback loop, with the brain instructing the endocrine system to release hormones when they fall below a particular set point.

Hypothalamus-Pituitary-Gonadal Axis

The feedback loop that regulates the sex hormones that drive puberty is known as the **hypothalamus-pituitary-gonadal axis (HPG)** (Figure 2.1). The endocrine system receives messages to control the levels of hormones in the body by the **hypothalamus**, a region at the base of the brain that is responsible for maintaining basic body functions such as eating, drinking, temperature, and hormone production. The hypothalamus releases **gonadotropin-releasing hormone (GnRH)**, which causes the **pituitary gland**, located adjacent to the hypothalamus, to stimulate the **gonads**, or sex glands (ovaries in females and testes in males) to mature, enlarge, and in turn

begin producing hormones themselves (Aylwin, Toro, Shirtcliff, & Lomniczi, 2019; Schulz, Molenda-Figueira, & Sisk, 2009). Levels of **testosterone**, a hormone responsible for male sex characteristics, and **estrogen**, responsible for female sex characteristics, increase in both boys and girls. However, testosterone is produced at a much higher rate in boys than girls and estrogen is produced at a much higher rate in girls than boys, leading to different patterns in reproductive development (Bogin, 2011). The physical maturation that comprises puberty is known as **gonadarche**.

Adrenarche

A separate but related hormonal process occurs prior to puberty, at about age 6 to 8, when a shift in hormones triggers **adrenarche**, the activation of the adrenal glands, which are located above the kidneys (Witchel & Topaloglu, 2019). The adrenal glands

---

FIGURE 2.1

Hypothalamus-Pituitary-Gonadal Axis

The Endocrine System

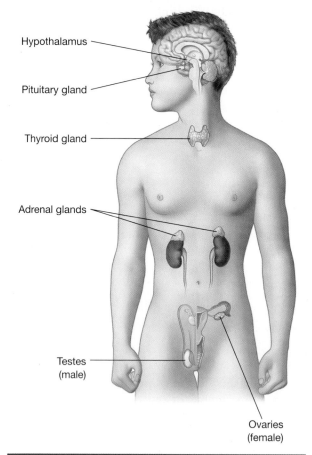

Source: Carolina Hrejsa/Body Scientific Intl

secrete low levels of testosterone and hormones that stimulate body growth, the eruption of the first permanent molars, and the development of body hair and odor (Auchus & Rainey, 2004; Utriainen, Laakso, Liimatta, Jaaskelainen, & Voutilainen, 2015). Adrenal hormones influence the body's metabolism, leading to an increase in fat that is needed to cause the onset of puberty, or sexual maturation. Although some of the body changes that accompany adrenarche are often associated with puberty, the two processes are independent (Del Giudice, 2018). Adrenarche is also thought to influence interests and behavior. For example, the brain converts adrenal androgens into estrogen and testosterone, feminizing and masculinizing hormones, which may influence the timing of initial sexual attraction (Campbell, 2011; Witchel & Topaloglu, 2019). Many adults recall their first memorable sexual attractions to peers occurring at about age 9 or 10 (Diamond, Bonner, & Dickenson, 2015).

The adrenal glands are also implicated in stress responses throughout the lifespan because they release cortisol, the hormone responsible for the "fight-or-flight" response. Adrenarche is thought to be a sensitive period in which adolescents are more vulnerable to stress and experience heightened cortisol responses (Del Giudice, Ellis, & Shirtcliff, 2011). This vulnerability is one of the reasons why mental health issues often emerge first in adolescence (Byrne et al., 2017). Stress responses acquired during adolescence, such as elevated cortisol secretion, may persist into adulthood and over the lifespan (Blakemore, Burnett, & Dahl, 2010).

Body Shape and Size

The first outward sign of puberty is the **adolescent growth spurt**, a rapid gain in height and weight that generally begins in girls at about age 10 (as early as age 7 and as late as 14) and in boys at about age 12 (as early as age 9 and as late as 16) (Tinggaard et al., 2012). The pattern and pace of growth, as shown in Figure 2.2, is similar across most children (Sanders et al., 2017). Girls begin their growth spurt about 2 years before boys, so 10- to 13-year-old girls tend to be taller, heavier, and stronger than boys their age. By starting their growth spurts 2 years later than girls, boys begin with an extra 2 years of prepubertal growth on which the adolescent growth spurt builds, leading boys to end up taller than girls (Yousefi et al., 2013). On average, the growth spurt lasts about 2 years, but growth in height continues at a more gradual pace, ending by about 16 in girls and 18 in boys. Adolescents gain a total of about 10 inches in height.

Different parts of the body grow at different rates. For example, the extremities grow first, the fingers and toes; then hands and feet; then arms and legs; and finally, the torso (Sheehy, Gasser, Molinari, & Largo,

Sequence of Physical Changes With Puberty

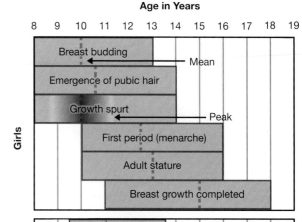
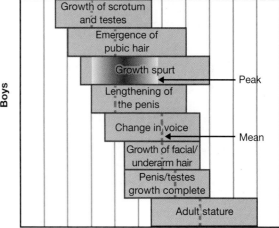

Source: Carolina Hrejsa/Body Scientific Intl

2009). Adolescents' bodies therefore tend to appear lanky and awkward, contributing to a temporary increase in clumsiness as adolescents attempt to control their quickly changing bodies. Adolescents' bodies become taller and heavier before their muscles grow stronger and their internal organs mature (DeRose & Brooks-Gunn, 2006; Seger & Thorstensson, 2000).

Sex differences in body shape emerge during the growth spurt. Boys and girls gain fat and muscle, but in different ratios. Girls gain more fat overall, particularly on their legs and hips, so that fat comes to comprise one-fourth of their body weight—nearly twice as much as that of boys. Boys gain more muscle than do girls, especially in their upper bodies, doubling their arm strength between ages 13 and 18 (Payne & Isaacs, 2016). Bone density increases in both boys and girls, and the respiratory and cardiovascular systems mature.

The adolescent growth spurt is accompanied by increases in lung size and capacity, leading adolescents to breathe more deeply. The heart doubles in size

Boys gain more muscle than girls, especially in their arms and upper body.
iStock.com/piyaset

and the total volume of blood in the body increases. These changes increase the amount of oxygen that circulates through the bloodstream to the muscles, improving physical performance and endurance. Boys become much better at taking in and using oxygen as their hearts and lungs grow larger and function more effectively and the number of red blood cells increases (Sadler, 2017). Consequently, once puberty has begun, boys generally tend to outperform girls in athletics (Tønnessen, Svendsen, Olsen, Guttormsen, & Haugen, 2015).

Secondary Sex Characteristics

Most people associate puberty with the development of **secondary sex characteristics**, body changes that indicate physical maturation but are not directly related to fertility. Examples of changes in secondary sex characteristics include breast development, deepening of the voice, growth of facial and body hair, and, for many, the emergence of acne (Hodges-Simeon, Gurven, Cárdenas, & Gaulin, 2013).

Rapid increases in estrogen cause the budding of breasts, which tends to accompany the growth spurt in

girls as the first signs of puberty (Emmanuel & Bokor, 2017). Testosterone causes boys' voices to deepen. As their voices change, boys may occasionally lose control over their voices and emit unpredictable changes in pitch often experienced as high squeaks (Hodges-Simeon et al., 2013). Girls' voices also deepen, but the change is not as noticeable as in boys. Oil and sweat glands become more active, resulting in body odor and acne (Sadler, 2017). Hair on the head, arms, and legs becomes darker, and pubic hair begins to grow, first as straight and downy, and later becomes coarse (Figures 2.3 and 2.4).

Primary Sex Characteristics

Maturation of the **primary sex characteristics**, the reproductive organs, is less noticeable than secondary sex characteristics but is the most important developmental change that accompanies puberty. In females, primary sex characteristics include the ovaries, fallopian tubes, uterus, and vagina. In males, they include the penis, testes, scrotum, seminal vesicles, and prostate gland. During puberty, the reproductive organs grow larger and mature.

The onset of menstruation marks sexual maturity in girls. **Menstruation** refers to the monthly shedding of the uterine lining, which has thickened in preparation for the implantation of a fertilized egg. **Menarche**, the first menstruation, occurs toward the end of puberty, yet most adolescents and adults view it as a critical marker of puberty because it occurs suddenly and is memorable (Brooks-Gunn & Ruble, 2013).

In North America, the average European American girl experiences menarche shortly before turning 13 and the average African American girl shortly after turning 12 (Emmanuel & Bokor, 2017). Generally, African American girls tend to be heavier and enter puberty about a year earlier, reaching pubertal milestones such as the growth spurt and menarche earlier than other girls (Emmanuel & Bokor, 2017).

FIGURE 2.3

Pubertal Stages for Penis and Pubic Hair Growth

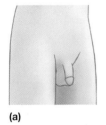  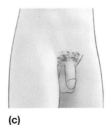  

(a)　　　　　(b)　　　　　(c)　　　　　(d)　　　　　(e)

Source: Carolina Hrejsa/Body Scientific Intl

FIGURE 2.4

Pubertal Stages for Breast and Pubic Hair Growth

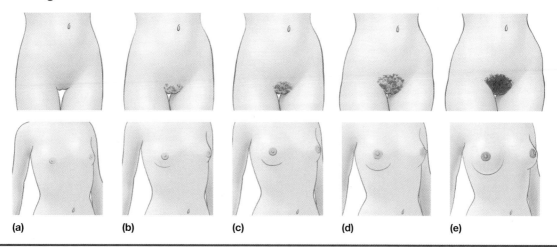

(a)　　　　　(b)　　　　　(c)　　　　　(d)　　　　　(e)

Source: Carolina Hrejsa/Body Scientific Intl

Hispanic American girls enter puberty at about the same time as African American girls, with some studies suggesting earlier menarche and others later (Biro et al., 2018; Deardorff, Abrams, Ekwaru, & Rehkopf, 2014). Frequently, during the first few months after menarche, menstruation takes place without ovulation, the ovaries' release of an ovum (Lacroix & Whitten, 2017). However, this period of temporary sterility is variable and unpredictable.

In boys, the first primary sex characteristic to emerge is the growth of the **testes**, the glands that produce sperm (Tinggaard et al., 2012). About a year later, the penis and scrotum enlarge, and pubic hair, a secondary sex characteristic, appears. As the penis grows, the prostate gland and seminal vesicles begin to produce **semen**, the fluid that contains sperm. At about age 13, boys demonstrate a principal sign of sexual maturation: the first ejaculation, known as **spermarche** (Gaddis & Brooks-Gunn, 1985; Tomova, Lalabonova, Robeva, & Kumanov, 2011). The first ejaculations contain few living sperm. Many boys experience spermarche in the form of **nocturnal emissions**, or wet dreams, involuntary ejaculations that are sometimes accompanied by erotic dreams.

REVIEW 2.1

1. What is the hypothalamus-pituitary-gonadal axis?

2. Describe adrenarche.

3. What triggers puberty?

4. What are some of the ways in which adolescents' bodies change?

5. Identify examples of primary and secondary sex characteristics.

THINKING IN CONTEXT 2.1

1. In what ways might pubertal changes, such as the growth spurt or emergence of secondary sex characteristics, influence adolescents' behavior?

2. What are some of the implications of sex differences in body growth? For example, might girls' earlier maturation contribute to sex differences in behavior? What are other social implications of pubertal growth?

APPLY 2.1

"Wow, I haven't seen her in a couple of months—and, wow, your daughter's growing so fast," remarked Sondra to her friend Tesa. "You may not have noticed, but your 9-year-old little girl does not look like a little girl," Sondra said. "I know. Her body is filling out very quickly, much faster than I'd like," Tesa replied.

1. What does Tesa's daughter need to know about her body? What should Tesa tell her daughter about puberty, if anything?

2. What information, if any, should schools provide children and preadolescents about puberty?

PSYCHOLOGICAL AND SOCIAL EFFECTS OF PUBERTY

Puberty, specifically menarche and spermarche, represents the transition to reproductive maturity. How do adolescents perceive these changes and how does puberty affect adolescents' lives?

Subjective Experience of Pubertal Events

Girls' experience is influenced by their knowledge about menstruation and their expectations (Brooks-Gunn & Ruble, 2013). Generations ago, girls received little to no information about menarche. Understandably, they were often surprised by it, viewed it negatively, and were often afraid (Costos, Ackerman, & Paradis, 2002). Today, surprise is often the first emotion girls express, but most girls are not frightened by menarche because they have been informed about puberty by health education classes and parents who are more willing to talk about pubertal development than parents in prior generations (Stidham-Hall, Moreau, & Trussell, 2012).

The extent to which adolescents discuss menarche and sexuality varies by context and culture. A study of 12- to 16-year-old Bangladeshi girls revealed that they generally were not informed about menarche, and over two-thirds reacted with fear (Bosch, Hutter, & van Ginneken, 2008). Their mothers also tended to lack an adequate understanding of pubertal processes. Other research has suggested that girls in low and middle income countries, such as India, Turkey, Pakistan, Nigeria, and Malaysia, often know little about menarche and, for religious and cultural reasons, may feel shame about menstruation (Behera, Sivakami, & Behera, 2015; Chandra-Mouli & Patel, 2017). In some cultures, girls can be excluded from interaction with others, including attending school, when they are menstruating. Girls who view menstruation negatively are at risk to experience menstruation negatively, with more menstrual symptoms and distress (Rembeck, Möller, & Gunnarsson, 2006).

We know less about boys' experience of puberty because they lack easily determined objective markers, such as menarche (Herman-Giddens et al., 2012). Research with small groups of adolescent boys suggests that most boys react positively to their first ejaculation, although many experience uneasiness and confusion, especially if they are uninformed about this pubertal change (Frankel, 2002; Stein & Reiser, 1994). Boys who know about ejaculation beforehand are more likely to show positive reactions, such as feeling pleasure, happiness, and pride. Unfortunately, many boys report that health education classes and parents generally do not discuss ejaculation (Omar, McElderry, & Zakharia, 2003; Stein & Reiser, 1994). Parents sometimes report discomfort talking with their sons about reproductive development, particularly ejaculation, because of the close link with sexual desire, sexuality, and masturbation (Frankel, 2002). Perhaps because of its sexual nature, boys are less likely to tell a friend about spermarche than girls are to discuss their own reproductive development (Downs & Fuller, 1991).

Sleep Patterns

Puberty entails many physical changes. One surprising change is a shift in adolescents' sleep patterns and preferred sleep schedule, known as a **delayed phase preference** (Carskadon, 2009; Crowley, Acebo, & Carskadon, 2007). Delayed phase preference is triggered by a change in the nightly release of **melatonin**, a hormone that influences sleep. Adolescents who have experienced puberty tend to show a nightly rise in melatonin (and sleep) about 2 hours later than those who have not begun puberty (Carskadon, Acebo, & Jenni, 2004). When adolescents are allowed to regulate their own sleep schedule, they tend to go to bed at about 1:00 a.m. and sleep until about 10:00 a.m. (Colrain & Baker, 2011). As a result, adolescents stay up later, miss out on sleep, and report sleepiness (Carskadon et al., 2004; Loessl et al., 2008). Adolescents need about 9 hours of sleep each night to support healthy development, but most get far less sleep. From ages 13 to 19, the average number of hours of sleep reported by adolescents in Western countries, such as the United States and Germany, tends to decrease from about 8 to 7 hours, with greater reductions in sleep with each year of age (Carskadon, 2009; Loessl et al., 2008).

Contextual factors also influence adolescents' sleep patterns. The tendency for adolescents to go to bed later has increased over the last 3 decades, along with the increased availability of television and electronic media that compete with sleep for adolescents' time (Bartel, Gradisar, & Williamson, 2015; Carskadon & Tarokh, 2014). Most adolescents have electronic devices such as cellphones, video games, and computers and many report using electronic devices in bed. Greater bedtime device use is associated with less sleep (Vernon, Modecki, & Barber, 2018). Screen use has biological implications for adolescents' sleep. Early in puberty, adolescents show more sensitivity to light and melatonin production is more easily suppressed by exposure to light in the evening (such as by the use of computer, tablet, and smartphone screens) (Crowley, Cain, Burns, Acebo, & Carskadon, 2015).

Poor sleep in adolescence is associated with anxiety, irritability, and depression (Fuligni, Arruda, Krull, &

Evening screen use is associated with poor sleep.
iStock.com/banusevim

Gonzales, 2018; Wong & Brower, 2012). It increases the probability of health problems, including illnesses, obesity, and accidents (Darchia & Cervena, 2014; Mitchell, Rodriguez, Schmitz, & Audrain-McGovern, 2013b). Poor sleep duration predicts less engagement in extracurricular school activities and declines in academic performance (Fuligni et al., 2018; Minges & Redeker, 2016). Sleep problems are also associated with risky behaviors, including cigarette smoking and substance use (Pieters et al., 2015; Telzer, Fuligni, Lieberman, & Galván, 2013; Wong, Robertson, & Dyson, 2015), and predict the onset of heavy drinking and marijuana use up to 5 years later (Miller, Janssen, & Jackson, 2017; Nguyen-Louie et al., 2018). Moreover, "catching up" on missed sleep by sleeping longer on the weekends may be ineffective in reducing the sleep deficit. For example, fluctuations in sleep length ("catching up") were associated with more internalizing and externalizing symptoms in a sample of Mexican American adolescents (Fuligni et al., 2018) and poor performance on attention tasks in a sample of Korean adolescents (Kim et al., 2011).

Most middle and high schools start earlier than elementary schools, often to allot time for after-school sports and activities. Earlier school starting times are associated with less total sleep and students generally do not make up for lost sleep on the weekends (Paksarian, Rudolph, He, & Merikangas, 2015). Delaying school start times improves student school attendance, grades, and disposition. For example, in one study, students reported getting 30 minutes more sleep each night and showed significant improvements in measures of adolescent alertness, mood, and health 3 months after a 50-minute delay in school start time (Owens, Belon, & Moss, 2010; Owens, Dearth-Wesley, Herman, Oakes, & Whitaker, 2017). A metanalysis suggested that when school times were delayed 25 and up to 60 minutes, total sleep time increased from 25 to as much as 77 minutes per weeknight (Minges & Redeker, 2016). Later start times were

associated with reduced student daytime sleepiness, depression, caffeine use, tardiness to class, and trouble staying awake. In 2017, the American Academy of Sleep Medicine (Watson et al., 2017a) issued a policy statement calling on communities, school boards, and educational institutions to implement start times of 8:30 a.m. or later for middle schools and high schools to ensure that every student arrives at school healthy, awake, alert, and ready to learn.

In addition to the school context, sleep is influenced by other contexts such as the home and family. For example, under contexts of family stress, more parental support and cohesive parent–child relationships are linked to longer sleep duration, less sleep variability, and less time spent awake during the night (Tsai et al., 2017). Relatedly, a study of adolescents showed that neighborhood factors, specifically greater perceived neighborhood cohesion, were associated with better sleep and the effect was greater for those of lower socioeconomic status, especially those with lower levels of maternal education (Troxel et al., 2017).

Parent–Adolescent Relationships

As adolescents begin puberty, parent–child interactions tend to change. Puberty is associated with an increase in conflict and distance in parent–child relationships, especially between adolescents and mothers (Ellis, Shirtcliff, Boyce, Deardorff, & Essex, 2011). Early pubertal changes such as the adolescent growth spurt are associated with a rise in negative parent–child interactions, such as complaining and anger, and a decline in positive interactions (Graber, Nichols, & Brooks-Gunn, 2010). The change in parent–child interactions varies with pubertal timing, occurring earlier in early maturers and later in late maturers. Although there is little recent research examining ethnic differences in these relationships, existing work suggests that these patterns tend to vary with ethnicity and sex (Sagrestano, McCormick, Paikoff, & Holmbeck, 1999). Specifically, one 7-year study of children from age 8.5 to 15.5 demonstrated that White girls show increases in lability, or fluctuations, in conflict with their mothers compared with Black or Hispanic girls (Marceau, Ram, & Susman, 2015). In contrast, both White and Black boys who matured more quickly tended to show more lability in conflict with their fathers than those who matured slowly.

However, puberty is one piece of the puzzle, as changing relationships between adolescents and parents are influenced by a variety of factors, as we will discuss in Chapter 8. As adolescents' bodies change, their peer relationships shift and they become interested in dating, potentially a source of conflict with parents. Moreover, parents' reactions to their teens' changing bodies, such as expectations for adolescents' help at home, worries about the potential dangers of dating and sexual relations, and feelings of loss for the child they once had, can influence their perceptions and interactions. As we will discuss in Chapter 8, parent–child relationships improve by the end of puberty, yet the relationships are different than they were in childhood.

REVIEW 2.2

1. Compare girls' and boys' experience of puberty.

2. How do adolescents' sleep patterns change with puberty and what are the implications of these changes?

3. Describe adolescents' relationships with parents during puberty.

. . . .

THINKING IN CONTEXT 2.2

1. How might adolescents' cognitive and social abilities influence their understanding and comfort with their changing bodies?

2. What role do interactions with others play in influencing adolescents' experience of puberty?

3. Do experiences at school and in the community influence adolescents' views of their changing bodies? Why or why not?

4. Do these factors influence boys and girls differently? Why or why not?

. . . .

APPLY 2.2

Fourteen-year-old Juan feels exhausted nearly every day. His alarm barely wakes him. After a few minutes of hearing Juan's alarm, his mother pounds on the door to his room and Juan finally gets out of bed. When Juan's mother is working the early shift, he often oversleeps and gets to school several periods late. Juan can hardly concentrate until about his third or fourth class of the day. Juan's mother reminds him to go to bed early; sometimes he tries, but he's usually wide awake until a few hours before he has to wake for school.

1. What are some of the possible reasons for Juan's sleep problems?

2. What can be done to help adolescents like Juan?

3. What advice do you have for Juan's mother?

4. What can she expect in the coming years?

. . . .

PUBERTAL TIMING

Casual observations of adolescents reveal that although most tend to progress through puberty at about the same time, some begin much earlier or later than others. Children who show signs of physical maturation before age 8 (in girls) or 9 (in boys) are considered early-maturing, whereas girls who begin puberty after age 13 and boys who begin after age 14 are considered late-maturing adolescents (Dorn, Dahl, Woodward, & Biro, 2006). Longitudinal research suggests that boys and girls who matured off-time, early or late relative to their peers, were more likely to show anxiety and depressed mood than their on-time peers in late adolescence and early adulthood (Mendle & Ferrero, 2012; Natsuaki, Biehl, Ge, & Xiaojia, 2009; Rudolph et al., 2014). Early maturation, in particular, poses challenges for both girls' and boys' adaptation (Stroud & Davila, 2016; Ullsperger & Nikolas, 2017).

Early Maturation

Adolescents who mature off-time relative to their peers are often treated differently by adults and peers, with consequences for their development. For example, adolescents who look older than their years are more likely to be treated in ways similar to older adolescents, which adolescents may perceive as stressful (Rudolph et al., 2014). Around the world, early-maturing boys and girls show higher rates of risky activity, including smoking, abusing alcohol and substances, and displaying aggressive behavior, than do their same-age peers (Mrug et al., 2014; Schelleman-Offermans, Knibbe, & Kuntsche, 2013; Skoog & Stattin, 2014).

Early maturation poses specific risks to girls' development. Girls who mature early relative to peers tend to feel less positive about their bodies, physical appearance, and menstruation itself and show higher rates of depression, anxiety, and low self-esteem than do girls who mature on time or late (Benoit, Lacourse, & Claes, 2013; Carter, 2015; Stojković, 2013). Although early-maturing girls are often popular, they are also more likely to be victims of rumor-spreading and sexual harassment, which is associated with feelings of depression, anxiety, and poor self-esteem (Carter, Halawah, & Trinh, 2018; Reynolds & Juvonen, 2011; Skoog, Özdemir, & Stattin, 2016). Early-maturing girls tend to date earlier than their peers, are at higher risk of dating violence, and experience more sexual harassment than their peers (Chen, Rothman, & Jaffee, 2017; Skoog & Özdemir, 2016). One recent study of African American and Caribbean Black girls found that girls who perceived their pubertal development as earlier than their same-aged peers tended to report more experiences with racial discrimination (Seaton & Carter, 2019). Early-maturing Black girls

Girls who mature earlier than their peers sometimes experience social difficulties, such as gossip.
iStock.com/fstop123

alcohol more frequently and in greater quantities, and becoming intoxicated more often than their on-time and late-maturing peers (Biehl, Natsuaki, & Ge, 2007; Schelleman-Offermans, Knibbe, & Kuntsche, 2013). Moreover, these patterns of problematic alcohol use often persist into late adolescence and early adulthood, suggesting that early pubertal maturation may hold long-term implications for young people's health.

Although all early-maturing adolescents tend to experience more problems, early-maturing girls are at higher risk for early sexual activity and for alcohol and substance use and abuse than boys (Ullsperger & Nikolas, 2017). Late maturation shows a different pattern of outcomes.

who attend schools where they are numerical minorities may experience heightened risk for discrimination, suggesting that the effects of pubertal timing may vary with race and ethnicity as well as peer and school context.

Interestingly, girls' view of their own early pubertal timing, whether they view themselves as maturing much earlier than their peers, is often only loosely related to their actual development (Dorn & Biro, 2011; Rasmussen et al., 2015). That is, girls are likely to hold inaccurate views of their bodies, seeing themselves are more or less developed than they are. Moreover, research suggests that girls' self-perceptions are not related to their peers' physical development; their views of their own physical development are independent of their peers' development (Kretsch, Mendle, Cance, & Harden, 2016a). Yet girls' views of their own physical development are often a better predictor of their age at first intercourse, as well as their engagement in sexual risk-taking and substance use and their likelihood of experiencing depression and anxiety, than actual pubertal development (Kretsch, Mendle, & Harden, 2016b; Moore, Harden, & Mendle, 2014).

In males, earlier timing of puberty historically has been viewed as advantageous because it conveys physical advantages for athletic activities. Early-maturing boys tend to be athletic, popular with peers, school leaders, and confident (Stojković, 2013). There is less research on boys than on girls, but it appears that early-maturing boys also experience some internalizing and externalizing symptoms (Rudolph et al., 2014; Stroud & Davila, 2016), especially when they judge their peer relationships as stressful (Benoit et al., 2013; Blumenthal, Leen-Feldner, Trainor, Babson, & Bunaciu, 2009). Early maturers tend to show higher rates of problematic drinking, including consuming

Late Maturation

In contrast to early maturation, the effects of late maturation tend to differ more dramatically for boys and girls. Late maturation appears to have a protective effect on girls with regard to depression (Negriff & Susman, 2011). In one study, late-maturing girls experienced less teasing about their appearance and lower rates of appearance-related anxiety compared with other girls (Zimmer-Gembeck, Webb, Farrell, & Waters, 2018). Findings regarding the effects of late maturation on boys are mixed and less consistent (Mendle & Ferrero, 2012). Late-maturing boys may experience more social and emotional difficulties. Similar to girls, perception may matter. For example, in one study, African American boys who perceived themselves as late maturers showed more symptoms of anxiety than their peers (Carter, 2015). During early adolescence, they may be less well liked by their peers and may be more likely than their peers to experience a poor body image, overall body dissatisfaction, and depression, but these effects tend to decline with physical maturation (Negriff & Susman, 2011). Other research suggests that late-maturing boys do not differ in anxiety or depression from their on-time peers (Crockett, Carlo, Wolff, & Hope, 2013; Marceau et al., 2011) or that it is only late-maturing boys with poor peer relationships who experience depression (Benoit et al., 2013).

Context and the Effects of Pubertal Timing

Contextual factors are thought to amplify the effects of pubertal timing on behavior (Natsuaki, Samuels, & Leve, 2015; Seaton & Carter, 2018). For example, some of the problems that early-maturing boys and girls experience arise because they tend to seek relationships with older peers who are more similar to them in physical maturity than their classmates (Kretsch et al, 2016a). Spending time with older peers makes early-maturing adolescents, especially girls, more likely to engage in age-inappropriate behaviors such as early and risky sexual activity (Baams, Dubas, Overbeek, & van Aken, 2015; Moore et al., 2014). The composition of the peer group may also matter. For example, in one study, early pubertal development was associated with a higher risk for experiencing adolescent dating abuse when the early-maturing girls' friendship groups comprised a higher percentage of boys but not when the friendship groups contained few boys (Chen et al., 2017).

The school context may also influence the effects of pubertal timing. For example, in one study, elementary school teachers shown drawings of girls at varying stages of pubertal development expected early-developing girls to have more academic and social problems relative to other girls (Carter, Mustafaa, & Leath, 2018). In addition, they expected Black early developers to experience more problems than White early developers, possibly suggesting that race and ethnicity may influence how early puberty is experienced by girls. Other research also suggests that racial identity can influence the effects of pubertal timing. In one study of Black adolescents, early-maturing girls were more likely to experience depressive symptoms when they attended mixed-race schools and believed that others held Blacks in poor regard (Seaton & Carter, 2018). The stress that accompanies perceived discrimination may pose serious risks to adaptation. In contrast, and perhaps surprisingly, a strong sense of racial identity was associated with increased depressive symptoms among late-maturing Black girls who attended schools with a mixed-race population. Late-maturing Black girls who identify with their race may value the earlier maturation common to Black girls and may feel dissatisfied with their bodies. Pubertal development influences girls' sense of self and may interact with their other self-relevant beliefs, as well as the social and racial contexts in which they are immersed, to influence their responses (Seaton & Carter, 2018).

REVIEW 2.3

1. Compare the effects of early maturation in boys and girls.
2. What are some of the effects of late maturation for boys and girls?
3. How might the peer and school context influence the effects of the timing of pubertal maturation?

THINKING IN CONTEXT 2.3

1. How might the neighborhood context influence how early and late maturation is experienced by boys and girls? Identify at least three influences in the neighborhood that might affect adolescents' experience of early and late maturation.

2. Consider the effect of neighborhood socioeconomic status. Might early- and late-maturing adolescents living in high, low, or middle income neighborhoods have different experiences? Why or why not?

3. How might the effects vary with race and ethnicity, factors that are associated with pubertal timing and also socioeconomic status?

APPLY 2.3

Sacha zips her sweatshirt up over her chest as she walks into class. "You look like you're wearing a potato sack," kids her friend Jana. "Everything you wear is so baggy," Jana says. Sacha moves to the back of the classroom and sits without saying a word. Later that day, she overhears her mother on the phone. "I don't know what to do about Sacha," her mother says. "She seems like a different kid. She's unsure of herself and I think she's depressed. But the biggest problem is that boy she's hanging out with. He's older—a senior. I don't think she's ready for a relationship and definitely not ready for sex! Sometimes I swear Sacha smells like beer."

1. Given what you know about pubertal development, how would you explain Sacha's behavior?

2. What role might pubertal timing have in this case, if any?

3. What should Sacha's mother know about girls' experience of puberty?

4. What advice do you have for Sacha's mother?

BIOLOGICAL AND CONTEXTUAL INFLUENCES ON PUBERTAL TIMING

In the school locker room, Monique quickly removes her T-shirt and jeans and speedily changes into her gym clothes. At 10 years old, Monique's adult-like figure sets her apart from her peers. Her friend Kaitlyn will not experience similar body growth until age 14. Why does the timing of puberty vary so dramatically for Monique and Kaitlyn? As we discussed, puberty is controlled by the HPG axis, which is responsible for regulating testosterone and estrogen, the hormones that drive puberty. These hormones circulate in the body before birth but they are maintained at a low level throughout infancy and much of childhood. In late childhood, however, the set point for estrogen and testosterone shifts and puberty begins. What triggers this shift? The timing of puberty reflects the interaction of biological and contextual influences.

Genetics

Genetics plays a role in puberty, but puberty is a complex trait influenced by many genes that interact with contextual factors (Day et al., 2017; Zhu, Kusa, & Chan, 2018). In support of the role of genetics, pubertal timing for both boys and girls tends to be similar to that of their parents (Wohlfahrt-Veje et al., 2016). Identical twins (who share 100% of their genes) experience menarche more closely in time than fraternal twins (who share only 50% of their genes) (Kretsch et al., 2016b).

Some children are genetically programmed to experience puberty earlier than others. Heredity sets the boundaries of pubertal timing, the earliest and latest age when we might begin puberty. Yet the onset of puberty and whether it is early or late relative to our inherited range is influenced by more than genes. Contextual influences and life experiences play a role in determining when a child begins puberty.

Nutrition and Health

The availability and consumption of calories and corresponding weight gain determines the onset of puberty (Das et al., 2017). Puberty is triggered by achieving a critical level of body weight, specifically body fat. From an evolutionary perspective, the link between body weight and the onset of reproductive maturation may be adaptive because it delays fertility when food and resources are scarce and unlikely to support offspring (Roa & Tena-Sempere, 2014). The ratio of body fat to weight is a particularly important influence on pubertal timing. Specifically, the accumulation of **leptin**, a protein found in fat, signals the brain to release **kisspeptin**, a brain chemical that stimulates the hypothalamic-pituitary-gonadal axis to increase the production and secretion of hormones (Aylwin et al., 2019; Manfredi-Lozano, Roa, & Tena-Sempere, 2018). Leptin receptors have been identified in the hypothalamus as well as in cells in the ovaries and testicles (Shalitin & Kiess, 2017). Girls with a greater **body mass index (BMI)**, especially those who are obese, mature earlier than do their peers, and girls who have a low percentage of body fat, whether from athletic training or severe dieting, often experience menarche late relative to other girls (Tomova, 2016; Villamor & Jansen, 2016). For example, research with

girls in 34 countries has shown that obesity predicted early puberty (Currie et al., 2012).

In contrast, extreme malnutrition can prevent the accumulation of adequate fat stores needed to support pubertal development so that menarche is delayed. In many parts of Africa, for example, menarche does not occur until age 14 to 17, several years later than in Western nations (Tunau, Adamu, Hassan, Ahmed, & Ekele, 2012). Similarly, some research suggests that weight affects the onset and tempo of puberty in boys, with higher BMI associated with earlier puberty (Lee et al., 2016; Song et al., 2016), but less so as compared with girls (Tinggaard et al., 2012), and the mechanism is not well understood (Cousminer et al., 2014). Swift declines in the age of menarche accompanied the rapid economic growth and advances in the standard of living in South Korea over the last half of the 20th century, illustrating the role of context in biological development (Sohn, 2016).

Stress

Adolescents' social contexts, especially exposure to stress, also influence pubertal timing (Joos, Wodzinski, Wadsworth, & Dorn, 2018). In fact, stress affects hormone production throughout the lifespan; it can trigger irregular ovulation and menstruation in females and reduce sperm production in males (Toufexis, Rivarola, Lara, & Viau, 2014). Early life stress and the experience of severe stress, such as the experience of sexual abuse and maltreatment, can speed the onset of menarche (Negriff, Blankson, & Trickett, 2015; Noll et al., 2017; Worthman, Dockray, & Marceau, 2019).

Similarly, poor family relationships, harsh parenting, family stress and conflict, parents' marital conflict, and anxiety are associated with early menarche in North American and European girls (Graber et al., 2010; Rickard, Frankenhuis, & Nettle, 2014). In industrialized countries such as the United States, Canada, and New Zealand, girls who are raised by single mothers experience puberty earlier than those raised in two-parent homes (Mendle et al., 2006).

In addition, the absence of a biological father and the presence of a biological unrelated male, such as a stepfather or a mother's live-in boyfriend, in the home is associated with earlier onset of menarche (Deardorff et al., 2011; Webster, Graber, Gesselman, Crosier, & Schember, 2014). Animal studies show a similar trend: The presence of a biologically related male delays reproductive maturation and functioning, while the presence of unrelated males speeds female reproductive maturation (Neberich, Penke, Lehnart, & Asendorpf, 2010). Household stress and economic adversity may hold similar implications for boys' pubertal development, speeding it (Sun, Mensah, Azzopardi, Patton, & Wake, 2017); however, there is much less research on boys' development (Joos et al., 2018).

Socioeconomic Status and Ethnicity

Contextual factors outside the home also influence pubertal timing. Adolescents who live in similar contextual conditions, especially those of socioeconomic advantage, reach menarche at about the same age, despite having different genetic backgrounds (Obeidallah, Brennan, Brooks-Gunn, & Earls, 2004). Low socioeconomic status (SES) is associated with early pubertal onset in the United States, Canada, and the United Kingdom and may account for some of the ethnic differences in pubertal timing (Kelly, Zilanawala, Sacker, Hiatt, & Viner, 2017; Mendle & Koch, 2019; Sun et al., 2017). For example, African American and Latina girls tend to reach menarche before White girls, but they are also disproportionately likely to live in low SES homes and neighborhoods. Ethnic differences in the timing of menarche are reduced or even disappear when researchers control for the influence of socioeconomic status (Deardorff et al., 2014; Obeidallah, Brennan, Brooks-Gunn, Kindlon, & Earls, 2000). That is, girls growing up in low SES contexts may experience more stress at home and the community and may have less access to healthy foods and opportunities for safe physical activity. In support of this view, girls' perceptions of neighborhood safety and their estimates of the likelihood that they will live to age 35 predicted early menarche (Amir, Jordan, & Bribiescas, 2016).

Secular Trend

The influence of contextual conditions and physical health in triggering puberty is thought to underlie the **secular trend**, or the lowering of the average age of puberty with each generation from prehistoric to the present times (Papadimitriou, 2016a) (Figure 2.5). Through the 18th century in Europe, puberty occurred as late as age 17; between 1860 and 1970, the age of menarche declined by about

FIGURE 2.5

Secular Trend in Girls' Pubertal Development, 1830–2010

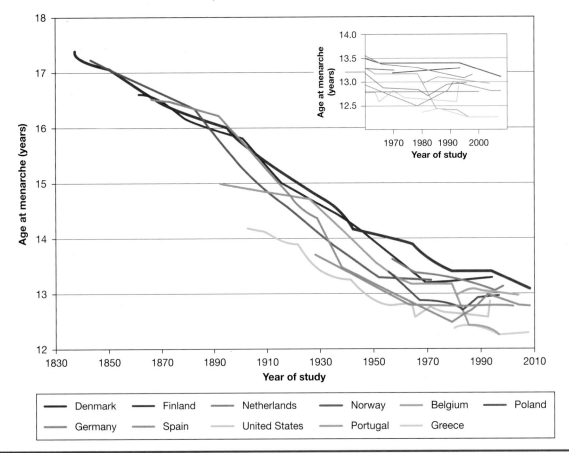

Source: Sørensen et al. (2012).

3 to 4 months per decade (Tanner, 1990). In China, the age at menarche declined from 14.25 in girls born before 1976 to 12.60 in girls born after 2000, with an estimated decline of 0.51 years per decade (Meng, Martinez, Holmstrom, Chung, & Cox, 2017). Boys in the United States and Canada begin puberty at least 1 to 1½ years earlier today than in the 1960s (Herman-Giddens, 2006; Herman-Giddens et al., 2012). Likewise, boys reached peak velocity of growth over 1 month earlier each decade between 1946 and 1991 (Bygdell, Vandenput, Ohlsson, & Kindblom, 2014). The secular trend parallels increases in the standard of living and average BMI among children in developed countries and is especially influenced by the growing problem of childhood obesity (Biro, Greenspan, & Galvez, 2012). There are some indications that the secular trend has slowed or stopped in most industrialized nations, but it is unclear when it will stop completely (Kleanthous, Dermitzaki, Papadimitriou, Papaevangelou, & Papadimitriou, 2017; Papadimitriou, 2016b). Girls have shown precocious puberty as early as age 5 (Scutti, 2015); however, it is unlikely that the average age of puberty will ever drop that low. Nevertheless, the secular trend poses challenges for young people and parents because the biological entry to adolescence is lowering at the same time as the passage to adulthood is lengthening, making the period of adolescence longer than ever before.

REVIEW 2.4

1. Discuss the contributions of genetics and health in pubertal timing.

2. How is the experience of stress related to pubertal timing?

3. How does pubertal timing vary with socioeconomic status and ethnicity?

4. How do contextual influences, such as socioeconomic status and historical time, affect pubertal development?

THINKING IN CONTEXT 2.4

1. If possible, ask a parent, grandparent, or other older relative about their pubertal timing. When did they experience the growth spurt, for example? How does their experience compare with your own, if at all? What might account for the similarities or differences?

2. In your view, which contextual factors are most relevant in influencing pubertal timing, generally?

APPLY 2.4

Wanda began a rapid growth spurt at about age 8. Her friend Clarissa entered her growth spurt just before she turned 14. What are some of the factors that might account for these differences in pubertal timing?

HEALTH IN ADOLESCENCE AND EMERGING ADULTHOOD

Adolescents continue to share many of the same health concerns they did as children, such as access to good nutrition and opportunities for physical activity, safe schools and neighborhoods, and health care. With puberty, adolescents experience new health issues, including adjusting to changing bodies, understanding sexuality, and promoting safe sex.

Nutrition

As boys and girls enter the adolescent growth spurt, their bodies require more energy and their caloric demands increase rapidly to about 2,200 and 2,700 calories a day for girls and boys, respectively (Jahns, Siega-Riz, & Popkin, 2001). Good nutrition is essential to support adolescents' growth, yet young people's diets tend to worsen as they enter adolescence (Frazier-Wood, Banfield, Liu, Davis, & Chang, 2015). Adolescents tend to consume only about one-half of the U.S. recommendations for vegetables, whole grains, and fruits (Banfield, Liu, Davis, Chang, & Frazier-Wood, 2016). In addition, adolescents tend to skip meals, especially breakfast, and drink less milk (Stang & Stotmeister, 2017; Vikraman, Fryar, & Ogden, 2015). One nationally representative sample of over 11,000 high school students showed that girls and Black and Hispanic adolescents are more likely to skip breakfast than boys and White non-Hispanic adolescents (Demissie, Eaton, Lowry, Nihiser, & Foltz, 2018). Skipping breakfast increased over high school, with eleventh- and twelfth-grade students more likely to skip breakfast than ninth- and tenth-grade students.

Fast food consumption tends to increase over adolescence and is associated with lower consumption of fruits and vegetables (Gopinath et al., 2016; Stang & Stotmeister, 2017). Fast food is high in calories; when adolescents eat a fast food meal, they do not appear to adjust their other meals to make up for the excess calories and instead consume more calories overall (Bowman, Gortmaker, Ebbeling, Pereira, & Ludwig, 2004). When a fast food restaurant is near school, students in the United States, United Kingdom, Australia, and Finland show more irregular eating habits, greater consumption of fast food, and higher rates of overweight and obesity (Janssen, Davies, Richardson, & Stevenson, 2018; Virtanen et al., 2015).

Family meals are an important way of establishing healthy eating habits. At home, U.S. children and adolescents who eat an evening meal with their parents tend to have healthier diets that include more fruits and vegetables and they tend to have a lower BMI than their peers who do not share family meals (Watts, Loth, Berge, Larson, & Neumark-Sztainer, 2017). Young people who participate in preparing and eating family meals at least once or twice a week tend to have healthier eating habits 5 years later, from early to middle adolescence through young adulthood (Berge et al., 2015; Berge, MacLehose, Larson, Laska, & Neumark-Sztainer, 2016). Research with families in the Netherlands, Poland, Portugal, and the United Kingdom suggests that family meals are associated with healthier eating habits and enhanced self-control over eating (de Wit et al., 2015). However, the frequency of family dinnertimes drops sharply between ages 9 and 14, and family dinners have become less common in recent decades (Walton & Spencer, 2009; Walton et al., 2016). When family meals are irregular, parents can encourage healthy eating by educating adolescents about nutrition, providing access to fruits and vegetables in the home, and modeling fruit and vegetable consumption and healthy eating habits (Watts et al., 2017).

Physical Activity and Exercise

Regular physical activity is an important component to health throughout life. In adolescence, physical activity promotes cardiovascular health, muscle strength, motor control, cognitive performance, mental health, and well-being (Esteban-Cornejo, Tejero-Gonzalez, Sallis, & Veiga, 2015; McMahon et al., 2017). Physical activity tends to decline beginning in middle childhood, at about age 7 (Farooq et al., 2018). Although some teens engage in competitive sports, average levels of physical activity decrease throughout adolescence, and many adolescents do not engage in regular exercise or activity (Dumith, Gigante, Domingues, & Kohl, 2011; Farooq et al., 2018). Most adolescents in the United States do not meet the federal recommendations of at least 60 minutes of moderate to vigorous physical activity every day. It is estimated that only about 8% of 12- to 15-year-old adolescents are active for 60 minutes per day on at least 5 days per week (Kann et al., 2014). Schools play a role in promoting physical fitness through physical education classes. Yet participation in physical education is highest among students in ninth grade, decreases among tenth- and eleventh-grade students, and is lowest among twelfth-grade students (Kann et al., 2014).

Longitudinal research with U.S. adolescents has shown that the reductions in physical activity during adolescence are consistent across contextual settings, whether rural or urban, and across SES (Metcalf, Hosking, Jeffery, Henley, & Wilkin, 2015). Adolescents of low SES are more likely to be sedentary and obese than their more affluent peers; this holds true for adolescents from a variety of developed nations, such as Canada, England, Finland, France, and the United States (Frederick, Snellman, & Putnam, 2014; Mielke, Brown, Nunes, Silva, & Hallal, 2017; Wang & Lim, 2012). Socioeconomic disparities may be influenced by opportunities for physical activity, such as the availability of safe parks and outdoor spaces, and opportunities for extracurricular activities in the school and community (Watts, Mason, Loth, Larson, & Neumark-Sztainer, 2016). After-school and community sports teams, for example, may be more prominent and available in middle income and affluent communities.

Obesity

Child and adolescent obesity has doubled in prevalence since the 1970s (Lobstein et al., 2015). Health care professionals determine whether someone's weight is in the healthy range by examining BMI, calculated as weight in kilograms/height in meters squared (kg/m²; World Health Organization, 2009). **Overweight** is defined as having a BMI at or above the 85th percentile for height and age, as indicated by the 2000 Centers for Disease Control and Prevention growth charts, and **obesity**

Family meals are associated with healthier eating habits in adolescence and young adulthood.

iStock.com/monkeybusinessimages

FIGURE 2.6

Overweight and Obesity in Adolescents Age 12 to 20, 1999–2016

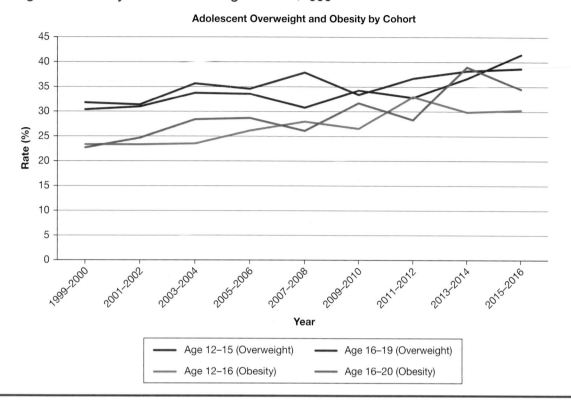

Adolescent Overweight and Obesity by Cohort

Legend:
- Age 12–15 (Overweight)
- Age 16–19 (Overweight)
- Age 12–16 (Obesity)
- Age 16–20 (Obesity)

Source: Skinner et al. (2018).

refers to a BMI at or above the 95th percentile (Skinner, Ravanbakht, Skelton, Perrin, & Armstrong, 2018; Skinner & Skelton, 2014). As shown in Figure 2.6, overweight and obesity become more common with age and the prevalence of each has increased since 1999.

Rising rates of overweight and obesity among adolescents are a problem not only in the United States but also in all other developed nations, including Australia, Canada, Denmark, Finland, Germany, Great Britain, Ireland, Japan, Hong Kong, and New Zealand (de Onis, Blössner, & Borghi, 2010; Janssen et al., 2005; Lobstein et al., 2015; Wang & Lim, 2012). Obesity is also becoming more common in developing nations, such as India, Pakistan, and China, as they adopt Western-style diets higher in meats, fats, and refined foods and as they show the increased snacking and decreased physical activity linked with watching television (Afshin, Reitsma, & Murray, 2017).

As shown in Figure 2.7, rates of obesity vary by race and ethnicity. Black and Hispanic youth show higher rates of obesity than non-Hispanic White youth and non-Hispanic Asian youth (Ogden et al., 2016). A BMI signifying overweight and obesity is generally more likely among girls, regardless of race or ethnicity. Considering both race and ethnicity, Black girls generally show higher rates of overweight and obesity than girls and boys of all ethnicities. Race and ethnicity tend to be interwoven with other contextual factors that may influence adolescents' health and BMI, such as socioeconomic status.

Generally speaking, adolescents in low SES homes are at higher risk for obesity than their peers who live in high SES homes (Chung et al., 2016). This holds true for adolescents from a variety of countries, such as Canada, England, Finland, France, Czechoslovakia, Australia, and the United States (Frederick, Snellman, & Putnam, 2014; Hardy et al., 2017; Sigmund et al., 2018; Wang, Jackson, Zhang, & Su, 2012; Wang & Lim, 2012). Research with North American youth suggests a complex relation between socioeconomic status and obesity. One longitudinal study of over 4,800 U.S. fifth- through seventh-grade students showed that those with the highest socioeconomic status were less likely to be obese than their peers at both time points (Fradkin et al., 2015). However, when ethnicity was considered, this pattern was confirmed for Latinx and White adolescents, but not Black adolescents. Growing up in a high SES home was associated with a lower risk of obesity in Latinx and White adolescents but was unrelated to obesity in African American

FIGURE 2.7

Prevalence of Obesity in U.S. Adolescents (Age 12–19), by Sex, Race, and Ethnicity, 2011–2014

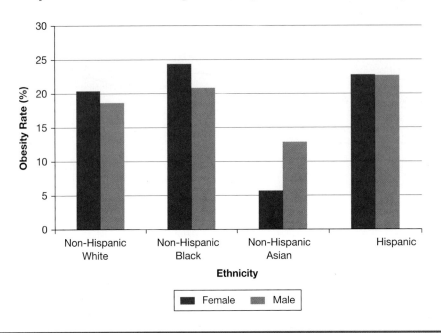

Source: Ogden et al. (2016).

adolescents. Thus, the health advantage associated with higher parental education and income may not apply consistently to boys and girls across all ethnic groups. Influences on young people's health, such as socioeconomic status, must be considered within the context of the broader social and physical environments in which youth live (Schreier & Chen, 2013). For example, the African American adolescents in the above study were less likely to report weight loss attempts than their peers (Fradkin et al., 2015). Cultural depictions of beauty may rival other contextual influences such as SES.

Other research suggests that genetic and contextual factors interact to influence BMI (Albuquerque, Nóbrega, Manco, & Padez, 2017; Goodarzi, 2018). For example, the effects of SES may vary with individuals' genetic predispositions. In one study, early adolescents who were carriers of a particular allele of the *OXTR* gene had greater BMI when reared in low SES environments but had the lowest BMI when reared in high SES homes (Bush et al., 2017). We are just beginning to examine the complex interactions among biology and context on obesity.

Contextual factors in the home and community, such as family dinners, the availability of healthy foods, and parks and opportunities for physical activity, are associated with nutrition, health eating, and exercising. Behavioral factors, specifically sedentary activities such as screen time—time spent in front of a television, computer, or electronic device screen watching videos, playing video games, and engaging with social media are risk factors for overweight and obesity in U.S., U.K., and Canadian adolescents (Herman, Hopman, & Sabiston, 2015; Mitchell, Rodriguez, Schmitz, & Audrain-McGovern, 2013a; Pearson et al., 2017). It is estimated that American adolescents spend over 11 hours each day in front of a screen (American Academy of Pediatrics & American Academy of Pediatrics Council on Communications and Media, 2013; Rideout, 2010).

Obesity in adolescence is a serious problem because the majority of obese youngsters, about 80%, do not outgrow obesity but instead become obese adults (Simmonds, Llewellyn, Owen, & Woolacott 2016). Adolescent obesity is associated with short- and long-term health problems, including heart disease, high blood pressure, orthopedic problems, and diabetes (Pulgarón, 2013). Obese adolescents are at risk for peer rejection, depression, low self-esteem, and body dissatisfaction (Gibson et al., 2008; Harrist et al., 2016; Pulgarón, 2013; Quek, Tam, Zhang, & Ho, 2017). Obese adolescents of all ethnicities are likely to report being teased or bullied at school (Bucchianeri, Eisenberg, & Neumark-Sztainer, 2013) and are likely to experience weight-related stigma from adults and peers (Pont, Puhl, Cook, & Slusser, 2017). The social correlates of overweight and obesity, such as weight-related teasing, hold long-term implications. Adolescents who are teased about their weight are more likely to have unhealthy eating habits and be overweight or obese as adults, 15 years later (Puhl et al., 2017). Moreover, weight-related stigma is associated with a variety of risk behaviors, including substance use, sexual risk-taking, and violence (Farhat, 2015).

Programs that effectively reduce obesity in adolescents target their screen time, increase their physical activity and time spent outdoors, and teach them about nutrition, reducing their consumption of high-calorie foods and increasing their consumption of fruits and vegetables (Bleich, Segal, Wu, Wilson, & Wang, 2013; Kumar & Kelly, 2017; Lobstein et al., 2015; Nowicka & Flodmark, 2007). For example, effective school programs couple education with opportunities to engage in an after-school exercise program (Pbert et al., 2016). At home, parents can increase the availability of healthy foods, discuss nutrition and health, and model healthy eating and an active lifestyle.

Eating Disorders

Adolescents' rapidly changing physique, coupled with media portrayals of the ideal woman as thin with few curves, leads many to become dissatisfied with their body image and the dissatisfaction often persists into emerging adulthood (Benowitz-Fredericks, Garcia, Massey, Vasagar, & Borzekowski, 2012). Girls who have a negative body image are at risk of developing **eating disorders**, mental disorders that are characterized by extreme over- or under-control of eating and behaviors intended to control weight such as compulsive exercise, dieting, or purging (American Psychiatric Association, 2013). Eating disorders, such as **anorexia nervosa**, **bulimia nervosa**, and **binge eating disorder**, pose serious challenges to health.

Anorexia Nervosa and Bulimia Nervosa

Anorexia nervosa and bulimia nervosa are both characterized by excessive concern about body weight and attempts to lose weight. However, they differ in how this concern is manifested. Those who suffer from anorexia nervosa starve themselves and sometimes engage in extreme exercise in order to achieve thinness and maintain a weight that is substantially lower than expected for their height and age (American Psychiatric Association, 2013). A distorted body image leads youth with anorexia to perceive themselves as "fat" despite their emaciated appearance, and they continue to lose weight (Gila, Castro, Cesena, & Toro, 2005; Hagman et al., 2015). Anorexia affects about 2% of girls 19 and younger; however, many more girls show similar poor eating behaviors (Smink, van Hoeken, & Hoek, 2013; Smink, van Hoeken, Oldehinkel, & Hoek, 2014).

Adolescents' rapidly changing physique is sometimes accompanied by body dissatisfaction and a distorted body image.
iStock.com/ronstik

Bulimia nervosa is characterized by recurrent episodes of *binge eating*—consuming an abnormally large amount of food (thousands of calories) in a single sitting coupled with a feeling of being out of control—followed by *purging*, inappropriate behavior designed to compensate for the binge, such as vomiting, excessive exercise, or use of laxatives (American Psychiatric Association, 2013). Individuals with bulimia nervosa experience extreme dissatisfaction with body image and attempt to lose weight, but they tend to have a body weight that is normal or high-normal (Golden et al., 2015). Bulimia is more common than anorexia, affecting between 1% and 5% of females across Western Europe and the United States (Kessler et al., 2013; Smink et al., 2014) and many more young people show symptoms of bulimia but remain undiagnosed (Keel, 2014).

Both anorexia and bulimia pose serious health risks. Girls with anorexia may lose 25% to 50% of their body weight (Berkman, Lohr, & Bulik, 2007). They may not experience menarche or may stop menstruating because menstruation is dependent on maintaining at least 15% to 18% body fat (Golden et al., 2015). Starvation and malnutrition not only contribute to extreme sensitivity to cold and to growth of fine hairs all over the body; they can also have serious health consequences such as bone loss, kidney failure, heart and brain damage, and even death (Golden et al., 2015; Reel, 2012). Side effects of bulimia nervosa include nutritional deficiencies. Repeated exposure to stomach acid causes tooth damage, ulcers and even holes in the mouth and esophagus, as well as an increased risk of cancers of the throat and esophagus (Katzman, 2005).

Anorexia and bulimia occur more often in both identical twins than in fraternal twins, indicating a genetic component (Bulik, Kleiman, & Yilmaz, 2016; Strober, Freeman, Lampert, Diamond, & Kaye, 2014). These disorders are more common in girls than boys, with a prevalence of about 6% compared with about 1%

(Raevuori, Keski-Rahkonen, & Hoek, 2014). Girls who compete in sports and activities that idealize lean figures, such as ballet, figure skating, gymnastics, and long-distance running, are at higher risk for disordered eating than are other girls (Nordin, Harris, & Cumming, 2003; Voelker, Gould, & Reel, 2014). Anorexia nervosa is associated with perfectionism and strict regulation of eating, and thus it may be viewed as a way to exert control and reduce negative mood states (Kaye, Wierenga, Bailer, Simmons, & Bischoff-Grethe, 2013; Tyrka, Graber, & Brooks-Gunn, 2000). Anorexia nervosa and bulimia nervosa are associated with altered neural activity in several limbic system structures and parts of the prefrontal cortex, responsible for aspects of emotion, rewards, and decision-making (Fuglset, Landrø, Reas, & Rø, 2016; Monteleone et al., 2018; Wang et al., 2017).

Anorexia nervosa and bulimia nervosa occur in all ethnic and socioeconomic groups in Western countries and are increasingly common in Asian and Arab cultures (Isomaa, Isomaa, Marttunen, Kaltiala-Heino, & Björkqvist, 2009; Keski-Rahkonen & Mustelin, 2016; Pike, Hoek, & Dunne, 2014; Thomas et al., 2015). In the United States, White and Latina girls, especially those of higher socioeconomic status, are at higher risk for low body image and eating disorders than are Black girls, who may be protected by cultural and media portrayals of African American women that value voluptuous figures (Smink et al., 2013). Some researchers suggest, however, that ethnic differences in eating disorders are not as large as they appear. Instead, eating disorders may exist in Black girls but remain undetected and undiagnosed because of barriers to diagnosis and treatment (Wilson, Grilo, & Vitousek, 2007). This is supported by research with adult women suggesting that the prevalence of anorexia nervosa is similar, but bulimia nervosa is more common in African American and Latina women than in White women (Marques et al., 2011). In addition, lesbian, gay, and bisexual (LGB) youth report higher rates of dangerous eating behaviors, such as fasting, using diet pills, and purging to control weight, than their heterosexual peers (Watson, Adjei, Saewyc, Homma, & Goodenow, 2017b). The experience of stigma and discrimination is associated with higher rates of disordered eating behaviors in LGB youth, whereas social support and connections to family, school, and peers are associated with lower levels of disordered eating (Watson et al., 2017b).

Anorexia nervosa and bulimia nervosa are difficult to treat. Research following adolescents over time suggests continuity in disordered eating patterns. In some studies, as many as three-quarters of adolescents diagnosed with an eating disorder continued to show symptoms 5 years later (Ackard, Fulkerson, & Neumark-Sztainer, 2011; Herpertz-Dahlmann et al., 2015). Standard treatment for anorexia includes hospitalization to remedy malnutrition and ensure weight gain, antianxiety or antidepressant medications, and individual and family therapy (Herpertz-Dahlmann, 2017). Therapy is designed to enhance girls' motivation to change and engage them as collaborators in treatment, providing them with a sense of control. Unfortunately, girls with anorexia tend to deny that there is a problem because they are unable to objectively perceive their bodies and they value thinness and restraint, making anorexia very resistant to treatment (Berkman et al., 2007). As a result, only about 50% of girls with anorexia make a full recovery and anorexia nervosa has the highest mortality rate of all mental disorders (Smink et al., 2013).

Bulimia tends to be more amenable to treatment because girls with bulimia often acknowledge that their behavior is not healthy. Girls with bulimia tend to feel guilty about binging and purging and are more likely than those with anorexia to seek help. Individual therapy, support groups, nutrition education, and anti-anxiety or antidepressant medications are the treatments of choice for bulimia nervosa (Hay & Bacaltchuk, 2007; le Grange & Schmidt, 2005). Individual and family-based therapy helps girls become aware of the thoughts and behaviors that cause and maintain their binging and purging behaviors, which decreases binge eating and vomiting and reduces the risk of relapse (Lock, 2011; Smink et al., 2013).

Binge Eating Disorder

It's not uncommon for people to use the word "binge" in reference to their eating (e.g., "I totally binged on pizza!"). Binge eating disorder, however, is not simply overeating. Binge eating is uncomfortable. It refers to eating an amount of food much larger than a similar person would eat in a discrete period (such as 2 hours). More important, it is associated with a sense of feeling out of control, as if one cannot stop or control what one is eating. The person eats more quickly, even when not hungry, and feels uncomfortably full. Binge eating typically occurs in private, out of embarrassment, and tends to be accompanied by a sense of guilt, shame, self-disgust, and depression afterward. Notably, the binge eating is not accompanied by compensatory behavior, such as exercising or purging, as with bulimia nervosa (Campbell & Peebles, 2014). Binge eating disorder is diagnosed when binges occur at least once a week for 3 months.

Binge eating disorder is the most prevalent eating disorder and may affect up to 5% of adolescents (Marzilli, Cerniglia, & Cimino, 2018). Although most research has examined adolescent girls, binge eating disorder may occur in 1% to 2% of boys. Similar rates of binge eating are seen in adolescents of all ethnicities (Rodgers, Watts, Austin, Haines, & Neumark-Sztainer, 2017). Binge eating disorder emerges more frequently in early adolescence and in emerging adulthood (Marzilli et al., 2018). Binge eating disorder often persists from adolescence into emerging adulthood and even into middle adulthood (Goldschmidt, Wall, Zhang, Loth, & Neumark-Sztainer, 2016).

Like other eating disorders, binge eating disorder is associated with internalizing thin body ideals, body dissatisfaction, dieting, and negative affect (Stice, Gau, Rohde, & Shaw, 2017). Experiencing negative emotions may increase the risk for binge eating, as high-calorie "comfort" foods may become more rewarding and enticing and binge eating may be rewarding and improve mood (Lavender et al., 2016). Binge eating is associated with chronic abdominal pain, obesity, diabetes, and other health problems associated with obesity, as well as anxiety, depression, and suicidality (Ágh et al., 2016; Forrest, Zuromski, Dodd, & Smith, 2017; Micali et al., 2015). Treatment for binge eating disorder addresses eating behaviors, patients' weight and shape concerns, and psychological conditions such as anxiety and depression (Berkman et al., 2015). A combination of medication and behavioral training can help adolescents with binge eating disorder manage emotions and learn long-term behavioral strategies for coping with strong emotions and drives.

Mortality

Although adolescence is a generally healthy time in which young people tend to report good or excellent health and low rates of illness, mortality, the death rate, rises in adolescence (Kochanek, Murphy, Xu, & Arias, 2017; U.S. Department of Health and Human Services, 2017). Adolescent mortality is largely influenced by the risky behavior that is common in adolescence and accompanies neurological development.

As shown in Figure 2.8, adolescent mortality showed an overall decline between 1999 and 2016 but has increased 12% since 2013. The increase in mortality is attributable to a rise in injury-related deaths. Specifically, about 70% of deaths of adolescents age 10 to 19 in 2016 were due to fatal injuries caused by unintentional injury (accident), suicide, and homicide. Each of these types of fatal injuries declined in prevalence from 1999 through 2013 and has since increased (Curtin, Heron, Miniño, & Warner, 2018). Boys and girls show similar patterns in death rates, with boys consistently showing about twice the mortality rate as girls.

As shown in Figure 2.9, older adolescents age 15 to 19 show higher rates of injury-related deaths than those age 10 to 14, but emerging adults age 20 to 24 show the highest rates of injury-related deaths. Fatal injuries—specifically, traffic accidents, suicide, unintentional poisoning, and homicide—remain the leading causes of death, respectively, into emerging adulthood.

Ethnic differences in mortality emerge in late adolescence, in both death rates and causes of fatal injuries. As shown in Figure 2.10, Black adolescents show dramatically higher rates of death by homicide than their peers. American Indian and Alaskan Native adolescents show the highest rates of unintentional injury and suicide as compared with other adolescents (Ballesteros, Williams, Mack, Simon, & Sleet, 2018). White non-Hispanic adolescents show higher rates of suicide than Black, Hispanic, and Asian

FIGURE 2.8

Total Injury and Noninjury Death Rates for Children and Adolescents Aged 10 to 19 Years: United States, 1999–2016

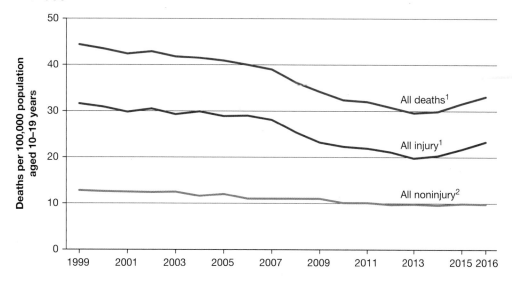

(Continued)

FIGURE 2.8   (Continued)

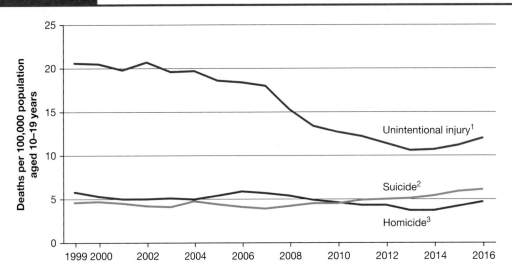

Source: Curtin et al. (2018).

FIGURE 2.9

Fatal Injuries in Adolescence and Emerging Adulthood, 1999–2016

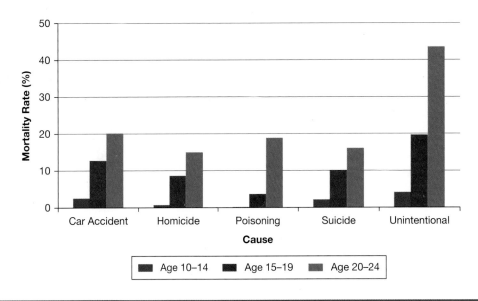

Source: Centers for Disease Control and Prevention (2017).

American and Pacific Islander American adolescents. Contextual factors contribute to ethnic differences in mortality rates during adolescence. Specifically, socioeconomic status and community factors place Black and American Indian/Alaskan Native youth, who are disproportionately at risk to live in low SES homes and communities, at risk for higher rates of mortality. Economic disadvantage is one of the most robust predictors of violence, especially in urban settings (Stansfield, Williams, & Parker, 2017). Violence

by Black adolescents may be fueled by insufficient home and neighborhood resources and exposure to violence and discrimination in the community (Rojas-Gaona, Hong, & Peguero, 2016). American Indian/Alaskan Native adolescents also experience high levels of poverty. The perception of discrimination, difficulty acculturating or integrating native customs and beliefs with popular culture, and feeling marginalized contribute to higher rates of suicide in American Indian/Alaskan Native adolescents (Jaramillo, Mello,

FIGURE 2.10

Fatal Injuries Among Youth Aged 10–19 Years, by Intent and Race, National Vital Statistics System, United States, 2013–2015

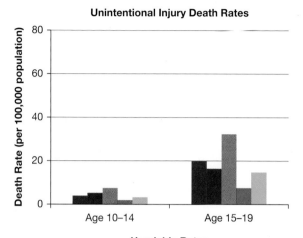

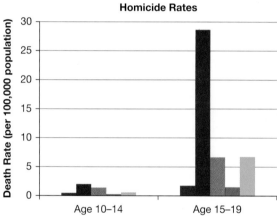

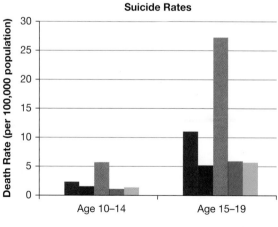

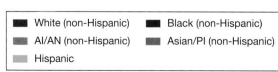

Source: Ballesteros et al. (2018).

& Worrell, 2016; Wyatt, Ung, Park, Kwon, & Trinh-Shevrin, 2015).

Health Promotion

The health behaviors established in adolescence tend to last well into adulthood. As a result, there is a growing emphasis on promoting healthy habits by improving access to health care and educating adolescents about health.

Health Care Access

Over the course of adolescence into emerging adulthood, young people become less likely to use health services. One recent study examined health care use by children, adolescents, and adults after the implementation of the Affordable Care Act in 2010, U.S. federal legislation designed to improve access to health insurance coverage (Spencer et al., 2018). From 2010 to 2016, rates of uninsured adolescents dropped from 8% to 5% in early adolescence (age 10 to 14) and 12% to 8% in late adolescence (age 15 to 18). The most dramatic changes were observed among emerging adults (age 19 to 25), dropping to 14% uninsured in 2016 from 34% in 2010. At all ages, but especially in emerging adulthood, young people were more likely to report having a regular source of medical care and having had a doctor or provider visit and in the past years, and they were less likely to report having unmet health needs in 2016 than in 2010. These findings suggest that improving access to health care can improve young people's use of health resources, with benefits for their health.

There are large economic disparities in health care access. Adolescents of color, especially those from low SES homes and communities, experience more difficulties with health care access than White adolescents (Yoshikawa, Aber, & Beardslee, 2012). Recent research suggests that sexual minority adolescents may be less likely to use health services than their heterosexual peers. For example, in one study, males who reported same-sex, bisexual, and questioning orientations (collectively referred to as sexual minority adolescents) were three times as likely as heterosexual males to report unmet medical needs in the past year (Luk, Gilman, Haynie, & Simons-Morton, 2017). Girls with a same-sex, bisexual, or questioning orientation were nearly twice as likely to have no routine checkup in the past year relative to heterosexual adolescents. Sexual minority adolescents are more likely than their heterosexual peers to report concerns discussing sexuality with health care providers (Fuzzell, Fedesco, Alexander, Fortenberry, & Shields, 2016). Some sexual minority adolescents report the sense that doctors seem uncomfortable discussing sexuality with them and feel isolated by noninclusive language used in the

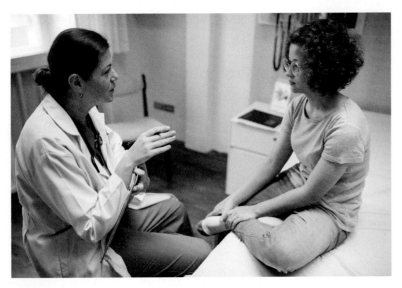

Health care providers can play an important role in promoting adolescents' health literacy.
iStock.com/Rawpixel

office and in conversations. Overall, physicians tend to discuss sexual behaviors and attractions rarely relative to other physical health topics, regardless of their patients' sexual orientation (Fuzzell, Shields, Alexander, & Fortenberry, 2017). In fact, communication about sexual topics tends to most frequently mention contraception and rarely discusses sexual attractions and orientations. Health care providers may miss out on important opportunities for helping the young people they treat.

Health Literacy

Adolescents' conceptions of health and health-related attitudes are important influences on their behaviors and have implications for health in adulthood (Michaelson, Pickett, Vandemeer, Taylor, & Davison, 2016). **Health literacy** refers to the knowledge, skills, and attitudes about health and the ability to obtain, process, and understand health information to make appropriate health decisions (Ghaddar, Valerio, Garcia, & Hansen, 2012; Manganello, 2008). Health literacy holds implications for individuals' ability to influence their own and others' health. For example, individuals with low levels of health literacy show poorer health (Peralta, Rowling, Samdal, Hipkins, & Dudley, 2017).

Adolescents and adults may conceptualize health in different ways. Adults often evaluate health based on the presence or absence of self-limiting health problems, but adolescents may emphasize different factors (Peralta et al., 2017). Adolescents tend to focus on specific behaviors and psychological states such as physical activity, nutrition, sense of well-being, and specific behaviors such as not smoking. For example, one study of Canadian adolescents born between 1995 and 2002 suggested that they viewed good health as individualized, different for everyone (Michaelson et al., 2016). They tended to explain that good health is subjective. Specifically, how one felt about one's health state and behaviors was considered fundamental in determining one's health. In this study, the majority of adolescents reported that their health was "good" or "excellent," despite often engaging in unhealthy behaviors, in line with the theme expressed by one participant: "You can be healthy without always being healthy." Adolescents may not accurately access their health.

Educators who seek to improve health literacy are challenged with teaching adolescents the basics of health, how their bodies work, and how to promote health, while balancing adolescents' preferred individualized views of health (Peralta et al., 2017). A customized view of health, recognizing that there are individual differences among adolescents, can help young people value individual differences in health needs and offer protection from unhealthy beliefs (e.g., that everyone's body should look the same) (Michaelson et al., 2016). However, a subjective one-size-does-not-fit-all approach to health can interfere with school and community health promotion efforts that educate students about universal influences on health, such as good nutrition and exercise, as well as the hazards of drug use. ●

REVIEW 2.5

1. What challenges do adolescents face in meeting their needs for nutrition and physical activity?

2. Identify influences on and correlates of overweight and obesity.

3. Distinguish among anorexia nervosa, bulimia nervosa, and binge eating disorder.

4. Discuss mortality and injury rates in causes of mortality in adolescence and emerging adulthood, including sex and ethnic differences.

5. How does health care access influence adolescent health and what is health literacy?

THINKING IN CONTEXT 2.5

1. How physically active were you as a child? Did you play a sport, ride a bike or skate, or play at a

playground? In what ways did your interests and activities change as you entered adolescence? Do your experiences match the finding that people often become less physically active in adolescence? Why or why not?

2. What are some of the influences that determine whether someone develops an eating disorder? Consider eating disorders from Bronfenbrenner's bioecological perspective (Chapter 1).

   a. How might adolescents' physical, cognitive, and socioemotional development influence their eating and health habits and the likelihood of developing an eating disorder?

   b. Identify factors at the microsystem and mesosystem levels that may influence the likelihood of developing an eating disorder. What role might interactions within the home, peer, and school context play?

   c. How might exosystem factors influence the development of eating disorders?

   d. What macrosystems are at play?

   e. Do you think these factors influence all three eating disorders (anorexia nervosa, bulimia nervosa, and binge eating disorder) in the same way? Explain.

APPLY 2.5

Imagine that you are a health teacher preparing a curriculum for middle school students.

1. What do they need to know about exercise and nutrition?

2. What should young adolescents know about eating disorders?

3. What other health information do you think is important to share?

4. How might you present this information?

5. Next, consider high school students. How might you present the material to older adolescents? Discuss similarities and differences in your approach.

CHAPTER SUMMARY

2.1 Summarize the physical changes that accompany puberty in boys and girls.

Puberty is the process by which adolescents become reproductively mature and it entails changes in growth and body shape, emergence of secondary sex characteristics, and, most importantly, maturation of primary sex characteristics. Adrenarche occurs prior to puberty, causing the adrenal glands to secrete low levels of testosterone that influence body growth and the development of body odor. Puberty is controlled by the hypothalamus-pituitary-gonadal axis, which influences and regulates hormone levels produced by the endocrine system. Puberty begins at about age 10 in girls and 12 in boys and the process lasts about 4 years, on average. Menarche, the onset of menstruation in girls, occurs on average at about age 13, with ethnic differences. Boys experience spermarche also at about age 13.

2.2 Describe adolescents' experience of puberty and its influence on their relationships with parents.

Girls' experience of puberty is influenced by their knowledge and expectations. The extent to which adolescents and parents discuss menarche and sexuality varies by context and culture. Less is known about boys' puberty, and their preexisting knowledge appears to influence their experience. With puberty, adolescents experience a shift in their preferred sleep schedule, or delayed phase preference. Sleep changes are also related to contextual factors, such as screen use and the home environment, and changes in sleep are associated with academic, health, and behavior problems. Puberty is associated with an increase in conflict and distance in parent–child relationships, especially between adolescents and mothers, that may vary with ethnicity and sex.

2.3 Examine the effects of pubertal timing on adolescents.

Girls who show signs of physical maturation before age 8 (or 9 in boys) are considered early-maturing, whereas girls who begin puberty after age 13 (or 14 in boys) are considered late-maturing adolescents. Adolescents who mature off-time relative to their peers are often treated differently, with consequences for their development. Early-maturing boys and girls show higher rates of risky activity, including smoking, abusing alcohol and substances, and displaying aggressive behavior, than do their same-age peers, perhaps because they tend to seek relationships with older peers. Early maturation is particularly challenging for girls. Early-maturing girls tend to feel less positive about their bodies and show higher rates of depression, anxiety, sexual harassment, and dating violence than do girls who mature on time or late. Early maturation has historically been viewed as advantageous for boys, but early-maturing boys may experience some internalizing and externalizing symptoms. Whereas late maturation has a protective effect on girls, it is associated with social and emotional difficulties in boys. Contextual factors, such as peers, the school context, and experience of stress, may amplify the effects of pubertal timing on behavior.

2.4 Analyze influences on pubertal timing.

Genetics plays a role in puberty, but puberty is a complex trait influenced by many genes that interact with contextual factors. Pubertal timing is similar in families, especially in identical twins as compared to fraternal twins. Some children are genetically programmed to experience puberty earlier than others. Heredity sets the boundaries of pubertal timing, but the onset of puberty is also influenced by individual and contextual factors such as ethnicity, nutrition and health, exposure to stress, parenting, and socioeconomic status. Puberty is triggered by achieving a critical level of body weight, specifically body fat. Increases in the standard of living and average BMI among children in developed countries over the last century have led to a lowering of the average age of puberty with each generation, known as the secular trend.

2.5 Discuss common health problems in adolescence and ways of promoting health.

The adolescent growth spurt demands energy as adolescents' caloric demands increase. Yet adolescents' diets tend to worsen. Although some adolescents engage in competitive sports, average levels of physical activity decline throughout adolescence and most adolescents in the United States do not meet the federal recommendations for physical activity. Obesity rates have increased over the past 4 decades, posing a variety of health problems. Several eating disorders become more common in adolescence, including anorexia nervosa, bulimia nervosa, and binge eating disorder. Mortality also rises in adolescence, most often due to a rise in injury-related death. Ethnic differences in mortality emerge in adolescence, in both death rates and causes of fatal injuries. Adolescents' health is also influenced by their access to health care. Over the course of adolescence, young people become less likely to use health services and there are large socioeconomic disparities in health care access. Health literacy refers to the knowledge, skills, and attitudes about health and the ability to obtain, process, and understand health information to make appropriate health decisions. Health literacy holds critical implications for adolescents' health and well-being.

KEY TERMS

adolescent growth spurt, 33

adrenarche, 32

anorexia nervosa, 47

binge eating disorder, 47

body mass index (BMI), 41

bulimia nervosa, 47

delayed phase preference, 36

eating disorders, 47

endocrine system, 32

estrogen, 32

gonadarche, 32

gonadotropin-releasing hormone (GnRH), 32

gonads, 32

health literacy, 52

hormones, 32

hypothalamus, 32

hypothalamus-pituitary-gonadal axis (HPG), 32

kisspeptin, 41

leptin, 41

melatonin, 36

menarche, 34

menstruation, 34

nocturnal emissions, 35

obesity, 44

overweight, 44

pituitary gland, 32

primary sex characteristics, 34

puberty, 31

secondary sex characteristics, 34

secular trend, 42

semen, 35

spermarche, 35

testes, 35

testosterone, 32

3 Cognitive Development

Learning Objectives

Chapter Contents

Adolescents think in new, very different ways than children. Their thinking gets faster, more streamlined, and becomes abstract. Adolescents can reason about ideas rather than focus only on objects. They can think about the nature of friendship—for example, what they value in a friend—and compare their friends' behavior to their values. Adolescents can take their friends' perspectives and use their understanding to provide meaningful support. Their skills in abstraction make adolescents more effective negotiators with parents, challenging parents in new ways that are sometimes surprising and frustrating. Advances in reasoning are, paradoxically, often accompanied by increases in risky behaviors that seemingly defy logic, such as dangerous skateboarding or acrobatic stunts. Adolescents are attracted to excitement, and they often act impulsively, seemingly without thinking, and make poor decisions. Frequently, adolescents' behavior does not reflect their reasoning abilities. Why the mismatch between thought and behavior? In this chapter, we examine adolescent thinking, the changes in the brain that underlie cognitive advances, and what they mean for adolescent behavior.

BRAIN DEVELOPMENT IN ADOLESCENCE

The radical changes in adolescents' thinking have their origins in brain development. The adolescent brain is a work in progress. Processes of neural development initiated before birth continue throughout childhood and increase in adolescence, leading to changes in brain structure and function that are reflected in adolescents' competencies and behaviors.

The Neuron

The brain is composed of cells called **neurons**. As shown in Figure 3.1, neurons have specialized structures that enable them to communicate with other neurons, sensory cells (including those responsible for vision and hearing), and motor cells (responsible for movement). Dendrites are branching receptors that receive chemical messages from other neurons (Markant & Thomas, 2013). The axon is a long tube-like structure that extends from the body of the neuron and carries signals to other neurons. When neural signals reach the tips of the axon, they signal the release of **neurotransmitters**, chemical messengers that cross the **synapse** or the gap between two neurons. There are many types of neurotransmitters that have varying effects on cognition and behavior. As they cross the synapse, neurotransmitters communicate with the dendrites of the next neuron (Carlson & Birkett, 2014). It is through this process that neurons communicate with other neurons. Neurons also communicate with sensory and motor cells. Some axons synapse with muscle cells and are responsible for movement. The dendrites of some neurons synapse with sensory cells, such as those in the eyes or ears, to transfer sensory information such as vision and hearing (Kolb, 2015).

Processes of Brain Development

The first neurons form early in prenatal development through a process called **neurogenesis**. A burst of neurogenesis continues into the first years of life in which the brain generates more neurons than we will ever need (Kolb, 2015). Over time, some of our neurons die, but neurogenesis continues throughout life, at a much slower pace (Spalding et al., 2013; Stiles et al., 2015). Adolescence is an important time for brain development because pubertal hormones lead to a second burst of neurogenesis,

---

FIGURE 3.1

The Neuron

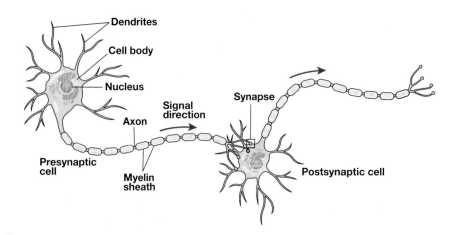

specifically in the **hippocampus**, which plays a role in memory and emotion. The rate of neurogenesis is about four times greater in adolescence than in adulthood (Hueston, Cryan, & Nolan, 2017). As the brain develops, new neurons are born in the hippocampus and migrate or travel along **glial cells** to the location of the brain where they will function (see Figure 3.2), such as the outer layer of the brain, known as the **cortex**. Glial cells are a second type of brain cell that outnumbers neurons 10 to 1 (Gibb & Kovalchuk, 2018). Glial cells nourish neurons and provide a physical structure to the brain (Zhang et al., 2010).

As new neurons migrate to the areas where they will function, they form synapses, connections with other neurons. This process is called **synaptogenesis** (Price, Jarman, Mason, & Kind, 2011). Additional synapses are created as dendrites grow and branch out (Kolb, 2015; Markant & Thomas, 2013). In early adolescence, the increase in sex hormones with puberty triggers a burst of synaptogenesis, resulting in a rapid increase of connections among neurons (Goddings, 2015; Sisk, 2017). Connections between the **prefrontal cortex** (responsible for planning and higher thinking) and various brain regions strengthen, permitting rapid communication, enhanced cognitive functioning, and greater behavioral control (Jolles, van Buchem, Crone, & Rombouts, 2011; Luna, Marek, Larsen, Tervo-Clemmens, & Chahal, 2015).

Another process, **myelination**, involves the glial cells producing and coating the axons of neurons with a fatty substance called myelin. Myelinated axons transmit neural impulses more quickly than unmyelinated axons (Markant & Thomas, 2013). Myelination predicts general cognitive function (Deoni et al., 2011). That is, with myelination, adolescents' thought and behavior becomes faster, more coordinated, and efficient (Chevalier et al., 2015). Myelination proceeds most rapidly from birth to age 4, first in the sensory and motor cortex in infancy, and continues through childhood into adolescence and emerging adulthood (Jessen, 2004; Qiu, Mori, & Miller, 2015). Myelination contributes to steady increases in the brain's white matter, especially in the prefrontal cortex and the **corpus callosum**, a thick band of nerve fibers that connect the left and right hemispheres, which increases up to 20% in size, speeding communication between the right and left hemispheres (Lebel & Deoni, 2018).

Brain development is not simply a matter of adding connections among neurons. It also entails **synaptic pruning**, reducing unused synapses in response to experience. Synaptic pruning occurs at an accelerated rate during adolescence and

FIGURE 3.2

Neural Migration

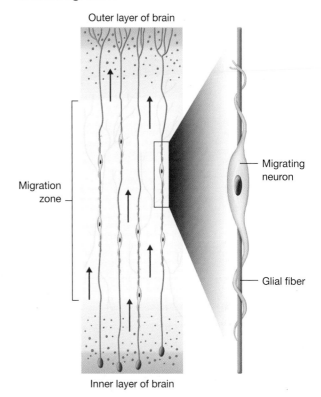

Neurons migrate along thin strands of glial cells.

Source: Adapted from illustration by Lydia Kibiuk, © 1995.

emerging adulthood (Giedd, 2018). Synaptic pruning decreases the volume of unmyelinated brain matter, thins and molds the prefrontal cortex, which is responsible for rational thought and executive function, and results in markedly more efficient cognition and neural functioning (Zhou, Lebel, Treit, Evans, & Beaulieu, 2015). These rapid changes and the corresponding shaping of the cortex make it likely that adolescence is a sensitive period for brain development (Fuhrmann, Knoll, & Blakemore, 2015); only in the first years of life are there as many rapid and significant changes.

Changes in Brain Structure and Function

The billions of neurons that comprise the brain are organized into structures that make up the cortex, the wrinkled outer layer of the brain, as well as subcortical ("below the cortex") structures. As shown in Figure 3.3, each lobe is specialized to a certain extent. In addition, the cortex is composed of two

FIGURE 3.3

The Human Brain

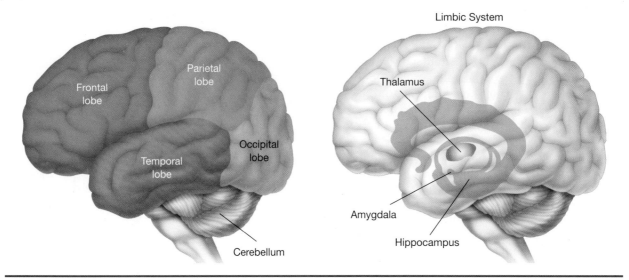

hemispheres that are joined by the corpus collosum. Although all four lobes appear on both hemispheres, the hemispheres are not identical. The right and left hemispheres are specialized for different functions, known as **lateralization**. For example, for most people, language is governed by the left hemisphere. Each hemisphere of the brain (and the parts of the brain that comprise each hemisphere) is specialized for particular functions and becomes more specialized with experience (Duboc, Dufourcq, Blader, & Roussigné, 2015).

Although it was once believed that brain development ended in childhood, advances in neuroimaging have revealed that brain structure and function changes dramatically during adolescence (Morris, Squeglia, Jacobus, & Silk, 2018). Research using functional magnetic resonance imaging (fMRI) scans has shown substantial growth and change in cortical and subcortical structures. For example, the **limbic system**, a set of subcortical structures responsible for emotion, undergoes a burst of development in response to pubertal hormones (Goddings et al., 2014; Sisk, 2017). The **amygdala**, a limbic structure that plays a role in fear learning, reward, aggression, and sexual behavior, increases in volume in childhood and peaks in growth at around 12 to 14 years of age. The hippocampus, also part of the limbic system, shows linear growth in adolescence, influencing learning, memory, and aspects of emotional function and stress reactivity. In contrast to the limbic system, which shows a burst of growth

in early adolescence, the prefrontal cortex continues to develop in emerging adulthood, into the mid-20s (Blakemore & Mills, 2014). The prefrontal cortex is the seat of reasoning, cognitive control, decision-making, and planning, suggesting that these sophisticated abilities continue to develop into emerging adulthood.

The overall volume of the cerebral cortex increases in early adolescence, peaking at about 10.5 years of age in girls and 14.5 in boys (Giedd et al., 2009). There are regional differences in the timing and pace of changes in brain volume. The parietal lobe and parts of the occipital lobe show volume reductions in late childhood and early adolescence as a result of pruning, whereas other parts of the cortex demonstrate an inverted "U" pattern of growth (Tamnes et al., 2017). For example, one analysis of people age 7 to 29 showed overall declines in brain volume over this period but increases in the surface area of the prefrontal and temporal cortex, followed by decreases in volume (Mills et al., 2016). Similar patterns of growth were discovered in a longitudinal analysis of participants from ages 3 to 19; the prefrontal cortex and other areas responsible for higher-order social cognitive and brain regulatory functions showed volume increases in early adolescence, followed by decreases in late adolescence (Vijayakumar et al., 2016).

Although the general trend is for an overall decline in cortical volume with pruning, the two main types of tissue in the brain, gray and white matter, show different developmental trajectories

FIGURE 3.4

Developmental Changes in Gray and White Matter Across Adolescence

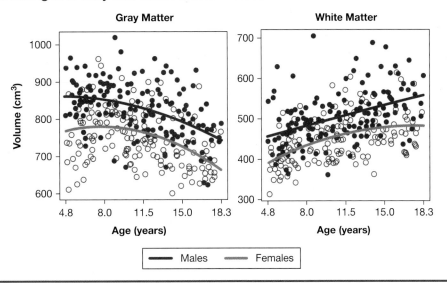

Source: Brain Development Cooperative Group (2012).

(see Figure 3.4). **Gray matter** includes unmyelinated axons, dendrites, glial cells, and blood vessels and tends to increase and reach its greatest volume in childhood, decreasing in adolescence and stabilizing in early adulthood (Mills & Tamnes, 2018). **White matter**, myelinated neurons, occupies about half of the brain; it increases linearly through adolescence, until about age 15, then is thought to decrease and stabilize in late adolescence and emerging adulthood (Lebel & Deoni, 2018). Some research suggests that gray and white matter may continue to develop well into adulthood. For example, observations of people age 7 to 60 as well as postmortem analyses suggested that a developmental trajectory of white matter increases until about age 43, followed by decline, and gray matter declines until age 40, followed by stability and degenerative (aging-related) decline (Sowell et al., 2003).

In addition to changes in structure, patterns of brain activity shift during adolescence. Functional connections between brain networks strengthen in early adolescence, leading to rapid increases in connectivity into middle adolescence, continuing into late adolescence, and slowing in emerging adulthood (see Figure 3.5, next page) (Dosenbach et al., 2010; Sherman et al., 2014). One study examined resting brain activity in males and females age 8 to 46 and found an exponential decrease in activity, halving it from adolescence to the age 35 and stabilizing in middle adulthood (Kundu et al., 2018). Although there was less overall activity, it was more focused and integrated rather than spread diffusely.

Experience and the Adolescent Brain

Throughout the lifespan, the brain retains **plasticity**, the ability to adapt its structure and function in response to environmental demands, experiences, and physiological changes (Nelson, 2011). The rapidly forming neural connections in adolescence make it especially plastic but also uniquely vulnerable to experience. Exposure to stress and substance use are two examples of risks to adolescent brain development.

Stress and Brain Development

Although exposure to stress has a detrimental effect on neurogenesis in adults, the effect on adolescents is less well studied. Research with rodents suggests that exposure to stress during adolescence may reduce neurogenesis in the hippocampus with potentially long-lasting effects for cognitive function (Hueston et al., 2017). Moreover, adolescents may be uniquely vulnerable to stress because the adolescent brain, especially the hippocampus, amygdala, and prefrontal cortex, is particularly sensitive to stress hormones (Romeo, 2017). Exposure to stress hormones is associated with reduced volume, reduced dendritic growth, and atrophy of dendrites and thereby synapses (Romeo, 2017; Tottenham & Galván, 2016).

Socioeconomic status is an important contextual factor associated with brain development from childhood through adolescence. In one cross-sectional study of 1,099 individuals aged 3 to 20 years, the

FIGURE 3.5

Connectivity Maturation in Adolescence and Emerging Adulthood

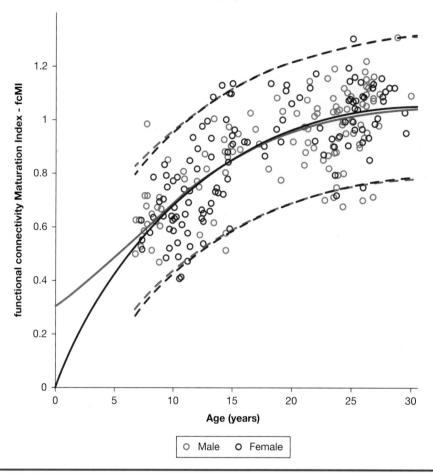

Source: Dosenbach et al. (2010).

Note: See source for more information on the graph details.

number of years of parental education was associated with larger cortical surface area in many brain regions involved in language, reading, social cognition, executive function, and spatial skills (Noble et al., 2015). Another study with participants aged 5 to 18 years showed an interaction between socioeconomic status (SES) and age on gray matter volume in the hippocampus and regions of the frontal and temporal lobes (Noble, Houston, Kan, & Sowell, 2012). As shown in Figure 3.6, in late adolescence, individuals with the highest SES show relatively larger volumes in the left inferior frontal gyrus (which has been implicated in the development of both phonologic and semantic processing, critical to language and reading ability), and the left superior temporal gyrus (related to the development of phonologic skill). SES disparities in volume development in these two regions increase with age, perhaps reflecting differences in language exposure over time, or the cumulative effect of home and school differences. These findings are based on cross-sectional analyses of a small sample, so

causality cannot be determined and additional research is needed to confirm these patterns of change. However, it appears that contextual factors such as exposure to stress and SES hold implications for brain development in adolescence.

Substance Use and Brain Development

In addition to stress, the adolescent brain is sensitive to the effects of substance use. Specifically, cross-sectional and longitudinal studies have shown abnormal gray and white matter trajectories in adolescent alcohol and substance users (Spear, 2018; Squeglia & Gray, 2016). In one prospective 8-year study of youth ages 12 to 24, those who transitioned to heavy drinking showed accelerated decreases in gray matter volume than light and nondrinkers (particularly in frontal and temporal regions) and attenuated increases in white matter volume over the follow-up, even after controlling for marijuana

FIGURE 3.6

Socioeconomic Status and Brain Development

(A)

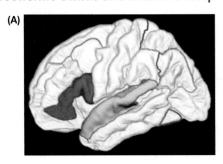

(B)

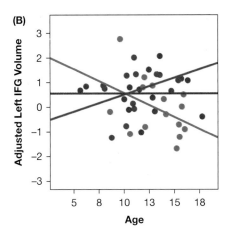

(C)

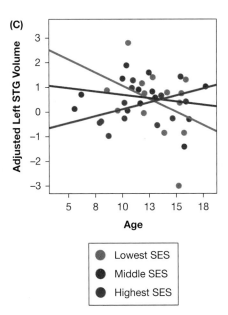

● Lowest SES
● Middle SES
● Highest SES

SES differences in brain development occur over childhood and adolescence. Adolescents from low SES homes show lower volume in the left inferior frontal gyrus (implicated in the development of both phonologic and semantic processing, critical to language and reading ability) and in the left superior temporal gyrus (related to the development of phonologic skill) compared with adolescents from high SES homes.

Source: Noble et al. (2012).

Longitudinal research suggests that marijuana use is harmful to the adolescent brain.
Tunatura/Shutterstock.com

and other substance use (Squeglia et al., 2015). This is consistent with other findings that heavy-drinking adolescents and emerging adults have systematically thinner and lower volume in the prefrontal cortex, attenuated white matter development, and altered neural activity, suggesting a toxic effect of consuming alcohol in large quantities on brain development (Cservenka & Brumback, 2017).

Marijuana use during adolescence is also associated with abnormalities in brain structure and patterns of activity and function (Takagi, Youssef, & Lorenzetti, 2016). Longitudinal data indicate that self-reported persistent marijuana use between 13 and 15 years is associated with a significant decline in IQ and the longer the period of use, the greater the decline in IQ (Meier et al., 2012). A recent longitudinal study tracked heavy-marijuana-using youth who also engaged in alcohol use from age 16 to 19 (Jacobus et al., 2015). Heavy marijuana users showed worsening performance on several cognitive domains when compared to nonusing youth, including worse performance on tests of complex attention, memory, processing speed, and visuospatial functioning. Earlier onset of marijuana use was associated with poorer processing speed and executive functioning by age 19, suggesting that initiation of marijuana use during early adolescence (before age 16) may be more harmful to the developing brain than later initiation (Jacobus et al., 2015). Research has consistently shown that recreational cannabis use before the age of 18 has been linked to gray matter atrophy (Battistella et al., 2014).

Brain Development and Behavior

We have seen that the limbic system, responsible for emotion, undergoes a burst of development well before the prefrontal cortex, responsible for judgment and executive control (Sisk, 2017). Full development entails the prefrontal cortex catching up to the early-developing limbic system. According to the

dual systems model, the different developmental timetables for these structures can account for many "typical" adolescent behaviors (Mills et al., 2014; Shulman et al., 2016). Let's take a closer look at how these changes influence adolescents' thought and behavior.

Socioemotional Perception

Parents often wonder whether they are speaking in a foreign language when their teens unexpectedly break off a conversation and storm away or when conflict arises over seemingly innocuous events. However, in a way, parents *are* speaking in a foreign language because adolescents' brains do not always lead them to accurately assess situations. Adolescents have difficulty identifying some emotions depicted in facial expressions. Specifically, in studies in which both adults and adolescents are shown photographs of people's faces depicting fear, adults tend to correctly identify the emotion shown in the photograph but many of the adolescents incorrectly identify the emotion as anger (Yurgelun-Todd, 2007). Why? fMRI scans indicate that when adults view facial expressions, both their limbic system and prefrontal cortex are active. Scans of adolescents' brains, however, reveal a highly active limbic system but relatively inactive prefrontal cortex relative to adults, suggesting that adolescents experience emotional activation with relatively little executive processing in response to facial stimuli indicating fear (Yurgelun-Todd, 2007).

When faced with emotionally arousing contexts and stimuli, adolescents tend to show exaggerated activity in the amygdala relative to adults and fewer functional connections between the prefrontal cortex and amygdala, suggesting that adolescents experience more emotional arousal yet less cortical processing and control than adults (Blakemore & Mills, 2014). The ability to control responses to emotionally triggering stimuli develops independently and after the ability to reason about neutral stimuli (Aïte et al., 2018). Generally, amygdala volume increases more in adolescent males than females (Dumontheil, 2016). It seems that adolescents are wired to experience strong emotional reactions and to misidentify emotions in others' facial expressions, which can make communication and social interactions difficult.

Generally speaking, performance on tasks measuring sensitivity to facial expressions improves steadily during the first decade of life but dips in early adolescence, increasing in late adolescence into emerging adulthood (Motta-Mena & Scherf, 2017). For example,

Although adolescents may find it difficult to process adult faces, they are better able to read the emotions of their peers.
iStock.com/SDI Productions

research with people ages 7 to 37 reveals developmental changes in brain activation with facial processing, with activity in parts of the frontal cortex increasing over childhood, then decreasing in early adolescence, and increasing again in late adolescence continuing into emerging adulthood (Cohen Kadosh, Johnson, Dick, Cohen Kadosh, & Blakemore, 2013). Face recognition, memory for faces, shows a similar pattern (Lawrence, Campbell, & Skuse, 2015). However, recent research suggests that adolescents are better able to process peer faces than adult faces, especially faces with a pubertal status similar to their own (Picci & Scherf, 2016). As the young adolescent's body prepares for sexual maturity, the brain's face processing system may become calibrated toward peers, potential reproductive partners, rather than caregivers.

Reward Perception

Most adults look back on their own adolescence and recall engaging in activities that included an element of risk or were even outright dangerous, such as racing bikes off ramps to soar through the air or driving at fast speeds. Risk-taking and adolescence go hand in hand, and the brain plays a large part in such behavior. In early adolescence, the balance of neurotransmitters shifts. At 9 to 10 years of age, the prefrontal cortex and limbic system experience a marked shift in levels of serotonin and dopamine, neurotransmitters that are associated with impulsivity, novelty seeking, and reward salience (Luna et al., 2015; Mills et al., 2014). Sensitivity to rewards peaks at the same time as adolescents experience difficulty with response inhibition, the ability to control a response. A heightened response to motivational cues coupled with immature behavioral control results in a bias toward immediate goals rather than long-term consequences (van Duijvenvoorde, Peters, Braams, & Crone, 2016). The shift is larger for boys than girls and is thought to make potentially rewarding stimuli even more rewarding for teens (Steinberg, 2008). As a result, risky situations, those that entail an element of danger, become enticing and experienced as thrills (Spielberg, Olino, Forbes, & Dahl, 2014). Adolescents may find themselves drawn to extreme sports, for example, enjoying the high and element of the unknown when they direct their skateboard into the air for a daring turn. These same mechanisms, adolescents' attraction to novelty and enhanced sensitivity to immediate rewards, serve to increase their vulnerability to the lure of drugs and alcohol (Bava & Tapert, 2010; Geier, 2013).

Developmental shifts in risky behavior are common among adolescents around the world (Duell et al., 2018). For example, one study examined adolescents in 11 countries in Africa, Asia, Europe, and the Americas and found that sensation seeking increased in preadolescence, peaked at around age 19, and declined thereafter (Steinberg et al., 2018). Risky activity is thought to decline in late adolescence in part because of increases in adolescents' self-regulatory capacities and the capacities for long-term planning that accompany maturation of the frontal cortex (Dumontheil, 2016). However, the imbalance between frontal and limbic activity and fine-tuning of behavioral control continues into emerging adulthood (Giedd, 2018).

Contextual factors, such as adult supervision, exposure to stressors, and impoverished communities, influence adolescents' brain development and hence their propensities for risk-taking (Scott, Duell, & Steinberg, 2018; Smith, Chein, & Steinberg, 2013; Tottenham & Galván, 2016). For example, one study of Australian adolescents revealed that neighborhood socioeconomic disadvantage was associated with altered brain development from early to late adolescence (Whittle et al., 2017). Positive parenting reduced the effects of family and neighborhood disadvantage, supporting the role of contextual factors as influences—risk and protective factors—for neural development. This conclusion is supported by other research suggesting that parenting influences the neural circuitry governing emotion (Morris, Criss, Silk, & Houltberg, 2017).

Decision-Making

Advances in cognition permit adolescents to engage in more complex thinking and approach decision-making in more sophisticated ways than children. Under laboratory conditions, adolescents are capable of demonstrating rational decision-making that is in line with their goals and is comparable to that of adults (Reyna & Rivers, 2008). For example,

comparisons of adolescents and adults' decisions on hypothetical dilemmas—such as whether to engage in substance use, have surgery, have sex, or drink and drive—show that adolescents and adults generate similar consequences to each decision option, spontaneously mention similar risks and benefits of each option, and rate the harmfulness of risks in similar ways (Furby & Beyth-Marom, 1992; Halpern-Felsher & Cauffman, 2001; Reyna & Farley, 2006). However, laboratory studies of decision-making usually present adolescents with hypothetical dilemmas that are very different from the everyday decisions they face.

Everyday decisions have personal relevance, require quick thinking, are emotional, and often are made in the presence and influence of others. Recall the developmental mismatch described by the dual systems model. Adolescents often feel strong emotions and impulses that they may be unable to regulate, due to the still-immature condition of their prefrontal cortex (Cohen & Casey, 2017). Therefore, laboratory studies of decision-making are less useful in understanding how young people compare with adults when they must make choices that are important or occur in stressful situations in which they must rely on experience, knowledge, and intuition (Steinberg, 2013). When faced with unfamiliar, emotionally charged situations, spur-of-the moment decisions, pressures to conform, poor self-control, and risk and benefit estimates that favor good short-term and bad long-term outcomes, adolescents tend to reason more poorly than adults (Albert, Chein, & Steinberg, 2013; Breiner et al., 2018). Adolescents are susceptible to risk-taking in situations of heightened emotional arousal (Figner, Mackinlay, Wilkening, & Weber, 2009; Mills et al., 2014).

Adolescents are more approach oriented to positive consequences and less responsive to negative consequences than are adults (Cauffman et al., 2010; Javadi, Schmidt, & Smolka, 2014). We have seen that adolescents are neurologically more sensitive to rewards than adults. Adolescents tend to place more importance on the potential benefits of decisions (e.g., social status, pleasure) than on the potential costs or risks (e.g., physical harm, short- and long-term health issues) (Javadi et al., 2014; Shulman & Cauffman, 2013). In the presence of rewards, adolescents show heightened activity in the brain systems that support reward processing and reduced activity in the areas responsible for inhibitory control, compared with adults (Paulsen, Hallquist, Geier, & Luna, 2014; Smith, Steinberg, Strang, & Chein, 2015). Risky activity is thought to decline in late adolescence in part because of increases in adolescents' self-regulatory capacities and their capacities for long-term planning that accompany maturation of the frontal cortex (Albert et al., 2013; Casey, 2015).

REVIEW 3.1

1. Identify the parts of the neuron.

2. What are four processes of neural development?

3. How do brain volume and patterns of brain activity shift in adolescence?

4. What are some of the effects of brain development on behavior?

5. List examples to illustrate the adolescent brain's vulnerability.

THINKING IN CONTEXT 3.1

1. How might the contexts in which we live—features of our home, school, peer, or neighborhood contexts—influence brain development in positive and negative ways? Provide three examples.

2. How might SES be associated with brain development? Explain your reasoning.

APPLY 3.1

As a child, Raul visited the local playground nearly every day. He loved the swings, especially swinging higher than the other kids. The monkey bars, however, were his favorite. Raul would climb to the top, holding on to the highest bar. Now at age 14, Raul can balance on the top bar, grasping only at air. He prefers climbing the fire escape on his building where he climbs to the roof and balances on the edge, six stories above the street. Raul saw his friend, Joaquin, jump from the rooftop to the rooftop next door, like Spiderman. "What a rush!" Joaquin shouts. Raul takes a deep breath and jumps across.

Consider the effects of brain development on behavior. Specifically, how can the processes and correlates of adolescent brain development account for Raul and Joaquin's behavior?

COGNITIVE-DEVELOPMENTAL THEORY

Brain development underlies all of the cognitive change adolescents experience. Explanations of process of cognitive change vary. Some developmental theorists emphasize abrupt cognitive changes, while others argue that the changes are much more gradual, as we discuss in the following sections.

Piaget's Cognitive-Developmental Theory

Piaget viewed children and adolescents as active participants in their own development. Individuals actively engage the world and through those interactions organize what they learn in ways that are uniquely theirs. Piaget proposed that individuals naturally strive to achieve a sense of cognitive equilibrium in which their thinking reflects the outside world. Because we constantly encounter new stimulation and information, this state of cognitive equilibrium is rare and fleeting. The drive for equilibrium and the discomfort that accompanies disequilibrium propel individuals though four stages of cognitive development from infancy through adolescence. With each advancing stage, individuals employ more sophisticated ways of thinking. Formal operational reasoning, the pinnacle of Piaget's stages, emerges in adolescence.

Formal Operational Reasoning

Fifteen-year-old Zuri spends much of her time learning about astronomy. She wonders about the existence of dark matter—cosmological matter that cannot be observed but is inferred by its gravitational pull on objects like planets and even galaxies. Zuri reads blogs written by astronomers and has started her own YouTube channel where she shares what she knows and comments on the best websites for teenagers who are interested in learning about the galaxy. Zuri's newfound ability and interest in considering complex, abstract phenomena illustrates the ways in which adolescents' thinking departs from children's.

In early adolescence, at about 11 years of age, individuals may enter the final stage of Piaget's scheme of cognitive development: formal operations. Formal operational reasoning entails the ability to think abstractly, logically, and systematically (Inhelder &

Formal operational reasoning influences adolescents' hobbies as they can now consider complex abstract phenomena.
Sergey Kamshylin/Shutterstock.com

Piaget, 1958). Whereas children in the concrete operational stage reason about specific things—that is, concepts that exist in reality, such as problems concerning how to equitably divide materials (e.g., dividing candies of different types into equal servings). Adolescents in the formal operational stage, however, reason about ideas, possibilities that do not exist in reality and that may have no tangible substance, such as whether it is possible to love equitably—to distribute love equally among several targets. Adolescents become capable of reasoning about their own thinking and even positing their own existence. Caleb, for instance, wonders, "I know I'm thinking. So, I'm thinking about my thinking . . . and I'm thinking about thinking about how I think. Now, how do I know that I am real? Am I just a thought?" The ability to think about possibilities beyond the here and now permits adolescents to plan about the future, make inferences from available information, and consider ways of solving potential but not yet real problems.

Formal operational thought enables adolescents to engage in **hypothetical–deductive reasoning**, or the ability to consider problems, generate and systematically test hypotheses, and draw conclusions. It is these abilities that underlie the scientific method (Chapter 1). The tasks that Piaget constructed to study formal operational reasoning test adolescents' abilities to use scientific reasoning to approach a problem by developing hypotheses and systematically testing them. For example, consider his famous pendulum task (Figure 3.7) (Inhelder & Piaget, 1958). Adolescents are presented with a pendulum and asked what determines the speed with which the pendulum swings. They are given materials and told that there are four variables to consider: (1) length of string (short, medium, long), (2) weight (light, medium, heavy), (3) height at which the weight is dropped, and (4) force with which the weight is dropped. Adolescents who display formal operational reasoning develop hypotheses that they systematically test. For example, they change one variable while holding the others constant (e.g., trying each of the lengths of string while keeping the weight, height, and force the same). Concrete operational children, on the other hand, do not proceed systematically and fail to test each variable independently. For example, concrete operational children might test a short string with a heavy weight, then try a long string and short weight. Solving the pendulum problem requires the scientific reasoning capacities that come with formal operational reasoning.

Evaluating Formal Operational Reasoning

Although Piaget believed that cognitive development is a universal process, individuals show varying abilities. For example, most adolescents and many adults do not display formal operational thinking in Piagetian

FIGURE 3.7

Measuring Formal Operations: The Pendulum Task

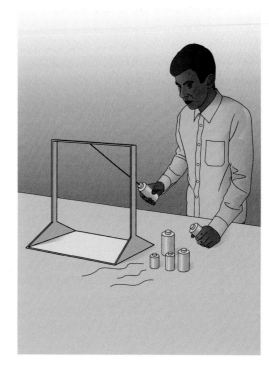

Children and adolescents are presented with a pendulum and are asked what determines the speed with which the pendulum swings. They are given materials and told that there are four variables to consider: Adolescents in formal operations systematically test each variable.

hypothetical–deductive tasks (Kuhn, 2013). Does this mean that they cannot think abstractly? Likely not. Piaget (1972) explained that opportunities to use formal operational reasoning influence its development. Individuals are more likely to show formal operational reasoning when considering material with which they have a great deal of experience. For example, completing college courses is associated with gains in propositional and statistical thought, skills that are often honed in college as well as measured in Piagetian tasks (Kuhn, 2012; Lehman & Nisbett, 1990). In one study in the early 1990s, adolescents from 10 to 15 years of age performed better on Piagetian tasks such as the pendulum task than adolescents had done over 2 decades before. The researchers attributed the difference to the fact that in France, where the studies were done, secondary education was less common in the earlier decades; therefore, adolescents had fewer opportunities to practice the reasoning measured by Piagetian tasks (Flieller, 1999).

Ultimately, the appearance of formal operational reasoning varies across individuals as well as within individuals because it is not consistent across intellectual areas. Instead, the appearance of formal operations varies with situation, task, context, and the individual's motivation (Birney & Sternberg, 2011; Labouvie-Vief, 2015; Marti & Rodríguez, 2012). Moreover, formal operational reasoning does not suddenly appear in early adolescence. Instead, cognitive change occurs gradually from childhood on, with gains in knowledge, experience, and information processing capacity (Keating, 2012; Moshman, 2011). Finally, most developmental scientists believe that we do not reach the peak of cognitive ability in adolescence. Most agree that cognitive development continues throughout adulthood.

Post-Formal Operational Reasoning in Emerging Adulthood

For Laniyah, a college junior majoring in biology, weighing hypotheses on evolutionary theory is easy. As she sees it, there is one account that is clearly more rational and supported by data than the others. However, like most emerging adults, Laniyah finds personal decisions much more difficult because many solutions are ambiguous with multiple options entailing both costs and benefits.

Post-Formal Reasoning

Although formal operational reasoning is the end point of Piaget's scheme, representing what he believed to be the most advanced form of reasoning, many researchers believe that there is much more to adult thinking than logical abstract reasoning. Researchers who adopt a cognitive-developmental perspective on cognitive development tend to agree that formal operations, Piaget's final stage of cognitive development does not adequately describe adult cognition. Instead, many emerging adults develop a more advanced form of thinking known as **post-formal reasoning**, which integrates abstract reasoning with practical considerations (Sinnott, 1998). Emerging adults who demonstrate post-formal reasoning recognize that most problems have multiple causes and solutions, that some solutions are better choices than others, and that all problems involve uncertainty. Attending college offers unique opportunities to develop advanced forms of reasoning.

When they enter college, individuals tend to view knowledge as a set of facts that hold true across people and contexts (King & Kitchener, 2015; Perry, 1970). Beginning college students tend to display **dualistic thinking**, in which knowledge and accounts of phenomena are viewed as either right or wrong with no in-between. Learning is often viewed as the collection of facts. Dualistic thinkers tend to have difficulty grasping that several contradictory arguments can each have supporting evidence. The entering college student may sit through class lectures, wondering, "Which theory is right?" and become frustrated when the professor explains that multiple theories each have various strengths and weaknesses.

With experience and exposure to multiple viewpoints, multiple arguments, and their inherent contradictions, emerging adults become aware of the diversity of viewpoints that exist in every area of study. Their thinking becomes more flexible and they appreciate that knowledge is not absolute, black or white, and right or wrong. **Relativistic thinking**, the next step in development, entails recognizing that most knowledge is relative, dependent on the situation and thinker (King & Kitchener, 2015; Perry, 1970). Relativistic thinkers recognize that beliefs are subjective, that there are multiple perspectives on a given issue, and that all perspectives are defensible, at least to a certain extent. At first, emerging adults in this stage may become overwhelmed by relativism—the great many opinions and options—and conclude that most topics are simply a matter of opinion and all views are correct. For example, they may conclude that all solutions to a problem are equally valid because it all depends on a person's perspective. The more mature thinker who displays **reflective judgment**, however, acknowledges the multiple options and carefully evaluates them to choose the most adequate solution. He or she recognizes that options and opinions can be evaluated—and generates criteria to do so (Sinnott, 2003). As shown in Table 3.1, reflective judgment is the most mature type of reasoning because it synthesizes contradictions among perspectives. Although reasoning tends to advance throughout the college years, ultimately few adults demonstrate reflective judgment (Hamer & van Rossum, 2017).

Social interaction is critical to the development of post-formal reasoning. Discussing and considering multiple perspectives and solutions to a problem can spur individuals to evaluate their own reasoning. When individuals are exposed to situations and reasoning that challenges their knowledge and belief systems, they may be motivated to consider the adequacy of their own reasoning processes and modify them as needed (Sandoval, Greene, & Bråten, 2016). Advancement to post-formal reasoning is associated with contextual factors—specifically, exposure to realistic but ambiguous problems with diverging information, as well as supportive guidance, such as that which is often a part of college education within Western cultures (Stahl, Ferguson, & Kienhues, 2016; Zeidler, Sadler, Applebaum, & Callahan, 2009).

Evaluating Post-Formal Reasoning

Given that post-formal reasoning is influenced by experience, not all emerging and young adults

TABLE 3.1

Post-Formal Reasoning

	UNDERSTANDING OF KNOWLEDGE	EXAMPLES FROM INTERVIEWS WITH EMERGING ADULTS
Dualistic thinking	Knowledge is a collection of facts, and a given idea is either right or wrong.	"… [T]heory might be convenient…, but …. The facts are what's there … and . . . should be the main thing." (Perry, 1970/1998)
Relativistic thinking	Knowledge is relative, dependent on the situation and thinker, and a matter of opinion and perspective.	"I really can't [choose a point of view] on this issue. It depends on your beliefs since there is no way of proving either one … I believe they're both the same as far as accuracy." (King & Kitchener, 2004, p. 6) "People think differently and so they attack the problem differently. Other theories could be as true as my own but based on different evidence." (King & Kitchener, 2004, p. 7)
Reflective judgment	Knowledge is a synthesis of contradictory information and perspectives whose evidence can be evaluated according to certain criteria.	"[When approaching a problem] there are probably several ways to do it. What are they? Which one's most efficient? Which one will give us the most accurate results?" (Marra & Palmer, 2004, p. 117) "One can judge an argument by how well thought-out the positions are, what kinds of reasoning and evidence are used to support it, and how consistent the way one argues on this topic is as compared with how one argues on other topics." (King & Kitchener, 2004, p. 7) "It is very difficult in this life to be sure. There are degrees of sureness. You come to a point at which you are sure enough for a personal stance on the issue." (King & Kitchener, 2004, p. 7)

Opportunities to practice post-formal reasoning vary with context and culture.
iStock.com/goc

and residential arrangements (Zhang, 1999). Experience in decision-making matters.

Some theorists argue that even in Western cultures, the most advanced level of post-formal reasoning (reflective judgment) may come only with graduate study and wrestling with challenging philosophical and practical problems (Hamer & van Rossum, 2017; King & Kitchener, 2015). Adults are more likely than adolescents and emerging adults to demonstrate post-formal reasoning, but not all adults reach the most advanced levels of reasoning (Commons & Richards, 2002; Sinnott, 2003). In fact, most do not. Similar to formal operational reasoning, people seem to show more mature reasoning when considering material and problems with which they have the greatest experience.

display it. For example, Chinese college students generally do not display the typical advancement from dualism to relativism to reflective judgment (Zhang, 2004). When compared with their U.S. counterparts, Chinese students tend to lack opportunities for making their own choices and decisions in many areas such as curricula, career choices, academic majors,

Although cognitive-developmental perspectives offer rich descriptions of how people think and what reasoning looks like across development, critics have argued that they provide little explanation of just how these changes occur (Brainerd, 1978; Halford,

1989). That is, what causes cognitive change? Most current research focuses on cognitive development changes that occur in information processing capacities, such as advances in attention, memory, and problem-solving—topics we discuss next.

REVIEW 3.2

1. What is formal operational reasoning and what are some criticisms of formal operational reasoning?

2. Differentiate dualistic thinking, realistic thinking, and reflective judgment.

3. What are some criticisms of post-formal reasoning?

• •

THINKING IN CONTEXT 3.2

1. In your view, is formal operational reasoning the norm in adolescence? To what extent do you think it characterizes the thinking of the average young adolescent at age 13, for example?

2. What factors might contribute to the development of formal operational reasoning?

3. Are these factors equally available or characteristic for all adolescents? Why or why not?

4. What conclusions do you draw about the nature of formal operational reasoning?

• •

APPLY 3.2

Patrick, Alicia, and Eduardo are working on a group project in a college-level psychology course. For their paper topic, they are tasked with writing a report on the most influential psychologist in history. Patrick states that there is one obvious answer. "The very first psychologist is Wilhelm Wundt because he opened the first experimental laboratory," Patrick explains. "It's a fact." Alicia disagrees, pointing to all of the theories in the class textbook: "All of these psychologists have created valuable theories. It's impossible to choose just one." Eduardo adds, "Yeah, there are lots of theories, but they all contradict each other. Let's find the theory that makes the most sense—whoever created that is the most influential psychologist."

1. What types of reasoning do Patrick, Alicia, and Eduardo display? Explain your choices.

2. Suppose you were the instructor in this class. How might you help your students advance in their reasoning?

• •

INFORMATION PROCESSING THEORY

Whereas Piaget's cognitive-developmental theory emphasizes abrupt stage changes in cognition, in which thought transforms quickly, information processing theorists pose a more gradual process of cognitive change.

Information Processing System

Even the casual observer will notice that adolescents are better at processing information than children. The information processing perspective poses that, throughout the lifespan, we manipulate information through a cognitive system composed of three mental stores: sensory register, working memory, and long-term memory. Figure 3.8 illustrates the information processing system. From childhood into adolescence, we get more proficient at using these stores.

FIGURE 3.8

Information Processing System

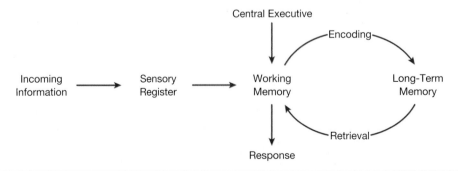

The **sensory register**, sometimes referred to as *sensory memory*, filters incoming sensory information. It holds incoming sensory information in its original form. For example, look at this page, then close your eyes. Did you "see" the page for a fraction of a second after you closed your eyes? That image, or icon, represents your sensory register. Information fades from sensory memory rapidly—sometimes in fractions of a second—if it is not processed. We take in much more sensory information than we process. Instead, much is discarded. But when we direct our **attention** or awareness to information, it passes to the next part of the information processing system, working memory.

Working memory is composed of a short-term store (sometimes called short-term memory) for holding information, a working space where information is processed or "worked on" by manipulating (considering), encoding (creating a memory), or retrieving (recalling), and the **central executive**, a control processor that regulates cognitive activities. Working memory is responsible for maintaining and processing information used in complex cognitive tasks (Gathercole, 1998). All of your thoughts—that is, all conscious mental activity—occur within working memory. For example, reading this paragraph, remembering what you have learned about memory in prior classes, and considering how this material applies to your own experience taps your working memory. Just as your thoughts are constantly changing, so are the contents of working memory. A core assumption of the information processing approach is the idea of limited capacity. We can only hold so much information in our mind, or in working memory, for so long. With development we get better at retaining information in working memory and use it in more efficient ways. The central executive directs the flow of information throughout the cognitive system (Baddeley, 2016). The central executive determines what is important to attend to (and when to stop attending to stimuli), combines new information with information already in working memory, and selects and applies strategies for manipulating the information in order to understand it, make decisions, and solve problems (Baddeley, 2012). Collectively, these cognitive activities are known as **executive function**.

As information is manipulated in working memory, it becomes more likely that it will enter long-term memory, the third mental store. **Long-term memory** is an unlimited store that holds information indefinitely. Information is not manipulated or processed in long-term memory; it is simply stored until it is retrieved to manipulate in working memory (e.g., remembering events and thinking about them). In adolescence, we amass a great deal of information, organize it in increasingly sophisticated ways, and encode and retrieve it more efficiently and with less effort.

Attention

Greater control over attention allows adolescents to deploy it selectively. Compared with children, adolescents show improvements in **selective attention**, focusing on one stimulus while tuning out others and remaining focused even as task demands change, as well as **divided attention**, attending to two stimuli at once (Hanania & Smith, 2010; Memmert, 2014). With increases in attention, adolescents are better able to hold material in working memory while taking in and processing new material (Barrouillet, Gavens, Vergauwe, Gaillard, & Camos, 2009). Improvements in the ability to monitor information and select the most important parts of it have important implications for classroom performance. Now students can concentrate on more complex tasks. For example, tenth-grader Leon can tune out his giggling friends to pay attention to what the teacher is saying. He can determine what is important and explain the material in his own words as he takes notes. He can shift his attention and focus on each speaker during class discussion and identify new ideas to add to his notes. Advances in information processing support adolescents' abilities to solve geometry problems, employ the scientific method, and solve other complex problems.

Working Memory and Executive Function

Neurological maturation leads to improvements in working memory throughout adolescence. Working memory reaches adult-like levels by about age 19 and continues to improve into the 20s (Isbell, Fukuda, Neville, & Vogel, 2015; Murty, Calabro, & Luna, 2016; Simmonds & Luna, 2015). Advances in working memory are largely driven by changes in the central executive. Advances in executive function permit individuals to effectively deploy their attention and memory to solve problems.

Adolescents become better able to determine what is important to attend to, combine new information with information already in working memory, and select and apply strategies for manipulating the information in order to understand it, make decisions, and solve problems (Andersson, 2008; Baddeley, 2016). Adolescents are more likely than children to use memory strategies such as organizing new material into patterns and connecting new material with what is already known (Camos, Barrouillet, & Barrouillet, 2018). Experience contributes to cognitive advances. Adolescents know more than children, permitting them more opportunities to associate new material with old and enhancing encoding and long-term memory (Keating, 2012). These advances in knowledge and strategy use result in more sophisticated, efficient, and quick thinking and learning. Now adolescents can retain more information at once, better integrate prior experiences and knowledge with new information, and combine information in more complex ways (Cowan et al., 2010; Gaillard, Barrouillet, Jarrold, & Camos, 2011). Specifically, brain development influences adolescents' growing capacities for executive function, permitting greater cognitive control and regulation of attention, thinking, and problem-solving (Carlson, Zelazo, & Faja, 2013; Crone, Peters, & Steinbeis, 2018).

An important aspect of executive function is **response inhibition**, the ability to control and stop responding to a stimulus (Carlson et al., 2013). The ability to control and inhibit responses advances through childhood but shows substantial gains in adolescence and increases through emerging adulthood (Crone et al., 2018; Zhai et al., 2015). Advances in response inhibition enable adolescents to adapt their responses to the situation. They can inhibit well-learned responses when they are inappropriate to the situation and thereby speed cognitive processing (Luna, Paulsen, Padmanabhan, & Geier, 2013). Response inhibition improves gradually in adolescence. Immature inhibitory processes can contribute to outbursts where it seems as if adolescents speak before considering their feelings or the potential consequences of their actions. The neurological changes that underlie response inhibition continue to develop into the 20s, and still-immature capacities for response inhibition are thought to underlie the risk-taking behavior common in adolescence (Luna et al., 2013; Müller & Kerns, 2015; Peeters et al., 2015).

Working memory and executive function improve with maturation and experience, but they are also influenced by contextual factors. For example, some research suggests that the experience of early life stress is associated with impaired inhibition in adolescence (Mueller et al., 2010). In addition, the development of executive function is associated with socioeconomic status, suggesting that adolescents in low SES homes and neighborhoods may experience greater challenges in developing the cognitive control capacities needed for good decision-making (Lawson, Hook, & Farah, 2018). A cross-sectional study of adolescents and emerging adults age 9 to 25 showed an inverse association of SES and executive function for individuals of all ethnicities (Last, Lawson, Breiner, Steinberg, & Farah, 2018). Adolescents from high income families show greater activation of the prefrontal cortex during working memory tasks than those from low-income families and prefrontal activity better predicted math achievement in high income adolescents (Finn et al., 2017). Contextual factors can also buffer the negative effects of low SES. For example, low SES adolescents who perceive greater academic support at school show better performance on executive function tasks, specifically inhibition, than their peers who perceive less support (Piccolo, Merz, & Noble, 2018).

Processing Speed

One important way in which adolescents' thinking improves is that it gets quicker (Kail, 2008). Older adolescents are able to process information to solve problems more quickly than younger adolescents, who are quicker than children. Processing speed reaches adult levels in middle to late adolescence, as early as 15 (Coyle, Pillow, Snyder, & Kochunov, 2011). Part of the gains in speed are biological in origin. Changes in the brain underlie many improvements in information processing capacities. As the structure of the prefrontal cortex changes, with decreases in gray matter and increases in white matter, cognition becomes markedly more efficient (Asato, Terwilliger, Woo, & Luna, 2010). Myelination underlies improvements in processing speed during childhood and adolescence, permitting quicker physical and cognitive responses (Silveri, Tzilos, & Yurgelun-Todd, 2008). Compared to children, adolescents not only show faster reaction speed in gym class, but they are also quicker at connecting ideas, making arguments, and drawing conclusions. Processing speed increases and

Just as adolescents' bodies become faster, their processing speed increases, enabling them to think more quickly and efficiently.
Sergey Novikov/Shutterstock.com

reaches adult levels at about age 15 and is associated with advances in working memory and cognition, especially reasoning (Coyle et al., 2011).

Advances in processing speed are also due to improvements in working memory and long-term memory. **Automaticity** is the amount of cognitive effort required to process the information; as processes become automatic, they require fewer resources and become quicker (Servant, Cassey, Woodman, & Logan, 2018). Automaticity is a function of experience. Adolescents become more efficient problem solvers as they get better at understanding how their mind works, or metacognition.

Metacognition

Not only are adolescents better at thinking than children, they are also more aware of their own thought process. Adolescents become capable of thinking about ideas and the nature of thinking itself, metacognition (Cowan et al., 2010; Gaillard et al., 2011; Murty et al., 2016). **Metacognition** refers to knowledge of how the mind works and the ability to control the mind. One study of adolescents and adults found that metacognitive ability develops dramatically between ages 11 and 17 (Weil et al., 2013). As metacognition develops, adolescents become better able to think about how their mind works—how they take in, manipulate, and store information (Ardila, 2013; van der Stel & Veenman, 2014). They can monitor their own thinking. They are better able to understand how they learn and remember and to choose and deploy strategies that enhance the representation, storage, and retrieval of information. Eleventh-grader Travis explains, "Studying for a biology exam is really different than studying for a history exam. In biology, I visualize the material, but when I study for history, I make up stories to help me remember it all." Travis illustrates the metacognitive skills that emerge in adolescence because he is able to evaluate his understanding, and he adjusts his strategies to the content by applying what helps him learn best. Adolescents' abilities to apply metacognition in real-world settings continue to develop into late adolescence and early adulthood.

The ability to think about one's thinking enables adolescents to reason about problems in new ways. By considering their own cognitive strategies and experimenting and reflecting on their experiences, adolescents begin to appreciate logical reasoning, which they increasingly apply to everyday situations (Ardila, 2013; van der Stel & Veenman, 2014). As adolescents become able to reason about reasoning, they show improvements in manipulating abstract ideas and engaging in the hypothetical–deductive thinking that is characteristic of scientific reasoning (Kuhn, 2013). The development of metacognition proficiency

is associated with gains in academic performance (van der Stel & Veenman, 2014).

REVIEW 3.3

1. Describe the parts of the information processing system.
2. Describe changes in and influences on working memory and executive function.
3. How do attention and processing speed change?
4. What is metacognition and how does it change during adolescence?

THINKING IN CONTEXT 3.3

Recall from Chapter 1 that different aspects of development interact. Consider connections between brain development and cognitive development.

1. Compare the changes that occur in the brain with those that occur in information processing abilities. How might cognition be influenced by physical development?
2. How might the changes in information processing abilities influence an adolescent's social interactions and socioemotional development?

APPLY 3.3

"Luciana pushes back on everything," complains her mother. "I say white, she immediately blurts out, 'black.' Sometimes I think she just can't stop the witty retorts to everything I say. Yet a lot of the time she makes sense, even when she's arguing against me."

1. Consider cognitive development from a parent's perspective. Provide examples of how advances in information processing abilities might influence parent–adolescent interactions, such as between Luciana and her mother.
2. What challenges and rewards might these pose for parents?
3. How have your cognitive advances influenced your relationships with your parents and other family members?

INDIVIDUAL DIFFERENCES IN INTELLIGENCE

So far, we have discussed processes of cognitive development that developmental scientists view as universal. For example, all healthy adolescents experience advances in processing speed and reasoning skills. Another perspective on cognitive development emphasizes identifying and explaining individual differences in intellectual abilities.

Measuring Intelligence

The first step in identifying individual differences in intellectual abilities is to define and measure intelligence. What is intelligence? Its nature has been debated for centuries. At its simplest, **intelligence** refers to an individual's ability to adapt to the world in which he or she lives (Sternberg, 2014). Intelligence is most commonly assessed through the use of **intelligence tests (IQ tests)**, which yield IQ scores that are intended to measure intellectual aptitude, an individual's capacity to learn.

The most widely used measures of intelligence today are a set of tests constructed by David Wechsler, who viewed intelligence as "the global capacity of a person to act purposefully, to think rationally, and to deal effectively with his environment" (Wechsler, 1944, p. 3). The Wechsler Intelligence Scale for Children (WISC-V) is designed for children aged 6 through 16 and the Wechsler Adult Intelligence Scale (WAIS-IV) is administered to individuals aged 16 and older. A 16-year-old adolescent may be administered either the WISC-V or WAIS-IV, based on the test administrator's judgment. Both tests are standardized on samples of individuals of various ages and who are geographically and ethnically representative of the total population of the United States, creating age-based norms that permit comparisons among people who are similar in age and ethnic background (Sattler, 2014).

The WISC-V and WAIS-IV are each composed of 10 subtests that comprise an overall measure of IQ as well as the following indices: verbal comprehension, visual spatial, working memory, and processing speed (Wechsler, 2014). The WISC-V also includes a fifth index, fluid reasoning (Wechsler, 2014) (Table 3.2). In addition to an overall IQ score, composite scores measure verbal and performance abilities. Verbal scores tap vocabulary and knowledge and factual information that is influenced by culture. The performance score tests nonverbal abilities, such as tasks that require the individual to arrange materials such as blocks and pictures and to complete mazes. Nonverbal tests are thought to be less influenced by culture. The nonverbal subtests require little language proficiency, which enables children with speech disorders and those who do not speak English to be fairly assessed. Knowing a person's IQ score tells you where that person stands in comparison with same-age peers (Bjorklund & Myers, 2015).

Cognitive Development and IQ

Changes in intelligence scores parallel cognitive development—specifically, information processing capacities. Working memory and processing speed are associated with intelligence in childhood, adolescence, and adulthood (Giofrè, Mammarella, & Cornoldi, 2013; Kail, 2000; Nussbaumer, Grabner, & Stern, 2015; Redick, Unsworth, Kelly, & Engle, 2012; Sheppard, 2008). Developments in attention, working memory, and processing speed predict gains in intelligence through late adolescence (Cuevas & Bell, 2013; Luttikhuizen dos Santos, de Kieviet, Königs, van Elburg, & Oosterlaan, 2013; Rose, Feldman, Jankowski, &

TABLE 3.2

Sample Items Measuring WISC-V and WAIS Indices

INDEX	SAMPLE ITEM
Verbal comprehension index	Vocabulary: What does amphibian mean?
Visual spatial index	Block design: In this timed task, individuals are shown a design composed of red-and-white bocks, are given a set of blocks, and are asked to put together the blocks in order to copy the design.
Working memory index	Digit span: Individuals are read lists of numbers and asked to repeat them as heard or in reverse order.
Processing speed index	Coding: In this timed task, individuals are shown a code that converts numbers into symbols and are asked to transcribe lists of numbers into code.
Fluid reasoning index (WISC-V only)	Matrix reasoning: Individuals are shown an array of pictures with one missing. They must select the picture that completes the array.

Van Rossem, 2012). The information processing skills that underlie intelligence, such as attention, working memory, and processing speed, are influenced by brain development.

Neurological development is linked with the development of intelligence. For example, brain volume and cortical thickness are positively associated with IQ in children and adults (Pietschnig, Penke, Wicherts, Zeiler, & Voracek, 2015; Ritchie et al., 2015). Likewise, meta-analyses have suggested that intelligence is associated with increased gray matter in parts of the brain responsible for processing sensory experiences (occipital and temporal cortex) and abstract cognitive processing (frontal cortex) (Basten, Hilger, & Fiebach, 2015). Research has also linked white, myelinated, matter with measures of general intelligence (Ritchie et al., 2015), largely through white matter's influence on processing speed (Penke et al., 2012) and working memory (Privado et al., 2014). Longitudinal research with adolescents from age 10 through 18 suggests that advances in IQ accompany an increase in the efficiency of brain networks (Koenis et al., 2018). Intelligence is thought to arise from the activity and interaction of brain regions in the frontal cortex, particularly the prefrontal cortex, responsible for executive function (Basten et al., 2015; Deary, Penke, & Johnson, 2010; Margolis et al., 2013). Recall that the prefrontal cortex undergoes a massive growth spurt in adolescence, which may contribute to advances in intelligence.

Group Differences in IQ

Examinations of large samples of children and adolescents have revealed a consistent and controversial finding of ethnic differences in IQ. African American children as a group tend to score 10 to 15 points below non-Hispanic White Americans on standardized IQ tests (Rindermann & Thompson, 2013). The IQ scores of Hispanic children as a group tend to fall between those of children of African American and non-Hispanic White descent, and the scores of Asian American children tend to fall at the same level or slightly higher than those of non-Hispanic White children (Neisser et al., 1996; Nisbett et al., 2013). However, average group differences are misleading because the overall distribution or pattern of scores among all children overlaps for children of all ethnicities. That is, there are more differences among African American and non-Hispanic White adolescents than between them. For example, at least 20% of African American students score higher on IQ than all other students, African American and non-Hispanic White (Flynn, 2008; Phillips, Crouse, & Ralph, 1998; Rindermann & Thompson, 2013). Like all facets of development, intelligence is influenced by dynamic interactions among individuals and their contexts.

Contextual Influences on IQ

SES is an important contextual factor associated with intelligence scores. In one longitudinal study of nearly

---

FIGURE 3.9

IQ Growth Curves, by Socioeconomic Status

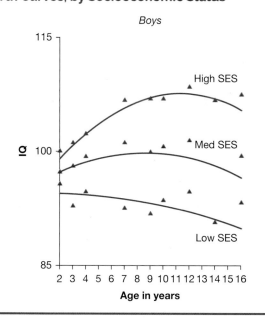

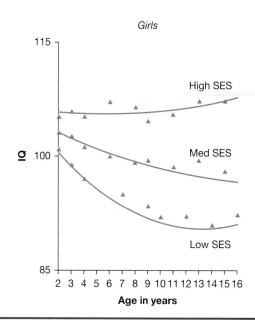

Source: von Stumm and Plomin (2015).

Adolescents from similar socioeconomic backgrounds tend to earn similar scores on IQ tests regardless of their race or ethnicity.
iStock.com/SolStock

15,000 U.K. children, SES was positively associated with IQ at age 2; children from lower SES backgrounds scored on average 6 IQ points lower (Figure 3.9). The difference nearly tripled by age 16 (to 15 points in boys and 17 in girls) (von Stumm & Plomin, 2015).

Research with U.S. children shows that those who are adopted from low SES homes to higher SES homes typically score 12 points higher than siblings who are raised by birth parents or adopted into lower SES homes (Duyme, Dumaret, & Tomkiewicz, 1999; Locurto, 1990). Children from similar middle class backgrounds tend to have similar IQ scores regardless of their race or ethnicity (Brooks-Gunn, Klebanov, & Duncan, 1996). In fact, ethnic differences are reduced and often disappear when socioeconomic differences are taken into account (Brooks-Gunn et al., 1996; Flynn, 2008; Ford, 2008; Rindermann & Thompson, 2013).

Why does SES matter? Contextual factors that accompany SES contribute to IQ. SES differences are accompanied by differences in living conditions, environmental stress, nutrition, school resources, stimulation, and life circumstances that influence IQ (Plomin & Deary, 2015; Turkheimer, Haley, Waldron, D'Onofrio, & Gottesman, 2003). The experience of discrimination influences cognitive and psychosocial factors related to IQ, such as self-concept, motivation, and academic achievement. Education and IQ interact dynamically. Exposure to education improves IQ. School provides children with exposure to information and ways of thinking that are valued by the majority culture and reflected in IQ tests. Yet IQ scores are a strong predictor of academic achievement. Adolescents with high IQs tend to earn higher-than-average grades at school and are more likely to stay in school (Mackintosh, 2011). Same-age children with more

years of schooling tend to have higher IQs than their less educated peers (Cliffordson & Gustafsson, 2008), and correlations between IQ and school achievement tests tend to increase with age (Sternberg, Grigorenko, & Bundy, 2001). In fact, IQ rises with each year spent in school, improves during the school year, between September and May, and drops over the summer vacation (Ceci, 1991, 1999; Huttenlocher, Levine, & Vevea, 1998). The seasonal drop in IQ scores each summer is larger for children from low SES homes (Nisbett et al., 2013). School itself provides children with opportunities to be exposed to information and ways of thinking that are valued by the majority culture and reflected in IQ tests. At the same time, the results of children's IQ tests influence the schooling that they receive because IQ tests serve as gatekeepers to gifted programs (Ford, 2008).

Alternative Views of Intelligence

Many researchers believe that there is more to intelligence than what IQ tests measure. If intelligence entails the ability to adapt to one's environment, it must include more than academic and analytical abilities. Researchers Howard Gardner and Robert Sternberg propose that intelligence takes many forms and intelligent people are able to adapt to everyday problems and situations.

Multiple Intelligences

A champion gymnast, elite musician, skilled painter, and excellent communicator have talents that are not measured by traditional IQ tests. Howard Gardner (2017) proposes that intelligence is best described as the ability to solve problems or create culturally valued products. Gardner's **multiple intelligence theory** describes eight independent kinds of intelligence, shown in Table 3.3. Each person is thought to have a unique pattern of intellectual strengths and weaknesses. A person may be gifted in athletics (bodily-kinesthetic intelligence), communication (verbal-linguistic intelligence), or music (musical intelligence), yet score low on traditional measures of IQ. The theory of multiple intelligences is an optimistic perspective that allows everyone to be intelligent in his or her own way, viewing intelligence as broader than book-learning and academic skills. If intelligence is multidimensional, as Gardner suggests, perhaps school curricula should target the many forms that

TABLE 3.3

Multiple Intelligences

INTELLIGENCE	DESCRIPTION
Verbal-linguistic intelligence	Ability to understand and use the meanings and subtleties of words ("word smarts")
Logical-mathematical intelligence	Ability to manipulate logic and numbers to solve problems ("number smarts")
Spatial intelligence	Ability to perceive the visual-spatial world accurately, to navigate an environment, and to judge spatial relationships ("spatial smarts")
Bodily-kinesthetic intelligence	Ability to move the body skillfully ("body smarts")
Musical intelligence	Ability to perceive and create patterns of pitch and melody ("music smarts")
Interpersonal intelligence	Ability to understand and communicate with others ("people smarts")
Intrapersonal intelligence	Ability to understand the self and regulate emotions ("self-smarts")
Naturalist intelligence	Ability to distinguish and classify elements of nature: animals, minerals, and plants ("nature smarts")

Source: Adapted from Gardner (2017).

intelligence may take and help students to develop a range of talents (Gardner, 2013).

According to Gardner (2017), each form of intelligence is biologically based and each develops on a different timetable. Assessing intelligence involves observing the products of each form of intelligence (e.g., how well a child can learn a tune, navigate an unfamiliar area, and learn dance steps). In practice, assessing multiple intelligences might entail multiple observations of a child in order to identify patterns of strengths and weaknesses and help them understand and achieve their potential (Gardner, 2016). This process is lengthy and may be nearly impossible to implement on a large scale (Barnett, Ceci, & Williams, 2006). The theory of multiple intelligences has led to a great deal of debate among intelligence theorists and researchers (Kaufman, Kaufman, & Plucker, 2013). Although the theory of multiple intelligences has been criticized as not being grounded in research (Waterhouse, 2006), neuroscientists have noted that each type of intelligence corresponds to specific neurological processes (Shearer & Karanian, 2017). The theory of multiple intelligences draws attention to the fact that IQ tests measure a specific set of mental abilities and ignore others.

Triarchic Theory of Intelligence

Similar to traditional views of intelligence, Robert Sternberg views it as the ability to adapt to the world (Sternberg, 1985). Specifically, he defines intelligence as a set of mental abilities that permits individuals to adapt to any context and to select and modify the sociocultural contexts in which they live and behave. According to Sternberg's **triarchic theory of intelligence**, there are three forms of intelligence that interact: analytical, creative, and practical (Sternberg, 2011). Individuals may have strengths in any or all of them.

Analytical intelligence refers to the ability to process information quickly and consider different solutions. It comprises information processing capacities, such as attention, information acquisition and processing, metacognition, and the ability to generate and apply strategies to solve problems. *Creative intelligence* refers to insightfulness (to display original thinking) and the ability to deal with novelty (to respond to new tasks efficiently). *Applied intelligence* influences how people interact with their surroundings: how well they evaluate their environment, selecting and modifying it and adapting it to fit their own needs and external demands. Intelligent people apply their analytical, creative, and applied abilities to suit the setting and problems at hand (Sternberg, 2011). Some situations require careful analysis, others the ability to think creatively, and yet others the ability to solve problems quickly in everyday settings. Many situations tap more than one form of intelligence.

Traditional IQ tests measure analytical ability, which is thought to be associated with school success. However, IQ tests do not measure creative and practical intelligence, which predict success outside of school. Some people are successful in everyday settings but less so in school settings, and therefore may obtain low scores on traditional IQ tests despite being successful in their careers and personal lives. In this way, traditional IQ tests can underestimate the intellectual strengths of some children. However, similar to multiple intelligence theory, the triarchic theory of intelligence is generally not used to measure adolescents' intellectual ability but remains a useful way of conceptualizing intelligence.

REVIEW 3.4

1. What is intelligence and how is it typically measured?

2. Describe contextual influences on group differences in IQ.

3. Compare multiple intelligence theory with the triarchic theory of intelligence.

. . . .

THINKING IN CONTEXT 3.4

1. What are some reasons why SES may be associated with IQ? How might we address these influences to aid adolescents?

2. Consider influences on IQ from a bioecological perspective. What microsystem and mesosystem factors contribute to adolescents' intellectual ability? Describe three exosystem factors that might influence IQ in adolescence. How might macrosystem factors influence adolescents' intellectual ability?

. . . .

APPLY 3.4

After 5 years of teaching high school, Octavia has decided to try something new. She knows that young people's thinking advances in adolescence. However, she has noticed that the students in her classes vary, with some much more advanced than others. Octavia believes that the differences in intelligence play a role in student performance. She would like to apply intelligence theory in her classroom. Provide advice. Specifically, address the following:

1. How do you define intelligence? What does it look like? How does an intelligent person behave or perform?

2. Apply your definition of intelligence in school settings. What should Octavia look for in class and out of class to determine a student's intelligence?

3. How should Octavia measure intelligence?

4. What can Octavia do to foster her students' intellectual ability?

. . . .

SOCIAL COGNITION

Adolescent development is inherently social. The physical, cognitive, and socioemotional changes of adolescence occur in a social world that influences and is influenced by adolescents' development. Adolescents' maturing cognitive abilities have special implications for **social cognition**, their thinking about people, social situations, and relationships.

Perspective Taking

Advances in reasoning and metacognition lead adolescents to understand themselves and others in new ways. Adolescents become better able to take others' perspectives, which has implications for social relationships (Carpendale & Lewis, 2015). According to Robert Selman (1980), **social perspective taking** ability follows a developmental path from extreme egocentrism in early childhood through mature perspective taking ability in late adolescence.

Similar to Piaget's ideas about cognition, Selman posed that individuals progress through several stages of social perspective taking. Children are often unable to separate their own perspective from others, believing that others hold their views. Preadolescents (age 8 to 10) tend to appreciate that others have different perspectives and consider that others' point of view offers a valuable window to interpreting their behavior. It is not until early adolescence (age 10 to 12) that individuals develop the abstract thinking needed to realize that other people can take *their* perspective. That is, adolescents become capable of **mutual perspective taking**, understanding that they take other people's point of view at the same time as others attempt to take their own point of view. Now adolescents can consider how their behavior appears to others (take a third person's perspective) and modify their behavior accordingly. By middle adolescence (age 12 to 15), **societal perspective taking** emerges and adolescents recognize that the social environment, including the larger society, influences people's perspectives and beliefs. Research has suggested that perspective taking ability develops from childhood into adolescence but may not closely follow the age-based timeline advocated by Selman. For example, Selman found that mutual perspective taking may emerge as early as 11 or as late as 20 (Selman, 1980). Other research suggests that the ability to use another's perspective in communication and decision-making continues to develop in late adolescence (Nilsen & Bacso, 2017).

Working memory is associated with perspective taking ability. Specifically, improvements in cognitive control influence social cognitive processing. For example, attending to another person's perspective when it differs from our own requires inhibiting or suppressing our own view, an effortful process that requires cognitive control resources in working memory (Kilford, Garrett, & Blakemore, 2016). A recent study showed that adolescents and adults were slower at tasks requiring perspective taking under conditions that use high levels of working memory (simultaneously remembering three 2-digit numbers) than when under low cognitive load (remembering one 3-digit number), suggesting that taking another's perspective is cognitively demanding (Mills, Dumontheil, Speekenbrink, & Blakemore, 2015). Research with 9- to 29-year-olds has shown that inhibitory control ability partly accounted for errors on a perspective taking task and above age-related variance (Kilford et al., 2016; Symeonidou, Dumontheil, Chow, & Breheny, 2016).

Advances in social perspective taking permit adolescents to better understand others as well as how they are perceived by others. Perspective taking is related to peer relations, friendship, and popularity (Nilsen & Bacso, 2017). Yet social perspective taking ability does not always influence behavior. One study of 12- to 17-year-old adolescents found that social perspective taking ability does not necessarily translate into use (Flannery & Smith, 2017). Similar to abstract thought, the ability to apply their understanding of other peoples' perspectives emerges gradually. Teenagers are prone to errors in reasoning and lapses in judgment, as evidenced by the emergence of adolescent egocentrism.

Adolescent Egocentrism

As adolescents get better at reasoning and metacognition, they often direct their abstract thinking abilities toward themselves. Although social perspective taking improves, it often develops slowly and even in a piecemeal fashion. When it comes to considering themselves, adolescents often have difficulty separating their own and others' perspectives. That is, adolescents find it difficult to distinguish their view of what others think of them from reality, what others actually think about them. They show **adolescent egocentrism**, a perspective taking error that is manifested in two phenomena: the **imaginary audience** and the **personal fable** (Elkind & Bowen, 1979).

The imaginary audience is experienced as self-consciousness, feeling as if all eyes are on them. Adolescents misdirect their own preoccupation about themselves toward others and assume that they are the focus of others' attention (Elkind & Bowen, 1979). In this way, the imaginary audience is an error in perspective taking. The imaginary audience fuels adolescents' concerns with their appearance and can make the slightest criticism sting painfully, as teens are convinced that all eyes are on them. The imaginary audience contributes to the heightened self-consciousness characteristic of adolescence (Alberts, Elkind, & Ginsberg, 2007).

Adolescents' preoccupation with themselves also leads them to believe that they are special, unique, and invulnerable—a belief known as the personal fable (Elkind & Bowen, 1979). They believe that their emotions, the highs of happiness and depths of despair that they feel, are different from and more intense than other people's emotions and that others simply do not understand. The invulnerability aspect of the personal fable may predispose adolescents to seek risks and leads them to believe that they are immune to the negative consequences of such risky activities as drug use, delinquency, and unsafe sex (Alberts et al., 2007).

Both the imaginary audience and the personal fable are thought to increase in early adolescence, peak in middle adolescence, and decline in late adolescence (Elkind & Bowen, 1979). Recent research suggests that adolescent egocentrism may persist into late adolescence and beyond (Schwartz, Maynard, & Uzelac, 2008). One study examined adolescents in 11 countries in Africa, Asia, Europe, and the Americas and found that sensation seeking increased in preadolescence, peaked at around age 19, and declined thereafter (Steinberg et al., 2018). Indeed, in one recent study, adolescents 13 to 16 showed similar levels of egocentrism as adults; they were just as likely as adults to believe that others could tell when they were lying and when they were nervous (Rai, Mitchell, Kadar, & Mackenzie, 2016). Moreover, for many adolescents (and adults), the audience is not imaginary. When posting to social media, many adolescents painstakingly consider their audience and play to them by sharing content to appear interesting, well liked, and attractive (Yau & Reich, 2018). ●

REVIEW 3.5

1. Define social perspective taking and describe the forms it takes in early and middle adolescence.

2. Differentiate between the imaginary audience and the personal fable.

• •

THINKING IN CONTEXT 3.5

1. What are some of the implications of advances in perspective taking for adolescents' relationships with friends? Romantic interests?

2. How might perspective taking influence the parent–adolescent relationship?

• •

APPLY 3.5

Rico's skateboard launched into the air, skidded down a railing, and landed cleanly on the sidewalk below—with Rico proudly on board. Certain that everyone has witnessed his success, Rico triumphantly pumps his fist in the air. He quickly takes a selfie holding his board and posts it online. Nearby, Mia perches on the fence, strikes just the right pose that's relaxed but flattering and cool, and snaps a selfie. "Ugh, everyone will think I look terrible," Mia laments, then plays with a photo filter and editor. She covers a few blemishes, contours her face, and whitens her teeth before uploading the photo to Snapchat.

1. Consider Rico and Mia's behavior from a social cognitive perspective. How might adolescent egocentrism account for their behavior?

2. What role might social media play in adolescent egocentrism? Alternatively, how might adolescent egocentrism be manifested in adolescents' social media activities?

· ·

CHAPTER SUMMARY

3.1 Discuss brain development in adolescence and its implications for behavior.

The brain is composed of neurons, cells that are specialized to communicate with other neurons, sensory cells, and motor cells. Processes of neural development include neurogenesis, synaptogenesis, synaptic pruning, and myelination. Puberty hormones trigger a burst of brain development, including increases in white matter and decreases in gray matter. Changes in the volume of the cortex, interconnections among neurons, and myelination influence the speed and efficiency of thought and the capacity for executive function. Adolescents' brains are plastic but also uniquely vulnerable to risks such as stress and substance use. According to the dual systems model, the limbic system undergoes a burst of development well ahead of the prefrontal cortex, and this difference in development can account for many common adolescent behaviors. Changes in the balance of neurotransmitters are associated with impulsivity and reward salience. A heightened response to motivational cues coupled with immature behavioral control results in a bias toward immediate goals rather than long-term consequences. When faced with unfamiliar, emotionally charged situations, spur-of-the moment decisions, pressures to conform, poor self-control, and risk and benefit estimates that favor good short-term and bad long-term outcomes, adolescents tend to reason more poorly than adults.

3.2 Describe formal operational and post-formal reasoning in adolescence and emerging adulthood.

Piaget proposed that individuals actively engage with the world and in adolescence become capable of formal operational reasoning, permitting hypothetical–deductive reasoning and the use of propositional logic. Although Piaget believed that cognitive development is a universal process, individuals show varying abilities and are more likely to show formal operational reasoning when considering material with which they have a great deal of experience. Researchers have proposed a more advanced form of thinking known as post-formal reasoning, which integrates abstract reasoning with practical consideration. Post-formal reasoning progresses through several stages from dualistic thinking, in which knowledge and accounts of phenomena are viewed as either right or wrong with no in-between, to more flexible relativistic thinking, and finally to reflective judgment, the recognition that there are multiple options and opinions that can be evaluated to choose the most adequate solution. Social interaction is critical to the development of post-formal reasoning as well as exposure to realistic but ambiguous problems with diverging information and supportive guidance. Given that post-formal reasoning is influenced by experience, not all emerging and young adults display it.

3.3 Summarize changes in information processing and cognitive function during adolescence.

The information processing system includes the sensory register, working memory, long-term memory, and processes such as attention, encoding, and retrieval. Adolescents gain greater control over attention, demonstrating divided and selective attention. They become better able to hold material in working memory while taking in and processing new material. Advances in working memory are driven by changes in the central executive, which influences the ability to deploy attention, monitor cognitive activities, inhibit responses, and engage in metacognition. Working memory and executive function improve with maturation and experience but are also influenced by contextual factors, such as stress, socioeconomic status, and perceived support. Processing speed improves with neural maturation and advances in executive function.

3.4 Describe ways in which intelligence has been defined and measured.

IQ tests, such as the WISC-V and WAIS-IV, measure intellectual aptitude and are often used to identify adolescents with special educational needs. Changes in intelligence scores parallel cognitive development—specifically, information processing capacities such as working memory and processing speed. IQ predicts school achievement, how long an adolescent will stay in school, and career attainment in adulthood. Persistent group differences are found in IQ scores, but contextual factors, such as socioeconomic status, living conditions, school resources, culture, and life circumstances, are thought to account for group differences. Multiple intelligence theory and the triarchic theory of intelligence conceptualize intelligence as entailing a broader range of skills than those measured by IQ tests.

3.5 Examine changes in social cognition over the adolescent years.

Advances in reasoning and metacognition lead adolescents to understand themselves and others in more complex ways, with implications for social relationships. Selman proposed that social perspective taking ability follows a developmental sequence. Mutual perspective taking, the understanding that individuals take other people's point of view at the same time as others attempt to take their own point of view, emerges in early adolescence. In middle adolescence, societal perspective taking enables adolescents to recognize that the social environment, including the larger society, influences people's perspectives and beliefs. Research has suggested that perspective taking ability develops from childhood into adolescence but may not closely follow the age-based timeline advocated by Selman. As reasoning and metacognition improve, adolescents often direct their abstract thinking abilities toward themselves, demonstrating adolescent egocentrism, a perspective taking error that is manifested in two phenomena: the imaginary audience and the personal fable.

KEY TERMS

adolescent egocentrism, 79

amygdala, 60

attention, 71

automaticity, 73

central executive, 71

corpus callosum, 59

cortex, 59

divided attention, 71

dual systems model, 64

dualistic thinking, 68

executive function, 71

glial cells, 59

gray matter, 61

hippocampus, 59

hypothetical–deductive reasoning, 67

imaginary audience, 79

intelligence, 74

intelligence tests (IQ tests), 74

lateralization, 60

limbic system, 60

long-term memory, 71

metacognition, 73

multiple intelligence theory, 76

mutual perspective taking, 78

myelination, 59

neurogenesis, 58

neurons, 58

neurotransmitters, 58

personal fable, 79

plasticity, 61

post-formal reasoning, 68

prefrontal cortex, 59

reflective judgment, 68

relativistic thinking, 68

response inhibition, 72

selective attention, 71

sensory register, 71

social cognition, 78

social perspective taking, 78

societal perspective taking, 78

synapse, 58

synaptic pruning, 59

synaptogenesis, 59

triarchic theory of intelligence, 77

white matter, 61

working memory, 71

PART 2

Psychosocial and Socioemotional Development

4

Self and Identity

Learning Objectives

Chapter Contents

Introspective, rebellious, smart, attractive, outgoing, shy . . . How do you describe yourself? How has your view of yourself changed over the years? Who are you and where are you going? This, of course, is a question that arises all throughout life, but it is in adolescence that this developmental task first arises. Adolescents construct a sense of self and identity, an understanding of who they are and who they hope to be. Adolescents' attempts at self-definition and discovery are influenced by their relationships with parents and peers, relationships that become more complex during the adolescent years. In this chapter we examine adolescents' changing understanding of themselves and the process of identity development.

SELF-CONCEPT

Adolescents' views of themselves are shaped by their cognitive capacities. With cognitive maturation, adolescents begin to think about the world—and themselves—in more complex ways. **Self-concept**, the traits and characteristics we attribute to ourselves, increases in breadth and depth (Harter, 2012a). Adolescents spend a great deal of time reflecting on themselves and engaging in introspective activities: writing in journals, composing poetry, snapping selfies, and posting messages, photos, and videos about their lives on social media. Although adults often view these activities as self-indulgent and egotistical, they help adolescents work through the important developmental task of constructing a more abstract, differentiated, and organized self-concept.

Changes in Self-Conceptions

Whereas children's self-descriptions tend to emphasize physical characteristics ("I'm a boy"), ownership ("I have a dog"), interests ("I like baseball"), and broad attributes ("I'm smart"), adolescents include abstract and complex labels in their self-descriptions (e.g., witty, intelligent). Adolescents learn that they can describe themselves in multiple ways that often are contradictory, such as being both silly and serious, and that they show different aspects of themselves to different people (e.g., parents, teachers, friends) (Harter, 2012a). Self-concept is domain specific, meaning that we hold different beliefs about ourselves across different areas or domains, such as academics, athletics, social abilities, and behavior, for example.

As young people recognize that their feelings, attitudes, and behaviors may change with the situation, they begin to use qualifiers in their self-descriptions (e.g., "I'm sort of shy"). Adolescents' awareness of the situational variability in their psychological and behavioral qualities is evident in statements such as, "I'm talkative with my friends. I like to debate them, but in class, I'm much quieter. I don't like it when everyone looks at me." Many young adolescents find these inconsistencies confusing and wonder who they really are, contributing to their challenge of forming a balanced and consistent sense of self.

Self-concept clarity refers to the extent to which adolescents' beliefs about themselves are clearly and consistently defined, expressed confidently, and enduring (Campbell et al., 1996). It is related to adjustment and well-being (Bleidorn & Ködding, 2013), including positive associations with self-esteem and emotional control, and negative associations with anxiety, depression, and loneliness (Bigler, Neimeyer, & Brown, 2001; Campbell et al., 1996; Frijns & Finkenauer, 2009; Schwartz, Klimstra, Luyckx, Hale, & Meeus, 2012; Van Dijk et al., 2014). Self concept clarity tends to increase slightly from early to middle adolescence, as cognitive advances help adolescents better understand themselves (Schwartz et al., 2011). Self-concept clarity can shift in response to life events, experiences, and transitions, such as from adolescence to emerging adulthood (Lodi-Smith, Spain, Cologgi, & Roberts, 2017). For example, a 6-year study of Dutch adolescents found declines in self-concept clarity from age 17 to 18, then linear increases through age 23 (as shown in Figure 4.1) (Crocetti et al., 2016). Common transitions in late adolescence, such as the move from high school to college, can induce temporary decreases in self-certainty as routines and relational ties (such as connections to high school friends) may weaken (Light & Visser, 2013). Navigating these transitions can spur young

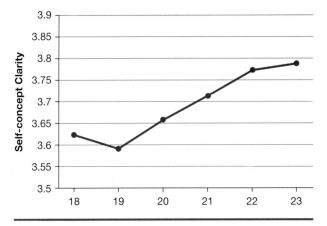

FIGURE 4.1

Changes in Self-Concept Clarity From Age 18 to 23

Source: Crocetti et al. (2016).

people to learn about themselves and view themselves in new ways, leading to a revised sense of self-concept and shifts in self-concept clarity.

Self-concept is influenced by experiences in the home, school, and community. At home, consistent parenting that is warm and firm can provide support, acceptance, and give-and-take to help adolescents develop a positive sense of self-concept—that is, a self-concept that includes positive attributes and traits (Van Dijk et al., 2014). Parents' sense of self-concept clarity tends to be transmitted to their adolescents through interactions and modeling (Crocetti, Rubini, Branje, Koot, & Meeus, 2016). At school, particularly among high school students, perceived teacher support predicts positive academic and behavioral self-concept (Dudovitz, Chung, & Wong, 2017). Adolescents' views of themselves reflect but also influence their behavior. For example, young adolescents' academic self-concept predicts their academic achievement in middle adolescence (Preckel, Niepel, Schneider, & Brunner, 2013). Participation in youth organizations, such as the Boys and Girls Clubs of America, has positive effects on the self-concept of young people, especially those reared in impoverished neighborhoods, because such organizations foster competence, positive socialization, and connections with the community (Quane & Rankin, 2006). Adolescents' evaluations of their self-concepts are the basis for self-esteem, as discussed later in this chapter (Harter, 2006; Marsh, Trautwein, Lüdtke, Köller, & Baumert, 2006).

Multiple Selves

Self-conceptions become more complicated as adolescents become able to consider the future, plan ahead, and imagine their future lives and how they might change over time. Adolescents identify a self that they aspire to be, the **ideal self**, which is characterized by traits that they value and hope to develop. The ideal self can be a source of motivation, a goal that prompts adolescents to adopt behaviors that will bring them closer to their ideal self. Adolescents' capacities for metacognition and self-reflection enable them to contrast the ideal self with the **real self**—their current personal characteristics. The degree of match between adolescents' aspirations and their current characteristics predicts well-being. Specifically, the greater the discrepancy between the ideal and real self, the more likely adolescents are to experience symptoms of depression, low self-esteem, and poor school grades (Ferguson, Hafen, & Laursen, 2010; Stevens, Lovejoy, & Pittman, 2014).

As they gain experience in romantic relationships and managing conflict, adolescents become less likely to show a false self to dating partners.
iStock.com/Martin Dimitrov

Advanced capacities for self-understanding coupled with the ability to take the perspective of others can lead adolescents to sometimes act inauthentically in social situations. Adolescents are more likely to show a **false self,** or present themselves in a way that they know is untrue, with dating partners and others they wish to impress and are least likely to act inauthentically with close friends (Harter, 2012a). The ability to apply conflict management skills to romantic relationships is inversely associated with false self behavior in high school students, suggesting that acting inauthentically in romantic relationships may be a way of avoiding conflict and potential romantic break-ups (Sippola, Buchanan, & Kehoe, 2007). False self behavior may be also motivated by feeling misunderstood by others, the fear that others may not understand or approve of their real selves, desire for approval, and the fear of losing a friend. Adolescents who frequently present a false self tend to perceive less support from parents and peers, report more depressive symptoms, and tend to show poor self-esteem.

Brain Development and Self-Concept

Thinking about one's self-concept is associated with specific patterns of neurological activity, suggesting that brain development may play a role in self-concept. Neuroimaging studies have shown developmental changes in regions of the brain thought to be important for the sense of self, specifically the medial prefrontal cortex (mPFC) (Mills, Lalonde, Clasen, Giedd, & Blakemore, 2014; Pfeifer & Peake,

2012). For example, in a longitudinal study of young adolescents age 10 and 13, participants completed a self-conceptions task in which they considered their own social skills and those of a familiar fictional character (for example, Harry Potter) (Pfeifer et al., 2013). The adolescents showed more activity in the mPFC when they considered themselves compared with others and mPFC activity increased from age 10 to 13. The mPFC is associated with processing information about the self (Northoff & Hayes, 2011) and also plays a role in reward and evaluation processes (Rangel, Camerer, & Montague, 2008), suggesting that adolescents may experience self-evaluation as rewarding.

In a similar study, 10-year-olds and adults completed a task examining the ability to retrieve information about the self (Pfeifer, Lieberman, & Dapretto, 2007). Participants judged whether phrases such as "I like to read just for fun" described either themselves or a familiar fictional character. The young adolescents showed more activity in the mPFC when retrieving information about themselves than did adults and the adults showed more activity in the lateral temporal cortex, which is associated with semantic memory. The adolescents' increased mPFC activity suggests that they were actively processing the task and engaging in self-reflection to construct self-descriptions, whereas the adults relied on memory to complete the task, perhaps because they have more extensive knowledge about themselves. The mPFC undergoes significant development in adolescence and is one of the last parts of the brain to develop (Mills, Goddings, Clasen, Giedd, & Blakemore, 2014). Overall mPFC activity increases between childhood and adolescence in response to self-knowledge and evaluation tasks, followed by a decrease from adolescence into adulthood as self-conceptions become established and more a matter of recall rather than construction (Blakemore, 2012).

Personality Traits

"I'm really introverted," explains Tasha, "I like hanging out with my friends, but I feel like I really need time to myself. I used to like to play by myself when I was little. I still do. That's just my personality." Like Tasha, most adolescents' self-conceptions include personality traits that they view as long lasting and stable. Researchers who study personality often share this view, applying a **five-factor model** to describe personality as composed of five clusters of personality traits (often referred to as the Big Five) (Costa, McCrae, & Löckenhoff, 2019; McCrae & Costa Jr., 2008). Based on extensive research on the nature of personality, conducted with multiple samples over several decades, the five-factor model collapses the many characteristics on which people differ into personality traits:

- *Openness to experience:* curious, explorative, and imaginative

- *Conscientiousness:* organized, responsible, and disciplined

- *Extraversion:* outgoing, active, and assertive

- *Agreeableness:* kind, helpful, and cooperative

- *Neuroticism:* anxious, irritable, and tense

The Big Five personality factors are thought to reflect inherited predispositions that persist throughout life, and a growing body of evidence supports their genetic origins (Penke, Denissen, & Miller, 2007; Power & Pluess, 2015). Personality is first manifested as temperament, a collection of inborn biological tendencies in mood, distractibility, and regularity. Temperament evolves into recognizable personality traits by early childhood that influence how emotions are experienced and expressed and how the child acts (Chen, Schmidt, Chen, & Schmidt, 2015; Shiner & DeYoung, 2013; Wängqvist, Lamb, Frisén, & Hwang, 2015). Personality traits become more distinctive with development and reflect the five-factor model (Wilson, Schalet, Hicks, & Zucker, 2013).

Longitudinal research following adolescents from age 12 to 22 suggests overall increases in agreeableness for both boys and girls, conscientiousness in girls, and openness in boys (Borghuis et al., 2017). The biological, social, and psychological transitions from childhood to adolescence appear to be accompanied by temporary dips in some aspects of personality maturity, lending credence to the stereotype of adolescent moodiness (Soto, John, Gosling, & Potter, 2011; Van den Akker, Deković, Asscher, & Prinzie,

2014). For example, in one study, boys showed a temporary dip in conscientiousness and girls showed a similar dip in emotional stability and extraversion (Borghuis et al., 2017). In addition, neuroticism tends to remain stable in adolescence and declines in emerging adulthood and both conscientiousness and agreeableness increase in emerging adulthood (Wängqvist et al., 2015).

Although there are predictable age-related shifts in Big Five traits, there are also individual differences in the pattern and magnitude of change (Graham & Lachman, 2012). Not all individuals follow the normative increase in conscientiousness scores over adulthood, for example. Some people change more than others, and some change in ways that are contrary to general population trends (McAdams & Olson, 2010). However, individuals' relative position with regard to traits does not change (Deary, Pattie, & Starr, 2013; Roberts & Mroczek, 2008). Individual differences in personality traits are highly stable over periods of time ranging from 3 to 30 years (McAdams & Olson, 2010; Wängqvist et al., 2015). For example, childhood personality ratings by teachers predict personality ratings in middle adulthood (Edmonds, Goldberg, Hampson, & Barckley, 2013; Hampson & Goldberg, 2006), as do personality ratings collected during adolescence (Morizot & Le Blanc, 2003).

In adolescence, personality scores predict a wide range of variables, including academic engagement, externalizing behavior, and substance use (Clark, Durbin, Hicks, Iacono, & McGue, 2016; Wilson et al., 2013). For example, youths low in agreeableness, low in conscientiousness, and high in neuroticism show higher rates of externalizing, or rule-breaking behaviors, whereas youths low in extroversion and high in neuroticism show higher rates of internalizing psychopathology, such as anxiety and depression (Caspi & Shiner, 2008; Tackett, 2006). Adolescents who are high in neuroticism show higher rates of victimization at school (Kulig, Cullen, Wilcox, & Chouhy, 2018). Adolescents' views of themselves reflect but also influence their behavior and their self-evaluations.

REVIEW 4.1

1. How does self-concept change in adolescence and what are some influences on self-concept?

2. Differentiate among the ideal, real, and false self.

3. How is brain development related to changes in self-concept?

4. Describe the Big Five traits and describe how they change, if at all, during adolescence.

• •

Recall from Chapter 1 that development is the result of dynamic interactions between individual and biological factors and the contexts in which individuals are embedded. Identify influences on self-concept within individuals and their contexts. How might these factors influence each other? Give three examples. Explain your choices.

● ●

At 7 years of age, Kenya wanted to be a soccer player and described herself as fast, strong, and coordinated. Yet try as she might, she couldn't score a goal. At age 9, Kenya spent a lot of time on the sidelines, watching her teammates and hoping the coach would send her onto the field. She started to dislike going to practice because she couldn't keep up during team runs. At age 12, Kenya didn't make the team. At first, she was crushed. She focused on her schoolwork and soon discovered that she was much better at math than her classmates. Kenya's teacher encouraged her to take a math placement test and Kenya's high score led her to be placed in an advanced algebra class. She continued to excel and decided that she wanted a career in science or math, but she wasn't sure which. Kenya did know, however, that if she wanted to date in high school, then she'd have to play down her smarts. Her friend told her that boys don't like girls who are smarter than them, so Kenya decided to purposely fail an exam to commiserate with Peter and, hopefully, date him.

1. Describe Kenya's self-concept. How has it changed?

2. Identify examples of Kenya's ideal, real, and false self.

3. Compare Kenya's development to normative development.

4. What role might Kenya's experiences and interactions have in her developing sense of self?

● ●

SELF-ESTEEM

Self-concept becomes more refined as adolescents become more aware of their characteristics and nature. Adolescents' complex thinking also influences how they evaluate their abilities. **Global self-esteem** refers to an individual's subjective evaluation of his or her worth as a person. Although there are developmental shifts in global self-esteem, it tends to show moderate rank stability over time. That is, individuals who show high self-esteem relative to their peers tend to retain this position or rank despite developmental shifts.

Developmental Changes in Self-Esteem

Global self-esteem shows reliable changes over the course of adolescence and emerging adulthood. Children often have unrealistically positive views of themselves and their abilities. With experience and interactions with parents, peers, teachers, and coaches, children develop more realistic views of themselves. Advances in perspective-taking abilities and self-reflection lead early adolescents to be more aware of others and often more self-conscious and self-critical. Self-esteem tends to decline in early adolescence, at about 11 years of age, reaching its lowest point at about 13 years of age, then rises (Orth, 2017). Likewise, self-esteem tends to become more unstable or volatile in early adolescence. Fluctuations in self-image increase over the transition to adolescence and tend to peak in early adolescence between age 12 and 14 (Thomaes, Poorthuis, & Nelemans, 2011). This pattern is true for both boys and girls, with girls tending to show lower self-esteem (von Soest, Wichstrøm, & Kvalem, 2016).

Declines in global self-esteem are influenced by the multiple transitions that young adolescents undergo, such as body changes and the emotions that accompany those changes, as well as adolescents' self-comparisons to their peers (Schaffhuser, Allemand, & Schwarz, 2017). Girls reach puberty earlier than boys; in addition, girls' pubertal transitions tend to accompany school transitions, which are associated with temporary declines in self-esteem. Most adolescents view themselves more positively as they progress from early adolescence through the high school years and these shifts in self-esteem are small for most adolescents (Bachman, O'Malley, Freedman-Doan, Trzesniewski, & Donnellan, 2011; von Soest et al., 2016).

Self-esteem may change in response to transitions, such as from high school to college and adolescence to emerging adulthood. For example, in a 4-year longitudinal study, college students' levels of self-esteem dropped substantially during the first semester of college, rebounded by the end of the first year, and then gradually increased over the next 3 years, to represent an overall increase in self-esteem from the beginning to the end of college (Chung et al., 2014). In this study, most students believed that their self-esteem increased during college and their perceptions tended to correspond with actual changes in their self-esteem scores, suggesting that emerging adults may view themselves accurately. As individuals progress through emerging adulthood, they gain competence and have increasing control over their everyday social contexts, which corresponds to increases in self-esteem (Orth & Robins, 2014). Self-esteem continues to increase from emerging adulthood through middle adulthood (Bleidorn et al., 2016).

FIGURE 4.2

Changes in Global Self-Esteem and Domain-Specific Self-Esteem in Adolescence

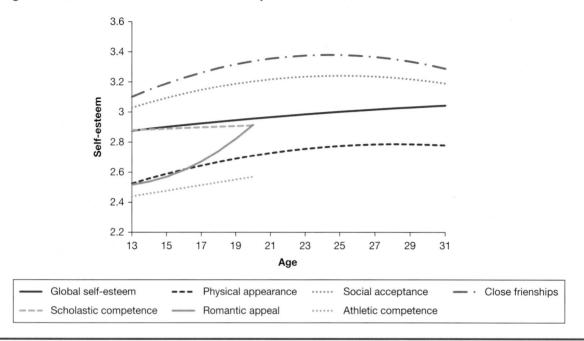

Source: von Soest, Wichstrøm, and Kvalem (2016).

Domain-Specific Self-Esteem

As self-conceptions become more differentiated, so do self-evaluations. Adolescents describe and evaluate themselves overall as well as in specific areas or domains, such as academics, athletic ability, and social competence (Harter, 2012b) (Figure 4.2). Adolescents develop a positive sense of self-esteem when they evaluate themselves favorably in the domains that they view as important. For example, sports accomplishments are more closely associated with physical self-esteem in adolescent athletes, who tend to highly value physical athleticism. Nonathletes tend to place less importance on athleticism (Wagnsson, Lindwall, & Gustafsson, 2014). Similarly, adolescents with high academic self-esteem tend to spend more time and effort on schoolwork, view academics as more important, and continue to demonstrate high academic achievement (Preckel et al., 2013).

The best domain-specific predictor of global self-esteem in adolescence is physical attractiveness, how adolescents feel about their appearance (Harter, 2006). Although evaluations of physical attractiveness are linked with global self-esteem for both boys and girls, the relationship is stronger for girls, perhaps reflecting the cultural

Success on the basketball court is rewarding and boosts self-esteem in adolescents who value athleticism.
iStock.com/monkeybusinessimages

Close-knit communities and churches tend to offer Black adolescents support, guidance, and positive connections with adults who bolster their high self-esteem, buffering the negative effects of racism and discrimination.
Jeffrey Isaac Greenberg 2/Alamy Stock Photo

emphasis on physical attractiveness for women (Bleidorn et al., 2016; von Soest et al., 2016). We have seen that girls tend to be more vulnerable to self-image problems than boys. With puberty, many girls develop a more negative body image than boys and tend to be less satisfied with their bodies (Andrew, Tiggemann, & Clark, 2016). Given the link between evaluations of physical attractiveness and global self-esteem, girls are at risk to experience low self-esteem relative to boys, reflecting commonly reported sex differences (Steiger, Allemand, Robins, & Fend, 2014).

Self-esteem in social domains, such as close relationships, also influences evaluations of global self-esteem. During adolescence and emerging adulthood, young people become more concerned and invested in social roles and relationships. Success in these roles influences self-evaluations. Self-esteem in social domains, such as close relationships and romantic appeal, tends to increase over adolescence and emerging adulthood, and these domains become more closely related with global esteem over time (Steiger et al., 2014; von Soest et al., 2016).

Racial and Ethnic Differences in Self-Esteem

Generally speaking, Black adolescents tend to have higher self-esteem than their peers of other ethnicities (see Figure 4.3) (Bachman et al., 2011; Erol & Orth, 2011). From early to late adolescence, the relative position of White and Hispanic adolescents shifts with dramatic increases in self-esteem among Hispanic adolescents relative to White students. Asian American adolescents tend to score particularly low on measures of self-esteem and much lower than their peers (Bachman et al., 2011). How do we account for ethnic differences in self-esteem?

Why, despite often perceiving racism and discrimination, do Black adolescents have high self-esteem relative to their peers? Close-knit Black communities offer young people support, guidance,

---

FIGURE 4.3

Self-Esteem in Black, White, and Hispanic Adolescents From Age 14 to 30

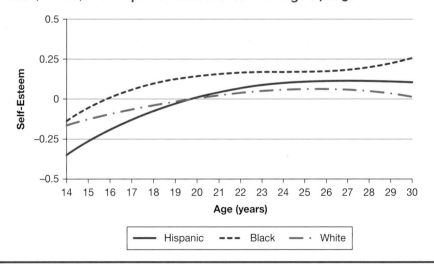

Source: Erol and Orth (2011).

and connections to adults who provide positive feedback. These connections are a source of support that influences Black adolescents' self-conceptions and their feelings of worth. Hispanic adolescents are immersed in similar communities that emphasize family ties that buffer the effect of negative experiences on adolescents' self-evaluations. Culture also plays a role in influencing Asian American adolescents' self-evaluations, which tend to be much lower than their peers. Asian cultures tend to emphasize interdependence and collectivism, valuing the community over the individual (Markus & Kitayama, 2010). Promoting self-esteem runs contrary to these values (Heine & Hamamura, 2007). We will return to this question in our discussion of ethnic-racial identity later in this chapter.

Correlates of Self-Esteem

Adolescents' sense of self-worth influences their behavior and well-being. Adolescents with high self-esteem tend to be more confident, more willing to reject advice they deem poor, more likely to speak up, and more sure of themselves (Baumeister & Vohs, 2018). They tend to respond more proactively to initial failure, either by trying again or by switching to a different line of strategy or goal that seems more promising (Baumeister & Vohs, 2018). Adolescents with high self-esteem have more self-compassion—they are kind to themselves and are more likely to perceive experiences and failures as opportunities for self-awareness rather than self-judge (Barry, Loflin, & Doucette, 2015).

Whereas favorable self-evaluations are associated with positive adjustment and sociability in adolescents of all socioeconomic status and ethnic groups, persistently low self-esteem is associated with adjustment difficulties that can extend throughout the lifespan (Orth, 2017). For example, one longitudinal study of over 1,500 adolescents age 12 to 16 years found that both level and change in self-esteem predicted depression at age 16 and, also 2 decades later, at 35 (Steiger et al., 2014). Those who entered adolescence with low self-esteem and whose self-esteem declined further during the adolescent years were more likely to show depression 2 decades later; this pattern held for both global and domain-specific self-esteem (physical appearance and academic competence). Self-esteem is also negatively associated with adolescent risky activity, including alcohol and substance use (Jackman & MacPhee, 2017; Oshri, Carlson, Kwon, Zeichner, & Wickrama, 2017). Individuals with low self-esteem may be less motivated to follow normative expectations and instead deviate from them in an effort to boost self-esteem (Lee, Seo, Torabi, Lohrmann, & Song, 2018). In support

of this, one longitudinal study showed that although low self-esteem predicted binge drinking and marijuana use at age 15, the relationship weakened over time with age such that by 21, when substance use is somewhat normative, self-esteem no longer predicted binge drinking and marijuana use (Lee et al., 2018).

Contextual Influences on Self-Esteem

Family and peers are important contexts for the development of self-esteem. Research suggests that the overall quality of the parent–adolescent relationship and parents' emotional availability are associated with higher estimates of self-worth and better adjustment in adolescents from the Netherlands, China, Australia, Germany, Italy, and the United States (Babore, Carlucci, Cataldi, Phares, & Trumello, 2017; Harris et al., 2015; Miconi, Moscardino, Ronconi, & Altoè, 2017; Wang & Sheikh-Khalil, 2014; Wouters, Doumen, Germeijs, Colpin, & Verschueren, 2013). Parents who adopt a warm, encouraging, but firm style of parenting are more likely to raise adolescents who display high self-esteem (Milevsky, Schlechter, Netter, & Keehn, 2007; Steinberg, 2001; Wouters et al., 2013). Self-esteem derived from parental relationships has long-term effects for adjustment. For example, in middle and high school students, maternal support predicts positive self-esteem, which, in turn, is negatively associated with problem behavior (Liu, Ksinan, & Vazsonyi, 2018). In contrast, parent–adolescent conflict and parental feedback that is critical, inconsistent, and not contingent on behavior predicts the development of poor self-esteem (Wang et al., 2016).

Peer acceptance appears to have a protective effect on self-esteem and can buffer the negative effects of a distant relationship with parents (Birkeland, Breivik, & Wold, 2014). Adolescents who feel supported and well-liked by peers tend to show high self-esteem (Vanhalst, Luyckx, Scholte, Engels, & Goossens, 2013). Positive attachments to peers predict self-esteem in adolescence and emerging adulthood and may have long-lasting effects on self-evaluations (Sánchez-Queija, Oliva, & Parra, 2017). For example, a longitudinal study that spanned 2 decades showed that peer approval during ages 12 to 16 predicted self-esteem in adolescence as well as at age 35 (Gruenenfelder-Steiger, Harris, & Fend, 2016). Other data collected over a 5-year period, beginning at about age 13, suggested that self-esteem predicted social support quality increasingly over time (Marshall, Parker, Ciarrochi, & Heaven, 2014). The direction of influence between peer relationships and self-esteem is difficult to interpret and complicated; it is likely a two-way relationship in which self-esteem influences and is influenced by social support.

Close relationships with peers and a sense of peer acceptance promote self-esteem.
iStock.com/DMEPhotography

social self-esteem were positively related across all three waves of data collection (Valkenburg et al., 2017). Social self-esteem increased social network use, suggesting that those who feel good about themselves use social media more and get more positive feedback, which increases self-esteem. Adolescents who are high in self-esteem may be less hesitant to communicate online and to share positive information about themselves, and by doing so enhance the likelihood that they receive positive feedback, which further boosts their self-esteem (Valkenburg et al., 2017). We examine adolescents' experience with social media in Chapter 11.

Self-esteem has long-term implications for romantic relationships. In late adolescence, self-esteem may influence young people's experiences with intimacy, which, in turn, predicts their feelings of self-worth (Van Petegem, Brenning, Baudat, Beyers, & Zimmer-Gembeck, 2018). For example, in longitudinal research conducted with over 9,000 late adolescent and young adult Germans, high self-esteem predicted starting a new relationship and low self-esteem predicted ending a relationship (Luciano & Orth, 2017). Moreover, beginning a relationship was associated with an increase in self-esteem, and the increase was sustained when the relationship was maintained for at least a year. A break-up predicted declines in self-esteem that disappeared after a year, even if the individual remained single. Our self-evaluations influence and are influenced by our social and romantic relationships.

Adolescents' self-esteem is also associated with their communication on social media (Valkenburg, Koutamanis, & Vossen, 2017). Receiving positive feedback from online peers is associated with rises in self-esteem and negative feedback or neglect is associated with self-esteem declines in preadolescents; however, subsequent peer approval is associated with recovery of self-esteem (Sander Thomaes et al., 2010). One 3-year study of 10- to 15-year-old adolescents found that social networking use and

Adolescents' interactions on social media both influence and are influenced by their self-esteem.
iStock.com/monkeybusinessimages

REVIEW 4.2

1. Describe the normative changes in self-esteem from childhood through adolescence.

2. Identify influences on global self-esteem.

3. What are some of the correlates of self-esteem?

4. How is self-esteem associated with individual differences, such as race and ethnicity, and social factors, such as interactions with others?

IDENTITY

As adolescents come to understand their own traits and characteristics, they begin to construct an identity, a sense of self that is coherent and consistent over time (Erikson, 1950). According to Erikson, to establish a sense of identity, individuals must consider their past and future and determine a sense of their values, beliefs, and goals with regard to vocation, politics, religion, and sexuality.

Identity Versus Role Confusion

Recall from Chapter 1 that Erik Erikson posited that each age in life has its own developmental task. In adolescence we face the crisis of identity versus identity diffusion. Our task is to determine who we are and who we would like to become. In devising an identity, young people integrate all that they know about themselves—their self-conceptions—along with their evaluations of themselves, to construct a self that is coherent and consistent over time (Erikson, 1950). **Identity achievement** represents the successful resolution of this process, establishing a coherent sense of self after exploring a range of possibilities. In establishing a sense of identity, individuals must consider their past and future and come to a sense of their values, beliefs, and goals with regard to vocation, politics, religion, and sexuality.

A key assumption of identity theory is that individuals must engage in an active process of exploring identity alternatives before committing to a particular identity (Meeus, 2011). Crucial to a successful identity search is having the time and space to do the hard work of figuring oneself out. Adolescents are best positioned to construct an identity when they experience what Erikson referred to as a **psychosocial moratorium**, a time-out period that provides more freedom and autonomy than childhood but is without the full autonomy and responsibilities of adulthood. This period allows adolescents the opportunity to explore possibilities of who they might become. They might sample careers, considering becoming an actor one week and a lawyer the next. Adolescents explore personalities and desires, trying out different personas and styles. Some adolescents examine their religion more closely and consider their own beliefs, perhaps learning about other religions. As adolescents explore possible identities, they identify choices and become increasingly confident about those choices over time.

Young people who successfully engage in this process emerge with a sense of identity—an understanding of who they are and where they are going. The unsuccessful resolution of the identity search is

Religion is an important aspect of identity for many adolescents.
iStock.com/elifranssens

confusion, in which one withdraws from the world, isolating oneself from loved ones, parents, and peers. Alternatively, confusion may take the form of immersing oneself into the peer world—of losing the self. Erikson's ideas about identity have influenced thinking in this area for the past half century and researchers have devised ways of measuring identity, permitting his ideas to be tested.

Identity development is a dynamic process in which individuals shifts between certainty to uncertainty as they explore identity alternatives and examine their feelings of commitment to a particular identity structure (Galliher, McLean, & Syed, 2017; Meeus, 2011). Adolescents navigate these shifts in certainty on a daily basis, moment-to-moment (Becht et al., 2017; Bosma & Kunnen, 2001). Many adolescents experience daily shifts in identity certainty that accompany shifts in circumstances and moods (Becht et al., 2016). As the uncertainty is experienced as discomfort, young people are highly motivated to seek resolution and reduce the discomfort. Longitudinal research following individuals from early to late adolescence suggests that adolescents' uncertainty in identity precedes commitment making at the within-person level from early to late adolescence for interpersonal identity (Becht et al., 2017). Contemporary research considers identity processes more specifically as exploration in breadth, exploration in depth, reconsideration of commitment, and identification with commitment (Galliher et al., 2017).

Identity Status

How do researchers study identity? Researchers study identity in large samples of people with the use of interview and survey measures. The most common approach is to classify individuals' progress in identity development into four categories known as **identity status**, the degree to which individuals have explored possible selves and whether they have committed to specific beliefs and goals (Marcia, 1966). The identity status model conceptualizes Erikson's ideas about identity development as entailing of exploration and commitment making.

Identity statuses reflect different ways that individuals view and respond to the world. Table 4.1 summarizes four identity statuses, or categories, describing a person's identity development. The least mature status is **identity diffusion** (not having explored or committed to a sense of self), characterized by pervasive uncertainty with little motive for resolution (Berzonsky & Kuk, 2000). Individuals who are in the **identity foreclosed** status have prematurely chosen an identity without having engaged in exploration; they tend to be inflexible and view the world in black and white, right and wrong, terms. The **moratorium status** involves an active exploration of ideas and a sense of openness to possibilities, coupled with some uncertainty. When uncertainty is experienced as discomfort, young people are highly motivated to seek resolution and reduce this discomfort. The fourth

TABLE 4.1

Identity Status

		COMMITMENT	
		PRESENT	ABSENT
EXPLORATION	PRESENT	**Identity Achievement** Commitment to an identity after exploring multiple possibilities. Associated with an active problem-solving style, high self-esteem, feelings of control, high moral reasoning, and positive views of work and school	**Moratorium** Active exploration of identity alternatives without having committed to an identity. Associated with openness to experience, an active problem-solving style, anxiety and discomfort, and experimentation with alcohol or substance use
	ABSENT	**Identity Foreclosure** Commitment to an identity without having explored multiple possibilities. Associated with avoiding reflection or exploration of identity alternatives, rigidity, and a lack of openness to new information and ideas, especially if they contract their position	**Identity Diffusion** Has neither committed to an identity nor explored alternatives. Associated with avoidance, tending to not solve personal problems in favor of letting issues decide themselves, academic difficulties, apathy, and alcohol and substance use

Sources: Marcia (1966) and Meeus (2011).

category, identity achievement status, requires that individuals construct a sense of self through reflection, critical examination, and exploring or trying out new ideas and belief systems and that they have formed a commitment to a particular set of ideas, values, and beliefs. Identity diffusion and foreclosure become less common in late adolescence, when moratorium and identity achievement are more prevalent.

Individuals' identity status refers to their identity situation at a given point in life (Kroger & Marcia, 2011). Young people typically shift among identity statuses over the adolescent years, but the specific pattern of identity development varies among adolescents (Meeus, 2011). Some adolescents remain in one identity status, such as identity moratorium, for the bulk of adolescence, while others experience multiple transitions in identity status. The most common shifts in identity status are from the least mature statuses, identity diffusion and identity foreclosure, to the most mature statuses, moratorium and achievement, in middle and late adolescence (Al-Owidha, Green, & Kroger, 2009; Yip, 2014). Many adolescents experience daily shifts in identity certainty that accompany shifts in circumstances and moods (Becht et al., 2016). Although some adolescents attain a sense of certainty in their commitments that persists through adolescence, variability is the norm (Becht et al., 2016). The overall proportion of young people in the moratorium status tends to increase during adolescence, peaking at about age 19 and declining over emerging adulthood as young people gradually commit to identities (Kroger, Martinussen, & Marcia, 2010). Emerging adulthood is a ripe time for identity development. In fact, longitudinal research with diverse samples has suggested that most young people enter emerging adulthood without substantial commitments and only about one-third have by age 29 (Kroger et al., 2010).

Although the task of forming an identity is first encountered during adolescence, it is often not resolved in adolescence and the resulting identity is still not final thereafter (Kroger, 2015; Kroger et al., 2010). Identity development continues through early adulthood even after achievement has been reached (Carlsson, Wängqvist, & Frisén, 2015). Changing life circumstances, contexts, and developmental needs spur identity development over adulthood. Adults often move in and out of identity statuses. For example, in one study of young adults, nearly half shifted identity statuses between ages 25 and 29, and all four

Adolescents explore various career options before committing to a vocational identity.
Jim West / Alamy Stock Photo

statuses were represented at both ages (Carlsson, Wängqvist, & Frisén, 2016).

Identity is not an all-or-nothing concept. People form a sense of identity in many different domains or areas and the relative salience of each domain can vary over development (McAdams & Zapata-Gietl, 2015). The pace and pattern of development varies across identity domains and adolescents with a strong sense of identity in one domain do not necessarily have a strong sense of identity in other domains (Goossens, 2001; Klimstra et al., 2016). For example, having chosen a career, an adolescent may demonstrate identity achievement with regard to vocation yet remain diffused with regard to political ideology, never having considered political affiliations. Some identity domains may remain unexplored. For example, persistent and increasing levels of identity diffusion have been commonly found in the political and religious domains, continuing through middle adulthood (Fadjukoff, Pulkkinen, & Kokko, 2016). Researchers often group different identity domains under two broad umbrella domains: interpersonal (i.e., friendships and dating) and ideological (i.e., occupation, religion, and politics) (Schwartz, 2001; Schwartz, Luyckx, & Crocetti, 2015). Frequently there is little convergence or overlap in identity processes in ideological and relational domains (Luyckx, Teppers, Klimstra, & Rassart, 2014). In one study of late adolescents, the interpersonal domains (relationships with friends, family, and dates) were most salient, but occupational identity was the only ideological realm that was salient (McLean, Syed, & Shucard, 2016). Relatedly, other research with emerging adults suggests that the relational domain is more closely correlated with global identity than occupational and ideological (Vosylis, Erentaitė, & Crocetti, 2018). We look to our relationships and contexts to make sense of ourselves.

Influences on Identity Development

Identity is constructed through our relationships and interactions with parents and peers. Relationships with parents are renegotiated as adolescents claim more and more autonomy, gaining space to develop their own sense of identity (Meeus & de Wied, 2007). When parents provide a sense of security along with autonomy, adolescents tend to be more comfortable exploring their world, using their parents are a secure base to which to return (Schwartz et al., 2015; Schwartz, Zamboanga, Luyckx, Meca, & Ritchie, 2013). Young people who feel connected to their parents, supported and accepted by them, but also feel encouraged to develop and voice their own views are more likely to engage in the exploration necessary to advance to the moratorium and achieved statuses. Adolescents who are not encouraged or permitted to explore are more likely to show the foreclosed status. For example, a 14-year-old in a family of doctors who has not considered any careers and comes to the decision, after much prodding by her parents and grandparents, that she wants to be a doctor may be in the identity foreclosed status. The degree of freedom afforded to adolescents for identity exploration varies with family and community contextual factors, such as socioeconomic status.

Adolescents from high socioeconomic status homes may have fewer responsibilities to work outside the home, may reside in communities with more extracurricular opportunities, and may be more likely to attend postsecondary education than their peers from low socioeconomic homes—all factors that support the exploration needed for identity achievement (Kroger, 2015; Spencer, Swanson, & Harpalani, 2015). Adolescents who do not receive support and encouragement to develop and express ideas are likely to experience identity diffusion, as they lack opportunities to seek out and make commitments to possible selves (Hall & Brassard, 2008; Reis & Youniss, 2004). Nearly 2,000 Dutch adolescents and parents surveyed over five waves showed that as adolescents commit to identities, their relationships with parents tend to improve (Crocetti, Branje, Rubini, Koot, & Meeus, 2017).

Peers also influence identity development as they serve as a mirror in which adolescents view their emerging identities, an audience to which they relay their self-narratives (McAdams & Zapata-Gietl, 2015). When adolescents feel supported and respected by peers, they feel more comfortable exploring identity alternatives (Ragelienė, 2016). As with parents, conflict with peers harms identity development as adolescents often feel less free to explore identity alternatives and lack a supportive peer group to offer input on identity alternatives, which holds negative implications for identity development, such as identity foreclosure or diffusion (Hall & Brassard, 2008). In emerging adulthood, romantic relationships are an important context for identity development as the attachment to partners provides security for exploration, similar to infants' secure base (Pittman, Keiley, Kerpelman, & Vaughn, 2011). Romantic partners influence each other reciprocally, illustrating some of the many interactions that occur between individuals and the people in their immediate contexts (Wängqvist, Carlsson, van der Lee, & Frisén, 2016).

Outcomes Associated With Identity Development

Identity achievement is associated with high self-esteem, a mature sense of self, feelings of control, high moral reasoning, and positive views of work and school (Jespersen, Kroger, & Martinussen, 2013; Spencer et al., 2015). In contrast, young people in the moratorium status often feel puzzled by the many choices before them (Lillevoll, Kroger, & Martinussen, 2013). The process of sorting through and determining commitments in the educational and relationship domains is stressful and is associated with negative mood and, at its extreme, can be paralyzing and curtail identity exploration (Crocetti, Klimstra, Keijsers, Hale, & Meeus, 2009; Klimstra et al., 2016). Young people who show identity foreclosure tend to take a rigid and inflexible stance. Unopen to new experiences, they avoid reflecting on their identity choice, and they reject information that may contradict their position.

Finally, while it is developmentally appropriate for early adolescents to have neither explored nor committed to a sense of identity, identity diffusion is uncommon by late adolescence and has been considered indicative of maladjustment (Kroger et al., 2010). Young people in identity diffusion keep life on hold; they don't seek the meaning-making experiences needed to form a sense of identity (Carlsson et al., 2016). Young people who show identity diffusion tend to use a cognitive style that is characterized by avoidance. Academic difficulties, general apathy, organization and time management problems, and alcohol and substance abuse are associated with identity diffusion and often precede it (Crocetti, Klimstra, Hale, Koot, & Meeus, 2013; Laghi, Baiocco, Lonigro, & Baumgartner, 2013). Research with Dutch adolescents followed from ages 14 to 18 suggests that engagement in delinquency is associated with identity diffusion, especially if the adolescent uses delinquent activities to assert independence (Mercer, Crocetti, Branje, van Lier, & Meeus, 2017). However, in-depth exploration of alternatives can predict advances in identity synthesis and a decline in delinquency. Identity is an ongoing construction over adolescence.

REVIEW 4.3

1. Explain Erikson's identity versus role confusion stage.

2. Define four identity statuses.

3. How does identity status change over time?

4. What are some influences on identity?

5. What are some outcomes associated with identity?

THINKING IN CONTEXT 4.3

1. How are adolescents' sense of self and identity influenced by other domains of development? In turn, how might other areas of development influence how adolescents view themselves? For example, consider aspects of physical and cognitive development, such as puberty and decision-making. Now how might adolescents' sense of identity influence other areas of development?

2. Identify contextual influences on the development of identity. In what ways do interactions with contextual influences, such as parents, peers, school, community, and societal forces, shape adolescents' emerging sense of identity?

3. Consider your identity in adolescence and now. What changes can you identify? Are there ways in which you remain the same? Explain. How have outside influences contributed to your development?

APPLY 4.3

Seventeen-year-old Leo entered the auditorium with some trepidation. Not only was it his first day of college, but Leo was a year younger than most students because he skipped a year of high school. Leo was nervous about sitting through orientation and meeting other first-year students. One activity required students to define themselves and their career goals and write their responses on a small sticky note to be posted on the wall. "I want to major in premed, go to medical school, and be a surgeon at a prestigious hospital, just like my mother," Leo wrote. Leo didn't look forward to taking the required general education classes. Later, after meeting his advisor to register for classes, Leo wondered why he should have to take classes in subjects that have nothing to do with medicine, like art, history, and English.

1. How would you describe Leo's identity?

2. In what ways might you expect it to change in the coming years?

3. What are some of the potential influences on Leo's identity development?

4. What advice would you give Leo?

ETHNIC-RACIAL IDENTITY

By middle childhood, many children begin to use ethnic and racial group terms as self-descriptors (Spencer & Markstrom-Adams, 1990; Umaña-Taylor et al., 2014). Children's understanding of ethnicity and race broadens as they enter adolescence. The cognitive and social advances that drive adolescents' quest to construct a sense of identity often spur exploration of their ethnic heritage. **Ethnic-racial identity** refers to a sense of membership to an ethnic or racial group including the attitudes, values, and culture associated

Adolescents of color often face the challenge of constructing positive ethnic-racial identities while confronting racism and discrimination.

Richard Levine / Alamy Stock Photo

with that group (whether Latinx, Asian American, African American, White, and so on) within a specific sociohistorical context (Phinney & Ong, 2007; Rivas-Drake et al., 2014; Umaña-Taylor, 2016b; Umaña-Taylor et al., 2014). As we have discussed, identity formation is a central developmental task for adolescents and emerging adults that is influenced by contextual factors. Many adolescents of color construct identities while immersed in contexts rife with racism and prejudice that are displayed as discrimination. Young people's sense of ethnic-racial identity influences the ways in which they experience, interpret, and respond to discrimination (Yip, 2018). The following sections often refer to the development of ethnic or racial identity. However, many individuals develop a sense of identity that includes both ethnicity and race (e.g., Black *and* Latinx).

Development of Ethnic-Racial Identity

Like other components of a sense of self, ethnic-racial identity develops and changes over time as individuals explore, gain experience, and make choices in various contexts. Adolescents explore their ethnic-racial identity by learning about the cultural practices associated with their ethnicity or race by reading, attending cultural events, and talking to members of their culture (Romero, Edwards, Fryberg, & Orduña, 2014). In addition to exploration, the process of ethnic-racial identity development involves internalizing values from one's ethnic and racial group (Hughes, Del Toro, & Way, 2017). As adolescents develop a sense of belonging to their cultural community, they may become committed to an ethnic-racial identity.

Similar to Marcia's identity status model, ethnic-racial identity can be described by three statuses (Phinney, 1989; Phinney & Ong, 2007). The *unexamined* status includes adolescents who have not explored the meaning of their ethnicity or race and show no clear personal understanding of or commitment to their race and ethnicity. The *exploration* status represents a moratorium in which the individual engages in an active search for information about the meaning of ethnic and racial group membership for them, without having committed. The a*chievement* status refers to having explored ethnicity or race, considering its meaning, and having accepted and internalized ethnicity or race as part of one's sense of self-identity. Ethnic-racial identity achievement results in commitment to and affirmation of one's ethnic or racial group as well as participation in identity-relevant contexts. That is, adolescents who demonstrate ethnic-racial identity achievement are engaged in their ethnic and racial community and participate in their culture.

During adolescence, young people progress from an unexplored and uncommitted ethnic-racial identity to a more secure one. Individuals move through the ethnic-racial identity generally, from unexamined, to exploration, to achieved in response to new experiences and opportunities for making meaning of their ethnicity or race (Phinney & Chavira, 1992). Early and middle adolescents tend to demonstrate a less clear and committed sense of ethnic-racial identity and engage in greater exploration compared with their older adolescent and young adult counterparts (Hughes et al., 2017). However, the ethnic-racial identity statuses are not stages. Instead, the development of ethnic-racial identity is cyclical in the sense that it is formed and reformulated throughout the life cycle (Hughes et al., 2017; Phinney & Ong, 2007). Individuals may regress to lower statuses as part of the normative identity development process (Syed, Azmitia, & Phinney, 2007). Thus, empirical studies have suggested that exploration and commitment begins in early adolescence but continues throughout early adulthood (Hughes et al., 2017).

Influences on Ethnic-Racial identity

The exploration and commitment process that is key to identity achievement also underlies establishment of a sense of ethnic-racial identity (Yip, 2014). Like other aspects of identity, ethnic-racial identity is influenced by family, peer, school, neighborhood, and societal contexts. Adolescents who learn about their culture, such as values, attitudes, language, and traditions, and regularly interact with parents and peers as members of a cultural community are more likely to construct a favorable ethnic-racial identity (Romero et al., 2014; White, Knight, Jensen, & Gonzales, 2018). For example, ethnic-racial identity is positively associated with an adolescent's proficiency in speaking his or her heritage language (Oh & Fuligni, 2010). Contexts that heighten awareness or salience of one's race or ethnicity, such as attending a large school with a diverse student population, may foster exploration and commitment of ethnic identity.

Adolescents may find it difficult to develop a feeling of cultural belonging and personal goals when the standards of the larger society are different from those of the culture of origin. For example, many Asian, Central American, and South American cultures emphasize collectivist values. Collectivist cultures stress commitment to family and community (Hofstede, 2001). Identity is fused with group membership. Children and adolescents reared in collectivist cultures understand themselves through their relationships, as sons and daughters, grandchildren, siblings, and community members. Individualist cultures, such as those in North America, Western Europe, and Australia, tend to value independence and autonomy. Identity development entails constructing a sense of self as an individual, based on one's unique characteristics and independent of others.

Parents

The family is a particularly important context for ethnic-racial identity formation, as close and warm family relationships are associated with more well-developed ethnic-racial identities (Umaña-Taylor et al., 2014). Parents promote ethnic, racial, and cultural socialization and pride by teaching children about the history, culture, and heritage associated with their ethnicity and race (Umaña-Taylor, 2016b). Parents who provide positive ethnic socialization messages promote a sense of group identity (Douglass & Umaña-Taylor, 2016).

Research suggests that there are group differences in ethnic socialization practices. Parents of color tend to engage in higher levels of ethnic socialization than White parents (Else-Quest & Morse, 2015; Harding, Hughes, & Way, 2017). In one study, Latinx and Asian American families reported engaging in more cultural socialization compared with White families (Kiang & Fuligni, 2009). Likewise, African American parents tend to engage in more ethnic socialization compared with White parents (Hughes & Chen, 1997). Black and Puerto Rican youth report higher levels of cultural socialization and preparation for bias than their White and Asian American peers (Hughes, Witherspoon, Rivas-Drake, & West-Bey, 2009b; Rivas-Drake, Hughes, & Way, 2009). Parents of African American youth tend to report more ethnic and cultural socialization than parents of White and Latinx youth, and they also report a greater emphasis on preparing their adolescents to manage bias than parents of youth from all other ethnic groups (Else-Quest & Morse, 2015). African American parents' socialization practices may buffer the effects of discrimination and racism on their adolescents' adjustment.

Ethnic socialization practices aim to pass down one's cultural heritage, traditions, and customs to children and often emphasize the experience of ethnic minority status. Cultural socialization, to the extent that it teaches youth about the traditions and history of their ethnic and racial group, is likely to foster ethnic-racial identity exploration and commitment (Nelson, Syed, Tran, Hu, & Lee, 2018; Sanchez, Whittaker, Hamilton, & Arango, 2017). For example, among Mexican-origin preadolescents, parental cultural socialization in fifth grade predicted the development of ethnic pride, affirming one's identity, in seventh grade (Hernández, Conger, Robins, Bacher, & Widaman, 2014). Similarly, Umaña-Taylor, Alfaro, Bámaca, and Guimond (2009) studied a predominantly Mexican-origin high school sample and found that high familial ethnic socialization during middle adolescence predicted increased exploration and ethnic-racial identity resolution 2 years later. Parental ethnic socialization also predicts ethnic-racial identity exploration and commitment in emerging adulthood (Nelson et al., 2018).

Adolescents' perception of their ethnic socialization, their view of the degree to which they adopt the customs and values of their culture, also predicts ethnic-racial identity (Hughes, Hagelskamp, Way, & Foust, 2009a). For example, Seaton, Yip, Morgan-Lopez, and Sellers (2012) found that African American adolescents' reports of perceived racial socialization were associated with their own ethnic identity exploration and commitment, as predicted likelihood of having an achieved ethnic identity status.

Sometimes, however, strong ethnic socialization messages from the family and ethnic community are perceived as pressure and stressful. Sometimes adolescents may experience discontinuity between the two worlds of home and ethnic community and school and society in general (Yoon et al., 2017). For example, parents who are immigrants may emphasize cultural socialization and devalue acculturation. Some may work long hours, with little time or energy to aid their children's adjustment. Parents who grew up as a member of a racial or ethnic majority in their home country or in a country that is ethnically homogeneous may be unaware of or lack the knowledge to help their children cope with the challenges of navigating two different cultures. Language barriers can prevent meaningful communication with teachers and school administrators (Boutakidis, Chao, & Rodríguez, 2011).

Alternatively, parents might restrict adolescents from participating in the larger culture out of fear that assimilation will undermine cultural values. One study of Vietnamese American adolescents living in an ethnic enclave in southern California provides an example. Most of the adolescents felt that their parents encouraged them to embrace their heritage, and make friends and engage in activities within the Vietnamese community, rather than become involved with the larger community of school and neighborhood (Vo-Jutabha, Dinh, McHale, & Valsiner, 2009). As one boy explained, "My parents expect me to speak Vietnamese consistently. Every now and then they just say that I forgot it and that I don't know how to speak it anymore. . . . Of course, I understand it and my parents expect me to be in a Viet Club or something. But I mean c'mon, really c'mon" (pp. 683–684). Another girl added, "I think living in the Asian community kinda stops me from branching out. I live in this area and all of my friends are mostly Asian and

I want to have other friends" (p. 680). Adolescents who perceive excessive parental pressure and restrictions might respond with rebellion and rejection of their ethnic heritage.

Peers

Similar to other aspects of identity, peers play a role in the development of an ethnic-racial identity. Adolescents may first be drawn to peers and make friendships based on superficial similarities, like appearance and perceived group membership in a race or ethnicity (see Chapter 9). Over time, more sophisticated processes, such as intimacy and identity, become important for sustaining the friendship. Indeed, a longitudinal study of sixth- and seventh-grade students found that having more diverse friends at the beginning of the academic year predicted increases in ethnic-racial identity exploration 1 year later (Rivas-Drake, Umaña-Taylor, Schaefer, & Medina, 2017). In addition, over time, adolescents' ethnic-racial identity becomes more like their peers. Exposure to an ethnically diverse friendship network may prompt greater engagement in activities that help adolescents learn about their own ethnic-racial background.

Other research supports the role of peers in ethnic-racial identity. Among African American adolescents, high levels of peer acceptance and popularity with African American peers are associated with a strong sense of ethnic identity (Rivas-Drake et al., 2014; Rock, Cole, Houshyar, Lythcott, & Prinstein, 2011). Similarly, college student friendship dyads tend to show similar levels of ethnic-racial identity exploration and commitment (Syed & Juan, 2012). Peers may support ethnic-racial identity development by communicating experiences and beliefs about ethnicity and race. For example, recent research with diverse emerging adults suggested that the messages that peers communicate about prejudice and discrimination predicted ethnic-racial identity commitment (Nelson et al., 2018). Peers provide a sense of community that can bolster young people's sense of commitment to an ethnic-racial identity and offer a buffer against stress from prejudice and discrimination.

Discrimination

Adolescents' developing cognitive abilities lead them to consider other people's perspectives with increasing complexity. Adolescents of color may become increasingly aware of and sensitive to negative stereotypes about their race or ethnicity, discrimination, and inequality. Negative messages, unequal treatment, and discrimination pose challenges to developing a positive sense of ethnic identity (McLean, Syed, Way, & Rogers, 2015). Adolescents from a variety of racial and ethnic groups, both native born and immigrant,

report experiences of discrimination on average one to two times a week (Hughes, Del Toro, Harding, Way, & Rarick, 2016; Umaña-Taylor, 2016a), which are associated with low self-esteem, depression, low social competence, behavior problems, and distress (Mrick & Mrtorell, 2011; Rivas-Drake et al., 2014; Wakefield & Hudley, 2007). For example, Mexican American youth who perceive and experience discrimination are less likely than other Mexican American youth to explore their ethnicity, feel positive feelings about their ethnicity, and incorporate a sense of ethnic identity (Romero & Roberts, 2003).

Some adolescents of color perceive discrimination in the classroom, such as feeling that their teachers call on them less, grade them more harshly, or discipline them more severely than other students. Discrimination at school has negative consequences for grades, academic self-concept, school engagement, and adjustment (Hood, Bradley, & Ferguson, 2017; McWhirter, Garcia, & Bines, 2018). For example, Navajo ninth- and tenth-grade adolescents who perceived discrimination showed poorer psychosocial adjustment and higher levels of substance use than their peers over a 1-year period (Galliher, Jones, & Dahl, 2011). Ethnic and racial minority adolescents often receive confusing messages to embrace their heritage while confronting discrimination, making the path to exploring and achieving ethnic identity challenging and painful (McLean et al., 2015).

Discrimination and ethnic-racial identity are interwoven. Adolescents' ethnic-racial identity and how they feel about their ethnic-racial group membership influences their perceptions and experiences of discrimination (Seaton, Yip, & Sellers, 2009). Young people who rate ethnicity/race as important to their overall sense of self, as well as those who are still in the process of exploring their identity, are more likely to report experiences with discrimination (Burrow & Ong, 2010; Pahl & Way, 2006). For instance, one study of Black and Hispanic college students found associations among ethnic identity exploration, ethnic identity affirmation, and perceived discrimination (Brittian et al., 2015). Correlational research is difficult to disentangle. Identifying with one's ethnic group may increase one's sensitivity to discrimination. Alternatively, the experience of discrimination may serve as an impetus to seek information about, and increase identification with, one's ethnic and racial group (Yip, 2018).

Although ethnic-racial identity exploration is associated with experiencing discrimination, a strong sense of ethnic-racial identity helps young people to reject negative views of their culture that are based on stereotypes (Rivas-Drake et al., 2014). Adolescents who report feeling positively about their ethnic-racial group membership report fewer experiences

Adolescents with a strong sense of ethnic-racial identity embrace their culture, such as these adolescents celebrating Dia de los Muertos.

Evelyn Orea/Alamy Stock Photo

with discrimination (Burrow & Ong, 2010). Longitudinal research with Hispanic immigrant adolescents in Miami and Los Angeles suggests that ethnic-racial identity exploration predicts perceptions of discrimination; adolescents who reported higher levels of ethnic-racial identity exploration reported more perceived discrimination 1 year later (Gonzales-Backen et al., 2018).

Ethnic-Racial Identity and Adjustment

A strong positive sense of ethnic-racial identity is an important contributor to well-being and is associated with school achievement in adolescents from diverse ethnicities, such as those of Mexican, Chinese, Latinx, African American, and European backgrounds (Adelabu, 2008; Fuligni, Witkow, & Garcia, 2005; Miller-Cotto & Byrnes, 2016). Adolescents who have achieved a strong sense of ethnic-racial identity tend to show better adjustment and coping skills as well as fewer emotional and behavior problems than do those who do not or only weakly identify with ethnicity or race (Kerpelman, Eryigit, & Stephens, 2008; Miller-Cotto & Byrnes, 2016; Mrick & Mrtorell, 2011; Nelson et al., 2018; Umaña-Taylor, 2016a; Zapolski, Fisher, Banks, Hensel, & Barnes-Najor, 2017). For example, African American and Afro-Caribbean college students with a more mature sense of ethnic-racial identity report engaging in less substance use and less risky alcohol use than their peers (Bowman Heads, Glover, Castillo, Blozis, & Kim, 2018). Adolescents who have achieved a strong sense of ethnic-racial identity tend to have high self-esteem, be optimistic, and view their ethnicity positively (Douglass & Umaña-Taylor, 2017; Gonzales-Backen, Bámaca-Colbert, & Allen,

2016; Williams, Aiyer, Durkee, & Tolan, 2014).

A strong sense of ethnic-racial identity can reduce the magnitude of the effects of racial discrimination on self-concept, academic achievement, and problem behaviors among African American, Latinx, and multiracial adolescents, as well as act as a buffer to stress, including discrimination stress (Douglass & Umaña-Taylor, 2016; Romero et al., 2014; Zapolski et al., 2017). For example, one sample of Asian American college students showed that ethnic-racial identity buffered the negative mental health effects of experiencing racial microaggressions (Choi, Lewis, Harwood, Mendenhall, & Huntt, 2017).

Over time, ethnic-racial identity becomes integrated with and interacts with other aspects of identity, such gender, career, and relationships, to create a coherent sense of self (Umaña-Taylor et al., 2014). Ethnic-racial identity continues to influence adjustment in adulthood (Syed et al., 2013). ●

REVIEW 4.4

1. What is ethnic-racial identity?

2. What patterns of change does ethnic-racial identity typically display?

3. Identify influences on ethnic-racial identity.

4. How is ethnic-racial identity related with adjustment?

THINKING IN CONTEXT 4.4

1. Consider your own sense of ethnic identity. Is ethnicity an important part of your sense of self? Why or why not?

2. Have you experienced shifts in your experience of ethnicity from childhood to adulthood?

3. What factors might influence whether an adolescent is aware and feels a sense of ethnic identity?

APPLY 4.4

Keenan never really paid attention to the ways in which he was different from his peers. Growing up in a predominantly White community, Keenan knew his skin was much darker than his friends, but everyone got along. When Keenan enrolled in a more diverse high school, however, he had his first experience with racism when an older student yelled out a racial slur. Keenan didn't know what to do, but this event made him aware of his race and of discrimination for the first time. As he learned more about his culture and about racism, Keenan realized that he had experienced discrimination in the past but didn't recognize it. Keenan became interested in African American culture and made new friends who shared his cultural heritage. His identity as an African American young

man has become an important part of Keenan's sense of identity.

1. Describe the changes in Keenan's ethnic-racial identity.

2. How might you classify Keenan's ethnic-racial identity?

3. What are some influences on his identity? What other contextual factors might influence Keenan's sense of ethnic-racial identity?

4. What outcomes might you predict for Keenan?

CHAPTER SUMMARY

4.1 Identify developmental changes in self-concept during adolescence.

Self-concept refers to the traits and characteristics we attribute to ourselves. With cognitive maturation, simple self-descriptions in childhood give way to abstract, often contradictory labels. Self-concept is domain specific and composed of the ideal and real self, as well as sometimes a false self. Thinking about one's self-concept is associated with specific patterns of brain activity in response to self-knowledge and evaluation tasks. Adolescents' Big Five personal characteristics are largely inborn but show age-related shifts and individual differences in the pattern and magnitude of change.

4.2 Discuss self-esteem in adolescence, including its influences and correlates.

Global self-esteem, an individual's subjective evaluation of his or her worth as a person, shows reliable changes from childhood through adolescence. Self-esteem tends to decline and fluctuations peak in early adolescence. Self-esteem becomes more differentiated and adolescents' self-esteem rises when adolescents evaluate themselves favorably in the domains that they view as important. Ethnic differences appear, with Black adolescents demonstrating higher levels of self-esteem than their peers, likely influenced by close-knit communities and support that helps to buffer the negative effects of racism and discrimination. Favorable self-evaluations are associated with positive adjustment and sociability in adolescents of all socioeconomic status and ethnic groups and persistently low self-esteem is associated with adjustment difficulties that can extend into adulthood.

4.3 Summarize the process of identity development, including influences on identity development and outcomes associated with it.

As adolescents come to understand their own traits and characteristics, they begin to construct an identity, a sense of self that is coherent and consistent over time. Identity achievement represents the successful resolution of this process, establishing a coherent

sense of self after exploring a range of possibilities. Adolescents must experience a psychosocial moratorium, a time-out period that allows adolescents the opportunity to explore possibilities of whom they might become. The identity status approach measures identity as entailing exploration and commitment making and categorizes adolescents into four statuses: moratorium, identity foreclosed, identity diffused, and identity achieved. People form a sense of identity in many different domains or areas and the relative salience of each domain can vary over development. Identity is constructed through our relationships and interactions with parents and peers. The degree of freedom afforded to adolescents for identity exploration varies with family and community contextual factors, such as socioeconomic status. Identity achievement is associated with high self-esteem, a mature sense of self, feelings of control, and high moral reasoning.

4.4 Describe ethnic-racial identity, its influences, and its role in adolescent adjustment.

Ethnic-racial identity refers to a sense of membership to an ethnic or racial group including the attitudes, values, and culture associated with that group within a specific sociohistorical context. Adolescents explore their ethnic-racial identity by learning about the cultural practices associated with their race. Similar to that of identity, ethnic-racial identity is characterized into three statuses: unexamined, exploration, and achievement. During adolescence, young people progress from an unexplored and uncommitted ethnic-racial identity to a more secure one. Individuals move through the ethnic-racial identity generally from unexamined, to exploration, to achieved in response to new experiences and opportunities for making meaning of their ethnicity or race. Adolescents who have achieved a strong sense of ethnic identity tend to show better adjustment and coping skills as well as fewer emotional and behavior problems than their peers. A strong sense of ethnic-racial identity can reduce the magnitude of the effects of racial discrimination.

KEY TERMS

ethnic-racial identity, 98

false self, 87

five-factor model, 88

global self-esteem, 89

ideal self, 87

identity achievement, 94

identity diffusion, 95

identity foreclosed, 95

identity status, 95

moratorium status, 95

psychosocial moratorium, 94

real self, 87

self-concept, 85

self-concept clarity, 86

5 Gender

Learning Objectives

Chapter Contents

In recent years, "gender reveal" parties have become popular among expectant couples who bat a piñata, pop a balloon, or cut a cake to reveal pink or blue ribbons, confetti, or icing reflecting the gender of their unborn child. Pink—it's a girl! Blue—it's a boy! What does gender mean for our development? In this chapter we examine common beliefs about gender, influences on gender, and the process of gender development in adolescence.

GENDER STEREOTYPES AND GENDER DIFFERENCES

What is gender and how it different from sex? Many people use the terms interchangeably, but to developmental scientists, sex and gender have distinct meanings. **Sex** is biological and determined by genetics—specifically, by the presence of a

Y chromosome in the 23rd pair of chromosomes that determine sex—and usually indicated by the appearance of an infant's genitals. **Gender**, on the other hand, is social: It is determined by socialization and the roles that the individual adopts. Most people naturally expect that men and women will behave differently according to their society's gender roles. These expectations sometimes reflect **gender stereotypes**, beliefs about the activities, attitudes, skills, and characteristics labeled as appropriate for males or females in a given culture. Gender stereotypes are exaggerated beliefs about what males and females should and should not do.

Gender Stereotypes

Throughout history, most societies have expected different behavior for males and females based on family and community needs. Expectations for women tend to derive from their traditional role as child bearer and caregiver (Best & Williams, 2001). Consequently, women were expected to be nurturing, kind, gentle, and sensitive to others. In contrast, men were expected to provide for and protect the family, requiring traits such as dominance, independence, strength, and power. Generalized expectations about the characteristics and activities of males and females reflect gender stereotypes and exist in most cultures. For example, adults in 30 countries generally agree on the instrumental and expressive traits thought to characterize males and females, respectively (Best & Williams, 2001; Guimond, Chatard, & Lorenzi-Cioldi, 2013; Lockenhoff et al., 2014). Likewise, emerging adults agreed that women should be cheerful, friendly, patient, and emotionally expressive, but not stubborn, intimidating, or arrogant; whereas men were expected to be ambitious, assertive, and have strong personalities, but not be emotional or approval seeking (Prentice & Carranza, 2002).

Over the past 3 decades, however, the roles and activities of women in Western countries have shifted, often in ways contrary to gender stereotypes. In 2016, women represented 47% of the U.S. workforce, compared to 38% in the mid-1980s (U.S. Bureau of Labor Statistics, 2019). Girls' participation in organized sports, traditionally the purview of males, has increased radically. For example, girls accounted for only 7% of high school athletes in 1971 to 1972; that number is now more than 40% (National Coalition for Women and Girls in Education, 2017). Women earned 40% of bachelor's degrees in the early 1980s compared with 57% today (National Center for Education Statistics, 2019). Despite these changes in women's activities, gender stereotypes in the United States have changed little over the past 3 decades. For example, a recent study compared adults surveyed in the early 1980s with those in the early 2010s and found no change in beliefs about expressive and instrumental traits (Haines, Deaux, & Lofaro, 2016). Across both time periods, women were rated as more communal than men and men as more instrumental than women. Adolescents tend to show similar patterns of judgments. An analysis of over 80 studies conducted in 29 countries over a 30-year period (1984 to 2014) suggests that early adolescents (age 10 to 14) endorse stereotypical gender roles, such as toughness, physical strength, and competitiveness for boys, and attractiveness, physical weakness, vulnerability, and compliance for girls (Kågesten et al., 2016). How do we acquire gender stereotypes?

Gender stereotypes emerge in early childhood and increase over childhood (Banse, Gawronski, Rebetez, Gutt, & Morton, 2010; Martin & Ruble, 2010). With cognitive and social development, adolescents' views about gender become more complex but most continue to endorse gender stereotypes (Brown & Stone, 2016). To date, most of the research on gender stereotyping has simply compared adolescents' judgments of hypothetical boys and girls. However, recent research from an intersectional perspective suggests that gender stereotyping is much more nuanced. For example, sixth- and eighth-grade students' beliefs about gender stereotypes varied with ethnicity and sexual orientation (Ghavami & Peplau, 2018). Specifically, girls on average were stereotyped as less aggressive, a masculine trait, than boys, but lesbian girls were viewed as most aggressive among girls and comparable to boys. Gay boys were stereotyped as least aggressive

Adolescents' views about gender become more complex and may vary with ethnicity and sexual orientation.

iStock.com/FG Trade

among boys, at levels similar to girls. Ethnicity also mattered. Gay African American and Latinx boys were rated less aggressive and lesbian Asian American and White girls were viewed as more aggressive than their heterosexual counterparts (Ghavami & Peplau, 2018). Gender stereotypes are complex and must be understood in concert with other social dimensions.

Gender Differences

Is there any truth to gender stereotypes? In short, no. Adolescent boys and girls certainly look different and they are treated differently, but a great body of research suggests that average sex differences in cognitive abilities and social behaviors are negligible at all ages (Hyde, 2014; Liben et al., 2013). Adolescent boys' and girls' abilities and behaviors overlap and there is a great deal of variability within each sex, more so than between the sexes (Blakemore, Berenbaum, & Liben, 2009; Hyde, 2016; Miller & Halpern, 2014). In other words, there are more differences among boys and among girls than there is between them. Thus, generalizations about males and females should be understood as referring to the average, but not necessarily to any individual boy or girl. The following sections examine compare boys' and girls' physical, cognitive, and socioemotional abilities.

Similarities and Differences in Physical Abilities

Throughout childhood, girls and boys are similar in weight and height and show similar rates of growth. Yet at all ages, even before birth, boys tend to be more physically active than girls, and this difference increases during childhood (Alexander & Wilcox, 2012; Leaper, 2013). Boys engage in more physical, active play, including rough-and-tumble interactions that involve playful aggression and overall body contact (Scott & Panksepp, 2003). As we have seen in Chapter 2, puberty triggers reproductive development and adolescent girls' and boys' bodies show different patterns of primary and secondary characteristics. After puberty, boys tend to be bigger, stronger, and faster than girls (Malina, Bouchard, & Bar-Or, 2004). Males continue to show more physical activity than females in adolescence and adulthood (Belcher et al., 2010; Colley et al., 2011).

Similarities and Differences in Cognitive Abilities

Boys and girls do not differ in intelligence, but research has recorded subtle differences in several specific cognitive tasks (Ardila, Rosselli, Matute, & Inozemtseva, 2011; Miller & Halpern, 2014). Sex differences in verbal ability emerge in infancy, as girls begin to talk earlier than boys and have a larger vocabulary

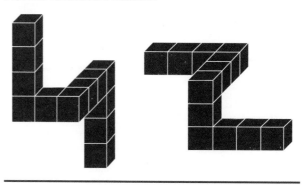

FIGURE 5.1

Mental Rotation Problem

than boys through age 5 (Bornstein et al., 2004). In all industrialized countries, girls show a small advantage on reading comprehension and verbal fluency tasks (Ardila et al., 2011; Miller & Halpern, 2014). From infancy, boys tend to perform better at spatial tasks, specifically those that measure mental rotation, the ability to recognize a stimulus that is rotated in space (see Figure 5.1) (Alexander & Wilcox, 2012; Quinn & Liben, 2014). Other spatial tasks show few to no differences (Hyde, 2016; Miller & Halpern, 2014).

Sex differences in math abilities are mixed. Girls perform better on tests of computational math (Hyde, 2014; Wei et al., 2012) and boys tend to perform better at word problems and tasks measuring mathematical reasoning (Byrnes & Takahira, 1993; Leahey & Guo, 2001). Yet boys and girls show similar understanding of math concepts (Hines, 2015). National standardized exams reveal no sex differences in math performance among U.S. eighth-graders (National Assessment of Educational Progress, 2019), but in high school boys tend to earn slightly higher scores on the mathematics portion of the Scholastic Aptitude Test (SAT) (College Board, 2018). The size of the difference in SAT scores has markedly decreased over the past 3 decades such that boys show a negligible advantage (Hyde, 2016; Lindberg, Hyde, Petersen, & Linn, 2010). Girls' advances in mathematics performance reflect the increasing emphasis by educational institutions, government, and industry on encouraging females to enter careers in the sciences (Ceci, Ginther, Kahn, & Williams, 2014; Dasgupta & Stout, 2014), supporting the role of socialization in girls' mathematics achievement.

Similarities and Differences in Socioemotional Abilities

From an early age, girls are better able to manage and express their emotions than boys (Weinberg, Tronick, Cohn, & Olson, 1999). While girls tend to express happiness and sadness more often than boys, boys

Today, girls are encouraged to succeed in mathematics and to consider careers in the sciences, once fields reserved for men.
iStock.com/skynesher

express more anger (Chaplin & Aldao, 2013). Girls also express shame and guilt more often than boys (Else-Quest, Higgins, Allison, & Morton, 2012). Girls are also more accurate at identifying facial expressions, such as happy or sad, than boys (Alexander & Wilcox, 2012; Thompson & Voyer, 2014).

It may not be surprising that girls and boys view themselves in different ways. Boys' believe that they are more competent in math, computers, and sports and girls' tend to view themselves as more competent in reading, music, English, art, and social studies (Harter, 2006). As we have discussed in prior chapters, adolescent girls tend to show lower self-esteem and a poorer body image than boys. Sex differences in depression emerge by around age 13 and increase throughout adolescence (Galambos, Berenbaum, & McHale, 2009). We examine depression in Chapter 13.

The most marked gender difference is in aggression. Beginning at preschool age and continuing through adolescence, boys tend to exhibit more physical aggression than girls (Card, Stucky, Sawalani, & Little, 2008; Ostrov & Godleski, 2010). Despite stereotypes about "mean girls," girls and boys show similar rates of verbal aggression and girls engage in relational aggression—excluding a peer from social activities, withdrawing friendship, spreading rumors, or humiliating the person— only slightly more often than boys (Else-Quest & Hyde, 2018; Perry & Pauletti, 2011).

Gender Roles

If there are more similarities than differences between boys and girls, why do beliefs about sex differences—that men and women come from "different planets," for example—persist? There is likely a cultural lag between societal changes, such as women's increasing levels of education, and gender beliefs (Diekman, Brown, Johnston, & Clark, 2010). The depth and durability of gender stereotypes means that even people who explicitly describe themselves as free of gender

stereotypes may be implicitly influenced by them (Rudman & Glick, 2001).

Masculinity, Femininity, and Androgyny

How do you view yourself? Do you believe that you have many masculine characteristics and few feminine characteristics, more feminine and fewer masculine characteristics, or do you have both masculine and feminine characteristics? In a classic study conducted in the 1970s, Sandra Bem examined college students' perceptions of gender roles for men and women. Students rated each characteristic as appropriate for a man or women or whether it is neutral, not associated with gender. The resulting measure, the Bem Sex Role Inventory (BSRI) (Bem, 1974), is the most commonly used measure of gender role perceptions. The BSRI includes scales for both masculine and feminine gender roles. The masculine gender role includes **instrumental traits** such as dominance, competitiveness, aggressiveness, and traits needed to act on the world and fulfill the traditional role of protector and provider for the family. The feminine gender role includes **expressive traits**, such as sympathetic, compassionate, and yielding, and traits that reflect women's roles as nurturers, such as sensitive to others and loves children. In addition, the BSRI includes a scale composed of neutral items not classified as masculine or feminine. Notably, Bem described the masculine and feminine gender roles as independent, meaning that individuals can show both masculine and feminine traits, known as **androgyny**. Table 5.1 illustrates sample items from the BSRI.

TABLE 5.1

Sample Items From the Bem Sex Role Inventory

MASCULINE	FEMININE	NEUTRAL
Aggressive	Affectionate	Adaptable
Ambitious	Cheerful	Conceited
Analytical	Childlike	Conscientious
Assertive	Does not use harsh language	Friendly
Competitive		Helpful
Has leadership abilities	Gentle	Likable
	Loves children	Reliable
Independent	Sensitive to the needs of others	Sincere
Strong personality		
Willing to take a stand	Soft spoken	Truthful
	Understanding	Unpredictable
Willing to take risks	Warm	

Source: Bem (1974).

Research with adults has shown that the greater repertoire of instrumental and expressive skills that accompanies the androgynous gender role permits them to adapt to a variety of situations with greater ease than do those who adopt either a masculine or feminine gender role (Lefkowitz & Zeldow, 2006; Pilar Matud, Bethencourt, & Ibáñez, 2014). The scant research on adolescents has suggested that androgyny is associated with fewer internalizing problems, such as anxiety and depression (Pauletti, Menon, Cooper, Aults, & Perry, 2017). However, the relation of androgyny and adaptation may vary with gender (and as we have discussed, likely other dimensions, such as sexual orientation). In girls, androgyny is associated with greater self-esteem relative to highly feminine or masculine gender roles, but boys who are masculine show higher self-esteem than their feminine or androgynous counterparts (Markstrom-Adams, 1989). Why do adolescent girls, but not boys, benefit from androgyny? Instrumental behaviors, such as assertiveness, enable girls to communicate their needs. However, boys are more heavily gender socialized from birth. In childhood, gender-atypical behavior is punished more in boys than girls (Hines, 2015). This pattern continues in adolescence. Adolescents, especially boys, who display gender-atypical behavior experience higher rates of bullying, social anxiety, and psychological distress than their gender-typical peers (Price, Olezeski, McMahon, & Hill, 2019; Smith & Juvonen, 2017; van Beusekom, Baams, Bos, Overbeek, & Sandfort, 2016).

Because of gender stereotypes, boys who identify as androgynous may face more social challenges to adaptation than girls.
Adolescent Content/Hanna Wentz/Getty Images

Gender Roles and Sexual Orientation

What does gender role—holding masculine, feminine, or androgynous characteristics—mean for sexuality? Is there a relationship between masculine or feminine traits and sexual orientation? Although television and media may depict gay men as overtly feminine and lesbian women as masculine, the relationship between gender nonconformity and sexual orientation is complex. Some studies suggest that gender nonconformity and sexual orientation are correlated and others suggest that they are independent (Martin-Storey, 2016). Most of the research suggesting a link between childhood gender nonconformity and sexual orientation is based on retrospective reports in which gay, lesbian, and heterosexual adults recall their childhood behavior (Li, Kung, & Hines, 2017). Retrospective reports may be susceptible to memory bias because our memories of past events are subtly influenced by our subsequent attitudes, behaviors, and experiences (Gottschalk, 2003). In contrast, prospective research follows participants over time, enabling researchers to study behaviors as they unfold.

Is childhood gendered behavior related to sexual orientation? One prospective study of over 4,500 children found that parent reports of gender-typed behavior at ages 4 and 5 predicted adolescents' self-reported sexual orientation at age 15 (Li et al., 2017). A larger study of over 10,000 middle and high school students surveyed again 7 and 14 years later, in emerging adulthood and early adulthood, respectively, found average group differences in gender nonconforming behavior as well as substantial individual variability (Kahn & Halpern, 2019). Although on average gay and lesbian participants reported more gender nonconforming behavior than their heterosexual counterparts, many gender nonconforming young people identified as heterosexual, suggesting that gender-typed behaviors vary among all sexual orientations. That is, sexual orientation cannot be inferred from gender-typed behavior. Both gay and heterosexual men may adopt a masculine gender role characterized by instrumental traits, a feminine gender role characterized by expressive traits, or both instrumental and expressive traits (androgyny). This is also true for lesbian women and bisexual men and women. We examine sexual orientation in Chapter 6.

REVIEW 5.1

1. Define sex and gender.

2. What are gender stereotypes?

3. Identify gender roles.

4. Describe gender differences in physical, cognitive, and socioemotional abilities.

. . . .

THINKING IN CONTEXT 5.1

What contextual factors might contribute to the differences and similarities we see in boys and girls?

. . . .

APPLY 5.1

In elementary school Marcel loved to write. He'd write short stories and post them online. In high school he enrolled in a writing class, one that his teacher said was unique because most high schools in the area didn't have writing courses. On the first day Marcel noticed that he was the only boy in class. Later that day he asked his friend to enroll in the class and keep him company. "Nope—writing's for girls. No one wants to date a guy who's 'in touch' with his feminine side," Marcel's friend explained. Marcel wondered if this was right and whether he was too girly. He hoped this didn't mean that girls would ignore him—or, even worse, that maybe his interests signaled that he wasn't attractive to girls.

1. Examine Marcel's situation and perspective. How are gender roles and stereotypes reflected in Marcel's concerns?

2. What advice would you give Marcel?

. . . .

INFLUENCES ON GENDERED BEHAVIOR

We have seen that, despite few sex differences in abilities, gender stereotypes are common and correspond to many people's behavior. How is gender transmitted to young people? Some explanations of gendered behavior rely on biology, others hinge on cognitive factors, and still others point to contextual influences.

Biological Influences on Gender in Adolescence

Biological explanations point to the role of evolution and look to sex differences in hormones and the brain

as contributors to psychological and behavioral functioning (Hines, 2015). From an evolutionary perspective, males and females' behavior adapted over centuries to the challenges they faced. As providers and protectors, males adapted to become aggressive and competitive because these traits were advantageous in securing, providing for, and protecting a mate and thereby passing along their genetic inheritance (Côté, 2009). Females became more nurturing as it was adaptive to care for the young to ensure that their genes survived to be passed along to the next generation. Gendered behavior promotes survival of the individual and species. In support of this evolutionary perspective, most mammalian species demonstrate a preference for same-sex playmates, males are more active and aggressive, and females are more nurturing (Beatty, 1992; de Waal, 1993).

Hormones also contribute to sex differences in interests and behaviors. Animal and human studies have demonstrated that early exposure to relatively high levels of testosterone promotes male-typical behavior development. When females are prenatally exposed to high levels of male sex hormones (e.g., in the case of congenital adrenal hyperplasia, a genetic disorder that causes excess androgen production beginning prenatally), they show more active play and fewer caregiving activities in early childhood compared with their female peers (Auyeung et al., 2009; Hines et al., 2016). Testosterone is linked with aggression. Higher levels of testosterone, prenatally and after birth, can account for boys' tendency to be more aggressive than girls. These differences then influence play styles; children choose to play with children who have similar styles, resulting in a preference

Children tend to choose same-sex playmates.
monkeybusinessimages/iStock

for same-sex playmates (Berenbaum, Blakemore, & Beltz, 2011). In this way, biological factors influence the behaviors that are associated with gender roles.

Puberty causes radical shifts in hormones that influence adolescents' brains and behavior. As we have discussed, pubertal hormones stimulate brain development (Goddings, Beltz, Peper, Crone, & Braams, 2019; Wierenga et al., 2018). Neural changes parallel pubertal timing, with peaks in cerebral volume and cortical and subcortical gray matter corresponding to increases in testosterone and occurring 1 to 2 years earlier in girls than boys (Herting & Sowell, 2017; Hines, 2011). Testosterone also plays a role in adolescents' increased sensitivity to rewards. Specifically, pubertal increases in testosterone are associated with increased activity in the nucleus accumbens, part of the brain's reward circuitry, in response to rewards in both males and females (Braams, van Duijvenvoorde, Peper, & Crone, 2015).

Testosterone also plays a role in threat perception. For example, one recent study examined connectivity between the amygdala and orbitofrontal cortex (OFC) in a sample of 11- and 12-year-old girls and boys matched for pubertal stage (Spielberg et al., 2015). Increases in testosterone were associated with reduced connectivity between the amygdala and OFC (part of the prefrontal cortex responsible for coordinating emotion, rewards, and decision-making) and, in turn, heightened reactivity to perceived threats. Other research has found the same pattern of reduced functional coupling between the amygdala and prefrontal cortex with higher testosterone levels and accompanied by increased reactivity and aggression (Nguyen et al., 2016; Peters, Jolles, Duijvenvoorde, Crone, & Peper, 2015). Overall, it appears that testosterone is associated with loosening the links between the amygdala and regulatory parts of cortex that characterizes the dual systems model (see Chapter 3). Given that boys experience greater changes in testosterone, they likely experience greater changes in aggression and threat reactivity. Other explanations for gender role development rely on understanding children and adolescents' thinking, as described in the next section.

Cognitive Influences on Gender in Adolescence

Cognitive development, individuals' capacity for thought and reasoning, influences how children and adolescents understand gender. According to the **cognitive-developmental theory of gender** (Kohlberg, 1966), children and adolescents' understanding of gender is constructed in the same manner as their understanding of the world: by interacting with people and things and thinking about their experiences. Young infants, by 3 to 4 months of age, distinguish between female and male faces (Quinn, Yahr, Kuhn, Slater, & Pascalis, 2002). By about 2 years of age, children develop a **gender identity**, an awareness of their sex (Bussey, 2013). Once children label themselves as male or female, they classify the world around them, as well as their own behaviors, according to those labels (e.g., like me, not like me) (Kohlberg, 1966). By 2 to 2½ years of age, once children have established gender identity, they show more interest in gender-appropriate toys (e.g., dolls for girls, cars for boys) and they show a preference for playing with children of their own sex (Zosuls et al., 2009). In this way, children construct their own understandings of what it means to be a boy or a girl and thereby begin to acquire gender roles (Levy & Carter, 1989).

Gender stability, the understanding that gender generally does not change, emerges at about age 3. However, children's grasp of gender tends to emphasize appearance and they therefore tend to believe that wearing a dress, for example, can change a child from boy to girl.

Between ages 3 and 5, after acquiring gender stability, children show an increase in stereotype knowledge, evaluate their own gender more positively, and tend to show more rigidly sex-typed behaviors (Halim et al., 2013). In one study of U.S. children from Mexican, Chinese, Dominican, and African American ethnic backgrounds, gender stereotypes held at age 4 predicted positive same-gender attitudes and gender-stereotyped behavior at age 5 (Halim, Ruble, Tamis-LeMonda, Shrout, & Amodio, 2017). The more positively children view their own gender, the more likely girls are to insist on wearing dresses and the more likely boys are to refuse to wear anything with a hint of femininity (Halim et al., 2014). In contrast, children with positive other-gender attitudes tend to have more flexible thoughts about gender appropriateness and less gender biased behavior (Halim et al., 2017).

Only as children come to understand Piagetian conservation tasks (see Chapter 3) do they come to realize that a boy will always be a boy, even if he changes his appearance, such as by growing long hair or wearing a skirt; and a girl will remain a girl no matter what she wears or which activities she chooses. **Gender constancy** refers to the child's understanding that gender does not change; that he or she will always be the same regardless of appearance, activities, or attitudes (Kohlberg, 1966). Awareness of the biological basis of gender, that a person's sex is a biological characteristic, occurs around 8 years of age (Ruble et al., 2007). Older children tend to develop more flexible and less stereotyped views of gender because they recognize that gender is independent of appearance and behavior. Gender-stereotypical preferences for movies and television programs decline from middle childhood to early adolescence (Kanka, Wagner, Buchmann, & Spiel, 2019).

Gender schema theory is another cognitive explanation of gender development that emphasizes information processing and environmental influences on gender (Martin, Ruble, & Szkrybalo, 2002). Once children develop the ability to label their sex, they begin to form a **gender schema**, a concept or a mental structure that organizes gender-related information and embodies their understanding of what it means to be a male or female (similar to Piaget's concept of schemes). A child's gender schema becomes an organizing principle and children notice more and more differences between males and females, such as preferred clothes, toys, and activities. Gender stereotypes are often incorporated into gender schemas because children tend to notice and emphasize differences. Children then use their gender schemas as guides for their behavior and attitudes, and gender typing occurs (Miller et al., 2006; Weisgram, 2016). In this way, gender development is influenced by self-socialization. In addition, children play with peers who engage in similar levels of gender-stereotyped activities (e.g., playing dress-up, playing with tools) and further socialize one another's gendered behavior and attitudes (Martin et al., 2013). Gender schemas influence our expectations for others' behavior as well as our own. As children's reasoning advances, they may become aware of the many similarities boys and girls share. Although their understanding of gender stereotypes persists, older children and adolescents may apply more complex gender schemas to their behavior.

From a cognitive perspective, in adolescence, advances in reasoning should contribute to more flexible and sophisticated views of gender. Yet, as we will discuss, gender stereotyping and gender-typed behavior persists, and some argue increases, in early adolescence (Priess & Lindberg, 2018). Why? Adolescents are immersed in a gendered world that influences their development.

Contextual Influences on Gender in Adolescence

A contextual approach to understanding gender development emphasizes individuals' constructions of gender through processes of social learning and interactions with the sociocultural context in which they are raised. Gender typing occurs through socialization and interactions with parents, peers, teachers, and culture (Hanish et al., 2013). Children internalize

expectations about gender-related behavior as they make gains in self-regulation, such that they feel good about themselves when their behavior is in accord with their internal standards and experience negative feelings when their behavior is not (Leaper, 2013).

Gender socialization begins in infancy, at home. From birth, boys and girls have different social experiences (Martin & Ruble, 2010). Parents perceive sons and daughters differently and have different expectations for them from birth. For example, parents often describe competition, achievement, and activity as important for sons and warmth, politeness, and closely supervised activities as important for daughters (Turner & Gervai, 1995). Boys tend to receive toys that emphasize action and competition, such as cars, trains, and sports equipment, and girls tend to receive toys that focus on cooperation, nurturance, and physical attractiveness, such as baby dolls, Easy-Bake Ovens, and play makeup (Hanish et al., 2013). Parents tend to encourage boys' independent play, demands for attention, and even attempts to take toys from other children, whereas parents tend to direct girls' play, provide assistance, refer to emotions, and encourage girls to participate in household tasks (Basow, 2008; Hines, 2015). Boys tend to be reinforced for independent behavior, whereas girls are reinforced for behavior emphasizing closeness and dependency.

As children enter adolescence, parents continue to foster autonomy in boys, allowing them more independence than girls. Parents tend to monitor and restrict adolescent girls' behavior more than boys, as girls are often viewed as more vulnerable (McHale, Crouter, & Whiteman, 2003). However, a recent examination of 126 studies suggests a cohort or generational shift in parents' behavior toward children and

Gender-typed behavior often increases in early adolescence.
imageBROKER / Alamy Stock Photo

adolescents (Endendijk, Groeneveld, Bakermans-Kranenburg, & Mesman, 2016). Specifically, studies published in the 1970s and 1980s reported that parents directed more autonomy-supportive strategies with boys than toward girls; yet from 1990 onward, parents directed somewhat more autonomy-supportive strategies with girls than toward boys. As parents' gender-related behavior and parenting strategies shift, adolescents' gendered behavior may shift. Adolescents whose parents express traditional attitudes toward gender roles are more likely to hold traditional attitudes themselves (Tenenbaum & Leaper, 2003).

The peer group also serves as a powerful influence on gender typing in young children. As early as age 3, peers reinforce gender-typed behavior with praise, imitation, or participation (Martin & Ruble, 2010). Girls and boys show different play styles that influence their choices of play partners and contribute to sex segregation (Martin, Fabes, Hanish, Leonard, & Dinella, 2011). Boys use more commands, threats, and force; girls use more gentle tactics, such as persuasion, acceptance, and verbal requests, which are effective with other girls but ignored by boys (Leaper, 2013; Leaper, Tenenbaum, & Shaffer, 1999). Children tend to disapprove of gender-atypical behavior, especially in boys, and gender-atypical behavior is associated with exclusion and peer victimization in adolescence (Roberts, Rosario, Slopen, Calzo, & Austin, 2013; Zosuls, Andrews, Martin, England, & Field, 2016).

Adolescents tend to encounter similar gender-related messages from parents, peers, and teachers (Galambos et al., 2009; Kågesten et al., 2016) as all are immersed in a larger set of interacting contexts of socialization agents. Teachers, often unwittingly, reinforce gender stereotypes, such as assuming that boys and girls have differing abilities in math, science, and English and differ in activity level (Leaper & Brown, 2018). At the level of the school, gender norm salience, the extent to which gender atypicality stands out and is accompanied by peer victimization, varies (Smith, Schacter, Enders, & Juvonen, 2018). Some schools show high gender norm salience characterized by greater peer victimization of gender-atypical adolescents. Other schools show less gender norm salience and the association of gender typicality and peer victimization is small or nonexistent. Gender norm salience is associated with depressed mood in boys, regardless of gender typicality, and boys reporting lower gender typicality experienced more loneliness and social anxiety in schools with more salient gender norms (Smith et al., 2018).

Popular children's media often confirms gender stereotypes.
SilverScreen / Alamy Stock Photo

Media influences on gender socialization begin early in life. Children's television, G-rated movies, and even coloring books tend to depict the world as gender stereotyped, such as by displaying more male than female characters, with male characters in action roles such as officers or soldiers in the military and female characters as more likely to have domestic roles and be in romantic relationships (England, Descartes, & Collier-Meek, 2011; Fitzpatrick & McPherson, 2010; Smith, Pieper, Granados, & Choueiti, 2010).

Adolescents are also exposed to gender stereotypes in media, including music and music videos, which are associated with gender-typed attitudes and behavior (Koletić, 2017; Peter & Valkenburg, 2009). One study of Dutch 13- to 16-year-old adolescents suggested that media preferences were associated with gender stereotypes such that girls and boys who reported preferring hip-hop and hard-house music were more likely to endorse gender stereotypes than their peers (ter Bogt, Engels, Bogers, & Kloosterman, 2010). Do media preferences influence gender stereotyping or do gendered interests influence media preferences? Correlational studies such as these cannot tell us about causality; however, media preferences and gendered interests likely influence each other. We examine the role of media in development in Chapter 11.

In addition to media, the larger culture and its many aspects also influence gender development in that most cultures emphasize gender differences. Some societies closely link activities and dress with gender; girls and boys may attend sex-segregated schools, wear contrasting types of school uniforms, and never interact (Beal, 1994). Societies vary in the types of behavior that are considered appropriate for men and women. For example, farming is a task for women in many parts of the world, but in North America it is men who are traditionally in charge of farming duties. The exact behaviors may vary across societies, but all societies have values regarding gender-appropriate behavior for males and females and all societies transmit these values to young children.

Sometimes adolescents experience conflicting cultural messages. One longitudinal study examined the role of acculturation in Mexican American adolescents' views of gender roles. Mexican American adolescents born in Mexico or the United States were followed from ages 13 to 20 (Updegraff et al., 2014). Among the adolescents born in Mexico, girls showed declines in traditional attitudes from early to late adolescence, but males' attitudes were stable over time. U.S.-born males and females did not differ in their traditional gender attitude trajectories, with both declining over time. Mexico-born adolescents' likely greater exposure to Mexican culture, wherein attitudes about men's and women's roles are generally quite traditional, may influence their views of gender roles (Cauce & Domenech-Rodríguez, 2002). Yet in this study, only Mexico-born males maintained their traditional gender role attitudes across adolescence (Updegraff et al., 2014). In addition, the differences in the trajectories of Mexico-born males versus females suggested that males may be less influenced by acculturation processes, which are expected to lead to less traditional gender role attitudes. One possibility is that traditional gender role values in Mexican American families are advantageous for males, as Latinx culture traditionally awards status and privilege (e.g., freedom to spend time outside the home) and fewer responsibilities (e.g., less involvement in housework) for adolescent and young adult males (Raffaelli & Ontai, 2004).

REVIEW 5.2

1. Identify biological influences on gendered behavior in adolescence.

2. How do cognitive theories account for gendered behavior in adolescence?

3. What are contextual influences on gendered behavior in adolescence?

• •

THINKING IN CONTEXT 5.2

Consider bioecological influences on gender development. Identify microsystem and mesosystem influences on gender. Give examples. How might exosystem factors influence gendered behavior? Macrosystem factors?

• •

APPLY 5.2

Thirteen-year-old Sam has consistently displayed gender-atypical behavior since childhood.

1. How might cognitive-developmental and gender schema theories account for Sam's behavior?

2. What challenges might Sam face?

3. In what ways might your responses differ if Sam is a boy or girl?

• •

GENDER TYPING AND GENDER IDENTITY

From birth we are immersed in a gendered world that influences how we understand ourselves, others, and our environment and experiences. **Gender typing**, the process of acquiring gendered behaviors, begins in infancy (Liben et al., 2013; Martin & Ruble, 2010).

Gender Typing in Infancy and Childhood

Young infants notice gender. By 3 months of age, infants can distinguish male and female faces (Quinn et al., 2002); by 6 months, they match male voices with male faces and female voices with female faces (Patterson & Werker, 2002). Young infants may not understand gender, but they show more interest in toys that match their biological sex. In one study of 3- to 8-month-old infants, boys looked longer at a toy truck than a doll, whereas girls looked longer at the doll (Alexander, Wilcox, & Woods, 2009).

At around 2 years, children label their own sex, referring to themselves as boy or girl (Campbell, Shirley, & Candy, 2004). As children develop a sense of gender, they actively seek information about gender, expand their knowledge of gender stereotypes, and demonstrate gender stereotyping in toy and play preferences, such as not playing with toys associated with the opposite sex even when there are no other toys available (Jadva, Hines, & Golombok, 2010; Zosuls et al., 2009). Preschoolers express their extensive knowledge of the activities and interests stereotyped for males and females as rigid rules about the behavior appropriate for boys and girls (Baker, Tisak, & Tisak, 2016; Blakemore et al., 2009). For example, most 3- and 4-year-old children agree that gender stereotypes for clothing (wearing a dress), hairstyle (long hair), and toys (Barbie doll and GI Joe) cannot be violated (Blakemore, 2003). Preschoolers expect males to be independent, forceful, and competitive, and females to be warm, nurturing, and expressive (Martin et al., 2013; Miller, Trautner, & Ruble, 2006; Tisak, Holub, &

Tisak, 2007). Children spend more time playing with same-sex peers and expect gender-stereotypical play from their peers

In middle childhood, knowledge of stereotypes expands to include beliefs about personality and achievement (Bussey, 2013; Serbin, Powlishta, & Gulko, 1993). Stereotypes influence children's preferences and views of their own abilities. For example, by age 6, girls are less likely than boys to believe that members of their gender are "really, really smart," lump more boys into the "really, really smart" category, and begin to avoid activities and games said to be for children who are "really, really smart" (Bian, Leslie, & Cimpian, 2017). Elementary school children describe reading, spelling, art, and music as appropriate subjects for girls and mathematics and athletics as for boys (Cvencek, Meltzoff, & Greenwald, 2011; Kurtz-Costes, Copping, Rowley, & Kinlaw, 2014; Passolunghi, Rueda Ferreira, & Tomasetto, 2014).

Gender rigidity tends to decline in middle to late childhood (Ruble et al., 2007; Trautner et al., 2005). Advances in cognitive development enable older children to understand that gender-stereotyped traits are associated with gender, not defined by gender (Banse et al., 2010; Martin et al., 2002). This trend toward flexibility in views of what males and females can do increases with age, with girls showing more flexible gender-stereotype beliefs than boys (Blakemore et al., 2009).

Gender Identity and Gender Typing in Adolescence

One of the most important developmental tasks of adolescence is identity development, forming a comprehensive sense of self. Recall from Chapter 4 that there are multiple dimensions to identity, such as vocation, interpersonal relationships, sexuality, and gender. Adolescents explore identity possibilities, eventually making commitments, in each area, often on different timetables. Gender identity is a particularly salient aspect of self for many adolescents.

Gender Identity in Adolescence

Children's gender identity is rooted in self-identification, generally as boy or girl, beliefs about appropriate behaviors for boys and girls, and adoption of gendered behavior. In preadolescence and early adolescence, gender identity expands to include four other components in addition to self-identification: *gender typicality* (the degree to which adolescents feel like a typical member of their gender group), *gender contentedness* (the degree to which adolescents are happy with their gender group), *felt pressure for gender conformity* (the degree to which adolescents feel pressure from parents, peers, and self for conformity to gender stereotypes), and *intergroup bias* (the extent to which adolescents believe that their own gender is superior to the other) (Egan & Perry, 2001). Through a process of personal reflection and input from others, adolescents judge and make commitments to each facet of gender identity. Individuals vary in how they proceed in considering the various facets of gender identity and when each is achieved (Perry & Pauletti, 2011). Like other aspects of identity, once established, these dimensions of gender identity are relatively stable but may undergo change over adolescence, emerging adulthood, and adulthood (Kornienko, Santos, Martin, & Granger, 2016).

Most of the research on gender identity in adolescence has focused on perceived gender typicality. Generally, the degree to which adolescents view themselves as typical of their gender predicts adolescent adjustment, including measures of mental health and popularity with peers, especially in boys (Egan & Perry, 2001; Jewell & Brown, 2014). Associations between gender typicality and adjustment are influenced by interactions with peers, especially peer acceptance and victimization (Menon, 2011; Smith & Leaper, 2006). For example, one longitudinal study found that low gender typicality in seventh grade was associated with peer victimization, which in turn predicted increased social anxiety and somatic problems (feeling physically ill) in eighth grade (Smith & Juvonen, 2017). Generally, adolescents who feel gender-atypical perceive pressure from parents and peers to act in gender-typical ways and tend to show more internalizing problems, such as anxiety, than their peers (Yunger, Carver, & Perry, 2004).

Gender Intensification in Adolescence

With the onset of puberty, physical development takes center stage. As their bodies mature and they look more like adults, adolescents are often treated differently by others and become acutely aware of their appearance and their gender. Some researchers argue that young people perceive greater social pressure to adhere to gender-stereotyped roles and behaviors in early adolescence, a phenomenon referred to as the **gender intensification hypothesis** (Galambos et al., 2009; Priess & Lindberg, 2018). Boys may feel greater pressure to become more masculine and less feminine and girls may experience the reverse, greater pressure to become more feminine and less masculine. Although gender flexibility tends to increase in late childhood (Banse et al., 2010), rigidity tends to rebound in early adolescence. For example, one meta-analysis of 30 years of research conducted in 29 countries found that young adolescent boys and girls tended to endorse gender-stereotyped norms such as toughness and competition as representative of masculinity and weakness and attractiveness as representative of femininity (Kågesten et al., 2016). Boys were more likely to endorse stereotypical gender norms and girls tended to express more flexible views of gender.

Although adolescents' thinking becomes more flexible and abstract, they often express stereotyped views about gender roles. Similar to young children, adolescents tend to negatively evaluate peers who violate expectations for gendered behavior, such as by engaging in behaviors or expressing interests stereotyped for the other sex (Alfieri, Ruble, & Higgins, 1996; Sigelman, Carr, & Begley, 1986; Toomey, Card, & Casper, 2014). Social pressures may drive adolescents toward more gender-stereotypic behavior (Galambos et al., 2009). As we will discuss in Chapter 9, the urge to conform to perceived peer pressure increases in early adolescence. Gender-consistent

Adolescent boys tend to perceive more social pressure to act in gender stereotypical ways.
iStock.com/bokan76

behavior may have social rewards. Boys who are perceived as less masculine and girls as less feminine than peers may feel less accepted, be less popular, and experience higher rates of victimization (Smith & Leaper, 2006; Toomey et al., 2014). Indeed, longitudinal surveys of adolescents conducted at the beginning and end of their first year of middle school found an increase in masculinity scripts for boys but not girls (Rogers, DeLay, & Martin, 2017). Longitudinal research with African American youth found that young girls and boys show knowledge of gender stereotypes, but from ages 9 to 15 they show declines in traditional gender attitudes that level off through age 18 (Lam, Stanik, & McHale, 2017). Some developmental scientists, however, question whether all adolescents experience gender intensification (Priess & Lindberg, 2018).

Research findings examining the gender intensity hypothesis are mixed. For example, Galambos, Almeida, and Petersen (1990) found that sex differences in instrumental (masculine) qualities, such as independence and leadership, increased in early adolescence, but sex differences in expressive (stereotypically feminine) qualities, such as sensitivity and kindness, did not. That is, boys endorsed more masculine qualities than girls over early adolescence, but gender differences in femininity remained the same; girls did not endorse more feminine qualities. Recall that boys tend to experience greater gender socialization pressure than girls. More recent longitudinal research found no increases in gender conformity for boys or girls between ages 11 and 15 (Priess, Lindberg, & Hyde, 2009). In the United States and other Western cultures, boys are free to be more expressive and girls are encouraged to be more independent than they were in the past (Steensma, Kreukels, de Vries, & Cohen-Kettenis, 2013). By late adolescence, even

young people who earlier displayed gender intensification tend to become more flexible in their thinking and adoption of gender roles.

Contextual Influences on Gender Typing in Adolescence

It is difficult to draw conclusions about gender typing in adolescence because gendered expectations and adolescents' responses and adjustment to gender typing likely vary with contextual factors and reflect the intersection of gender, ethnicity, and socioeconomic status (Buckley, 2018). Boys' adherence to the norms of masculinity varies, with some boys clinging tightly to traditional masculine ideologies and others deviating from these gender expectations (Santos, Galligan, Pahlke, & Fabes, 2013; Way et al., 2014). The experience of gender is filtered through and interacts with other social identities, such as race (Rogers, Scott, & Way, 2015; Shields, 2008). For example, both race and gender tend to be particularly salient and interrelated for Black adolescent males (Cunningham, Swanson, & Hayes, 2013; Ghavami & Peplau, 2013). In response to a history of slavery, poverty, and ongoing discrimination, Black adolescent boys may feel pressure to adopt a hypermasculine role. An extreme instrumental role characterized by toughness, aggressiveness, detachment, and strength may protect Black boys' sense of self and self-esteem in light of injustices and can help them cope with the anger and fear that accompanies discrimination (Buckley, 2018; Seaton, 2007; Spencer, Fegley, Harpalani, & Seaton, 2004).

Yet current research with Black male youth also suggests variability in gender typicality. In one study, Black males examined at three points from the beginning of ninth grade to the end of tenth grade found that the centrality of gender to their sense of identity declined, contrary to gender intensification theory and the literature on hypermasculinity (Rogers et al., 2015). However, these findings were likely influenced by the boys' context—an all-male high school. Incoming ninth-grade students may have experienced the school context as threatening and responded with heightened levels of masculinity that declined to normal levels as the adolescents adjusted to the new school (Rogers et al., 2015). Black adolescent boys may adopt a hypermasculine gender role as a reactive coping strategy to negative experiences in community and school contexts, suggesting that hypermasculinity may be defensive, in response to challenging contexts, rather than normative (Cunningham et al., 2013). More recent research found that male Black high school students endorsed both feminine and masculine characteristics (androgynous) than endorsed a stereotypical sex-typed masculine role and androgyny was associated with a positive self-concept (Buckley, 2018). In reality, it is likely that Black adolescent males experience a range of gender identities in response to different contexts and experiences.

As individualistic cultures value independence, assertiveness, and other traditionally masculine characteristics, some have argued that girls may also experience pressure to adopt qualities deemed masculine (for example, as "tomboys") (Ahlqvist, Halim, Greulich, Lurye, & Ruble, 2013). As explained by one adolescent girl, "We're supposed to look like girls, but act like boys" (Rogers, Yang, Way, Weinberg, & Bennet, 2019). Gendered expectations also vary with ethnicity and socioeconomic status. Black girls and Latinas may be more likely than White girls to perceive pressure to adopt masculine qualities (Ghavami & Peplau, 2013). For example, the ideology of the "strong Black woman" who is tough, resilient, and self-sufficient is often perceived as an ideal for Black women and self-endorsed by Black adult women (Donovan & West, 2015; Thomas, Witherspoon, & Speight, 2004). Historically, in the United States, economic necessity has made women of color more likely to participate in the workplace than White women, requiring the adoption of instrumental characteristics such as strength and tenacity to succeed, making femininity a privileged status out of reach to poor women of color. In support of this, in one recent study, Black girls and Latinas and girls from lower socioeconomic classes reported higher levels of adherence to norms of masculinity (masculine autonomy, toughness, and stoicism) with their peers

Girls raised in cultures that value independence, assertiveness, and other traditionally masculine characteristics may feel pressure to adopt qualities deemed as such, like being tough or a "tomboy."
iStock.com/kali9

compared to White girls and those from higher socioeconomic backgrounds (Rogers et al., 2019). Higher levels of adherence to masculine norms were associated with lower levels of psychological (self-esteem, depressive symptoms) and social (peer support and conflict) well-being among White, Latina, and Black early adolescent girls assessed at both seventh and eighth grades (Rogers et al., 2019).

Research with diverse samples of U.S. adolescents suggests that a masculine gender script may pose challenges to boys' and girls' adjustment. It is thought that masculine ideologies clash with the human need and desire for mutually supportive relationships (Way et al., 2014). For example, conformity to a traditional masculine role was associated with depressive symptoms and decreased academic engagement in one sample of middle school boys and girls (Rogers et al., 2017). In contrast, androgyny is associated with psychological well-being in diverse samples of adolescents (Buckley, 2018; Bukowski, Panarello, & Santo, 2017). Internalizing a flexible gender role is considered to be advantageous because a person can feel equally comfortable performing instrumental and communal roles and functions (Markstrom-Adams, 1989). Both boys and girls can be strong, assertive, warm, and communicative.

REVIEW 5.3

1. Describe processes of gender typing in childhood and adolescence.

2. Explain the gender intensification hypothesis.

3. What are some contextual influences on gender typing in adolescence?

THINKING IN CONTEXT 5.3

How might gender be influenced by other domains of development? Specifically, how might physical development influence gender typing? In what ways might cognitive development influence gender typing? What socioemotional developments influence gender typing?

● ●

APPLY 5.3

Fifteen-year-old Dwayne is proud that he completed 20 pull-ups. He hangs out with his friends in the neighborhood. They often challenge each other to perform physical feats, such as a series of stunts like climbing fences, balancing on railings, and riding on car bumpers. Some of these activities scare Dwayne but he doesn't dare let his fear show. Instead he gets pumped up and charges ahead. Dwayne's mother has noticed that he's much more interested in keeping face and she worries that he won't back down from fights or other challenges. She also worries because she suspects that Dwayne starts some of those fights.

1. Given what you know about Dwayne, describe his gender identity and the extent to which he displays gender typing.

2. Identify potential influences on Dwayne's gender identity.

3. How do you expect Dwayne's gender identity to shift in the coming years, if at all?

4. What advice do you have for Dwayne's mother?

● ●

TRANSGENDER IDENTITY

Our discussion of gender and gender identity thus far has emphasized **cisgender** development—that is, development in adolescents whose gender identity matches their sex assigned at birth (usually based on the appearance of their external genitalia), also known as *natal sex*. The vast majority of research examining gender socialization and gender identity examines how boys and girls adopt the identities that correspond to their natal sex (Olson & Gülgöz, 2018). Researchers increasingly are becoming critical of the gender binary, or the emphasis on two distinct genders: male and female (Hyde, Bigler, Joel, Tate, & van Anders, 2019). Instead many argue that gender is fluid. Increasing attention has been directed at individuals whose gender identity does not match their natal sex, most often **transgender** individuals (Dickey, Hendricks, & Bockting, 2016). Transgender individuals' self-identified gender differs from the gender assigned at birth. A transgender woman identifies as female but was assigned a male gender at birth, and a transgender man identifies as male but was assigned a female gender at birth. The body of research on gender development to date has focused on cisgender individuals (Dickey et al., 2016; Olson & Gülgöz, 2018). We know relatively little about transgender individuals and their development.

Although transgender issues are receiving increasing attention in the media and courts, a transgender identity is rare. About .5% to 1% of the population of adolescents and adults identify themselves as transgender (Crissman, Berger, Graham, & Dalton, 2017; Gates, 2011; Zucker, 2017), although the true figure may be higher. One nationally representative survey of adolescents in New Zealand (nearly 8,200 individuals) found that 1.2% of participants identified themselves as transgender and 2.5% reported not being sure about their gender (Clark et al., 2014). Although the prevalence of transgender identity is still not well documented, the vast majority of adolescents adopt a gender identity that is congruent with their biological sex.

Gender Nonconforming and Transgender Children

In the past, transgender children were often viewed as confused, delayed, or simply rebellious. Research, however, suggests that transgender children are similar to gender conforming children. For example, like gender-typical children, transgender children show preferences for peers, toys, and clothing typically associated with their expressed gender, choose stereotypically gendered outfits, and say that they are more similar to children of their expressed gender than to children of the other gender (Fast & Olson, 2018). One study compared 5- to 12-year-old transgender children, their cisgender siblings, and a group of unrelated cisgender children on self-report and implicit, less controllable, measures of gender identity and preferences (Olson, Key, & Eaton, 2015). When transgender children's responses were considered in light of their natal sex, their responses differed radically from the cisgender children and did not conform to the gender-stereotyped behavior typical of children their age. However, when transgender children's responses were evaluated in terms of their expressed gender, their self-reports and implicit, less controllable, preferences were indistinguishable from those of other children when matched by gender identity. Transgender children showed a clear preference for peers and objects endorsed by peers who shared their expressed gender and demonstrated an explicit and implicit identity that aligned with their expressed gender, suggesting that their gender identity was deeply felt and genuine. In middle to late childhood, transgender children tend to show more flexible views of gender stereotypes than cisgender children. For example, one study suggested that 6- to 8-year-old transgender children and their siblings were less likely to endorse gender stereotypes than unrelated children and viewed gender nonconformity as more acceptable in peers (Olson & Enright, 2018).

Parents, peers, and teachers tend to discourage gender nonconformity in children, especially boys who show interest in girls' activities and toys (Halpern & Perry-Jenkins, 2016; Martin et al., 2013). Transgender children typically resist such pressure, insisting on their true gender identity. Not all gender nonconforming children develop a transgender identity (Deardorff, Hoyt, Carter, & Shirtcliff, 2019; Ristori & Steensma, 2016). That is, many gender nonconforming children ultimately develop a gender identity that is consistent with their natal sex. It is difficult to predict whether a gender nonconforming child will develop a transgender identity, but gender nonconforming children whose gender identity is very intense are more likely to retain that identity over time and are less likely to identify with their natal sex (Steensma, McGuire, Kreukels, Beekman, & Cohen-Kettenis, 2013). It is estimated that nearly 50% of transgender youth identify as such before age 12 and many report knowing before age 8 and some as early as preschool (Deardorff et al., 2019; Fast & Olson, 2018; Olson, 2016).

Transgender Adolescents

The physical changes of puberty transform adolescents' bodies and pose unique stressors to transgender adolescents' adjustment. Transgender adolescents often experience heightened distress and risks for adjustment with the onset of puberty, especially when their bodies change in ways that do not align with their gender identity (Vance, Ehrensaft, & Rosenthal, 2014). Recall the gender intensification hypothesis, which poses that the physical changes with puberty are associated with increased social pressure to conform to gender standards. Transgendered adolescents who feel pressure to conform to their natal sex may be particularly prone to adjustment problems. As compared with their gender normative peers, transgender adolescents experience elevated distress during adolescence and experience higher rates of mental health problems compared with their cisgender peers, including self-harm, depression, anxiety, and suicidality (Becerra-Culqui et al., 2018; Connolly, Zervos, Barone, Johnson, & Joseph, 2016; Mustanski & Liu, 2013; Russell & Fish, 2016; Toomey, Syvertsen, & Shramko, 2018). Transgender adolescents commonly

Jazz Jennings, a transgender woman, YouTube personality, model, and LGBT rights activist, identified as transgender in early childhood and biologically transitioned in late adolescence.
Michael Stewart / Contributor

experience harassment, discrimination, and higher levels of peer victimization than their cisgender peers (Birkett, Newcomb, & Mustanski, 2015; Hatchel, Valido, De Pedro, Huang, & Espelage, 2019; Mustanski, Andrews, & Puckett, 2016).

Contextual Influences on Adjustment of Transgender Adolescents

Adolescents' acceptance and adjustment to a transgender identity varies with individual and contextual factors, such as whether the adolescent has transitioned, and the degree of available support.

Gender Affirming Support

Gender identity, like other facets of identity, is influenced by interactions with others. The reactions and support children and adolescents receive in response to their emerging gender identity, influences their adjustment. While in the past parents may have ignored young and older children's wishes or outright prohibited them from adopting a transgender identity, some parents today adopt a different approach, permitting their children to "socially transition" to the gender identity that feels right to the child. A **social gender transition** entails changing the child's everyday experience to match their gender identity. It includes activities such as changing the pronoun used to describe a child, perhaps the child's name, and the child's appearance, including hair and clothing. Social transitioning is reversible and gives children the opportunity to live according to their chosen gender identity rather than their natal sex.

Whether or not parents should support children and adolescents' desire to socially transition and live presenting as their gender identity is hotly debated (Steensma & Cohen-Kettenis, 2011; Zucker, Wood, Singh, & Bradley, 2012). One of the few studies of socially transitioned transgender children prior to puberty suggested that they are no more likely to experience depression and anxiety as gender-consistent children (Olson, Durwood, DeMeules, & McLaughlin, 2016). Research with adolescents affirms that social transitioning is associated with better mental health outcomes, including lower rates of anxiety and depression (Durwood, McLaughlin, & Olson, 2017; Ryan, Russell, Huebner, Diaz, & Sanchez, 2010; Simons, Schrager, Clark, Belzer, & Olson, 2013). Parental support of transgender adolescents' social transitions, such as by using the adolescent's preferred pronouns and name, is associated with positive mental health (Russell, Pollitt, Li, & Grossman, 2018; Ryan et al., 2010). A sense of acceptance and the ability to live as one's perceived gender may buffer the stresses that tend to accompany gender nonconformity.

Although much of the research examines the damaging effects of peer victimization (Hatchel et al., 2019; Shiffman et al., 2016), peer relationships can also promote health and adjustment. When transgender adolescents feel supported by peers, they report a positive sense of self and fewer mental health problems (Johns, Beltran, Armstrong, Jayne, & Barrios, 2018). There is generally less research on the positive effects of peers on adjustment in transgender adolescents but research examining LGB samples suggests that social support from peers has a protective effect on adolescent development (Birkett et al., 2015; Ybarra, Mitchell, Palmer, & Reisner, 2015). In addition, some transgender adolescents seek support through online peer interactions and communities, which can buffer the negative effects of victimization (Allen, Watson, & VanMattson, 2020; Ybarra et al., 2015).

At school, relationships with supportive teachers can help transgender adolescents feel safer and are associated with less absenteeism (McGuire, Anderson, Toomey, & Russell, 2010; Seelman, Forge, Walls, & Bridges, 2015). Transgender students who attend schools with clear policies against bullying, LGBT inclusive curricula, and the presence of a gay-straight alliance (GSA) or other gender inclusive student group tend to report feeling more connected to adults at school and school itself, as well as report feeling safer at school and more engaged (Hazel, Walls, & Pomerantz, 2018; Ioverno, Belser, Baiocco, Grossman, & Russell, 2016; Marx & Kettrey, 2016). Schools with gender affirming policies can aid transgender adolescents' adjustment, but many students do not attend schools with such policies. For example, a national survey of over 23,000 U.S. secondary students found that only about 20% of LGBTQ students reported being taught positive representations about LGBTQ people, history, or events in their school (Kosciw, Greytak, Zongrone, Caitlin Clark, & Truong, 2018). In addition, only about half of U.S. secondary students report the availability of a GSA in their school (Kosciw et al., 2018). The school context offers important opportunities to support transgender students and to reduce the incidence of peer victimization; however, many adolescents attend schools with few resources.

Gender Affirming Health Care

In contrast to a social gender transition in which adolescents adopt the likeness associated with their gender identity, a **biological gender transition** is a medical process. It typically involves both developmental changes (body changes that are induced by hormone therapy) and permanent changes to the external genitals (accomplished by means of gender reassignment surgery). Older children who identify as transgender, in consultation with their parents and pediatrician, may take medication to delay the onset of puberty and the reproductive maturation that goes with it. Postponing puberty provides children with additional time to socially transition, decide whether biological transition is the right decision for them, and make a mature, informed decision.

In recent years, the popularity and demand for medication to delay the onset of puberty has increased (Lopez, Solomon, Boulware, & Christison-Lagay, 2018). Endocrinologists (physicians who specialize in the endocrine system and hormones) prescribe **puberty suppressors**, medication that inhibits sex hormones and prevents the onset of pubertal changes. Puberty suppression prevents the development of cisgender sex characteristics, is reversible, and affords transgender adolescents and their parents and medical team the time needed to explore and understand transgender adolescents' gender identity and develop coping skills (Panagiotakopoulos, 2018). Some research has suggested that puberty suppression is safe and associated with positive mental health outcomes in transgender adolescents (Bonifacio, Maser, Stadelman, & Palmert, 2019; Schagen, Cohen-Kettenis, Delemarre-van de Waal, & Hannema, 2016); however, there have been no large long-term studies to date to inform professional practice (Mahfouda, Moore, Siafarikas, Zepf, & Lin, 2017). Medical and social interventions to support adolescents' gender transitions are often accompanied by psychological interventions in which psychologists, social workers, and other health providers work to help families support adolescents' social transition (Connolly et al., 2016; Durwood et al., 2017; Olson et al., 2016).

However, many transgender adolescents lack access to medical and social interventions because services are not widely available and are often limited to cities (Shumer & Spack, 2013). In addition, transgender adolescents report less use of health care, have fewer physician visits and health checkups, and report their health more poorly than do their cisgender peers, suggesting that they may have fewer opportunities to interact with health care professionals who can offer assistance (Rider, McMorris, Gower, Coleman, & Eisenberg, 2018). Adolescents and their parents report many barriers to gender affirming care, such as the availability of medical care sensitive to transgender adolescents' needs, a general lack of education about treatment options, experience of bias, fear of rejection, and, especially, economic barriers (Gridley et al., 2016; Puckett, Cleary, Rossman, Mustanski, & Newcomb, 2018). Medical interventions, such as puberty suppression medication, are expensive and often not covered by medical insurance (Stevens, Gomez-Lobo, & Pine-Twaddell, 2015). Adolescents from low socioeconomic status homes and communities with fewer health resources are less likely to obtain gender affirming care (Safer & Chan, 2019). ●

REVIEW 5.4

1. Define cisgender and transgender.
2. Discuss gender development in transgender children.
3. What challenges do transgender individuals face with puberty?
4. What are examples of gender affirming support?
5. What are some of the effects of gender affirming support and gender affirming health care?
6. What are some of the challenges of providing gender affirming health care for transgender adolescents?

THINKING IN CONTEXT 5.4

Consider influences on whether transgender adolescents socially transition to their gender identity. What factors at home might determine whether adolescents seek to transition socially? What role might peers play? The school context? Consider the larger environment. How might neighborhoods and towns vary in the support provided to transgender adolescents? To what degree do you think support exists at the macrosystem level? Why? Explain.

APPLY 5.4

Although they were aware of Brooklyn's gender nonconformity, Brooklyn's parents have just learned that their 11-year-old has a transgender identity.

1. What are some important issues of which Brooklyn's parents should be aware?
2. What challenges might Brooklyn and their parents face? What are some potential risks to Brooklyn's development?
3. Might Brooklyn's experience as a transgender adolescent vary depending on whether Brooklyn was assigned a male or female gender at birth? Explain your reasoning.
4. How can parents and others support Brooklyn? What are some pros and cons of gender affirming support? Explain.

CHAPTER SUMMARY

5.1 Compare gender stereotypes, gender differences, and gender roles.

Gender is determined by socialization and the roles that the individual adopts. Gender stereotypes are beliefs about the activities, attitudes, skills, and characteristics labeled as appropriate for males or females in a given culture. Gender stereotypes emerge in childhood and exist in most cultures. Adolescents' views of gender become more complex, yet most continue to endorse gender stereotypes. Adolescent boys' and girls' cognitive and social abilities and behaviors overlap and there is a great deal of variability within each sex, more so than between the sexes. The most marked gender difference is in aggression. Gender roles consist of combinations of instrumental and expressive traits. Androgynous adolescents report both masculine and feminine traits and tend to show fewer internalizing problems, such as anxiety and depression. Most notably, sexual orientation cannot be inferred from gender-typed behavior.

5.2 Evaluate the influences of biological, contextual, and cognitive factors on gendered behavior.

Biological explanations emphasize the role of evolution and look to sex differences in hormones and the brain as contributors to psychological and behavioral functioning. The cognitive-developmental theory of gender poses that adolescents' understanding of gender is constructed in the same way as their understanding of the world. Gender identity forms, followed by gender stability and gender constancy. Adolescents create gender schemas that organize and influence their thinking. Contextual influences on gender development include parents and the home context, peers, school settings, and neighborhood and emphasize individuals' constructions of gender through processes of social learning and interactions with the sociocultural context in which they are raised. Gender typing occurs through socialization and interactions with parents, peers, teachers, media, and cultural influences.

5.3 **Describe processes of gender typing and gender identity in adolescence.**

Gender typing, the process of acquiring gendered behaviors, begins in infancy. As children develop a sense of gender, they actively seek information about gender and they tend to demonstrate gender stereotyping in toy and play preferences. Although gender flexibility tends to increase in late childhood, gender rigidity tends to rebound in early adolescence when young people perceive greater social pressure to adhere to gender-stereotyped roles and behaviors, known as the gender intensification hypothesis. Research examining the gender intensity hypothesis is mixed. By late adolescence, most people become more flexible in their thinking and adoption of gender roles. It is difficult to draw conclusions about the effects of gender typing in adolescence because gendered expectations and adolescents' responses and adjustment to gender typing likely vary with contextual factors and reflect the intersection of gender, ethnicity, and socioeconomic status.

5.4 **Discuss the development of transgender identity and influences on adjustment in transgender adolescents.**

Transgender individuals' self-identified gender differs from the gender assigned at birth. Research suggests that gender development is similar in transgender children and gender conforming children, such as showing preferences for peers, toys, and clothing typically associated with their expressed gender. In middle to late childhood, transgender children tend to show more flexible views of gender stereotypes than cisgender children. Transgender adolescents often experience heightened distress and risks for adjustment with the onset of puberty, especially when their bodies change in ways that do not align with their gender identity. They also experience higher rates of mental health problems compared with their cisgender peers. Adjustment varies with individual and contextual factors, such as whether the adolescent has transitioned, and the level of gender affirming support. The availability of gender affirming health care varies and many transgender adolescents lack access to care.

KEY TERMS

androgyny, 110

biological gender transition, 122

cisgender, 120

cognitive-developmental theory of gender, 113

expressive traits, 110

gender, 108

gender constancy, 113

gender identity, 113

gender intensification hypothesis, 117

gender schema, 114

gender schema theory, 114

gender stability, 113

gender stereotypes, 108

gender typing, 116

instrumental traits, 110

puberty suppressors, 122

sex, 107

social gender transition, 121

transgender, 120

iStock.com/Martin Dimitrov

6

Sexuality

Learning Objectives

6.1 Examine patterns of sexual activity in adolescence.

6.2 Discuss biological and contextual influences on sexual activity in adolescence.

6.3 Summarize risks to adolescents' sexual health.

6.4 Compare approaches to sexuality education.

Chapter Contents

Raging hormones. Sexualized images in social media. Do adolescents suffer from "sex on the brain"? Sexual activity during adolescence receives a great deal of attention in the media and from parents, educators, and policy makers. Fears about sex-crazed teenagers abound. Recall from Chapter 1 that sexuality is a developmental task for adolescence. Sexuality includes the understanding and expression of sexual feelings and behaviors, including feelings and appraisals about oneself as a sexual being and attitudes and behaviors regarding sex (McClelland & Tolman, 2014). With the hormonal changes of puberty, both boys and girls experience an increase in sex drive and sexual interest (Fortenberry, 2013). Social context influences how biological urges are channeled into behavior and adolescents' conceptions of sexuality. In this chapter we examine the development of sexuality during adolescence.

SEXUAL ACTIVITY DURING ADOLESCENCE

Adolescents are often depicted in media as driven by hormones and immersed in media that lead them to be obsessed with sex. How sexually active are adolescents? This question is difficult to answer because studying sensitive topics, such as sexuality, is challenging. Recall from Chapter 1 that research with minors generally requires parental consent. Yet researchers who study sexuality argue that requiring parental consent can interfere with adolescents' participation (Flores, McKinney, Arscott, & Barroso, 2018). Adolescents may fear that their parents will learn about their sexual activity. Lesbian, gay, bisexual, queer, and transgender adolescents may fear being "outed" before they are ready to

Sexual relationships tend to emerge within the context of romantic relationships.
istock.com/Chalffy

share their sexuality with parents, family, and friends (Macapagal, Coventry, Arbeit, Fisher, & Mustanski, 2017). Many adolescents report that they would not participate in research about sexual topics if parental permission were required (Nelson, Carey, & Fisher, 2019). Researchers therefore face the challenge of protecting adolescents' rights to privacy and protecting them from potential harms from participation, while recognizing parents' desires to learn about their children's responses and have a say in whether their child participates in research (Brawner & Sutton, 2018). The World Health Organization notes that adolescents have the right to share information, to be informed about pertinent issues related to themselves, and to privacy, but these rights must be balanced against researchers' obligations to disclose information to protect adolescents from harm and to act within adolescents' best interests (Singh, Siddiqi, Parameshwar, & Chandra-Mouli, 2019). Therefore, studying adolescent sexuality is challenging. We have learned a great deal, as discussed in the following sections, but there is much more to learn.

Prevalence of Sexual Activity in Adolescence

Most of the research on adolescent sexuality tends to focus on intercourse, leaving gaps in our knowledge about the range of sexual activity milestones young people experience (Diamond & Savin-Williams, 2009). Sexual behaviors tend to progress from handholding to kissing, to touching through clothes and under clothes, to oral sex, and then to genital intercourse (de Graaf, Vanwesenbeeck, Meijer, Woertman, & Meeus, 2009). A sample of over 11,000 U.K. adolescents revealed that nearly two-thirds engage in light intimate activities, such as holding hands, kissing on the mouth, or hugging (Kelly, Zilanawala, Tanton, Lewis, & Mercer, 2019). Adolescents are about as

likely to engage in oral sex as vaginal intercourse, with male and female high school students showing similar rates of oral sex (Copen, Chandra, & Martinez, 2012; Lefkowitz, Vasilenko, & Leavitt, 2016). Oral sex does not seem to be a substitute for vaginal sex, as the majority of over 12,000 adolescents in one sample initiated oral sex after first experiencing vaginal intercourse, and about one-half initiated oral sex a year or more after the onset of vaginal sex (Haydon, Herring, Prinstein, & Halpern, 2012).

Contrary to the stereotypes of promiscuous sex-obsessed adolescents, most young people have sexual intercourse for the first time at about age 17 (Guttmacher Institute, 2017). Many adults are surprised to learn that the percentage of high school students who have ever had sexual intercourse is at an all-time low, from 54% in 1991 to 40% in 2017 (Kann et al., 2018; Witwer, Jones, & Lindberg, 2018). An important trend over the past 3 decades is that fewer adolescents initiate sexual activity in the early years of high school. As shown in Figure 6.1, between 1991 and 2015, sexual activity declined for ninth- and tenth-grade students but not eleventh- and twelfth-grade students (Child Trends, 2017). By the time they graduate, 57% of high school students report having had sexual intercourse (Witwer et al., 2018). Only about a third of high school students, however, report being sexually active, defined as within the previous 3 months (Child Trends, 2017).

As shown in Figure 6.2, the proportion of adolescents who have ever engaged in sexual intercourse declined from 2005 to 2015. This trend is especially visible among Black adolescents and, to a lesser extent, among Hispanic adolescents, but not among White adolescents (Ethier, Kann, & McManus, 2018). Racial and ethnic differences in adolescent sexual activity are intertwined with the socioeconomic and contextual factors that are correlated with race and ethnicity. Early sexual activity and greater sexual experience are more common in adolescents reared in stressful contexts, such as low socioeconomic status homes and neighborhoods where community ties are weak (Carlson, McNulty, Bellair, & Watts, 2014; Warner, 2018). For example, in one study of middle school students, experiencing a direct threat of violence in the school or community predicted early sexual initiation (Coyle, Guinosso, Glassman, Anderson, & Wilson, 2017). In addition, racial differences in rates of pubertal maturation influence sexual activity, with African American girls experiencing puberty earlier than other girls, and early maturation is a risk factor for early sexual activity, as we will discuss later in this chapter (Carlson et al., 2014; Moore, Harden, & Mendle, 2014). It is unclear why adolescents of color have experienced greater declines in sexual initiation and activity than White adolescents; however, racial and ethnic differences remain.

FIGURE 6.1

Percentage of Students in Grades 9 Through 12 Who Report Ever Having Had Sexual Intercourse, 1991–2015

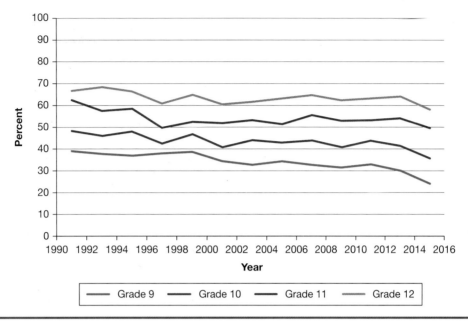

Source: Child Trends (2017).

FIGURE 6.2

Ethnic Differences in Sexual Initiation, 2005–2015

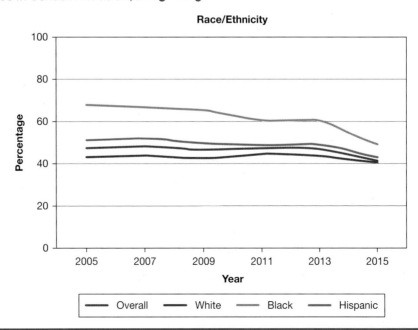

Source: Ethier et al. (2018).

Early Sexual Activity and Adolescent Adjustment

Understanding and becoming comfortable with one's sexuality is a developmental task for adolescents (see Chapter 1). In late adolescence, sexual activity is associated with positive self-esteem and well-being (Goodson, Buhi, & Dunsmore, 2006; Vrangalova & Savin-Williams, 2011) and is not associated with psychological problems such as anxiety or depression or problem behavior (Harries, Paglia, Redden, & Grant, 2018). Although initiating sexual activity in the later high school years is not associated with poor adjustment, early sexual initiation (prior to age 16) poses risks to development. Early sexual activity is associated with attitudes that are more accepting of risk-taking and engaging in more risk behaviors, such as sexual risks, alcohol and substance use, poor academic achievement, and delinquency, as well as having a larger number of sex partners, relative to peers (Finer & Philbin, 2013; Harries et al., 2018; Lara & Abdo, 2016; McLeod & Knight, 2010; Warner, 2018).

The long-term effects of early initiation of sexual intercourse are less well understood. Some research suggests a higher risk for sexually transmitted infections (STIs) and depression in early adulthood (Vasilenko, Kugler, & Rice, 2016). Other work suggests no link with depression and that the risks are simply those that accompany sexual activity (Epstein et al., 2018). A recent study suggests that the negative effects of early sexual initiation may be temporary (Wesche, Kreager, Lefkowitz, & Siennick, 2017). The researchers found that sexual initiation was associated with internalizing symptoms, such as anxiety and depression, for girls who initiated sexual activity prior to age 15, but not for boys or for teens who initiated sexual activity later. Moreover, there was no difference in internalizing symptoms among girls 1 year later for those who initiated sexual activity early and those who initiated sexual activity on-time, suggesting that early sexual initiation may not produce lasting detriments to girls' mental health (Wesche et al., 2017).

Risk factors for early sexual activity in U.S. teens are early pubertal maturation, poor parental monitoring, and poor parent–adolescent communication (McClelland & Tolman, 2014; Negriff, Susman, & Trickett, 2011; Nogueira Avelar e Silva, van de Bongardt, van de Looij-Jansen, Wijtzes, & Raat, 2016). Authoritative parenting, regularly shared family activities (e.g., outings, game nights, or shared dinners), parental monitoring, and parental knowledge are

Close relationships with parents are associated with lower rates of sexual activity.
iStock.com/kate_sept2004

associated with lower rates of sexual activity (Dittus et al., 2015; Huang, Murphy, & Hser, 2011). Having sexually active peers and perceiving positive attitudes about sex among schoolmates predict initiation and greater levels of sexual activity and a greater number of sexual partners (Coley, Lombardi, Lynch, Mahalik, & Sims, 2013; Moore et al., 2014; White & Warner, 2015). In addition, adolescents' perceptions of the sexual norms in their neighborhood, as well as siblings' sexual activity, are associated with age of initiation, casual sex, and the number of sexual partners, even after controlling for neighborhood demographic risk factors (Almy et al., 2016; Warner, Giordano, Manning, & Longmore, 2011).

Lesbian, Gay, and Bisexual Adolescents

The developmental tasks of identity and sexuality intersect because adolescents are driven to understand the sexual feelings they experience and they integrate their understanding into their sense of self (McClelland & Tolman, 2014). As we discussed in Chapter 4, adolescents are faced with constructing an identity, a sense of self. They question and explore their views in a variety of domains, such as career, relationships, gender, and sexuality. Many youth experience a period of questioning in which they explore their sexual feelings, are uncertain of their sexual interests, and attempt to determine their **sexual orientation**.

Sexual Orientation

Sexual orientation refers to an enduring pattern of emotional, romantic, and sexual attraction to opposite-sex partners (heterosexual), same-sex partners (gay or lesbian), or partners of both sexes (bisexual) (Greenberg, 2017). Recall from Chapter 5 that adolescents who identify as transgender do not identify with their natal sex but instead adopt an alternative gender identity (Diamond, Bonner, & Dickenson, 2015). Transgender is distinct from sexual orientation. That is, a transgender identity does not signify sexual orientation, whether one is gay, lesbian, or bisexual (Bosse & Chiodo, 2016). However, research on the intersection of transgender identity and sexual orientation is rare. Consequently, many researchers study transgender adolescents alongside LGB adolescents (Galupo, Davis, Grynkiewicz, & Mitchell, 2014). Wherever possible, the following discussion distinguishes LGB and transgender adolescents.

The process of determining sexual orientation often entails exploring and considering alternatives. For example, many preadolescents and young adolescents engage in sex play with members of the same sex, yet ultimately develop a cisgender orientation. Many researchers today view sexual orientation as a dynamic spectrum, ranging from exclusive opposite-sex attraction and relations to exclusive same-sex attraction and relations, with multiple sexual orientations in between (Bailey et al., 2016; Savin-Williams, 2016). Many people are attracted to both sexes and attractions vary over time (Kaestle, 2019). For example, one longitudinal study followed nearly 14,000 youth from ages 12 to 33 and found three general patterns

of sexual attraction: heterosexual (88%), mostly heterosexual (10%), and LGB (2%) (Calzo, Masyn, Austin, Jun, & Corliss, 2017). Sexual attraction does not always match behavior; many people experience attractions that they do not act on. In addition, a small minority of people report an asexual orientation, feeling no sexual attraction whatsoever (Greaves et al., 2017; Van Houdenhove, Gijs, T'Sjoen, & Enzlin, 2015). Figure 6.3 illustrates the sexual identities reported by high school students in 2015.

Moreover, reporting of same-sex attraction and behavior among adolescents and emerging adults is not stable. Longitudinal data with more than 10,000 seventh- to twelfth-grade students over a 6-year period revealed some migration over time in both directions—from opposite-sex attraction and behavior to same-sex attraction and behavior and vice versa (Saewyc, 2011). However, stability develops over time. Over 12,000 emerging adults (ages 18 to 24) surveyed over a 6-year period revealed that stability of sexual orientation was more common than change, especially among emerging adults who identified strongly as heterosexual or gay or lesbian (as compared with bisexual, which was the most unstable category) (Savin-Williams, Joyner, & Rieger, 2012). After a period of questioning and exploration, adolescents may commit to a sexual orientation and integrate their sexuality into their overall sense of identity. However, adoption of a sexual orientation is not a linear process.

FIGURE 6.3

Percentage of High School Students by Sexual Identity, 2015

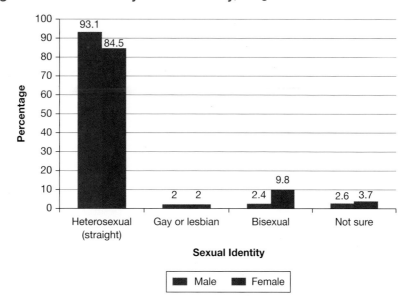

Source: Kann et al. (2016).

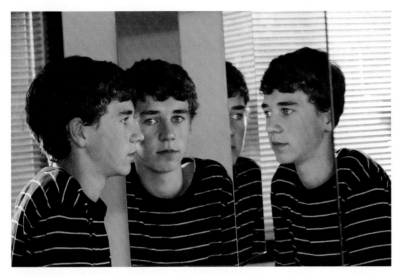

Sexual attraction can be confusing for adolescents.
iStock.com/Pixel_Pig

Developmental Transitions in LGB Adolescents

Many adolescents with same-sex attractions report as children feeling aware that they were different from their peers, perhaps because they showed different interests or behavior. The sense of feeling different tends to intensify with age. Young people tend to experience their first same-sex attraction during adrenarche, typically between ages 7 and 9 (Savin-Williams & Cohen, 2015). With puberty, sexual feelings emerge, often with confusing results. The onset of sexual activity can precede, co-occur, or follow self-identification as gay or lesbian; however, most often first sex typically occurs after, not before, young people recognize that they are gay or lesbian. For example, in one study of nearly 1,300 gay and lesbian adults, only about one-quarter of gay and lesbian youth had sex prior to self-identification; typically, there was a 1-year gap between identifying and engaging in first sex (Calzo, Antonucci, Mays, & Cochran, 2011). Although it was once thought that same-sex sexual experiences served to test or confirm a lesbian or gay identity (Cass, 1979), it instead appears that young people often embrace a lesbian or gay identity prior to experiencing same-sex behavior (Drasin et al., 2008; Floyd & Bakeman, 2006).

The first same-sex encounter typically occurs with a friend or someone the adolescent is dating, although gay boys are more likely than lesbian girls to have first sex within the context of a purely sexual encounter (Savin-Williams & Cohen, 2015). Most gay and lesbian adolescents do not participate exclusively in same-sex behavior (Diamond & Savin-Williams, 2009). Reasons for heterosexual dating and activities include the desire to experiment or have

fun, pressure from peers or parents, alcohol intoxication or substance use, and genuine sexual desire. The earlier adolescents identify as lesbian or gay, the less likely they are to have heterosexual sex (Drasin et al., 2008).

In North America and many developed countries, young people are disclosing their sexual orientation—"coming out" as gay or lesbian—at earlier ages than in prior generations, likely due to an increasingly inviting, positive cultural context for LGB young people (Calzo et al., 2011; Lucassen et al., 2015). Coming out to others entails many ongoing decisions about whether, when, and how to reveal their sexuality to family, friends, and new acquaintances (Cohen & Savin-Williams, 1996).

On average, young people come out just prior to high school graduation (Savin-Williams & Cohen, 2015). Research suggests that some sexual minority youth may disclose their sexuality starting at around age 14 or 15, yet many wait until late adolescence or emerging adulthood (Calzo et al., 2017; Savin-Williams & Ream, 2003). Both boys and girls tend to first disclose to a female best friend, followed by another LGB person, close sibling, or male friend. Young people delay disclosing to parents not because parents are deemed unimportant, but precisely because of their importance; young people report wanting to be certain about their sexuality before they initiate this highly significant disclosure (Savin-Williams, 2001). Despite stereotypes, adolescents who come out to a parent are rarely met with ongoing condemnation, severe negative response, or expulsion (Savin-Williams, Dubé, & Dube, 1998). Most receive responses that range from neutral to positive (Samarova, Shilo, & Diamond, 2014). Adolescents who anticipate negative responses from parents are less likely to disclose their sexual orientation to them and may become emotionally distant (Ueno, 2005).

Accepting reactions from parents and peers can buffer the psychological and behavioral risks that accompany perceived discrimination (Birkett, Newcomb, & Mustanski, 2015; Rosario, Schrimshaw, & Hunter, 2009). Developmental scientists have come to conclude that disclosing a sexual minority identity can be a positive event that facilitates the development of identity, self-esteem, and psychological health and can often reduce distress, anxiety, and depression (Juster, Smith, Ouellet, Sindi, & Lupien, 2013; Ueno, 2005; Vincke & van Heeringen, 2002). It can also be a means for obtaining social support and interpersonal closeness (Kosciw, Palmer, & Kull, 2015;

Legate, Ryan, & Weinstein, 2012; Savin-Williams & Cohen, 2015).

Risks and Supports for LGBT Adolescents

Constructing an identity as a young person who is lesbian, gay, bisexual, or transgender can be complicated by the prejudice and discrimination that many LGBT youth experience in their schools and communities. LGBT adolescents experience more harassment and victimization by peers and report a more hostile peer environment than their heterosexual peers (Robinson & Espelage, 2013). Perceived discrimination and victimization by peers contributes to LGBT adolescents' increased risk for psychological and behavioral problems, such as depression, self-harm, suicide, running away, poor academic performance, substance use, and risky sexual practices (Barnett, Molock, Nieves-Lugo, & Zea, 2019; Collier, van Beusekom, Bos, & Sandfort, 2013; Haas et al., 2011; Plöderl et al., 2013).

GSAs are a source of support for all students, regardless of sexual orientation.
iStock.com/wundervisuals

Support from parents and peers can buffer the negative effects of stigmatization and victimization for LGBT individuals (Birkett et al., 2015). For example, one study of a national sample of over 7,800 LGBT secondary school students revealed that adolescents who had come "out" were more likely to experience peer victimization but also reported higher self-esteem and fewer depressive symptoms than their "closeted" peers (Kosciw et al., 2015). Specifically, support from parents and, to a lesser extent, peers is associated with high self-esteem and positive adjustment (McConnell, Birkett, & Mustanski, 2016; Watson, Grossman, & Russell, 2019). Thus, being out may increase the risk of victimization but also offer support that promotes resilience.

Within the school setting, supports such as knowledgeable teachers and counselors, vigilance against bullying, and the presence of gay–straight alliance (GSA) student groups aid LGBT students' adjustment (Gower et al., 2018). GSAs are an important source of support and education for students, because GSAs help sexual minority students connect with peers, reduce hopelessness, and are associated with lower suicide attempts (Davis, Royne Stafford, & Pullig, 2014). Students in schools that have GSAs show lower rates of student truancy, smoking, drinking, suicide attempts, and casual sex than do those in schools without GSAs, with this difference being more sizable for LGBT than heterosexual youth (Baams, Pollitt, Laub, & Russell,

2018; Day, Ioverno, & Russell, 2019; Poteat, Sinclair, DiGiovanni, Koenig, & Russell, 2013). GSAs may offer benefits to all students. For example, perceived GSA support predicts greater well-being in racial and ethnic minority students, regardless of sexual orientation (Poteat et al., 2015). In addition to in-person support from parents, peers, and GSAs, LGBT adolescents often turn to the Internet as a source of information and exploration by learning about sexual orientation, communicating with other LGBT people, and finding support from others (Harper, Serrano, Bruce, & Bauermeister, 2016)

REVIEW 6.1

1. How common is sexual activity in adolescence?

2. Describe age and ethnic differences in sexual activity.

3. Identify correlates of and risk factors for early sexual activity.

4. What are some risks and supports that influence the adjustment of LGBT adolescents?

THINKING IN CONTEXT 6.1

1. How might biological, cognitive, and socioemotional factors (such as pubertal timing, abstract thinking, and social and identity development) influence the timing of adolescent sexual activity?

2. Do you expect girls and boys to adjust in similar ways and at similar rates? Why or why not?

INFLUENCES ON SEXUAL ACTIVITY

Sexual activity rises in adolescence, but why? What influences adolescents' sexual interests and activity? Like other aspects of development, sexuality is influenced by both biology and context.

Biological Influences

Many people believe that adolescents are victims of "raging hormones" that cause their interests in sex and engagement in sexual activity to skyrocket. What is the role of biology in adolescent sexuality? Recall from Chapter 2 that adrenarche, the maturation of the adrenal glands, occurs in late childhood and the accompanying release of androgens triggers some of the physical changes associated with puberty, such as an increase in body hair and odor. These hormonal changes are associated with a rise in erotic interests. Many adults recall their first memorable sexual attractions to peers occurring at about age 10 (Diamond et al., 2015).

Adolescents' interests in sexual activity increase as they begin and progress through puberty. Both boys and girls experience increases in testosterone during puberty, with boys experiencing a much greater surge. Testosterone levels are associated with sexual fantasies in both boys and girls; however, testosterone's relation with behavior varies by sex (Fortenberry, 2013). Pubertal changes in testosterone influence the timing of sexual initiation and the frequency of sexual activity in boys. For example, early-maturing boys in one study reported dating and sexual intercourse at the earliest age, followed by average maturers and late maturers (Halpern, Udry, & Suchindran, 1998). Girls' interests in sex are also associated with testosterone (Halpern, Udry, & Suchindran, 1997) but contextual factors, such as peers, play a larger role in girls' sexual activity (Pringle et al., 2017).

Testosterone influences sexual urges and sexual activity through its effect on the brain. Recall from Chapter 3 that testosterone triggers brain development. Parts of the limbic system, specifically the nucleus accumbens and amygdala, play a role in social information processing. These subcortical regions have testosterone receptors and testosterone plays a role in changes in information social processing associated with romance and sexual cognitions (Ernst, Romeo, & Andersen, 2009; Suleiman, Galván, Harden, & Dahl, 2017). Adolescents have stronger subcortical responses to social stimuli than adults, combined with prefrontal development that is still incomplete. This imbalance is thought to contribute to adolescents' emotional and behavioral changes (Shulman et al., 2016). There is a heightened motivation to seek out highly arousing, slightly scary, highly rewarding, and novel experiences, and increases in sensation seeking make adolescents more likely to find these high-intensity experiences, such as having a first crush or engaging in a first kiss, enjoyable (Spielberg, Olino, Forbes, & Dahl, 2014). Having a crush and beginning a romantic relationship is especially engaging and neurologically rewarding, because it's all new.

However, the increased importance of sexuality in adolescence is not due only to puberty. Emerging cognitive abilities such as hypothetical thinking, perspective taking, self-consciousness, and decision-making lead adolescents to be curious, reflective, and introspective about sexual feelings and behavior. The social recognition of sexuality as a task for adolescence also influences their experience. Contextual factors also matter.

Contextual Influences

Sexual activity is influenced by the myriad of interacting contexts in which adolescents are embedded.

Parents

What role do parents play in adolescent sexual activity? Close, supportive, and communicative relationships with parents are associated with many positive outcomes and lower rates of problem behaviors, including risky sexual activity. Adolescents who report close relationships with parents tend to initiate sex at a later age and report lower rates of sexual activity overall than their peers with poor relationships with their parents (Longmore, Eng, Giordano, & Manning, 2009; van de Bongardt, de Graaf, Reitz, & Deković, 2014). Warm parenting, regularly shared family activities (e.g., outings, game nights, or shared dinners), and parental monitoring of adolescents' activities are associated with lower rates of sexual activity and fewer sexual partners (Dittus et al., 2015; Huang, Murphy, & Hser, 2011; McElwain & Booth-LaForce, 2006). In contrast, parental psychological control, attempts to control the adolescent's thoughts or beliefs through manipulation or intimidation, is associated with internalizing and externalizing problems, such as risky behavior, specifically sexual risk-taking (Kerpelman, McElwain, Pittman, & Adler-Baeder, 2016; Pinquart, 2017). The effects of parenting behaviors on adolescent sexuality vary with the sex of the parent and child. One longitudinal study found that rapid increases in mother-adolescent conflict from childhood into adolescence predicts initiating sexual intercourse by age 15 in girls; boys' early sexual activity is related

Parent–adolescent discussion about sex predicts safe sex, but parents often report engaging in more discussions with their youth about sex, while adolescents report having fewer of these talks with their parents.
iStock.com/SDI Productions

to rapid declines in father-adolescent closeness and increases in father-adolescent conflict (McElwain & Bub, 2018).

Parents may also influence their adolescents' sexual behavior through discussions about sexuality; however, about one-quarter of adolescents report that they have not discussed sexual topics with a parent (Widman, Choukas-Bradley, Helms, Golin, & Prinstein, 2014). A lack of knowledge about sexual topics or embarrassment may prevent parents from discussing sex with their adolescent (Heller & Johnson, 2010; Jerman & Constantine, 2010). For instance, in a study about family planning discussions, parents generally reported little knowledge about contraceptives and little understanding of risks and side effects (Akers, Holland, & Bost, 2011). Sometimes adolescents are aware of their parents' poor knowledge about sex-related topics and attribute the lack of sex communication to parents not being knowledgeable about sex-related topics (Widman, Choukas-Bradley, Noar, Nesi, & Garrett, 2016b). Some adolescents avoid discussing sex with their parents out of fear that they may be viewed as sexually active, be judged, and face punishment.

Most parents report general communication about sex rather than discussing specific topics (Flores & Barroso, 2017; Widman et al., 2014). The overall tone of discussions influences their effect. For example, girls report that a parent's negative emotional tone hindered their ability and interest in talking about sex, while a positive tone led to further discussions about sex (Aronowitz & Agbeshie, 2012). Adolescents tend to dismiss scare tactics, such as when parents emphasize consequences and cautionary statements, with the underlying message prohibiting sex, often being sexually prohibitive without

the positive and pleasurable aspects of sex (Akers, Schwarz, Borrero, & Corbie-Smith, 2010; Jerman & Constantine, 2010). One-sided discussions are often influenced by parents' concerns about sending mixed signals when discussing sex with children and fears that the information might be misconstrued as permission to have sex and promote adolescent sexual activity (Wilson, Dalberth, Koo, & Gard, 2010). However, longitudinal research following nearly 15,000 adolescents to adulthood suggests that greater parental warnings regarding potential negative consequences of sexual activity predicted higher rather than lower partner accumulation (Coley et al., 2013).

Interestingly, adolescents and parents often have different perspectives on their communication about sex. Parents typically report more incidents of having the sex talk, while children report fewer instances (Fitzharris & Werner-Wilson, 2004). In reality, in the United States most parent–adolescent discussions about sex are one-time events or several short episodes that are punctuated by frustration and unease (Aronowitz & Agbeshie, 2012; Flores & Barroso, 2017).

Does talking about sex influence adolescents' behavior? In some ways, yes, and in others, no. When parents and children communicate about sexuality—specifically, when they have open conversations characterized by warmth, support, and humor—adolescents tend to show a later onset of sexual activity and engage in less sexual risk-taking than their peers (Lefkowitz & Stoppa, 2006; Lohman & Billings, 2008; Trejos-Castillo & Vazsonyi, 2009; Widman et al., 2016b). A meta-analysis of 50 studies with over 25,000 adolescents found a positive association between parent–adolescent sexual communication and safer sex behavior among youth, including use of condoms and contraceptives, with stronger effects for girls than boys and for communication with mothers versus fathers (Widman et al., 2016b). However, communication about risky sexual activity is associated with engaging in safer sex, but it does *not* prevent sexual activity itself (Widman et al., 2016b). Why? Sexual exploration and experimentation is a normative developmental task for adolescents and sexual intercourse is common in late adolescence.

Peers communicate messages about sex in person and online.
iStock.com/MarioGuti

Peers

Another important contextual influence on adolescent sexual activity is the peer group (Sieving, Eisenberg, Pettingell, & Skay, 2006). However, it is not simply peer behavior that matters. Adolescents' perception of peer activity is a particularly important predictor of sexual activity (van de Bongardt, Reitz, Sandfort, & Deković, 2015). Adolescents who perceive their peers as more sexually active believe that they have positive attitudes about and are more approving of sexual activity, are more likely to initiate sexual activity, engage in sex more frequently, and accumulate a greater number of sexual partners than those with peers who are less sexually active (Coley et al., 2013; Coley, Kull, & Carrano, 2014; White & Warner, 2015). Similarly, adolescents who believe that their peers engage in more risky sexual behavior tend to be more likely to engage in such behavior themselves (van de Bongardt et al., 2015).

One recent experiment examined the relation of peer influence on adolescents' reports of sexual activity. In this study, adolescents reported their sexual activity and expectations about the rewards of sexual activity, as well as their intentions to engage in sex in the future (Widman, Choukas-Bradley, Helms, & Prinstein, 2016a). The adolescents then participated in an Internet chat room where they believed they were chatting with peers, but "peer" responses were generated by a computer program. Adolescents reported a greater intention to engage in sexual activity in the future when they believed peers could see their responses than when their responses were private. In addition, boys and girls who expected more positive social rewards for sexual behavior were more likely to report intentions to engage in sex when they believed their responses were public than when they were private. In this laboratory study, adolescents' reported intentions for sexual activity varied with their exposure to peers. It is unclear whether these

findings extend to adolescents' behavior; however, adolescents' self-reported sexual activity tends to correlate with their beliefs about peer behavior (van de Bongardt et al., 2015).

Generally, adolescents' sexual activity tends to be more strongly related to sexual behavior of close friends than of other peers (Jaccard, Blanton, & Dodge, 2005). Yet the direction of peer influence is debated. Longitudinal studies suggest that similarities in adolescent-peer behavior are the result of adolescents selecting peers who share similar interests. That is, adolescents associate with peers who share similar beliefs about sexual activity rather than being socialized or pressured by peers (van de Bongardt et al., 2015).

Neighborhood and Community

Neighborhood and community resources are also associated with sexual activity and its negative outcomes in adolescence. Neighborhood disadvantage is an exosystem factor that is associated with early sexual activity, risky sexual activity, and adolescent pregnancy and birth (Carlson et al., 2014; Lindberg & Orr, 2011; Warner et al., 2011). Economic disadvantage affects community resources that support adolescents and families, such as schools, local voluntary organizations, recreational options, access to health care, and informal neighborhood networks. Population turnover and neighborhood disorder and violence can interfere with the development of social ties among residents and identification with the community, interfering with a community's cohesion and collective self-efficacy, or sense of control (Cuellar, Jones, & Sterrett, 2013). Poor community cohesion and collective self-efficacy contributes to a diminished capacity and willingness to supervise adolescents in the community (Sampson, 1997). Neighborhood disorder and disadvantage can also interfere with family routines and reduce opportunities for parent–child communication (Decker et al., 2018).

Neighborhood socioeconomic characteristics contribute to ethnic and racial differences in adolescent sexual initiation and activity (Brewster, 1994; Dupéré, Lacourse, Willms, Tremblay, & Leventhal, 2008). For example, we have seen that African American adolescents experience higher risk of early timing of sexual initiation and higher rates of sexual activity and risky sexual activity. Families of color are disproportionately likely to live in neighborhoods characterized by disadvantage and chaos—factors that increase the risk of early and risky sexual activity as well as influence health and community resources that can protect adolescents against risk (Carlson et al., 2014; Cubbin, Brindis, Jain, Santelli, & Braveman, 2010; Warner et al., 2011).

Other contextual factors that may influence adolescent sexual behavior include exposure to sexually themed material in television, movies, music, and video games, as well as interactions on social media. We examine the effects of media on adolescent behavior, including sexuality, in Chapter 11.

REVIEW 6.2

1. What are some biological influences on sexual activity in adolescence?

2. How is parent–adolescent communication associated with adolescents' sexual activity?

3. How do peer and neighborhood factors influence sexual activity in adolescence?

THINKING IN CONTEXT 6.2

A counselor at the local high school has asked you for advice on how to reduce sexual activity in high school students.

1. Explain the difference between sexual activity and risky sexual activity with regard to influences and adolescent adjustment.

2. In your view, what are the most important factors to address in order to reduce risky sexual activity?

3. Give advice to the counselor. What can be done to reduce risky sexual activity in high school students?

4. How might your response change if the counselor worked with middle school students?

APPLY 6.2

"Kids will do what they want to do when it comes to sex. Parents don't matter. It's simple biology—hormones," explains Rita. Her friend Noreen agrees, "And talking about sex just sends the message that it's okay."

1. What is the role of biological factors in sexual activity?

2. Considering the research on sexual activity in adolescence, do parents matter? Why or why not? If so, how?

3. What other factors matter in influencing sexual activity in adolescents?

4. What advice might you give Rita and Noreen?

RISKY SEXUAL ACTIVITY AND PROBLEMS

Although some sexual activity is normative in late adolescence, risky sexual activity poses risks to adolescents' health and well-being.

Contraceptive Use

Most sexually active high school students report using contraceptives. For example, in 2017, 84% of sexually active girls and 90% of boys reported using contraceptives at last intercourse (Witwer et al., 2018). Contraceptive use varies with gender, race, and ethnicity. In 2017, 24% of Black, 21% of Hispanic, and 12% of White sexually active girls reported not using a method of contraception at last intercourse, as compared with 10% of Black, 15% of Hispanic, and 7% of White sexually active boys. These differences may be influenced by gender stereotypes that sexual activity is more appropriate for boys than girls. Ethnic differences in contraceptive use might be associated with socioeconomic differences and access to contraception as well as cultural differences in views of sexuality. Among adolescents who use contraceptives, the condom is the most popular method (Guttmacher Institute, 2014).

Many adolescents use contraceptives only sporadically and not consistently (Pazol et al., 2015). About one-half of high school students report using a condom at last intercourse (Witwer et al., 2018). Common reasons given for not using contraceptives include not planning to have sex, the belief that pregnancy is unlikely, and difficulty communicating and negotiating the use of condoms (Johnson, Sieving, Pettingell, & McRee, 2015).

Adolescents' knowledge of and access to contraceptives are the best predictors of contraceptive use. Frequently adolescents encounter information about contraceptives in health and sexual education class at school (Maziarz, Dake, & Glassman, 2019). Boys and girls with more reproductive knowledge report greater use of contraceptives and more consistent use of contraceptives (Jaramillo, Buhi, Elder, & Corliss, 2017). Students who receive HIV education are more likely than their peers to report using a condom. Unsurprisingly, adolescents who have access to condoms are more likely to use them. However, in one recent survey of nearly 800 high school superintendents, only 7% of schools offered condoms to high school students (Demissie, Clayton, & Dunville, 2019).

Parents also play a role in promoting safe sex. Research suggests that parents who are warm, set firm boundaries, and engage in open discussions about sex and contraception are associated with increased contraceptive use (Bersamin et al., 2008; Widman et al., 2016a). We know less about LGBT adolescents' communication with parents about safe sex. In one small sample of boys, many reported engaging in little communication about sexual topics with parents and the belief that parents knew little about LGBT-specific information (Flores, Docherty, Relf, McKinney, & Barroso, 2019). Research with parents of LGBT adolescents suggests that many feel that a lack of LGBT-specific sexuality poses a barrier to communicating with their adolescent (Newcomb, Feinstein, Matson, Macapagal, & Mustanski, 2018).

Adolescents who have access to condoms are more likely to use them.
Bloomberg/Contributor/Getty Images

Sexually Transmitted Infections

With sexual activity comes the risk of transmitting or acquiring STIs, infections passed from one individual to another through sexual contact. STIs may be caused by viruses, bacteria, or parasites. In 2017, STIs—specifically, cases of chlamydia, gonorrhea, and syphilis—reached an all-time high in the United States (Centers for Disease Control and Prevention, 2018b). Although they represent only 25% of the sexually active population, 15- to 24-year-olds account for over half of all STI diagnoses each year. Untreated STIs can result in sterility and serious, even life-threatening, illnesses such as cancer. Despite the high risk for acquiring STIs among youth, only one-third of adolescent girls and less than half (45%) of young women ages 19 to 25 report that they have discussed STIs with their health care providers (Kaiser Family Foundation, 2014).

Human papillomavirus (HPV) is the most common STI diagnosed in people of all ages. There are several types of HPV, and some can cause cancer in different areas of the body—most commonly, cervical cancer in women (McQuillan, Kruszon-Moran, Markowitz, Unger, & Paulose-Ram, 2017). The U.S. Centers for Disease Control and Prevention recommends HPV vaccinations for males and females starting at age 11. In 2017, 68% of adolescents age 13 to 17 received at least one dose of the vaccine against HPV, but only 51% completed the recommended regimen of three doses (54% of girls and 49% of boys) (Walker et al., 2019). Health care experts believe that HPV vaccination rates are low, compared to other vaccinations, because of vaccine cost and the belief that giving the vaccine might condone sexual activity (Holman et al., 2014).

The most serious STI is **human immunodeficiency virus (HIV)**, which causes acquired immune deficiency syndrome (AIDS). Adolescents and emerging adults aged 13 to 24 represented over one in five new HIV/AIDS diagnoses in 2017 (Centers for Disease Control and Prevention, 2018a). Symptoms of AIDS, specifically a deterioration of the immune system, occur about 8 to 10 years after infection with HIV. Although most adolescents (about 85% of high school students) receive education and demonstrate basic knowledge about HIV/AIDS, most underestimate their own risks, know little about other STIs, and are not knowledgeable about how to protect themselves from STIs (Kann et al., 2014). The three ways to avoid STIs are to abstain from sex; to be in a long-term, mutually monogamous relationship with a partner who has been tested and does not have any STIs; or to use condoms consistently and correctly.

Adolescent Pregnancy and Parenthood

In 2017, the birth rate among 15- to 19-year-old girls in the United States was 18.8 per 1,000 girls, down from a high of 117 per 1,000 in 1990 (Martin, Hamilton, & Osterman, 2018). The decline in adolescent birth rates can be attributed to an increase in contraceptive use (Lindberg, Santelli, & Desai, 2016). Despite overall declines over the past 2 decades, the United States continues to have one of the highest teen birth rates in the developed world (Sedgh, Finer, Bankole, Eilers, & Singh, 2015). In addition, ethnic and socioeconomic disparities place vulnerable teens at heightened risk for adolescent pregnancy and birth. Hispanic, African American, and American Indian/Alaska Native adolescents, as well as those from low socioeconomic status homes and communities (both rural and urban), have the highest adolescent birth rates in the United States (Burrus, 2018). As shown in Figure 6.4, although birth rates have declined dramatically since the 1980s, the birth rate for Hispanic and Black girls is over twice that for non-Hispanic White girls (Child Trends, 2019).

The risks for adolescent parenthood are much the same as for early sexual activity. For example, girls who experience menarche early, relative to peers, tend to engage in sexual behavior earlier than their same-age peers and experience higher risks of pregnancy (De Genna, Larkby, & Cornelius, 2011). Similarly, poor academic achievement, delinquency, substance use, depression, and affiliation with deviant peers are risk factors for early sexual activity and adolescent pregnancy (Carlson et al., 2014; Fortenberry, 2013). Low socioeconomic status homes and neighborhoods are associated with a higher risk of adolescent pregnancy, likely influenced by lack of access to health services, after-school activities, and weak community ties. Recall that adolescents reared in stressful contexts tend to engage in sexual activity at earlier ages than their peers, and early sexual activity increases the risk of adverse outcomes such as pregnancy. In addition, low levels of parental warmth and monitoring influence early sexual activity and the risk for adolescent childbirth. Girls are much more likely to become pregnant when they have an older sister who experienced adolescent pregnancy (Wall-Wieler, Roos, & Nickel, 2016). The home context can also serve a

---

FIGURE 6.4

Birth Rates for Adolescents Aged 15 to 19, 1960–2017

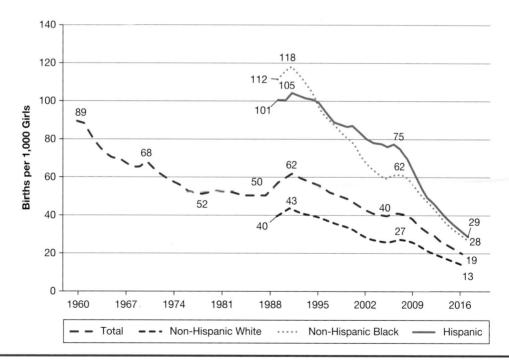

Source: Child Trends (2019).

protective role. Involved and firm parenting during early adolescence can buffer the effects of multiple home and community risk factors on the likelihood of early sexual activity and adolescent pregnancy (East, Khoo, Reyes, & Coughlin, 2006).

Adolescent mothers are less likely than their peers to achieve many of the typical markers of adulthood on-time, such as completing high school, entering a stable marriage, and becoming financially and residentially independent (Taylor, 2009). A lack of resources such as child care, housing, and financial support is associated with poor educational outcomes; adolescents with child care and financial resources tend to show higher educational attainment (Casares, Lahiff, Eskenazi, & Halpern-Felsher, 2010). Although adolescent

Adolescent mothers often experience heightened stress that can make it challenging to care for their infants.
Catchlight Visual Services/Alamy Stock Photo

pregnancy is associated with negative outcomes, the risk factors for adolescent pregnancy are also those that place youth at risk for negative adult outcomes in general, such as extreme poverty, family instability, and few educational and community supports (Oxford et al., 2005). It is therefore difficult to determine the degree to which outcomes are caused by adolescent pregnancy itself or the contextual conditions that are associated with it. Adolescent fathers are similar to adolescent mothers in that they are more likely than their peers to have poor academic performance, higher school dropout rates, finite financial resources, and lowered income potential (Kiselica & Kiselica, 2014).

Infants born to adolescent mothers are at risk for preterm birth and low birth weight (Jeha, Usta, Ghulmiyyah, & Nassar, 2015). Children of adolescent mothers tend to be at risk for a variety of negative developmental outcomes such as conduct and emotional problems, cognitive and developmental delays, and poor academic achievement (Baudry, Tarabulsy, Atkinson, Pearson, & St-Pierre, 2017; Rafferty, Griffin, & Lodise, 2011; Tang, Davis-Kean, Chen, & Sexton, 2016). These outcomes are influenced by the characteristics of adolescents who are likely to become mothers, as well as the consequences of having a child at a young age (e.g., low level of maternal education, low socioeconomic status, frequent caretaker and residence changes, poor parenting) (De Genna et al., 2011; Rafferty et al., 2011). Adolescent mothers tend to experience heightened stress that influences their interactions with their infants. Maternal cortisol levels, a physiological response to stress, are associated with increased cortisol in infants, suggesting that the stress of adolescent parenting may have negative effects on mothers and infants' physical functioning

and well-being (Hendrix, Stowe, Newport, & Brennan, 2018). However, there is variability in outcomes. Many children of adolescent mothers demonstrate resilience and adjustment despite these risks (Levine, Emery, & Pollack, 2007). Positive adjustment is predicted by secure attachment, low maternal depressive symptoms, and positive parenting on the part of the mother, characterized by warmth, discussion, and stimulation.

Adolescent parents are more likely to be successful parents when they have a range of supports—economic, educational, and social. Effective supports for adolescent parents include access to health care and affordable child care, encouragement to stay in school, and training in vocational skills, parenting skills, and coping skills (Easterbrooks, Chaudhuri, Bartlett, & Copeman, 2011). For example, interventions that emphasize promoting high-quality parent–infant interactions are associated with positive cognitive development in infants (Baudry et al., 2017). Social support predicts increased parenting self-efficacy and parental satisfaction (Angley, Divney, Magriples, & Kershaw, 2015; Umaña-Taylor, Guimond, Updegraff, & Jahromi, 2013). Adolescent parents who experience positive family interactions and support tend to demonstrate greater parenting competence and satisfaction (Angley et al., 2015). Relationships with adults who are close, are supportive, and provide guidance predict completing high school. Adolescent parents who share caregiving with their mothers or other adults learn as apprentices and become increasingly competent at parenting over time (Oberlander, Black, & Starr, 2007). Adolescent parents also benefit from relationships with adults who are sensitive not only to their needs as parents but also to their own developmental needs for autonomy and support.

Sexual Coercion

Healthy sexual activity is consensual sexual activity. It is estimated that about one in three women experience nonconsensual sexual activity; that is, they experience sexual assault or rape over their lifetime (Smith et al., 2017). **Rape** refers to nonconsensual sexual penetration of the body by the body part of another person or object (Federal Bureau of Investigation, 2015), while **sexual assault** is a broader term referring to a wide variety of nonconsensual sexual contact or behavior. Nonconsensual is the key to identifying sexual assault: It includes instances in which the victim is coerced by fear tactics, such as threats or use of physical harm, or is incapable of giving consent due to the influence of drugs or alcohol or because of age. Emerging adulthood is a particularly vulnerable time. It is estimated that between 20% and 30% of emerging adult women experience nonconsensual sexual activity; that is, they experience sexual assault or rape (Fedina, Holmes, & Backes, 2018; Mellins et al., 2017). Most victims are young, with nearly 80% experiencing sexual assault prior to age 25; 40% of victims are under the age of 18 (Breiding et al., 2014). Although adolescence seems to be a period of high risk, college is also a vulnerable time. In a large, cross-sectional survey of campus sexual assault, 20% of undergraduate women indicated that they had been a victim of sexual assault since beginning college (Basile et al., 2016; Krebs, Lindquist, Warner, Fisher, & Martin, 2009).

Adolescents are most likely to be assaulted by someone they know (Breiding, Chen, & Black, 2014; Sinozich & Langton, 2014). The commonly used term "date rape" for nonconsensual sexual activity with an acquaintance downplays the severity of sexual assault. Many cases of date rape are premeditated and involve slipping powerful sedatives such as rohypnol (roofie) into a young person's drink. The drug makes the victim drowsy, unconscious, or unable to move and often causes her to not recall the event the next day. When alcohol is involved, victims may blame themselves for drinking (Hock, 2015). Many victims wrongly assume that they sent "mixed signals" or that things "got out of hand."

Underreporting of rape is high. The actual number of incidents is hard to determine, but one study found that only about 20% of rapes had been reported to the police (Sinozich & Langton, 2014). Sometimes victims believe that their attacker will deny the rape or believe that no assault occurred. Victims may want to avoid being judged negatively by friends, peers, or future potential dating partners. Most victims tell a friend and the support they receive often influences help-seeking and well-being (Lichty & Gowen, 2018). Many victims do not acknowledge rape or sexual assault, but instead refer to it as miscommunication or sexual activities that "got out of hand." One meta-analysis of 28 studies (with almost 6,000 participants) found that two-thirds of women rape survivors, particularly those who experienced acquaintance rape, did not acknowledge that they had been raped (Wilson & Miller, 2016). Instead, they used more benign labels such as "bad sex" or "miscommunication."

Survivors of sexual assault have a higher than average risk of developing post-traumatic stress disorder (PTSD), anxiety, and depression and of abusing alcohol and other substances (Carey, Norris, Durney, Shepardson, & Carey, 2018; Kirkner, Relyea, & Ullman, 2018). Women's attributions for the assault influence their adjustment. Women who blame themselves for the assault tend to experience more adjustment difficulties, including a higher risk for depression, whereas support from family and friends influences positive adjustment (Orchowski, Untied, & Gidycz, 2013; Sigurvinsdottir & Ullman, 2015; Vickerman & Margolin, 2009).

Contextual influences, such as the prevalence of rape myths, can affect the prevalence of sexual assault. High school students' endorsement of rape myths (such as "girls don't really mean no") and perceived peer endorsement of myths was associated with engaging in dating aggression (Collibee, Rizzo, Bleiweiss, & Orchowski, 2019). Among college students, men tend to be more accepting of rape myths than are women and are more likely to cling to them following date rape education classes (Maxwell & Scott, 2014; Stewart, 2014). Gender-role stereotyping may contribute to the prevalence of sexual assault, as cultural stereotypes of men's and women's roles, encouraging dominance, aggression, and competition in males and passivity in females, may support attitudes that are accepting of sexual violence. Research with college students has shown that students who are highly gender stereotyped and believe in strict gender roles are more likely than their peers to blame sexual assault survivors, express attitudes condoning nonconsensual sex, and be aroused by depictions of rape (Lambert & Raichle, 2000; Malamuth, Addison, & Koss, 2000). Boys and men who engage in sexual assault tend to interpret women's behavior inaccurately, often perceiving warmth and friendliness as indicating sexual interest (Perilloux, Easton, & Buss, 2012). They buy into rape myths, such as the belief that a victim "asked for it" by dressing attractively or behaving flirtatiously; that nonconsensual sex with a romantic partner, friend, or acquaintance cannot be considered rape; or that men are driven to commit rape by uncontrollable sexual impulses (Malamuth et al., 2000). Effective sexual assault prevention educates men and women about gender socialization, describes the nature and impact of sexual violence, debunks rape myths, and offers suggestions on how to intervene as a bystander (Stewart, 2014). In women, effective sexual assault prevention includes helping women assess assault risk from acquaintances, overcome emotional barriers in acknowledging danger, and engage in effective verbal and physical self-defense (Senn et al., 2015). Teaching adolescents about sexual consent is an important way of educating adolescents about the relationship dynamic of sexual activity and protecting them against unwanted sexual activity. We examine methods of teaching adolescents about consent later in this chapter.

REVIEW 6.3

1. What factors are associated with condom use?

2. Give some examples of STIs and describe how they can be avoided.

3. What are some correlates and outcomes of adolescent parenthood for parents and children?

4. How might contextual factors influence the prevalence of sexual assault?

· ·

THINKING IN CONTEXT 6.3

Consider adolescent pregnancy from a bioecological perspective (see Chapter 1). Identify factors at each bioecological level that might contribute to the risk of adolescent pregnancy. Specifically:

1. Identify at least three microsystem and mesosystem factors.

2. How might the exosystem contribute to the risk for adolescent pregnancy? Give two examples.

3. What role does the macrosystem play in influencing the risk of adolescent pregnancy?

· ·

APPLY 6.3

"That was some party! Way to end the school year!" Morena exclaimed. "I'm so glad my parents finally let me stay home alone for the weekend!"

"My head is killing me. What happened last night?" asked Keanna.

"You don't remember? You were hanging out with that senior guy, Matt. You two looked very cozy," Morena teased.

"Really? I remember talking early in the evening, but that's it," Keanna explained.

"You guys went into my bedroom. I found you sleeping there this morning. You really don't remember?"

"Guess it was bad sex—if there was sex. I don't know."

"That's really weird. I didn't see you drink much last night. Maybe you got roofied?"

"I don't know. I hope not."

1. Discuss the prevalence and nature of sexual assault.

2. What concerns might Keanna have about the risks and negative consequences of sexual assault?

3. Discuss ways of preventing assault.

· ·

SEXUALITY EDUCATION

Adolescents' learn about sex in a variety of ways—through interactions with parents and peers, media, and, often, at school. Sexuality education, however, is not federally mandated or regulated. Only about half of states require schools to provide sex education, but over two-thirds require HIV education (Guttmacher Institute, 2019). Debates over the content of sexuality education have centered primarily on whether instruction should emphasize abstinence until marriage or promote medically accurate information on a broad range of topics related to sexuality, often referred to as comprehensive sex education.

Abstinence Only Until Marriage

Over the past 2 decades, the U.S. federal government has spent about $2 billion on sexual education programs for adolescents that emphasize abstinence from sex outside of marriage. **Abstinence-only-until-marriage programs** teach social, psychological, and health gains that come with abstaining from sexual activity and convey the expectation that young people will abstain from sexual activity outside of marriage and that sexual activity outside of marriage is "likely to have harmful psychological and physical effects" (Social Security Administration, 1996). These programs instruct adolescents on the benefits of abstinence but do not provide information about safe sex.

Are abstinence-only-until-marriage programs effective? A large body of scientific evidence has demonstrated that programs promoting abstinence only until marriage, without information about sexuality and safe sex, are ineffective (Breuner, Mattson, & Commitee on Psychosocial Aspects of Child and Family Health, 2016). Research has suggested that abstinence-only-until-marriage programs do not delay initiation of sexual intercourse or reduce the frequency of sexual activity, numbers of sexual partners, contraception use, or safe sex (Santelli et al., 2017). One recent systematic review of the literature summarized the results of 224 controlled trials of school-based sex education programs and concluded that abstinence-only interventions did not promote

Comprehensive sexual education programs emphasize the overall health of adolescents.
iStock.com/michaeljung

positive changes in sexual initiation or other sexual behaviors (Denford, Abraham, Campbell, & Busse, 2017). In some states, abstinence-only-until-marriage programs are associated with increased birth rates (Fox, Himmelstein, Khalid, & Howell, 2019).

Why? Many adolescents who intend to be abstinent fail to do so. Recall that adolescents often have difficulty controlling impulses in situations that are emotionally charged. Abstinence-only education programs do not provide adolescents with information about sexuality and safe sex. Unfortunately, when adolescent abstainers initiate intercourse, many fail to use condoms and contraception to protect themselves (Paik, Sanchagrin, & Heimer, 2016; Santelli et al., 2017). Therefore, user failure with abstinence is high.

Some health care professionals and researchers have argued that by not providing medically accurate information about sexuality and safe sex, abstinence-only-until-marriage programs are harmful and threaten fundamental human rights to health, information, and life (American College of Obstetricians and Gynecologists., 2016; American Public Health Association., 2006; Breuner et al., 2016; Santelli, Ott, Lyon, Rogers, & Summers, 2006). Young people need access to accurate and comprehensive sexual health information to protect their health and lives.

Comprehensive Sex Education

According to the Sexuality Information and Education Council of the United States, comprehensive sex education is part of an overall school health education approach, emphasizing age-appropriate physical, mental, emotional and social dimensions of human sexuality (Future of Sex Education Initiative, 2012). Comprehensive sexual programs emphasize the overall health of adolescents. Components of comprehensive sex education programs include the following (Panchaud & Anderson, 2014):

Promote sexual and reproductive health

- Anatomy, reproduction; how to use contraception; pregnancy options and information; understanding STIs, including transmission, symptoms, and prevention
- Virginity; abstinence and faithfulness; social expectations
- Self-esteem and empowerment; myths and stereotypes about sex

Promote sexual rights

- Discussion of social, cultural, and ethical barriers to exercising rights related to sexual and reproductive health; understanding advocacy and choice
- Understanding that sexuality and culture are diverse and dynamic and include various practices and norms
- Understanding consent and the right to have sex only when an individual is ready; the right to freely express and explore one's sexuality in a safe, healthy, and pleasurable way

Promote a positive approach to sexuality and well-being

- A positive approach to young people's sexuality; understanding that sex should be enjoyable and consensual; understanding that sex is much more than just sexual intercourse; sexuality as part of a healthy and normal life
- Sexual well-being; safer sex practices and pleasure; interpersonal communication; the diversity of sexuality; consent; alcohol, drugs, and the implications of their use

Prevent violence

- Exploring the various types of violence toward men and women and how they manifest, particularly gender-based violence; nonconsensual sex and understanding what is unacceptable

Promote diversity

- Recognizing and understanding the range of diversity (e.g., faith, culture, ethnicity, socioeconomic status, ability/disability, and sexual orientation); a positive view of diversity; recognizing discrimination and its damaging effects and managing it; promoting equality

Promote healthy relationships

- Different types of relationships; that relationships are constantly changing; emotions; intimacy; rights and responsibilities; power dynamics
- Recognizing healthy and unhealthy or coercive relationships; communication, trust, and honesty in relationships; peer pressure and social norms; that love and sex are not the same

Comprehensive sexuality education programs promote healthy adolescent development and provide medically accurate information, including information about safe sex (Future of Sex Education Initiative, 2012). Systematic reviews consistently find that comprehensive sexuality education programs tend to show efficacy in delaying initiation of intercourse in addition to promoting other protective behaviors such as condom use (Breuner et al., 2016).

Public opinion polls in the United States suggest strong support for comprehensive approaches to sex education that include information about abstinence and education about sexuality, condoms, and contraception, as well as access to condoms and contraception for sexually active adolescents (Santelli et al., 2017). One recent study of more than 1,600 parents revealed that over 90% place high importance on sex education in both middle and high school, including topics in sex education such as puberty, healthy relationships, abstinence, sexually transmitted diseases, and birth control (Kantor & Levitz, 2017). Likewise, health professionals have overwhelmingly supported comprehensive sexuality education (American College of Obstetricians and Gynecologists, 2016; American Public Health Association., 2014; APA Council of Representatives, 1996; Breuner et al., 2016; Hagan et al., 2001). ●

REVIEW 6.4

1. Describe characteristics and effectiveness of abstinence-only-until-marriage education programs.

2. Discuss characteristics of comprehensive sexuality education.

THINKING IN CONTEXT 6.4

1. How do physical, cognitive, and socioemotional development influence adolescents' ability to understand and implement information from sex education programs? For example, consider brain development, cognition, and identity development.

2. How might adolescents' interactions at home, with peers, and in the community influence how they understand and implement sex education messages?

3. Describe your experience with sexuality education, if any. How would you describe the educational approach? What were characteristics of the program, lessons, activities, or assignments? In your view, how effective was the approach? How might you improve it?

APPLY 6.4

As an expert in adolescent sexuality, you have been asked to design an effective sexuality education program.

1. How would you structure your program? Would it be conducted in class or by some other means?

2. What topics would you teach? What are the important points within each topic?

3. Brainstorm two activities or assignments to help students learn the concepts you deem important.

4. How might your choice of topics and activities or assignments vary depending on students' grade—for example, seventh, ninth, or eleventh grade?

CHAPTER SUMMARY

6.1 Examine patterns of sexual activity in adolescence.

Most young people have sexual intercourse for the first time at about age 17. The proportion of high school students who have ever had sexual intercourse is at an all-time low. Initiating sexual activity in the later high school years is not associated with poor adjustment; however, early sexual initiation, prior to age 16, poses risks to development, including alcohol and substance use, poor academic achievement, delinquency, and risky sex. Risk factors for early sexual activity include early pubertal maturation, poor parental monitoring, poor parent–adolescent communication, and perceiving peer and neighborhood attitudes and norms as supportive of sexual activity. Young people tend to disclose their sexual orientation at earlier ages than in prior generations, likely due to an increasingly

inviting, positive cultural context for LGB young people. On average, young people come out just prior to high school graduation. Accepting reactions from parents and peers as well as the presence of gay–straight alliances at school can buffer the psychological and behavioral risks that accompany perceived discrimination.

6.2 Discuss biological and contextual influences on sexual activity in adolescence.

Increases in testosterone are associated with sexual fantasies in both boys and girls, but girls' sexual behavior is more closely linked to contextual factors than boys. Warm parenting, regularly shared family activities, and parental monitoring of adolescents' activities are associated with lower rates of sexual activity and fewer sexual partners.

Adolescents tend to show a later onset of sexual activity and engage in less sexual risk-taking than their peers when parents and children communicate about sexuality with warmth, support, and humor. Parent–child communication about risky sexual activity is associated with engaging in safer sex but does *not* prevent sexual activity itself. Adolescents who perceive their peers as more sexually active believe that they have positive attitudes about and are more approving of sexual activity and are more likely to initiate sexual activity, engage in sex more frequently, and accumulate a greater number of sexual partners than those with peers who are less sexually active. Neighborhood disadvantage is associated with early sexual activity, risky sexual activity, and adolescent pregnancy and birth because it affects community resources that support adolescents and families, such as schools, local voluntary organizations, recreational options, access to health care, and informal neighborhood networks.

6.3 Summarize risks to adolescents' sexual health.

Adolescents' knowledge of and access to contraceptives are the best predictors of contraceptive use; however, 15- to 24-year-olds account for over half of all STI diagnoses each year. Despite overall declines over the past 2 decades, the United States continues to have one of the highest teen birth rates in the developed world. The risks for adolescent parenthood are much the same as for early sexual activity. Adolescent mothers are less likely than their peers to achieve many of the typical markers of adulthood on-time. Children of adolescent mothers tend to be at risk for negative developmental outcomes such as conduct and emotional problems, cognitive and developmental delays, and poor academic achievement. Positive adjustment is predicted by secure attachment, low maternal depressive symptoms, and positive parenting on the part of the mother, characterized by warmth, discussion, and stimulation. Adolescent parents are more likely to be successful parents when they have a range of supports—economic, educational, and social. It is estimated that about one in three women experience sexual assault or rape over their lifetime. Adolescents are most likely to be assaulted by someone they know and underreporting of rape is high. Survivors of sexual assault have a higher than average risk of developing post-traumatic stress disorder, anxiety, and depression and of abusing alcohol and other substances.

6.4 Compare approaches to sexuality education.

Abstinence-only-until-marriage programs teach social, psychological, and health gains that come with abstaining from sexual activity and convey the expectation that young people will abstain from sexual activity outside of marriage. Research has suggested that abstinence-only-until-marriage programs do not delay initiation of sexual intercourse or reduce the frequency of sexual activity, numbers of sexual partners, contraception use, or safe sex. Comprehensive sex education is part of an overall school health education approach emphasizing age-appropriate physical, mental, emotional, and social dimensions of human sexuality. Comprehensive sexuality education programs promote healthy adolescent development and provide medically accurate information, including information about safe sex. Systematic reviews consistently find that comprehensive sexuality education programs tend to show efficacy in delaying initiation of intercourse in addition to promoting other protective behaviors such as condom use.

KEY TERMS

abstinence-only-until-marriage programs, 142

human immunodeficiency virus (HIV), 138

human papillomavirus (HPV), 138

rape, 141

sexual assault, 141

sexual orientation, 130

7

Morality, Religion, and Values

Learning Objectives

Chapter Contents

One of the simplest ways to describe adolescence is as a period of becoming. Adolescents are faced with many developmental tasks, such as establishing a sense of identity and becoming autonomous. As we discussed in Chapter 1, autonomy is multidimensional, with emotional, cognitive, and behavioral components (Zimmer-Gembeck & Collins, 2003). Adolescents seek emotional autonomy, or to individuate, from parents, and work toward behavioral autonomy, the ability to regulate their own behavior. In this chapter we examine aspects of the third dimension of autonomy: **cognitive autonomy**, which refers to independent decision-making, an internalized sense of right and wrong, the capacity to voice opinions, and a personal value system (Beckert, 2007). Adolescents' emerging cognitive autonomy influences how they reason about moral, prosocial, religious, and civic issues.

MORAL DEVELOPMENT

We encounter the need to make moral decisions every day. Is it ever acceptable to cut the line at the grocery store? Park in a fire lane? Tell a white lie? Our capacity to think about everyday moral dilemmas such as these emerges early in life (Skitka, Bauman, & Mullen, 2016). **Moral reasoning**, how we view and make judgments about issues of rights and justice in our social world, develops and grows rapidly with advances in cognitive development, social experience, and opportunities to consider issues of fairness.

Moral Reasoning

Kohlberg (1976) proposed that moral reasoning reflects cognitive development and is organized into three broad levels, each with two substages. Beginning in early childhood and persisting until about age 9, children demonstrate what Kohlberg called **preconventional reasoning**. Kohlberg argued that young children's behavior is governed by self-interest, the desire to gain rewards and avoid punishments ("Don't steal because you don't want to go to jail"). Moral behavior is a response to external pressure, and children's reasoning illustrates their difficulty in taking another person's perspective. Instead, young children's moral reasoning is motivated by their desires. The preconventional level comprises two stages, in which children move from avoiding punishment as a motivator of moral judgments (Stage 1) to self-interest, rewards, and concern about what others can do for them (Stage 2).

At about age 9 or 10, children transition to the second level of Kohlberg's scheme, **conventional moral reasoning**. Children are now able to take others' perspectives and are motivated by reciprocity, seeking to be accepted and avoid disapproval. Rules maintain relationships. Children uphold rules in order to please others, gain affection, and be a good person—honest, caring, and nice (Stage 3). Their behavior is motivated by the Golden Rule: "Do unto others as you would have them do unto you." In adolescence, perspective taking expands beyond individuals to include society's rules (Stage 4). Adolescents accept rules as a tool to maintain social order and believe that everyone has a duty to uphold the rules. Reasoning is no longer influenced by relationships and a desire to be a good person. Instead, rules are universal and must be enforced for everyone. Many people demonstrate conventional reasoning throughout their lives.

Not until adolescence, according to Kohlberg, do people become capable of demonstrating the most advanced moral thinking, **postconventional moral reasoning**, which entails autonomous decision-making from moral principles that value respect for individual rights above all else. Postconventional moral thinkers recognize that their self-chosen principles of fairness and justice may sometimes conflict with the law. As they enter postconventional moral reasoning, individuals view laws and rules as flexible and part of the social contract or agreement meant to further human interests (Stage 5). Laws and rules are to be followed as they bring good to people, but laws can be changed if they are inconsistent with the needs and rights of the majority. Sometimes, if laws are unjust—if they harm more people than they protect—they can be broken. The final, most advanced and most rare, stage of reasoning, Stage 6, is based on abstract ethical principles that are universal, valid for all people regardless of law, such as equality and respect for human dignity. Although advances in cognitive development make postconventional reasoning possible, the highest forms of postconventional reasoning are rare.

Lawrence Kohlberg's cognitive-developmental theory posited that moral reasoning progresses through three levels.
Lee Lockwood/Contributor/Getty Images

Assessing Moral Reasoning

Much of Kohlberg's theory was based on longitudinal research with a group of boys, ages 10, 13, and 16, who were periodically interviewed over 3 decades (Kohlberg, 1969). Kohlberg discovered that the boys' reasoning progressed through sequential stages and in a predictable order. Kohlberg measured moral reasoning by presenting individuals with hypothetical dilemmas such as the following:

> Near death, a woman with cancer learns of a drug that may save her. The woman's husband, Heinz, approaches the druggist who created the drug, but the druggist refuses to sell the drug for anything less than $2,000. After borrowing from everyone he knows, Heinz has only scraped together $1,000. Heinz asks the druggist to let him have the drug for $1,000 and he will pay him the rest later. The druggist says that it is his right to make money from the drug he developed and refuses to sell it to Heinz. Desperate for the drug, Heinz breaks into the druggist's store and steals the drug. Should Heinz have done that? Why or why not? (Kohlberg, 1969)

The Heinz dilemma is the most popular example of the hypothetical conflicts that Kohlberg used to study moral development. These problems examine how people make decisions when fairness and people's rights are pitted against obedience to authority and law. Participants' explanations of how they arrived at their decisions reveal developmental shifts through three broad levels of reasoning that correspond to cognitive development.

At the preconventional level, decisions are influenced by self-interest, the desire to gain rewards and avoid punishments. Children might respond that Heinz should not steal the drug because he will go to prison, or that he should steal the drug to avoid his wife's anger or to receive her affection. Conventional moral reasoning is socially driven. School-age children might argue that Heinz should steal the drug because good people help their wives or because it is his duty as a husband. Alternatively, they might say that Heinz should not steal the drug because good people do not steal or because following rules maintains social order; what would happen if everyone stole? At the postconventional level of reasoning, adolescents might explain that, although stealing is against the law, laws are intended to help people and, in this case, stealing the drug is intended to help Heinz's wife. Moreover, the value of a life is exponentially greater than that of the drug, suggesting that Heinz should steal the drug.

A great deal of research has confirmed that individuals proceed through the first four stages of moral reasoning in a slow, gradual, and predictable fashion (Boom, Wouters, & Keller, 2007; Dawson, 2002). Specifically, reasoning at the preconventional level decreases by early adolescence. Conventional reasoning, specifically Stage 3, increases through middle adolescence, and Stage 4 reasoning increases in middle to late adolescence and becomes typical of most individuals by early adulthood. Research suggests that few people advance beyond conventional (Stage 4) moral reasoning. Postconventional reasoning is rare in adults and appears as Stage 5 reasoning (Kohlberg, Levine, & Hewer, 1983). Research generally has not supported the existence of Stage 6, the hypothesized most advanced type of moral reasoning; however, Stage 6 represents an end goal state to which human development strives (Kohlberg & Ryncarz, 1990).

Kohlberg's theory of moral reasoning has led to 5 decades of research. Most of the research conducted has examined the role of social interaction in promoting development, the role of gender and culture, and the link between reasoning and behavior.

Social Interaction and Moral Reasoning

Moral development occurs within parent, peer, and school contexts and is influenced by social development. Social interactions offer important

opportunities for the development of moral reasoning. High-quality parent–child relationships predict advanced moral reasoning (Malti & Latzko, 2010). Reasoning advances when adolescents have opportunities to engage in discussions that are characterized by mutual perspective taking. Engaging adolescents in discussion about personal experiences, local issues, and media events—while presenting alternative points of view and asking questions—advances reasoning. For example, a parent might ask, "Why do you think he did that? Was there something else that he could have done? How do you think other people interpret his actions?" Issue-focused discussions that present adolescents with reasoning that is slightly more advanced than their own prompts them to compare their reasoning with the new reasoning and often internalize the new reasoning, advancing their moral reasoning to a new level.

Parents who engage their children in discussion, listen with sensitivity, ask for children's input, praise them, engage them with questioning, and use humor promote the development of moral reasoning (Carlo, Mestre, Samper, Tur, & Armenta, 2011b). Likewise, interactions with peers in which adolescents confront one another with differing perspectives and engage each other with in-depth discussions promote the development of moral reasoning (Power, Higgins, & Kohlberg, 1989). Adolescents who report having more close friendships in which they engage in deep conversations tend to show more advanced moral reasoning than do teens who have little social contact (Schonert-Reichl, 1999). They also report feeling positive emotions when they make unselfish moral decisions (Malti, Keller, & Buchmann, 2013). Moral reasoning is inherently social. Some have argued, however, that the social basis of morality means that men and women should reason in very different ways.

Gender and Moral Reasoning

A popular criticism of Kohlberg's theory of moral reasoning arises because his initial research was conducted with samples of boys. Early research that studied both men and women suggested gender differences in moral reasoning, with men typically showing Stage 4 reasoning, characterized by concerns about law and order, and women showing Stage 3 reasoning, characterized by concerns about maintaining relationships (Poppen, 1974). Carol Gilligan (1982) argued that Kohlberg's theory neglected a distinctively feminine mode of moral reasoning, a **care orientation**, which is characterized by empathy, a desire to maintain relationships, and a responsibility not to cause harm. As Gilligan explains, the care orientation contrasts with the distinctively masculine mode of moral reasoning, a **justice orientation**, which is based on the abstract principles of fairness and individualism captured by

Kohlberg. Care and justice represent frameworks modified by experience that influence how people interpret and resolve moral problems.

Although most people are capable of raising both justice and care concerns in describing moral dilemmas, Gilligan argued that care reasoning was thought to be used predominantly by women and justice reasoning by men (Gilligan & Attanucci, 1988). In agreement with Gilligan, most researchers acknowledge that more than one mode of moral reasoning exists (Kohlberg et al., 1983) but instead argue that moral orientations are not linked with gender (Knox, Fagley, & Miller, 2004). Boys, girls, men, and women display similar reasoning that combines concerns of justice (e.g., being fair) with those of care (e.g., being supportive and helpful), and when there are sex differences, they are very small (Jaffee & Hyde, 2000; Weisz & Black, 2002). The most mature forms of moral reasoning incorporate both justice and care concerns.

Adolescents of different cultures can apply both care and justice reasoning. These Hong Kong adolescents protest in favor of democracy, suggesting a justice orientation.
Anthony Kwan / Stringer/Getty Images

Culture and Moral Reasoning

Cross-cultural studies of Kohlberg's theory show that the sequence appears in all cultures but that people in non-Western cultures rarely score above the conventional level—specifically, Stage 3 (Gibbs, Basinger, Grime, & Snarey, 2007). Like cognitive capacities, morality and appropriate responses to ethical dilemmas are defined by each society and its cultural perspectives. Whereas Western cultures tend to emphasize the rights of the individual (justice-based reasoning), non-Western cultures tend to value collectivism, focusing on human interdependence (care-based reasoning). Individuals in collectivist cultures tend to define moral dilemmas in terms of the responsibility to the entire community rather than simply to the individual (Miller, 2018). Such emphasis on the needs of others is characteristic of Stage 3 in Kohlberg's scheme. However, because moral values are relative to the cultural context, Stage 3 reasoning is an advanced form of reasoning in collectivist cultures because it embodies what is most valued in these cultures, concepts such as interdependence and relationships.

Despite cross-cultural differences, individuals in many cultures show similarities in reasoning. For example, one study examined Chinese and Canadian 12- to 19-year-old adolescents' views of the fairness of various forms of democratic and nondemocratic government (Helwig, Arnold, Tan, & Boyd, 2007). Adolescents from both China and Canada preferred democratic forms of government and appealed to

fundamental democratic justice principles such as representation, voice, and majority rule to support their judgments, suggesting that adolescents in collectivist cultures are able to reason with justice principles in particular contexts. In addition, similar age-related patterns in judgments and reasoning were found across cultures and across diverse regions within China. It appears that the development of moral reasoning progresses in a similar pattern across cultures. People of different cultures are able to reason using both care and justice orientations even though cultures tend to vary in the weight they assign moral orientations, emphasizing one over another.

Moral Reasoning and Behavior

Moral reasoning explains how people think about issues of justice, but reasoning is only moderately related to behavior (Colby & Damon, 1992). People often behave in ways they know they should not. For example, an adolescent who explains that stealing and cheating are wrong may slip a pack of gum into her pocket and leave a store without paying or may peek at a classmate's paper during an exam. Like other decisions, ethical conflicts experienced in real life are complex, accompanied by intense emotions, social obligations, and practical considerations, which lead people to act in ways that contradict their judgments (Walker, 2004).

With advances in moral reasoning, adolescents are more likely to act in ways that are in line with their beliefs (Smetana, Jambon, & Ball, 2013). For example, adolescents who demonstrate higher levels of moral reasoning are more likely to share with and help others and are less likely to engage in antisocial behavior such as cheating, aggression, or delinquency (Brugman, 2010; Comunian & Gielen, 2000). Although adolescents who show low levels of moral reasoning are thought to be at greater risk for delinquency, findings are mixed in this area. Some studies find that low levels of reasoning predict delinquency, and others show no relationship (Leenders & Brugman, 2005; Tarry & Emler, 2007). Perhaps the degree to which moral reasoning is associated with behavior varies with whether adolescents perceive the behavior as a moral issue or simply a social convention or a personal choice (Berkowitz & Begun, 1994; Brugman, 2010). Adolescents, particularly early adolescents, tend to overwhelmingly label behaviors as personal choices. Adolescents' moral development influences behaviors they label as moral decisions but not those viewed as social conventions or personal choices. Adolescents who engage in delinquency are more likely than other adolescents to view delinquent behaviors as issues of social convention or personal choice rather than moral issues, suggesting that their level of moral maturity is not an influence on their delinquent behavior because they do not label the behavior as entailing a moral decision (Kuther & Higgins-D'Alessandro, 2000; Leenders & Brugman, 2005). Another perspective on moral development focuses on the drive to help others and engage in prosocial behavior, which we discuss next.

REVIEW 7.1

1. Describe three levels of moral reasoning.

2. How is moral reasoning assessed?

3. How do social interaction and contextual factors influence moral reasoning?

4. To what degree does moral reasoning influence behavior?

THINKING IN CONTEXT 7.1

1. How might other aspects of development, such as brain development and cognitive development, influence moral development?

2. How might contextual factors influence moral reasoning? For example, consider whether socioeconomic status in the home and community influences the development of moral reasoning. Do race, ethnicity, and culture matter? Why or why not?

APPLY 7.1

When asked why it's wrong to steal, 12-year-old James replies, "Because you'll get caught and go to jail!"

1. What type of reasoning does James display?

2. Compare James's response with what young adolescents typically show in Kohlberg's model.

3. Identify influences on James's reasoning.

4. How might you expect James's reasoning to change?

PROSOCIAL DEVELOPMENT

Over the course of adolescence, young people think about moral issues in more complex ways and their orientation toward helping others undergoes similar developmental shifts. **Prosocial behavior**, voluntary behavior intended to benefit another, emerges in infancy and becomes more common and complex throughout childhood into adolescence (Eisenberg, Spinrad, & Knafo-Noam, 2015). Adolescents' increasing social mobility, coupled with advanced cognitive capacities in comparison to younger children, presents them with more opportunities to engage in prosocial behavior. Prosocial behavior is positively related to social competence and academic outcomes and may be a protective factor against problem behaviors (Carlo et al., 2014; Xiao, Hashi, Korous, & Eisenberg, 2019).

Developmental Shifts in Prosocial Reasoning

Prosocial reasoning, or thinking and decision-making about helping others, tends to improve in adolescence (Eisenberg, Cumberland, Guthrie, Murphy, & Shepard, 2005). Prosocial behavior, however, shows more mixed changes over adolescence. Self-reported prosocial behavior tends to decline in early adolescence and rebound in middle to late adolescence (Carlo, Padilla-Walker, & Nielson, 2015; Luengo Kanacri, Pastorelli, Eisenberg, Zuffianò, & Caprara, 2013). In addition to self-reports, prosocial behavior is often studied in the laboratory through the use of economic games in which adolescents must decide how much of a given quantity, such as coins, tokens, or candy, to give to others. Research using this paradigm has shown that adolescents' giving behavior depends on the target. Generally adolescents report higher mean levels of prosocial behavior toward friends than toward either parents or strangers (Güroglu, van den Bos, & Crone, 2014; Padilla-Walker & Christensen, 2011). Prosocial behavior toward family tends to remain stable or decrease over time, while prosocial behavior toward friends increases over time (Padilla-Walker, Dyer, Yorgason, Fraser, & Coyne, 2015b).

Girls and boys are more alike than different. Whereas some studies suggest no gender differences in prosocial behavior (Barry, Lui, & Anderson, 2017),

Adolescents who participate in research on prosocial development are often asked to sort—and then share—coins.
iStock.com/kate_sept2004

others suggest small gender differences in some types of prosocial behavior (Xiao et al., 2019). For example, girls tend to donate more than boys regardless of target (Espinosa & Kovářík, 2015; Padilla-Walker, Carlo, & Memmott-Elison, 2018). Girls tend to report higher levels of altruistic prosocial behavior (performed without expectation of self-reward), emotional prosocial behavior (performed under emotionally evocative situations), and compliant prosocial behavior (in response to a direct request of assistance from others) (Eberly-Lewis & Coetzee, 2015; Hardy & Carlo, 2005). Boys tend to report more public prosocial behavior, behavior enacted in front of others. These differences reflect traditional gender roles, with girls socialized to nurture and care for others and boys to inhibit emotional responding in factor of instrumental actions. Recall that some early adolescents experience gender intensification, in which their gender-related beliefs and behaviors are magnified (see Chapter 5), perhaps influencing gender differences in prosocial responding (Van der Graaff, Carlo, Crocetti, Koot, & Branje, 2018).

Cognitive, emotional, and social development influence the display of prosocial behavior in adolescence. Abstract reasoning enables adolescents to engage in perspective taking and advances in emotion understanding contribute to **empathic concern**, the ability to understand and feel concern for another's emotional experience (Eisenberg et al., 2015). Individual differences in perspective taking in 12- to 17-year-old adolescents predict their giving behavior in economic games (Güroglu et al., 2014). Perspective taking and empathic concern facilitate positive peer relationships and prosocial behavior. As adolescents become more peer oriented, increasing interactions with peers, developing more intimate relationships

with peers, and becoming more interested in romantic relationships, their behaviors tend to become more other oriented, with opportunities for prosocial behavior (Wentzel, 2014). In turn, engaging in prosocial behavior may foster adolescents' tendency to show perspective taking and empathic concern as well as improve relations with peers (Van der Graaff et al., 2018).

Developmental changes also pose challenges for adolescents' prosocial behavior. For example, brain maturation influences how adolescents perceive and process their own and others' emotions (see Chapter 3). Adolescents' attention and sensitivity to others' emotions may temporarily decline and their prosocial tendencies may decrease (Padilla-Walker & Christensen, 2011). Brain development also influences adolescents' ability to regulate their emotions and behavior. Prosocial behavior increases as self-regulation improves (Luengo Kanacri et al., 2013; Padilla-Walker et al., 2015b).

Social Influences on Prosocial Behavior

Adolescents' prosocial behavior is influenced by their interactions with others, especially parents. For example, authoritative parenting is associated with higher rates of prosocial behavior in fifth-, tenth-, and twelfth-grade students, as compared with parenting that is less warm and involved (Carlo, White, Streit, Knight, & Zeiders, 2018). Warm parent–child relationships promote prosocial behavior and some research suggests that maternal warmth is especially influential (Carlo et al., 2011b; Padilla-Walker et al., 2015b). However, recent research with nearly 1,200 families (consisting of mothers, fathers, and children) from nine countries suggests that both mother and father acceptance are positively associated with child prosocial behavior in preadolescence and early adolescence (Putnick et al., 2018). In addition, adolescents' prosocial behavior predicted mother and father acceptance, suggesting bidirectional relations over time.

Similar to relationships with parents, close high-quality friendships predict prosocial behavior (Silke, Brady, Boylan, & Dolan, 2018). The peer group influences prosocial behavior through modeling and communicating values. Adolescents whose peers model prosocial behaviors, promote prosocial values and norms, or discourage deviant/aggressive behavior also show higher levels of a variety of prosocial

Adolescents often engage in prosocial behaviors, such as volunteer work, together.
iStock.com/Daisy-Daisy

behaviors (Farrell, Thompson, & Mehari, 2017). Peers also influence adolescent behavior by providing feedback. In one study, 12- to 16-year-old adolescents made decisions about the allocation of coins between themselves and a group of anonymous peers who provided either prosocial feedback (liking the decision to give more coins to others), antisocial feedback (liking the decision to keep more coins to oneself), or no feedback (van Hoorn, van Dijk, Meuwese, Rieffe, & Crone, 2016). As shown in Figure 7.1, prosocial behavior increased after prosocial feedback and decreased after antisocial feedback; when no feedback was provided, prosocial behavior remained stable and did not change over multiple consecutive decisions. Peers influence adolescents' prosocial behavior in both positive and negative ways.

Prosocial Behavior and Developmental Outcomes

Prosocial behavior is associated with many positive developmental outcomes in adolescence, including self-esteem, social competence, social approval from peers and teachers, academic achievement, and high-quality relationships (Eisenberg et al., 2015; Padilla-Walker et al., 2018; Wentzel, 2014). Moreover, prosocial behavior is negatively associated with internalizing and externalizing problems such as anxiety, depression, aggression, risky behaviors, substance use, delinquency, and association with deviant peers (Carlo, Crockett, Wilkinson, & Beal, 2011a; Carlo et al., 2014; Laible, McGinley, Carlo, Augustine, & Murphy, 2014; Padilla-Walker, Carlo, & Nielson, 2015a).

Prosocial behavior is not simply negatively associated with problem behavior—it may have a protective effect on problem behavior. For example,

FIGURE 7.1

Adolescent Prosocial Behavior in Response to Peer Feedback

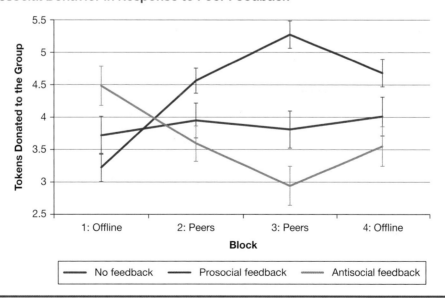

Source: van Hoorn et al. (2016).

one 3-year longitudinal study of early adolescents found that prior prosocial behavior toward family members and strangers predicted fewer problem behaviors 2 years later (Carlo et al., 2015). Prosocial behavior over the 3-year transition from elementary to middle school was associated with lower levels of peer rejection (Zimmer-Gembeck, Geiger, & Crick, 2005). Prosocial behavior at age 14 years predicted lower aggression at age 19 years (Caprara, Barbaranelli, Pastorelli, Bandura, & Zimbardo, 2000), and research following over 2,000 adolescents from age 12 to 19 found that prosocial behavior was a buffer against delinquency, risky sexual behavior, and drug use, especially for girls (Ludwig & Pittman, 1999). The protective effect of prosocial behavior may occur through the peer group as adolescents who show prosocial behavior are less likely to affiliate with deviant peers (Carlo et al., 2014). For many adolescents, religion is another contributor to prosocial reasoning and behavior.

REVIEW 7.2

1. What patterns of change do prosocial reasoning and prosocial behavior display in adolescence?

2. How do parents and peers influence prosocial behavior?

3. What are correlates of prosocial behavior?

• •

THINKING IN CONTEXT 7.2

Compare moral reasoning with prosocial reasoning. What patterns of change do moral and prosocial reasoning display?

1. What are their influences?

2. To what degree can one occur without the other, in your view? That is, is it possible to show low moral reasoning and high prosocial behavior? Or high moral reasoning and low prosocial behavior?

3. Why or why not?

• •

APPLY 7.2

Suppose Mr. Trouba, a seventh-grade teacher, wanted to improve the prosocial reasoning—and especially the behavior—of his students. How can Mr. Trouba help his students become more sensitive and kinder to each other?

• •

RELIGION AND RELIGIOSITY

Cognitive and social changes contribute to adolescents' emerging cognitive autonomy, with corresponding shifts in moral and prosocial reasoning over the course of adolescence. These processes also influence adolescents' understanding of religion and the meaning they ascribe to it. Specifically, **religiosity**, which is religious practice, including religious affiliation and participation in its prescribed rituals and practices, may change over adolescence (King & Boyatzis, 2015). A related concept, **spirituality**, refers to a personal search for answers to ultimate questions about life, such as its meaning, and about transcendent others, such as God. Religiosity and spirituality are distinct concepts that sometimes overlap. Young adolescents might practice religion in the sense that they attend church and participate in religious instruction, but they may not consider its meaning and may not be spiritual. Older adolescents' sense of religiosity may include a spiritual search for meaning, demonstrating both religiosity and spirituality. Some adolescents are spiritual but not religious; they search for meaning in life without engaging in religious practice.

Adolescent Development and Religion

One large-scale survey of adolescents and emerging adults age 12 to 25 across eight countries and five continents revealed that over three-quarters report identifying with some religious affiliation and two-thirds report following God or a higher power as an important life goal (Benson, Scales, Syvertsen, & Roehlkepartain, 2012). Despite this, adolescents' reports of religious affiliation tend to decline from twelfth grade to 4 years out of high school (Chan, Tsai, & Fuligni, 2015). Religious practice, including attendance at religious services, also declines into late adolescence and emerging adulthood (Hardie, Pearce, & Denton, 2016; Park et al., 2008). Although this time in life is marked by a decline in adherence to any single faith tradition, religion remains important to young people (Smith & Snell, 2009). Most adolescents' religious beliefs become less rigid and more flexible; for example, many report viewing God as a creator and promoter of goodness and fairness yet peripheral to daily life unless a problem arose (Barry, Nelson, & Abo-Zena, 2018). Over the transition to emerging adulthood, young people tend to become more spiritual and less religious (Smith & Snell, 2009). Religious practice tends to rebound as young adults adopt adult roles, such as marrying and having children (Barry et al., 2018).

Like other forms of cognitive autonomy, adolescents' thinking about religion is influenced by their advances in cognitive development. Abstract cognitive schemes enable adolescents to consider metaphysical concepts, such as the existence of God, and engage in metacognition to evaluate their own understanding and beliefs (Labouvie-Vief, 2006). Adolescents can integrate and weigh information from multiple sources with their emotions and experiences to construct personal religious beliefs. For many adolescents, religiosity becomes less about rituals and practices, such as attending religious services, and more about spirituality, searching for answers to life's meaning and establishing beliefs (Lopez, Huynh, & Fuligni, 2011).

Adolescents who have close relationships with their parents are more likely to attend worship services with them.
iStock.com/Mlenny

Adolescents are faced with the psychosocial task of coming to a sense of self. They are concerned with questions of who they are, not just in relation to others, but may wonder about life's greater meaning and their reason for being. Religion is a medium for exploring these questions (Ream & Savin-Williams, 2006). For some, religion can be a remedy for the instability characteristic of adolescence. Determining how religion fits into one's life is an aspect of identity development (Erikson, 1959). Identity development entails exploration, a quest to identify and commit to values and beliefs about many issues, including religion. In Western countries, religious identity often becomes a focus in adolescence and proceeds toward achievement in emerging adulthood (Meeus, Iedema, Helsen, & Vollebergh, 1999). As young people move toward identity resolution, religiosity tends to increase (Duriez, Smits, & Goossens, 2008).

Influences on Religious Socialization

Parents play an important role in religious socialization. Most U.S. adolescents tend to share similar religious beliefs, are oriented toward the same general religious traditions, and attend religious service at similar frequency as their parents (Smith & Snell, 2009). Parents serve as models, engaging in religious practices such as including religious discussions, praying at family meals, reading sacred texts as a family, and participating in other family rituals (Barry et al., 2018; Dollahite & Thatcher, 2008; Layton, Dollahite, & Hardy, 2011). Parents may also channel their adolescent toward particular activities, such as

religious youth groups, in order to promote their religious development.

Parenting also influences adolescents' religious practice. That is, the quality of parent–adolescent relationships influences the effectiveness of parental religious socialization. Adolescents who have close relationships with both parents are more likely than other adolescents to attend weekly worship services with their families (Day et al., 2009). Positive parent–child relationships and an authoritative parenting style predict adolescent religiosity (Gunnoe & Moore, 2002; Power & McKinney, 2013). Adolescents with secure attachments to their parents or who rate their relationship with their parents positively tend to show similar levels of religiosity as their parents (Ream & Savin-Williams, 2006). Adolescents with insecure attachments, on the other hand, tend to show a mismatch to their parents' level of religiosity. Some insecurely attached adolescents might disaffiliate with religion to break from religious but dysfunctional family relationships. Others might seek religion-based attachments that were lacking in their family systems, developing strong attachment to religious figures, for example (Granqvist, 2002; King & Roeser, 2009).

Religious beliefs and practices are also modeled and socialized through peer relationships. Adolescents tend to affiliate with peers who share similar interests and values, which extends to religious beliefs, especially among highly religious adolescents (French, Purwono, & Rodkin, 2012; Smith & Snell, 2009). Religious groups can be contexts to support friendship formation through activities and social gatherings. Some adolescents look to friendships as valuable spiritual guides (Birkinshaw, 2015).

Through shared activities, adolescents tend to socialize one another, becoming more similar in values, attitudes, and behaviors—religious and otherwise.

Religiosity and Adjustment

Religiosity is associated with a range of positive psychosocial and behavioral outcomes, such as high self-esteem, greater prosocial behavior, higher well-being, and academic achievement (Barry et al., 2018; Hardy & King, 2019; Yonker, Schnabelrauch, & DeHaan, 2012). Perhaps more importantly, religiosity is negatively associated with, and may serve a protective role against, adjustment and behavior problems, including depression, substance use, delinquency, and sexual risk-taking (Hardy & King, 2019; Kim-Spoon, McCullough, Bickel, Farley, & Longo, 2015; Peviani, Brieant, Holmes, King-Casas, & Kim-Spoon, 2019; Sinha, Cnaan, & Gelles, 2007). For example, in one study of African American adolescents followed from age 12 to 18, religiosity served a protective role against the effect of stressful life events, such as neighborhood disorganization, violence, and discrimination, on depression over time (Lee & Neblett, 2019). Religiosity shows a similar protective effect for the relation of negative peer experiences (e.g., peer victimization) and internalizing symptoms (Helms et al., 2015) and the effect of parental substance use on adolescent substance use (Peviani et al., 2019).

Factors that promote religiosity, such as supportive parent and peer relationships, are also known to protect adolescents against risk. In one study, highly religious parents were more likely to engage in effective parenting practices, such as communication, warmth, and monitoring, than their less religious peers (Snider, Clements, & Vazsonyi, 2004). Part of the buffering effect of religiosity on adjustment and risky behavior occurs through religiosity's positive influence on parenting and the parent–child relationship (Goeke-Morey & Cummings, 2017). For example, in one longitudinal study of African American adolescents and their parents, parental religiosity predicted authoritative parenting and adolescent religiosity, which in turn were negatively associated with affiliating with sexually permissive peers and engaging in risky sexual activity in girls (Landor, Simons, Simons, Brody, & Gibbons, 2011). In boys, although parental religiosity predicted authoritative parenting and adolescent religiosity, authoritative parenting was not associated with risky sexual activity, suggesting gender differences in sexual socialization regardless of parent religiosity.

The religious community provides a network of social support and opportunities for high-quality social relationships that may serve a protective role for adolescents. Social support from a religious community is negatively associated with risky behaviors,

including alcohol and substance use (Holder et al., 2000; Peviani et al., 2019). Religiosity and participation in religious communities may promote healthy behaviors in adolescents by fostering emotion regulation (Vishkin, Bigman, & Tamir, 2014). Achieving the goals and standards articulated by religious communities, such as regular attendance at religious services and participation in prosocial community groups, encourages adolescents to monitor and regulate their behavior, promoting self-control (Holmes, Kim-Spoon, & Deater-Deckard, 2016; McCullough & Willoughby, 2009). Indeed, research with early adolescents suggests that religiosity is inversely associated with substance use and other risk behaviors through its influence on executive function and self-regulation mechanisms, including the ability to resist impulses and delay gratification (Holmes, Brieant, King-Casas, & Kim-Spoon, 2019; Kim-Spoon et al., 2015).

REVIEW 7.3

1. Differentiate religiosity and spirituality.

2. How does religiosity shift over adolescence?

3. How do interactions with others influence adolescents' religious socialization?

4. How is religiosity related to adolescent adjustment and what accounts for the relationship?

· ·

THINKING IN CONTEXT 7.3

Consider the process of identity development (Chapter 4).

1. What forms might identity exploration and commitment take when it comes to religious identity?

2. How might adolescents explore their religious identity?

3. What might moratorium, identity achievement, identity foreclosure, and identity diffusion look like?

· ·

APPLY 7.3

Thirteen-year-old Ramon explains, "I don't want to go to church. It's a waste of time."

1. How typical is Ramon, as a young adolescent?

2. How do adolescents' religious views typically change over the course of adolescence?

3. How might interactions with others influence Ramon's desire to attend religious services?

4. What might be the effects of a poor sense of religiosity in adolescence?

5. What should Ramon's parents do, if anything. Why?

. . . .

CIVIC DEVELOPMENT AND ENGAGEMENT

In adolescence, moral and prosocial reasoning often include a sense of social responsibility, a personal commitment to contribute to community and society (Wray-Lake & Syvertsen, 2011). **Civic engagement** refers to a broad range of activities related to involvement in the community or society at large, including community-oriented activity (e.g., volunteerism), consciousness raising (e.g., increasing awareness and voicing political opinions in public forums), and activities intended to influence political outcomes (e.g., campaigning, voicing opinions to political representatives, protesting, and voting) (Lerner, Wang, Champine, Warren, & Erickson, 2014; Wray-Lake, Metzger, & Syvertsen, 2017). **Civic development** refers to the skills, knowledge, and motivation to participate in community and political life (Malin, Ballard, & Damon, 2015). Even activities that are not explicitly "civic" or political, such as membership in academic, artistic, or athletic clubs/teams, could develop skills related to effective civic engagement later in life (McFarland & Thomas, 2006).

Adolescent Development and Civic Engagement

Adolescents' understanding of social responsibility and their sense of civic purpose is influenced by their cognitive abilities, moral reasoning, and prosocial development. Reasoning about abstract principles such as justice and equality may lead adolescents to consider their role in the community in new ways. Improvements in perspective taking mean that adolescents can attend to others' experiences, emotions, and suffering, which can lead to more nuanced thinking about causes such as injustice and inequality (Hoffman, 2000; Kohlberg, 1969). The underlying motivation for civic purpose is the moral value associated with social responsibility, such as helping others, fairness, justice, equality, and rights (Wray-Lake & Syvertsen, 2011). For example, in one study of nearly 2,500 adolescents ranging in age from 8 to 20, social responsibility and civic skills were associated with empathy, future orientation, and prosocial reasoning (Metzger et al., 2018).

Civic development is also an aspect of identity as adolescents develop an understanding of larger societal systems and their place in those systems (Hart, Donnelly, Youniss, & Atkins, 2007; Rubin, 2007). Generally, young people develop civic purpose in response to local issues, specifically those that impact their family, friends, and neighbors, or issues that impact a community that they identify with, such as an immigrant community or the lesbian, gay, bisexual, and transgender (LGBT) community (Malin et al., 2015). Identity exploration may take the form of civic engagement in which adolescents sample and test different beliefs. For some adolescents, political engagement fulfills preferences for risk. For example, in one study, late adolescents with greater preferences for risk engaged in higher levels of participation in civic activities, such as donating to a campaign, writing government officials, boycotting, and protesting (Oosterhoff & Wray-Lake, 2019). Participation in civic activities strengthens civic identity and civic participation becomes a sustained commitment when civic concerns are incorporated into one's identity. A sense of civic identity can motivate and sustain civic participation and commitment during difficult times, leading to an enduring civic commitment and lasting impact on civic engagement in adulthood (Malin et al., 2015; Youniss, McLellan, & Yates, 1997).

Although commitment to civic engagement in adulthood is predicted by participation in civic activity in adolescence (Hart et al., 2007; McFarland & Thomas, 2006), the path often is not straightforward in U.S. adolescents. Community service requirements in many high schools get adolescents engaged in civic life and correlate with later participation in both political and community activity (Hart et al., 2007), but civic

Civic development may take the form of political engagement.
Chris Fitzgerald/Candidate Photos/Newscom

engagement tends to decline from high school into emerging adulthood for U.S. adolescents of all backgrounds (Malin, Han, & Liauw, 2017). Civic engagement tends to rise again after emerging adulthood, as young people take on adult roles (Finlay, Flanagan, & Wray-Lake, 2011; Jennings & Stoker, 2004).

Civic engagement is associated with a range of positive outcomes such as academic achievement, identity achievement, life satisfaction, and social competence and is negatively associated with delinquency and antisocial behavior (Kirshner, 2007; Mahatmya, Owen, & Carter, 2018; Pancer, Pratt, Hunsberger, & Alisat, 2007; Scales, Benson, Roehlkepartain, Sesma, & van Dulmen, 2006). Engaging in civic activities offers opportunities to interact with peers and adults in working together to address social problems, aiding adolescents in developing the social and emotional skills and resources needed in adulthood. Civic engagement offers adolescents a chance to contribute, provide care, and find meaning—and may also provide a sense of psychological empowerment or control, which are associated with academic success, political engagement, and general well-being (Ballard & Syme, 2016). Civic engagement can also be a form of identity exploration through which adolescents learn about themselves and others around them and solidify their values. There are long-term positive correlates of adolescent civic engagement, such as lower levels of depression and less risk-taking behavior in early adulthood (Ballard, Hoyt, & Pachucki, 2019).

Influences on Civic Engagement

Socialization plays an important role in civic development as many adolescents are first invited to participate in civic activities by someone with more experience (Malin et al., 2015; McIntosh & Youniss, 2010). Civic socialization also may occur at home in families that model civic engagement or in schools with a democratic school climate (Andolina, Jenkins, Zukin, & Keeter, 2003; Flanagan, Cumsille, Gill, & Gallay, 2007; Jennings, Stoker, & Bowers, 2009).

Family social capital and civic socialization practices influence civic involvement (Lenzi, Vieno, Santinello, Nation, & Voight, 2014a; White & Mistry, 2016). Adolescents from families with high parental education and high SES show consistently higher rates of civic involvement than their peers (Penner, Dovidio, Piliavin, & Schroeder, 2005; Watts & Flanagan, 2007). Parental civic engagement predicts adolescent civic development (Lenzi et al., 2014a). Adolescents who participate in community service tend to have parents who volunteer and talk about volunteering and giving (Ottoni-Wilhelm, Estell, & Perdue, 2014). When parents recruit their children into community service, it transmits prosocial values, including the meaning of service and its effect on others (White &

Mistry, 2016). Parental encouragement and modeling of volunteer work predict sympathy, feeling compassion for another person, and adolescents' volunteer work (McGinley, Lipperman-Kreda, Byrnes, & Carlo, 2010; van Goethem, van Hoof, van Aken, Orobio de Castro, & Raaijmakers, 2014).

Adolescents also learn civic values at school. For many adolescents, high school provides opportunities to engage in meaningful community service, leadership, and organized activities. Contact with adults is important because adolescents might not readily identify their interests as political or civic or might not be able to connect their interests to civic opportunities. However, this potential largely depends on the presence of adults who are paying attention to students' interests, keeping alert to possible political and civic strengths, and seeking ways that students can develop their interests (Lenzi et al., 2014b).

Community service offers adolescents opportunities to better understand themselves as they interact with a heterogeneous group of people in their community who likely differ from them in age, ethnicity, religion, or social class (Flanagan, Kim, Collura, & Kopish, 2015; Yates & Youniss, 1996). Community service holds the potential to enhance sensitivity toward others. Compared to their nonvolunteer peers, early adolescents who do community volunteer work are more likely to identify similarities between themselves and disadvantaged groups, are less likely to stereotype outgroups, and are more likely to believe that people are capable of change (Flanagan et al., 2015; Karafantis & Levy, 2004). Moreover, the quality of civic learning experiences may have a greater impact than simply whether or not students were involved in civic activities, suggesting that there is more to civic development than early civic participation. In one study, justice-oriented service that exposed students to social inequities was more likely than general helping activities to raise students' awareness of civic issues and support long-term civic commitment (Metz, McLellan, & Youniss, 2003). In another study, participation in activities rated as high quality, in which students solved real-world problems, interacted with perspectives different from their own, and analyzed the experience, had a more lasting impact on civic engagement than low-quality participation (Ferreira, Azevedo, & Menezes, 2012).

The qualities of the school climate play a role in adolescents' civic engagement. One study of middle school students found that more positive perceptions of school climate were positively related to school connectedness and this, in turn, was positively associated with civic engagement (Guillaume, Jagers, & Rivas-Drake, 2015). Ideally, schools create a democratic climate for teachers and students to converse about controversial issues and opportunities to practice democratic skills (Flanagan et al., 2007). Schools that provide a supportive and democratic climate buffer negative effects of poor neighborhood contexts—those in high poverty neighborhoods experience greater gains in civic involvement when the school curriculum more intentionally incorporates civic education and experiences (Lenzi et al., 2014b; Wilkenfeld, 2009).

Adolescents' experiences, especially those with justice, influence their civic development. Adolescents from low SES communities and those of color may experience a disconnect between civic ideals and the reality of their lives (Malin et al., 2017; Rubin, 2007). The experience of racial and SES inequalities can shape their view of themselves as members of society and citizens and influence civic identity. The gap between values and experience can drive youth to take action and to develop civic purpose. For example, although research with adults suggests that income inequality is associated with less civic engagement, one study of over 12,000 U.S. 15-year-olds suggests that the reverse may be true for adolescents (Godfrey & Cherng, 2016). Specifically, adolescents—especially those of low SES and of color—who lived in counties with high income inequality (large differences in SES) reported greater beliefs in the importance of helping others and higher rates of volunteering than those in counties with low income inequality (fewer differences in SES).

Experiences with racism and discrimination pose challenges to adolescents' developing understanding of justice and, in some cases, can spur civic engagement. For example, one adolescent describes her experiences as an African American girl from a low income community as an emotional trigger to take civic action:

> Even though we say everybody's free in America and everyone is equal, because I was born in a certain social and economic status, I've not had the freedom of opportunity . . . Injustices really . . . make me angry. I feel like when you get angry about something, you're really called to do something about it, so I'm really proactive. So if I see an injustice . . . I try to figure out a way that we can work together . . . to try to change the issue. (Malin et al., 2015)

Forms of civic engagement in adolescence tend to vary with SES and race/ethnicity. High SES youth tend to participate more in traditional forms of civic engagement, such as campaigning, running for student government, and volunteering. Low SES youth tend to be more active in issue-based activity on issues of concern pertaining to the community environments in which they live (Ballard et al., 2019). Youth in groups that traditionally experience exclusion or marginalization in society might be motivated to civic activity that supports the economic and political interests of their group more so than the interests of broader society (Sánchez-Jankowski, 2002). Expressive political activities are key to organizing an effective community response to a social issue or concern. For example, a study of high school seniors found that African American and Latinx students were more engaged in expressive political activity than their peers and were more likely to sustain their involvement in expressive political activities 2 years later compared to other groups (Malin et al., 2017). ●

Civic engagement can take many forms, from campaigning to protests.
Chip Somodevilla / Staff/Getty Images

REVIEW 7.4

1. Explain how civic engagement shifts over adolescence.

2. Identify two types of development that influence civic development.

3. Describe correlates of civic engagement.

. . . .

THINKING IN CONTEXT 7.4

Why are some adolescents more interested in civic activities such as volunteer work or political activism (such as participating in marches)? Consider civic development from a bioecological framework.

1. Identify microsystem and mesosystem factors that might contribute to an adolescent's interest in civic activities.

2. How might factors in the community and other exosystem factors influence adolescents? Might adolescents from different contexts, such as high and low SES neighborhoods, have different opportunities for and experiences with civic engagement? Why or why not?

3. Identify macrosystem influences.

. . . .

APPLY 7.4

Sixteen-year-old Rafael explains, "I want to make a difference but I don't know how. Student government is dumb. Students can't change anything at the school. I want to do something that really matters. What should I do?"

1. Discuss Rafael's drive to make a difference. How does it reflect adolescent development?

2. What advice do you give Rafael? Is it possible for an adolescent to make a difference?

3. How can others—parents, peers, teachers, and/or school—influence Rafael's civic development?

. . . .

CHAPTER SUMMARY

7.1 Discuss the process of moral development and its influence on behavior.

Beginning in early childhood and persisting until about age 9, children demonstrate what Kohlberg called preconventional reasoning, governed by self-interest, which is the desire to gain rewards and avoid punishments. At about age 9 or 10, children transition to conventional moral reasoning, can take others' perspectives, and are motivated by reciprocity and the desire to maintain social order. Postconventional moral reasoning, autonomous decision-making from universal moral principles that value respect for individual rights above all else, becomes possible in adolescence. Social interactions in the home, peer, and school contexts offer important opportunities for the development of moral reasoning. Reasoning advances when adolescents have opportunities to engage in discussions that are characterized by mutual perspective taking. Although Kohlberg's theory emphasizes justice concerns, most people also report care-oriented concerns and most mature forms of moral reasoning incorporate both justice and care concerns. Cross-cultural research suggests that reasoning progresses in a similar pattern across cultures. People of different cultures reason using both care and justice orientations even though cultures tend to vary in the weight they assign to justice and care concerns. With advances in moral reasoning, adolescents are more likely to act in ways that are in line with their beliefs.

7.2 Examine influences and outcomes of prosocial development.

Prosocial reasoning tends to improve in adolescence but prosocial behavior shows more mixed changes over adolescence. Prosocial behavior toward family tends to remain stable or decrease over time, while prosocial behavior toward friends increases. Cognitive, emotional, and social development influence the display of prosocial behavior in adolescence. Warm relationships with parents and peers promote prosocial behavior. The peer group also influences prosocial behavior through modeling and

communicating values. Prosocial behavior is associated with many positive developmental outcomes in adolescence, including self-esteem, social competence, social approval from peers and teachers, academic achievement, and high-quality relationships. Prosocial behavior is negatively associated with internalizing and externalizing problems such as anxiety, depression, aggression, risky behaviors, substance use, and delinquency.

7.3 Summarize influences on religiosity and adjustment in adolescence.

Adolescents' reports of religious affiliation tend to decline but religion tends to remain important to young people. Adolescents' thinking about religion is influenced by their advances in cognitive development. Most adolescents' religious beliefs become less rigid and more flexible. Religious practice tends to rebound as individuals adopt adult roles. Parents play an important role in religious socialization. Religious beliefs and practices are also modeled and socialized through peer relationships. The religious community provides a network of social support and opportunities for high-quality social relationships that may serve a protective role for adolescents. Social support from a religious community is negatively associated with risky behaviors, including alcohol and substance use. Religiosity is associated with a range of positive psychosocial and behavioral outcomes, such as high self-esteem, greater prosocial behavior, higher well-being, and academic achievement. Religiosity is negatively associated with adjustment and behavior problems, including depression, substance use, delinquency, and sexual risk-taking.

7.4 Discuss the development of civic engagement in adolescence.

Adolescents' understanding of social responsibility and their sense of civic purpose is influenced by their cognitive abilities, moral reasoning, and prosocial development. Civic engagement tends to decline from high school into emerging adulthood and rise again as young people take on adult roles. Civic engagement is associated with a range of positive outcomes such as academic achievement, identity achievement, life satisfaction, and social competence and is negatively associated with delinquency and antisocial behavior. Civic socialization occurs at home, school, and in the peer group and community. Adolescents' experiences, especially those with justice, influence their civic development.

KEY TERMS

care orientation, 149

civic development, 157

civic engagement, 157

cognitive autonomy, 147

conventional moral reasoning, 148

empathic concern, 152

justice orientation, 149

moral reasoning, 147

postconventional moral reasoning, 148

preconventional reasoning, 148

prosocial behavior, 151

religiosity, 154

spirituality, 154

PART 3

Contexts of Development

8 Family Context

Learning Objectives

8.1 Explain family systems theory and the interactions among family systems.

8.2 Describe adolescents' relationships with their parents, attachment, and emotional autonomy.

8.3 Summarize what is known about parenting style in adolescence.

8.4 Discuss common family transitions, such as divorce, remarriage, adoption, foster care, and others.

Chapter Contents

Adolescents are immersed in a variety of contexts that influence their development. The most obvious—and influential—is the family. In this chapter we examine the role of the family context in development.

THE FAMILY AS A SYSTEM

As we have seen throughout this book, adolescents are active participants in their development. That is, they are not only influenced by the contexts in which they are immersed, such as family, but they influence those contexts as well. This view is consistent with **family systems theory**, which emphasizes the interactive and bidirectional nature of relationships within families. Each member of the family both affects and is affected by the other members. As family members interact with each other over time, the interactions come to reflect stable patterns of behavior and the family system reaches a state of equilibrium, a balance (Gavazzi, 2013). However, changes in any individual or relationship can lead to changes in the others. As family members develop (e.g., when adolescents undergo puberty) or the family experiences shifting circumstances (e.g., a divorce, move, or change in SES), the equilibrium is disrupted. Therefore, the rapid changes that adolescents experience influence the entire family and their interactions.

Changing Adolescent

How do the biological, cognitive, and socioemotional changes that adolescents undergo influence parents? With puberty, adolescents' bodies take on adult proportions and functions, leading adolescents to be increasingly treated like adults. Adolescents often find these changes stressful, but so do parents. For example, as pubertal changes peak, conflict with parents tends to rise and parent–child relationships become more volatile—with many ups and downs (Collins & Steinberg, 2006; Marceau, Ram, & Susman, 2015).

Adolescent cognitive development plays a special role in parent–child interactions. With cognitive maturation, adolescents become able to reason as never before. They are more likely to expect parents to provide reasons for rules and they can counter parental arguments, often with sound rationales. Parents are often surprised by their adolescents' new abilities to argue. Those who were used to explaining rules by stating "Because I said so" are likely to experience this change as stressful.

Socioemotional tasks such as identity development lead adolescents to explore and consider many options in areas such as sexuality, friendships and romantic relationships, career, and others. Frequently adolescents explore and consider options that parents may find distasteful, which is potentially a cause of conflict. As adolescents' attention turns to their peers, they seek distance from their parents and seek to become independent, important tasks for adolescents that parents may find challenging, partly because parents are undergoing their own changes as they enter and progress through middle adulthood.

Changing Parent

Human development is a lifelong process. Parents age as their children do, and they face unique developmental needs (Bornstein, 2015). In 2014, the median age for first birth was 26 for women (up from about age 25 in 2000) (Matthews & Hamilton, 2002, 2016). Most parents are around age 40 when their first child enters adolescence. Age 40 also marks the transition to middle adulthood. Like all transitions, entering midlife is often stressful but adults vary dramatically in their experiences. Although some theorists and pop culture describe the transition to middle adulthood as entailing a midlife crisis, similar to discussions of adolescent storm and stress, this is likely more myth than truth because research suggests that a midlife crisis is the exception rather than the rule (Robinson & Wright, 2013).

Both parents and adolescents experience physical changes, but on different trajectories. As adolescents reach physical maturity, their bodies take on adult proportions, and they show increases in strength, speed, and endurance. In contrast, in middle adulthood, physical strength, speed, and endurance tend to decline and body mass tends to increase. Exercise and lifestyle can offset these changes, but adults' bodies show very different patterns of change than their children. Not surprisingly, midlife parents tend to become more aware of their own aging. Generally speaking, adults of many cultures tend to associate negative physical and mental traits with old age (Löckenhoff et al., 2009) and negative attitudes toward old age tend to peak in midlife (Davis & Friedrich, 2010; McBride & Hays, 2012). Midlife adults' awareness of aging and their attitudes about aging hold implications for their sense of self and their views of their aging process (Kornadt & Rothermund, 2015).

Similar to adolescents, adults often revisit and revise their sense of identity. Midlife changes often trigger reflection, the tendency to look back on accomplishments in light of youthful goals. Turning points in life, such as a child's entry to adolescence, as well as normative age-related changes can prompt growth and change in adults' identity (Kuther & Burnell, 2019; Moen & Wethington, 1999). Self-reported sense of meaning in life tends to increase in midlife and predicts well-being, self-reported health, life satisfaction, and enthusiasm for life (Heintzelman & King, 2014; Ko, Hooker, Geldhof, & McAdams, 2016). Adults who have found a sense of meaning in life perceive their lives as having inherent value or worth, which can influence how they navigate other developmental tasks such as consolidating a sense of identity.

Just as adolescents' expectations of parents change, so do parents' expectations for their children's behavior. In Chapter 1 we discussed the common stereotypes about adolescents. Consistent with the notion that adolescence is a time of "storm and

Both adolescents—and their parents—undergo developmental changes.
iStock.com/Vesnaandjic

stress" (Arnett, 1999; Hall, 1904), parents and others hold stereotypes of adolescent behavior that are more negative than stereotypes of younger children (Buchanan & Holmbeck, 1998; Holmbeck & Hill, 1988). These stereotypes, or category-based beliefs, can influence parents' expectations for their own children (i.e., target-based expectations) independent of the child's actual current and past behavior. Thus, parents' expectations, which ultimately have the potential to influence the way parents react to and interact with their children, might shift in a negative direction during adolescence (Glatz & Buchanan, 2015). Moreover, parents' views of their own parenting efficacy shifts, declining as children move from early to middle adolescence, and might be a normative development as children reach an age at which they gain more autonomy (Glatz & Buchanan, 2015).

Adolescent and parent development interacts and influences all members of the family system, disrupting the equilibrium achieved in childhood. Next we consider adolescents' interactions with siblings.

Siblings

Of all of the close relationships formed over life, the sibling relationship is among the longest lasting, with implications for adjustment and well-being all throughout life (Lindell & Campione-Barr, 2017). From a family systems perspective, parents, siblings, and adolescents interact dynamically, each relationship influencing the others. Our discussion so far has focused on the parent–adolescent relationship; however, adolescents' relationships with their parents influence their relationships with siblings. Adolescents with close and warm relationships with parents tend to also have positive sibling relationships characterized by less conflict than those with less warm parental relationships (East, 2009; Ruff, Durtschi, & Day, 2018). The processes of autonomy seeking that increase distance between parents and adolescents also influence the sibling relationship.

In most families, siblings have a natural hierarchy, influenced by age. Older siblings generally are physically, socially, and cognitively advantaged over their younger siblings, are considered more capable than their siblings, and are often involved in the caretaking of siblings. Therefore, older siblings tend to have greater power than younger siblings (Tucker, Updegraff, & Baril, 2010). The largest power discrepancies between siblings appear to be present during childhood and early adolescence and decrease in magnitude as siblings move through adolescence.

Parents remain a source of support for adolescents.
iStock.com/doble-d

Older siblings serve as sources of advice and role models for both positive and negative behaviors (East, 2009; McHale, Updegraff, & Whiteman, 2012). Siblings engage in similar levels of risk behaviors, such as delinquency and externalizing problems, alcohol and other substance use, and sexual attitudes and behaviors during adolescence (Huijsmans, Eichelsheim, Weerman, Branje, & Meeus, 2019; Samek, Rueter, Keyes, McGue, & Iacono, 2015; Wheeler et al., 2016). Siblings shape adolescents' expectancies about what behaviors are popular or desirable through modeling, self-disclosure, and even coaching and encouragement (Whiteman, Jensen, & McHale, 2017). Siblings also exert a positive influence on each other. Sibling support is associated with academic engagement and school achievement (Wang, Degol, & Amemiya, 2019).

Over adolescence, the family network shifts to a more peripheral position (including siblings) and peers become more central (Gavazzi, 2013). As adolescents seek greater autonomy from the family and spend more time with peers, they spend less time with siblings and the emotional intensity of the relationship (positive and negative), as well as the involvement, declines (McHale et al., 2012). Although adolescents tend to spend less time with siblings, younger siblings' drive for equality often results in increased conflict, especially during early adolescence (Lindell & Campione-Barr, 2017). Generally, sibling relationships become more egalitarian with age and development. As younger siblings become more equally matched in these capacities with their older siblings, the expectation that interactions will become more equal increases (Campione-Barr, 2017).

Ultimately, the quality of the sibling relationships influences adolescents' well-being (Solmeyer, McHale, & Crouter, 2014). Sibling conflict is a risk factor for problem behaviors. Adolescents who engage their siblings in excessive arguments or deliberately attempt to bother or harm a sibling may apply this interpersonal approach in other relationships, making it more likely that they will be involved with similarly aggressive peers (Gallagher, Updegraff, Padilla, & McHale, 2018). In contrast, sibling relationships offer opportunities to learn about intimacy. High-quality sibling relationships are associated with romantic competence in late adolescence (Doughty, McHale, & Feinberg, 2015).

REVIEW 8.1

1. Describe family systems theory.

2. Give examples of how adolescents and parents influence each other.

3. Describe sibling relationships in adolescence.

. . . .

THINKING IN CONTEXT 8.1

Describe your family system.

1. Who are the members and where does each fall along the lifespan?

2. How do they influence you?

3. How has their influence changed over time, as they have developed or as you have developed?

4. How has your development influenced your family members?

. . . .

APPLY 8.1

Maura observes that, until recently, her daughters Karolyn (age 9) and Kayla (age 13) were inseparable. Now all they do is argue. "There they go, yelling again," she thinks. "You took my seat!" cries Karolyn. "It's mine!" shouts Kayla. "Kayla, let your little sister sit on the couch!" Maura yells to her daughter. "You always take her side!" Kayla cries back.

Maura thinks to herself, "No matter what I say, someone will be unhappy. I thought infancy and toddlerhood were the hardest stages to parent. It just doesn't get better. They grow older and get smarter—and it all just gets harder. No one seems to appreciate that I'm a person too."

1. How common are sibling relationships similar to that of Kayla and Karolyn? How do you expect their relationship to change as they grow older?

2. What is the role of their mother, Maura, in their interactions?

3. Describe this family's interactions from the family systems perspective.

. . . .

PARENT–ADOLESCENT RELATIONSHIPS

From middle childhood into adolescence, parents must adapt their parenting strategies to their children's developing capacities for reason and their desire for independence. Physically, adolescents appear more mature. They also can demonstrate better self-understanding and more rational decision-making and problem-solving, creating a foundation for parents to treat adolescents less like children and grant them more decision-making responsibility. As they advance cognitively and develop a more complicated sense of self, adolescents strive for more adult-like relationships with their parents and reduce their reliance on parents. Adolescence marks a change in parent–child relationships. The parenting challenge of adolescence is to offer increasing opportunities for adolescents to develop and practice autonomy while providing protection from danger and the consequences of poor decisions (Kobak, Abbott, Zisk, & Bounoua, 2017). Parents may doubt their own importance to their adolescent children, but a large body of research shows that parents play a critical role in adolescent development alongside that of peers.

Parent–Adolescent Conflict

Leroy's mother orders, "Clean your room," but Leroy snaps back, "It's my room. I can have it my way!" Conflict between parents and adolescents tends to rise in early adolescence as adolescents begin to seek autonomy and begin to recognize that their parents are fallible and are capable of good and bad decisions. Conflict peaks in middle adolescence and declines from middle to late adolescence and emerging adulthood as young people become more independent and begin to better understand their parents as people (Branje, Laursen, & Collins, 2013). For example, in one longitudinal study, about 14% of participants reported turbulent relationships with parents characterized by low support and high conflict in early adolescence (age 12), rising to 29% at about age 16 and declining to 10% by around age 20 (Hadiwijaya, Klimstra, Vermunt, Branje, & Meeus, 2017). Most teenagers reported that the nature of their relationships with parents did not change. Although conflict rises during early adolescence, the majority of adolescents and parents continue to have warm, close, communicative relationships characterized by love and respect.

Parent–adolescent conflict is generally innocuous bickering over mundane matters: small arguments over the details of life, such as household responsibilities, privileges, relationships, curfews, cleaning of the adolescent's bedroom, choices of media, or music volume (Van Doorn, Branje, & Meeus, 2011). Conflicts over religious, political, or social issues occur less frequently, as do conflicts concerning other potentially sensitive topics (e.g., substance use, dating, sexual relationships) (Renk, Liljequist, Simpson, & Phares, 2005). Adolescents report having three or four conflicts or disagreements with parents over the course of a typical day, but they also report having one or two conflicts with friends (Adams & Laursen, 2007). Conflict is sometimes related to contextual influences, such as culture. For example, in one study of Arab American adolescents, the larger acculturation gap between parents and adolescents (as perceived by adolescents), the greater the conflict (Goforth, Pham, & Oka, 2015). Despite coming from cultural traditions that emphasize family solidarity and parental respect, adolescents from immigrant families argue with their parents as frequently as do their peers from nonimmigrant families (Chung, Flook, & Fuligni, 2009; Fuligni & Tsai, 2015).

Severe parent–adolescent conflict occurs in some families. Like many aspects of development, there tends to be continuity in parenting and parent–child relationships (Huey, Hiatt, Laursen, Burk, & Rubin, 2017). Patterns of harsh verbal discipline (yelling, threatening, punishment, shaming) and insensitive parenting established in early childhood tend to persist and worsen in middle childhood and adolescence (Lansford, Staples, Bates, Pettit, & Dodge, 2013). Frequent arguments charged with negative emotion are harmful to adolescents (Huey et al., 2017). In adolescents of all ethnicities—African American, Latinx, Asian, and White—parent–adolescent conflict is associated with internalizing problems such as depression, externalizing problems such as aggression and delinquency, and social problems such as social withdrawal and poor conflict resolution with peers, poor school achievement, and, among girls, early sexual activity (Hofer et al., 2013; Moreno, Janssen, Cox, Colby, & Jackson, 2017; Skinner & McHale, 2016; Weymouth, Buehler, Zhou, & Henson, 2016).

Although severe conflict is harmful, some conflict is conducive to adolescent development, helping adolescents learn to regulate emotions and resolve conflicts (Branje, 2018). Parent–adolescent conflict that is coupled with acceptance, respect, and autonomy promotes adolescent development.

Parental Monitoring

One way in which parents balance granting autonomy to their adolescents with protecting them is through **parental monitoring**, being aware of their teens' whereabouts and companions. Parental monitoring is associated with overall well-being in adolescents, including academic achievement, delayed sexual initiation, and low levels of substance use and delinquent activity in youth of all ethnicities (Ethier,

Harper, Hoo, & Dittus, 2016; Lopez-Tamayo, LaVome Robinson, Lambert, Jason, & Ialongo, 2016; Malczyk & Lawson, 2017). Effective parental monitoring is accompanied by warmth and is balanced with respect for adolescents' autonomy and privacy. When parents monitor too closely, in ways that adolescents perceive as intrusive, adolescents are likely to conceal their activities from their parents and continue to do so over time (Rote & Smetana, 2016). In middle SES adolescents, intrusive parental monitoring is positively associated with delinquency as well as increases in delinquency over time (Kerr, Stattin, & Burk, 2010; Willoughby & Hamza, 2011). However, adolescents who live in poor, high-risk communities tend to benefit from more active and restrictive forms of parental monitoring, such as daily discussions about activities and behavioral limit setting (Bendezú, Pinderhughes, Hurley, McMahon, & Racz, 2018; Burton & Jarrett, 2000). These adaptive strategies are a response to unique threats and are thought to help protect youth from dangers looming in their communities.

Parental monitoring occurs within the context of ongoing parent–adolescent relationships in which parents and adolescents are mutually influential. Yet parents and adolescents often differ in their perception of parental monitoring. Studies that have measured parental monitoring simultaneously from both parent and adolescent perspectives tend to find only small to moderate positive associations between parents' and adolescents' reports (Lippold, Greenberg, & Feinberg, 2011; Reynolds, MacPherson, Matusiewicz, Schreiber, & Lejuez, 2011), indicating substantial discrepancies. When parents' and adolescents' reports of monitoring are used as simultaneous predictors of outcomes, adolescents' reports tend to be more strongly predictive of alcohol and marijuana use and sexual risk (Abar, Jackson, Colby, & Barnett, 2015). Moreover, adolescents' perceptions of monitoring and their subsequent behavior influence parents (Keijsers, 2016).

What is considered effective parental monitoring changes as adolescents grow older. From middle to late adolescence, parental knowledge and control declines as adolescents establish a private sphere, become more secretive, and disclose less (Masche, 2010; Wang, Dishion, Stormshak, & Willett, 2011). However, adolescent and parents' perceptions of parental monitoring remain mismatched, with parents, but not adolescents, reporting declines in parental solicitation of information from adolescents (Lionetti et al., 2019).

Attachment

Although parent–adolescent relationships change, there is also continuity. The emotional bonds established in childhood persist into adolescence.

Attachment refers to a lasting emotional tie between two people who each strive to maintain closeness and sustain the relationship. Attachment relationships serve as an important backdrop for emotional and social development. Our earliest attachments are with our primary caregivers. Attachment is an innate adaptive behavior that, from an evolutionary standpoint, may have evolved because the attachment bond between caregivers and infants ensures that the two will remain in close proximity, thereby aiding the survival of the infant and, ultimately, the species (Bowlby, 1969, 1988). The formation of an attachment bond is crucial for infants' development because it enables infants to begin to explore the world, using their attachment figure as a secure base, or foundation, to return to when frightened. Attachment is activated during times of stress. When a child feels sick, frightened, or threatened in any way, the child seeks closeness to the caregiver. When a child feels safe and secure, attachment figures provide a secure base from which to explore the world. Security in times of stress and facilitation of exploration are two functions of the system.

The attachment bond developed during infancy and toddlerhood becomes represented as an **internal working model of attachment**, which includes the children's expectations about whether they are worthy of love, whether their attachment figures will be available during times of distress, and how they will be treated. Attachments may be classified as secure or insecure. Children who have a *secure attachment* tend to be confident and emotionally expressive and can display both positive and negative emotions. When upset, they are easily soothed by parents, who tend to be sensitive to their needs. There are three types of insecure attachments, representing different strategies for interacting with caregivers (Ainsworth, Blehar, Waters, & Wall, 1978). Children with an *insecure avoidant attachment* minimize contact with caregivers and attachment behavior. They tend to show minimal distress in stressful situations and generally do not rely on their caregivers for support. Children who show an *insecure resistant attachment* tend to be difficult to soothe by parents and may show anger at the same time as they cling to parents, seemingly preoccupied with parents. Children with a *disorganized attachment* tend lack a clear a consistent strategy to relate to parents. They may appear scared and act unpredictably in stressful situations.

Attachment remains important throughout life. Positive attachment experiences lead to confidence in oneself and the availability of sensitive others (Bretherton & Munholland, 2016). In adolescence, secure attachment is positively associated with self-esteem, emotional health, ego resiliency, academic performance, emotion regulation, and increased social competence as shown by a greater sense of social acceptance and higher quality of peer relationships and friendships (Keizer, Helmerhorst, & van Rijn-van Gelderen, 2019; Sroufe, 2016; Stern & Cassidy, 2018).

Insecurely attached adolescents may view themselves as unworthy of love and the social world as negative and untrustworthy. They tend to be less able to regulate their emotions and experience more negative emotions and behavior problems than adolescents with a secure attachment (Cooke, Kochendorfer, Stuart-Parrigon, Koehn, & Kerns, 2018; de Vries, Hoeve, Stams, & Asscher, 2016). Individuals with insecure resistant and insecure avoidant attachment experience a heightened risk for depression, as they tend to view their attachment figures as unavailable and develop a negative self-image, low self-esteem, and a reduced sense of self-control. Insecure resistant attachment is also associated with anxiety as parents of resistant children may be either rejecting or overprotective, resulting in less exploration and more fearfulness. Insecure avoidant and disorganized attachment are associated with increased risk of aggression, delinquency, substance use, and other risk behaviors (Buist, 2018).

Experience with attachment figures over time influences adolescents' internal working models of self, which is used in engaging new relationships (Bowlby, 1973; Bretherton & Munholland, 2016). Attachment tends to be stable throughout adolescence; however, as adolescents become more independent, their attachment relationships change in form, function, and security (Jones et al., 2018).

Although adolescents tend to increase emotional distance from parents, parents remain an important source of support for adolescents with secure attachments.

iStock.com/monkeybusinessimages

Adolescents seek emotional autonomy from parents, to be separate but remain emotionally close.
iStock.com/monkeybusinessimages

Adolescents and parents renegotiate their relationship and their positions and roles in the family. As we have discussed, most adolescents experience increased conflict with parents and greater feelings of insecurity. Generally, the quality of adolescent-parent attachment tends to temporarily decrease from early to middle adolescence, followed by a gradual increase until late adolescence (Buist, 2018). In one study, adolescents followed from age 10 to 14 tended to increasingly view parents as rejecting (Ammaniti, Van Ijzendoorn, Speranza, & Tambelli, 2000). Similarly, as adolescents showed increasing autonomy, they tended to restrict the expression of attachment sentiments, such as sharing hugs or expressing love for parents (Scharf & Mayseless, 2007; Scharf, Mayseless, & Kivenson-Baron, 2004). Even securely attached adolescents tend to increase emotional distance from parents, preferring peers to parents for attachment functions such as proximity seeking and separation protest and even secure base (Buist, 2018). Distancing and conflict with parents, weakening the attachment and emotional investment in parents, promote self-reliance and emotional autonomy, as discussed next.

Emotional Autonomy

Adolescents' sense of attachment and the parent-adolescent relationship are central influences on the development of **emotional autonomy**, establishing adult-like emotional relationships with parents (Steinberg & Silverberg, 1986). Although early perspectives on emotional autonomy emphasized detaching from parents and relinquishing close ties to them (Freud, 1958), today it is generally recognized that healthy autonomy is a process of **individuation** in which adolescents gradually come to see themselves as separate from parents and become less dependent on parents (Blos, 1967).

Individuation is the gradual, progressive sharpening of one's sense of self as autonomous, competent, and separate from one's parents. In addition to individuation, emotional autonomy entails a process of **deidealization**, during which adolescents begin to view their parents as imperfect versus all-knowing and all-powerful. Deidealization comes with increased cognitive maturity, as adolescents gain the capacity to see their parents in both positive and negative ways (Steinberg & Silverberg, 1986). Generally middle to older adolescents (ages 15 to 17) are much less likely than younger adolescents or preteens to endorse items suggesting that their parents are perfect (Beyers & Goossens, 1999; Levpušček, 2006). Similarly, increased deidealization with age is also seen in measures of "positive identification"; older teens are less likely than younger teens to report the desire to be exactly like their parents (Gutman & Eccles, 2007).

Attachment plays a role in autonomy development. Secure adolescents should also be better able to use their parents as a base from which to confidently and autonomously explore the world around them, returning to parents for comfort, support, and advice when the limits of their competence are reached (Belsky & Cassidy, 1994). Secure attachment tends to co-occur with a parenting style and parent-adolescent relationship qualities that support and promote autonomy. For example, secure teens and young adults perceive their families as more involved and supportive and as granting them more psychological autonomy than insecure teens (Allen & Miga, 2010). In healthy families, parent-adolescent relationships become transformed but not detached.

Emotional autonomy spills over to influence peer relationships. Adolescents who are better able to individuate, balancing attachment and autonomy with parents, are also better able to do so in their peer relationships, both friendship and romantic (Allen & Loeb, 2015; Moilanen & Manuel, 2017).

REVIEW 8.2

1. Describe the nature of parent–adolescent conflict in adolescence.

2. What is parental monitoring and why do it?

3. What is an internal working model of attachment? How does it influence adolescent development?

4. Describe the development of emotional autonomy in adolescence.

• •

THINKING IN CONTEXT 8.2

1. How might contextual influences, especially at the exosystem and macrosystem levels of Bronfenbrenner's bioecological theory, influence parent–adolescent relationships? Give three examples.

2. What factors might increase the level of conflict between adolescents and parents?

3. Under what conditions might you expect low conflict between adolescents and parents?

4. Reflect on your experience as an adolescent. How do your experiences compare with research findings about parent–adolescent relationships?

• •

APPLY 8.2

"Jason stopped giving me hugs, even when I'm away for several days on business tips," Mayra complained to her friend. Mayra continued, "And the constant arguing…about everything. He refuses to clean his room, wants to eat dinner in front of his game rather than at the table with us, and won't keep a normal bedtime. I feel like I'm constantly fighting these small battles over dumb stuff."

Mayra's friend commiserated, "My daughter is the same. But we fight about makeup—she insists on wearing gobs of black eyeshadow. And she wants a nose ring. Mayra, my friend, buckle up because I don't think we'll get hugs, or maybe even smiles, for a few years."

1. Compare Mayra and her friend's experience with what we know about parent–adolescent relationships.

2. In what ways might Jason's behavior reflect processes of attachment and emotional autonomy?

3. Is Mayra and her friend's experience as parents of adolescents normal? Why or why not?

• •

PARENTING STYLES

Parents vary in how they interact with and socialize their adolescents. Researcher Diana Baumrind (1971, 2013) proposed that parents' behavior reflects combinations of responsiveness and demandingness. **Responsiveness** refers to the degree to which parents are accepting of their adolescents, responding to them with warmth, sensitivity, and support. Parents also vary in **demandingness**, the degree to which they expect mature behavior from their adolescents. Patterns of responsiveness and demandingness are displayed as **parenting styles**, enduring sets of parenting behaviors that occur across situations to form childrearing climates. These behaviors combine warmth and acceptance with limits and rule setting in various degrees.

Parenting Styles and Their Correlates

Parents who use an **authoritarian parenting style** emphasize behavioral control and obedience over warmth. Parents with an authoritarian style are less accepting and supportive and exert strong control over adolescents' behavior and generally restrict their autonomy. Adolescents are to conform to parental rules without question, simply "because I say so." Authoritarian parents value compliance and discourage, or even forbid, independent decision-making and behavior.

Authoritarian parenting's emphasis on psychological control and punishment (e.g., "my way or the highway") is associated with poor adjustment (Milevsky, 2016). Psychological control inhibits the development of autonomy and is to be linked with low self-esteem, depression, low academic competence, and antisocial behavior in adolescence through early adulthood in young people from Africa, Asia, Europe, the Middle East, and the Americas (Bornstein & Putnick, 2018; Griffith & Grolnick, 2013; Lansford, Laird, Pettit, Bates, & Dodge, 2014; Uji, Sakamoto, Adachi, & Kitamura, 2013). Moreover, it is adolescents' perceptions of negative or controlling parenting behavior, rather than parents' own views, that predict behavior problems (Dimler, Natsuaki, Hastings, Zahn-Waxler, & Klimes-Dougan, 2017). In adolescence, authoritarian parenting is associated with less curiosity, passivity, and low self-esteem (Pinquart & Gerke, 2019). A recent meta-analysis of over 1,400 studies concluded that harsh parenting and psychological control show the strongest associations with behavior problems in childhood and adolescence (Pinquart, 2017). Moreover, parents and adolescents influence each other. As parenting becomes harsher, adolescents tend to display more behavior problems, which may increase negative interactions with parents.

Parents who adopt a **permissive parenting style** are warm, accepting, and indulgent, with few behavioral expectations. Parents with a permissive style emphasize self-expression and autonomy and do not set many rules. When rules are set, they often are not enforced or are enforced inconsistently. Adolescents generally monitor their own behavior and make their own decisions. For example, adolescents may come and go, without a curfew. Autonomy is not granted gradually and in developmentally appropriate ways in permissive households. Instead, adolescents are permitted to make their own decisions at any early age, often before they are able. Adolescents reared in permissive homes are more likely to show immaturity, have difficulty with self-control, and are more likely to conform to peers (Moilanen, Rasmussen, & Padilla-Walker, 2015). Adolescents raised by permissive parents tend to be impulsive, show less task persistence, have low levels of school achievement, and have more behavior problems, including delinquency (Hoeve, Dubas, Gerris, van der Laan, & Smeenk, 2011; Llorca, Richaud, & Malonda, 2017). In short, a permissive parenting style interferes with the development of self-regulatory skills that are needed to develop academic and behavioral competence in childhood and adolescence.

Parents with an **indifferent parenting style** focus on their own needs rather than those of their children. Parents who are under stress, emotionally detached, or depressed often lack time or energy to devote to their children, putting them at risk for an indifferent parenting style (Baumrind, 2013). Indifferent parents provide little support or warmth, exert little control, and fail to recognize their children's need for affection and direction. At the extreme, indifferent parenting is neglectful and a form of child maltreatment. Indifferent parenting is associated with poor mental health, depression, and delinquency and has negative consequences for all aspects of development (Givertz, 2015; Hoeve et al., 2011; Maccoby & Martin, 1983).

The most positive developmental outcomes are associated with what Baumrind termed the **authoritative parenting style**. Authoritative parents are warm and sensitive to adolescents' needs but also are firm in their expectations that adolescents conform to appropriate standards of behavior. While exerting firm, reasonable control, they engage their adolescents in discussions about standards and grant them developmentally appropriate levels of autonomy, permitting decision-making that is appropriate to the adolescent's abilities (Baumrind, 2013). When a rule is violated, authoritative parents explain what the adolescent did wrong and impose limited, developmentally appropriate punishments that are closely connected to the misdeed. Authoritative parents value

Parents who adopt an authoritarian style value obedience and control and restrict adolescents' autonomy.
LightField Studios/Shutterstock.com

and foster adolescents' individuality. They encourage their children to have their own interests, opinions, and decisions, but ultimately, they control their adolescents' behavior.

Adolescents of authoritative parents display confidence, self-esteem, social skills, curiosity, and high academic achievement, and they score higher on measures of executive functioning; these positive effects persist throughout childhood into adolescence (Fay-Stammbach, Hawes, & Meredith, 2014; Sosic-Vasic et al., 2017). Across ethnic and socioeconomic groups and in countries around the world, multiple studies have found that authoritative parenting fosters autonomy, self-reliance, self-esteem, a positive view of the value of work, academic competence, and lower levels of delinquency, substance use, and risky behaviors in adolescents (Bornstein & Putnick, 2018; McKinney & Renk, 2011; Uji et al., 2013). Parents in a given household often share a common parenting style, but when they do not, the presence of authoritative parenting in at least one parent buffers the negative outcomes associated with the other style and predicts positive adjustment (Hoeve et al., 2011; McKinney & Renk, 2011).

Why is authoritative parenting successful? The high levels of responsiveness communicate acceptance, which is associated with reduced levels of depression, psychological disorders, and behavior problems (Pinquart, 2017). Authoritative parents value their adolescents' input and combine open discussion and joint decision-making with firm but fair limit setting, which helps adolescents feel valued, respected, and encouraged to think for themselves (Hart, Coates, & Smith-Bynum, 2019; Lamb & Lewis, 2015). In this way, authoritative parents balance control, rules, and boundaries, with autonomy, opportunities to develop independence. Moreover, autonomy is granted gradually as adolescents mature, in line with their developing capacities.

Culture, Context, and Parenting

Given its combination of acceptance, autonomy granting, and appropriate behavioral limits, authoritative parenting is associated with positive outcomes in adolescents of all ethnic and socioeconomic groups and in countries around the world (Bornstein & Putnick, 2018; McKinney & Renk, 2011; Uji et al., 2013). Yet the impact of parenting styles may vary with contextual factors, such as socioeconomic status and the neighborhood in which the family is embedded (Assadi et al., 2007; Brody & Flor, 1998). There is not just one effective way to parent. Instead, some researchers argue that there are many cultural variations in parenting, and the effectiveness of disciplinary techniques may differ by cultural context (Cauce, 2008).

Is strict control always harmful? Researchers have identified a disciplinary style common in African American families that combines strict parental control with affection (Tamis-LeMonda, Briggs, McClowry, & Snow, 2009). This style stresses obedience and views strict control as important in helping children develop self-control and attentiveness. African American parents who use controlling strategies tend to raise adolescents who are more cognitively mature and socially competent than their peers who are raised in other ways. This difference is particularly apparent in adolescents reared in low income homes and communities, where vigilant, strict parenting enhances their safety (Weis & Toolis, 2010). Whereas strict control and discipline is associated with behavioral problems in European American children, it appears to protect some African American children from conduct problems in adolescence (Lansford, Deater-Deckard, Dodge, Bates, & Pettit, 2004). The warmth and affection buffer some of the negative consequences of strictness (McLoyd & Smith, 2002; Stacks, Oshio, Gerard, & Roe, 2009). Adolescents' perception of parental discipline and intention is important in determining its effect. Adolescents evaluate parental behavior in light of their culture and the emotional tone of the relationship. African American and low income adolescents reared in homes with strict but warm parents often see this style of discipline as indicative of concern about their well-being (Lee et al., 2016). However, research with socioeconomically diverse African American adolescent–mother pairs revealed that adolescents of authoritative mothers reported higher levels of closeness and warmth in relationships with mothers (Hart et al., 2019). In addition, authoritative parenting was associated with better relationships regardless of SES.

In the United States, it is often difficult to disentangle the effects of culture and neighborhood context on parenting behaviors because African American and other families of color are disproportionately represented in disadvantaged neighborhoods. Does strict discipline embody cultural beliefs about parenting? Or is it a response to raising children in a disadvantaged environment (Murry, Brody, Simons, Cutrona, & Gibbons, 2008)? Parental perceptions of danger and their own distress influence how they parent (Cuellar, Jones, & Sterrett, 2013). Parenting behaviors, including discipline, must be considered within a cultural and environmental context, as parenting is not "one size fits all" (Sorkhabi, 2005).

REVIEW 8.3

1. Describe four parenting styles and their correlates.

2. How do the effects of parenting behaviors, such as strict control, vary with context?

. . . .

THINKING IN CONTEXT 8.3

Consider the changing parent–adolescent relationship from the family systems perspective.

1. What aspects of adolescent development may influence parents' reactions and parenting style?

2. What developmental changes might parents experience that may influence their parenting style and interactions with their adolescent children?

3. Explain how adolescents and parents influence each other.

4. What is the role of contextual factors, such as neighborhood, in parent–adolescent interactions and relationships? Give examples.

. . . .

APPLY 8.3

Mak pressed the phone to his ear and looked at the police officer, who instructed, "Tell your mother what you did and that she can pick you up at the station."
"Oh boy, breaking into a store. Mom's going to have a fit. At least I'm not arrested. I'm getting off with a warning," Mak thought to himself as he pressed the phone to his ear and heard his mother answer the phone on the other end.

Contrast how four styles of parenting might respond to Mak's call. Specifically, describe each parenting style. For each, give an example of how a parent might react and what the parent might say or do in response to Mak's behavior.

. . . .

FAMILIES AND FAMILY TRANSITIONS

Adolescents grow up in many different kinds of living situations and families. Some are raised in two-parent intact homes, but many adolescents experience family transitions such as divorce and remarriage. Other adolescents experience different circumstances, such as being adopted, living in foster homes, or living with family members who are undocumented immigrants.

Exposure to parental conflict predicts adolescents' adjustment to divorce.
iStock.com/skynesher

Divorced and Divorcing Families

For many decades, it was assumed that divorce caused significant and irreparable harm to adolescents. Today most researchers agree that, like other transitions, divorce poses challenges to adolescents' adjustment. On average, adolescents whose parents divorce are at risk for more internalizing problems (such as anxiety and depression), externalizing behaviors (such as delinquent activity), poor academic achievement, and problematic social relationships than those whose parents do not divorce (Lansford, 2018). However, these effects are small in magnitude, are often transient, and are not universal (Amato & Anthony, 2014; Weaver & Schofield, 2015). Difficulties are most common immediately after parents separate, but most adolescents show improved adjustment within 2 years after the divorce (Lamb, 2012). The majority of adolescents with divorced parents show no long-term adjustment problems in adulthood (Oldehinkel et al., 2009). Divorce is not a discrete event in a family's experience. Adolescents' adjustment to divorce is related to processes before and after the transition, such as exposure to conflict between parents, disruptions in parenting, parental distress, changes in household circumstances, and individual differences (Weaver & Schofield, 2015).

Interparental Conflict

Adjustment challenges often begin well before the divorce is announced, because parental divorce tends to be preceded by a period of tension, often characterized by increases in conflict between parents (Amato, 2010). Exposure to high levels of interparental conflict before and during divorce impairs adolescents' emotional, psychological, and behavioral adaptation, which, in turn, predicts poor long-term outcomes and adjustment difficulties (Harold, Aitken, & Shelton, 2007; van der Wal, Finkenauer, & Visser, 2019). High

levels of conflict are particularly stressful to adolescents, especially if they feel caught between parents or forced to take sides. Adolescents exposed to interparental conflict that includes screaming, insulting, hitting, or threatening are more likely to show problems such as depression, aggression, and acting-out behaviors (Lansford, 2018; Lucas-Thompson, Lunkenheimer, & Dumitrache, 2017). Adolescents exposed to chronic interparental conflict tend to show increased physiological arousal and an elevated stress response (Davidson, O'Hara, & Beck, 2014; Davies & Martin, 2014). The dissolution of a high-conflict marriage can reduce adolescents' exposure to daily conflict, improving adjustment. In contrast, the dissolution of a low-conflict marriage may come as a surprise and result in a greater sense of loss.

Disrupted Parenting

A family systems perspective suggests that conflict between parents spills over to influence parent–adolescent relationships. For example, parents' well-being may play a role in adolescents' adjustment. Divorce poses adjustment challenges for parents and increases the risk for depression, anxiety, and stress, which influences their ability to parent well (Lansford, 2018). Divorce disrupts parents' ability to parent well, which in turn influences adolescent adjustment. As they struggle with their own adaptation, parents tend to feel less efficacious in monitoring and disciplining their children (Amato, Kane, & James, 2011). Generally, low levels of monitoring are associated with academic and behavior problems (Bendezú et al., 2018).

Parent–adolescent conflict often increases after divorce, discipline becomes less consistent, and parents experience more conflict and less cohesion in their relationships with their children than prior to divorce (Amato et al., 2011; Wallerstein & Lewis, 2004). Yet positive relationships can serve a protective function in adolescent adjustment. Parents who cope well are able to maintain high-quality relationships. Moreover, just as exposure to interparental conflict prior to the divorce influences adjustment, so do parenting practices. Adolescents show worse adjustment when their parents engage in more problematic parenting practices prior to the divorce (Murry & Lippold, 2018). Harmful family processes, such as parental conflict, poor parent–child interactions, and ineffective parenting strategies, take a toll on children's emotional and psychological health and can precede parental divorce by as much as 8 to 12 years (Amato, 2010; Potter, 2010).

Socioeconomic Changes

Divorce is often accompanied by socioeconomic transitions. After divorce, adolescents most often live with their mothers and may experience a drop in household income that influences their adjustment (Bratberg & Tjøtta, 2008; White & Rogers, 2000). Fewer financial resources can be disruptive, leading to changes in residence, such as a move to more affordable housing, causing additional changes in adolescents' school, community, and circle of friends and often reducing adolescents' access to social support. Financial hardships may lead to emotional and behavioral difficulties that link divorce and adjustment.

Variations in child, parent, and family characteristics and contexts influence children's adjustment to parental divorce. Boys are more likely to show behavior problems and delinquent activity immediately after parental separation and divorce (Malone et al., 2004). Girls tend to respond with anxiety and depression (Amato & Sobolewski, 2001; Størksen, Røysamb, Moum, & Tambs, 2005). It may not be surprising that young adolescents show heightened risk for adjustment given the many simultaneous physical, cognitive, and social changes they experience, such as puberty and school transitions, for example. It is important to remember that problems tend to be transient and most adolescents show improved adjustment within 2 years after the divorce, suggesting that the majority of children of divorce are resilient (Lamb, 2012). Moreover, when researchers take into account the quality of parenting and children's exposure to conflict, the link between parental divorce and children's adjustment lessens, suggesting that parenting strategies and relationships are more important influences on children's adjustment than divorce (Bing, Nelson, & Wesolowski, 2009; Whiteside & Becker, 2000).

Blended Families

About 15% of U.S. children live in a **blended family**: a family composed of a biological parent and a nonrelated adult, most commonly a mother and stepfather (Pew Research Center, 2015). Blended families, also sometimes referred to as *stepfamilies* or *reconstituted families*, present children with new challenges and adjustments, as the multiple transitions entailed by divorce and remarriage are stressful. It is often difficult for blended families to integrate and balance the many relationships among custodial, noncustodial, and stepparents, in addition to grandparents and extended family members (Dupuis, 2010). There is the potential for adolescents to experience family conflict on multiple levels, between birth parents, birth and stepparents, and among stepsiblings (and their conflicts with parents and stepparents). Many adults look back on their parents' remarriage as more stressful than the divorce itself (Ahrons, 2007).

Adolescents tend to display more difficulties in adjusting to remarriage than do younger children (Hennon, Hildenbrand, & Schedle, 2008; Ram & Hou, 2003). Both boys and girls tend to experience psychological distress in adjusting to remarriage; however, they may direct their distress in different ways. Living with a stepparent is associated with physical aggression, destructive behaviors, and other behavior problems among boys, and indirect, passive, and not easily noticeable aggression among girls that often appears as anxiety or depression. Adapting to a new authority figure and parenting and discipline style is challenging, especially if it differs from one's parents.

The developmental transitions and tasks of adolescence pose challenges for adjusting to parental remarriage. Multiple stressors, such as puberty, entry to middle and high school, and peer processes, intersect with divorce-related stressors, such as parental conflict and residential moves, to influence how adolescents approach and adjust to stepparents. Changes in family processes may affect adolescents' sense of attachment and parents' support of autonomy, with implications for the development of emotional autonomy and individuation as well as parent and peer relationships.

Overall, blended families adapt more easily and children show better adjustment when stepparents build a warm friendship with the child and adopt their new roles slowly rather than rushing or forcing relationships (Doodson & Morley, 2006). However, stepmothers often find that their role is challenging and ill defined, especially if a nonresident biological mother retains close and frequent contact with the children (Greeff & Du Toit, 2009). Stepmothers tend to report more depressive symptoms and parenting stress, and they tend to enjoy the parenting role less than do biological mothers (Shapiro, 2014; Shapiro & Stewart, 2011). How well adults adjust to the role of stepparent is influenced by the support of the biological parent as well as the children's perception of their relationship with the stepparent and willingness to accept the adult into the family (Jensen & Howard, 2015). When stepparents are warm and involved and do not exert authority too soon, children usually adjust quickly. After a challenging transition, many couples adjust to their roles as spouses and parents, and interactions with stepchildren improve (Jensen & Howard, 2015). The difficulties that stepparenting entails—especially child-parent conflicts—are among the reasons that the divorce rate is higher in couples with stepchildren (DeLongis & Zwicker, 2017; Teachman, 2008).

Same-Sex Parented Families

More than 3 decades of research conducted in the United States, the United

Children and adolescents raised by lesbian mothers or gay fathers do not differ from other children on measures of emotional and social development.
iStock.com/DragonImages

Kingdom, Belgium, and the Netherlands has failed to reveal important differences in the adjustment or development of children and adolescents reared by same-sex couples compared with those reared by other couples (Fedewa, Black, & Ahn, 2014; Patterson, 2017; Perrin & Siegel, 2013). Specifically, children and adolescents raised by lesbian mothers or gay fathers do not differ from other children on measures of emotional development, such as empathy and emotion regulation (Bos, Knox, van Rijn-van Gelderen, & Gartrell, 2016; Farr, 2017). Instead, some studies have suggested that children raised by gay and lesbian parents may score higher in some aspects of social and academic competence, as well as show fewer social and behavioral problems and lower levels of aggression, than other children (Golombok et al., 2014, 2018; Miller, Kors, & Macfie, 2017). Moreover, children raised by lesbian mothers and gay fathers show similar patterns of gender identity and gender role development as children raised by heterosexual parents—they are not more likely to identify as gay or lesbian in adulthood (Fedewa et al., 2014; Tasker & Patterson, 2007). Researchers have concluded that a family's social and economic resources, the strength of the relationships among members of the family, and the presence of stigma are far more important variables than parental gender or sexual orientation in affecting children's development and well-being (Farr, 2017; Perrin & Siegel, 2013).

Adoptive Families

Our understanding of adoptive families with adolescents is limited because most research focuses on children. Generally, adoptive children tend to be raised by parents with higher levels of education and income than other parents, spend more time with their parents, and have more educational resources than other children (Zill, 2015). Despite these advantages, longitudinal research suggests that adoption is associated with lower academic achievement across childhood, adolescence, and emerging adulthood compared with nonadopted comparison groups (Brown, Waters, & Shelton, 2017). Adopted children show greater psychological problems and adjustment difficulties than their nonadoptive peers, in some cases persisting into adulthood (Palacios & Brodzinsky, 2010). Early adolescence is a peak risk period given the multiple transitions adolescents undergo (Brooker, Berenbaum, Bricker, Corley, & Wadsworth, 2012). In addition, cognitive advances may lead adolescents to consider their adoptive status in more complicated ways and apply their hypothetical reasoning to their lives, including their biological and adoptive parents. Despite these findings, it is critical to note that the magnitude of differences is small; the majority of adopted adolescents function within the normal range of adjustment (Grotevant & McDermott, 2014; Levesque, 2018).

Transracial adoption, in which a child (typically of color) is adopted to parents of a different race (most often White), accounts for about one-quarter of adoptions (Marr, 2017). As adolescents, all children struggle to come to a sense of identity, to figure out who they are. This struggle may be especially challenging for transracial adopted children and internationally adopted children who may wonder about their ethnic or racial culture and, for internationally adopted children, homeland (Rosnati et al., 2015; Wiley, 2017). Research reviews suggest that racial and ethnic socialization is associated with healthy adoptee outcomes (Montgomery & Jordan, 2018). Parents who assume a multicultural perspective and provide opportunities for their children to learn about their birth culture support adopted children's development and promote healthy outcomes (Pinderhughes, Zhang, & Agerbak, 2015). Parents can foster their adoptive children's ethnic and racial socialization by exposing children to their racial and ethnic heritage and providing opportunities for children to learn about and interact with people who identify with their birth race and ethnicity (Hrapczynski & Leslie, 2018).

Internationally adopted children seek to understand their birth culture and integrate their birth and adopted cultures into their sense of self (Grotevant, Lo, Fiorenzo, & Dunbar, 2017). A positive sense of ethnic identity is associated with positive outcomes such as self-esteem in international adoptees (Mohanty, 2015). Although there are individual differences in the degree of resilience and in functioning across developmental domains, adopted children overall show great developmental gains and resilience in physical, cognitive, and emotional development (Misca, 2014; Palacios, Román, Moreno, León, & Peñarrubia, 2014; Wilson & Weaver, 2009).

For many children, emotional differences are transitional. Research has suggested that most children show resilience in the years after adoption, but some issues continue (Palacios & Brodzinsky, 2010). Those who develop a close bond with adoptive parents tend to show better emotional understanding and regulation, social competence, and also self-esteem (Juffer & van IJzendoorn, 2007). This is true also of children who have experienced emotional neglect, and those effects hold regardless of age of adoption (Barone, Lionetti, & Green, 2017).

Foster Care

Foster care is a child welfare arrangement in which a child is temporarily placed outside the home because the parents are unable to provide care or safety. Although intended as a temporary placement, many adolescents remain in the foster care system for months and years. Adolescents experience risks for adjustment prior to entering foster care, such as maltreatment, abandonment, family breakdown, or parental substance abuse (Leloux-Opmeer, Kuiper, Swaab, & Scholte, 2016). Many have preexisting problems, including poor health, emotional, cognitive, and behavioral problems, and problems at school (Farruggia, Germo, & Solomon, 2018). Transitions pose challenges for adjustments, and adolescents in foster care experience multiple transitions in and out of care, such as when parents are deemed able to care for them, as well as from foster home to foster home. Mental health problems are common among foster youth, with as many as 66% of adolescents in foster care receiving a lifetime diagnosis for mental health disorders (Havlicek, Garcia, & Smith, 2013; McMillen et al., 2005).

The majority of adolescents in foster care for a long period of time transition to independence because they "age out" of the foster care system. Once they reach adulthood (age 18 to 21 depending on the state), they exit the system regardless of their readiness. About 18,000 adolescents face this transition annually each year (Administration for Children and Families, 2019). Although many are eager to leave foster care, the transition is difficult. Many adolescents are unprepared because they have not experienced normative increases in autonomy coupled with support. Emancipated youth experience high rates of homelessness, especially upon leaving care. High homelessness rates are likely the result of many emancipated youth lacking the social ties that many young adults rely on like living at home and being financially supported by parents (Bender, Yang, Ferguson, & Thompson, 2015). The academic problems common among adolescents in foster care lead many to drop out of high school. Most have difficulty finding employment and experience extended financial challenges. Given problems with housing, employment, and education, many young adults who age out of foster care have high rates of psychological behavioral and social problems (Farruggia et al., 2018).

Families With Undocumented Members

About 5.5 million minor children in the United States live with at least one immigrant parent who is undocumented—that is, without the legal right to be in the United States—and 4.5 million of these young people are U.S.-born citizens (Yoshikawa, Kholoptseva, & Suárez-Orozco, 2013). Families with undocumented members face multiple challenges, such as severe financial stress, fear of deportation, inadequate means to higher education, and heightened uncertainty about the future (Abrego & Gonzales, 2010; Talleyrand & Vojtech, 2018).

Adolescents in homes with undocumented family members often live in fear of the detention and removal of a parent and, perhaps not surprisingly, tend to show higher levels of anxiety and depressive symptoms than other adolescents (Kam, Gasiorek, Pines, & Fazio, 2018). An undocumented parent's removal from the home has profound consequences for the family. The loss of a parent's income can be economically devastating. Emotional consequences

Adolescents who are U.S.-born citizens with parents who are undocumented immigrants face unique adustment challenges.
James Tsukano/Alamy Stock Photo

for adolescents include coping with distressed relatives while managing their own distress. Some adolescents may take on adult roles in the family, such as responsibility for siblings, in the wake of one or more parents' detention and removal. Adolescents may be encouraged to stay at home and remain out of school during removal proceedings, potentially influencing their academic achievement and peer relationships. Many adolescents develop fear of authority figures. Feelings of fear, isolation, anger, and hopelessness can interfere with healthy development.

When adolescents are undocumented themselves, the cognitive and socioemotional changes of adolescence often bring a heightened awareness of their undocumented status. Recall from Chapter 4 that ethnic identity, the extent to which adolescents identify with and affirm their ethnic heritage, is a protective factor associated with positive mental health and academic outcomes (Rivas-Drake et al., 2014). For many adolescents, ethnic identity is a valuable resource for coping with stress related to acculturation. However, ethnic identity may not serve as a protective factor for Latinx youth who experience unauthorized legal status and may view their ethnic group as unwanted and rejected by society. That is, undocumented youth are at risk of developing a negative ethnic identity due to the stress, stigma, and politicization associated with their unauthorized status (Rodriguez, 2017; Suárez-Orozco, 2017). In addition, adolescents with undocumented status face practical challenges in balancing normative social experiences, such as driving, working, and planning for college, with the barriers posed by undocumented status. Difficulties

in access to drivers' licenses, college, and employment block adolescents' economic and educational progress in late adolescence, preventing adolescents with undocumented status from advancing from poverty (Abrego & Gonzales, 2010; Talleyrand & Vojtech, 2018). Ultimately, adolescents with undocumented status face challenges that can impact their psychological and economic well-being throughout adulthood. ●

REVIEW 8.4

1. Describe three processes by which divorce influences adolescents' development.

2. What are some influences on adolescents' adjustment in blended families?

3. Describe adolescents' adjustment to adoption.

4. What challenges do adolescents who are out of the foster care system face?

5. What difficulties do adolescents with undocumented family members experience?

THINKING IN CONTEXT 8.4

Adolescents thrive across a range of different types of family circumstances.

1. Considering the various family circumstances discussed, identify general risk factors for poor adjustment.

2. What individual and contextual factors are associated with positive adjustment, generally?

APPLY 8.4

Fourteen-year-old Casey's parents are getting divorced.

1. What changes might Casey expect?

2. What factors might influence Casey's development and adjustment?

3. Suppose one of Casey's parents remarried, forming a blended household with children from another marriage. What factors might influence Casey's adjustment?

CHAPTER SUMMARY

8.1 **Explain family systems theory and the interactions among family systems.**

The family systems theory emphasizes the interactive and bidirectional nature of relationships within families. As family members interact with each other over time, the interactions come to reflect stable patterns of behavior, reaching a state of equilibrium. Each member of the family—parents, adolescents, and siblings—undergoes developmental changes that influence the family system. However, changes in any individual or relationship can disrupt the equilibrium.

8.2 **Describe adolescents' relationships with their parents, attachment, and emotional autonomy.**

Conflict between parents and adolescents tends to rise in early adolescence, peak in middle adolescence, and decline from middle to late adolescence. Attachment bonds established in childhood persist into adolescence; however, as adolescents become more independent, their attachment relationships change in form, function, and security. Generally, the quality of adolescent–parent attachment tends to temporarily decrease from early to middle adolescence, followed by a gradual increase until late adolescence. Even securely attached adolescents tend to increase emotional distance from parents, preferring peers to parents for attachment functions such as proximity seeking and separation protest and even secure base. Adolescents' sense of attachment and the parent–adolescent relationship are central influences on the development of emotional autonomy, establishing adult-like emotional relationships with parents. Healthy autonomy is a process of individuation in which adolescents gradually come to see themselves as separate from parents and become less dependent on parents. In addition to individuation, emotional autonomy entails a process of deidealization, during which adolescents begin to view their parents as imperfect versus all-knowing and all-powerful.

8.3 **Summarize what is known about parenting style in adolescence.**

Patterns of parental responsiveness and demandingness are displayed as parenting styles. Parents who use an authoritarian parenting style emphasize behavioral control and obedience over warmth. Parents who adopt a permissive parenting style are warm, accepting, and indulgent, with few behavioral expectations or limits. Indifferent parents provide little support or warmth and exert little control. Authoritarian, permissive, and indifferent parenting are associated with poor adjustment. Authoritative parents are warm and sensitive to adolescents' needs but also are firm in their expectations that adolescents conform to appropriate standards of behavior. Authoritative parents value and foster adolescents' individuality. They encourage their children to have their own interests, opinions, and decisions, but ultimately, they control their adolescents' behavior. Across ethnic and socioeconomic groups and in countries around the world, multiple studies have found that authoritative parenting fosters autonomy, self-reliance, self-esteem, a positive view of the value of work, academic competence, and lower levels of delinquency, substance use, and risky behaviors in adolescents. Yet the impact of parenting styles may vary with contextual factors, such as socioeconomic status and neighborhood in which the family is embedded.

8.4 **Discuss common family transitions, such as divorce, remarriage, adoption, foster care, and others.**

Today most researchers agree that, like other transitions, divorce poses challenges to adolescents' adjustment. On average, adolescents whose parents divorce are at risk for more internalizing problems, externalizing behaviors, poor academic achievement, and problematic social relationships than those whose parents do not divorce, but these effects are small in magnitude, are often transient, and are not universal. Adolescents' adjustment to divorce is related to processes before and after the transition, specifically exposure to conflict between parents, disruptions in parenting, parental distress, changes in household circumstances, and individual differences. Likewise, blended families present adolescents with new challenges and adjustments. Adoptive adolescents tend to experience more psychological problems and adjustment difficulties than their nonadoptive peers, but the magnitude of differences is small; the majority of adopted adolescents function within the normal range of adjustment. Adolescents in foster care experience risks for adjustment prior to entering foster care, and many have preexisting problems that influence their adjustment. Those who age out of foster care are at high risk for adjustment difficulties. Adolescents with undocumented family members or who are undocumented themselves show higher levels of anxiety and depressive symptoms than other adolescents and face challenges that can impact their psychological and economic well-being throughout adulthood.

KEY TERMS

attachment, 170

authoritarian parenting style, 172

authoritative parenting style, 173

blended family, 176

deidealization, 171

demandingness, 172

9

Peer Context

Learning Objectives

9.1 Discuss the nature of friendship in adolescence.

9.2 Examine characteristics of the peer group and the impact of popularity, rejection, and victimization on development.

9.3 Discuss adolescents' susceptibility to peer influence.

9.4 Summarize what we know about dating in adolescence, including developmental trends and relation with adjustment.

Chapter Contents

The most easily recognizable influence on adolescents, and that which gets the most attention from adults and the media, is the peer group. Each week, adolescents spend up to about twice as much time with peers than parents and they spend many more hours interacting with friends online (Brown & Larson, 2009). In this chapter, we examine the role of the peer context in development.

FRIENDSHIP

"Best friends forever!" shouted Lexa as her friend snapped a selfie and agreed, "BFFs!" In adolescence, friendship is a close dyadic relationship characterized by a shared history, sense of commitment, and companionship. About 60% to 80% of adolescents have at least one same-sex reciprocal friendship and the typical adolescent has four to six close friends (French & Cheung, 2018). Adolescent friendships are characterized by intimacy, self-disclosure, trust, and loyalty (Bowker & Ramsay, 2018). Adolescents expect their friends to be there for them, stand up for them, and not share their secrets or harm them. Adolescent friendships tend to include cooperation, sharing, intimacy, and affirmation, which reflect their emerging capacities for perspective taking, social sensitivity, empathy, and social skills (Poulin & Chan, 2010).

Over the course of adolescence, the number of friendships declines and conceptions of friendship deepen, moving from a focus on proximity and common activities to an appreciation of character traits (Gomez, Iyer, Batto, & Jensen-Campbell, 2011). Adolescents develop a more abstract understanding of the reciprocal nature of friendship, placing greater importance on intimacy and self-disclosure.

High-quality friendships characterized by sharing, intimacy, and open communication tend to endure over time (Hiatt, Laursen, Mooney, & Rubin, 2015).

Similarities Among Friends

Friendships tend to be characterized by **homophily**, similarity (Rubin, Fredstrom, & Bowker, 2008). Adolescents tend to form friendships with others who are like them. Friends tend to be similar in demographics, such as age, ethnicity, and socioeconomic status (Bowker & Ramsay, 2018; Laursen, 2017). Close friends and best friends tend to be similar in orientation toward risky activity, such as willingness to try drugs and engage in delinquency and dangerous behaviors such as unprotected sex (de Water, Burk, Cillessen, & Scheres, 2017; Hiatt, Laursen, Stattin, & Kerr, 2017; Scalco, Trucco, Coffman, & Colder, 2015). Adolescent friends tend to share interests, such as tastes in music; they are also similar in academic achievement, educational aspirations, and political beliefs; and they show similar trends in psychosocial development, such as identity status (Markiewicz & Doyle, 2016; Shin & Ryan, 2014). Through interaction, friends tend to become even more similar to each other (Scalco et al., 2015).

Sometimes, however, middle and older adolescents choose friends who are different from them, which encourages them to consider new perspectives. Cross-ethnic friendships, for example, are less common than same-ethnic friendships but are associated with unique benefits. Adolescent members of cross-ethnic friendships show declines in racial prejudice over time (Titzmann, Brenick, & Silbereisen, 2015). Having friends of other ethnicities can serve as a buffer, reducing the negative effects of discrimination on adjustment (Benner & Wang, 2017). Ethnic minority adolescents with cross-ethnic friends perceive less discrimination, vulnerability, and relational victimization and show higher rates of self-esteem and well-being over time than those without cross-ethnic friends (Bagci, Rutland, Kumashiro, Smith, & Blumberg, 2014; Graham, Munniksma, & Juvonen, 2014; Kawabata & Crick, 2011).

Sex Differences in Friendship

Boys and girls interact with their friends in different ways. Adolescent boys tend to have larger peer groups than girls. Boys get together for activities, usually sports and competitive games, and tend to be more social and vocal in groups as compared with one-on-one situations. Boys tend to excel at being fun companions, coping with a friend who violates an expectation, and sustaining friendships within the context of having other friends (Rose & Asher, 2017). In contrast, most girls tend to prefer one-on-one interactions and often spend their time together talking, sharing thoughts and feelings, and supporting each other. Although girls tend to have fewer friendships and their friendships are of shorter duration, girls rate their friendships as more intimate, more caring, and more important than boys do (Erdley & Day, 2017).

Girls tend to associate intimacy, especially self-disclosure, with friendship quality. Sharing personal issues, problems, and feelings with supportive friends is a mark of friendship quality. High rates of self-disclosure, however, may pose risks to girls' mental health when girls co-ruminate on personal problems and rehash and focus on their distress, increasing the risk of depression (Rose, Schwartz-Mette, Glick, Smith, & Luebbe, 2014). At the same time, although co-rumination poses risks, it increases friendship quality among girls.

In early adolescence, boys and girls tend to prefer same-sex peers as close friends; as they progress through adolescence, other-sex friendships become more common and are rated as more important (Bowker & Ramsay, 2018). Other-sex friendships can help adolescents learn about how boys and girls approach relationships and might help with later romantic relationships. Perhaps because of the sex differences in interaction patterns, boys tend to rate their friendships with girls more positively than those with other boys (Rose & Asher, 2017). Yet other-sex friendships may influence boys and girls in different ways; one study suggested that opposite-sex friendships were associated with an increase in smoking in girls and a decrease in drinking in boys (Mrug, Borch, & Cillessen, 2011).

Boys' friendships tend to center around activities, such as sports.
Harold Cunningham/Contributor/Getty Images

Girls' friendships tend to emphasize intimacy and self-disclosure, such as sharing secrets.
iStock.com/South_agency

Friendship Stability

Friendships become more stable and enduring over the course of adolescence. Although most early adolescents describe their friendships as high quality, many of these friendships do not last the school year. About one-third to one-half of friendships in early adolescence are unstable, with young people regularly losing friends and making new friendships (Poulin & Chan, 2010). After early adolescence, friendships become more stable, with young people retaining the majority of their friendships over the course of a school year.

Just as compatibility influences friendship formation, it also predicts friendship stability. In one study, adolescent friend pairs who differed in peer acceptance, physical aggression, and school competence in seventh grade were more likely to dissolve their friendship during high school than were dyads who were more similar in social and academic abilities and traits (Hartl, Laursen, & Cillessen, 2015). Enduring friendships also show similarity in mental health. In one recent study, adolescent friendship dyads who showed dissimilar patterns of anxiety and depression (for example, one adolescent reporting many symptoms and the other reporting few) were more likely to break up between Grades 7 and 12 than were those with similar levels of internalizing symptoms (Guimond, Laursen, Hartl, & Cillessen, 2019). Enduring friendships are characterized by homophily in traits, abilities, and even mental health.

Friendships dissolve for a variety of reasons. Although conflict is associated with friendship dissolution, conflict management strategies are better predictors of friendship dissolution and are even more important than relationship quality (Bowker & Ramsay,

2018). Specifically, the ability for a friendship dyad to deal with conflict directly rather than minimize or ignore it predicts stability (Bowker, 2004).

Friendship dissolution may have serious consequences for adolescents who are unable to replace the friendship. Some adolescents who experience disruption and loss of close friendships have problems with depression, loneliness, guilt, anger, anxiety, and acting-out behaviors, yet adolescents with psychosocial problems are also at risk to experience friendship loss and, in turn, show poor adjustment (Rubin, Bukowski, & Bowker, 2015). Many adolescents replace "lost" friendships with "new" friendships. In one study of fifth-graders, losing a friend was associated with adjustment difficulties only when the lost friendship was not replaced by a new friendship. For these adolescents, the lost and new friendships were largely interchangeable (Wojslawowicz Bowker, Rubin, Burgess, Booth-Laforce, & Rose-Krasnor, 2006).

An estimated 15% to 20% of young people are chronically friendless or consistently without a mutual best friend (Rubin et al., 2015). Lacking a best friend itself is not necessarily harmful or associated with problems (Klima & Repetti, 2008). However, adolescents without friends tend to report feeling more lonely than other children, especially when they desire friends (Lodder, Scholte, Goossens, & Verhagen, 2017). Friendless adolescents may lack social skills or might direct their friendship toward others who are unlikely to reciprocate (Bowker et al., 2010). Adolescents who are lonely are more likely to experience social anxiety, which may interfere with their ability to form friendships (Maes et al., 2019).

Friendship and Adolescent Development

Adolescents navigate multiple developmental tasks and friendships play a role in each—the development of identity, autonomy, and intimacy. Close supportive friendships offer adolescents a safe environment for self-exploration and identity formation (Erikson, 1959). Friends also play a role in adolescents' drive for emotional autonomy from parents (see Chapter 8). As adolescents separate from parents, the peer group becomes an important attachment figure and provides acceptance and validation (Nickerson & Nagle, 2005). Adolescents' attachment to parents and their internal working model of self derived from these attachments tend to remain stable over time and influence peer relationships (Jones et al.,

2018). Adolescents tend to show similar patterns of attachment strategies and relationships with parents and peers (Sroufe, 2016). For example, adolescents with secure attachments to parents tend to form friendships that are more harmonious, intimate, and responsive compared to adolescents with insecure attachments to parents (Bauminger, Finzi-Dottan, Chason, & Har-Even, 2008). Insecure attachment to parents poses risks for problematic peer relationships (Booth-Laforce et al., 2006). The developmental tasks of establishing autonomy and intimacy are intertwined because adolescents must develop the capacity for mature intimacy in friendships and romantic relationships while simultaneously maintaining close and autonomous relationships with parents (Scharf, Mayseless, & Kivenson-Baron, 2004). Adolescents' close friendships and developing capacities for intimacy influence and are influenced by their internal working models of self.

Friends who are supportive and empathetic help adolescents manage stress.
iStock.com/FatCamera

Intimacy first develops within the context of close platonic (nonromantic) friendships (Sullivan, 1953). Intimate friendships involve shared activities, mutual disclosure, and reciprocal feelings of satisfaction with the relationship. According to theorist Harry Stack Sullivan, friendship quality plays an important role in intimacy development because loyalty, mutual commitment, and trust provide a framework for self-disclosure, for adolescents to share their personal experiences and private thoughts and feelings with friends (Erdley & Day, 2017). Self-disclosure increases dramatically during adolescence, providing opportunities for adolescents to develop sensitivity and concern about others' welfare (Bauminger et al., 2008). The feeling of being understood, validated, and cared for that accompanies self-disclosure promotes the development of intimacy (Sullivan, 1953; Van Petegem, Brenning, Baudat, Beyers, & Zimmer-Gembeck, 2018).

Close, intimate, and stable friendships support adolescents' development and adjustment (French & Cheung, 2018). By communicating with others and forming mutually self-disclosing supportive relationships, adolescents develop perspective taking, empathy, self-concept, and a sense of identity. Adolescents who describe their friendships as compassionate, disclosing, and satisfying also tend to report being more competent, more sociable, less hostile, less anxious, less depressed, and having higher self-esteem when compared to peers involved in less intimate friendships (Bauminger et al., 2008; Bowker & Ramsay,

2018). Friends who are supportive and empathetic encourage prosocial behavior, promote psychological health, reduce the risk of delinquency, and help adolescents manage stress, such as the challenges of school transitions, experiences with bullying, or poor relationships with parents (Hiatt et al., 2015; Roach, 2018; Wentzel, 2014). First established within the context of same-sex platonic friendships, intimacy is increasingly sought in romantic relationships over the course of adolescence (Sullivan, 1953). The quality of intimate relationships and attachments to parents and peers influences adolescents' experiences with intimacy in romantic relationships (Kochendorfer & Kerns, 2017).

REVIEW 9.1

1. What are examples of homophily in adolescent friendship?

2. How do boys' and girls' friendships differ?

3. Under what conditions might friendships endure? What might influence their dissolution?

4. How is friendship related to developmental tasks of adolescence, such as identity, autonomy, and intimacy?

THINKING IN CONTEXT 9.1

What are some of the reasons why boys and girls interact with their friends differently? Recall the biological and contextual influences on gender discussed in Chapter 5. How might these account for sex differences in friendship?

1. Identify physical or biological factors that might influence boys' and girls' differing interaction styles.

2. How might contextual factors such as the aspects of the school environment and neighborhood influence how boys and girls interact?

3. To what degree do you think the media, including social media, influence sex differences in friendship, if at all? Explain.

• •

APPLY 9.1

"You've been friends so long, you're like two peas in a pod," Sophia's mother said, smiling as Sophia and her friend Chelsea entered the room. "And today even our outfits match," Sophia responded. The girls went to Sophia's room and began their homework. Now eighth-graders, Sophia and Chelsea have been friends since Chelsea moved into the house next door in first grade.

1. What kinds of similarities do you expect close friends like Sophia and Chelsea to share? Why?

2. How do you expect Sophia and Chelsea's friendship to change over time?

3. What developmental purposes do friendships such as Sophia and Chelsea's serve?

• •

PEER GROUP

Friendships change from childhood to adolescence and so does the nature of the peer group. Adolescents spend less time with parents and other adults in favor of peers. The peer group is increasingly unsupervised as adolescents become more mobile and are granted more autonomy. Friendships tend to be sex segregated in early adolescence, but the peer group becomes more mixed as adolescents transition to high school (Lam, McHale, & Crouter, 2014). Small tight-knit friendship groups continue to be a vehicle for interpersonal interaction. However, cognitive and social advances enable adolescents to think about their peers in new ways, clustering them into groups based on styles of dress, interests, and behavior.

Cliques and Crowds

During adolescence, one-on-one friendships tend to expand into tightly knit peer groups of anywhere from three to about nine but most commonly around five members who are close friends. These close-knit, friendship-based groups are known as **cliques**. Like most close friends, members of cliques tend to share similarities such as demographics and attitudes (Lansford et al., 2009). Cliques are a context for adolescents' social interactions. The behavior and values that clique members share derive from interactions among the group members. For example, a norm of spending time exercising together and snacking afterward, as well as valuing health and avoiding smoking, alcohol, and drugs, may emerge in a clique whose members are athletes. Belonging to a peer group provides adolescents with a sense of inclusion, worth, support, and companionship (Ellis & Zarbatany, 2017).

In early adolescence, cliques tend to be sex segregated, with some composed of boys and others composed of girls. Girls' groups tend to be smaller than boys' groups, but both are similarly close (Gest, Davidson, Rulison, Moody, & Welsh, 2007). By mid-adolescence, cliques become mixed and form the basis for dating. A mixed-sex group of friends provides opportunities for adolescents to learn how to interact with others of the opposite sex in a safe, nonromantic context (Connolly, Craig, Goldberg, & Pepler, 2004). By late adolescence, especially after high school graduation, mixed-sex cliques tend to split up as adolescents enter college, the workforce, and other post–high school activities (Connolly, Craig, Goldberg, A., & Pepler, 1999).

In contrast with cliques, which are an expansion of intimate friendships, **crowds** are larger and looser groups based on shared characteristics, interests, and reputation (Cross & Fletcher, 2009). The emergence of crowds is tied to cognitive development as young

By mid-adolescence, cliques become mixed groupings of boys and girls.
iStock.com/FatCamera

adolescents notice patterns of characteristics of traits and behaviors in their peers. Adolescent crowds have been found in nearly all U.S. secondary schools large enough to have multiple social groups (Cross, 2018). Crowds are identifiable by commonalities in dress, interests, and preferences for activities. Common categories of peer groups include populars/elites (high in social status), athletes/jocks (athletically oriented), academics/brains (academically oriented), and partiers (highly social; care little about academics). Other types of crowds include nonconformists (unconventional in dress and music), deviants (defiant; engage in delinquent activity), and normals (not clearly distinct on any particular trait) (Delsing, ter Bogt, Engels, & Meeus, 2007; Sussman, Pokhrel, Ashmore, & Brown, 2007; Verkooijen, de Vries, & Nielsen, 2007). Populars and jocks are generally rated by adolescents as higher in social status than brains and partiers (Helms et al., 2014). As adolescents recognize their peers as members of crowds, they learn the social organization of their school, such as the relative hierarchy of crowds.

Crowd membership is based on an adolescent's image or reputation among peers (Cross & Fletcher, 2009). Rather than voluntarily "joining" a crowd, adolescents usually are sorted into crowds based on their peers' perception of their appearance and interests. Crowds are therefore not based on friendship or interaction. Members of a crowd may or may not interact with one another; however, because of similarities in appearance, activities, and perceived attitudes, their peers consider them members of the same group. Crowds differentiate young people on the basis of behaviors such as sexual activity, academic achievement, psychiatric symptoms, and health risks such as alcohol and substance use (Jordan et al., 2018; Van Hoorn, Crone, & Van Leijenhorst, 2017).

Some adolescents may use a particular crowd as a reference group and model their behavior and appearance accordingly, but adolescents do not always accurately perceive their own crowd status (Verkooijen et al., 2007). In one study, about one-half of students placed themselves in a crowd different from that assigned by peers—generally most tended to label themselves as normals or as not having a crowd. Only about 20% of adolescents classified in the low status crowds, such as brains, agreed with their peers on their crowd status (Brown, Bank, & Steinberg, 2008). Adolescents who did not perceive themselves as part of a low status crowd showed higher self-esteem than did adolescents who agreed with their crowd placement.

In middle adolescence, as their cognitive and social capacities become more sophisticated, adolescents begin to classify their peers in more complex ways and hybrid crowds emerge, such as popular-jocks and partier-jocks (Cross, 2018). As with cliques, crowds decline in late adolescence, especially after young people leave high school. However, recent research suggests that crowds may persist beyond high school. College students self-identify into crowds along four dimensions: social, scholastic, athletic, and counterculture, with social and counterculture affiliation predicting drug use (Hopmeyer & Medovoy, 2017). In contrast, populars, the most social affiliation in adolescent samples, tend to engage in relatively few risk behaviors (Jordan et al., 2018), suggesting that norms regarding substance use may shift from adolescence into emerging adulthood.

Popularity

Some adolescents are labeled by peers as **popular**. They tend to receive more attention from their peers than other adolescents. Do you recall popular adolescents from your high school? What characteristics did the popular teens share? Were they well liked by their classmates? It is likely that some of the popular peers you recall were quite likable and others were not particularly likable. This observation reflects the finding that there are two types of popularity: one based on peer acceptance and the other based on peer status. These two forms of popularity can co-occur but they generally have distinct profiles and characteristics (Parkhurst & Hopmeyer, 1998).

Sociometric popularity refers to being widely liked and accepted by peers. Researchers assess

Popular teens tend to receive more attention from their peers than other adolescents.
iStock.com/SolStock

sociometric popularity with surveys asking adolescents to nominate peers who they "like the most" or "want to spend the most time with." Adolescents who are sociometrically popular are viewed positively by peers and are frequently preferred over other students as activity partners, academic helpers, and possible friends (Ryan & Shin, 2018). Popular adolescents tend to have a variety of positive characteristics, including helpfulness, trustworthiness, and assertiveness (Kornbluh & Neal, 2016). These well-liked adolescents tend to be cooperative, prosocial, and kind and they have high-quality peer friendships at school and tend to do well academically (Cillessen & van den Berg, 2012). They are interpersonally skilled and their friends tend to rate their interactions with them

Relational aggression includes the intent to harm others by manipulating their relationships and social status among peers.
iStock.com/Highwaystarz-Photography

more favorably than the friends of less widely liked peers (Allen, Porter, McFarland, Marsh, & McElhaney, 2005). Popular adolescents are good at reading social situations, problem-solving, conflict resolution, and emotion regulation. In addition, adolescents who are widely liked by peers tend to receive more social opportunities and develop greater social competence, higher-quality friendships, and greater psychosocial well-being (Ferguson & Ryan, 2019).

Not all popular adolescents are well liked, however. A second form of popularity, **perceived popularity**, refers to peer status and denotes high prestige, visibility, and dominance within the peer context (Ryan & Shin, 2018). Perceived popularity, typically assessed by adolescents nominating peers who they think are "popular," is characterized by both positive and negative attributes. Generally, adolescents who are perceived as popular among their peers tend to be socially skilled and have characteristics valued by peers, such as attractiveness, athleticism, and visibility (Cillessen & van den Berg, 2012). Similar to sociometrically popular adolescents, those who are perceived as popular by peers tend to be interpersonally skilled; however, perceived popular adolescents tend to resort to manipulation, coercion, and aggression to maintain and enhance their status among peers (Rodkin & Roisman, 2010). Specifically, perceived popular adolescents tend to use instrumental aggression, directing aggression strategically to achieve goals such as increasing one's social status (Gangel, Keane, Calkins, Shanahan, & O'Brien, 2017). Perceived popularity is associated with risky behaviors such as alcohol and substance use and antisocial activity (Andrews, Hanish, & Santos, 2017; Dumas, Davis, & Ellis, 2019; Fujimoto & Valente, 2015).

Perceived popular adolescents' aggression is often expressed as **relational aggression**, intents to harm others by manipulating their relationships and social status among peers or by excluding them or withdrawing friendship. Relational aggression is not confined to girls' friendships; boys use it too (Juvonen, Wang, & Espinoza, 2013). Effectively employing relational aggression by spreading rumors, gossiping, and excluding peers to reduce their social standing and improve one's own status requires social skill (Ferguson & Ryan, 2019). Aggressive adolescents who are less socially skilled or have poor emotion regulation abilities are more likely to have difficulty with peers and experience risk of peer rejection (Dijkstra, Berger, & Lindenberg, 2011).

Peer Rejection

Some adolescents with poor social skills experience **peer rejection** and tend to be disliked and shunned by their peers. Rejected adolescents tend to show three patterns of behavior, characterized by combinations of aggression and withdrawal (Pope & Bierman, 1999; Prinstein & La Greca, 2004). Some rejected adolescents are aggressive. Aggressive adolescents experience heightened peer rejection because they tend to be confrontational, hostile toward others, impulsive, or hyperactive and have difficulty regulating their emotions (Ettekal & Ladd, 2015). They enter peer groups in destructive ways that disrupt the group's interaction or activity and direct attention to themselves. Aggressive-rejected adolescents tend to have difficulty taking the perspective of others, and they tend to react aggressively to slights by peers, quickly assuming hostile intentions (Lansford,

Malone, Dodge, Pettit, & Bates, 2010). Adolescents whose parents show little warmth and use coercive discipline and threats are likely to threaten others, have poor social skills, show aggressive behavior, and are more likely to be rejected by peers (Kuppens, Laurent, Heyvaert, & Onghena, 2013; Lansford, Laird, Pettit, Bates, & Dodge, 2014).

Other rejected adolescents are withdrawn, passive, timid, anxious, and socially awkward. Withdrawn adolescents tend to isolate themselves from peers, rarely initiate contact with peers, and speak less frequently than their peers (Rubin, Coplan, & Bowker, 2009). They tend to spend most of their time alone and on the periphery of the social scene, often because of shyness or social anxiety. When socially withdrawn adolescents experience peer rejection, they tend to become more withdrawn and even more disliked by their peers (Coplan et al., 2013; Ladd, 2006). Withdrawn-rejected adolescents, however, are as likely as their peers to have a best friend and those with a best friend tend to show more positive psychological adjustment (Markovic & Bowker, 2017; Rubin, Wojslawowicz, Rose-Krasnor, Booth-LaForce, & Burgess, 2006).

Aggressive adolescents and withdrawn adolescents are similar in that they misinterpret other people's behaviors and motives, have trouble understanding and regulating their emotions, are poor listeners, and are less socially competent than other adolescents (Ladd & Kochenderfer-Ladd, 2016). A third group of rejected adolescents are both aggressive and withdrawn. In addition to being confrontational and experiencing difficulty controlling their aggression and hostility, adolescents who are both aggressive and withdrawn tend to be socially awkward and anxious and avoid making friendships with other adolescents. Adolescents who are both aggressive and withdrawn are at greatest risk for peer rejection.

Peer rejection is associated with short- and long-term problems such as loneliness, anxiety, depression, low self-esteem, low academic achievement, delinquency, and school dropout (Bierman, Kalvin, & Heinrichs, 2014; Cooley & Fite, 2016; Fite, Hendrickson, Rubens, Gabrielli, & Evans, 2013; Menting, Koot, & van Lier, 2014). Chronic peer rejection is associated with high levels of activity in regions of the brain linked with detecting and experiencing the emotional distress caused by social exclusion. Moreover, the experience of chronic rejection in childhood is associated with heightened neural responses to exclusion in adolescence (Will, van Lier, Crone, & Güroğlu, 2016). Peer rejection further hinders social development by depriving adolescents of opportunities to learn and practice social and relationship skills such as resolving conflict and regulating emotions. Adolescents who are rejected by peers are at heightened risk for victimization by peers.

Peer Victimization

Peer victimization, also known as bullying, refers to an ongoing interaction in which an adolescent repeatedly attempts to inflict harm on another adolescent through physical, verbal, or social means by hitting, name-calling, teasing, shunning, or humiliating the other adolescent, for example (Olweus, 2013). About 20% to 25% of high school students report experiencing bullying in person (cyberbullying, a type of relational bullying carried out by electronic means, often accompanies in-person bullying and is discussed in Chapter 11). Generally, peer victimization tends to peak in early adolescence, typically during middle school (i.e., age 12 to 15 years), and tends to decrease by the end of high school (Hymel & Swearer, 2015).

Adolescents who are withdrawn experience heightened risk for not only peer rejection but also for victimization by peers. Adolescents who are victimized are often perceived as different from their peers, or as more quiet, cautious, and inhibited (Juvonen & Graham, 2014). Many victim characteristics, including nonassertive styles of interacting with peers, shyness, passivity, and social withdrawal, as well as anxiety, depression, and poor emotional control, are present prior to victimization and are amplified by victimization (Perren, Ettekal, & Ladd, 2013). Many adolescents respond to peer victimization by avoiding contact with peers, such as by not going to school or refusing to go to certain places (Waasdorp & Bradshaw, 2011). Others may respond to victimization in ways that reinforce bullies, such as by becoming defensive, crying, and further withdrawing. Not all victims of bullying are passive and withdrawn, however. Adolescents who are aggressive may respond with hostility and may lash out impulsively and with poor self-control, potentially escalating the problem and inviting aggressive exchanges with others (Arseneault, 2018; Swearer & Hymel, 2015; van Dijk, Poorthuis, & Malti, 2017).

Experiencing repeated victimization is associated with negative emotional, academic, and behavioral correlates that may persist into adulthood. Adjustment problems include anxiety, depression, suicidal ideation, poor health, and heightened alcohol and substance use (Kretschmer, Veenstra, Deković, & Oldehinkel, 2017; Moore et al., 2017). Peer victimization is associated with poor academic performance (Hysing et al., 2019; Wolke & Lereya, 2015), which can have life-long consequences because academic achievement influences educational and career opportunities such as admission to college. Unfortunately, many of the factors that increase adolescents' risk of peer victimization, such as social withdrawal, passivity, and anxiety, influence adolescents' responses and may interfere with their adjustment to victimization (Shetgiri, Lin, & Flores, 2013).

Reducing peer victimization is challenging because it occurs within a system of peers, teachers, and contexts, both in and out of school. Successful interventions with children and preadolescents address multiple perspectives, including victims, bullies, and schools (Nese, Horner, Dickey, Stiller, & Tomlanovich, 2014). Interventions may aid adolescents in acquiring relationship skills and teaching them how to address conflict and respond to victimization (Olweus & Limber, 2010). Helping adolescents learn to identify, understand, and manage their and other people's emotions, as well as direct anger in safe and appropriate ways, helps all adolescents (Hutson, Kelly, & Militello, 2018). Teachers can influence the classroom climate by becoming aware of bullying, being willing to intervene, and fostering an atmosphere of warm and respectful communication (Cornell, Shukla, & Konold, 2015; Espelage, Low, & Jimerson, 2014). Class norms can influence whether bystanders—adolescents who witness episodes of bullying but do not act—intervene (Pozzoli, Gini, & Vieno, 2012). Classmates can be encouraged to support one another when bullying events occur and encourage bullies to stop.

Intervention strategies, such as those just described, are effective with children and preadolescents, but research suggests that they are not effective, and may even increase bullying, in middle school, from about seventh grade onward (Yeager, Fong, Lee, & Espelage, 2015). Why are bullying interventions ineffective and even harmful with adolescents? The nature of peer victimization changes from childhood to adolescence, generally becoming less easily observed. Physical and verbal aggression, such as hitting and name-calling, tends to decline from childhood into adolescence, whereas less observable relational aggression tends to increase (Troop-Gordon, 2017). For example, one adolescent notes

> Our high school isn't like any school in the movies. Jocks don't throw freshmen into the trashcan, or dunk nerds' heads into the toilet. Bullies aren't people who punish physically, but are mostly just people who ignore and exclude others. (Yeager, Dahl, & Dweck, 2018, p. 4)

Interventions to combat bullying in younger groups tend to focus on the more observable forms of bullying common in childhood. The relational bullying more common in adolescence is much less visible and often goes unnoticed by adults. Existing interventions for bullying may not address the reasons for peer victimization in adolescence. For example, antibullying interventions for children tend to emphasize social and emotional skills. However, adolescents often victimize others through relational aggression, not because they lack social and emotional regulation skills but because relational aggression enhances their social status (Yeager et al., 2018). Recall that perceived popular adolescents tend to employ relational aggression to achieve their goals. In this way, relational aggression can be an effective tool to raise one's status relative to peers. It is difficult to design effective interventions to target behaviors that adolescents find useful; therefore, peer victimization is a complicated problem to treat.

REVIEW 9.2

1. Differentiate cliques from crowds.

2. Describe two types of popularity.

3. What are characteristics of adolescents at risk for peer rejection?

4. What are some influences and correlates of peer victimization?

THINKING IN CONTEXT 9.2

Think back to your own early adolescence, when you were in eighth grade.

1. Do you remember students who were popular? Why were they popular? What were they like? Did they participate in specific activities, like athletics? Explain.

2. Next, consider your experiences in tenth grade. Can you identify students who were popular? Why were they popular? What characteristics did they share?

3. What similarities and differences did the popular tenth-graders share with the popular students in eighth grade? Do you notice any differences?

4. Do you recall students who were rejected? What were some of their characteristics? Consider both eighth-grade and tenth-grade peers.

5. What similarities and differences do rejected eighth-grade and tenth-grade students share?

APPLY 9.2

In an attempt to reduce bullying and other negative peer interactions, Principal Richter decided to ban cliques and crowds from the high school. The school counselor sighed in exasperation, "With all due respect, Principal Richter, it is impossible to ban cliques and crowds." The principal shook his head and replied, "At best, cliques leave kids feeling left out. At worst, they're the source of bullying. We stop cliques and we stop bullying." The counselor repeated, "It's impossible to prevent adolescent cliques and crowds from forming and cliques and crowds aren't necessarily harmful anyway,"

1. Describe the characteristics of cliques and crowds.

2. Why do cliques and crowds form? How is their formation linked with adolescent development?

3. Is it possible to ban or eliminate cliques and crowds? Why or why not?

4. What would you tell Principal Richter?

5. Provide suggestions for Principal Richter for improving peer interactions and reducing bullying.

PEER INFLUENCE

We have seen that the peer group rises in importance in early adolescence. Peers are a source of friendship and tightly knit cliques offer adolescents support and opportunities for social interaction. Despite its benefits, the peer group is often a source of concern for adults who worry about its influence on adolescents. The term *peer pressure* evokes an image of a lone adolescent struggling against a mass of peers goading them to engage in undesirable behaviors, but the pressure to conform to peers is often quite subtle and varies among adolescents.

Pressure to Conform

Generally, the pressure to conform to peers rises in early adolescence, peaks at about age 14, and declines through age 18 and after (see Figure 9.1; Steinberg & Monahan, 2007). Adolescents experience the greatest pressure to conform to day-to-day activities and personal choices such as appearance (clothing, hairstyle,

makeup) and music. Peer influence occurs within the context of friendship. Friends tend to share similarities because adolescents tend to select friends on the basis of shared interests; through the shared activities and norms of friendship, adolescents tend to become more similar to their friends (Erdley & Day, 2017). Are similarities among friends the result of pressure to conform or of mutual socialization?

Adolescents' reports of risky behavior such as smoking and unsafe sexual activity correlate with their peers' behaviors (Choukas-Bradley, Giletta, Widman, Cohen, & Prinstein, 2014; Daspe, Arbel, Ramos, Shapiro, & Margolin, 2019; van de Bongardt, Reitz, Sandfort, & Deković, 2014). However, risky behaviors tend to occur in the presence of peers, raising the question of whether adolescents' risky behavior is the result of conforming to peer influence or whether it is simply a shared activity. Longitudinal research suggests that adolescents tend to select peers who engage in similar behaviors and friends' behaviors become more similar over time (Gremmen, Dijkstra, Steglich, & Veenstra, 2017). Despite this, there are clear developmental trends in risky activity among adolescents and their peers over time suggesting that young adolescents are more susceptible to peer influence than older adolescents, especially for antisocial behaviors such as delinquent activity, peaking at about age 14 (Sumter, Bokhorst, & Westenberg, 2018).

Influences on Susceptibility to Peer Influence

Why does susceptibility to peer influence show a U-shaped curve, rising in early adolescence and falling from middle to late adolescence? First, peers become more important in early adolescence. As adolescents

FIGURE 9.1

Age Differences in Resistance to Peer Influence

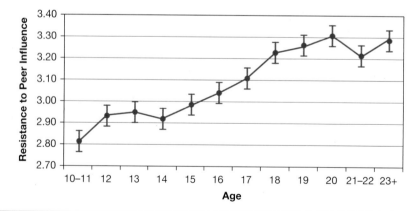

Source: Obtained with permission from Steinberg and Monahan (2007, p. 1536).

strive for emotional autonomy from parents, attachments become extended to close friends who become a source of intimacy. Peer approval becomes more important and adolescents become more susceptible to their influence. Peer influence takes place within friendship cliques (Ellis & Zarbatany, 2017).

Second, brain development may play a role in the shifting influence of peers. Recall from Chapter 3 that adolescents show increased neurosensitivity to rewards, which influences risky behavior. Research suggests that peers themselves are experienced as rewarding (Albert, Chein, & Steinberg, 2013). In one study, adolescents who completed a computer-simulated driving task in the presence of peers showed greater activity in parts of the brain responsible for reward than did those who completed the task alone, and they also took more risks in the driving task (Chein, Albert, O'Brien, Uckert, & Steinberg, 2011). Moreover, adolescents engage in more risk in laboratory tasks when they simply believe that an unknown peer is watching them, suggesting that adolescents are primed to seek peer approval, even among unknown peers (Weigard, Chein, Albert, Smith, & Steinberg, 2014). Indeed, research suggests that adolescents naturally engage in more risk in the presence of peers, even without encouragement (Van Hoorn et al., 2017). Interestingly, this is also true of adolescent mice, bred to consume alcohol, who drink more in the presence of peers than do adult mice (Logue, Chein, Gould, Holliday, & Steinberg, 2014).

Third, adolescents may be more likely to conform to peers to improve their status among peers and to avoid rejection. High status adolescents, specifically those who are perceived as popular, tend to engage in risky behaviors such as alcohol and substance use and antisocial activity (Andrews et al., 2017; Dumas et al., 2019; Fujimoto & Valente, 2015). The social risk of being rejected by peers outweighs other potentially negative outcomes of decisions, such as threats to one's health or the prospect of getting caught (Blakemore, 2018). Adolescents may conform to gain approval among high status peers. In one study, adolescents who believed they were chatting online with an adolescent described as either high status or low status were more likely to rate risky behaviors as acceptable when the behaviors were endorsed by high status (popular) peers compared with low status peers (Choukas-Bradley et al., 2014). It is not simply peer behavior that influences adolescent behavior, but it is adolescents' perceptions of peer behavior, as well as beliefs about peers' activity, that predict engaging in risky activities such as smoking, alcohol use, and marijuana use (Duan, Chou, Andreeva, & Pentz, 2009). Adolescents tend to misperceive peer norms, assuming that risky behaviors are more common among peers; some

Adolescents often misperceive the norm and believe that substance use is more common among peers than it is.
iStock.com/Rattankun Thongbun

also assume that their behavior reflects the norm (Scalco, Meisel, & Colder, 2016).

Finally, there are individual differences in the susceptibility to peer influence. Young people vary in how they perceive and respond to peer pressure based on factors such as age, personal characteristics, and context, such as the presence of norms. Adolescents are especially vulnerable to the negative effects of peer pressure during transitions such as entering a new school and undergoing puberty (Brechwald & Prinstein, 2011) and when they are uncertain of their status in the peer group (Ellis & Zarbatany, 2017). Personality factors such as sensitivity to social evaluation predict susceptibility, yet we also know that adolescence is a time of heightened sensitivity to social evaluation as indicated by patterns of brain activity (Blakemore, 2018). Adolescents are more likely to conform to best friends' behavior when they share a high-quality and satisfying relationship (Hiatt et al., 2017).

Peer Influence on Prosocial Behavior

Peer pressure is not always negative. Adolescents also report pressure from their friends to engage in prosocial and positive behaviors such as getting good grades, performing well athletically, getting along with parents, and avoiding smoking (Brown et al., 2008; Farrell, Thompson, & Mehari, 2017; Hofmann & Müller, 2018; Wentzel, 2014). In laboratory experiments, adolescents were likely to show prosocial behavior, such as sharing coins with others, after believing that anonymous peers approved of their prosocial actions (van Hoorn, van Dijk, Meuwese, Rieffe, & Crone, 2016). Adolescents aged 12 to 15 years are more likely to volunteer to help others in their community if they believe other students in their school volunteer (Choukas-Bradley, Giletta, Cohen, & Prinstein, 2015). Peer relationships are a positive force on adolescent development. Ultimately, susceptibility to peer influence tends to decline with advances in psychosocial maturity that support **behavioral autonomy**, the ability to make and carry out one's own decisions, withstanding pressure from others.

REVIEW 9.3

1. How does susceptibility to peer influence shift over adolescence?

2. What are some reasons for the increasing susceptibility to peer influence?

. . . .

THINKING IN CONTEXT 9.3

1. To what extent do you think susceptibility to peer influence varies with context, such as home, school, and neighborhood?

2. In what contexts are adolescents most likely to encounter pressure from peers?

3. For what kinds of activities might adolescents encounter the most pressure to conform? Explain.

. . . .

APPLY 9.3

"Aunt Aretha, they're my friends. No one pressures me to do anything," 15-year-old Darnell assured his worried aunt. "Sure, there's always stuff going on. And you might feel dumb if you're the only one not participating, but there's no peer pressure," he said.

"Then explain your nose ring," she replied.

"I think it's cool," replied Darnell.

"Every one of your friends has one. Are you going to follow and do whatever they do?" Aunt Aretha asked.

Later Aunt Aretha clucks to herself, "It's all about peer pressure. Teens will do anything their friends pressure them to do—especially act out. Peer pressure is always present and intense. Kids are doomed."

1. What is the nature of peer pressure in adolescence? How does it change?

2. Do all adolescents experience similar levels of pressure to conform? Explain.

3. Who is right, Darnell or Aunt Aretha?

. . . .

DATING

Establishing romantic relationships, dating, is part of the adolescent experience. The development of intimacy is an important psychosocial task for adolescents, typically carried out through friendship in early adolescence and increasingly through romantic relationships throughout adolescence.

Prevalence of Dating

Romantic relationships are common in adolescence, but dating has become less common over the past 3 decades. About two-thirds of adolescents age 13 to 17 report that they have not dated or experienced a romantic relationship (Lenhart, 2015). As shown in Figure 9.2, the proportion of twelfth-grade students who report that they do not date more than tripled between 1992 and 2017, from 15% to 49% (Child Trends, 2019). The proportion of tenth-graders who do not date doubled during that time period and not dating increased among eighth-graders by one-quarter.

Adolescents who date do so less frequently than in prior decades. The declines in dating coincide with the rise of social media and video technology that permits face-to-face contact from a distance. It may be that in-person dating has transitioned to electronic forms (Twenge & Park, 2019). Some are concerned because, as we will see, dating serves developmental purposes. Although adolescents can interact with one another online, online communication cannot replace in-person contact. For example, frequent use of technology-based communication with romantic partners is associated with lower social competence, especially among boys (Nesi, Widman, Choukas-Bradley, & Prinstein, 2017). Romantic relationships become more common with age. In one study of emerging adults, they reported an average of 10.5 relationships before they were age 25, suggesting that romantic exploration may be shifting to emerging adulthood rather than adolescence (Furman, Collibee, Lantagne, & Golden, 2019).

What do adolescents seek in romantic partners? Adolescents report that they place most emphasis on positive personality characteristics, such as reliability, honesty, and kindness; the relative importance of different characteristics is quite similar for males and females, although males rate attractiveness as relatively more important (Ha, Overbeek, & Engels, 2010). Like friendship, romantic partners tend to share similarities prior to dating, such as in physical attractiveness, popularity, academic achievement, and race (Furman & Rose, 2015; Simon, Aikins, & Prinstein, 2008).

Developmental Shifts in Dating

Generally speaking, adolescents' orientation toward romantic relationships progresses over the course of adolescence. In early adolescence, from about age 11 to 13, young people become interested in the concept of romance, tend to develop crushes, and focus

FIGURE 9.2

Percentage of Eighth-, Tenth-, and Twelfth-Graders Who Report They Never Date: Selected Years, 1976–2017

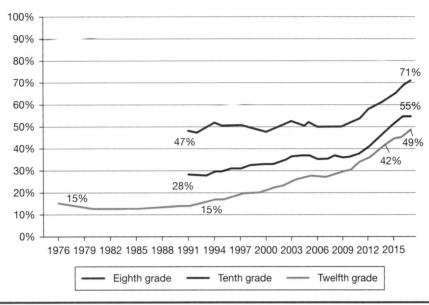

Source: Child Trends (2019).

their conversations with close friends on potential romances (Connolly & McIsaac, 2011). Adolescents begin to consider their potential as romantic partners, incorporating their growing understanding into their self-concepts. Many do not interact with their crush and romance relationships, if they occur, are short but often raise an adolescent's status in the peer group. Adolescents who experience puberty early relative to peers are more likely to date early, and they tend to experience adjustment difficulties (Low & Shortt, 2017), as discussed later in this chapter.

In middle adolescence, from about age 14 to 16, romantic relationships tend to occur within a group context and through casual dating. Dating typically begins through the intermingling of mixed-sex peer groups (for example, at parties and dances), progresses to group dating and casual relationships, and finally, leads to one-on-one dating and romantic relationships (Connolly, Nguyen, Pepler, Craig, & Jiang, 2013). Adolescents with larger social networks and greater access to opposite-sex peers tend to date more than those who are less social. However, some research suggests that adolescents date outside of their friendship networks and that preexisting friendships are not likely to transform into romantic relationships (Kreager, Molloy, Moody, & Feinberg, 2016). Dating relationships may bridge friendship networks, potentially exposing adolescents to new sets of peers.

In middle adolescence, young people continue to learn about themselves as romantic partners and the peer group provides feedback that influences adolescents' developing self-conceptions and identities as romantic partners. The peer group serves as a type of "secure" base from which adolescents experiment with involvement in dating relationships more fluidly (Connolly et al., 2004). The emotional qualities of relationships emerge and adolescents often become preoccupied by their feelings and the passion expressed in the relationship. Romantic relationships are longer than in early adolescence but generally last a few months (Connolly & McIsaac, 2011). In late adolescence at about age 17 or 18, relationships tend to occur outside of peer groups (Furman & Rose, 2015). Relationships may become more serious in the sense that they become characterized by emotional bonds, they become a source of intimacy, and commitment is valued.

Reasons for Dating

Why do adolescents date? Dating may serve different purposes at different ages. Across all ages, dating can be a source of fun and recreation through engaging in shared activities. In early adolescence, dating can be a way of establishing status in the peer group, especially when adolescents' dates are of high social status or popularity. There is also

Adolescents who are attracted to the same sex are more likely to have same-sex romantic relationships today than in prior generations, but we know little about dating in LGBT adolescents.
Per-Anders Pettersson/Contributor/Getty Images

Dating in LGBT Youth

Discussions of romantic relationships in adolescence tend to focus on heterosexual relationships. We know little about romantic relationship development in LGBT youth. Adolescents today who are attracted to the same sex are more likely to have same-sex romantic relationships than in prior generations. However, romantic relationships among sexual minority youth may be less public, because of concerns of being stigmatized or being unprepared to come out to family. Adolescents with same-sex interest frequently date other-sex adolescents for a variety of reasons, such as exploration, attraction, social pressure, a desire to conceal, or because they are not ready to come out (Savin-Williams, 2019; Ybarra, Price-Feeney, & Mitchell, 2019). Similar to gender differences in friendship, girls' same-sex relationships tend to be closer and more intimate than boys' (Furman et al., 2019). Although we know little about LGBT dating, it is clear that we cannot generalize from heterosexual youth.

Dating and Psychosocial Adjustment

Just as the functions of dating change with age, so do the relations with adaptive functioning. In middle and late adolescence, romantic relationships are associated with positive self-concept, expectations for success in relationships, fewer feelings of alienation, and good physical and mental health (Connolly & McIsaac, 2011). Romantic partners can be an important source of social support and self-esteem for adolescents (Luciano & Orth, 2017). However, early dating relative to peers, prior to age 15, is associated with higher rates of alcohol and substance use, smoking delinquency, and low academic competence, as well as depression, especially in girls (Connolly et al., 2013; Furman & Collibee, 2014). Dating off-time may interfere with developmental tasks, such as identity development, and adolescents who date early may not be able to handle the emotional demands of these relationships.

some evidence that popular adolescents are more likely to date than their less popular peers (Little & Welsh, 2018). Through romantic relationships, adolescents learn social and interpersonal skills, how to get along with others, and how to resolve conflicts. Just as adolescents direct their attachments toward peers and they seek autonomy from parents, romantic partners can be a source of emotional support (Furman & Rose, 2015).

Romantic relationships are an especially important context for intimacy development in boys. As we have discussed, boys' friendships tend to center on activities and are generally less intimate than girls' friendships, which tend to be fewer in number but more focused on self-disclosure. Girls express intimacy in their romantic relationships with boys, aiding boys in developing intimacy (Buhrmester & Furman, 1987). Adolescents' capacity for romantic intimacy develops slowly and is influenced by the quality of their experiences with intimacy in friendships and their attachments to parents and peers (van de Bongardt, Yu, Deković, & Meeus, 2015). Specifically, one longitudinal study showed that attachment to parents and friendship quality at 10 years of age predicted being in a relationship and relationship quality at ages 12 and 15 (Kochendorfer & Kerns, 2017). Through romantic relationships, adolescents can learn to share, be sensitive to others' needs, and develop the capacity for intimacy. Close romantic relationships provide opportunities to develop and practice sensitivity, cooperation, empathy, and social support, as well as to aid in identity development. Generally, feelings of passionate love, emotional rewards of dating, perceived support, and dating confidence increase over adolescence (Little & Welsh, 2018).

The association between early dating and risky behaviors may not be causal but might instead reflect a general tendency to engage in risk-taking and behaviors appropriate for older adolescents. For example, early dating may be linked with both an orientation toward delinquency and a greater likelihood of delinquent partners (Low & Shortt, 2017). It is likely that risky activity and early dating are influenced by a set of risk factors such as early pubertal development, low parental monitoring, and family instability (Ethier, Harper, Hoo, & Dittus, 2016; Moore, Harden, & Mendle, 2014). Similarities draw partners to each other and their behavior, including risk behaviors such as substance use and delinquency, becomes more similar over time (DeLay, Laursen, Bukowski, Kerr, & Stattin, 2016; Monahan, Dmitrieva, & Cauffman, 2014).

Although positive relationships with a romantic partner are associated with benefits, navigating relationship dynamics is often challenging for adolescents because of their inexperience. Romantic relationship dynamics can be highly variable and emotionally intense, such that romantic involvement can present significant coping challenges (Ha, Dishion, Overbeek, Burk, & Engels, 2014; Larson, Clore, & Wood, 1999). With still-maturing cognitive and socioemotional capabilities, the novelty of these strong feelings may heighten risks for psychological difficulties. Furthermore, relationship dynamics require high-level communication and problem-solving skills, which may still be developing for adolescents (Rogers, Ha, Updegraff, & Iida, 2018). Therefore, most adolescents are likely to be inconsistent in their application of these skills in their day-to-day lives and the interpersonal and emotional complexity of a romantic relationship may present a considerable coping challenge (Furman, 2018).

Although adolescents have experienced relationship conflicts within friendships, their romantic partner conflicts are different. Conflicts in a romantic context may be uniquely challenging given the powerful emotional aspects that differentiate romantic from peer relationships (Furman & Shomaker, 2008). Indeed, conflicts and negative relationship quality happen more frequently with romantic partners than with friends (Kochendorfer & Kerns, 2019) and, unlike conflicts with friends, are more likely to be handled with maladaptive strategies such as avoidance and coercion (Rogers et al., 2018; Shulman, Tuval-Mashiach, Levran, & Anbar, 2006). However, for many adolescents, such competencies do not come easily; conflicts are more often challenging than not. For example, observational work has demonstrated that adolescents can struggle so much in the midst of romantic conflict that they often resort to coping strategies that exacerbate relationship problems (Ha et al., 2014). Similar principles also likely apply to romantic-related feelings, particularly negative feelings. Romantic-related emotions constitute a significant portion of dating adolescents' daily emotional lives and are very strongly felt (Furman & Shomaker, 2008; Larson et al., 1999). Intense, negative feelings such as jealousy and doubtfulness may also present coping challenges and leave adolescents vulnerable to fluctuations in their negative mood states (Rogers et al., 2018).

Romantic experiences in adolescence are often continuous with romantic experiences in adulthood, suggesting that building romantic relationships is an important developmental task for adolescents (Collins et al., 2009). Adolescents who date fewer partners and experience better quality dating relationships in middle adolescence tend to demonstrate smoother partner interactions and relationship processes in young adulthood (e.g., negotiating conflict, appropriate caregiving) compared with their peers who are more indiscriminate in their choice of dates (Madsen & Collins, 2011).

Adolescent romantic relationships can have consequences for functioning later in life. For example, in one longitudinal study, high-quality romantic relationships at age 17 were associated with fewer externalizing problems, such as substance use and antisocial behavior, in early adulthood at ages 25 to 27 (Kansky & Allen, 2018). Poor relationships, however, predicted increased levels of anxiety and depression in early adulthood. Causality cannot be assumed. It is likely that interpersonal and developmental characteristics that led to poor relationships in adolescence also influenced poor functioning in adulthood.

Dating Violence

Dating violence, the actual or threatened physical or sexual violence or psychological abuse directed toward a current or former boyfriend, girlfriend, or dating partner, is surprisingly prevalent during adolescence. Like adult domestic violence, adolescent dating violence occurs in youth of all socioeconomic, ethnic, and religious groups (Herrman, 2009). On average, about 20% of high school students have experienced physical violence, and 9% have experienced sexual violence, within a dating relationship (Wincentak, Connolly, & Card, 2017). Both males and females perpetrate dating violence at roughly equal rates and within the context of relationships of mutual partner aggression in which both partners perpetrate and sustain the aggression (Sears, Byers, & Price, 2007; Williams, Connolly, Pepler, Laporte, & Craig, 2008). Girls are more likely to inflict psychological abuse and minor physical abuse (slapping, throwing objects, pinching), and boys are more likely to inflict more severe types of physical abuse, such as punching, as well as sexual abuse, making girls more likely to suffer physical wounds than boys. Physical violence tends to occur alongside other problematic relationship dynamics and behaviors such as verbal conflict, jealousy, and accusations of "cheating" (Giordano, Soto, Manning, & Longmore, 2010).

Risk factors for engaging in dating violence include difficulty with anger management, poor interpersonal skills, early involvement with antisocial peers, a history of problematic relationships with parents and peers, exposure to family violence and community violence, and child maltreatment (Foshee et al., 2014, 2015; Vagi et al., 2013). Many of the risk factors for dating victimization are also outcomes of dating violence, such as depression, anxiety, negative interactions with family and friends, low self-esteem, and substance use, making it difficult to determine causality (Collibee, Furman, & Shoop, 2019; Exner-Cortens, Eckenrode, & Rothman, 2013; Niolon et al., 2015).

Victims of dating violence in adolescence are more likely to experience intimate partner violence in adulthood. Individuals vary over time in their risk for engaging in relationship violence, suggesting that risk for violence may sometimes be tied to the specific relationship and interpersonal risk factors shared by partners (Furman et al., 2019). In this way, risk may be dynamic and varies within an individual, making it important to know not only who is at risk (i.e., a between-person effect) but also the individual is at risk (i.e., within-person effects) in order to identify optimal times to intervene.

Adolescent dating violence is less likely to be reported than adult domestic violence. Only about 1 in 11 cases is reported to adults or authorities (Herrman, 2009). In addition, only one-third of adolescents report that they would intervene if they became aware of a peer's involvement in dating violence, predominately believing that dating violence is the couple's own private business (Weisz & Black, 2008). Encouraging close relationships with parents is an important way of preventing dating violence because adolescents learn about romantic relationships by observing and reflecting on the behaviors of others. Adolescent girls who are close with their parents are more likely to recognize unhealthy relationships, are less likely to be victimized by dating violence, and are more likely to seek help (Leadbeater, Banister, Ellis, & Yeung, 2008).

Developmental interventions to address adolescent dating violence are often housed within high schools. Interventions have been successful in increasing teens' awareness of dating violence, helping them to identify violence, and shifting teens' attitudes to be less supportive of violence in dating relationships (Fellmeth, Heffernan, Nurse, Habibula, & Sethi, 2013). However, school-based programs are generally not successful at reducing the incidence of violence in adolescents' dating relationships (De La Rue, Polanin,

Espelage, & Pigott, 2017). It is likely that adolescents must learn skills to change their behavior. Successful interventions help adolescents build skills in regulating their emotions, communicating effectively, and resolving conflicts (Rizzo et al., 2018; Smith-Darden, Kernsmith, Reidy, & Cortina, 2017). ●

REVIEW 9.4

1. Discuss trends in the prevalence of dating.

2. Why do adolescents date?

3. How is dating related to adjustment?

4. What are some predictors of dating violence?

THINKING IN CONTEXT 9.4

1. How does physical, cognitive, and socioemotional development contribute to an adolescent's capacity for dating and romantic relationships? Give two examples for each.

2. What are some reasons why we know little about dating in LGBT adolescents?

3. Specifically, consider the development of sexual orientation, described in Chapter 6. What developmental reasons might contribute to our lack of knowledge?

4. What might be entailed in conducting research to learn about LGBT youth? Consider research design, from Chapter 1. Also, what are some ethical challenges that might arise when studying LGBT youth?

APPLY 9.4

"You won't be allowed to date until you're 20," Tabitha's dad says. Twelve-year-old Tabitha hopes that her dad is kidding but he's said this before. Provide an argument, referring to what we know about dating in adolescence, such as its prevalence and role in development and adjustment, as to why Tabitha should be allowed to date earlier.

CHAPTER SUMMARY

9.1 Discuss the nature of friendship in adolescence.

Adolescent friendships are characterized by intimacy, self-disclosure, and trust. Over the course of adolescence, the number of friendships declines and conceptions of friendship deepen. Friendships tend to be characterized by homophily,

similarity in demographics, and orientation toward risky activity. Adolescent boys tend to have larger peer groups than girls, who tend to prefer talking, sharing thoughts and feelings, and supporting each other. Although girls tend to have fewer friendships and their friendships are of shorter duration, girls rate their friendships as more intimate, more caring, and more important than boys do. As they progress through adolescence, other-sex friendships become more common and are rated as more important. Friendships become more stable and enduring over the course of adolescence but dissolve for a variety of reasons. Adolescents navigate multiple developmental tasks and friendships play a role in each—the development of identity, autonomy, and intimacy.

9.2 Examine characteristics of the peer group and the impact of popularity, rejection, and victimization on development.

During adolescence, one-on-one friendships tend to expand into tightly knit cliques of close friends that tend to share similarities such as demographics and attitudes. Cliques tend to be sex segregated in early adolescence, but they become mixed by mid-adolescence and form the basis for dating. In contrast with cliques, which are an expansion of intimate friendships, crowds are larger and looser groups based on shared characteristics, interests, and reputation. Sociometric popularity refers to being widely liked and accepted by peers and is associated with positive characteristics, including helpfulness, trustworthiness, assertiveness, and interpersonal skills. A second form of popularity, perceived popularity, refers to peer status and denotes high prestige, visibility, and dominance within the peer context. Some adolescents with poor social skills experience peer rejection and tend to be disliked and shunned by their peers. Rejected adolescents tend to show patterns of behavior characterized by combinations of aggression and withdrawal. Peer rejection is associated with short- and long-term problems, such as loneliness, anxiety, depression, low self-esteem, low academic achievement, delinquency, and heightened risk for victimization by peers, which is also associated with adjustment problems.

9.3 Discuss adolescents' susceptibility to peer influence.

The pressure to conform to peers shows a U-shaped curve, rising in early adolescence and falling from middle to late adolescence. Peer influence occurs within the context of friendship and adolescents experience the greatest pressure to conform to day-to-day activities and personal choices. Adolescents experience pressure to conform to risky activities but also prosocial behavior.

9.4 Summarize what we know about dating in adolescence, including developmental trends and relation with adjustment.

Romantic relationships are common in adolescence, but adolescent dating has declined over the past 3 decades. Like friendship, romantic partners tend to share similarities prior to dating, such as in physical attractiveness, popularity, academic achievement, and race. Dating serves many purposes, including offering adolescents opportunities for fun and recreation, providing ways of establishing peer status, learning interpersonal skills, and developing intimacy. In middle and late adolescence, romantic relationships are associated with positive self-concept, expectations for success in relationships, fewer feelings of alienation, and good physical and mental health. However, early dating relative to peers, prior to age 15, is associated with higher rates of alcohol and substance use, smoking delinquency, and low academic competence, as well as depression, especially in girls. Dating off-time may interfere with developmental tasks, such as identity development, and adolescents who date early may not be able to handle the emotional demands of these relationships. Dating violence, the actual or threatened physical or sexual violence or psychological abuse directed toward a current or former boyfriend, girlfriend, or dating partner, is surprisingly prevalent during adolescence but less likely to be reported than in adulthood. Many of the risk factors for dating victimization are also outcomes of dating violence, such as depression, anxiety, negative interactions with family and friends, low self-esteem, and substance use. Victims of dating violence in adolescence are more likely to experience intimate partner violence in adulthood.

KEY TERMS

behavioral autonomy, 194

clique, 187

crowd, 187

dating violence, 197

homophily, 184

peer rejection, 189

peer victimization, 190

perceived popularity, 189

popular, 188

relational aggression, 189

sociometric popularity, 188

10

School and Work Contexts

Learning Objectives

10.1 Discuss achievement attributions and motivation, including their influences.

10.2 Examine correlates of school transitions and contextual influences on academic achievement in adolescence.

10.3 Identify common developmental disabilities and specific learning disorders experienced by adolescents and ways of addressing their educational needs.

10.4 Contrast the experience of college-bound and noncollege-bound youth.

Chapter Contents

In a typical U.S. secondary school, the bell rings and students stream from the crowded hallway into classrooms to sit at desks as class begins. Adolescent development unfolds within the school context, whether it is learning in class, socializing at lunch, or exercising during physical education or in after-school athletics. Adolescents spend their weekdays at school, which comprises 10 months of the year.

This chapter examines adolescents' interactions and development within the school and work contexts.

ACHIEVEMENT MOTIVATION

As we consider adolescents' academic performance within the school context, it is tempting to emphasize the link from school to adolescents—that is, to focus on how schools influence adolescents. However, similar to other contexts, adolescents influence the school context just as they are influenced by it. Adolescents play a role in their experiences at school and their academic performance through their views of their own abilities and competencies. **Achievement motivation** refers to the willingness to persist at challenging tasks and meet high standards of accomplishment (Wigfield et al., 2015a). Achievement motivation is a powerful predictor of academic success, beyond intelligence, cognitive abilities, and prior performance (Steinmayr, Weidinger, Schwinger, & Spinath, 2019). How adolescents explain their own successes and failures is important for sustaining motivation and ultimately influencing their own achievement.

Achievement Attributions

How we account for our successes and failures, and how we explain them to ourselves, influences our subsequent behavior and our views of ourselves. Performance can be attributed to causes that vary in internality, controllability, and stability (Wigfield et al., 2015a). Some adolescents gravitate toward **internal attributions**, emphasizing their own role in outcomes, such as succeeding or failing on an exam based on internal factors such as ability or skill. Other adolescents rely on **external attributions**, causes that emphasize external factors, such as an easy or difficult exam, to explain their performance. Adolescents also vary in how controllable they view their performance. Some may emphasize controllable factors such as study habits and choice of study techniques to explain succeeding on an exam, while others attribute their performance to uncontrollable factors such as luck or inborn ability. In addition to attributing success or failure to causes that vary in internality and controllability, adolescents also vary in their mindset, the degree to which they believe that their abilities and characteristics are modifiable (Dweck, 2017; Dweck & Yeager, 2019). Some show a **growth mindset**, viewing their skills and characteristics as malleable or changeable. In contrast, others show a **fixed mindset**, believing that their characteristics are enduring and unchangeable.

Adolescents who adopt internal, controllable explanations of performance and a growth mindset tend to have a strong **mastery orientation**, a belief that success stems from effort and applying strategies well (Haimovitz & Dweck, 2017). When faced with challenges, adolescents who are mastery oriented focus on changing or adapting their behavior (Muenks, Wigfield, & Eccles, 2018). They are able to bounce back from failure and take steps to improve their performance, such as learning study strategies to boost their exam scores.

Other adolescents respond to success and failure in maladaptive ways, by attributing success to external, uncontrollable factors such as luck. Even worse, they tend to attribute failure to internal factors such as ability, adopting a **learned helplessness orientation** that combines a fixed mindset and the attribution of poor performance to internal uncontrollable factors. Adolescents who experience learned helplessness are overwhelmed by challenges, are overly self-critical, feel incompetent, and avoid challenging tasks (Dweck & Yeager, 2019; Yeager & Dweck, 2012). A learned helplessness orientation can perpetuate poor performance. Poor performance, in turn, can confirm adolescents' negative views of their ability and their sense of helplessness.

A mastery orientation has been shown to predict subsequent classroom engagement and higher grades among high school students (Ciarrochi, Heaven, & Davies, 2007; Heaven & Ciarrochi, 2008; Hwang, Reyes, & Eccles, 2019; Rattan, Savani, Chugh, & Dweck, 2015). Students with a mastery orientation are more likely to seek help from teachers and in turn show higher academic performance (Duchesne, Larose, & Feng, 2019). The relation of attributions and achievement is bidirectional. For example, one longitudinal study that examined Australian adolescents through middle school and high school confirmed that a learned helplessness orientation was associated with poor school performance, and poor performance was in turn associated with subsequent attributions of helplessness (Chan & Moore, 2006). In another study, African American adolescents' attributions and school performance were assessed in Grades 8 and 11 (Swinton, Kurtz-Costes, Rowley, & Okeke-Adeyanju, 2011). Attributions for math successes and failures became more negative in the high school years, and early negative attributions about math predicted lower math engagement 3 years later. Research with college students has supported relations between attributions and achievement outcomes (Hsieh & Schallert, 2008). For example, students' causal attributions at college entry predict later grade point averages in college (Perry, Stupnisky, Daniels, & Haynes, 2008).

Contextual Influences on Achievement Attributions and Motivation

Our views about our abilities and our explanations for our successes and failures are influenced by our interactions with the people around us. The contexts in which we are immersed, including factors such as parents and teachers, socioeconomic status (SES), and culture, also play a role in shaping our views of our abilities.

Parents

Parents influence their children's achievement through their own beliefs and attitudes about ability. For example, preadolescents raised by parents with a fixed view of abilities tend to view their own ability as fixed and unchangeable and are more likely to show a learned helplessness orientation (Pomerantz & Dong, 2006). When parents believe that ability cannot be changed, they tend to provide few opportunities for their children to improve and may ignore positive changes that their children show. In addition, failing to provide opportunities to problem-solve or intervening when a child tries a challenging task may inhibit children's desire to succeed and may foster helplessness (Orkin, May, & Wolf, 2017).

Parenting styles also have an effect. Warm and supportive parenting can help adolescents to recognize their worth and appreciate their own competence. Authoritative parents who promote their adolescents' autonomy, encourage them to explore their environment, and permit them to take an active role in solving their own problems foster a mastery orientation (Raftery, Grolnick, & Flamm, 2012). In contrast, excessive control and harsh criticism can damage adolescents' motivation. Adolescents who believe that they receive strong emotional support from their parents are more likely to pursue mastery goals, are less likely to pursue performance-avoidance goals, feel lower test anxiety, and attain higher levels of academic achievement (Song, Bong, Lee, & Kim, 2015).

Parents also influence children through the home context they provide. SES influences adolescents' motivation through the availability of opportunities and resources and through parents' behavior. Research has shown that young people who grow up in high SES families are more likely than their middle or low SES peers to show a greater mastery orientation and higher levels of achievement motivation, as well as better academic performance and greater involvement in organized activities after school (Wigfield et al., 2015a). Adolescents require not only opportunities to try new things but also parents who are aware of and able to take advantage of opportunities (Archer et al., 2012; Simpkins, Delgado, Price, Quach, & Starbuck, 2013). Parents in low SES families often work jobs that involve long hours, rotating and nonstandard shifts, and high physical demands. As a result, many low SES parents lack the energy and time to devote to fostering adolescents' extracurricular activities and they may be unaware of opportunities or unable to take advantage of them (Parra-Cardona, Cordova, Holtrop, Villarruel, & Wieling, 2008).

Teachers

Like parents, teachers support a mastery orientation in students when they are warm and helpful and when they attribute students' failure to lack of effort (Wentzel, 2002). Students who believe that their teachers provide a positive learning environment tend to work harder in class and show higher achievement than students who lack this belief (Song et al., 2015; Wigfield, Muenks, & Rosenzweig, 2015b). When students view their teachers as unsupportive, they are more likely to attribute their performance to external factors, such as luck or the teacher, and to withdraw from class participation. As students' achievement declines, they further doubt their abilities, creating a vicious cycle between helpless attributions and poor achievement. Teachers who relate failure back to their students' effort, are supportive of their students, and stress learning goals over performance goals are more likely to have mastery-oriented students (Meece, Anderman, & Anderman, 2006). The characteristics of effective schools, discussed later in this chapter, support the development of positive attributions of ability.

Peers

The peer group influences achievement motivation through adolescents' beliefs about their friends' behavior and attitudes as well as their perception of implicit norms of the group (Ryan & Patrick, 2001). Adolescents tend to affiliate with students who share their academic competence and orientation and become more similar over time through their interactions (Gremmen, Dijkstra,

Warm and supportive parenting can help adolescents to recognize their worth and appreciate their own competence.
iStock.com/MStudioImages

Steglich, & Veenstra, 2017; Rambaran et al., 2017). Peer orientation predicts adolescents' achievement motivation. Adolescents who have best friends who value academics are likely to have high achievement motivation and adolescents who view their friends as resistant to classroom norms are likely to have poor achievement motivation (Nelson & DeBacker, 2008). Peer norms that value a growth mindset support the growth mindset in adolescents (Yeager et al., 2019). Perceived acceptance by peers is positively associated with achievement motivation. Middle and high school students who feel valued and respected by peers and who have high-quality friendships are likely to have high achievement motivation (Nelson & DeBacker, 2008). Adolescent students who perceived stronger emotional support from their peers reported stronger mastery goals, weaker performance-avoidance goals, and lower test anxiety (Song et al., 2015).

Adolescents who have close friends who value academics are likely to have high achievement motivation and perform well at school.
iStock.com/SolStock

Cultural Influences

Culture has an important bearing on adolescents' achievement attributions and motivation through its influence on parenting and family processes. For example, among Latinx families, familism is protective of academic outcomes. Latinx American college students who report higher levels of familism tend to demonstrate higher levels of intrinsic motivation and earn higher grades than their peers who lack a strong sense of familism (Próspero, Russell, & Vohra-Gupta, 2012). Similarly, a study of Mexican American male college students found that a strong sense of familism was accompanied by parental encouragement concerning college and was positively related to persistence in college over time (Ojeda, Navarro, & Morales, 2011).

Internal attributions for success tend to be more common in Westerners and may be less common among people of other cultural backgrounds (Reyna, 2008). One study of over 5,300 New Zealand students in Grades 10 and 11 found ethnic differences in students' attributions of the role of family in their academic performance (McClure et al., 2011). Students from the Pacific Islands (e.g., Samoa and Tonga) rated family as a particularly important influence on their best grades and rated family, teacher, luck, and friends as more important for their best marks than did European, Asian, or Maori (indigenous) students. Moreover, Maori and other Pacific Islander students were less likely to adopt internal attributions (e.g., ability, effort) for their best and worst marks compared with European and Asian students.

Parents in many Asian countries tend to hold a growth mindset and to view the application of effort as a moral responsibility (Pomerantz, Ng, Cheung, & Qu, 2014). Parents in many Asian cultures tend to focus more on children's failure in order to encourage them to make corrections. North American parents, on the other hand, tend to pay attention to children's success and its relevance for self-esteem. For example, when U.S. and Chinese mothers watched their fourth- and fifth-grade students solve a puzzle, the U.S. mothers offered more praise after the child succeeded, but the Chinese mothers tended to point out poor performance and offer task-oriented statements to make the child try harder (e.g., "You only got 7 of 10"). After the mothers left the room, the children continued to play, and the Chinese children showed greater improvements in performance than the U.S. children (Ng, Pomerantz, & Lam, 2007).

Cultures also vary in the use and perception of criticism and praise. Students from some cultures may feel uncomfortable with praise because it singles them out from the group and, by implication, elevates them above their peers (Markus & Kitayama, 1991). Some students may be more motivated by critical feedback because their goal is to meet the expectations of their teachers and/or family (Pomerantz et al., 2014).

REVIEW 10.1

1. Differentiate among two types of attributions and mindsets.

2. Compare a mastery orientation with a learned helplessness orientation.

3. How do contextual influences contribute to achievement attributions and motivation?

. . . .

THINKING IN CONTEXT 10.1

1. Recall that friendships are characterized by homophily (Chapter 9). To what degree does this apply to achievement motivation? Think back to your friends in middle or high school. Did you share similarities in how you approached challenging tasks? Did you attribute your successes in similar ways or did you differ? Do friends influence achievement motivation? Explain.

2. In what ways might factors such as gender, ethnicity or race, and socioeconomic status contribute to adolescents' mindset and achievement orientation? Explain your reasoning.

3. Adolescents receive messages about their abilities at home, school, and in their interactions with others in the neighborhood. Give examples.

. . . .

APPLY 10.1

Chris's stomach churned as the professor distributed graded exams. "I need to pass this test or my grade is toast," Chris thought to himself. Upon receiving his exam, Chris sighed, "Oh no! D? I pulled an all-nighter to study for this. What a waste of time," he complained to his friend. "It wasn't exactly an all-nighter, Chris," his friend reminded him. "Don't you remember that epic game of *League of Legions*? We were all online until at least 3 a.m." Chris shrugged his shoulders and said, "Still, I studied for this exam. My grade should be higher. The questions were all tricky with multiple correct answers. No one could do well with questions like these." "I don't know, Chris. Some questions were hard, but I got a B+," his friend responded.

1. Describe Chris's achievement attributions.

2. Suppose Chris had a fixed mindset. How might he account for his poor grade?

3. How might Chris account for his grade with a growth mindset?

4. How would you characterize Chris's achievement orientation? Why?

5. What are some influences on mastery orientation? What might help Chris?

. . . .

SCHOOL TRANSITIONS AND ACADEMIC ACHIEVEMENT

Apart from the home context, school is the most relevant and immediate context in which adolescents live. The structure of schools in the United States has changed dramatically since the mid-20th century. In past generations, students made only one school transition, or change of schools: from elementary school (kindergarten to Grade 8) to high school (Grades 9 to 12). Today, students make more school transitions than ever before. Junior high schools, typically comprising students in Grades 7, 8, and 9, were created in the 1960s and were modeled after high schools, serving as mini-high schools. In the late 1970s and 1980s, educators began to recognize that young adolescents have different educational needs than middle and older adolescents, and junior high schools began to be converted and organized into middle schools of Grades 5 or 6 through 8 or 9 (Byrnes & Ruby, 2007). Middle schools are designed to provide more flexibility and autonomy than elementary schools while encouraging strong ties to adults, such as teachers and parents, as well as offering active learning that takes advantage of and stimulates young adolescents' emerging capacities for abstract reasoning (National Middle School Association, 2003).

Shifting Contexts

The transition from elementary to middle school, and from middle school to high school, entails a complete shift in contexts, including environments, teachers, standards, support, and, often, peers. School transitions tend to coincide with many developmental and contextual changes. Many young people experience puberty during the transition to middle school. Changing thought capacities, self-perceptions, and relationships as well as new responsibilities and opportunities for independence influence how adolescents adapt to school transitions. For example, as friendships become more important, they may be disrupted when friends transition into different schools. Most adolescents experience the many changes that accompany school transitions as stressful, and academic achievement tends to decline during the transition to middle school and high school (Booth & Gerard, 2014; Felmlee, McMillan, Inara Rodis, & Osgood, 2018). In addition, student engagement and motivation tends to decline and feelings of loneliness, anxiety, depression, and stress tend to rise (Akos, Rose, & Orthner, 2014; Benner, 2011; Goldstein, Boxer, & Rudolph, 2015).

Grades tend to decline with each school transition, and students who experience more school transitions tend to perform more poorly than peers who have changed schools less often (Rudolph, Lambert, Clark, & Kurlakowsky, 2001; Seidman, Lambert, Allen, & Aber, 2003). For example, young adolescents enrolled in K–8 schools tend to score higher in academic achievement, specifically math and reading, than do those in middle school who have changed

Students who experience greater stress with school transitions tend to show greater drops in motivation and academic achievement that persists.
mooremedia / Shutterstock.com

schools from elementary to middle school (Byrnes & Ruby, 2007). Larger cumulative declines in academic achievement are seen when students make two school transitions before high school (elementary to middle school and middle to high school) compared with one (K–8 elementary school to high school) (Crockett, Petersen, Graber, Schulenberg, & Ebata, 1989), although some research disputes the size of this difference (Weiss & Bearman, 2007). During transitions, students may experience an increase in anxiety or depression that may manifest as poor school attendance, lower grades, and behavior problems in school (Coelho, Marchante, & Jimerson, 2017; Duchesne et al., 2019). For most students, these adjustment difficulties are temporary and their achievement recovers within 1 to 2 years as they adapt to their new schools (Crosnoe & Benner, 2015). However, students who perceive the school transition as more stressful than do their peers tend to show greater drops in motivation and academic achievement and less connectedness to school that persists well beyond the school transition (Goldstein et al., 2015). In addition, students with lower academic ability or lower self-esteem and those who are unprepared for middle or high school appear to be particularly vulnerable to poorer school and peer transitions, which have been associated with depressive symptoms (Coelho et al., 2017).

Stage-Environment Fit

Why are school transitions vulnerable periods for adolescents? According to researcher Jacqueline Eccles, negative effects of school transitions occur when there is little **stage-environment fit**. That is, adolescents experience difficulties when there is a poor match between their developmental needs and what the school environment affords in its organization and characteristics (Eccles & Roeser, 2011). The school environment, teachers, and standards change with each transition. Middle schools were intended to be tailored to the needs of early adolescents, yet research suggests that many students view their middle school experiences less positively than their elementary school experiences (Byrnes & Ruby, 2007; Roeser, Eccles, & Sameroff, 2000; Wigfield & Eccles, 1994).

As adolescents enter middle school and then high school, they are confronted with more stringent academic standards and evaluation becomes more frequent and formal than in elementary school. At the same time, many students feel that they receive less support from teachers (Mueller & Anderman, 2010). Students commonly report feeling less connected to middle school teachers than elementary school teachers and view their middle school teachers as less friendly, supportive, and fair (Way, Reddy, & Rhodes, 2007). High school students often report that they receive less personal attention from teachers, more class lectures, fewer hands-on demonstration activities, and fewer opportunities to participate in class discussions and group decision-making than they did in middle school (Gentle-Genitty, 2009; Seidman, Aber, & French, 2004).

Although it is tempting to blame adolescents' views about school on poor perspective taking or an immature prefrontal cortex, research suggests that many teachers' views corroborate them. For example, middle and junior high school teachers hold different beliefs about students than do elementary school teachers, even when they teach students of the same chronological age (Midgley, Anderman, & Hicks, 1995). They are less likely to report trusting their students and are more likely to emphasize discipline than their peers who teach elementary school. Teachers' belief in their abilities as teachers declines with each grade into secondary school (Eccles & Roeser, 2015). Teachers' sense of competence predicts high expectations for students, which in turn predicts student success. This decline is greater for teachers in low SES communities, likely influenced by access to resources and the increased stressors that may accompany low SES (Cooper, Kurtz-Costes, & Rowley, 2010), adding to the challenges that at-risk students face. As a result, middle school classrooms tend to be characterized by a greater emphasis on teacher control, offer fewer opportunities for student decision-making and autonomy, and involve more frequent and formal evaluations than those in elementary school (Eccles & Roeser, 2015).

Teachers' beliefs in their competence influences their interactions with students and teaching effectiveness.
iStock.com/shironosov

Teachers become more stringent, less personal, and more directive at the same time as young people value independence. Adolescents need more guidance and assistance with academic, social, and mental health issues just as teachers report feeling less responsibility for students' problems. The mismatch of adolescents' changing developmental needs and school resources contributes to declines in academic performance, motivation, and overall functioning (Booth & Gerard, 2014). Many students may feel more lonely and anxious, and they may report depressive symptoms (Benner, Boyle, & Bakhtiari, 2017; Coelho et al., 2017). For example, one sample of predominantly White middle income students found that declines in teacher support across the high school transition are associated with increases in depression from Grades 8 to 9 (Barber & Olsen, 2004). Vulnerable students, such as those from low income families or those who require special education services, tend to show a larger interruption in academic achievement (Akos et al., 2014).

Some adolescents face greater risks with school transitions than others. Changes in school demographics, particularly a mismatch between the ethnic composition of elementary and middle school or middle school and high school, can pose challenges to adolescents' adjustment (Douglass, Yip, & Shelton, 2014). Recent research suggests that students of all ethnicities, including African American, Latinx, Asian, and White adolescents, fare best in diverse schools with ethnic groups of relatively equal size (Juvonen, Kogachi, & Graham, 2018). Students in diverse schools reported feeling safer, less victimized, and less lonely; they also perceived teachers as fairer and reported more favorable attitudes toward students of other ethnicities. One study of over 900 students entering high school found that students who experienced more ethnic incongruence from middle to high school, a mismatch in demographics, reported declining feelings of connectedness to school over time and increasing worries about their academic success (Benner & Graham, 2009). Students who moved to high schools with fewer students who were ethnically similar to themselves were most likely to experience a disconnect, as were African American male students. This is of particular concern because African American adolescents tend to experience more risk factors related to academic achievement, tend to have more difficulties in school transitions, and are more likely to fall behind during school transitions than adolescents of other ethnicities (Burchinal, Roberts, Zeisel, Hennon, & Hooper, 2006). Similarly, Latinx students tend to be more sensitive to changes in the school climate and experience school transitions as more challenging than do non-Hispanic White students (Espinoza & Juvonen, 2011). One recent study found that students' academic risk during the transition to high school varied with their academic standing in middle school and their ethnicity (Sutton, Langenkamp, Muller, & Schiller, 2018). In this study with a large national sample of adolescents, Black boys and Latina girls who were high achieving in middle school tended to experience the greatest losses in achievement over the transition to high school and White girls tended to show the greatest continuity in academic status between middle school and high school. Risks to academic achievement tend to accumulate over time, with disadvantaged students facing disproportionate risks to achievement as they are often less prepared to meet the heightened demands of high school.

Promoting Stage-Environment Fit

The best student outcomes occur when schools closely match adolescents' developmental needs. Small, tight-knit middle schools may reduce the alienation that some students experience during the school transitions (Crosnoe & Benner, 2015). Small schools may also foster strong teacher–student relationships through more opportunities for teachers to interact with a smaller student base. Close relationships may help teachers feel comfortable providing opportunities for adolescents to have autonomy in classroom interactions and assignments while providing strong support. Adolescents who report high levels of teacher support and feel connected to their schools tend to show better academic achievement and better emotional health, including lower rates of depressive and anxiety symptoms (Kidger, Araya, Donovan, & Gunnell, 2012).

Teachers can play a large role in helping adolescents during school transitions by working to construct a context that supports students' psychological needs (Eccles & Roeser, 2011; Madjar & Cohen-Malayev, 2016). Those who provide a high-quality classroom environment, including emotional support, autonomy, positive relationships with their students, and greater teaching self-efficacy, show less decline in student achievement (Alley, 2019; Holas & Huston, 2012; Yu, Li, Wang, & Zhang, 2016). Students who perceive support from teachers tend to show higher self-esteem and fewer depressive symptoms (Madjar & Cohen-Malayev, 2016). A sense of school belonging is associated with positive school engagement, conduct, and psychological well-being (Demanet & van Houtte, 2012; Neel & Fuligni, 2013). Students who are able to forge positive relationships with new sets of teachers and peers and maintain positive relationships with friends from elementary or middle school who transition with them tend to show better adjustment to school transitions (Benner et al., 2017). Schools can build students' feelings of school belonging by helping them make connections with teachers and students in their new school contexts.

Adolescents' success in navigating school transitions is also influenced by their experiences outside of school. Adolescents are most vulnerable to the negative effects of school transitions when they lack the social and emotional resources to cope with multiple stressors. Young people who report feeling supported by their families and having many friends are less bothered by day-to-day stressors and experience

school transitions with few problems (Kingery, Erdley, & Marshall, 2011; Rueger, Chen, Jenkins, & Choe, 2014). Finally, as in other aspects of development, expectations matter. Adolescents who expect a positive transition to secondary school are more likely to report experiencing a positive experience and are at lower risk of school dropout (Waters, Lester, & Cross, 2014).

Contextual Influences on Academic Achievement

Adolescents' abilities, motivation, and attributions influence their success at school, but a host of contextual factors also play a role in their academic performance, including parents, peers, schools, and communities.

Parents

Close parent–adolescent relationships serve as an important support for academic motivation and performance from childhood through adolescence for young people at all socioeconomic levels (Dotterer, Lowe, & McHale, 2014). As in other areas of development, both the overly harsh parenting characterized by the authoritarian parenting style and the lax, permissive parenting style are associated with poor academic performance. Likewise, adolescents reared by uninvolved parents tend to show the poorest school grades (Gonzalez & Wolters, 2006; Heaven & Ciarrochi, 2008). Authoritative parenting, in contrast, is associated with academic achievement in U.S. adolescents of all ethnicities as well as in adolescents in many countries, including Argentina, Australia, Canada, China, Hong Kong, Iran, Pakistan, and Scotland (Assadi et al., 2007; Gonzalez & Wolters, 2006; Pinquart, 2017; Spera, 2005).

When parents use the authoritative style, they are open to discussion, involve their adolescents in joint decision-making, and firmly but fairly monitor their adolescents' behavior and set limits. This style of parenting helps adolescents feel valued, respected, and encouraged to think for themselves (Dornbusch, Ritter, Mont-Reynaud, & Chen, 1990; Spera, 2005). Adolescents are learning to regulate their emotions and behavior and to set, work toward, and achieve educational goals (Aunola & Stattin, 2000; Moilanen, Rasmussen, & Padilla-Walker, 2015). Authoritative parenting supports these developments.

Parents can promote high academic achievement in middle and high school students by setting high but realistic expectations and being

Strong connections with teachers can increase adolescents' sense of school belonging.
iStock.com/fstop123

active and involved—for example, by knowing their teens' teachers, monitoring progress, ensuring that their teens are taking challenging and appropriate classes, and expressing high expectations (Benner, 2011; Boonk, Gijselaers, Ritzen, & Brand-Gruwel, 2018; Karbach, Gottschling, Spengler, Hegewald, & Spinath, 2013). Parent–school involvement predicts academic achievement for adolescents, regardless of SES and ethnicity, but may be particularly beneficial for more disadvantaged youth such as those from low SES families or with poorer prior achievement (Benner, Boyle, & Sadler, 2016; Castro et al., 2015). By being involved in the school, parents communicate the importance of education; they also model academic engagement and problem-solving, which can help protect against dropout.

Peers

Peer relationships and interactions also influence adolescents' school experiences and academic achievement. Adolescents tend to choose friends who share interests and similarities, such as academic achievement (Véronneau, Vitaro, Brendgen, Dishion, & Tremblay, 2010). Friends mutually influence each other, becoming more similar through socialization (Gremmen et al., 2017). Peer support can be a protective factor for adolescents at risk. For example, research with African American students has shown peer support to be related to emotional engagement in school and, indirectly, to academic outcomes (Golden, Griffin, Metzger, & Cooper, 2018). Adolescents who viewed their peers as having high academic values reported engaging in greater school effort. Students' grades become more similar over time in response to their connectedness (Gremmen et al., 2017). One study of middle adolescents suggested that friends tended to exert a positive influence on one another to increase achievement (Rambaran et al., 2017).

Schools

Schools influence adolescents' academic achievement in a variety of ways. Perhaps most obviously, effective schools adopt a rigorous curriculum that meets state and federal education guidelines and includes topics that students cover as well as the cognitive skills they must demonstrate during each course (Rutledge, Cohen-Vogel, Osborne-Lampkin, & Roberts, 2015). One curricular choice is whether to group students by ability, known as **tracking**. Given what we

have discussed about expectations and achievement motivation, it is likely not surprising that grouping adolescents by ability influences their academic expectations (Karlson, 2015). Students in lower tracks tend to be viewed more poorly by other students and also view themselves more poorly (Legette, 2018). Some research has suggested that students in lower-achieving tracks are more likely to have lower-quality teachers (Kalogrides, Loeb, & Béteille, 2013). Effective schools emphasize inclusive education and work to ensure that all students have access to advanced courses.

The curriculum describes what students will learn, but quality instruction is at the heart of effective education. Instruction refers to the teaching strategies and practices that teachers employ to help students learn. Good teachers are well prepared, use individualized strategies, encourage higher-order thinking, and couple rigor with warmth (Borich, 2017). Quality instruction engages students, supports learning, and constructs a classroom climate where students are encouraged to try and are allowed to fail without negative consequences. Effective schools foster personalized learning connections, strong positive connections among adults and students that enable teachers to meet students' individual needs and develop students' sense of belonging (Burden & Byrd, 2019; Yager, Diedrichs, Ricciardelli, & Halliwell, 2013). Students who feel a sense of belonging to the school as a whole and experience meaningful, positive connections with adults and students are more likely to persist and be motivated academically (Neel & Fuligni, 2013). The

Adolescents' participation in extracurricular activities is associated with academic success and well-being.
iStock.com/lissart

school social context provides students with opportunities for positive and productive interactions with their teachers and peers (Wang & Hofkens, 2019).

Extracurricular activities play a role in developing personalized learning connections in high schools. Adolescents' participation in school-sponsored extracurricular activities is associated with academic success and psychosocial well-being (Im, Hughes, Cao, & Kwok, 2016). Such activities provide opportunities to develop supportive networks (such as mentoring relationships with coaches and other adults) that increase student connectedness, which has a positive relationship with achievement and staying in school (Booth & Gerard, 2014; Mahoney, 2014; Morris, 2016).

The most effective schools have a culture of learning and professional behavior and hold high expectations for teachers and students (Preston, Goldring, Guthrie, Ramsey, & Huff, 2017). These schools clearly state expectations for student behavior and academic performance, encourage adolescents to assume responsibility for their own learning, and encourage teachers to promote a collaborative culture to foster student success and efficacy. Effective schools press for and celebrate academic achievements, model success for teachers and students, and enable communication among teachers, students, and families (Rutledge et al., 2015). Adults and students internalize these cultural values and work together to achieve shared goals of creating a supportive learning community of adults and students.

In effective schools, teachers are supported by effective school leadership. School principals influence student learning through their support of teachers, working conditions, and learning climate. Studies also suggest that schools whose leaders organize their schools by articulating an explicit school vision, generating high expectations and goals for all students, and monitoring their schools' performance through regular use of data and frequent classroom observations are linked to increases in their students' learning (Preston et al., 2017). Principals' effects on student learning are also likely influenced by their efforts to improve teacher motivation, working conditions, and the school learning climate as well as to hire high-quality personnel.

Finally, effective schools develop connections with the community in which they are immersed, between the school, parents, and the larger community. These schools have high parental involvement and are attuned to the socioeconomic, cultural, and language needs of parents and students (Rutledge et al., 2015).

Neighborhood/Community

Adolescents and schools are immersed in neighborhoods or communities that influence their functioning and opportunities. Communities high in poverty tend to be poorly maintained, have high crime rates, and provide inadequate or limited access to resources, such as public transportation, sufficient street lights, and grocery and other stores, for adolescents and their families who live there (Gordon & Cui, 2018; Hopson & Lee, 2011). Community socioeconomic disadvantage is negatively associated with academic achievement in adolescence. Compared to their peers living in more affluent communities, adolescents living in less advantaged communities experience lower academic achievement, including lower scores on standardized tests, lower math and reading scores, and lower grade point averages (Gordon, 2016). Lower achievement among adolescents residing in disadvantaged communities is likely a reflection of the limited resources of that community, such as schools with fewer resources (Devenish, Hooley, & Mellor, 2017). They are also less likely to have access to broadband Internet and a laptop or desktop computer at home, which could be used to aid them with completing school work (Anderson & Jiang, 2018).

Adolescents living in disadvantaged communities may be exposed to widespread environmental inequities, such as community violence, which may further disrupt their academic and developmental progress. Exposure to community violence has negative effects on adolescent well-being and academic achievement (King & Mrug, 2018). Adolescents who live in communities of chronic violence may experience repeated trauma and post-traumatic stress symptoms, such as sleep disturbances, problems with memory and concentration, and intrusive thoughts—all of which can create challenges to their motivation and success in school (Jain & Cohen, 2013; Wright, Austin, Booth, & Kliewer, 2016).

Other contextual factors can buffer the negative effects of community disadvantage. For example, a positive school climate can compensate for community risk factors such as low SES and violence on academic achievement (Kennedy & Ceballo, 2014; Voisin, Kim, & Hong, 2018). Parental involvement and monitoring are protective factors associated with adolescent adjustment and higher school bonding (Wang, Hill, & Hofkens, 2014). Father involvement in education and especially father–adolescent relationship quality determines the effects of various individual and community-level factors and the developmental outcomes of adolescents (Gordon, 2016; Voisin et al., 2018).

REVIEW 10.2

1. How does academic functioning and adjustment typically shift over school transitions?

2. What is stage-environment fit and how can it be promoted?

3. How do parents contribute to academic achievement?

4. Identity ways in which effective schools influence adolescent academic achievement.

5. What are some ways in which community factors contribute to adolescent academic achievement?

• •

THINKING IN CONTEXT 10.2

1. Given what you know about physical, cognitive, and socioemotional development in boys and girls, would you expect gender differences in adjustment during school transitions? Why or why not? Under what circumstances might you expect boys and girls to have greater difficulties? Provide examples referring to aspects of physical, cognitive, and socioemotional development.

2. Think back to your experience transitioning to middle or high school. In what ways was the new school different from the old school? How did you feel about the changes? To what degree were they challenging? How did your parents, teachers, and school assist you in adjusting to the new environment?

3. Imagine that you are the parent of a fifth-grader about to enter middle school. What can you do to promote your child's adjustment?

• •

APPLY 10.2

Imagine that you are about to conduct a workshop with parents of fifth-grade students who will soon enter middle school.

1. Describe common challenges that boys and girls encounter as they enter middle school and explain why they occur.

2. Provide advice for parents to help their children adjust to middle school.

3. After the workshop, the middle school principal asks you to provide advice to teachers and staff. What can teachers do to ease their students' transition?

4. What can the principal do? Suggest ways that the school rules or environment can be modified to improve students' adjustment.

• •

ADOLESCENTS WITH DEVELOPMENTAL DISABILITIES AND SPECIFIC LEARNING DISORDERS

School systems must meet the needs of a diverse population of adolescents, many with unique educational needs. Adolescents with intellectual and learning disabilities require sensitive educational support to advance their learning.

Intellectual Disability

Intellectual disability is a neurodevelopmental disorder in which a child shows significant deficits in cognition (as defined by an IQ below 70) and in age-appropriate adaptive skills to such a degree that he or she requires ongoing support to adapt to everyday living (American Psychiatric Association, 2013). Difficulty in adaptation—the inability to appropriately modify one's behavior in light of situational demands—is essential to a diagnosis of intellectual disability (American Association on Intellectual and Developmental Disabilities, 2010). About 1% to 2% of people in the United States are diagnosed with intellectual disability (McKenzie, Milton, Smith, & Ouellette-Kuntz, 2016).

Individuals with intellectual disability show delayed development—that is, the pattern and sequence of development follows a typical order but at a slower rate and with limitations with respect to the final level of achievement. As children, individuals with intellectual disability are usually slower to use words and speak in complete sentences; their social development is sometimes delayed; and they may be slow to learn to dress and feed themselves. Children and adolescents with intellectual disabilities may experience more behavioral problems than other children, such as explosive outbursts, temper tantrums, and physically aggressive or self-injurious behavior, because their ability to communicate, understand, and control their emotional impulses and frustrations is impaired (Shea, 2012). Many adolescents with intellectual disabilities experience bullying (Tipton-Fisler, Rodriguez, Zeedyk, & Blacher, 2018). Social skills are challenging for many adolescents with disabilities; however, interventions can help improve their social competence (Carter, 2018). Friendship is an important source of support, improving quality of life for adolescents with disabilities (Sigstad, 2016). However, adolescents with intellectual deficits tend to show greater susceptibility to peer influence and greater risk-taking than other adolescents, likely influenced by the greater deficits in cognitive control (Bexkens et al., 2019; Bexkens, Jansen, Van der Molen, & Huizenga, 2016).

There are many causes of intellectual disability. It is estimated that genetic causes may be responsible for approximately one-fourth to one-half of identified intellectual disability cases (Srour & Shevell, 2014). Other biological influences include Down syndrome, metabolic disorders such as phenylketonuria, and mutations. Contextual factors include neglect, childbirth trauma, and factors associated with poverty, such as lack of access to health care and poor nutrition

With support, adolescents with developmental disabilities can succeed in classroom settings.
iStock.com/SolStock

(Heikura et al., 2008; Schalock, 2015). Furthermore, many cases of intellectual disability have no identifiable cause.

Autism Spectrum Disorders

Autism spectrum disorders (ASD) are a family of neurodevelopmental disorders that range in severity and are characterized by deficits in social communication and a tendency to engage in repetitive behaviors (Hall, 2018). About 1 in 68 U.S. children are diagnosed with ASD, with males about four times as likely to be diagnosed than females (Masi, DeMayo, Glozier, & Guastella, 2017). The social and communication impairments vary widely from minor difficulties in social comprehension and perspective taking to the inability to use nonverbal or spoken language. A common characteristic of ASD is repetitive behavior, such as rocking, hand-flapping, twirling, and repeating sounds, words, or phrases. Sensory dysfunction may accompany ASD, in which individuals perceive visual, auditory, and tactile stimulation as intense and even painful. Some adolescents with ASD are intellectually disabled; others show average or above-average intelligence (Hall, 2018). Adolescents with ASD often show difficulties with working memory, requiring additional time to process information (Wang et al., 2017). They may benefit from instruction that emphasizes modeling, hands-on activities, and concrete examples and teaches skills for generalizing learning from one setting or problem to another (Lewis, Wheeler, & Carter, 2017).

There is evidence for a hereditary influence on ASD but it is likely epigenetic, the result of multiple interacting genes and environmental factors rather than a single gene (Eshraghi et al., 2018; Sandin et al., 2017). Some of the genes associated with ASD influence the availability of proteins that affect synaptic strength or number and neural connectivity in the brain (Bourgeron, 2015). ASD is associated with atypical brain connectivity (Hahamy, Behrmann, & Malach, 2015). The sensorimotor areas of the brain tend to show heightened connectivity, perhaps accounting for the sensory difficulties and motor features associated with ASD (Hull et al., 2017; Khan et al., 2015). The brain areas responsible for inhibitory control, or self-regulation, tend to show less connectivity, suggesting that adolescents with ASD may experience difficulty controlling impulses (Voorhies et al., 2018). The areas of the brain implicated for facial expression involved in social behavior, emotion, social communication, and theory of mind show reduced and less efficient connectivity within and between each area (Cheng, Rolls, Gu, Zhang, & Feng, 2015; Dajani & Uddin, 2016; Doyle-Thomas et al., 2015). Collectively, these neurological differences mean that children with ASD may find it difficult to consider mental states and take other people's perspectives, which are essential to communication and relationship formation (Kana et al., 2015; Senju, 2012).

Adolescents with ASD tend to experience difficulty forming and maintaining peer relationships, a core developmental task of adolescence (Picci & Scherf, 2015). They tend to spend less time with peers and more time with parents and other adults compared with typically developing adolescents (Kuo, Orsmond, Cohn, & Coster, 2013). Parents often arrange and support friendships for adolescents with ASD. In one study, about half of friendships involving an adolescent with ASD emerged in the context of a prearranged setting and less than 10% of friendships involved reciprocal peer activities outside of an organized or prearranged setting (Orsmond, Krauss, & Seltzer, 2004). In addition to experiencing difficulty forming friendships, adolescents with ASD are more likely than their peers to experience peer rejection, with nearly half experiencing bullying (Cappadocia, Weiss, & Pepler, 2012; Sterzing, Shattuck, Narendorf, Wagner, & Cooper, 2012). Notably, given their difficulty forming and maintaining high-quality peer friendships, adolescents with ASD likely do not have the social support that is protective against the effects of peer rejection for other adolescents (Schwartz, Lansford, Dodge, Pettit, & Bates, 2014; Tipton-Fisler et al., 2018). Their difficulty in forming

There is growing awareness of the abilities and needs of adolescents with ASD.
David Grossman / Alamy Stock Photo

peer relationships, a central task of adolescence, may place adolescents with ASD at heightened risk for developing depression or anxiety (Kuusikko et al., 2008; McPheeters, Davis, Navarre, & Scott, 2011).

Attention-Deficit/ Hyperactivity Disorder

Attention-deficit/hyperactivity disorder (ADHD) is a neurodevelopmental disorder characterized by persistent difficulties with attention and/or hyperactivity/impulsivity that interferes with performance and behavior in school and daily life (Hinshaw, 2018). Difficulty with attention and distractibility may manifest, such as failing to attend to details, making careless mistakes, not appearing to listen when spoken to directly, not following through on instructions, or difficulty organizing tasks or activities. Impulsivity may include frequent fidgeting, squirming in one's seat, and leaving one's seat in class; running in situations where it is not appropriate; talking excessively, often blurting out an answer before a question is completed; and having trouble waiting a turn. While most young people show one or two symptoms of inattention or hyperactivity at some point in their development, a diagnosis of ADHD requires a consistent display of a minimum number of specific symptoms over a 6-month period, and the symptoms must interfere with behavior in daily life (Hinshaw, 2018). In adolescence, the difficulty in attentional control and impulsivity associated with ADHD may manifest in impulsive decision-making and difficulty delaying gratification (Patros et al., 2016), which is associated with greater risk-taking and externalizing behavior than in peers without ADHD (Li, 2019).

ADHD is associated with differences in brain development—specifically, structural abnormalities in the parts of the brain responsible for attentional and motor control (Jacobson et al., 2018). ADHD has biological causes and is nearly 80% heritable, or genetic (Aguiar, Eubig, & Schantz, 2010; Schachar, 2014). Research studying identical twins in which only one twin was diagnosed with ADHD has suggested a role for epigenetics in determining the degree to which genetic propensities are expressed (Chen et al., 2018). Environmental influences on ADHD include premature birth, maternal smoking, drug and alcohol use, lead exposure, and brain injuries (Tarver, Daley, & Sayal, 2014; Thapar, Cooper, Eyre, & Langley, 2013).

Stimulant medication is the most common treatment for ADHD. Stimulant medication increases activity in the parts of the brain that are responsible for attention, self-control, and behavior inhibition (Hawk et al., 2018). Behavioral interventions can help adolescents learn strategies to manage impulses and hyperactivity, direct their attention, and monitor their behavior (Evans, Owens, Wymbs, & Ray, 2018).

Specific Learning Disorder

Once referred to as learning disability, the fifth edition of the *Diagnostic and Statistical Manual of Mental Disorders* replaced this term with **specific learning disorder (SLD)**. SLDs are diagnosed in children who demonstrate a measurable discrepancy between aptitude and achievement in a particular academic area given their age, intelligence, and amount of schooling (American Psychiatric Association, 2013). Individuals with SLDs have difficulty with academic achievement despite having normal intelligence and sensory function. An estimated one in five elementary and secondary school students in the United States has an SLD (Horowitz, Rawe, & Whittaker, 2017). There are several SLDs that influence reading, writing skills, and mathematics ability and other cognitive skills.

Developmental dyslexia is the most commonly diagnosed SLD. Adolescents with developmental dyslexia tend to be bright yet show difficulty reading, with reading achievement below that predicted by age or IQ. Individuals with dyslexia demonstrate age-inappropriate difficulty in matching letters to sounds and difficulty with word recognition and spelling despite adequate instruction and intelligence and intact sensory abilities (Peterson & Pennington, 2012; Ramus, 2014). Dyslexia is estimated to affect 5% to nearly 18% of the school population, boys and girls equally.

Dyslexia is influenced by genetics (Carrion-Castillo, Franke, & Fisher, 2013). Individuals with dyslexia have a neurologically based difficulty in processing speech sounds. During speech tasks, they use different regions of the brain than others and they often have difficulty recognizing that words consist of small units of sound strung together and represented visually by letters (Lonigan, 2015; Schurz et al., 2015). Abnormalities in the brain areas responsible for reading can be seen in 11-year-olds with dyslexia but not in young children who have not been exposed to reading, suggesting that the brain abnormalities associated with dyslexia occur after reading commences (Clark et al., 2014). Successful interventions include not only training in phonics but also supporting emerging skills by linking letters, sounds, and words through writing and reading from developmentally appropriate texts (Snowling, 2013).

Providing adolescents with different types of pens and pencils can help those with dysgraphia.
iStock.com/portishead1

Another common SLD is **developmental dyscalculia**, a disorder that affects mathematics ability. Adolescents with developmental dyscalculia find it challenging to learn mathematical concepts such as counting, addition, and subtraction, and they often have a poor understanding of math concepts and tend to use ineffective strategies for solving math problems (Kucian & von Aster, 2015; Rapin, 2016). Many adolescents with developmental dyscalculia experience mathematics anxiety, which can further interfere with their learning (Devine, Hill, Carey, & Szucs, 2018). Dyscalculia is thought to affect about 5% of students and is not well understood (Kaufmann et al., 2013). Research suggests that it is influenced by brain functioning and difficulty with working memory and executive function, specifically visuospatial short-term memory and inhibitory function (Menon, 2016; Watson & Gable, 2013). Adolescents with dyscalculia are usually given intensive practice to help them understand numbers and mathematical concepts, but there is much to learn about this disorder (Fuchs, Malone, Schumacher, Namkung, & Wang, 2017; Kucian & von Aster, 2015).

Developmental dysgraphia is a disorder that affects writing abilities. It may appear as difficulties with spelling, poor handwriting, and trouble conveying thoughts on paper, leading a child to show writing performance below that expected based on a child's class level (Döhla & Heim, 2016). The prevalence for developmental writing disorders is about 7% to 15% of adolescents, with boys being more affected than girls (Horowitz et al., 2017). Similar to dyslexia, adolescents with dysgraphia experience difficulties with working memory and executive function, especially response inhibition; however, fMRI scans suggest different patterns of brain connectivity (Richards et al., 2015). Recent research suggests higher rates of dysgraphia in adolescents diagnosed with ADHD or ASD, disorders that share commonalities in executive function such as difficulty in impulse control (Mayes, Breaux, Calhoun, & Frye, 2019; Mayes, Frye, Breaux, & Calhoun, 2018).

Writing relies on motor and sensory skills, in addition to cognition. Adolescents with dysgraphia may hold their pencil in a tight awkward grip, show poor body posture while writing, and produce illegible handwriting. They may avoid writing tasks, get easily tired while writing, omit words in sentences, and have difficulty organizing and conveying ideas on paper. Teachers may identify adolescents with dysgraphia when they notice a large discrepancy between adolescents' understanding demonstrated by speech compared with written work.

Teachers and parents can help adolescents with dysgraphia by focusing on the sensory and motor aspects of the disorder (Berninger & Wolf, 2009). Encourage adolescents to experiment with different types of pens and pencils to find a comfortable tool. Permit them to write in print or cursive letters, whichever is most comfortable. Exercises to improve hand strength can help. In addition, adolescents with dysgraphia often benefit from the use of a keyboard, which is often easier than manipulating a pen; however, a keyboard should not completely replace handwriting. Like other SLDs, managing dysgraphia often requires learning and practicing skills.

Accommodating the Educational Needs of Adolescents With Developmental Disabilities

School systems must meet the needs of a diverse population of children, many with special educational needs. Adolescents with developmental disabilities require assistance to help them overcome obstacles to learning. **Special education** is tailored to individuals' specific needs. It is individually planned, specialized, goal directed, and guided by student performance (Heward, 2018). In the United States and Canada, legislation mandates that children and adolescents with disabilities are to be placed in the "least restrictive" environment, or classrooms that are as similar as possible to classrooms for children without learning disabilities. Whenever possible, they are to be educated in the general classroom, with their peers, for all or part of the day. Teachers must be sensitive to the special needs of students with developmental disabilities and provide additional instruction and extra time for them to complete assignments. When children are placed in classrooms with peers of all abilities, they have multiple opportunities to learn from peers and may be better prepared to learn and work alongside people of all abilities.

A special education approach known as **inclusion** integrates students with developmental disabilities in the classroom with nondisabled peers and provides them with a teacher or paraprofessional specially trained to meet their needs (Mastropieri & Scruggs, 2017). Inclusion may take different forms for different children or may vary depending on academic subject. For example, one student with a developmental disability may attend class with peers all day, receiving additional handouts, guidance, or extra time to complete assignments. Another student might be placed in a classroom with nondisabled peers but may receive individualized instruction for part of the day (or for a specific subject) in a resource room (Salend, 2015).

Adolescents' responses to inclusion vary with the severity of their disabilities as well as the quality and quantity of support provided in the classroom (Lewis et al., 2017). Most experts agree that inclusion works best when students receive instruction in a resource room that meets their specialized needs for part of the school day and the peer classroom for the rest of the school day (Heward, 2018). Students with developmental disabilities report preferring combining time in the regular classroom with time in a resource room with a teacher who is trained to meet their learning needs (Vaughn & Klingner, 1998). Interaction with peers and cooperative learning assignments that require students to work together to achieve academic goals help students with disabilities learn social skills and form friendships with peers.

Although adolescents with developmental disabilities learn strategies to succeed, the disabilities themselves and the academic and social challenges posed by them do not disappear. Like all students, those with disabilities must adapt their learning strategies as they gain competence. Parents and teachers who are sensitive to students' changing needs will be better able to help them. Parents and teachers are most helpful when they understand that learning disabilities are not a matter of intelligence or choice but rather a function of brain differences and when they help adolescents to learn to monitor their learning and behavior.

REVIEW 10.3

1. Define intellectual disability and list its correlates.
2. Differentiate autism spectrum disorders from attention-deficit/hyperactivity disorder.
3. Discuss the characteristics of three specific learning disorders.
4. What are some ways in which schools can accommodate the educational needs of adolescents with developmental disabilities?

THINKING IN CONTEXT 10.3

1. Consider the characteristics of the common developmental disabilities and specific learning disorders we have discussed. How might you design a classroom environment that accommodates these needs as well as students without disabilities? What are the challenges of this task? What commonalities do students require to succeed?
2. In what ways might developmental disabilities affect students outside the classroom? How might disabilities influence interactions with peers?
3. Many adults are concerned with impulsivity and risky behavior in adolescence. How might developmental disabilities and SLDs influence adolescent behavior?

APPLY 10.3

Several students with SLDs have enrolled in Ms. Kakko's tenth-grade math class. She is dedicated to ensuring that all students in her class have the opportunity to learn but is unfamiliar with SLDs.

1. What SLDs might Ms. Kakko encounter? Describe characteristics of each.

2. How might students with each type of SLD perform in a math class?

3. How can Ms. Kakko help her new students transition to the class, academically and socially?

• •

ADOLESCENT WORK AND EDUCATION

The majority of adolescents graduate high school and most enter postsecondary education for at least a period. Next we examine adolescents' work experiences and their experiences after leaving high school.

Adolescent Employment

Working at a part-time job during high school is commonplace in the United States and Canada, with over half of high school students reporting working at some point during the school year (Bachman, Johnston, & O'Malley, 2014). Labor force surveys report fewer employed adolescents than in prior generations, but many of the jobs held by teens are "off the books" and unrecorded (U.S. Bureau of Labor Statistics, 2015). Regardless, adolescent employment today is at its lowest level since World War II (see Figure 10.1; Desilver, 2019).

Most U.S. adolescents who work come from middle-SES families and seek part-time employment as a source of spending money (Bachman, Staff, O'Malley, & Freedman-Doan, 2013). Black adolescents are less likely to work than White adolescents, likely because Black adolescents are more likely to live in economically depressed areas with fewer job opportunities (McLoyd & Hallman, 2018).

Although both adults and adolescents tend to view working as an opportunity to develop a sense of responsibility, research suggests more mixed findings (Monahan, Lee, & Steinberg, 2011). For example, one area of responsibility that working is believed to affect is money management (i.e., a job may provide opportunities to learn how to budget, save, and spend wisely), yet most teens spend their earnings on personal expenses, such as clothes, and experience premature affluence—they get used to a luxurious standard of living before they have financial responsibilities (Bachman et al., 2013). Young adults who experience premature affluence in their teen years may be less satisfied with their financial situation than are their peers did not work during high school.

The effects of employment on adolescent well-being largely depend on the hours worked and the quality of the work experience (Hwang & Domina, 2017; Rauscher, Wegman, Wooding, Davis, & Junkin, 2013). About half of employed adolescents work 15 or

---

FIGURE 10.1

Employment of Adolescents and Adults in the United States, 1948–2018

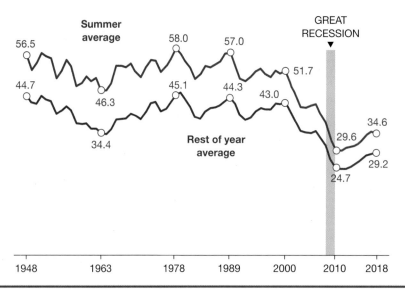

% of 16- to 19-year-olds who are employed

Source: Desilver (2019).

Adolescents who work may experience premature affluence.
iStock.com/urbazon

fewer hours per week (Bachman et al., 2014). Working few hours (15 or less) appears to have little positive or negative effect on adolescents' academic or psychosocial functioning (Monahan et al., 2011). On the other hand, working more than 20 hours each week, common to about one-third of employed adolescents (Bachman et al., 2014), is associated with many poor outcomes, such as poor school attendance, performance, and motivation; risk of school dropout; and problem behaviors such as smoking, alcohol and substance use, early sexual activity, and delinquency; and overall perceived quality of life (Bachman et al., 2013; Graves, Mackelprang, Barbosa-Leiker, Miller, & Li, 2017; Graves et al., 2019; Rocheleau, 2018; Staff, Vaneseltine, Woolnough, Silver, & Burrington, 2012; Staff et al., 2019). The negative effects of working long hours are especially evident for young and middle adolescents in eighth and tenth grade compared with twelfth-grade students who may show fewer negative outcomes of intense work (Hwang & Domina, 2017).

The effects of adolescent employment may vary with race and SES. For example, some research suggests that the negative effects of long hours of employment are most evident for White and middle-class adolescents but are associated with fewer disadvantages for Hispanic and African American adolescents from low income families (Bachman et al., 2013; Hwang & Domina, 2017). However, low SES adolescents of color tend to experience more difficulty obtaining jobs than their White and affluent peers because they are more likely to live in low SES communities with more limited local job markets, tend to have social networks with fewer individuals who can connect adolescents to job opportunities, and are more likely to experience discrimination that interferes with employment (Hwang & Domina, 2017; McLoyd & Hallman, 2018). Adolescents of color who are successful in finding and maintaining employment under difficult contextual conditions likely have psychosocial assets, such as self-reliance, self-control, and postsecondary education aspirations, that are associated with positive outcomes despite employment (Hwang & Domina, 2017; McLoyd & Hallman, 2018). Yet other research suggests that working long hours is associated with detrimental developmental outcomes for youth regardless of neighborhood context, and youth from disadvantaged contexts are most likely to work intense hours (Kingston & Rose, 2015; Staff et al., 2019).

In addition to the number of hours worked, the extent to which adolescents benefit from employment is influenced by the particular qualities of the work; not all types of work are beneficial. The most common jobs available to adolescents often entail repetitive simple tasks, such as microwaving meals at a fast food restaurant (Steinberg, Fegley, & Dornbusch, 1993). Adolescents often report that their jobs are repetitive with few opportunities for self-direction, stressful, and the belief that their jobs were not preparing them for their kind of work they hope to do in the future (Rauscher et al., 2013). Adolescent workers often have little contact with adults—their coworkers tend to be teens; supervisors tend to be not much older than they are; and customers, if the job is in food service or retail, tend to be adolescents (Greenberger & Steinberg, 1986). Working long hours, especially in settings with little contact with adults, may deprive adolescents of contact with supportive resources, such as family, school, and community contacts (Rocheleau, 2018).

However, adolescent work can be a positive experience if it entails limited hours and if it includes educational and vocational training opportunities and contact with adults (Greene & Staff, 2012; Mortimer & Johnson, 1998). Work settings that emphasize vocational skills, such as answering phones and communicating with clients as a receptionist, and in which adolescents interact with, work alongside, and help adults tend to promote positive attitudes toward work as well as academic motivation and achievement and are negatively associated with delinquency and drug and alcohol use (Rauscher et al., 2013; Staff & Uggen, 2003).

School Dropout

School dropout rates in the United States have reached historic lows, with dramatic decreases for African American and Hispanic adolescents (see Figure 10.2). Nevertheless, each year, about 6% of high school students drop out of school (National Center for Education Statistics, 2017b). Students of low SES are at high risk of school dropout, and minority and immigrant students are particularly vulnerable.

Students with behavior and substance use problems are most at risk for school dropout, but many who drop out simply have academic problems, skip classes with increasing frequency, and disengage emotionally and behaviorally (Bowers & Sprott, 2012; Henry, Knight, & Thornberry, 2012; Wang & Fredricks, 2014). Lack of parental involvement places students at risk for school dropout; when parents respond to poor grades with anger and punishment, this can further reduce adolescents' academic motivation and feelings of connectedness to school (Alivernini & Lucidi, 2011). Many of the unfavorable characteristics that students report of their high schools predict dropout, including large schools, few opportunities to form personal relationships with teachers or to speak out in class, poor emotional and academic support from teachers, and poor peer relationships and bullying (Freeman & Simonsen, 2015; Frostad, Pijl, & Mjaavatn, 2014; Jia, Konold, & Cornell, 2016).

Students who are engaged in and attached to school and who participate in many school-related activities are less likely to drop out than their less engaged peers (Janosz, Archambault, Morizot, & Pagani, 2008; Mahoney, 2014). Conversely, feelings of anonymity at school increase the risk of dropping out. Students who experience academic difficulties may be more vulnerable than their peers to the structural changes that are common during school transitions.

Although dropout is often the result of extended difficulties, there are multiple paths to dropout. Many students show few problems until a particularly disruptive event or situation, such as severe peer victimization, health problems, family instability, or long work hours, impairs their coping skills (Dupere et al., 2015). For example, a study comparing Canadian students who were recent dropouts, at-risk students who remained in school, and average students found that dropouts were over three times more likely to have experienced recent acute stressors, suggesting that it may be these acute stressors that place students at increased risk for dropout, over and above existing contextual risks (Dupéré et al., 2018).

As adults, high school dropouts experience higher rates of unemployment and, when hired, earn less than high school graduates throughout adulthood. Young people who have dropped out of school have the option of taking a high school equivalency test, the General Educational Development exam (GED).

FIGURE 10.2

Percentage of Grade 10 to 12 Dropouts Among Persons 15 Through 24 Years Old, by Race/Ethnicity: October 1976 Through 2016

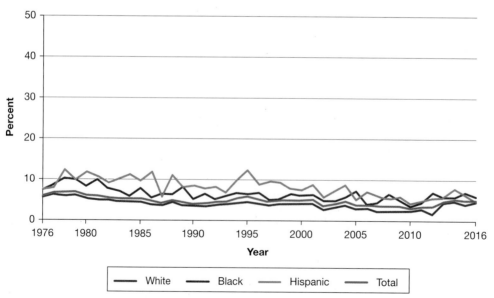

Source: National Center for Education Statistics (2017b).

The GED was developed in the late 1940s to certify that returning World War II veterans who had left high school to serve in the military were ready for college or the labor market. Although passing the GED exam can signify that a young person has accumulated the knowledge entailed in earning a high school diploma, GED holders do not fare as well as regular high school graduates in the labor market, and they tend to get much less postsecondary education (Tyler & Lofstrom, 2009).

Attending College

Attending college, at least for a time, has become a normative experience for emerging adults. In 2015, 69% of high school graduates in the United States enrolled in 2- or 4-year colleges (National Center for Education Statistics, 2017c). Students enroll in college to learn about a specific field of study (i.e., a major) and to prepare for careers, but attending college is also associated with many positive developmental outcomes.

College students encounter a wealth of new experiences and opportunities for autonomy, ideas, and social demands.
iStock.com/Andrei Stanescu

Developmental Impact of Attending College

Adults of all ages often view their college years as highly influential in shaping their thoughts, values, and worldview (Patton, Renn, Guido-DiBrito, & Quaye, 2016). In addition to academic learning, college presents young people with various perspectives and encourages experimentation with alternative behavior, beliefs, and values. College students encounter a wealth of new experiences and opportunities for autonomy, ideas, and social demands. College courses often require students to construct arguments and solve complex problems, fostering the development of post-formal reasoning (King & Kitchener, 2015). Attending college is associated with advances in moral reasoning, identity development, and social development (Lapsley & Hardy, 2017; Patton et al., 2016). In addition to intellectual growth, college students show advances in social development (Hassan, 2008). The expanded worldview that accompanies college attendance is displayed in young people's tolerance of diversity and their interest in subjects such as art, literature, and philosophy.

The positive impact of attending college is not simply a matter of the type of college one attends; research indicates that all institutions—public and private, selective and open enrollment—advance cognitive and psychological development

(Mayhew et al., 2016). In addition, students at 2-year community colleges show similar cognitive and academic gains to those of their peers at 4-year institutions (Monaghan & Attewell, 2015). Rather than the type of institution attended, developmental outcomes are most influenced by student involvement in campus life and peer interaction in academic and social contexts. Students who are active in campus life and feel a sense of belonging tend to show greater educational attainment (Mayhew et al., 2016). Students who live in residence halls have more opportunities to interact with peers and become involved in the academic and social aspects of campus life, and they show the greatest cognitive gains in the college years (Bronkema & Bowman, 2017).

Despite these benefits, however, many students do not complete college. Only about two-thirds of students who enroll in 4-year institutions graduate within 6 years and one-third of students enrolled at 2-year institutions graduate within 3 years (National Center for Education Statistics, 2017e). Generally, student attrition is highest in colleges with open enrollment and those with relatively low admission requirements.

Transition to College

How a student handles the transition to college itself predicts the likelihood of dropping out. While most students find the transition to college challenging, some fail to realize or act upon the fact that they are expected to take the initiative in requesting help as they face new demands. Such demands are not only academic (e.g., more difficult coursework) but also social (e.g., changes in living situation, whether a move to a dorm room or off-campus housing) and personal, including new psychological demands for autonomy, motivation, study skills, and self-management (Cleary, Walter, & Jackson, 2011).

Students' transition to college and success in college are also influenced by the college environment (Fischer, 2007). Institutions that are responsive to the academic, social, and cultural needs of students help them adjust to college and, ultimately, succeed (Mayhew et al., 2016). Reaching out to at-risk students during the first weeks of college can help them feel connected to the institution. Social connection, communication skills, motivation, and study skills are associated with retention (Robbins, Allen, Casillas, Peterson, & Le, 2006). Students who live on campus, see faculty as concerned with their development, establish relationships with faculty and other students, and become involved in campus life are more likely to succeed and graduate from college (Mayhew et al., 2016). Colleges and universities can provide opportunities for faculty and students to interact and form connections, help students develop study skills, and assist students in getting involved on campus. When students feel that they are part of a campus community, they are more likely to persist and graduate.

First-Generation College Students

Students whose parents do not have 4-year degrees are known as first-generation college students. About one-third of students are first-generation students (Skomsvold, 2014). First-generation college students experience a higher risk of dropout than students with parents who have earned 4-year degrees. Students of color and those of low SES are disproportionately likely to be first-generation college students. In 2016, about 14% of all college students enrolled in the United States were African American and 18% were Hispanic (compared with 57% White) (National Center for Education Statistics, 2017d).

With few family and peer models of how to succeed in college, first-generation and minority students may feel isolated and find it difficult to understand and adjust to the college student role and expectations (Collier & Morgan, 2008; Orbe, 2008). Compared with White students and those whose parents attended college, they may be assigned to more remedial coursework; trail in the number of credits they earn in the first year of college; have difficulty deciding on a major; and be less active in campus, academic, and social activities—all of which are risk factors for college dropout (Aronson, 2008; Walpole, 2008).

First-generation students tend to be less active in campus and extracurricular activities and less academically prepared than their peers, two factors that often aid students in adjusting to college and

are risk factors for college dropout (Feldman, 2017). In addition, first-generation college students often face economic circumstances that interfere with their ability to participate on campus. For example, first-generation students are more likely than their peers to be enrolled part-time, to hold a job, and to have mixed feelings about college (Ward, Siegel, & Davenport, 2012). With few family and peer models of how to succeed in college, first-generation and minority students may feel isolated and find it difficult to understand and adjust to the college student role and expectations. First-generation students report having fewer opportunities to talk about their negative experiences and are more likely to feel guilty about their educational achievement (Jury et al., 2017).

Many students experience a cultural mismatch between their college environment and their sense of self and the communities in which they identify (Phillips, Stephens, & Townsend, 2016). Many first-generation college students live in families and communities characterized by norms of interdependence, where community members "look out" for one another, which often contrasts with the norms of independence that are prevalent in college environments (Stephens, Fryberg, Markus, Johnson, & Covarrubias, 2012). For example, one study of Latinx first-generation students revealed that many experienced conflicts between their home and school values and responsibilities that interfered with their academic achievement and sense of well-being. Conflicts included providing assistance to family versus doing academic work and allocating funds to the family or for travel to see family versus allocating money for educational expenses (Vasquez-Salgado, Greenfield, & Burgos-Cienfuegos, 2015). Likewise, some Latinx students report feeling guilt for attending college and not offering their families daily assistance (Covarrubias & Fryberg, 2015). Among low SES first-generation college students, a sense of ethnic identity and maternal support predicted career expectations and, in turn, school engagement—the behavior needed to achieve vocational goals (Kantamneni, McCain, Shada, Hellwege, & Tate, 2018). Other research with college students in the Philippines showed that parent and teacher support predicted career optimism (Garcia, Restubog, Bordia, Bordia, & Roxas, 2015). Parental expectations and encouragement for academic success and pursuit of high-status occupations also predict vocational choice and success (Maier, 2005).

Noncollege-Bound Youth

Although most young people express the desire to go to college, only 34% of adults in 2017 held college degrees by age 25 (National Center for Education

Statistics, 2017a). Each year, about one-third of high school graduates in the United States transition from high school to work without attending college. While some academically well-prepared students report forgoing college because of a desire to work or a lack of interest in academics, many cite economic barriers, such as the high cost of college or the need to support their family, as reasons for nonattendance (Bozick & DeLuca, 2011). The population of noncollege-bound youth has been referred to in the literature as "forgotten" by educators, scholars, and policymakers, because relatively few resources are directed toward learning about them or assisting them compared with college-bound young adults.

Young adults who enter the workforce immediately after high school have fewer work opportunities than those of prior generations. In 2018, the rate of unemployment for high school graduates was twice that of bachelor's degree holders (Torpey, 2019). In addition, many young people with high school degrees spend their first working years in jobs that are similar to those they held in high school: unskilled, with low pay and little security (Rosenbaum & Person, 2003). As illustrated in Figure 10.3, at all ages high school graduates earn less and are more likely to be unemployed than peers with college degrees.

The curricula of most secondary schools tend to be oriented toward college-bound students, and counseling tends to focus on helping students gain admission to college (Krei & Rosenbaum, 2000). Over the past 3 decades, secondary education has shifted toward emphasizing academics and reducing vocational training, leaving young adults who do not attend college ill prepared for the job market (Symonds, Schwartz, & Ferguson, 2011). A solution proposed in the Pathways to Prosperity report from Harvard Graduate School of Education is for the U.S. educational system to support multiple pathways in the transition to adulthood (Ferguson & Lamback, 2014; Symonds et al., 2011). Opportunities for vocational training and to obtain relevant work experience will help young people try out careers and get relevant training for specific jobs.

The U.S. Department of Labor and many states have established a series of registered apprenticeships that combine on-the-job training with theoretical and practical classroom instruction to prepare young people to work in a variety of settings. About 150,000 companies and organizations serve as program sponsors in the Apprenticeship USA registered program, training about 410,000 young people in over 1,000 occupations in industries such as construction, manufacturing, health care, information technology, energy, telecommunications, and more (U.S. Department of Labor, 2015). Apprentices receive on-the-job training and instruction by employers, and they earn wages

FIGURE 10.3

Median Weekly Earnings and Unemployment by Educational Attainment, 2018 (Age 25 and Older)

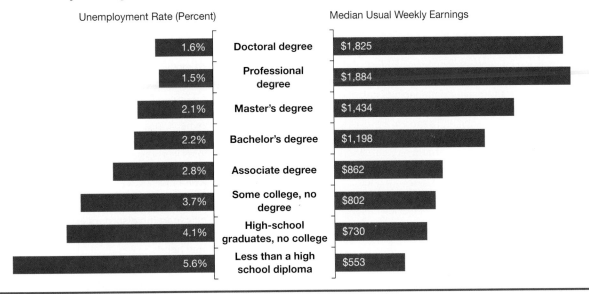

Source: U.S. Bureau of Labor Statistics, Current Population Survey.

Note: Earnings are for full-time wage and salary workers.

during training. The programs must meet national standards for registration with the U.S. Department of Labor and training results in an industry-recognized credential. Apprentices who complete the program are often hired by their placement employers; this is a win-win solution for the program alumni as well as for the employers, which benefit by hiring employees who have acquired the specific skills they need ●

REVIEW 10.4

1. What are typical patterns and correlates of adolescent employment?

2. What are predictors and consequences of school dropout?

3. How does attending college influence development?

4. Why is the transition to college important?

5. What are common experiences of first-generation college students?

6. What challenges do noncollege-bound youth face?

THINKING IN CONTEXT 10.4

1. Did you work in high school? Describe your job and the surrounding context. How do your experiences compare with the research findings?

2. What was your experience as a first-year college student? How well were you prepared for the changes? What were some of the challenges? How did you overcome them?

APPLY 10.4

During first-year orientation, Latisha listens to the group leaders. The students take turns, introducing themselves and sharing something about themselves. When it is Latisha's turn, she says, "My name is Latisha and I'm excited about college." As the next student begins her introduction, Latisha thinks to herself, "That was lame, but I'm so nervous I couldn't think of anything else. Everyone here looks like they belong. Everyone else knows what they're doing. Starting college is a really big deal to me. I don't want everyone to know that I'm the first of my family to go to college."

1. What do we know about the transition to college, generally?

2. What factors predict a successful college transition?

3. What challenges do first-generation students experience?

4. What are ways of supporting new college students and first-generation college students?

CHAPTER SUMMARY

10.1   Discuss achievement attributions and motivation, including their influences.

Achievement motivation, the willingness to persist at challenging tasks and meet high standards of accomplishment, is a powerful predictor of academic success, beyond intelligence, cognitive abilities, and prior performance. Performance can be attributed to causes that vary in internality, controllability, stability, and mindset. Adolescents who adopt internal, controllable explanations of performance and a growth mindset tend to have a strong mastery orientation, a belief that success stems from effort and applying strategies well. Others attribute failure to internal factors such as ability, adopting a learned helplessness orientation that combines a fixed mindset, and the attribution of poor performance to internal uncontrollable factors. A mastery orientation has been shown to predict subsequent classroom engagement and higher grades among high school students. The contexts in which we are immersed, including factors such as parents and teachers, socioeconomic status, and culture, also play a role in shaping our views of our abilities.

10.2   Examine correlates of school transitions and contextual influences on academic achievement in adolescence.

Most adolescents experience the many changes that accompany school transitions as stressful, and academic achievement and motivation tends to decline during the transition to middle school and high school. Grades tend to decline with each school transition. The negative effects of school transitions occur when there is little stage-environment fit, when there is a poor match between adolescents' developmental needs and what the school environment affords in its organization and characteristics. Parents, peers, schools, and neighborhoods influence academic achievement.

10.3   Identify common developmental disabilities and specific learning disorders experienced by adolescents and ways of addressing their educational needs.

Adolescents with intellectual disability show delayed development and difficulty adapting. Adolescents with autism spectrum disorders tend to experience deficits in social communication and a tendency to engage in repetitive behaviors, with or without intellectual disability. Both adolescents with intellectual disabilities and those with autism experience greater susceptibility to peers and risks for peer rejection. Adolescents with attention-deficit/ hyperactivity disorder experience difficulties with attention and impulsivity that interferes with school performance and increases the risk of impulsive risk-taking and externalizing behavior. Several specific learning disorders are common: developmental dyslexia, developmental dyscalculia, and developmental dysgraphia. Adolescents with developmental disabilities require assistance, such as special education, to help them overcome obstacles to learning.

10.4 Contrast the experience of college-bound and noncollege-bound youth.

School dropout rates in the United States have reached historic lows, but about 6% of high school students drop out of school each year. Adults of all ages often view their college years as highly influential in shaping their thoughts, values, and worldview. College students encounter a wealth of new experiences and opportunities for autonomy, ideas, and social demands. Attending college is associated with advances in moral reasoning, identity development, and social development. How a student handles the transition to college itself predicts the likelihood of dropping out, as does the quality of support from the college or university. First-generation college students experience higher risk of dropout. Young adults who enter the workforce immediately after high school have fewer work opportunities than those of prior generations and an unemployment rate about twice that of bachelor's degree holders. The curricula of most secondary schools tend to be oriented toward college-bound students, and counseling tends to focus on helping students gain admission to college, leaving young adults who do not attend college ill prepared for the job market.

KEY TERMS

achievement motivation, 202

attention-deficit/hyperactivity disorder (ADHD), 213

autism spectrum disorders (ASD), 212

developmental dyscalculia, 214

developmental dysgraphia, 214

developmental dyslexia, 213

external attribution, 202

fixed mindset, 202

growth mindset, 202

inclusion, 215

internal attribution, 202

learned helplessness orientation, 202

mastery orientation, 202

special education, 215

specific learning disorder (SLD), 213

stage-environment fit, 206

tracking, 209

11

Media and Online Contexts

Learning Objectives

11.1 Describe theories of media influence and adolescent development.

11.2 Analyze the effects of exposure to media with violent, sexual, and substance use themes on adolescent development.

11.3 Examine the relationship of social media and adolescent development.

11.4 Describe media literacy and recommendations for promoting media literacy in adolescents.

Chapter Contents

Adolescents are immersed in a media-filled world through interactions with television, magazines, books, movies, advertisements, video games, social media, and the Internet. Video games and social media receive a great deal of attention as potential triggers for violent and sexual behavior. However, concerns about media influence on adolescent behavior are not new. In the 1950s, concern centered on comic books and a U.S. Senate Judiciary Subcommittee was formed to evaluate the dangers of comic books to child and adolescent development. As noted in the hearing:

I would like to point out to you one other crime comic book which we have found to be particularly injurious to the ethical development of children and those are the Superman comic books. They [sic] arose in children phantasies of sadistic joy in seeing other people punished over and over again while you yourself remain immune. We have called it the Superman complex. (Comic Book Legal Defense Fund, 2019)

The U.S. Senate Judiciary hearing resulted in the formation of the Comic Magazine Association of America, which instituted the Comics Code Authority, a censorship code that sanitized the content of comics until the 2000s.

Concerns about the effects of exposure to media on development have persisted. Movies and television have remained in the spotlight since their invention. The potential influence of music lyrics has received attention since the 1950s, when adults worried about Elvis Presley and, later, the Beatles, heavy metal music in the 1980s, and rap music through today. Most recent are concerns about the potential for video games to incite violence. How does media influence development? Is it a powerful lure for adolescents? In this chapter we examine media use and its effects in adolescence.

UNDERSTANDING ADOLESCENTS' USE OF MEDIA

Although screen media receives the lion's share of attention from parents, educators, and professionals, adolescents also interact with nonscreen media such as print and audio media. For example, about two-thirds of adolescents report listening to music each day (Rideout, 2015). Adolescents' screen media activities include watching television, movies, and online videos; playing video, computer, and mobile games; using social media; and using the Internet, as discussed next.

Media Use in Adolescence

In total, adolescents between the ages of 13 and 18 spend a staggering 9 hours a day, over half of their waking hours, using entertainment media, including about 6½ hours of screen media (Figure 11.1). However, there are large individual differences in screen use. For instance, similar numbers of adolescents report using screen media for 2 hours or less a day (23%) and over 8 hours a day (26%) (Rideout, 2015).

The most common type of screen media is television, used by most adolescents each day (66%). Nearly half of adolescents age 13 to 18 (45%) report using social

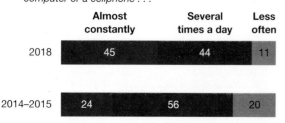

FIGURE 11.1

Screen Media Use in Adolescents

45% of teens say they're online almost constantly

% of U.S. teens who say they use the internet, either on a computer or a cellphone . . .

	Almost constantly	Several times a day	Less often
2018	45	44	11
2014–2015	24	56	20

Source: Anderson, Monica, and Jingjing Jiang. "Teens, Social Media & Technology 2018." Pew Research Center, Washington, DC (May 31, 2018). https://www.pewresearch.org/internet/2018/05/31/teens-social-media-technology-2018/.

media and about a third report watching online videos (34%) and playing mobile games (27%) every day (Rideout, 2015). Despite these trends, adolescents vary in media preferences and the time spent on media. Recent research has suggested five distinct patterns of screen use in adolescence. As shown in Figure 11.2, 26% of adolescents can be categorized as heavy viewers, spending about 6½ hours a day watching television. Other adolescents spend much of their screen time playing video games; gamers (20% of adolescents) tend to spend about 2½ hours day playing video games (Rideout, 2015). Boys and girls tend to report different media preferences. Girls are more likely to report listening to music as their favorite media activity (37%), whereas boys report playing video games (27%) and listening to music (22%) as preferred activities.

One type of screen use is of particular concern to parents, educators, and developmental scientists: social media. About 80% of adolescents report using social media and the frequency of social media use has skyrocketed over the past decade. As shown in Figure 11.3, the proportion of adolescents who report using social media multiple times a day has doubled, from 34% in 2012 to 70% in 2018. Over a third (38%) report using social media multiple times an hour (and 16% report using it "almost constantly"). The rise in social media use is linked with the proliferation of smartphones. The proportion of adolescents who own smartphones has more than doubled between 2012 to 2018, from 41% to 95% (Anderson & Jiang, 2018a; Rideout & Robb, 2018). Smartphones offer adolescents unprecedented access to digital media, including social media. We examine social media in more detail later in this chapter.

Theories of Media Influence

Media is an integral part of most adolescents' (and adults') days. A common concern of parents, educators, and policy makers that, ironically, often appears in media outlets, is that exposure to media may have harmful effects on adolescents. How does media use affect adolescents' thoughts and behavior? There are several theoretical explanations for media effects.

According to **cultivation theory**, exposure to media influences adolescents' thinking, shapes their attitudes, and affects their behavior (Gerbner et al., 2002). Repeated exposure to media promotes the belief that the messages conveyed by media apply to the real world. Television and other media are thought to have gradual long-term effects on their audience, influencing adolescents' attitudes, interests, and beliefs about society. From this perspective, media shapes adolescents' beliefs and behavior, and adolescents therefore reproduce what they see on television and in video games and other media. According to cultivation theory, adolescents who watch violent

Adolescents' Patterns of Media Use per Day

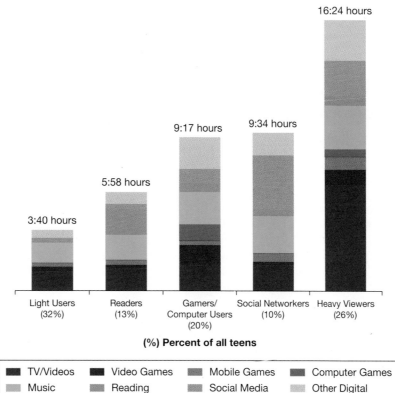

Time spent with each type of media

(%) Percent of all teens

Light Users (32%) · Readers (13%) · Gamers/Computer Users (20%) · Social Networkers (10%) · Heavy Viewers (26%)

3:40 hours · 5:58 hours · 9:17 hours · 9:34 hours · 16:24 hours

Legend: TV/Videos · Video Games · Mobile Games · Computer Games · Music · Reading · Social Media · Other Digital

Source: Rideout (2015).

Social Media and Digital Device Use, 2012 Versus 2018

Percent of 13- to 17-year-olds who:

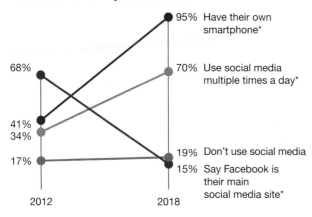

95% Have their own smartphone*
70% Use social media multiple times a day*
68%
41%
34%
19% Don't use social media
17%
15% Say Facebook is their main social media site*

2012 — 2018

*Differences over time are statistically significant at $p < .05$.

Sources: Anderson and Jiang (2018a) and Rideout and Robb (2018).

media or play violent games are at risk for engaging in violence.

A related view, social learning theory (discussed in Chapter 1), explains behavior as learned through observation. Specifically, adolescents observe models of behavior and, if motivated, reproduce that behavior. Individuals are likely to repeat a behavior when they attend to it, recall it, and perceive it as rewarding or fun. Adolescents imitate behavior that they see frequently performed and accompanied by rewards. Therefore, adolescents who observe violent models being rewarded on television, such as the "good guy" gunning down the "bad guys" and receiving accolades, are more likely to engage in similar aggressive acts.

Do adolescents simply mirror what they see? Both cultivation theory and social learning theory view adolescents as shaped by the media they consume. From these perspectives, viewing media that has violent or sexual themes makes adolescents more likely to engage in violent behavior or sexual activity. Other theories of media influence pose that, rather than being passively influenced by the media

Media influence is a two-way process whereby media also influences adolescents.
iStock.com/cagkansayin

they consume, adolescents actively select the media they watch. From this view, correlations between adolescent behavior and media exposure occur because adolescents choose media that they find interesting. For example, the **uses and gratifications theory** focuses on individual differences as influences on media use and its effects (Katz, Blumler, & Gurevitch, 1973; Rubin, 2002). Media fulfills a variety of purposes or needs, such as providing information, social bonding, opportunities to learn about oneself, and entertainment. Adolescents' specific characteristics and interests determine their needs and what they seek from media. Some characteristics lead adolescents to prefer specific media, such as that depicting violence or sex. Adolescents are satisfied when their needs are met. Therefore, adolescents interested in violence or sex seek out violent or sexy media that fulfills their interests and needs.

The theories we have discussed thus far pose one-way effects of media: media influences adolescents' behavior in cultivation and social learning theories, and adolescents' interests and behavior influence the media they select in uses and gratifications theory. Development, however, is much more complex. Adolescents both influence and are influenced by their contexts. The **media practice model** acknowledges these complex bidirectional relationships (Steele & Brown, 1995). Similar to uses and gratifications theory, the media practice model poses that adolescents' motivations or needs influence the media they select and how they attend to it. Adolescents' self-understanding and sense of identity are central to their interactions with media and media interactions in turn

influence their sense of who they are. Adolescents process media cognitively and emotionally. Adolescents use media to enhance their mood, cope with difficult feelings, make a statement about their identity, and imagine possible selves. They prefer characters they can relate to and match who they are or would like to be. Media influence is a two-way process whereby media also influences adolescents. As adolescents interact with media, they face the challenging task of balancing their already formed beliefs and world views with the sometimes contradictory messages and beliefs conveyed by media (Steele & Brown, 1995). The media practice model explains media use as an active process of self-construction, offering opportunities for identity development.

Media Use and Positive Development

Discussions about the effects of media on adolescent development tend to focus on the potential harms of media use. However, media use also offers benefits to development. For example, playing video games offers opportunities for exploration, cognitive challenge, relaxation, and, often, interaction with peers (Adachi & Willoughby, 2016; Przybylski, 2014). Playing video games is associated with advances in visuospatial abilities, attentional control, memory, executive function, and problem-solving skills (Bavelier & Davidson, 2013; Boot, Blakely, & Simons, 2011).

Internet and social media use provide adolescents opportunities to gather information, practice skills, and interact with peers. The ability to acquire, interpret, and apply information acquired from

Electronic media use is sometimes a shared activity in which adolescents share photos and gather information such as online reviews to decide on activities, such as what movie to see.
iStock.com/fstop123

screens—computers, tablets, and smartphones—is essential for success in all of the contexts in which adolescents are immersed. Gathering information to make decisions about whether to purchase an item or dine at a restaurant, interpreting the tone and content of text messages and emails, evaluating media stories, and determining whether to believe social media messages are life skills for today's information age. Because of this, recent research suggests that digital screen use at moderate levels is not intrinsically harmful and may be advantageous in a connected world (Orben & Przybylski, 2019; Przybylski & Weinstein, 2017). The overuse of screens, however, may displace important activities, such as school work, athletic activities, or social functions. In this sense, screen use may display a "Goldilocks effect" where, just as in the "Goldilocks and the Three Bears" fable, there is a level of screen use that is "just right" for adolescent development. Too little screen use might deprive adolescents of cognitive and social opportunities and too much might interfere with developmental tasks (Przybylski & Weinstein, 2017). However, the content of adolescents' screen media use may determine its effects on development, as discussed next.

REVIEW 11.1

1. Describe patterns of screen use in adolescence.

2. Explain three theories of media influence in adolescence.

3. Identify ways in which media can positively influence adolescent development.

THINKING IN CONTEXT 11.1

1. What media do you use, screen and nonscreen? How much time do you spend interacting with media?

2. How has your media use changed from childhood to adolescence to now? Consider the types of media, time spent on media, and characteristics of media.

3. In your view, does exposure to media affect adolescents? Why or why not?

4. Evaluate the three theories of media use. Which do you prefer? Why?

APPLY 11.1

Sixteen-year-old Carolyn has been homeschooled since the age of 5. In hopes of protecting her from the dangers of the outside world, Carolyn's parents ban the use of television and other forms of digital media. They believe that today's teenagers are glued to glowing screens all day, like zombies, with negative effects for development. For entertainment, Carolyn plays card games, writes stories, reads vintage books, and writes snail-mail letters to keep in contact with her extended family.

1. To what degree is Carolyn's parents' view of adolescent media use accurate?

2. Describe some of the ways that media use might positively effect Carolyn's development.

3. Considering what you know about Carolyn's parents, which theory of media influence do you think they would agree with and why?

EFFECTS OF EXPOSURE TO ADULT THEMES IN MEDIA

Since the comic book scare of the 1950s, discussed at the beginning of this chapter, and likely since the advent of media itself, adults have wondered about the effects of media consumption in adolescence. Specifically, adults are concerned about whether exposure to media that depicts adult themes, such as violence, sex, and substance use, is harmful. The answer to this question is complicated because it may vary with the type of media and the content.

Violence

Most of the attention on the effects of media on adolescents has focused on the effects of exposure to violence in media. Violence is prevalent in television and movies and has increased over the decades. For example, an analysis of 22 films in the popular James Bond movie franchise, spanning 4 decades, found that violence rates doubled from 1962 to 2008 (McAnally, Robertson, Strasburger, & Hancox, 2013). Likewise, an analysis of a cross-section of television shows rated for children, adolescents, and adults found that violence was pervasive, occurring in 70% of episodes overall and for 2.3 seconds per minute of each episode (Gabrielli, Traore, Stoolmiller, Bergamini, & Sargent, 2016). How does exposure to media violence influence adolescents?

Television

Generally speaking, we know more about the effects of exposure to violence on television in children than adolescents. Exposure to media violence in childhood has been associated with aggressive behavior in adolescence and adulthood (C. A. Anderson et al., 2003; Huesmann, 2007). Specifically, regular exposure to media violence in middle childhood predicts increased aggressiveness in adolescence and young adulthood (Eisner & Malti, 2015). For example, a classic study of children examined annually over 3 years in middle childhood found increasing rates of aggression in children who watched more television violence (Huesmann & Eron, 1986; Huesmann, Lagerspetz, & Eron, 1984). In this study, the children were most likely to act aggressively when they identified with the aggressor and perceived the violence as realistic. Fifteen years later, the children who habitually watched more television violence were more aggressive as young adults (Huesmann, Moise-Titus, Podolski, & Eron, 2003). The effects of exposure to television violence is gradual and is likely cumulative over time (Krahé, 2012). Children exposed to violence regularly are more likely to be desensitized to its effects and view aggression as more acceptable than children who watch less violent television (Calvert, 2015).

Most of the research on the effects of exposure to television violence examines children. Exposure to television violence is less likely to influence adolescent behavior than children's behavior (Browne & Hamilton-Giachritsis, 2005). Adolescents have more advanced cognitive abilities than children, including the ability to reason, they reflect on what they see, and they show more sophisticated moral reasoning. These capacities likely influence how adolescents view and respond to televised violence. Although adolescents are less likely to show violent behavior in response to television violence, viewing television violence may influence their attitudes toward violence, desensitizing them to the effects of violence and leading them to think aggressive thoughts and expect hostile and aggressive behavior from others (Calvert, 2015; Wiedeman, Black, Dolle, Finney, & Coker, 2015).

Television violence is associated with aggressive behavior in children and aggressive thoughts in adolescents; however, these conclusions are based on correlational research. Recall from Chapter 1 that correlations measure the relationship among variables, but they do not tell us about causality. Without controlling variables, there is no way to determine whether exposure to television violence increases aggression, whether aggressive adolescents watch more violent programs, or whether other, unmeasured, variables are at work (Slater, Henry, Swaim, & Anderson, 2003). Other factors, such as experiences at home, with peers, at school, and in the community, influence violence. Family factors, such as harsh parenting, maltreatment, and exposure to domestic violence are especially important predictors aggressive behavior in adolescence (Labella & Masten, 2018). Within the peer context, adolescents who feel rejected by their peers tend to report higher levels of anger and frustration and show more lenient moral judgments of antisocial media content, which was associated with a greater preference for antisocial YouTube clips (Plaisier & Konijn, 2013). In addition, personality factors, such as a predisposition toward aggression, also influence adolescents' choice of media (Rydell, 2016). Recall from the media practice model that adolescents select media that match their interests. Therefore, more aggressive adolescents tend to prefer more violent media that those who are less aggressive (Breuer, Vogelgesang, Quandt, & Festl, 2015). After considering their predispositions and the interactions adolescents experience in their immediate contexts, the effects of exposure to television violence on behavior tends to be small (Browne & Hamilton-Giachritsis, 2005).

Many popular television shows, such as *American Horror Story*, **contain a great deal of violence.**
TCD/Prod.DB / Alamy Stock Photo

Video Games

We have seen that viewing television violence is associated with aggressive cognition and has small effects on adolescents' behavior. What about video games? Video game players are immersed in a realistic world in which they shoot and kill zombies, "bad guys," and sometimes innocent people and "good guys." Does enacting violent scenarios in video games make adolescents more aggressive? A 2011 U.S. Supreme Court case, *Brown v. Entertainment Merchants Association*, examined this question and whether to limit adolescents' access to violent video games. The Supreme Court evaluated research summarized by psychologists, physicians, and other researchers and health professionals and concluded that the evidence on video game violence was not persuasive and could not justify the strict guidelines for scrutiny needed to regulate adolescents' access to violent video games (Ferguson, 2013). A growing body of research examines the effect of playing violent video games, with similar conclusions. For example, a study of adolescents and emerging adults who played shooter games, in which players hunt and "shoot" animated people, found that exposure to shooter games did not predict adolescent conduct disorder or criminal behavior (Smith, Ferguson, & Beaver, 2018). Another study of preadolescents surveyed at ages 7 to 11 and again 1 year later found that violent gaming was not associated with increases in aggressive behavior or problems (Lobel, Engels, Stone, Burk, & Granic, 2017).

Yet some researchers disagree, arguing that findings on video game violence are mixed. For example, a recent analysis of literature by the Workgroup on Media Violence and Violent Video Games reported evidence of short-term harmful effects as well as long-term harmful effects, such as increasing aggressive thoughts, angry feelings, physiologic arousal, aggressive behavior, desensitization to violence, and decreases in prosocial behavior (e.g., helping others) and empathy (Anderson et al., 2017). Likewise, the American Psychological Association Task Force on Violent Media reviewed the body of research and concluded that exposure to violent video games was associated with aggressive thoughts, affect, and behavior as well as physiological arousal, increased

desensitization to violence, and less empathy (Calvert et al., 2017).

Other researchers have noted, however, that sales of violent video games rose at the same time as violent behavior declined (see Figure 11.4; Ferguson, 2013). If playing violent video games triggered violent behavior, the rise in sales would be accompanied by a similar rise in violence. Instead, a body of research suggests that the effects of violent video games tend to be overestimated and are at about zero (Hilgard, Engelhardt, & Rouder, 2017). For example, a comprehensive review of the literature on violent video games showed that video games might have small relationships to aggressive behavior, reduced prosocial behavior, reduced academic performance, and attention-deficit symptoms and problems but the effects are negligible or nonexistent once other variables, such as family factors, are considered (DeCamp & Ferguson, 2017; Ferguson, 2015). As with the research on television violence, these studies are correlational. A multitude of interactions in the family, peer, school, and neighborhood contexts contribute to adolescent violence.

In line with the media practice model, individual differences, such as personality factors and interests, also matter. Adolescents who are more aggressive are likely to seek out media with aggressive or violent content (Saleem, Anderson, & Gentile, 2012; Wiedeman et al., 2015). In other words, individuals with aggressive tendencies tend to choose video games that reflect those tendencies, which in turn

FIGURE 11.4

Youth Violence and Violent Video Game Sales Data

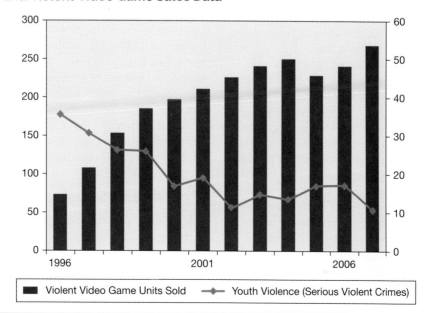

Source: Ferguson (2013) and sources therein.

might reinforce aggressive tendencies (Slater et al., 2003). Although adolescents who are not generally aggressive can still be negatively influenced by violent media, research has shown that children and adolescents who are generally more aggressive tend to be more strongly influenced by exposure to violent media (Wiedeman et al., 2015). One longitudinal study found that for 14- to 17-year-old adolescents physical aggression predicted the later use of violent video games rather than the reverse, suggesting that adolescents select video games that match their interests (in this case, aggressive; Breuer et al., 2015). This is supported by research with college students that suggests that more aggressive people may seek out competitive video games to a greater extent than less aggressive people (Adachi & Willoughby, 2016). Adolescents who feel excluded may also experience heightened preferences for violent games; the combination of exclusion and violent game playing fuels aggressive inclinations (Plaisier & Konijn, 2013).

Sexualized depictions of women in media can skew adolescent attitudes on sex, relationships, and their sense of self.
Xavier ROSSI / Contributor / Getty Images

Sex

Sexual content is nearly inescapable on television. It is estimated that nearly three-quarters of television programs include some form of sexual content (including talking about sex, passionate kissing, intimate touching, and explicit sexual intercourse) (Roberts, Henriksen, & Foehr, 2009). It is widely assumed that adolescents' exposure to sexual content on television and other forms of media influences their sexual activity. Is this true? Perhaps not surprisingly, the answer to this question is complicated.

Some studies have suggested that exposure to sexy media predicts the initiation of sexual activity in adolescents (Collins, Martino, Elliott, & Miu, 2011; O'Hara, Gibbons, Gerrard, Li, & Sargent, 2012). For example, in one study, 2,000 adolescents aged 12 to 17 reported on their sexual behavior and how often they watched a list of programs that varied in sexual content. One year later, the researchers found that adolescents who saw more sex on television were more likely to initiate intercourse than adolescents who saw less (Collins et al., 2004). Subsequent research that examined a multitude of factors, however, has suggested that exposure to sexy media does not influence sexual activity. In a 3-year study of adolescents aged 14 to 16, overall exposure to sexual content on television did not predict having had sex (Gottfried, Vaala, Bleakley, Hennessy, & Jordan, 2013). Likewise, a large meta-analysis found that when other factors are controlled, the association between media and sexual behavior is small and negligible (Ferguson, Nielsen, & Markey, 2016). Adolescents differ in experiences and interests. Adolescents who are more interested in sex tend to choose media that has more sexual content (Steinberg & Monahan, 2011).

Similar to findings concerning exposure to violence, although sexy media may not cause adolescents to engage in sexual behavior, exposure to sexual content on television is associated with greater acceptance of stereotypical and casual attitudes about sex (Ward & Friedman, 2006). Television and movies tend to emphasize sex as a recreational activity, a casual leisure activity. Sex is frequently depicted as occurring outside of committed relationships, with little mention of contraception and sexually transmitted infections (STIs). Television, movies, music videos, and other media with sexual content tend to portray women as sexual objects, emphasizing their physical appearance and sexual appeal. Men, on the other hand, are portrayed as sex-motivated predators whose status is enhanced by their success with women. Repeated exposure to sexual stereotypes can influence adolescents' attitudes about sex.

Alcohol and Substance Use

Adolescents are exposed to substance-related content in television, movies, and advertising (Collins et al., 2016; Jackson, Janssen, & Gabrielli, 2018). Unlike the more mixed findings with regard to violent and sexual content, research has shown that exposure to alcohol content in marketing and the media increases the risk of drinking from early adolescence through early adulthood (Anderson, de Bruijn, Angus, Gordon, &

Hastings, 2009; Jernigan, Noel, Landon, Thornton, & Lobstein, 2017). Exposure to alcohol advertising may lead to an earlier initiation of drinking, increase consumption among under-age drinkers, and increase the risk of problem drinking, including binge drinking (Grenard, Dent, & Stacy, 2013; Morgenstern et al., 2014). Likewise, exposure to e-cigarette content is associated with e-cigarette use in adolescents and young adults as well as with greater susceptibility and curiosity about trying e-cigarettes among adolescents who have never used e-cigarettes (Mantey, Cooper, Clendennen, Pasch, & Perry, 2016; Portnoy, Wu, Tworek, Chen, & Borek, 2014).

Media campaigns may increase adolescents' knowledge about substances, but they do not always affect adolescents' behavior.
geogphotos / Alamy Stock Photo

Popular music lyrics and music videos tend to portray the positive consequences of substance use (Cranwell, Britton, & Bains, 2017; Cranwell et al., 2015). Beliefs that substance use will result in positive outcomes such as having fun and making friends influence substance use and are one way that media messages about substance use influence adolescents' use (Collins et al., 2017). Adolescents who have positive expectations about the benefits of smoking, for example, are more likely to start smoking then their peers (Creamer, Delk, Case, Perry, & Harrell, 2018). Media portrayals of substance use often make it appear normative, making adolescents believe that substance use is widespread and that their peers ("everyone") engage in substance use (Elmore, Scull, & Kupersmidt, 2017). Media messages about substance use thereby socialize adolescents to believe that substance use is more prevalent among their peers than it actually is (Jackson et al., 2018). Believing that substance use is common among peers places adolescents at risk of initiating and maintaining substance use. Mass media campaigns to address substance use are often delivered as short advertisements and aim to educate the audience about the dangers of substance use and present positive role models who reject substance use. These campaigns tend to show mixed findings. Whereas mass media campaigns about alcohol use, for example, are often recalled and may influence knowledge, there is little evidence that they reduce alcohol consumption (Young et al., 2018). Some campaigns were associated with increases in substance use by adolescents, whereas others show no effect (Allara, Ferri, Bo, Gasparrini, & Faggiano, 2015).

As we have discussed, one of the challenges of studying media effects is the difficulty of determining cause and effect. Without conducting an experiment and manipulating the media that adolescents see, we cannot establish causality—that exposure to media influenced behavior. Adolescents' preferences and interests influence the media they choose and their subsequent behavior. Adolescents' interests also determine the messages to which they attend. It is conceivable that an adolescent who is curious about substance use and interested in risky behaviors might be more likely to notice and attend to media that displays substance use than an adolescent with different interests. In turn, adolescents who are curious about substance use, interested in risky behavior, and prefer media displaying substance use may be more likely to initiate and sustain substance use than peers. Disentangling the interactive effects of media, adolescents' preferences, and adolescents' behavior is challenging.

REVIEW 11.2

1. What are the effects of exposure to television violence in adolescents, as compared with children?

2. Describe the effects of playing violent video games on adolescent development.

3. In what ways might exposure to sexy media influence adolescent behavior?

4. How does exposure to substance-related content in media affect adolescents?

• •

THINKING IN CONTEXT 11.2

Think about the media that you have consumed today. Consider advertisements, social media posts, and other media.

1. What messages did you encounter about alcohol and substance use? Describe the content of those messages.

2. In your view, how accurate are the messages?

3. Considering cognitive and social development, how might a young adolescent interpret them? An older adolescent?

· ·

APPLY 11.2

At 10 years old Dara received a video game console and discovered a new game that involved shooting bad guys. Now 13, Dara immediately starts playing video games after she returns home from school. Dara feels that playing games is a great way to let off steam after a long school day, especially when she's angry after being snubbed by a classmate. Dara's mother observed that the shooting games have become more and more graphic each year, and Dara is glued to the screen all afternoon, evening, and weekend.

Dara's mother worries about her constant video game playing. The other day she asked Dara to put the game away and finish her homework as well as some household tasks, like doing the dishes. Dara flew into a rage, "No! You can't tell me what to do!" and furiously slammed her bedroom door. Dara threw her cup across her bedroom, spilling soda everywhere.

Dara's mother wondered to herself, "That's quite an outburst! I wonder if that video game gets her hyped up. I watched violent movies when I was a teenager. They're nothing like the games Dara plays. So realistic, it's scary."

1. Considering the research on violent media use in adolescence, should Dara's mother worry about Dara's video game use? Might it influence her behavior? Why or why not?

2. How might physical, cognitive, and socioemotional development play a role in Dara's media use and her reaction to her mother's request?

3. What developmental changes is Dara experiencing in each of these areas that might influence her response to her mother? How might these factors influence her media use?

· ·

SOCIAL MEDIA AND ADOLESCENT DEVELOPMENT

Social media is part of the fabric of daily life for adolescents and adults. It has transformed adolescents' social lives in ways that affect their cognitive, social, and emotional development. Although much of the research to date has examined the potentially harmful effects of social media on adolescents, social media is simply another context in which adolescents interact, with both positive and negative influences.

Social Media and Positive Development

Social media use is nearly universal (Anderson & Jiang, 2018b). Although adults often express concerns about the dangers of social media, it serves developmental functions for adolescents. Adolescents use social media to develop and maintain friendships (Uhls, Ellison, & Subrahmanyam, 2017). Decades ago, adolescents wrote lengthy notes on paper to friends to read in class and spent hours talking on the phone with friends each day (often causing friction with parents and siblings in homes with only one phone!). Today's adolescents aren't any different, but the means of communication have changed. Virtually all adolescents report interacting with offline friends on social media and most report sharing their usernames with new friends to stay in touch.

Social media offers new opportunities for developing the capacity for intimacy. For example, in one study of over 3,000 early adolescents, social media use was positively linked with reports of friendship quality and bonding (Antheunis, Schouten, & Krahmer, 2016). Adolescents share their thoughts and emotions with friends and offer friends support through communication on social media platforms. Adolescents report that they feel better connected to their friends through social media activity and know more about friends' lives and their feelings (Anderson & Jiang, 2018b; Lenhart, 2015).

Adolescents also report that interactions on social media make them feel like they have people who will support them through tough times (Uhls et al., 2017). Most obviously, communicating in writing, whether as texts or social media posts, differs from face-to-face communication. Many people find it easier to self-disclose on a screen where they can carefully compose and edit their message and deliver it without the potential discomfort that accompanies a real-time interpersonal interaction. Indeed, adolescents report more opportunities for self-disclosure on social media than in real life (Best, Manktelow, & Taylor, 2014). Although adults may be concerned that social media may interfere with social development and offline interpersonal communication, adolescents view their social media use positively. Adolescents tend to associate their social media use with positive rather than negative emotions, such as feeling included rather than excluded or feeling confident rather than insecure (see Figure 11.5; Anderson & Jiang, 2018b).

Social media offers opportunities for identity development. Recall that identity development is a

FIGURE 11.5

Adolescents' Feelings About Social Media Use and Emotions

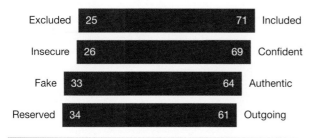

% of U.S. teens who say that social media makes them feel more . . .

Source: Anderson and Jiang (2018b).

constructive process in which the individual explores, tries out possible selves, interacts with the social world, and commits to identities (Erikson, 1959). Social media allows adolescents to engage in selective self-presentation, posting certain photographs and text that reflect their burgeoning identities, gaining feedback from their peers on such presentations, and engaging in social comparison with the self-presentations of their peers (Wood, Bukowski, & Lis, 2016). Adolescents can experiment by revealing and expressing different characteristics that represent different selves, such aspects of real, ideal, and false selves, and their multiple intersecting identities (Michikyan & Suárez-Orozco, 2016). Most adolescents agree that people get to show different sides of themselves on social media that they cannot show offline (Lenhart, 2015) and most adolescents (and adults) carefully plan how they will present themselves (Nesi, Choukas-Bradley, & Prinstein, 2018a).

In addition, social media may have a special role in identity and intimacy development for adolescents who are marginalized or who are questioning their identity. Access to diverse peers in other geographic locations can help adolescents find like-minded peers and those with similar experiences and interests. Adolescents in isolated communities or who feel different from peers can connect with similar peers, making social connections and friendships that may be unavailable offline (Nesi et al., 2018a). For example, adolescents attempting to understand their gender and sexual identities may learn about themselves through online interactions with other questioning peers (Michikyan & Suárez-Orozco, 2016). Through social media interactions with similar peers, adolescents without offline friends can feel less lonely and more confident. The majority of adolescents report that social media sites are a positive contribution to their lives (Uhls et al., 2017).

Social Media and Adolescent Problems

Adolescent development unfolds in the variety of interacting contexts in which adolescents are embedded. The developmental factors that place adolescents at risk for problems may work differently in different contexts. Most of the research examining the effects of social media has focused on its potentially negative effects, with mixed results. For example, heavy use of social media has been associated with depressive symptoms and low self-esteem (Bányai et al., 2017), but other research suggests that the overall correlation between social media use and depression is small (McCrae, Gettings, & Purssell, 2017). One 3-year longitudinal study of fifth-, seventh-, and ninth-grade students found no consistent relationships between social media use and depressive symptoms (Houghton et al., 2018). Likewise in longitudinal research following adolescents and emerging adults over 2 and 6 years, respectively, social media use did not predict depressive symptoms (Heffer, Good, Daly, MacDonell, & Willoughby, 2019). Other research examines the effects of social media on body image and peer relationships, including cyberbullying and sexting, conducted through text or social media.

Body Image

We have seen that adolescents engage with a great deal of media—traditional, such as magazines, and new, such as social media—and this exposure can have implications for their development and functioning. For example, fashion magazines and the advertisements in those magazines may send an inflated message of the importance of thinness and attractiveness. Research has shown that reading fashion magazines is associated with poor body image and unhealthy weight control behaviors (Benowitz-Fredericks, Garcia, Massey, Vasagar, & Borzekowski, 2012).

Today's media messages are nearly inescapable as they arrive through Instagram and other social media sites and include the images of not just models and celebrities but also peers. Exposure to idealized thin bodies, whether in traditional or new media, leads to greater focus on the body and higher body dissatisfaction (Fardouly & Vartanian, 2016; Grogan, 2016). Preadolescent and adolescent girls who spend more time on social media experience a greater drive for thinness, internalization of the thin ideal, and body surveillance, and they report more frequent dieting than their peers (Tiggemann & Slater, 2013, 2014).

Appearance comparisons to peers may be particularly influential for body image (Fardouly & Vartanian, 2016). Adolescents commonly use apps and digital tools to manipulate and tweak their appearance in pictures, creating an idealized self, with potentially negative consequences for peers. For example, high school girls were exposed to either original or retouched and reshaped Instagram selfies in one study. Girls preferred the manipulated images and showed lower body image after viewing the manipulated images as compared with the original (Kleemans, Daalmans, Carbaat, & Anschütz, 2018). Girls who regularly share photos on social media, and especially those who engage in greater manipulation of shared photos, tend to overemphasize body shape and weight, internalize the thin ideal, and show more body dissatisfaction (McLean, Paxton, Wertheim, & Masters, 2015).

One study of high school students found that greater social media use predicted greater body dissatisfaction and increased appearance-related discussions with peers 18 months later (de Vries, Peter, de Graaf, & Nikken, 2016). However, body dissatisfaction did not predict social media usage, suggesting that social media use precedes body image issues. Research with other samples suggests that it is not the total time on social media that matters but the time allocated to photo activity that is associated with greater thin ideal internalization, self-objectification, weight dissatisfaction, and drive for thinness (Meier & Gray, 2014). Again, it is worth noting that these conclusions are based on correlational data. It is difficult to determine the direction of effects, but it is plausible that there is a bidirectional relationship whereby adolescents with high thin ideal internalization and body dissatisfaction are driven to interact more heavily with photo-related features and this frequent appearance-related activity acts to reinforce or increase existing body image issues.

In today's connected world, adolescents are vulnerable to new and ever-present forms of cyberbullying.
iStock.com/Tassii

Cyberbullying

Perhaps the most studied problem associated with social media use is **cyberbullying**, repeated online assaults via social media, email, texting, or other electronic means. It is estimated that between 5% and 15% of adolescents experience cyberbullying (Modecki, Minchin, Harbaugh, Guerra, & Runions, 2014; Zycha, Ortega-Ruiza, & Del Rey, 2015). Some scholars have proposed that online victimization is simply traditional bullying that occurs online, that technology provides a new context for old behaviors, and that adolescent cyberbullying can be understood by studying traditional, offline bullying (Olweus, 2012). However, cyberbullying is distinct from in-person bullying in many ways.

Whereas traditional in-person bullying tends to occur at or near school, cyberbullying is asynchronous, meaning that it does not require the presence of the victim. It can happen at any time, so adolescents can never fully escape the potential for victimization, perhaps leading to feelings of powerlessness (Dooley, Pyżalski, & Cross, 2009). Whereas adolescents may have once perceived the home environment as a "sanctuary" from bullying, the availability of social media means that this is no longer the case (Slonje & Smith, 2008). Additionally, the ability to aggress against peers at night, outside of adult supervision is especially notable (Runions, 2013). This lack of control and asynchronous quality means that many victims perceive cyberbullying as more harsh and uncontrollable than traditional forms of bullying (Nesi, Choukas-Bradley, & Prinstein, 2018b). The features of the online environment create a context in which individuals are more likely to say or do things that they would not do in a face-to-face setting. Perpetrators likely cannot observe the verbal or facial cues of victims and may not receive immediate feedback from peers, which might worsen the cyberbullying.

Adolescents' responses to cyberbullying are commonly passive, with a pervasive lack of awareness or confidence that anything can be done to stop it. There is a consistent relationship between cyberbullying and depression and suicide ideation (Hamm et al., 2015; Zycha et al., 2015). Cyberbullying is also associated with anxiety, behavior problems, poor well-being, and poor life satisfaction (Fahy et al., 2016; Kim, Colwell, Kata, Boyle, & Georgiades, 2018; Sung Hong et al., 2016). It is difficult for adults to prevent and intervene with cyberbullying because they are frequently unaware that it is happening.

Sexting

Just as social media and electronic communication, such as texting, are a means for adolescent social and intimacy development, they may also play a role in sexual behavior. About a third of U.S. adolescents report engaging in **sexting**, sending or receiving sexually explicit images (Madigan, Ly, Rash, Van Ouytsel, & Temple, 2018). There are conflicting reports on whether girls or boys are more likely to be involved in sexting, with some researchers concluding that girls are more likely to send images and boys to receive, yet other studies suggest that there are no gender differences (Barrense-Dias, Berchtold, Surís, & Akre, 2017).

For many adolescents, engagement in sexting might never lead to any negative consequences. However, sexting can carry certain risks, especially when a sexually explicit text, image, or video is shared beyond the intended audience. Images forwarded beyond the intended recipient may lead to bullying victimization (e.g., name-calling) and can damage the victim's reputation psychological well-being, as well as negatively affect their perception of school safety (Van Ouytsel, Madigan, Ponnet, Walrave, & Temple, 2019; Van Ouytsel, Walrave, Ponnet, & Heirman, 2015). Especially in the case of sexually explicit images, this could lead to reputation damage and to subsequent bullying and cyberbullying victimization. Sexts may be distributed or posted online by a former partner after the end of a romantic relationship, out of revenge, or they can be misused by others, with coercing intent (e.g., victims can be forced to engage in other sexual acts by being threatened that the sexting content would be released if they don't comply). The sending of sexting images also comes with legal consequences. In some countries, such as the United States or Australia, the creation, sending, storing, or sharing of sexts could be prosecuted under child pornography laws, even when all parties involved are minors (Van Ouytsel, Walrave, Ponnet, & Temple, 2018). Sexting has implications for adolescent development, especially adolescents' engagement in risky activities.

Adolescent sexting is associated with sexual activity (Handschuh, La Cross, & Smaldone, 2019; Kosenko, Luurs, & Binder, 2017; Temple & Choi, 2014; Van Ouytsel et al., 2019). The research to date relies on correlational data, which can tell us about relationships but not causes. Therefore, although we know that sexting is linked with sexual behavior, it is unclear whether sexting precedes or follows engagement in sexual activity. It may be that sexting is a way of introducing sex into a relationship or the reverse that having sex increases the level of comfort in sharing nude images (Temple et al., 2012). One longitudinal study found that sending naked pictures of oneself was associated with being sexually active 1 year later (Temple & Choi, 2014). Notably, although the odds of having sex were significantly higher among adolescents who reported earlier sexting, the difference was small. Adolescents might use sexting as a first step toward actual sexual contact (Van Ouytsel et al., 2019).

Whether sexting is associated with risky sexual activity is debated. Some research suggests that sexting is associated with unprotected sex and having multiple partners (Dake, Price, Maziarz, & Ward, 2012; Van Ouytsel et al., 2015). Other work suggests no relation (Rice et al., 2012; Temple & Choi, 2014) or a relation between sexting and number of sexual partners for girls but not boys (Temple et al., 2012). However, the correlational nature of the studies makes it difficult to determine whether engagement in sexting actually leads to risky sexual activity at a later point in time or whether adolescents who engage in risky sexual activities also engage in sexting. The relation between sexting and risky sexual activity may vary with age, with worse effects for adolescents who engage in sexting earlier than peers (Mori, Temple, Browne, & Madigan, 2019). For example, among middle school students, those who engage in sexting are much more likely than their peers to report being sexually active (Houck et al., 2014; Rice et al., 2014). Recall that early sexual activity is associated with delinquent and sex risk behaviors, including an increased likelihood of being forced to have sex, multiple partners, STIs, and teenage pregnancy (Rice et al., 2014). Sexting may indicate that an adolescent is at risk for developing a variety of problems.

Sexting is associated with other risky activities such as smoking, alcohol use, binge drinking, and marijuana use (Barrense-Dias et al., 2017; Dake et al., 2012; Ševčíková, 2016; Van Ouytsel et al., 2015, 2018). Similar to other risky behaviors, sexting is associated with impulsivity and difficulty inhibiting behaviors (Barrense-Dias et al., 2017; Temple et al., 2014). Recall from Chapter 3 that changes in impulsivity correspond to adolescent brain development. According to the dual systems model, the development of the prefrontal cortex, responsible for executive function and impulse control, lags behind development of the limbic system, involved in emotion (Shulman et al., 2016; Steinberg, 2010). Adolescent risk behavior tends to increase as parts of the limbic system develop and the excitement that accompanies risks tends to become more reinforcing. These changes likely influence adolescents' sexing behavior. In addition, recall that peers rise in importance and adolescents become more susceptible to peer influence, partly due to brain development (Albert, Chein, & Steinberg, 2013). As peer group norms become more important to adolescents, they are more influenced by peer pressure, which may make them more likely to engage in risk behaviors such as the sending of sexually explicit photographs. Indeed, several studies have found that youth who engage in sexting are more likely to perceive that their friends approve of sexting and less likely if they perceive them to be negative (Van Ouytsel, Ponnet, Walrave, & d'Haenens, 2017; Walrave, Heirman, & Hallam, 2014). In this way, sexting may represent normative development and is similar to other common risk behaviors.

Sexting may also play a role in intimacy development. Most adolescents engage in sexting within the context of a dating or romantic relationship or in hopes of establishing a romantic relationship (Lenhart, 2009; Temple et al., 2012). Sexting may be viewed as a way to sustain intimacy in established couples (Van Ouytsel et al., 2019). Sexting might act as a way of introducing sex into a relationship or signaling one's readiness to increase sexual intimacy (Temple & Choi, 2014). Sexting might also be an alternative to engaging in physical intercourse as the behavior is "safe" in the sense that it does not run the risk of pregnancy or sexually transmitted diseases and does not require synchronous in-person or online meeting. However, like other sexual activities, sexting may occur under pressure. Adolescents may participate because they feel pressured or coerced by their romantic partner, because they feel that it is expected of them, or because they are scared that their partner will otherwise end the relationship (Choi, Van Ouytsel, & Temple, 2016).

In sum, sexting appears to be a newer type of risk behavior, influenced by the developmental factors that accompany other risk behaviors. Some experts believe that sexting, when conducted with mutual consent, can be considered a normal part of adolescent development, fulfilling needs for sexual expression, self-presentation, and experimentation and acting as a venue for expressing intimacy (Van Ouytsel et al., 2019; Ybarra & Mitchell, 2014).

REVIEW 11.3

1. How might social media use promote adolescent development?

2. What are some problems associated with social media use?

3. To what degree is sexting related with sexual activity in adolescence?

THINKING IN CONTEXT 11.3

1. What is your experience with social media? What apps, if any, do you use? Do you think your use of social media affects your thoughts, emotions, or behavior? Explain.

2. Why do you think that many adults focus on the negative aspects of social media? How valid are these messages?

3. How might you convince others of the positive aspects of social media use?

4. What challenges might you face in spreading your message?

APPLY 11.3

Mariela scrolls through her social media feed, clicking "like" on an image of a cute puppy, her friend's new dress, and her baby cousin. Next to her, her best friend Roselle clicks "like" on a photo of a skinny social media influencer, a social media star with a huge audience. "Liking the girl with the thigh gap again?" asks Mariela. "That's my goal—a thigh gap and a rib outline," Roselle clicks through the photos and then peruses the influencer's followers. She points to her phone and says, "See? These girls have both—thigh gaps and rib outlines. They're my body goals." Mariela agrees, "Who doesn't want to be skinny? But don't you think some of those images are fake?" Roselle shakes her head, "I don't care if they are. All I know is that I need that thigh gap if I'm going to share pics with Trevone." Mariela laughed, "He hasn't even asked you out yet!" "But he will . . . when he sees my thigh gap," Roselle giggles.

1. Compare Mariela and Roselle's use of social media.

2. What are some correlates of their social media use?

3. Compare Mariela and Roselle's experiences with what is known about the relationship between social media use and body image in adolescence.

4. How might Roselle's social media use affect her romantic relationships? How common are interactions such as these?

MEDIA LITERACY

Adolescents take in a great deal of information from a wide variety of traditional and new media sources. Through digital media—advertising, viral videos, social media, memes, online news, video games, and more—adolescents today are bombarded with more information than any generation to date. The concept of "fake news" has received a lot of attention in recent years. Fake news is just as it sounds—misinformation, hoaxes, propaganda, or deliberate dissemination of false information via media. How do adolescents make sense of the onslaught of information? How do they learn to distinguish reliable sources of information from fake news? This ability is increasingly referred to as media literacy.

What Is Media Literacy?

Traditionally, the term *literacy* referred to reading literacy, the ability to read and write. Today, parents, educators, researchers, and policy makers are increasingly concerned with a second type of literacy, **media literacy**, the ability to identify different types of media and understand the messages they are sending (Common Sense Media, 2019). More specifically, the National Association for Media Literacy Education defines media literacy as "the ability to access, analyze, evaluate, and communicate information in a variety of forms, including print and non-print messages" (National Association for Media Literacy Education, 2019).

Just as reading literacy develops slowly, from recognizing letters to identifying and understanding the meaning of words and sentences, media literacy, too, develops gradually with advances in cognitive development that help adolescents recognize media messages, consider different perspectives, and critically evaluate media messages. Media literacy entails the ability to understand not simply the surface content of any medium—print, audio, video, or other—but also the deeper, underlying messages. Processing the underlying messages of media content requires the cognitive and socioemotional skills to consider the source of a message, what may have been omitted, and what potential motives underly messages. Media literacy enables adolescents to successfully navigate, read, write, and participate in online spaces and digital media, critical skills for social, academic, and career success (Turner et al., 2017).

Promoting Media Literacy

Media literacy instruction can help adolescents develop the skills to critically evaluate media messages, such as those they might encounter on social media, news websites, and other Internet sources. Media literacy instruction emphasizes several goals (Common Sense Media, 2019). Media literate individuals are able to:

- **Identify point of view.** Every author has a perspective that influences their message. What is the author's goal? Helping adolescents appreciate authors' points of view and goals can help adolescents identify what they know and their own perspective.

- **Be smart consumers.** Adolescents learn how to critically evaluate information to determine its credibility. Media literacy helps adolescents identify the persuasive nature of advertising and marketing techniques.

- **Be responsible media creators.** Adolescents who are media literate can recognize their own point of view and are aware of the messages they create. Creating media responsibly means being truthful, being aware of persuasive techniques, and understanding how a message might affect others.

Media literacy interventions seek to equip young people with critical thinking skills to consider the motives of media creators, potential influences of media messages, and credibility of messages. Adolescents also learn how to apply their critical thinking skills to create a personal understanding of media messages. Programs intended to increase media literacy include content such as raising critical awareness of the positive and negative messages transmitted by media, how media affect people, motivations behind advertising, and ways to respond to media through advocacy. Media literacy helps adolescents combat the influence of unhealthy or deceptive information contained in media messages. It increases skepticism toward media messages by strengthening adolescents' critical thinking and reflection skills to determine the veracity of messages and make effective decisions (Austin & Pinkleton, 2016; McLean, Paxton, & Wertheim, 2016).

One example of a successful media literacy intervention is Media Aware Relationships (MAR), a program that seeks to help adolescents understand the influence media has on their decisions about relationships and sexual health, including pregnancy, STI prevention, and dating violence (Scull, Malik, & Kupersmidt, 2014). In several lessons, adolescents learn the basic concepts of media literacy and apply them to analyze gender stereotypes in media messages depicting sex, relationships, and alcohol use. Adolescents who completed the Media Aware Relationships curriculum demonstrated greater skepticism of media messages about sex, were better at deciphering underlying themes in media, and were more likely to judge media portrayals of sexual relationships as unrealistic. Other media literacy programs focus on helping adolescents critically evaluate media messages about alcohol and substance use and realistic body shapes and sizes (Austin & Pinkleton, 2016; McLean et al., 2016).

Generally speaking, meta-analyses of media literacy interventions suggest that they are effective in improving media literacy skills, such as media knowledge, skepticism, and perceived realism of media content (Jeong, Cho, & Hwang, 2012). Media literacy interventions that focus on risk behaviors, such as substance use, tend to be associated with reductions in adolescents' reports of positive attitudes toward risk behaviors and intention to engage in risk behaviors, but show a smaller effect on behavior (Vahedi, Sibalis, & Sutherland, 2018). Media literacy intervention effects on behavior tend to be small because adolescent behavior is influenced by a larger web of individual and contextual factors.

Media Policies

Medical and mental health organizations, such as the American Academy of Pediatrics and the American Psychological Association, agree that unmonitored media use, especially screen use, can pose risks to children and adolescents' development. Screens, however, are everywhere. It is difficult to determine how to help adolescents develop healthy media habits. Professional associations agree on these general recommendations:

- Discourage entertainment media while doing homework.

- Remove electronic devices from the bedroom.

- No screen use for 1 hour before bed.

- Designate media-free family times, such as at dinner.

- Designate media-free places, such as bedrooms.

- Co-view media with adolescents. Discuss the content and themes.

- Determine and enforce time limits for entertainment media.

- Communicate with adolescents about online safety and citizenship, such as treating others with respect, avoiding cyberbullying, and protecting privacy and safety.

The American Academy of Pediatrics encourages parents and adolescents to create a "Family Media Use Plan," a document that addresses what type of and how much media are used and what media behaviors are appropriate for each person in the home (American Academy of Pediatrics, n.d.). This plan should be revisited frequently and revised as needed. Specifically, to construct a family media plan, parents and adolescents:

- Decide what places in the home should be screen-free zones (such as a bedroom or the kitchen).

- Decide what time of day devices like televisions, phones, computers, games, or other electronics are off-limits.

- Choose device curfews and specify where devices will be charged.

- Plan for shared recreational screen time by choosing what media parents and adolescents

will view together and when co-viewing will occur.

- Consider how offline recreational time will be spent (e.g., reading, being with friends, etc.).

- Plan for shared offline recreational time by choosing ways adolescents and parents will share offline time.

- Agree on good digital manners (e.g., no screens at the dinner table).

- Agree on ways to protect privacy and promote safe online activities.

There are benefits and risks to media use at all ages. A family media plan helps parents and adolescents to consider their media preferences and use—and to make plans to ensure that they have time to view media as well as the time offline to develop physical, cognitive, and social competencies. A family media plan also addresses parents' use of media to serve as a model for their children but also to help adults manage their own media use to encourage healthy media limits and opportunities to interact with their adolescents. ●

REVIEW 11.4

1. What skills contribute to media literacy?

2. Describe some ways to promote media literacy.

3. What are some recommendations for adolescent media use?

4. What are some recommendations for adolescent media use?

· ·

THINKING IN CONTEXT 11.4

What developmental factors influence adolescents' media literacy? Consider physical, cognitive, and socioemotional development. How might these influence adolescents' ability to understand the media messages they encounter?

· ·

APPLY 11.4

Seventeen-year-old Devin walks into his 13-year-old sister's room. "You're just in time to see them make up and kiss," she says as she points to the couple on television. "That's the kind of guy I want." Devin replies, "You do know that's made up, right? Real relationships aren't like that." "Of course they are. Couples break up and make up all the time. It's easy," she responds. "TV makes it look easier than it is, sis. Trust me, relationships take more time to develop and more work to sustain," he advised.

1. Describe some of the differences in Devin's and his sister's perspectives.

2. How skilled do you think Devin's sister is in media literacy? Why or why not?

3. How might you help Devin's sister improve her media literacy skills?

· ·

CHAPTER SUMMARY

11.1 Describe theories of media influence and adolescent development.

Adolescents' screen media activities include watching entertainment, playing games, and using social media and the Internet. On average, adolescents spend about 9 hours a day using entertainment media, but there are individual differences in screen use. Cultivation theory and social learning theory view adolescents as shaped by the media they consume. According to uses and gratifications theory, adolescents select media that meet their interests and needs. The media practice model views media influence as a bidirectional process in which adolescents' characteristics influence their choice of media and media influence is a self-constructive process. Moderate media use has benefits for adolescents.

11.2 Analyze the effects of exposure to media with violent, sexual, and substance use themes on adolescent development.

Research on the effects of exposure to media with adult themes is mixed. Television violence is associated with aggressive thoughts in adolescents, but not behavior. Violent video games show small associations with aggressive behavior, reduced prosocial behavior, reduced academic performance, and attention problems, but the effects are negligible once other variables are considered. Similarly, when outside influences are controlled, exposure to sexy media shows only a small association with sexual activity. Exposure to sexual content on television, however, is associated with greater acceptance of stereotypical and casual attitudes about sex. Unlike the more mixed findings

with regard to violent and sexual content, research has shown that exposure to alcohol and substance use content in marketing and the media increases the risk of substance use from early adolescence through early adulthood.

11.3 Examine the relationship of social media and adolescent development.

Social media use serves developmental functions for adolescents, such as in the realms of intimacy and identity development. When adolescents engage in appearance comparisons and view unhealthy body images on social media, they may be at higher risk for poor body image. Social media presents new opportunities for peer victimization in the form of cyberbullying, which poses risks to adolescents' well-being. Adolescents who engage in sexting are more likely to engage in risky behaviors; however, sexting may also play a role in intimacy development.

11.4 Describe media literacy and recommendations for promoting media literacy in adolescents.

Media literacy develops gradually with advances in cognitive development that help adolescents recognize and critically evaluate media messages. Programs intended to promote media literacy help raise adolescents' awareness of the messages transmitted by media, how media affect people, motivations behind advertising, and ways to respond to media through advocacy. Parents and adolescents can create a family media plan that addresses the types and amount of media appropriate for each person in the home.

KEY TERMS

cultivation theory, 226

cyberbullying, 236

media literacy, 239

media practice model, 228

sexting, 237

uses and gratifications theory, 228

PART 4

Problems in Development

CHAPTER 12.

Socioemotional and Behavioral Problems During Adolescence

12

Socioemotional and Behavioral Problems During Adolescence

Learning Objectives

12.1 Discuss substance use in adolescence, including its prevalence, correlates, and risk and protective factors.

12.2 Summarize influences, correlates, and treatment of depression, suicide, and nonsuicidal self-injury.

12.3 Discuss the trajectory of delinquency and influences on delinquency in adolescence.

12.4 Discuss the concept of resilience and the positive youth development approach to fostering adaptation in adolescence.

Chapter Contents

By now you are well aware that stereotypes about adolescence abound. Recall from Chapter 1 that G. Stanley Hall (1905) described adolescence as a period of storm and stress characterized by turbulent moods, volatile relationships with parents, and antisocial behavior. Research, however, has softened this view, demonstrating that extreme storm and stress is not the norm and is not indicative of healthy development (Buchanan & Bruton, 2016). Although adolescents are more likely to experiment with risky activities such as substance use and acting-out behaviors, these activities are often transient, and most young people progress through adolescence without experiencing significant problems. A minority of adolescents, however, encounter significant socioemotional and behavioral problems.

In this chapter, we examine problems that may occur in adolescence relating to substance use and internalizing and externalizing problems. **Internalizing problems**, such as depression and anxiety, occur when an adolescent directs the problem or emotional stress inward. In contrast, **externalizing problems** occur when adolescents direct or turn their emotional stress outward. Frequently even serious problems are transient, both rising and falling in adolescence. Sometimes, however, problems persist into adulthood. In these cases, the problems often began prior to adolescence, as discussed in the following sections.

SUBSTANCE USE

The physical, cognitive, and socioemotional changes adolescents undergo, including changes in appearance and increases in introspection, identity exploration, and an interest in individuating from parents, facilitate experimentation and may predispose adolescents to initiate use of substances such as tobacco, alcohol, and cannabis, or marijuana.

Prevalence of Substance Use

Nearly half of U.S. teens have tried an illicit drug and about two-thirds have tried alcohol by the time they leave high school, as shown in Figure 12.1. There are cohort trends in substance use. For example, from 1991 to 2019, adolescents' reports of having used alcohol or been drunk within the past year declined, whereas marijuana use increased (Figure 12.2). Over this period, adolescents rated regular marijuana use as less harmful, perceived it as more available, and expressed less disapproval of regular use (Johnston et al., 2019). Another interesting trend concerns cigarette smoking and e-cigarette use or vaping. Among twelfth-grade students, the 30-day prevalence of smoking declined dramatically from 28% in 1991 to 6% in 2019, considered a great success by health advocates. However, vaping emerged in the early 2010s and quickly rose in popularity among adolescents. In 2019, 12% of eighth-graders, 25% of tenth-graders, and 31% of twelfth-graders reported vaping within the past 30 days.

Tobacco, alcohol, and marijuana are typically the first addictive substances that youth try. For this reason, some have referred to them as **gateway drugs** because they tend to precede use of other illicit substances (Kandel & Kandel, 2015; Lynskey & Agrawal, 2018). However, it is important to note that not every adolescent who tries smoking, for example, progresses to other substances. The prevalence statistics suggest that most adolescents do not.

Experimentation with alcohol, tobacco, and marijuana use—that is, "trying out" these substances—is so common that it may be considered normative for North American adolescents. Recall that adolescents' brains are wired to seek novel experiences and sensations. The limbic system and prefrontal cortex develop

---

FIGURE 12.1

Lifetime Versus 30-Day Prevalence of Use of Various Drugs for Eighth-, Tenth-, and Twelfth-Graders

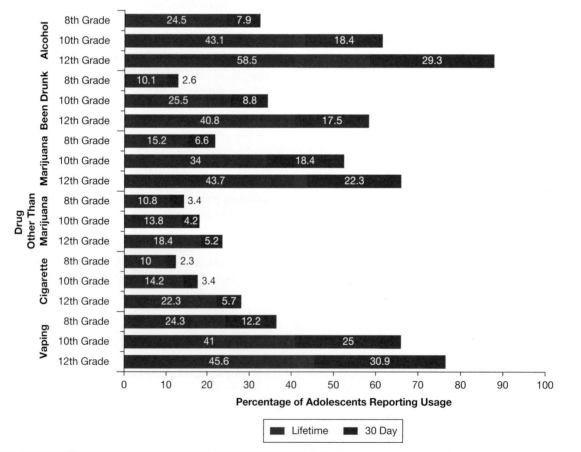

Source: Johnston et al. (2019).

FIGURE 12.2

Trends Change in 30-Day Prevalence for Twelfth-Graders Only

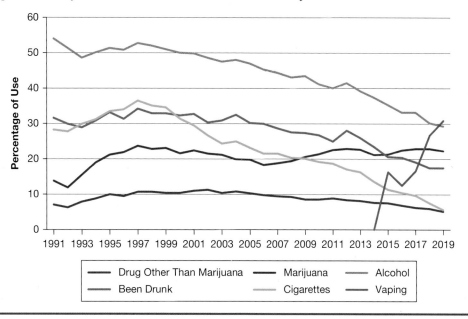

Source: Johnston et al. (2019).

on different timetables and changes in responsivity to dopamine cause adolescents' decisions to favor immediate rewards over longer-term consequences (Geier, 2013; Strang, Chein, & Steinberg, 2013). Rates of experimentation rise during the adolescent years into emerging adulthood, when alcohol and substance use tends to peak, followed by a decline as young people adopt adult roles (Miech et al., 2017).

Perhaps surprising to some adults is that a limited amount of experimentation with drugs and alcohol is positively associated with adjustment, psychosocial health, and well-being in middle and older adolescents (Mason & Spoth, 2011). Why? Alcohol and substance use may serve a developmental function in middle and late adolescence, such as a way of asserting independence and autonomy from parents, sustaining peer relationships, and learning about oneself (Englund et al., 2013; Rulison, Patrick, & Maggs, 2015). Notice, however, that many more adolescents have tried a given substance ("experimented" with it) than use it regularly.

Correlates and Outcomes of Substance Use

Experimentation with tobacco, alcohol, and marijuana, although somewhat normative, is associated with negative consequences, such as motor impairment, unintentional injuries, and motor vehicle accidents,

as well as risks for overdose, dependence, and abuse. Alcohol and substance use are associated with negative consequences that can interfere with adolescents' development, such as academic problems, unwanted sexual encounters, risky sexual activity, externalizing problems such as aggression and delinquency, and internalizing problems such as anxiety, depression, and suicide (Coffey & Patton, 2016; Marshall, 2014; Spear, 2018). Adolescents, however, may view the negative consequences of substance use differently than adults. In one recent study, 14- and 15-year-old adolescents who engaged in more risky drinking reported experiencing more negative consequences such as saying or doing embarrassing things, regretting sexual experiences, or experiencing impairments in performing schoolwork, problems with parents or friends, accidents or injuries, hangovers, vomiting, and memory lapses (Wicki et al., 2018). Yet adolescents who experienced a negative consequence were consistently also willing to experience it in the future, suggesting that adolescents may see the experience of negative consequences as a necessary evil to attain the positive consequences.

Alcohol use is associated with changes in the structure and function of the adolescent brain. Compared with those who do not use alcohol, adolescents who drink alcohol moderately show smaller brain volumes and gray matter density in areas responsible for executive control, including parts of the temporal and parietal lobes, hippocampus, and especially the frontal cortex (Cservenka & Brumback, 2017; Müller-Oehring et al., 2018; Silveri, Dager, Cohen-Gilbert, & Sneider, 2016; Squeglia et al., 2015). Changes in the brain associated with alcohol use also contribute to cognitive impairments. For example, heavy drinking is associated with reduced frontal cortex response during working memory tasks, slower information processing, and reductions in attention, visuospatial functioning, and problem-solving (Carbia et al., 2017; Feldstein Ewing, Sakhardande, & Blakemore, 2014). Executive function, working memory, and learning suffer—and adolescents become less well able to regulate their behavior. Recall that executive control influences higher-level cognitive functions such as planning, directing attention, and decision-making, as well as response inhibition and the ability to resist temptation, such as the rewards that come with risky but exciting activities such as drinking.

Alcohol and cannabis use tend to co-occur, making it difficult to disentangle the independent effects of each.
iStock.com/rez-art

At the same time, some research suggests that pre-existing individual differences, such as poor functioning in tests of inhibition and working memory, smaller gray and white matter volume, and altered brain activation, are not only influenced by substance use but also place adolescents at risk for heavy substance use (Brumback et al., 2016; Squeglia & Gray, 2016).

There is a strong dose-response relationship for alcohol effects: greater consumption of alcohol predicts decreased brain volume and less white matter integrity (Cservenka & Brumback, 2017; Silveri et al., 2016). The effects of adolescent alcohol use on brain function may be long lasting because alcohol use is associated with impaired neurogenesis and long-term reductions in synaptic connections and memory in animals (Spear, 2018; Tapia-Rojas et al., 2017). Yet there is room for optimism because some research has shown that the adolescent brain can increase in volume and show improved executive function when alcohol use is discontinued (Lisdahl, Gilbart, Wright, & Shollenbarger, 2013). The extent and limits of this rebound effect are unclear.

Whereas regular alcohol use is associated predominantly with deficits in attention and executive function, regular cannabis use is associated with a broad set of neurocognitive deficits in attention, learning and memory, processing speed, visuospatial functioning, and executive control (Lisdahl et al., 2013; Meruelo, Castro, Cota, & Tapert, 2017). Alcohol and cannabis use tend to co-occur, making it difficult to disentangle the independent effects of each; however, like alcohol use, regular cannabis use is associated

with brain alterations, including reduced brain and gray matter volumes in the frontal lobe, followed by the parietal and temporal lobes (Lopez-Larson et al., 2012; Takagi, Youssef, & Lorenzetti, 2016). Early onset of cannabis use, before age 18 and especially prior to age 16, is associated with more severe neurocognitive consequences, especially in learning, memory, and executive function (Lubman, Cheetham, & Yücel, 2015; Silveri et al., 2016). One study suggests that cognitive function improved after 3 weeks of abstention, but attention deficits remained (Hanson et al., 2010). It is unknown whether abstinence over a long period is associated with a rebound in function. Other research suggests that attention, verbal and working memory, and processing speed remain impaired up to 2 months later (Hanson, Thayer, & Tapert, 2014; Winward, Hanson, Tapert, & Brown, 2014). Given the plasticity of the brain, some recovery of neurological function after abstention is expected, but the degree of recovery it not clear (Meruelo et al., 2017).

Risk and Protective Factors for Substance Abuse

Adolescents are particularly vulnerable to alcohol abuse because they show reduced sensitivity to the effects of alcohol that serve as cues in adults to limit their intake, such as motor impairment, sedation, social impairment, and quietness or distress (Spear, 2018). They develop a tolerance and are at risk for developing dependence for alcohol more quickly than adults (Simons, Wills, & Neal, 2014).

Adolescents at risk for abusing alcohol and substances tend to begin drinking earlier than their peers

(Palmer et al., 2009). Adolescents who begin drinking before age 15 are up to six times more likely to develop alcohol dependence over their lifetime than those who remain abstinent from alcohol use until age 21 (National Institute on Drug Abuse, 2017). Most adults who have a substance use disorder report using substances before age 18 and develop their disorder by age 20, highlighting the importance of delaying initiation of substance use for as long as possible (Gray & Squeglia, 2018). In addition, adolescents with a family history of substance use disorders are especially at risk for substance-related problems (Cservenka, 2016). A recent meta-analysis of twin and adoption studies found that alcohol use disorder has genetic links (Verhulst, Neale, & Kendler, 2015); however, specific genes have not been identified (Hart & Kranzler, 2015; Tawa, Hall, & Lohoff, 2016) and substance disorders likely have epigenetic links (Berkel & Pandey, 2017), suggesting an important role for context (Gray & Squeglia, 2018).

Adolescents' relationship with their parents influences their use of alcohol and other substances. Adolescents are at reduced risk of developing alcohol and substance abuse problems if their parents are involved, warm, supportive, and aware of their children's whereabouts and friends. How parents communicate about alcohol and substance use influences adolescent use. Some research suggests that strict rules for drinking, higher levels of cautionary communication messages, and punishment for drinking are associated with lower odds of alcohol use (Cox, Janssen, Lopez-Vergara, Barnett, & Jackson, 2018). Other work suggests that it is more complicated. The quality of discussion matters. For example, parental lectures about the dangers of alcohol and substance use that emphasize only rules and consequences are often ineffective (Carver, Elliott, Kennedy, & Hanley, 2017). Parent-adolescent conversations about substance use are more effective when they are two sided, in which adolescents feel they are being listened to and contributing rather than being lectured. In addition, there appears to be a difference between enforcing rules and simply talking about them: when parents enforce rules around substance use, young people report lower use; however, when parents just talk to their adolescents about rules without actually making an attempt to enforce the rules, adolescents are more likely to drink alcohol, smoke, or use drugs (Carver et al., 2017).

Parents also influence adolescent drinking and substance use through modeling. Adolescents whose parents drink regularly are at increased risk for using alcohol themselves (Alati et al., 2014). Witnessing parents drink alcohol may lead adolescents to drink and/or adopt norms permissive of alcohol use and engage in more alcohol use (Duncan, Duncan, & Strycker, 2006; van der Vorst, Vermulst, Meeus, Deković, & Engels, 2009). Parental drinking levels are also associated with the severity of adolescent drinking, as heavy episodic parental drinking has been linked to both earlier and heavier alcohol use among adolescents (Cox et al., 2018; Vermeulen-Smit et al., 2012).

Other contextual factors, such as low socioeconomic status, family members with poor mental health, drug abuse within the community, disadvantaged neighborhoods, and early exposure to traumatic life events, increase the risk of alcohol and substance abuse in adolescence (Chaplin et al., 2012; Dube et al., 2006; Trucco, Colder, Wieczorek, Lengua, & Hawk, 2014). In addition, adolescents who have mental health problems, have difficulty with self-regulation, or are victims of physical or sexual abuse are at higher risk of alcohol and drug abuse than their peers. However, perhaps the most direct influences on adolescents are their peers' drinking or substance abuse behavior, their perceptions of peer support for such use, and their access to alcohol and substances (Brooks-Russell, Simons-Morton, Haynie, Farhat, & Wang, 2014; Leung, Toumbourou, & Hemphill, 2014).

The normative nature of alcohol and substance use experimentation makes preventing alcohol and substance use challenging. Effective prevention programs target parents by encouraging that they be warm and supportive, set rules, and be aware of their adolescents' activities. Effective alcohol and substance abuse prevention and treatment programs educate adolescents about the health risks of substance use and teach skills such as how to resist pressure from peers, how to refuse offers, and how to build their coping and self-regulatory capacities (Windle & Zucker, 2010). Given the role of peers in experimentation, effective programs help adolescents to develop accurate perceptions of peer norms, that substance use is less common among their peers and that peers are less accepting of substance use than they believe (Pedersen et al., 2017).

REVIEW 12.1

1. Why are some substances called gateway drugs?

2. How common is substance use in adolescence?

3. What are some correlates of substance use in adolescence?

4. What are some risk and protective factors for substance use?

• •

THINKING IN CONTEXT 12.1

Are there potential dangers of viewing some experimentation with alcohol and substance use as common and simply a part of growing up? Explain.

• •

APPLY 12.1

"He's just drinking a little beer. No big deal. We did that, remember?" Ryan's father reminded his mother. "But he's been missing school. How do we know it isn't serious?" asked Ryan's mother.

1. Discuss what we know about substance use in adolescence.

2. What are some characteristics that signify an adolescent's risk for substance use problems?

3. What are some risks of Ryan's alcohol use for his development?

4. Should Ryan's parents worry? Explain.

DEPRESSION, SUICIDE, AND NONSUICIDAL SELF-INJURY

Internalizing problems occur when adolescents turn their emotional distress inward. Some internalizing problems, such as anxiety, tend to emerge in childhood (Beesdo, Knappe, & Pine, 2009). Others, such as depression, begin in adolescence.

Depression

The moody, sulking teenager is a popular stereotype of adolescence rooted in G. Stanley Hall's depiction of adolescence as a period of storm and stress.

Occasionally feeling sad is normal for people of all ages, including adolescents. About one-third of adolescents report having felt sad or hopeless enough to temporarily stop engaging in their usual activities for up to 2 weeks (Department of Health and Human Services, 2019; Kann et al., 2014). A smaller number of adolescents, about 13% of 12- to 17-year-olds in the United States, meet the criteria to be diagnosed with **major depressive disorder**, a mental illness described in Table 12.1 (American Psychiatric Association, 2013; National Institute of Mental Health, 2019). Only 2% to 8% experience chronic depression that persists over months and years (Substance Abuse and Mental Health Services Administration, 2013). Many more adolescents, however, experience some symptoms of depression. The belief that depression is a typical part of adolescence is dangerous because parents, teachers, and other adults may view symptoms of depression as normal and temporary, rather than mental illness.

Depressive symptoms and rates of depression rise in early to middle adolescence and sex differences emerge, with girls reporting depression twice as often as boys (Petersen et al., 2018; Thapar, Collishaw, Pine, & Thapar, 2012). We have seen that adolescent girls experience puberty earlier than boys and pubertal changes influence how girls are perceived and treated by others. They are more likely to experience a poor body image and lower self-esteem compared with boys (Bachman, O'Malley, Freedman-Doan, Trzesniewski, & Donnellan, 2011). Puberty often coincides with school transitions, which poses challenges to adjustment. Although close friendships can protect

TABLE 12.1

DSM-5 Diagnostic Criteria for Major Depressive Disorder

The primary feature of major depressive disorder is the experience of either depressed mood or marked loss of interest of pleasure in all or almost all activities most of the day and nearly every day for a 2-week period. In addition, four of the following symptoms must appear over the same 2-week period:

- Significant weight loss when not dieting or weight gain or change in appetite
- Difficulty sleeping or sleeping too much
- Psychomotor agitation or retardation
- Fatigue or loss of energy nearly every day
- Feelings of worthlessness or excessive or inappropriate guilt
- Diminished ability to think or concentrate, or indecisiveness
- Recurrent thoughts of death, recurrent suicidal ideation, or a suicide attempt

The symptoms must distress or impair social, academic, or occupational functioning.

Source: Adapted from the *Diagnostic and Statistical Manual of Mental Disorders*, Fifth Edition, (Copyright 2013).

Depressive symptoms and rates of depression rise in early to middle adolescence as sex differences emerge, with girls reporting depression twice as often as boys. Girls who experience body dissatisfaction are at higher risk for depression.
iStock.com/MachineHeadz

Genetic factors play a role in depression as they influence the brain regions responsible for emotion regulation and stress responses as well as the production of neurotransmitters (Maughan, Collishaw, & Stringaris, 2013). Longitudinal research demonstrates a role for epigenetics in depression during adolescence. For example, in one study, boys with a specific neurotransmitter allele showed severe symptoms of depression in the presence of poor family support but showed positive outcomes in the presence of high family support (Li, Berk, & Lee, 2013). The allele may increase reactivity to both negative and positive family influences, serving as a risk factor in an unsupportive family context but a protective factor when coupled with family support.

Contextual factors, such as those that accompany low socioeconomic status and the extended experience of stress, also influence depression (Uddin, Jansen, & Telzer, 2017). Relationships with parents influence adolescents' responses to stressful life events. Nurturing responses and secure attachment can reduce adolescents' stress reactivity (Kuhlman, Olson, & Lopez-Duran, 2014). Sensitivity to stress coupled with an insecure attachment to parents increases adolescents' vulnerability to the negative emotional effects of social challenges such as bullying, family conflict, and peer problems, all of which are associated with depressive symptoms in adolescence (Shore, Toumbourou, Lewis, & Kremer, 2018). Parents can foster emotion regulation (Brumariu, 2015). The longitudinal effects of stressful life events on depression are buffered by parent–child closeness and worsened by parental depression (Ge, Natsuaki, Neiderhiser, & Reiss, 2009; Natsuaki et al., 2014). Family support is a particularly robust protective factor against depression (Rueger, Chen, Jenkins, & Choe, 2014).

Peers also play a role in adolescent depression. One meta-analysis of over 300 studies suggests that support from the general peer group, such as classmates, is inversely associated with depression and, surprisingly, was a greater predictor of adolescent depression than were close friendships (Rueger, Malecki, Pyun, Aycock, & Coyle, 2016). It may be that the broader network of supportive peer relationships provides youth with generalized socially rewarding positive experiences and a sense of predictability in their peer environment (Durlak, Weissberg, Dymnicki, Taylor, & Schellinger, 2011). In contrast, close friendships provide social support, but negative aspects of close friend interactions, such as co-rumination, may attenuate the benefits of close friend support (Rueger et al., 2016). **Co-rumination**, excessively discussing and rehashing problems, speculating about problems, and focusing on negative affect with a close friend, predicts increases in adolescents' depressive symptoms over time, including the onset

girls, girls are more likely than boys to ruminate with their friends (Rose, Schwartz-Mette, Glick, Smith, & Luebbe, 2014) and may be more sensitive to negative interpersonal interactions (Frost, Hoyt, Chung, & Adam, 2015), increasing the risk of depression.

The changes in body shape that accompany puberty, as well as adolescents' feelings about those changes and the reactions of others, may influence adolescents' depressive symptoms. Puberty also triggers neurological changes that may also place adolescents at risk for depressive symptoms and depression. Development of the limbic system may increase adolescents' sensitivity to stress and influence how they interpret others' emotions and behavior (Byrne et al., 2017). Other neurological changes make adolescents more sensitive to rewards, including social rewards such as from positive interactions with peers and the thrill that accompanies taking risks (van Duijvenvoorde, Peters, Braams, & Crone, 2016). Depressive symptoms may rise when adolescents do not experience the rewards they crave.

of major depression (Cohen, So, Hankin, & Young, 2019; Schwartz-Mette & Smith, 2018).

Cultural factors may also play a role in influencing adolescents' susceptibility to depression. Some adolescents find a discrepancy between their level of acculturation and that of their first-generation immigrant parents as stressful. Poor parental acculturation is linked with adolescent depression when adolescent–parent relationships are poor (Kim, Qi, Jing, Xuan, & Ui Jeong, 2009). For example, in one study, Chinese immigrant parents whose level of acculturation differed from their adolescent children tended to show more unsupportive parenting practices and the adolescents reported greater feelings of alienation (Kim, Chen, Wang, Shen, & Orozco-Lapray, 2013). Likewise, Vietnamese fathers who were less acculturated to the United States used more authoritarian parenting methods that fit their society, but their adolescents tended to experience more depression (Nguyen, Kim, Weiss, Ngo, & Lau, 2018). Latinx adolescents who experienced a discrepancy in acculturation compared with their parents also were at risk for depression (Howell et al., 2017; Nair, Roche, & White, 2018). As young people acculturate, they may challenge traditional attitudes and beliefs of their immigrant parents, leading to greater family conflict and emotional distress.

Depression is treated in a variety of ways that include therapy and the provision of antidepressant medication (Brent, 2009). Therapy that is designed to help the adolescent be more self-aware, identify harmful patterns of thinking and change them is especially effective and can be administered in school or community settings (Shirk, Gudmundsen, Kaplinski, & McMakin, 2008). Parent and teacher education about the signs of depression is an essential first step.

Suicide

Intense and long-lasting depression can lead to thoughts of **suicide**, death caused by self-directed injuries with the intent to die. In 2017, suicide was the second leading cause of death for adolescents and emerging adults age 10 to 24 (Curtin & Heron, 2019). It is a top-three leading cause of death for adolescents in many other Western countries, including Canada, the United Kingdom, and Australia (Australian Institute of Health and Welfare, 2016; Centers for Disease

TABLE 12.2

Suicide Warning Signs

Any of the following behaviors can serve as a warning sign of increased suicide risk:

- Change in eating and sleeping habits
- Withdrawal from friends, family, and regular activities
- Violent actions, rebellious behavior, or running away
- Drug and alcohol use, especially changes in use
- Unusual neglect of personal appearance
- Marked personality change
- Persistent boredom, difficulty concentrating, or a decline in the quality of schoolwork
- Frequent complaints about physical symptoms, such as stomachaches, headaches, and fatigue
- Loss of interest in pleasurable activities
- Complaints of being a bad person or feeling rotten inside
- Verbal hints with statements such as the following: "I won't be a problem for you much longer." "Nothing matters." "It's no use." "I won't see you again."
- Affairs are in order—for example, giving away favorite possessions, cleaning his or her room, and throwing away important belongings
- Suddenly cheerful after a period of depression
- Signs of psychosis (hallucinations or bizarre thoughts)
- *Most important:* Stating "I want to kill myself," or "I'm going to commit suicide."

Source: Adapted from American Academy of Child and Adolescent Psychiatry (2018).

Control and Prevention, 2017; Office for National Statistics, 2015; Statistics Canada, 2015). Moreover, the U.S. suicide rate for adolescents and emerging adults has increased by over one-third between 2007 and 2017, from 6.8% to 10.6% (Curtin & Heron, 2019). About 17% of high school students report suicidal ideation, thinking seriously about committing suicide in the past year (Child Trends Databank, 2019). Girls are more likely to report suicidal ideation (22%) than boys (17%). About 7% of high school students attempt suicide (9% girls and 5% boys) and about one-third of these attempts are serious enough to require medical attention. Large gender differences exist in suicide. Although females display higher rates of depression and make more suicide attempts, males are four times more likely to succeed in committing suicide (Xu, Kochanek, Murphy, & Arias, 2014). Girls tend to choose suicide methods that are slow and passive and that they are likely to be revived from, such as overdoses of pills. Boys tend to choose methods that are quick and irreversible, such as firearms. The methods correspond to gender roles that expect males to be active, decisive, aggressive, and less open to discussing emotions than females (Canetto & Sakinofsky, 1998; Hepper, Dornan, & Lynch, 2012). Preventing suicide relies on recognizing and treating depression and symptoms of suicide, such as those listed in Table 12.2.

Some adolescents who commit suicide first express their depression and frustration through antisocial activity such as bullying, fighting, stealing, substance abuse, and risk-taking (Cash, Bridge, & McNamara, 2018; Fergusson, Woodward, & Horwood, 2000). In addition to the risk factors for depression, suicide is also associated with poor peer relationships, specifically victimization by peers (Bauman, Toomey, & Walker, 2013; Stewart, Valeri, Esposito, & Auerbach, 2018). LGBT youth, especially male and bisexual youth, experience an exceptionally high risk for suicide, with three to four times as many attempts as other youth (Grossman, Park, & Russell, 2016; Miranda-Mendizábal et al., 2017; Pompili et al., 2014). In one national study, one-third to one-half of adolescents who identified as transgender reported a suicide attempt (Toomey, Syvertsen, & Shramko, 2018). LGBT adolescents who attempt suicide often list family conflict, peer rejection, and inner conflict about their sexuality as influences on their attempts (Liu & Mustanski, 2012; Mustanski & Liu, 2013; Russell & Fish, 2016).

Adolescents may be more likely to attempt suicide following the suicide of a friend or peer in the community.
iStock.com/RichLegg

Adolescents are more likely to attempt suicide following the suicide of a friend or peer in the community, known as **suicide contagion** (Haw, Hawton, Niedzwiedz, & Platt, 2013; Nanayakkara, Misch, Chang, & Henry, 2013). Risk for suicide can be transmitted through direct exposure, for example, the suicide of a friend, or through indirect exposure, such as through media reports or fictional portrayals. In one study of 48 communities with youth suicide clusters, media coverage, specifically newspaper coverage, was the strongest predictor of initiating the cluster (Gould, Kleinman, Lake, Forman, & Midle, 2014). One mechanism for suicide contagion comes from misperceiving descriptive norms. That is, adolescents who believe that suicide and suicide ideation are more widespread among peers than in reality are more likely to report suicide ideation and attempts (Hawton et al., 2020). Internet and social media platforms provide useful ways for young people to memorialize the deceased and both communicate and seek support; however, the immediate and unmonitored nature of social media can spread misinformation rapidly. Social media messages can also unintentionally reinforce adolescents' beliefs that suicide is a normal response to pain.

Although school-based suicide prevention programs tend to increase awareness and knowledge about suicide, they are not associated with lower rates of suicide (Cusimano & Sameem, 2011). Counseling and peer support groups can be provided by schools and community centers (Corrieri et al., 2014). The availability and advertisement of telephone hotlines can help adolescents in immediate danger of suicide. After a suicide, those around the adolescent require immediate support and assistance in working through their grief and anger. The availability of support and counseling to all adolescents within the school and community after a suicide is important given the accompanied increased risk for suicide among other adolescents in the community (Gould, Jamieson, & Romer, 2003; Haw et al., 2013).

Nonsuicidal Self-Injury

Some adolescents display internalizing problems by harming themselves. **Nonsuicidal self-injury**, or self-harm, is self-injurious behavior designed to cause harm, not death. Although self-harm may indicate serious psychological disorders, it is also fairly common among adolescents in Western countries, with lifetime prevalence rates of 13% to 23% of adolescents in the United States, Canada, Australia, and Western Europe (Klemera, Brooks, Chester, Magnusson, & Spencer, 2017; Muehlenkamp, Claes, Havertape, & Plener, 2012). Rates may be even higher because most self-harming adolescents do not seek help or medical attention for their injuries (Hall & Place, 2010). Most adolescents who engage in self-harm behaviors do so a few times, and most do not show recurring self-harm. Self-harm behaviors, particularly cutting, tend to emerge between ages 12 and 15, on average at about age 13 (Bjärehed, Wångby-Lundh, & Lundh, 2012). Girls are more likely than boys to report harming themselves, most commonly by cutting but also hitting, biting, or burning, but there are no differences on the basis of ethnicity or socioeconomic status (Klemera et al., 2017; Nock, Prinstein, & Sterba, 2009).

Some research has linked self-injurious behavior with impulsivity, perhaps accounting for the onset in early adolescence, when impulsivity tends to rise (Lockwood, Daley, Townsend, & Sayal, 2017; Stanford, Jones, & Hudson, 2017). Psychological and behavioral difficulties such as anxiety, depression, antisocial behavior, and poor problem-solving skills are also associated with self-harm (Bjärehed et al., 2012; Marshall, Tilton-Weaver, & Stattin, 2013). Adolescents who self-harm tend to report being more confused about their emotions, experiencing difficulty recognizing and responding to them, and being more reluctant to express their feelings and thoughts to others (Bjärehed et al., 2012; Nock et al., 2009). Common reasons that adolescents endorse for self-harm include depression, feeling alone, anger, self-dislike, and inadequacy.

Social problems and a difficulty forming close relationships are common among adolescents who self-harm (Ross, Heath, & Toste, 2009). Social risk factors include high family conflict, poor parent–adolescent communication, low levels of support, and intense conflict with peers and bullying (Claes, Luyckx, Baetens, Van de Ven, & Witteman, 2015; Fisher et al., 2012; Giletta, Burk, Scholte, Engels, & Prinstein, 2013). Yet positive parental involvement and support and close friendships can buffer adolescents against social risks for self-harm (Klemera et al., 2017).

Adolescents who repeatedly engage in cutting and other acts of self-harm tend to report that the act relieves emotional pain, reducing negative emotions (Scoliers et al., 2009; Selby, Nock, & Kranzler, 2014). Interestingly, self-harming adolescents tend to show little or no pain during the harm episode (Nock et al., 2009). Instead, the act of cutting or other self-harming behavior produces a sense of relief and satisfaction for adolescents who repeatedly self-harm. Soon, they tend to value self-harm as an effective way of relieving anxiety and negative emotions, making it a difficult habit to break (Madge et al., 2008; Selby et al., 2014).

The fifth edition of the *Diagnostic and Statistical Manual of Mental Disorders*, or DSM-5 (American Psychiatric Association, 2013), includes a diagnosis for severe self-harm: nonsuicidal self-injury—self-injurious behavior that occurs with the expectation of relief from a negative feeling—to solve an interpersonal problem, or to feel better, and interpersonal difficulty and negative feelings of thoughts, premeditation, or rumination on nonsuicidal self-injury. Many adolescents who self-harm receive treatment similar to other internalizing disorders, including a combination of medication, therapy, and behavioral treatment. However, repeated self-harming behaviors are difficult to treat because the relief they produce is reinforcing to adolescents, making psychologists and other treatment providers' work challenging (Bentley, Nock, & Barlow, 2014; Nock, 2009).

REVIEW 12.2

1. How are puberty and other biological factors related to depression?

2. How are parents and peers associated with adolescents' risk for depression?

3. What are risk factors for suicide?

4. What characteristics are associated with an increased risk for nonsuicidal self-injury?

· ·

THINKING IN CONTEXT 12.2

1. Adolescents' friendships can be a powerful source of support, protecting them from depression. However, research suggests that some aspects of friendship can worsen symptoms of depression. Discuss, providing examples.

2. In your experience, can friendships both help and hurt adolescents with internalizing problems like depression? Explain

· ·

APPLY 12.2

Professor Gee believes that adolescents are "wired" for depression and other internalizing problems, that they are developmentally and biologically primed. Professor Evans, on the other hand, believes that internalizing problems are the result of social factors in adolescents' home, peer, school, and community contexts. What do you think? Who is correct? Why? Explain your response.

· ·

DELINQUENCY

During adolescence, young people experiment with new ideas, activities, and limits. For many adolescents, experimentation includes an increase in externalizing problems (e.g., acting out) and **delinquency**, criminal behavior conducted by juveniles (e.g., vandalism, shoplifting, theft, and violence). Delinquent activity includes **status offenses**, activities that are illegal due to being underage, such as truancy, running away, and drinking (Woolard & Scott, 2009). **Index offenses**, on the other hand, are illegal regardless of age and include a range of criminal acts, such as theft, assault, robbery, rape, and homicide. Most adolescents engage in status offenses; fewer commit index offenses.

TABLE 12.3

DSM-5 Diagnostic Criteria for Conduct Disorder

The essential feature of conduct disorder is a repetitive and persistent pattern of behavior in which the basic rights of others or major age-appropriate societal norms or rules are violated. At least three of the following 15 criteria must be present in the past 12 months, with at least one criterion present in the past 6 months:

Aggression or Physical Cruelty to People and Animals

- Often bullies, threatens, or intimidates others
- Often initiates physical fights
- Has used a weapon that can cause serious physical harm to others (e.g., a bat, brick, broken bottle, knife, gun)
- Has been physically cruel to animals
- Has stolen while confronting a victim (e.g., mugging, purse snatching, extortion, armed robbery)
- Has forced someone into sexual activity

Destruction of Property

- Has deliberately engaged in fire setting with the intention of causing serious damage
- Has deliberately destroyed others' property (other than by fire setting)

Deceitfulness or Theft

- Has broken into someone else's house, building, or car
- Often lies to obtain goods or favors or to avoid obligations (i.e., "cons" others)
- Has stolen items of nontrivial value without confronting a victim (e.g., shoplifting, but without breaking and entering; forgery)

Serious Violations of Rules

- Often stays out at night despite parental prohibitions, beginning before age 13 years
- Has run away from home overnight at least twice while living in the parental or parental surrogate home, or once without returning for a lengthy period
- Is often truant from school, beginning before age 13 years

The disturbance in behavior must impair social, academic, or occupational functioning.

Source: Reprinted with permission from the *Diagnostic and Statistical Manual of Mental Disorders*, Fifth Edition, (Copyright 2013). American Psychiatric Association.

A minority of adolescents engage in serious externalizing problems that meet the clinical diagnosis of conduct disorder (see Table 12.3). **Conduct disorder** refers to a persistent pattern of antisocial activity that violates the rights of others and social norms and interferes with an individual's functioning in the home, peer, school, or work context (American Psychological Association, 2013). About 2% to 10% of adolescents have conduct disorder, which is six times more common in boys than girls (Fairchild et al., 2019; Taubner, Gablonski, & Fonagy, 2019). Conduct disorder that emerges in adolescence, especially cases with few or mild symptoms, often abates by adulthood and individuals show adequate adjustment to adult roles. Child-onset conduct disorder, however, tends to manifest in more severe behaviors and predicts a worse prognosis and an increased risk of criminal behavior and substance-related disorders in adulthood. The majority of antisocial behavior in adolescence takes the form of transient experimentation with delinquent activity and is not indicative of conduct disorder.

Prevalence of Delinquency

Nearly all young people engage in at least one delinquent or illegal act, such as vandalism, during the adolescent years, without coming into police contact (Flannery, Hussey, & Jefferis, 2005). In one study, boys admitted to engaging in, on average, three delinquent acts and girls reported one delinquent act between ages 10 and 20, yet nearly none of the adolescents had been arrested (Fergusson & Horwood, 2002). In 2018, adolescents younger than the age of 18 accounted for about 7% of police arrests in the United States, including 10% of violent crime, 11% of property crimes, and 5% of drug violations (Federal Bureau of Investigation, 2019).

As shown in Figure 12.3, juvenile arrests have declined dramatically over the past 4 decades but there are large ethnic and racial differences in arrest rates (Office of Juvenile Justice and Delinquency Prevention, 2019). African American youth are disproportionately likely to be arrested compared with White youth, and Asian American youth are least likely to be arrested (Federal Bureau of Investigation, 2019; Office of Juvenile Justice and Delinquency Prevention, 2019). By one estimate, Latinx and Hispanic youth show similar arrest rates as White youth (Andersen, 2015). In a recent national analysis of postarrest handling decisions by police (such as whether to release the adolescent or process the arrest and refer the adolescent to the court system), Hispanic and Latinx adolescents were more likely to be referred to the court for less severe charges, such as trespassing or loitering, than White adolescents (Claus, Vidal, & Harmon, 2017). However, there were no ethnic differences in referrals for more severe charges such as violence, weapons, and drug offenses. Differences in arrest rates may be influenced by the greater surveillance of the low socioeconomic communities in which youth of color are likely to live and adolescents' access to fewer community resources.

Trajectory of Delinquent Activity

As shown in Figure 12.4, most antisocial and criminal activity is limited to the adolescent years and does not continue into adulthood (Piquero & Moffitt, 2013). That is most adolescents demonstrate a pattern of delinquent behavior referred to as **adolescence-limited antisocial behavior** (Moffitt, 2017). As the name suggests, adolescence-limited antisocial activity tends to both increase and decrease during adolescence. Specifically, puberty is associated with a rise in antisocial behavior, which is sustained by affiliation with similar peers. Adolescents tend to find peer interaction highly rewarding, providing a context for antisocial activity. With advances in cognition, especially executive function and impulse control, as well as moral reasoning, emotion regulation, social skills, and empathy, antisocial activity declines (Monahan, Steinberg, Cauffman, & Mulvey, 2013). That is, most adolescents tend to show an increase in delinquent activity that is limited to the adolescent years, rising in early adolescence or middle adolescence and declining in late adolescence.

Although mild delinquency is common, adolescents who engage in serious crime, such as robbery and violent crimes, are at risk to become

Some delinquent acts, such as vandalism, are common during the adolescent years.
iStock.com/hanohiki

FIGURE 12.3

Arrest Rates per 100,000 Persons Age 10 to 17, 1980–2018

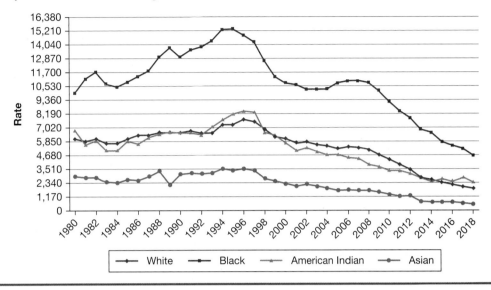

Source: Office of Juvenile Justice and Delinquency Prevention (2019).

FIGURE 12.4

Age–Crime Curve

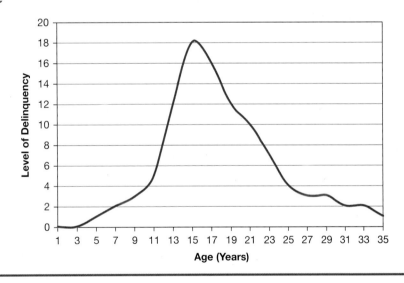

Source: Delisi (2015).

repeat offenders who continue criminal activity into adulthood, demonstrating a second trajectory of delinquent activity, **life-course persistent antisocial behavior**. Typically, life-course persistent antisocial behavior begins in childhood, rises and takes more severe forms in adolescence, and continues into adulthood (Moffitt, 2017). Individuals who show life-course

persistent antisocial behavior often have their first contacts with the criminal justice system by age 12 or earlier (Baglivio, Jackowski, Greenwald, & Howell, 2014) and they often meet the diagnostic criteria for conduct disorder, yet are frequently undetected.

Other researchers pose several trajectories for adolescent delinquency (Nagin, 2016). For example, one longitudinal study of African American adolescent boys from age 10 to 19 showed several patterns of change, illustrated in Figure 12.5 (Evans, Simons, & Simons, 2014). At age 10, higher rates of delinquency were associated with having deviant friends, poor parenting, and perceiving discrimination. An increasing trajectory of delinquent activity across adolescence was associated with increasing adversity, including increasing contact with deviant peers, greater increases in discrimination, low-quality parenting, and, for late starters, a greater number of family transitions. Adolescents who showed a decline in delinquency tended to report less discrimination and more authoritative parenting than their peers.

Risk Factors for Delinquent Activity

Although most antisocial behavior by young people is limited to adolescence, not all adolescents engage in delinquent or antisocial acts. Delinquent activity is more common among those with a greater drive for sensation seeking (Mann et al., 2016). The home and peer contexts play a large role in antisocial behavior. Specifically, poor parental monitoring is associated with poor school performance and affiliating with antisocial peers (Bendezú, Pinderhughes, Hurley, McMahon, & Racz, 2018; Lopez-Tamayo, LaVome Robinson, Lambert, Jason, & Ialongo, 2016).

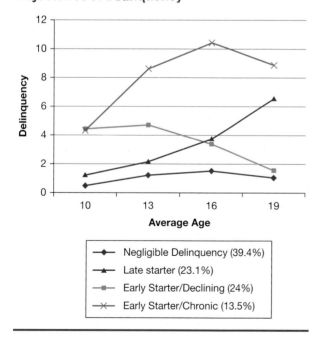

FIGURE 12.5

Trajectories of Delinquency

Average Age

- ◆ Negligible Delinquency (39.4%)
- ▲ Late starter (23.1%)
- ■ Early Starter/Declining (24%)
- ✕ Early Starter/Chronic (13.5%)

Source: Evans et al. (2014).

Unstructured time with peers, such as hanging out, is associated with risky activity, including delinquency (Hoeben, Meldrum, Walker, & Young, 2016; Lee, Lewis, Kataoka, Schenke, & Vandell, 2018). Susceptibility to peer influence increases the risk of engaging in risky activities, including delinquency (Choukas-Bradley, Giletta, Widman, Cohen, & Prinstein, 2014). Although there are individual differences in susceptibility to peer influence, recall that susceptibility tends to increase in early adolescence and decline in late adolescence, similar to adolescence-limited antisocial behavior (Steinberg & Monahan, 2007).

Serious antisocial behavior that persists into adulthood, life-course persistent antisocial activity, is associated with biological and individual risk factors coupled with challenging home and community contexts (Figure 12.6) (Dishion & Patterson, 2016). Some individual characteristics that predict antisocial activity, such as aggression, sensitivity to stimuli, sensation seeking, and self-regulation, have biological underpinnings (Mann et al., 2016; Manuck & McCaffery, 2014; Miyake & Friedman, 2012; Veroude et al., 2016). One study that followed a sample of boys for 38 years found substantial differences among boys whose antisocial activity was limited to the adolescent years compared with those whose activity persisted throughout adulthood (Moffitt, 2018). Specifically, life-course persistent antisocial behavior was associated with family factors (such as harsh discipline, family conflict, family transitions, socioeconomic status, and maternal mental health), cognitive and academic problems, association with delinquent peers, and, especially, difficult temperament characterized by hyperactivity, fighting, and difficulty getting along with peers.

Parenting that is inconsistent, controlling, and accompanied by harsh punishment, as well as parenting that is negligent and low in monitoring, can magnify impulsive, defiant, and aggressive tendencies in adolescents (Chen, Voisin, & Jacobson, 2013; Harris-McKoy & Cui, 2012). We have also seen that peers are an important influence on adolescent behavior; interaction with antisocial peers is positively associated with risky and antisocial behavior (Farrell, Thompson, & Mehari, 2017; Samek, Hicks, Keyes, Iacono, & McGue, 2017)

Contextual factors in the community also matter. Communities of pervasive poverty are characterized by limited educational, recreational, and employment activities, coupled with access to drugs and firearms, opportunities to witness and be victimized by violence, and offers of protection and companionship by gangs that engage in criminal acts—all of which contribute to the onset of antisocial behavior (Chen et al., 2013). Exposure to high levels of community violence predicts delinquent activity (Jain & Cohen, 2013). Low income communities tend to have schools that

FIGURE 12.6

Influences on Chronic, Life-Course Persistent Antisocial Activity

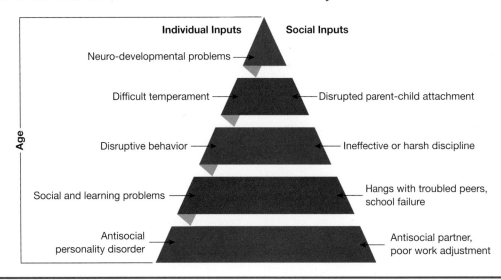

Source: Moffitt (2018).

struggle to meet students' educational and developmental needs, with crowding, limited resources, and overtaxed teachers (Flannery et al., 2005). Young people who experience individual, home, and community risk factors for antisocial behavior tend to associate with similarly troubled peers, a pattern that tends to increase delinquent activity as well as chronic delinquency (Evans et al., 2014).

Intervening in Delinquent Activity

Preventing and intervening in delinquency requires examining individual, family, and community factors. At the level of the individual, we can help adolescents learn skills to manage their emotions, regulate their behavior, and resist the pressure to conform to peers. Training parents in discipline, communication, and monitoring fosters healthy parent–child relationships, which buffers young people who are at risk for delinquency (Bowman, Prelow, & Weaver, 2007; Dopp, Borduin, White, & Kuppens, 2017; Piquero et al., 2016). High-quality teachers, teacher support, resources, and economic aid foster an educational environment that protects young people from risks for antisocial behavior. A 3-year longitudinal study following adolescents of low income single mothers transitioning

off welfare showed that involvement in school activities protects adolescents from some of the negative effects of low income contexts and is associated with lower levels of delinquency over time (Mahatmya & Lohman, 2011). Prevention is most effective in childhood, bolstering children's skills, relationships, and self-control before a pattern of antisocial and delinquent activity develops (Mazerolle, Patterson, DeBaryshe, & Ramsey, 2015; Moffitt et al., 2011).

Once patterns of criminal activity are established, intervention is challenging because it entails breaking

Adolescents who are involved in extracurricular activities, for example, theatre, are less likely to engage in delinquency.
iStock.com/monkeybusinessimages

patterns of behavior and the social interactions that sustain it. Adolescents who engage in delinquency may be reluctant to participate because they may not view themselves as having a problem. Instead they view themselves as required to participate in interventions by their parents, schools, and, especially, the court system. The most successful approach to intervening in delinquency is known as **multisystemic therapy (MST)**, which targets several bioecological systems, including the home, school, and neighborhood (Henggeler & Schaeffer, 2018; Vidal, Steeger, Caron, Lasher, & Connell, 2017; Zajac, Randall, & Swenson, 2015). Parents learn skills for interacting with, monitoring, and disciplining their adolescents. Multisystemic therapists and teams address barriers such as parental mental health problems, substance abuse, and poor parenting skills. MST interventions target the peer contexts, coaching parents to get involved with adolescents' peer group, help adolescents reduce their associations with deviant peers, promote prosocial activities, and improve school disengagement. Parents are coached to develop positive relationships with teachers and school administrators to improve home–school communication and facilitate academic success. Job training and vocational counseling for adolescents, and sometimes parents, can help adolescents envision and plan for a successful future.

REVIEW 12.3

1. Differentiate two patterns of delinquent activity.
2. What are risk factors for delinquent activity?
3. Describe a successful approach for intervening in delinquency.

THINKING IN CONTEXT 12.3

How might adults distinguish normative delinquent activity that declines with age from atypical delinquent activity that continues and escalates?

APPLY 12.3

Consider delinquent activity from a bioecological perspective.

1. What are some factors within the adolescent that might influence delinquent activity? Identify three.
2. Provide three examples of factors at the level of the microsystem and mesosystem that might contribute to delinquency.

3. Describe three exosystem factors that might contribute to delinquency.
4. What is the role of the macrosystem in delinquency?

RESILIENCE

Adolescence is a period of biological, cognitive, and socioemotional transitions. Adolescents are immersed in a myriad of shifting contexts that influence and are influenced by them. Individual characteristics and the contexts in which adolescents are embedded pose both opportunities and risks for development. **Risk factors** are individual and contextual variables associated with a higher likelihood of negative outcomes. In contrast, contexts also include **protective factors**, which may reduce or protect the adolescents from the poor outcomes associated with adverse circumstances.

Risk and Protective Factors

Contextual risk factors that many adolescents face include child maltreatment, neighborhood violence, mental health and substance abuse problems at home and in the community, poverty, homelessness, and war (Luthar et al., 2015; Masten & Cicchetti, 2016). Risk factors are cumulative; the more risks individuals face, the more difficult it is for them to adjust (Ungar, 2015). In one study, the adjustment of adolescents exposed to war in Bosnia varied with the extent to which they witnessed the atrocities of war, such as death, violence, and forced displacement; higher rates of PTSD and mental health and learning problems accompanied greater exposure to risk factors (Benson et al., 2011). In all contexts, poor responses to adversity include psychological, behavioral, and health problems, including anxiety, depression, frequent illnesses and hospitalizations, poor academic achievement, and delinquent activity (Cutuli et al., 2017). Each of these, in turn, poses cascading risks to future development and adjustment.

Culture can influence how risk and protective factors manifest. In one striking example, over 5,000 Aboriginal children and adolescents who participated in the Western Australian Aboriginal Child Health Survey showed that risk factors such as harsh parenting, family violence, and caregiver unemployment cumulatively predicted adjustment problems (Hopkins, Taylor, D'Antoine, & Zubrick, 2012). For these young people, living in a high SES neighborhood and demonstrating more knowledge of their culture were associated with *lower* levels of resilience to adversity. These unusual results can be accounted for by examining their context. About 90% of Aboriginal people lived in lower SES neighborhoods. Growing up in a more economically advantaged community may separate a child from social supports and expose the child to prejudice. Likewise, in this instance, Aboriginal adolescents' knowledge of their culture, as members of a minority group who are ostracized from the larger community, may create heightened sensitivity to oppression and lead to higher levels of depression and delinquency.

Adaptation

Adolescents from all cultures show a range of outcomes in response to adversity. Many outcomes are negative, such as internalizing and externalizing problems and poor academic achievement. However, some children and adolescents exposed to intense stressors, such as maltreatment, display little trauma and are able to manage their anxiety to succeed at home and school to show high self-esteem, low levels of depression, and few behavioral problems (Cicchetti, 2016; Pérez-González, Guilera, Pereda, & Jarne, 2017). These adolescents display **resilience**, the ability to respond or perform positively in the face of adversity, to achieve despite the presence of disadvantages, or to significantly exceed expectations given poor home, school, and community circumstances (Masten, 2016).

Adaptation to adversity is a dynamic process involving interactions among individuals' developmental capacities and their changing context, which includes both risk factors and protective factors. Protective factors are critical to adaptation because they may help shield children from risk factors, buffering the poor outcomes that accompany adverse circumstances and contexts. For example, warm relationships with caregivers and other adults, active engagement at school and in the community, participation in routines, and church attendance are protective factors that promote adjustment and can reduce the negative outcomes associated with adversity (Masten & Monn, 2015; Ungar, 2015).

Protective factors may arise from within the individual, from the family or extended family, and from the community (Pérez-González et al., 2017; Traub & Boynton-Jarrett, 2017). Resilient individuals tend to have personal characteristics that protect them from adversity and help them learn from experience, such as an easy temperament, a sense of competence, self-control, good information processing and problem-solving skills, friendliness, and empathy (Afifi & MacMillan, 2011; Domhardt, Münzer, Fegert, & Goldbeck, 2015; Marriott, Hamilton-Giachritsis, & Harrop, 2014). A fundamental characteristic of resilience is the ability

TABLE 12.4

Characteristics of Resilience

INDIVIDUAL COMPETENCIES	FAMILY COMPETENCIES AND CHARACTERISTICS	SCHOOL AND COMMUNITY CHARACTERISTICS
• Coping skills • Easy temperament • Emotion regulation abilities • Good cognitive abilities • Intelligence • Positive outlook • Positive self-concept • Religiosity • Self-efficacy (feeling of control over one's destiny) • Talents valued by others	• Close relationships with parents and caregivers • Organized home • Parental involvement in children's education • Positive family climate • Postsecondary education of parents • Provision of support • Religiosity and engagement with the church • Socioeconomic advantage • Warm but assertive parenting	• Access to local churches • After-school programs • Availability of emergency services • Mentoring programs and opportunities to form relationships with adults • Health care availability • Instruction in conflict management • Opportunity to develop and practice leadership skills • Peer programs, such as big brother/big sister programs • Programs to assist developing self-management skills • Public safety • Support networks outside of the family, such as supportive adults and peers • Ties to prosocial organizations • Well-funded schools with highly qualified teachers • Youth programs

to regulate one's emotions and behavior (Eisenberg et al., 2010). Resilient individuals also have a proactive orientation, take initiative, believe in their own effectiveness, and have a positive sense of self (Luthar et al., 2015; Pérez-González et al., 2017).

Avenues for fostering resilience include promoting adolescents' strengths and bolstering their executive function skills, self-appraisals, and sense of efficacy, or feelings of control (Ellis, Bianchi, Griskevicius, & Frankenhuis, 2017; Traub & Boynton-Jarrett, 2017). Resilience is accompanied by strong and supportive relationships with caregivers or adults who provide warm guidance and firm support (Domhardt et al., 2015; Labella, Narayan, McCormick, Desjardins, & Masten, 2019). Programs help bolster adolescents by targeting parents' mental health and self-care skills, aiding parents in establishing routines, promoting parenting skills, and helping parents understand the impact of trauma on their children (Masten & Monn, 2015; Ungar, 2015). Table 12.4 illustrates characteristics that are associated with resilience. Resilient adolescents illustrate an important finding: exposure to adversity does not necessarily lead to maladjustment; many adolescents thrive despite challenging experiences.

Positive Youth Development

Throughout much of history, developmental scientists who study adolescence tended to emphasize treating problems, such as those we have discussed. However, for the majority of adolescents, when problem behaviors occur they are mild and temporary, and most adolescents do not experience serious problems (Boyer & Byrnes, 2016; Lerner et al., 2015). Rather than emphasizing deficits and problems, today developmental scientists view adolescence as a period of growth and plasticity. Developmental scientists thereby focus on promoting healthy development in children and adolescents rather than simply treating problems. The **positive youth development (PYD)** approach seeks to discover and promote positive qualities that contribute to adolescents' ability to adapt and engage in constructive interactions with their complex and changing contexts (Lerner et al., 2019). Specifically, developmental assets, positive influences on adaptation, can be found within the individual and context. Table 12.5 illustrates some developmental assets within the individual and context. Interventions that promote PYD target both the individual and context.

PYD interventions are commonly implemented at school and involve practices and policies that help students and adults acquire and apply knowledge, skills, and attitudes that enhance personal development, social relationships, ethical behavior, and productive work (Ciocanel, Power, Eriksen, & Gillings, 2017; Taylor, Oberle, Durlak, & Weissberg, 2017). School-based PYD interventions promote asset development by focusing on interrelated cognitive, emotional, and behavioral competencies that are important for success in school

TABLE 12.5

Developmental Assets for Positive Youth Development

INDIVIDUAL	CONTEXT
• Self-regulation	• Family support
• Planning and decision-making competence	• Positive family communication
• Interpersonal competence	• Parental monitoring
• Conflict resolution	• Positive relationships with other adults
• School engagement	• High expectations from adults
• Hopeful expectations for the future	• Caring school climate
• Spirituality	• Parents' involvement in school
• Achievement motivation	• Organized out-of-school programs
• Self-esteem	• Neighborhood members monitor children in the community
• Sense of purpose	• Availability of youth programs
	• Supportive religious community
	• Availability of libraries and other community resources
	• Neighborhood safety

Sources: Adapted from Lerner et al. (2019) and Search Institute (2017).

The PYD approach promotes developmental assets that enable adolescents to adapt and engage in constructive interactions with the contexts in which they are embedded.
iStock.com/Motortion

and life, such as self-awareness (e.g., recognizing emotions, strengths and limitations, and values), self-management (e.g., regulating emotions and behaviors), social awareness (e.g., taking the perspective of and empathizing with others from diverse backgrounds and cultures), relationship skills (e.g., establishing and maintaining healthy relationships), and responsible decision-making (e.g., making constructive choices across varied situations).

PYD interventions applied in family, school, and community settings have shown success in promoting positive development in a broad range of developmental assets, such as self-control, interpersonal skills, problem-solving, the quality of their peer and adult relationships, commitment to schooling, and academic achievement (Ciocanel et al., 2017; Eichas, Ferrer-Wreder, & Olsson, 2019). Advances in social and emotional competencies are positively associated with social and academic adjustment and are also associated with fewer behavioral problems and emotional distress (Domitrovich, Durlak, Staley, & Weissberg, 2017; Osher et al., 2016; Weissberg, 2019). Frequently, PYD interventions are associated with decreases in substance use, negative risk-taking, and problem behaviors, suggesting that in addition to promoting positive outcomes, PYD interventions may protect against negative outcomes (Ciocanel et al., 2017; Waid & Uhrich, 2019). Moreover, the positive effects of interventions tend to persist up to at least 4 years (Taylor et al., 2017). ●

REVIEW 12.4

1. Give examples of risk and protective factors.

2. What is resilience?

3. What is the positive youth development approach?

· ·

THINKING IN CONTEXT 12.4

Suppose that you are an intervention researcher planning a program to promote resilience and positive development in adolescents.

1. What specific traits or abilities would you seek to improve? That is, what abilities do you think best support resilience? Explain your choices.

2. How can you help adolescents develop skills that promote resilience? What activities, lessons, or techniques might you use?

3. What skills should parents have to help their adolescents? What skills would you seek to promote in parents?

4. What would you tell teachers and school principals? What skills and characteristics can promote resilience in adolescents?

5. What neighborhood and community factors support resilience in adolescence? Suppose you had access to community leaders; what advice would you give?

· ·

APPLY 12.4

We all are immersed in a dynamic web of risk and protective factors for our development. Consider your own development.

1. What are some risks you have experienced, factors that might make adaptation more challenging? Identify three.

2. What protective factors have you experienced, factors that encourage adaptation? Identify three.

· ·

CHAPTER SUMMARY

12.1 **Discuss substance use in adolescence, including its prevalence, correlates, and risk and protective factors.**

Although they are often referred to as gateway drugs, not every adolescent who tries tobacco, alcohol, and marijuana progresses to other substances. A limited amount of experimentation with drugs and alcohol is positively associated with adjustment because this may serve developmental functions in middle and late adolescence. However, experimentation with tobacco, alcohol, and marijuana is associated with short- and long-term negative consequences that can interfere with adolescents' development, including changes in the brain and cognition. Adolescents are particularly vulnerable to alcohol abuse because they show reduced sensitivity to the effects of alcohol that serve as cues in adults to limit their intake and they develop a tolerance for alcohol more quickly than adults. Risk factors for alcohol and substance abuse include early start, a family history of substance use disorders, poor relationships with parents, peer use, and contextual factors such as low socioeconomic status, drug abuse within the community, disadvantaged neighborhoods, and early exposure to traumatic life events. Effective prevention programs target parents, educate adolescents about the health risks of substance use and teach skills, and help adolescents to develop accurate perceptions of peer norms.

12.2 Summarize influences, correlates, and treatment of depression, suicide, and nonsuicidal self-injury.

Depressive symptoms and rates of depression rise in early to middle adolescence, with girls reporting depression twice as often as boys. Depression is associated with biological factors such as pubertal and neurological changes, epigenetics, and contextual factors such as parent and peer support, acculturation, socioeconomic status, and the extended experience of stress. Depression is treated in a variety of ways that include therapy and the provision of antidepressant medication and education for parents and teachers. Suicide is a leading cause of death. In addition to the risk factors for depression, suicide is also associated with problems in peer relationships. Adolescents are more likely to attempt suicide following the suicide of a friend or peer in the community, known as suicide contagion. Although school-based suicide prevention programs tend to increase awareness and knowledge about suicide, they are not associated with lower rates of suicide. Some adolescents display internalizing problems by engaging in nonsuicidal self-injury. Impulsivity and psychological and behavioral difficulties, such as anxiety, depression, antisocial behavior, and poor problem-solving skills, as well as social problems are associated with self-harm. Nonsuicidal self-injury is difficult to treat because adolescents do not tend to view it as a problem.

12.3 Discuss the trajectory of delinquency and influences on delinquency in adolescence.

For many adolescents, experimentation includes an increase in delinquency. Most adolescents engage in status offenses; fewer commit index offenses. Most antisocial activity represents adolescence-limited antisocial behavior, increasing and decreasing during adolescence. A second trajectory of delinquent activity, life-course persistent antisocial behavior, begins in childhood, rises and takes more severe forms in adolescence, and continues into adulthood. Individual characteristics that predict antisocial activity include aggression, sensitivity to stimuli, sensation seeking, and self-regulation. The home, peer, and community contexts play a large role in antisocial behavior, specifically in the form of harsh parenting, poor parental monitoring, affiliating with antisocial peers, unstructured time with peers, and exposure to poverty and violence. Preventing and intervening in delinquency requires examining individual, family, and community factors, including multisystemic therapy.

12.4 Discuss the concept of resilience and the positive youth development approach to fostering adaptation in adolescence.

Resilience refers to the ability to respond or perform positively in the face of adversity, to achieve despite the presence of disadvantages, or to significantly exceed expectations given poor home, school, and community circumstances. Resilience is influenced by the interaction of risk factors, individual and contextual variables associated with a higher likelihood of negative outcomes, and protective factors, which may reduce or protect the adolescents from the poor outcomes associated with adverse circumstances. Adaptation to adversity is a dynamic process involving interactions among individuals' developmental capacities and their changing context, which includes both risk factors and protective factors. Avenues for fostering resilience include promoting adolescents' strengths and bolstering their executive function skills, self-appraisals, and sense of efficacy, or feelings of control. The positive youth development approach seeks to discover and promote positive qualities that contribute to adolescents' ability to adapt and engage in constructive interactions with their complex and changing contexts.

KEY TERMS

adolescence-limited antisocial behavior, 256

conduct disorder, 256

co-rumination, 251

delinquency, 255

externalizing problems, 245

gateway drugs, 246

index offenses, 255

internalizing problems, 245

life-course persistent antisocial behavior, 257

major depressive disorder, 250

multisystemic therapy (MST), 260

GLOSSARY

abstinence-only-until-marriage programs: An approach to sex education that emphasizes the benefits of abstinence from sexual activity outside of marriage; these programs generally do not provide information about safe sex.

achievement motivation: The willingness to persist at challenging tasks and meet high standards of accomplishment.

adolescence: A period in life representing a transition from childhood to adulthood.

adolescence-limited antisocial behavior: The most common pattern of criminal behavior, which increases and decreases during adolescence.

adolescent egocentrism: An error in perspective taking that includes the imaginary audience and personal fable.

adolescent growth spurt: The first outward sign of puberty; refers to a rapid gain in height and weight that generally begins in girls at about age 10 and in boys about age 12.

adrenarche: Refers to the maturation of adrenal glands.

amygdala: A brain structure that is part of the limbic system and plays a role in emotion, especially fear and anger.

androgyny: The gender identity of those who score high on both instrumental and expressive traits.

anorexia nervosa: An eating disorder characterized by compulsive starvation and extreme weight loss and accompanied by a distorted body image.

applied developmental science: A field that studies lifespan interactions between individuals and the contexts in which they live and applies research findings to real-world settings, such as to influence social policy and create interventions.

assent: Minor children and adolescents' agreement to participate in research.

attachment: A lasting emotional tie between two individuals.

attention: The ability to direct one's awareness.

attention-deficit/hyperactivity disorder (ADHD): A condition characterized by persistent difficulties with attention and/or impulsivity that interfere with performance and behavior in school and daily life.

authoritarian parenting style: An approach to childrearing that emphasizes high behavioral control and low levels of warmth and autonomy granting.

authoritative parenting style: An approach to childrearing in which parents are warm and sensitive to children's needs, grant appropriate autonomy, and exert firm control.

autism spectrum disorders (ASD): Refers to a family of disorders that range in severity and are marked by social and communication deficits, often accompanied by restrictive and repetitive behaviors.

automaticity: The degree of cognitive effort required to process information; as processes become automatic, they require fewer resources and become quicker.

autonomy: The ability to make and carry out decisions independently.

behavioral autonomy: The ability to control impulses, resist pressure from others, and make and carry out decisions.

behaviorism: A theoretical approach that studies how observable behavior is controlled by the physical and social environment through conditioning.

beneficence and nonmaleficence: The ethical principle that requires researchers to adhere to the dual responsibilities to do good and to avoid doing harm.

binge eating disorder: An eating disorder characterized by binges accompanied by a sense of feeling out of control, without compensatory behavior such as purging.

bioecological systems theory: A theory introduced by Bronfenbrenner that emphasizes the role of context in development, positing that contexts are organized into a series of systems in which individuals are embedded and that interact with one another and the person to influence development.

biological gender transition: A medical process that typically involves both developmental changes (body changes that are induced by hormone therapy) and permanent changes to the external genitals (accomplished by means of gender reassignment surgery).

blended family: A family composed of a biological parent and a nonrelated adult, most commonly a mother and stepfather.

body mass index (BMI): A measure of body fat based on weight in kilograms divided by height in meters squared (kg/m^2).

bulimia nervosa: An eating disorder characterized by recurrent episodes of binge eating and subsequent purging usually by induced vomiting and the use of laxatives.

care orientation: Gilligan's feminine mode of moral reasoning, characterized by a desire to maintain relationships and a responsibility to avoid hurting others.

case study: An in-depth examination of a single individual or small group of individuals.

central executive: In information processing, the part of our mental system that directs the flow of information and regulates cognitive activities such as attention, action, and problem solving.

chronosystem: In bioecological systems theory, refers to how people and contexts change over time.

cisgender: The condition in which an individual's gender identity matches their sex assigned at birth (usually based on the appearance of their external genitalia); also known as natal sex.

civic development: Refers to the skills, knowledge, and motivation to participate in community and political life.

civic engagement: Refers to a broad range of activities related to involvement in the community or society at large, including community-oriented activity, consciousness raising, and activities intended to influence political outcomes.

clique: A tight-knit peer group of about three to eight close friends who share similarities such as demographics and attitudes.

cognitive autonomy: Refers to the ability to make independent decisions, develop a personal value system of right and wrong, and voice opinions.

cognitive development: Maturation of mental processes and tools individuals use to obtain knowledge, think, and solve problems.

cognitive schema: A mental representation, such as concepts, ideas, and ways of interacting with the world.

cognitive-developmental perspective: A perspective posited by Piaget that views individuals as active explorers of their world, learning by interacting with the world around them, and describes cognitive development as progressing through stages.

cognitive-developmental theory of gender: Children and adolescents' understanding of gender is constructed in the same manner as their understanding of the world: by interacting with people and things and thinking about their experiences.

cohort: A generation of people born at the same time, influenced by the same historical and cultural conditions.

comprehensive sex education: An approach to sex education that views sex education as part of an overall school health education approach, emphasizing age-appropriate physical, mental, emotional, and social dimensions of human sexuality, including instruction in safe sex.

computerized tomography (CT): Compiles multiple X-ray images to create a three-dimensional picture of a person's brain, providing images of brain structures, bone, brain vasculature, and tissue.

conduct disorder: A DSM-5 (*Diagnostic and Statistical Manual of Mental Disorders*, fifth edition) diagnosis that refers to a persistent pattern of antisocial activity that violates the rights of others and social norms and interferes with an individual's functioning in the home, peer, school, or work context.

confidentiality: In research, a promise by a researcher that a participant's responses will be kept confidential and will not be disclosed to others.

context: Unique conditions in which a person develops, including aspects of the physical and social environment such as family, neighborhood, culture, and historical time period.

conventional moral reasoning: The second level of Kohlberg's theory in which moral decisions are based on conforming to social rules.

corpus callosum: A thick band of nerve fibers that connect the left and right hemispheres.

correlational research: A research design that measures relationships among participants' measured characteristics, behaviors, and development.

cortex: The outermost part of the brain containing the greatest numbers of neurons and accounting for thought and consciousness.

corumination: A dyad's excessive discussion, speculation, and focus on problems and negative affect.

cross-sectional research study: A developmental research design that compares people of different ages at a single point in time to infer age differences.

crowd: A large group of adolescents based on perceived shared characteristics, interests, and reputation.

cultivation theory: A theory of media influence that states that repeated exposure to media influences adolescents' thinking, shapes their attitudes, and affects their behavior.

culture: A set of customs, knowledge, attitudes, and values shared by a group of people and learned through interactions with group members.

cyberbullying: Bullying, or repeated acts intended to hurt a victim, carried via electronic means such as text messaging, posting in chat rooms and discussion boards, and creating websites and blogs.

data: Information scientists collect to study phenomena.

dating violence: The actual or threatened physical or sexual violence or psychological abuse directed toward a current or former boyfriend girlfriend or dating partner.

deidealization: An emotional autonomy process in which adolescents begin to view their parents as imperfect versus all-knowing and all-powerful.

delayed phase preference: A change in pubertal hormone levels that causes adolescents' sleep patterns to shift such that they tend to remain awake late at night and are groggy early in the morning.

delinquency: Criminal behavior conducted by juveniles.

demandingness: The degree to which parents expect mature behavior from their adolescents.

dependent variable: The behavior under study in an experiment; it is expected to be affected by changes in the independent variable.

developmental dyscalculia: A specific learning disorder that affects mathematics ability.

developmental dysgraphia: A specific learning disorder that affects writing ability.

developmental dyslexia: The most commonly diagnosed specific learning disorder, characterized by difficulty in matching letters to sounds and difficulty with word recognition and spelling.

developmental science: The scientific study of lifespan development.

diffusion tensor imaging (DTI): Uses an MRI machine to track how water molecules move in and around the fibers connecting different parts of the brain.

divided attention: Attending to two stimuli at once.

dual systems model: A model of the brain consisting of two systems, one emotional and the other rational, that develop on different timeframes, accounting for typical adolescent behavior.

dualistic thinking: Polar reasoning in which knowledge and accounts of phenomena are viewed as absolute facts, either right or wrong with no in-between.

early adolescence: The period of adolescence from age 10 to 14, corresponding roughly to the middle or junior high school years in the U.S. school system.

eating disorders: Mental disorders that are characterized by extreme over- or under-control of eating and behaviors intended to control weight such as compulsive exercise, dieting, or purging. Includes anorexia nervosa, bulimia nervosa, and binge eating disorder.

electroencephalography (EEG): Measures electrical activity patterns produced by the brain via electrodes placed on the scalp.

emerging adulthood: An extended transition to adulthood that takes place from ages 18 to 25, in which a young person is no longer an adolescent yet has not assumed the roles that comprise adulthood.

emotional autonomy: Refers to becoming self-reliant and less emotionally dependent on others, especially parents.

emotion regulation: The ability to adjust and control our emotional state to influence how and when emotions are expressed.

empathic concern: The ability to understand and feel concern for another's emotional experience.

endocrine system: Body system that produces and regulates levels of hormones to influence body processes.

estrogen: The primary female sex hormone responsible for development and regulation of the female reproductive system and secondary sex characteristics.

ethnic-racial identity: Sense of membership to an ethnic or racial group including the attitudes, values, and culture associated with that group.

executive function: The set of cognitive operations that support planning, decision-making, and goal-setting abilities, such as the ability to control attention, coordinate information in working memory, and inhibit impulses.

exosystem: In bioecological systems theory, social settings in which an individual does not participate but have an indirect influence on development.

experimental research: A research design that permits inferences about cause and effect by exerting control, systematically manipulating a variable, and studying the effects on measured variables.

expressive traits: Traits associated with communing with others, such as caring, nurturing, and expressing emotions; also referred to as stereotypical feminine traits.

external attribution: An attribution emphasizing the role of external factors in outcomes, such as task difficulty or luck.

externalizing problems: Occur when adolescents direct or turn their emotional stress outward, such as acting out and delinquent behavior.

false self: When individuals present themselves in a way that they know is untrue.

family systems theory: A theoretical perspective that emphasizes the interactive and bidirectional nature of dyadic relationships within families.

five-factor model: Also known as the Big 5; five clusters of personality traits that reflect an inherited predisposition that is stable throughout life: openness, conscientiousness, extroversion, agreeableness, and neuroticism.

fixed mindset: Viewing one's skills and characteristics as enduring and unchangeable.

formal operational reasoning: Piaget's fourth stage of cognitive development, characterized by abstract, logical, and systematic thinking.

foster care: A child welfare arrangement where a child is temporarily placed outside the home because the parents are unable to provide care or safety.

functional magnetic resonance imaging (fMRI): A method of measuring brain activity using a powerful magnet that uses radio waves to measure blood oxygen level.

gateway drugs: Substances, typically tobacco, alcohol, and marijuana, that tend to precede use of other illicit substances.

gender: The adoption of male or female characteristics.

gender constancy: A child's understanding of the biological permanence of gender and that it does not change regardless of appearance, activities, or attitudes.

gender identity: Awareness of oneself as a male or female.

gender intensification hypothesis: Theory suggesting that early adolescence young people perceive greater social pressure to adhere to gender-stereotyped roles and behaviors.

gender schema: A concept or a mental structure that organizes gender-related information and embodies their understanding of what it means to be a male or female and is used as a guide to attitudes and behaviors.

gender schema theory: A cognitive explanation of gender development that emphasizes information processing and environmental influences on gender.

gender stability: In Kohlberg's view, young children's recognition that gender does not change over time, although it is not yet understood as a biological construct but rather based on external traits and behaviors.

gender stereotypes: Refer to broad generalized judgments of the activities, attitudes, skills, and characteristics deemed appropriate for males or females in a given culture.

gender typing: The process in which young children acquire the characteristics and attitudes that are considered appropriate for males or females.

glial cell: A type of brain cell that nourishes neurons and provides structure to the brain.

global self-esteem: An overall evaluation of self-worth.

gonad: A sex gland; ovary in females and testis in males.

gonadarche: The physical maturation that comprises puberty.

gonadotropin-releasing hormone (GnRH): Released by the hypothalamus, causes the pituitary gland to stimulate the gonads to mature, enlarge, and in turn to begin producing hormones.

gray matter: Includes unmyelinated axons, dendrites, glial cells, and blood vessels.

growth mindset: Viewing one's skills and characteristics as malleable or changeable.

health literacy: The knowledge, skills, and attitudes about health and the ability to obtain, process, and understand health information to make appropriate health decisions.

hippocampus: Part of the brain that plays a role in memory and emotion.

homophily: Similarity.

hormone: A chemical that is produced and secreted into the bloodstream to affect and influence physiological functions.

human immunodeficiency virus (HIV): The most serious sexually transmitted infection, which causes acquired immune deficiency syndrome (AIDS).

human papillomavirus (HPV): The most common type of sexually transmitted infection diagnosed in people of all ages; comprises several types, some of which can cause cancer in different areas of the body (e.g., cervical cancer in women).

hypothalamus: A region at the base of the brain that is responsible for maintaining basic body functions such as eating, drinking, temperature, and the production of hormones.

hypothalamus-pituitary-gonadal axis (HPG): Feedback loop that regulates the sex hormones that drive puberty.

hypothetical–deductive reasoning: The ability to consider propositions and probabilities, generate and systematically test hypotheses, and draw conclusions.

ideal self: A sense of self that is characterized by traits that one values.

identity: A coherent organized sense of self that includes values, attitudes, and goals to which one is committed.

identity achievement: The identity state that requires that individuals construct a sense of self through reflection, critical examination, and exploring or trying out new ideas and belief systems.

identity development: Refers to forming a sense of self.

identity diffusion: The identity state in which an individual has not undergone exploration or committed to self-chosen values and goals.

identity foreclosed: The degree to which individuals have explored possible selves and whether they have committed to specific beliefs and goals, assessed by administering interview and survey measures, and categorized into four identity statuses.

identity status: Categories describing the degree to which individuals have explored possible selves and whether they have committed to specific beliefs and goals.

imaginary audience: A manifestation of adolescent egocentrism in which they assume that they are the focus of others' attention.

inclusion: The approach in which children with learning disabilities learn alongside other children in the regular classroom for all or part of the day, accompanied by additional educational support of a teacher or paraprofessional who is specially trained to meet their needs.

independent variable: The factor proposed to change the behavior under study in an experiment; it is systematically manipulated during an experiment.

index offenses: Acts that are illegal regardless of age, such as theft and assault.

indifferent parenting style: A childrearing style characterized by low levels of warmth and acceptance coupled with little control or discipline.

individuation: A process in which adolescents gradually come to see themselves as separate from parents and become less dependent on them.

information processing theory: A perspective that uses a computer analogy to describe how the mind receives information and manipulates, stores, recalls, and uses it to solve problems.

informed consent: A participant's informed (knowledge of the scope of the research and potential harm and benefits of participating), rational, and voluntary agreement to participate in a study.

instrumental traits: Traits associated with acting on the world; also referred to as stereotypical masculine traits.

integrity: Ethical principle that researchers be accurate, honest, and truthful in their work by being mindful of the promises they make to participants and making every effort to keep their promises.

intelligence: An individual's ability to adapt to the environment.

intelligence test (IQ test): A test designed to measure the aptitude to learn at school; intellectual aptitude.

internal attribution: An attribution emphasizing one's role in the outcome based on internal factors, such as ability or skill.

internal working model of attachment: A set of expectations about one's worthiness of love and the availability of attachment figures during times of distress.

internalizing problems: Occur when an adolescent directs the problem or emotional stress inward, such as depression and anxiety.

intersectionality: Individuals' unique experiences and perspectives are influenced by the dynamic interrelations of social categories, such as gender, race and ethnicity, sexual orientation, and ability, as well as social factors, such as socioeconomic status.

intimacy: The ability to form and sustain close relationships.

justice: The ethical principle that the risks and benefits of research participation must be spread equitably across individuals and groups.

justice orientation: A male mode of moral reasoning proposed by Gilligan that emphasizes the abstract principles of fairness and individualism.

kisspeptin: Brain chemical that stimulates the hypothalamic-pituitary-gonadal axis to increase the production and secretion of hormones.

late adolescence: The period of adolescence from age 16 to 18, corresponding to the later high school years.

lateralization: The process by which the two hemispheres of the brain become specialized to carry out different functions.

learned helplessness orientation: An orientation characterized by a fixed mindset and the attribution of poor performance to internal factors.

leptin: A protein found in fat that signals the brain to release kisspeptin.

life-course persistent antisocial behavior: Pattern of criminal behavior that begins in childhood, rises and takes more severe forms in adolescence, and continues into adulthood.

limbic system: A collection of brain structures responsible for emotion.

longitudinal research study: A developmental study in which one group of participants is studied repeatedly to infer age changes.

long-term memory: The component of the information processing system that is an unlimited store that holds information indefinitely, until it is retrieved to manipulate working memory.

macrosystem: In bioecological systems theory, the sociohistorical context—cultural values and laws in which the microsystem, mesosystem, and exosystem are embedded, posing indirect influences on individuals.

major depressive disorder: A mental illness defined by the DSM-5 characterized by symptoms such as the experience of either depressed mood at least a 2-week period.

mastery orientation: A belief that success stems from trying hard and that failures are influenced by factors that can be controlled, like effort.

media literacy: The ability to identify different types of media and understand the messages they are sending.

media practice model: A theory of media influence emphasizes media use as a process of self construction; adolescents' motivations influences their media use and media also influences adolescents.

melatonin: A hormone that influences sleep.

menarche: A girl's first menstrual period.

menstruation: Monthly shedding of the uterine lining, which has thickened in preparation for the implantation of a fertilized egg.

mesosystem: In bioecological systems theory, the relations and interactions among microsystems.

metacognition: The ability to think about thinking; knowledge of how the mind works.

microsystem: In bioecological systems theory, the innermost level of context, which includes an individual's immediate physical and social environment.

middle adolescence: The period of adolescence from age 14 to 16, corresponding to the first half of high school in the United States.

moral reasoning: How we view and make judgments about issues of rights and justice in their social world.

moratorium status: The identity state that includes active exploration of ideas and a sense of openness to possibilities, coupled with some uncertainty.

multiple intelligence theory: Gardner's proposition that human intelligence is composed of a varied set of abilities.

multisystemic therapy (MST): Approach to intervening in delinquency that targets several bioecological systems, addressing barriers in each, including the home, school, and neighborhood.

mutual perspective taking: Individuals' understanding that they take other people's point of view at the same time as others attempt to take their own point of view.

myelination: The process in which neurons are coated in a fatty substance, myelin, which contributes to faster neural communication.

naturalistic observation: A research method in which a researcher views and records an individual's behavior in natural, real-world settings.

neurogenesis: The production of new neurons.

neuron: A nerve cell that stores and transmits information; billions of neurons comprise the brain.

neurotransmitter: A chemical messenger that crosses the synapse or the gap between two neurons.

nocturnal emissions: Involuntary ejaculations that are sometimes accompanied by erotic dreams.

nonsuicidal self-injury: Deliberate and voluntary physical personal injury that is non-life-threatening and is without any conscious suicidal intent.

obesity: In children, defined as having a body mass index at or above the 95th percentile for height and age.

observational learning: Learning that occurs by watching and imitating models, as posited by social learning theory.

ontogenetic development: Refers to the changes that take place in the individual, the center of the bioecological model.

open-ended interview: A research method in which a researcher asks a participant questions using a flexible, conversational style and may vary the order of questions, probe, and ask follow-up questions based on the participant's responses.

operant conditioning: A form of learning in which behavior increases or decreases based on environmental consequences.

overweight: Defined as having a body mass index at or above the 85th percentile for height and age.

parental monitoring: Parents' awareness of their children's activities, whereabouts, and companions.

parenting styles: Enduring sets of childrearing behaviors a parent uses across situations to form a childrearing climate.

passive consent: A type of consent procedure in which parents are notified about the research and must reply if they do *not* want their child to participate.

peer rejection: An ongoing interaction in which a child is deliberately excluded by peers.

peer victimization: An ongoing interaction in which a child becomes a frequent target of physical, verbal, or social harm by another child or children; also known as bullying.

perceived popularity: A form of popularity based on peer status and denotes high prestige, visibility, and dominance within the peer context.

permissive parenting style: A childrearing approach characterized by high levels of warmth and low levels of control or discipline.

personal fable: A manifestation of adolescent egocentrism in which adolescents believe their thoughts, feelings, and experiences are more special and unique than anyone else's, as well as the sense that they are invulnerable.

physical development: Body maturation, including body size, proportion, appearance, health, and perceptual abilities.

pituitary gland: The gland that stimulates the gonads to mature, enlarge, and begin producing hormones themselves.

plasticity: A characteristic of development that refers to malleability or openness to change in response to experience.

popular: When an individual who receives many positive ratings from peers indicating that they are accepted and valued by peers.

positive youth development (PYD): An approach to intervention that emphasizes promoting positive qualities that contribute to adolescents' ability to adapt and engage in constructive interactions with their complex and changing contexts.

positron emission tomography (PET): A measure of brain activity that involves injecting a small dose of radioactive material into the participant's bloodstream to monitor the flow of blood in the brain.

postconventional moral reasoning: Kohlberg's third level of moral reasoning emphasizing autonomous decision-making based on principles such as valuing human dignity.

post-formal reasoning: A stage of cognitive development proposed to follow Piaget's formal operational stage. Thinking and problem solving is restructured in adulthood to integrate abstract reasoning with practical considerations, recognizing that most problems have multiple causes and solutions, some solutions are better than others, and all problems involve uncertainty.

preconventional reasoning: Kohlberg's first level of reasoning in which young children's behavior is governed by punishment and gaining rewards.

prefrontal cortex: Located in the front of the brain, responsible for higher thought, such as planning, goal setting, controlling impulses, and using cognitive skills and memory to solve problems.

primary sex characteristics: The reproductive organs; in females, this includes the ovaries, fallopian tubes, uterus, and vagina, and in males, this includes the penis, testes, scrotum, seminal vesicles, and prostate gland.

prosocial behavior: Actions that are oriented toward others for the pure sake of helping, without a reward.

protective factor: A variable that is thought to reduce the poor outcomes associated with adverse circumstances.

psychoanalytic theory: A perspective introduced by Freud that development and behavior is stage-like and influenced by inner drives, memories, and conflicts of which an individual is unaware and cannot control.

psychosocial moratorium: In Erikson's theory, a period in which the individual is free to explore identity possibilities before committing to an identity.

puberty: The biological transition to adulthood, in which hormones cause the body to physically mature and permit sexual reproduction.

puberty suppressors: Medication that inhibits sex hormones and prevents the onset of pubertal changes.

punishment: In operant conditioning, the process in which a behavior is followed by an aversive or unpleasant outcome that decreases the likelihood of a response.

questionnaire: A research method in which researchers use a survey or set of questions to collect data from large samples of people.

rape: Refers to nonconsensual sexual penetration of the body by the body part of another person or object.

real self: An individual's current personal characteristics.

reciprocal determinism: A perspective positing that individuals and the environment interact and influence each other.

reflective judgment: Mature type of reasoning that synthesizes contradictions among perspectives.

reinforcement: In operant conditioning, the process by which a behavior is followed by a desirable outcome that increases the likelihood of a response.

relational aggression: Harming someone through nonphysical acts aimed at harming a person's connections with others, such as by exclusion and rumor spreading.

relativistic thinking: Type of reasoning in which knowledge is viewed as subjective and dependent on the situation.

religiosity: Religious practice, including religious affiliation and participation in its prescribed rituals and practices.

resilience: The ability to adapt to adversity.

respect for autonomy: Researchers' ethical obligation to respect participants' ability to make and implement decisions, applied through the use of informed consent.

response inhibition: The ability to control and stop responding to a stimulus.

responsibility: The ethical principle that researchers must adhere to professional standards of conduct and clarify their obligations and roles to others.

responsiveness: The degree to which parents are accepting of their adolescents, responding to them with warmth, sensitivity, and support.

risk factors: Individual or contextual challenges that tax an individual's coping capacities and can evoke psychological stress.

secondary sex characteristics: Physical traits that indicate sexual maturity but are not directly related to fertility, such as breast development and the growth of body hair.

secular trend: The change from one generation to the next in an aspect of development, such as body size or in the timing of puberty.

selective attention: The ability to focus on relevant stimuli and ignore others.

self-concept: The set of attributes, abilities, and characteristics that a person uses to describe and define himself or herself.

self-concept clarity: The extent to which adolescents' beliefs about themselves are clearly and consistently defined, expressed confidently, and enduring.

semen: The fluid that contains sperm.

sensory register: Sometimes referred to as sensory memory, filters sensory information as it enters the mind, holding incoming sensory information in its original form.

sequential research design: A developmental design in which multiple groups of participants of different ages are followed over time, combining cross-sectional and longitudinal research.

sex: Biological and determined by genetics—specifically, by the presence of a Y chromosome in the 23rd pair of chromosomes that determine sex—and usually indicated by the appearance of an infant's genitals.

sexting: The exchange of explicit sexual messages or images via mobile phone.

sexual assault: A broader term than rape, refers to a wide variety of nonconsensual sexual contact or behavior.

sexual orientation: A term that refers to whether someone is sexually attracted to others of the same sex, opposite sex, or both.

sexuality: The understanding and expression of sexual feelings and behaviors.

social cognition: Thinking about people, social situations, and relationships.

social gender transition: Entails changing the child's everyday experience to match their gender identity.

social learning theory: An approach that emphasizes the role of modeling and observational learning over people's behavior in addition to reinforcement and punishment.

social perspective taking: The ability to take other peoples' perspectives or point of view.

societal perspective taking: The recognition that the social environment, including the larger society, influences people's perspectives and beliefs.

sociocultural theory: Vygotsky's theory that individuals acquire culturally relevant ways of thinking through social interactions with members of their culture.

socioemotional development: Maturation of social and emotional functioning, which includes changes in personality, emotions, personal perceptions, social skills, and interpersonal relationships.

sociometric popularity: A form of popularity based on peer nomination; being widely liked and accepted by peers.

special education: Education tailored to meet the needs of a child with special needs, such as a specific learning disability.

specific learning disorder (SLD): Diagnosed in children who demonstrate a measurable discrepancy between aptitude and achievement in a particular academic area given their age, intelligence, and amount of schooling.

spermarche: A boy's first ejaculation of sperm.

spirituality: Refers to a personal search for answers to ultimate questions about life, such as its meaning, and about transcendent others, such as God.

stage-environment fit: Refers to the match between the characteristics and supports of the school environment and the developing person's needs and capacities; influences well-being.

status offenses: Activities that are illegal due to being underage, such as truancy, running away, and drinking.

structured interview: A research method in which each participant is asked the same set of questions in the same way.

structured observation: An observational measure in which an individual's behavior is viewed and recorded in a controlled environment; a situation created by the experimenter.

suicide: Death caused by self-directed injuries with the intent to die.

suicide contagion: The tendency for the prevalence of suicide to rise in a school or community following a suicide death.

synapse: The intersection or gap between the axon of one neuron and the dendrites of other neurons; the gap that neurotransmitters must cross.

synaptic pruning: The process by which synapses, neural connections that are seldom used, disappear.

synaptogenesis: The process in which neurons form synapses and increase connections between neurons.

testes: The glands that produce sperm.

testosterone: The primary male sex hormone responsible for development and regulation of the male reproductive system and secondary sex characteristics.

theory: An organized set of observations to describe, explain, and predict a phenomenon.

tracking: A curricular choice in students grouped by ability,

transgender: Denotes when a person's sense of identity and gender do not correspond to that person's biological sex.

transracial adoption: The circumstance in which a child is adopted to parents of a different race

triarchic theory of intelligence: Sternberg's theory positing three independent forms of intelligence: analytical, creative, and applied.

uses and gratifications theory: A theory of media influence that states that adolescents seek out media that meet their interests and needs.

white matter: Myelinated neurons.

working memory: The component of the information processing system that holds and processes information that is being manipulated, encoded, or retrieved and is responsible for maintaining and processing information used in cognitive tasks.

REFERENCES

CHAPTER 1

Aizer, A. (2017). The role of children's health in the intergenerational transmission of economic status. *Child Development Perspectives, 11*(3), 167–172. https://doi.org/10.1111/cdep.12231

American Psychological Association. (2010). *Ethical principles of psychologists and code of conduct*. Retrieved from http://www.apa.org/ethics/code/principles.pdf

Aries, P., & van den Berg, J. H. (1978). Centuries of childhood. In J. Beck, C. Jenks, N. Keddie, and M. Young (Eds.), *Towards sociology of education* (pp. 37–47). Piscataway, NJ: Transaction Inc.

Arnett, J. J. (1999). Adolescent storm and stress, reconsidered. *The American Psychologist, 54*(5), 317–326. https://doi.org/10.1037/0003-066X.54.5.317

Arnett, J. J. (2006). G. Stanley Hall's adolescence: Brilliance and nonsense. *History of Psychology, 9*(3), 186–197. https://doi.org/10.1037/1093-4510.9.3.186

Arnett, J. J. (Ed.). (2015). *The Oxford handbook of emerging adulthood* (Vol. 1). Oxford, England: Oxford University Press. https://doi.org/10.1093/oxfordhb/9780199795574.001.0001

Arnett, J. J., & Padilla-Walker, L. M. (2015). Brief report: Danish emerging adults' conceptions of adulthood. *Journal of Adolescence, 38*, 39–44. https://doi.org/10.1016/J.ADOLESCENCE.2014.10.011

Arnett, J. J., & Schwab, J. (2012). *The Clark University poll of emerging adults: Thriving, struggling, and hopeful*. Retrieved from http://www2.clarku.edu/clark-poll-emerging-adults/pdfs/clark-university-poll-emerging-adults-findings.pdf

Arnett, J. J., Žukauskienė, R., & Sugimura, K. (2014). The new life stage of emerging adulthood at ages 18–29 years: Implications for mental health. *The Lancet Psychiatry, 1*(7), 569–576. https://doi.org/10.1016/S2215-0366(14)00080-7

Baltes, P. B., Lindenberger, U., & Staudinger, U. M. (2006). Life span theory in developmental psychology. In R. M. Lerner (Ed.), *Handbook of child psychology, Vol. 1: Theoretical models of human development* (6th ed., pp. 569–664). Hoboken, NJ: John Wiley & Sons.

Bandettini, P. A. (2012). Twenty years of functional MRI: The science and the stories. *NeuroImage, 62*(2), 575–588. https://doi.org/10.1016/j.neuroimage.2012.04.026

Bandura, A. (2010). Vicarious learning. In D. Matsumoto (Ed.), *Cambridge dictionary of psychology* (p. 344). New York, NY: Cambridge University Press.

Bandura, A. (2011). But what about that gigantic elephant in the room? In R. Arkin (Ed.), *Most underappreciated: 50 prominent social psychologists describe their most unloved work.* (pp. 51–59). New York, NY: Oxford University Press.

Bandura, A. (2012). Social cognitive theory. In P. A. M. Van Lange, A. W. Kruglanski, & E. T. Higgins (Eds.), *Handbook of theories of social psychology* (Vol. 1, pp. 349–373). Thousand Oaks, CA: Sage.

Bargh, J. A. (2013). Our unconscious mind. *Scientific American, 310*(1), 30–37. https://doi.org/10.1038/scientificamerican0114-30

Bass, R. W., Brown, D. D., Laurson, K. R., & Coleman, M. M. (2013). Physical fitness and academic performance in middle school students. *Acta Paediatrica, 102*(8), 832–837. https://doi.org/10.1111/apa.12278

Baxter, K. (2008). *The modern age: Turn-of-the-century American culture and the invention of adolescence*. Tuscaloosa, AL: University of Alabama Press.

Birney, D. P., & Sternberg, R. J. (2011). The development of cognitive abilities. In M. H. Bornstein & M. E. Lamb (Eds.), *Developmental science: An advanced textbook* (6th ed., pp. 353–388). New York, NY: Psychology Press.

Boyer, T. W., & Byrnes, J. P. (2016). Risk-taking. In J. R. Levesque (Ed.), *Encyclopedia of adolescence* (pp. 1–5). Cham, Switzerland: Springer. https://doi.org/10.1007/978-3-319-32132-5_15-2

Braams, B. R., & Crone, E. A. (2017). Longitudinal changes in social brain development: Processing outcomes for friend and self. *Child Development, 88*(6), 1952–1965. https://doi.org/10.1111/cdev.12665

Brawner, B. M., Volpe, E. M., Stewart, J. M., & Gomes, M. M. (2013). Attitudes and beliefs toward biobehavioural research participation: Voices and concerns of urban adolescent females receiving outpatient mental health treatment. *Annals of Human Biology, 40*(6), 485–495. https://doi.org/10.3109/03014460.2013.806590

Bronfenbrenner, U., & Morris, P. A. (2006). The bioecological model of human development. In R. M. Lerner & W. Damon (Eds.), *Handbook of child psychology* (Vol. 1, pp. 793–828). Hoboken, NJ: John Wiley & Sons.

Buchanan, C. M., & Bruton, J. H. (2016). Storm and stress. In J. R. Levesque (Ed.), *Encyclopedia of adolescence* (pp. 1–12). Cham, Switzerland: Springer. https://doi.org/10.1007/978-3-319-32132-5_111-2

Callaghan, T., & Corbit, J. (2015). The development of symbolic representation. In R. M. Lerner (Ed.), *Handbook of child psychology and developmental science* (7th ed., pp. 1–46). Hoboken, NJ: John Wiley & Sons. https://doi.org/10.1002/9781118963418.childpsy207

Centers for Disease Control and Prevention. (2018). *Youth Risk Behavior Surveillance System (YRBSS) overview. 2016*. Atlanta, GA: Author.

Cierniak, R. (2011). Some words about the history of computed tomography. In *X-ray computed tomography in biomedical engineering* (pp. 7–19). London, England: Springer. https://doi.org/10.1007/978-0-85729-027-4_2

Coplan, R. J., Ooi, L. L., & Nocita, G. (2015). When one is company and two is a crowd: Why some children prefer solitude. *Child Development Perspectives, 9*(3), 133–137. https://doi.org/10.1111/cdep.12131

Côté, J. E. (2014). The dangerous myth of emerging adulthood: An evidence-based critique of a flawed developmental theory. *Applied Developmental Science, 18*(4), 177–188. https://doi.org/10.1080/10888691.2014.954451

Crain, T. (2016). The unity of unconsciousness. *Proceedings of the Aristotelian Society, 117*(1), 1–21. https://doi.org/10.1093/arisoc/aox001

Crane, S., & Broome, M. E. (2017). Understanding ethical issues of research participation from the perspective of participating children and adolescents: A systematic review. *Worldviews on Evidence-Based Nursing, 14*(3), 200–209. https://doi.org/10.1111/wvn.12209

Crenshaw, K. (1989). Demarginalizing the intersection of race and sex: A Black feminist critique of antidiscrimination doctrine, feminist theory and antiracist politics. *University of Chicago Legal Forum*, 139. Retrieved from https://heinonline.org/HOL/LandingPage?handle=hein.journals/uchclf1989&div=10&id=&page=

Curtis, A. C. (2015). Defining adolescence. *Journal of Adolescent and Family Health*, 7(2), 40. Retrieved from https://scholar.utc.edu/jafh/vol7/iss2/2

du Bois-Reymond, M. (2015). Emerging adulthood theory and social class. In J. J. Arnett (Ed.), *The Oxford handbook of emerging adulthood* (Vol. 1, 47–61). Oxford, England: Oxford University Press. https://doi.org/10.1093/oxfordhb/9780199795574.013.37

Eisenberg, M. E., Spry, E., & Patton, G. C. (2015). From emerging to established: Longitudinal patterns in the timing of transition events among Australian emerging adults. *Emerging Adulthood*, 3(4), 277–281. https://doi.org/10.1177/2167696815574639

Erikson, E. H. (1950). *Childhood and society* (2nd ed.). New York, NY: Norton.

Feurer, C., Burkhouse, K. L., Siegle, G., & Gibb, B. E. (2017). Increased pupil dilation to angry faces predicts interpersonal stress generation in offspring of depressed mothers. *Journal of Child Psychology and Psychiatry*, 58(8), 950–957. https://doi.org/10.1111/jcpp.12739

Fisher, C. B., Higgins-D'Alessandro, A., Rau, J. M., Kuther, T. L., & Belanger, S. (1996). Referring and reporting research participants at risk: Views from urban adolescents. *Child Development*, 67(5), 2086–2100. https://doi.org/10.1111/j.1467-8624.1996.tb01845.x

Garrison, E. G., & Kobor, P. C. (2002). Weathering a political storm: A contextual perspective on a psychological research controversy. *American Psychologist*, 57(3), 165–175.

Gauvain, M. (2018). From developmental psychologist to water scientist and back again: The role of interdisciplinary research in developmental science. *Child Development Perspectives*, 12(1), 45–50. https://doi.org/10.1111/cdep.12255

Gentile, D. A., Bender, P. K., & Anderson, C. A. (2017). Violent video game effects on salivary cortisol, arousal, and aggressive thoughts in children. *Computers in Human Behavior*, 70, 39–43. https://doi.org/10.1016/j.chb.2016.12.045

Ghavami, N., Katsiaficas, D., & Rogers, L. O. (2016). Toward an intersectional approach in developmental science: The role of race, gender, sexual orientation, and immigrant status. *Advances in Child Development and Behavior*, 50, 31–73. https://doi.org/10.1016/BS.ACDB.2015.12.001

Godfrey, E. B., & Burson, E. (2018). Interrogating the intersections: How intersectional perspectives can inform developmental scholarship on critical consciousness. *New Directions for Child and Adolescent Development*, 2018(161), 17–38. https://doi.org/10.1002/cad.20246

Golinkoff, R. M., Hirsh-Pasek, K., Grob, R., & Schlesinger, M. (2017). "Oh, the places you'll go" by bringing developmental science into the world! *Child Development*, 88(5), 1403–1408. https://doi.org/10.1111/cdev.12929

Göllner, R., Roberts, B. W., Damian, R. I., Lüdtke, O., Jonkmann, K., & Trautwein, U. (2017). Whose "storm and stress" is it? Parent and child reports of personality development in the transition to early adolescence. *Journal of Personality*, 85(3), 376–387. https://doi.org/10.1111/jopy.12246

Halford, G. S., & Andrews, G. (2011). Information-processing models of cognitive development. In U. Goswami (Ed.), *The Wiley-Blackwell handbook of childhood cognitive development* (2nd ed., pp. 697–721). Hoboken, NJ: John Wiley & Sons.

Hall, G. S. (1904). *Adolescence*. New York, NY: Appleton.

Havighurst, R. J. (1972). *Developmental tasks and education*. New York, NY: McKay Company.

Hendry, L. B., & Kloep, M. (2010). How universal is emerging adulthood? An empirical example. *Journal of Youth Studies*, 13(2), 169–179. https://doi.org/10.1080/13676260903295067

Henrich, J., Heine, S. J., & Norenzayan, A. (2010). The weirdest people in the world? *Behavioral and Brain Sciences*, 33(2–3), 61–83. https://doi.org/10.1017/S0140525X0999152X

Hines, A. R., & Paulson, S. E. (2006). Parents' and teachers' perceptions of adolescent storm and stress: Relations with parenting and teaching styles. *Adolescence*, 41(164), 597–614. Retrieved from http://www.ncbi.nlm.nih.gov/pubmed/17240769

Hiriscau, I. E., Stingelin-Giles, N., Stadler, C., Schmeck, K., & Reiter-Theil, S. (2014). A right to confidentiality or a duty to disclose? Ethical guidance for conducting prevention research with children and adolescents. *European Child & Adolescent Psychiatry*, 23(6), 409–416. https://doi.org/10.1007/s00787-014-0526-y

Hollenstein, T., & Lougheed, J. P. (2013). Beyond storm and stress: Typicality, transactions, timing, and temperament to account for adolescent change. *The American Psychologist*, 68(6), 444–454. https://doi.org/10.1037/a0033586

Huston, A. C. (2018). A life at the intersection of science and social issues. *Child Development Perspectives*, 12(2), 75–79. https://doi.org/10.1111/cdep.12265

Jaeger, E. L. (2016). Negotiating complexity: A bioecological systems perspective on literacy development. *Human Development*, 59(4), 163–187. https://doi.org/10.1159/000448743

Kett, J. F. (2003). Reflections on the history of adolescence in America. *The History of the Family*, 8(3), 355–373. https://doi.org/10.1016/S1081-602X(03)00042-3

Kuruvilla, S., Bustreo, F., Kuo, T., Mishra, C., Taylor, K., Fogstad, H., . . . Costello, A. (2016). The Global Strategy for Women's, Children's and Adolescents' Health (2016–2030): A roadmap based on evidence and country experience. *Bulletin of the World Health Organization*, 94(5), 398–400. https://doi.org/10.2471/BLT.16.170431

Lapsley, D. K., Enright, R. D., & Serlin, R. C. (1985). Toward a theoretical perspective on the legislation of adolescence. *The Journal of Early Adolescence*, 5(4), 441–466. https://doi.org/10.1177/0272431685054004

Lerner, R. M., Buckingham, M. H., Champine, R. B., Greenman, K. N., Warren, D. J. A., Weiner, M. B., . . . Weiner, M. B. (2015a). Positive development among diverse youth. In R. A. Scott, S. M. Kosslyn, & M. Buchmann (Eds.), *Emerging trends in the social and behavioral sciences* (pp. 1–14). Hoboken, NJ: John Wiley & Sons. https://doi.org/10.1002/9781118900772.etrds0260

Lerner, R. M., Johnson, S. K., & Buckingham, M. H. (2015b). Relational developmental systems-based theories and the study of children and families: Lerner and Spanier (1978) revisited. *Journal of Family Theory & Review*, 7(2), 83–104. https://doi.org/10.1111/jftr.12067

Lerner, R. M., & Steinberg, L. (2009). The scientific study of adolescent development. In *Handbook of adolescent psychology* (pp. 1–12). Hoboken, NJ: John Wiley & Sons. https://doi.org/10.1002/9780470479193.adlpsy001002

Lilienfeld, S. O. (2002). When worlds collide. Social science, politics, and the Rind et al. (1998). *Child sexual abuse meta-analysis. The American Psychologist*, 57(3), 176–188. https://doi.org/10.1037/0003-066X.57.3.176

Linders, A. (2017). Deconstructing adolescence. In A. L. Cherry, V. Baltag, & M. E. Dillon (Eds.), *International handbook on adolescent health and development* (pp. 15–28). Cham, Switzerland: Springer. https://doi.org/10.1007/978-3-319-40743-2_2

Luna, B., Marek, S., Larsen, B., Tervo-Clemmens, B., & Chahal, R. (2015). An integrative model of the maturation of cognitive control. *Annual Review of Neuroscience*, 38(1), 151–170. https://doi.org/10.1146/annurev-neuro-071714-034054

Macapagal, K., Coventry, R., Arbeit, M. R., Fisher, C. B., & Mustanski, B. (2017). "I won't out myself just to do a survey": Sexual and gender minority adolescents' perspectives on the risks and benefits of sex research. *Archives of Sexual Behavior*, 46(5), 1393–1409. https://doi.org/10.1007/s10508-016-0784-5

Maggs, J. L., Jager, J., Patrick, M. E., & Schulenberg, J. (2012). Social role patterning in early adulthood in the USA: Adolescent predictors and concurrent wellbeing across four distinct configurations. *Longitudinal and Life Course Studies*, *3*(2), 190–210. https://doi.org/10.14301/llcs.v3i2.183

Markus, H. R., & Kitayama, S. (2010). Cultures and selves: A cycle of mutual constitution. *Perspectives on Psychological Science*, *5*(4), 420–430. https://doi.org/10.1177/1745691610375557

Mehl, M. R. (2017). The electronically activated recorder (EAR). *Current Directions in Psychological Science*, *26*(2), 184–190. https://doi.org/10.1177/0963721416680611

Miech, R. A., Johnston, L. D., O'Malley, P. M., Bachman, J. G., Schulenberg, J. E., & Patrick, M. E. (2017). *Monitoring the Future national survey results on drug use, 1975–2016: Volume I, Secondary school students*. Retrieved from http://www.monitoringthefuture.org/pubs/monographs/mtf-vol1_2016.pdf

Miller, P. H. (2016). *Theories of developmental psychology* (6th ed.). New York, NY: Worth.

Mistry, J., Li, J., Yoshikawa, H., Tseng, V., Tirrell, J., Kiang, L., . . . Wang, Y. (2016). An integrated conceptual framework for the development of Asian American children and youth. *Child Development*, *87*(4), 1014–1032. https://doi.org/10.1111/cdev.12577

Mitchell, L. L., & Syed, M. (2015). Does college matter for emerging adulthood? Comparing developmental trajectories of educational groups. *Journal of Youth and Adolescence*, *44*(11), 2012–2027. https://doi.org/10.1007/s10964-015-0330-0

Müller, U., Kerns, K., Müller, U., & Kerns, K. (2015). The development of executive function. In R. M. Lerner (Ed.), *Handbook of child psychology and developmental science* (7th ed., pp. 1–53). Hoboken, NJ: John Wiley & Sons. https://doi.org/10.1002/9781118963418.childpsy214

National Center for Education Statistics, Digest of Education Statistics. (2017). Enrollment in Grades 9 through 12 in public and private schools compared with population 14 to 17 years of age: Selected years, 1889–90 through fall 2017. *Digest of Education Statistics, 2016*. Retrieved from https://nces.ed.gov/programs/digest/d17/tables/dt17_201.20.asp

Nelson, L. J. (2009). An examination of emerging adulthood in Romanian college students. *International Journal of Behavioral Development*, *33*(5), 402–411. https://doi.org/10.1177/0165025409340093

Nielsen, M., Haun, D., Kärtner, J., & Legare, C. H. (2017). The persistent sampling bias in developmental psychology: A call to action. *Journal of Experimental Child Psychology*, *162*, 31–38. https://doi.org/10.1016/J.JECP.2017.04.017

Offer, D., Ostrov, E., Howard, K. I., & Atkinson, R. (1988). *The teenage world: Adolescents' self-image in ten countries* (Vol. 11). New York, NY: Springer.

Oulton, K., Gibson, F., Sell, D., Williams, A., Pratt, L., & Wray, J. (2016). Assent for children's participation in research: Why it matters and making it meaningful. *Child: Care, Health and Development*, *42*(4), 588–597. https://doi.org/10.1111/cch.12344

Portnow, L. H., Vaillancourt, D. E., & Okun, M. S. (2013). The history of cerebral PET scanning: From physiology to cutting-edge technology. *Neurology*, *80*(10), 952–956. https://doi.org/10.1212/WNL.0b013e318285c135

Qu, Y., Pomerantz, E. M., McCormick, E., & Telzer, E. H. (2018). Youth's conceptions of adolescence predict longitudinal changes in prefrontal cortex activation and risk taking during adolescence. *Child Development*, *89*(3), 773–783. https://doi.org/10.1111/cdev.13017

Qu, Y., Pomerantz, E. M., Wang, M., Cheung, C., & Cimpian, A. (2016). Conceptions of adolescence: Implications for differences in engagement in school over early adolescence in the United States and China. *Journal of Youth and Adolescence*, *45*(7), 1512–1526. https://doi.org/10.1007/s10964-016-0492-4

Ravert, R. D., Stoddard, N. A., & Donnellan, M. B. (2018). A content analysis of the methods used to study emerging adults in six developmental journals from 2013 to 2015. *Emerging Adulthood*, *6*(3), 151–158. https://doi.org/10.1177/2167696817720011

Rind, B., Tromovitch, P., & Bauserman, R. (1998). A meta-analytic examination of assumed properties of child sexual abuse using college samples. *Psychological Bulletin*, *124*(1), 22–53.

Ristic, J., & Enns, J. T. (2015). Attentional development. In R. M. Lerner (Ed.), *Handbook of child psychology and developmental science* (7th ed., pp. 1–45). Hoboken, NJ: John Wiley & Sons. https://doi.org/10.1002/9781118963418.childpsy205

Rogoff, B. (2016). Culture and participation: A paradigm shift. *Current Opinion in Psychology*, *8*, 182–189. https://doi.org/10.1016/j.copsyc.2015.12.002

Rogoff, B., Moore, L. C., Correa-Chavez, M., & Dexter, A. L. (2014). Children develop cultural repertoires through engaging in everyday routines and practices. In J. Grusec & P. Hastings (Eds.), *Handbook of socialization: Theory and research* (pp. 472–498). New York, NY: Guilford.

Roy, A. L. (2018). Intersectional ecologies: Positioning intersectionality in settings-level research. *New Directions for Child and Adolescent Development*, *2018*(161), 57–74. https://doi.org/10.1002/cad.20248

Sawyer, S. M., Azzopardi, P. S., Wickremarathne, D., & Patton, G. C. (2018). The age of adolescence. *The Lancet Child & Adolescent Health*, *2*(3), 223–228. https://doi.org/10.1016/S2352-4642(18)30022-1

Schwartz, S. J. (2016). Turning point for a turning point. *Emerging Adulthood*, *4*(5), 307–317. https://doi.org/10.1177/2167696815624640

Schwartz, S. J., Zamboanga, B. L., Luyckx, K., Meca, A., & Ritchie, R. A. (2013). Identity in emerging adulthood: Reviewing the field and looking forward. *Emerging Adulthood*, *1*(2), 96–113. https://doi.org/10.1177/2167696813479781

Sharkey, J. D., Reed, L. A., & Felix, E. D. (2017). Dating and sexual violence research in the schools: Balancing protection of confidentiality with supporting the welfare of survivors. *American Journal of Community Psychology*, *60*(3–4), 361–367. https://doi.org/10.1002/ajcp.12186

Simons, S. S. H., Cillessen, A. H. N., & de Weerth, C. (2017). Cortisol stress responses and children's behavioral functioning at school. *Developmental Psychobiology*, *59*(2), 217–224. https://doi.org/10.1002/dev.21484

Sirsch, U., Dreher, E., Mayr, E., & Willinger, U. (2009). What does it take to be an adult in Austria? Views of adulthood in Austrian adolescents, emerging adults, and adults. *Journal of Adolescent Research*, *24*(3), 275–292.

Soares, J. M., Marques, P., Alves, V., & Sousa, N. (2013). A hitchhiker's guide to diffusion tensor imaging. *Frontiers in Neuroscience*, *7*, 31. https://doi.org/10.3389/fnins.2013.00031

Society for Research in Child Development. (2007). *Ethical standards in research*. Retrieved from http://www.srcd.org/about-us/ethical-standards-research

Swanson, J. A. (2016). Trends in literature about emerging adulthood. *Emerging Adulthood*, *4*(6), 391–402. https://doi.org/10.1177/2167696816630468

Syed, M. (2015). Emerging adulthood: Developmental stage, theory, or nonsense? In J. J. Arnett (Ed.), *The Oxford handbook of emerging adulthood* (pp. 11–25). Oxford, England: Oxford University Press. https://doi.org/10.1093/oxfordhb/9780199795574.013.9

Syed, M., & Ajayi, A. A. (2018). Promises and pitfalls in the integration of intersectionality with development science. *New Directions for Child and Adolescent Development*, *2018*(161), 109–117. https://doi.org/10.1002/cad.20250

Syed, M., & Mitchell, L. L. (2014). How race and ethnicity shape emerging adulthood. In J. J. Arnett (Ed.), *The Oxford handbook of emerging adulthood* (pp. 87–101). Oxford, England: Oxford University Press. https://doi.org/10.1093/oxfordhb/9780199795574.013.005

Syed, M., Santos, C., Yoo, H. C., & Juang, L. P. (2018). Invisibility of racial/ethnic minorities in developmental science: Implications for research and institutional practices. *American Psychologist*, 73(6), 812–826. https://doi.org/10.1037/amp0000294

Tait, A. R., & Geisser, M. E. (2017). Development of a consensus operational definition of child assent for research. *BMC Medical Ethics*, 18(1), 41. https://doi.org/10.1186/s12910-017-0199-4

Tobin, E. T., Kane, H. S., Saleh, D. J., Naar-King, S., Poowuttikul, P., Secord, E., . . . Slatcher, R. B. (2015). Naturalistically observed conflict and youth asthma symptoms. *Health Psychology*, 34(6), 622–631. https://doi.org/10.1037/hea0000138

Tudge, J. R. H., Payir, A., Merçon-Vargas, E., Cao, H., Liang, Y., Li, J., & O'Brien, L. (2016). Still misused after all these years? A reevaluation of the uses of Bronfenbrenner's bioecological theory of human development. *Journal of Family Theory & Review*, 8(4), 427–445. https://doi.org/10.1111/jftr.12165

U.S. Bureau of the Census. (2017). Historical Marital Status Tables: Table MS-2. Estimated Median Age at First Marriage, by Sex: 1890 to the Present. Retrieved from https://www.census.gov/data/tables/time-series/demo/families/marital.html

U.S. Bureau of the Census. (2018). *America's families and living arrangements: 2017*. Retrieved from https://www.census.gov/data/tables/2017/demo/families/cps-2017.html

Vélez-Agosto, N. M., Soto-Crespo, J. G., Vizcarrondo-Oppenheimer, M., Vega-Molina, S., & García Coll, C. (2017). Bronfenbrenner's bioecological theory revision: Moving culture from the macro into the micro. *Perspectives on Psychological Science*, 12(5), 900–910. https://doi.org/10.1177/1745691617704397

Vraga, E., Bode, L., & Troller-Renfree, S. (2016). Beyond self-reports: Using eye tracking to measure topic and style differences in attention to social media content. *Communication Methods and Measures*, 10(2–3), 149–164. https://doi.org/10.1080/19312458.2016.1150443

Vygotsky, L. S. (1978). *Mind in society: The development of higher psychological processes*. Cambridge, MA: Harvard University Press.

Westen, D. (1998). The scientific legacy of Sigmund Freud: Toward a psychodynamically informed psychological science. *Psychological Bulletin*, 124, 333–371.

Wood, D., Crapnell, T., Lau, L., Bennett, A., Lotstein, D., Ferris, M., & Kuo, A. (2018). Emerging adulthood as a critical stage in the life course. In N. Halfon, C. B. Forrest, R. M. Lerner, & E. M. Faustman (Eds.), *Handbook of life course health development* (pp. 123–143). Cham, Switzerland: Springer. https://doi.org/10.1007/978-3-319-47143-3_7

World Health Organization. (1977). *Health needs of adolescents*. Geneva, Switzerland: Author. Retrieved from http://bases.bireme.br/cgi-bin/wxislind.exe/iah/online/?IsisScript=iah/iah.xis&src=google&base=PAHO&lang=p&nextAction=lnk&exprSearch=1596&indexSearch=ID

Yoshikawa, H., Mistry, R., & Wang, Y. (2016). Advancing methods in research on Asian American children and youth. *Child Development*, 87(4), 1033–1050. https://doi.org/10.1111/cdev.12576

Youniss, J. (2006). G. Stanley Hall and his times: Too much so, yet not enough. *History of Psychology*, 9(3), 224–235. https://doi.org/10.1037/1093-4510.9.3.224

CHAPTER 2

Ackard, D. M., Fulkerson, J. A., & Neumark-Sztainer, D. (2011). Stability of eating disorder diagnostic classifications in adolescents: Five-year longitudinal findings from a population-based study. *Eating Disorders*, 19(4), 308–322. https://doi.org/10.1080/10640266.2011.584804

Afshin, A., Reitsma, M. B., & Murray, C. J. L. (2017). Health effects of overweight and obesity in 195 countries. *The New England Journal of Medicine*, 377(15), 1496–1497. https://doi.org/10.1056/NEJMc1710026

Ágh, T., Kovács, G., Supina, D., Pawaskar, M., Herman, B. K., Vokó, Z., & Sheehan, D. V. (2016). A systematic review of the health-related quality of life and economic burdens of anorexia nervosa, bulimia nervosa, and binge eating disorder. *Eating and Weight Disorders - Studies on Anorexia, Bulimia and Obesity*, 21(3), 353–364. https://doi.org/10.1007/s40519-016-0264-x

Albuquerque, D., Nóbrega, C., Manco, L., & Padez, C. (2017). The contribution of genetics and environment to obesity. *British Medical Bulletin*, 123(1), 159–173. https://doi.org/10.1093/bmb/ldx022

American Academy of Pediatrics & American Academy of Pediatrics Council on Communications and Media. (2013). Children, adolescents, and the media. *Pediatrics*, 132(5), 958–961. https://doi.org/10.1542/peds.2013-2656

American Psychiatric Association. (2013). *Diagnostic and statistical manual of mental disorders* (5th ed.). Washington, DC: Author.

Amir, D., Jordan, M. R., & Bribiescas, R. G. (2016). A longitudinal assessment of associations between adolescent environment, adversity perception, and economic status on fertility and age of menarche. *PLoS ONE*, 11(6), e0155883. https://doi.org/10.1371/journal.pone.0155883

Auchus, R. J., & Rainey, W. E. (2004). Adrenarche - physiology, biochemistry and human disease. *Clinical Endocrinology*, 60(3), 288–296. https://doi.org/10.1046/j.1365-2265.2003.01858.x

Aylwin, C. F., Toro, C. A., Shirtcliff, E., & Lomniczi, A. (2019). Emerging genetic and epigenetic mechanisms underlying pubertal maturation in adolescence. *Journal of Research on Adolescence*, 29(1), 54–79. https://doi.org/10.1111/jora.12385

Baams, L., Dubas, J. S., Overbeek, G., & van Aken, M. A. G. (2015). Transitions in body and behavior: A meta-analytic study on the relationship between pubertal development and adolescent sexual behavior. *The Journal of Adolescent Health*, 56(6), 586–598. https://doi.org/10.1016/j.jadohealth.2014.11.019

Ballesteros, M. F., Williams, D. D., Mack, K. A., Simon, T. R., & Sleet, D. A. (2018). The epidemiology of unintentional and violence-related injury morbidity and mortality among children and adolescents in the United States. *International Journal of Environmental Research and Public Health*, 15(4), 616. https://doi.org/10.3390/ijerph15040616

Banfield, E. C., Liu, Y., Davis, J. S., Chang, S., & Frazier-Wood, A. C. (2016). Poor adherence to US dietary guidelines for children and adolescents in the National Health and Nutrition Examination Survey population. *Journal of the Academy of Nutrition and Dietetics*, 116(1), 21–27. https://doi.org/10.1016/j.jand.2015.08.010

Bartel, K. A., Gradisar, M., & Williamson, P. (2015). Protective and risk factors for adolescent sleep: A meta-analytic review. *Sleep Medicine Reviews*, 21, 72–85. https://doi.org/10.1016/j.smrv.2014.08.002

Behera, D., Sivakami, M., & Behera, M. R. (2015). Menarche and menstruation in rural adolescent girls in Maharashtra, India. *Journal of Health Management*, 17(4), 510–519. https://doi.org/10.1177/0972063415612581

Benoit, A., Lacourse, E., & Claes, M. (2013). Pubertal timing and depressive symptoms in late adolescence: The moderating role of individual, peer, and parental factors. *Development and Psychopathology*, 25(2), 455–471. https://doi.org/10.1017/S0954579412001174

Benowitz-Fredericks, C. A., Garcia, K., Massey, M., Vasagar, B., & Borzekowski, D. L. G. (2012). Body image, eating disorders, and the relationship to adolescent media use. *Pediatric Clinics of North America*, 59(3), 693–704, ix. https://doi.org/10.1016/j.pcl.2012.03.017

Berenbaum, S. A., Beltz, A. M., & Corley, R. (2015). The importance of puberty for adolescent development: Conceptualization and measurement. *Advances in Child Development and Behavior*, *48*, 53–92. https://doi.org/10.1016/BS.ACDB.2014.11.002

Berge, J. M., MacLehose, R. F., Larson, N., Laska, M., & Neumark-Sztainer, D. (2016). Family food preparation and its effects on adolescent dietary quality and eating patterns. *Journal of Adolescent Health*, *59*(5), 530–536. https://doi.org/10.1016/j.jadohealth.2016.06.007

Berge, J. M., Wall, M., Hsueh, T.-F., Fulkerson, J. A., Larson, N., & Neumark-Sztainer, D. (2015). The protective role of family meals for youth obesity: 10-year longitudinal associations. *The Journal of Pediatrics*, *166*(2), 296–301. https://doi.org/10.1016/j.jpeds.2014.08.030

Berkman, N. D., Brownley, K. A., Peat, C. M., Lohr, K. N., Cullen, K. E., Morgan, L. C., . . . Bulik, C. M. (2015). *Management and outcomes of binge-eating disorder*. Comparative Effectiveness Review No. 160. Rockville, MD: Agency for Healthcare Research and Quality. Retrieved from http://www.ncbi.nlm.nih.gov/pubmed/26764442

Berkman, N. D., Lohr, K. N., & Bulik, C. M. (2007). Outcomes of eating disorders: A systematic review of the literature. *International Journal of Eating Disorders*, *40*(4), 293–309.

Biehl, M., Natsuaki, M., & Ge, X. (2007). The influence of pubertal timing on alcohol use and heavy drinking trajectories. *Journal of Youth & Adolescence*, *36*(2), 153–167. https://doi.org/10.1007/s10964-006-9120-z

Biro, F. M., Greenspan, L. C., & Galvez, M. P. (2012). Puberty in girls of the 21st century. *Journal of Pediatric and Adolescent Gynecology*, *25*(5), 289–294. https://doi.org/10.1016/j.jpag.2012.05.009

Biro, F. M., Pajak, A., Wolff, M. S., Pinney, S. M., Windham, G. C., Galvez, M. P., . . . Teitelbaum, S. L. (2018). Age of menarche in a longitudinal US cohort. *Journal of Pediatric and Adolescent Gynecology*, *31*(4), 339–345. https://doi.org/10.1016/j.jpag.2018.05.002

Blakemore, S.-J., Burnett, S., & Dahl, R. E. (2010). The role of puberty in the developing adolescent brain. *Human Brain Mapping*, *31*(6), 926–933. https://doi.org/10.1002/hbm.21052

Bleich, S. N., Segal, J., Wu, Y., Wilson, R., & Wang, Y. (2013). Systematic review of community-based childhood obesity prevention studies. *Pediatrics*, *132*(1), 201–210. https://doi.org/10.1542/peds.2013-0886

Blumenthal, H., Leen-Feldner, E. W., Trainor, C. D., Babson, K. A., & Bunaciu, L. (2009). Interactive roles of pubertal timing and peer relations in predicting social anxiety symptoms among youth. *Journal of Adolescent Health*, *44*(4), 401–403. https://doi.org/10.1016/j.jadohealth.2008.08.023

Bogin, B. (2011). Puberty and adolescence: An evolutionary perspective. In *Encyclopedia of adolescence* (pp. 275–286). San Diego, CA: Academic Press. https://doi.org/10.1016/B978-0-12-373951-3.00033-8

Bosch, A. M., Hutter, I., & van Ginneken, J. K. (2008). Perceptions of adolescents and their mothers on reproductive and sexual development in Matlab, Bangladesh. *International Journal of Adolescent Medicine and Health*, *20*(3), 329–342. https://doi.org/10.1515/ijamh.2008.20.3.329

Bowman, S. A., Gortmaker, S. L., Ebbeling, C. B., Pereira, M. A., & Ludwig, D. S. (2004). Effects of fast-food consumption on energy intake and diet quality among children in a national household survey. *Pediatrics*, *113*(1), 112–118. https://doi.org/10.1542/peds.113.1.112

Brooks-Gunn, J., & Ruble, D. N. (2013). Developmental processes in the experience of menarche. In A. Baum, J. E. Singer, and J. L. Singer (Eds.), *Issues in child health and adolescent health: Handbook of psychology and health* (pp. 117–148). New York, NY: Psychology Press.

Bucchianeri, M. M., Eisenberg, M. E., & Neumark-Sztainer, D. (2013). Weightism, racism, classism, and sexism: Shared forms of harassment in adolescents. *Journal of Adolescent Health*, *53*(1), 47–53. https://doi.org/10.1016/J.JADOHEALTH.2013.01.006

Bulik, C. M., Kleiman, S. C., & Yilmaz, Z. (2016). Genetic epidemiology of eating disorders. *Current Opinion in Psychiatry*, *29*(6), 383–388. https://doi.org/10.1097/YCO.0000000000000275

Bush, N. R., Allison, A. L., Miller, A. L., Deardorff, J., Adler, N. E., & Boyce, W. T. (2017). Socioeconomic disparities in childhood obesity risk: Association with an oxytocin receptor polymorphism. *JAMA Pediatrics*, *171*(1), 61. https://doi.org/10.1001/jamapediatrics.2016.2332

Bygdell, M., Vandenput, L., Ohlsson, C., & Kindblom, J. M. (2014). A secular trend for pubertal timing in Swedish Men Born 1946-1991: The BEST Cohort: Puberty: From bench to bedside. *ENDO Meetings*. Retrieved from http://press.endocrine.org/doi/abs/10.1210/endo-meetings.2014.PE.10.OR11-3

Byrne, M. L., Whittle, S., Vijayakumar, N., Dennison, M., Simmons, J. G., & Allen, N. B. (2017). A systematic review of adrenarche as a sensitive period in neurobiological development and mental health. *Developmental Cognitive Neuroscience*, *25*, 12–28. https://doi.org/10.1016/J.DCN.2016.12.004

Campbell, B. C. (2011). Adrenarche and middle childhood. *Human Nature*, *22*(3), 327–349. https://doi.org/10.1007/s12110-011-9120-x

Campbell, K., & Peebles, R. (2014). Eating disorders in children and adolescents: State of the art review. *Pediatrics*, *134*(3), 582–592. https://doi.org/10.1542/peds.2014-0194

Carskadon, M. A. (2009). Adolescents and sleep: Why teens can't get enough of a good thing. *Brown University Child & Adolescent Behavior Letter*, *25*(4), 1–6.

Carskadon, M. A., Acebo, C., & Jenni, O. G. (2004). Regulation of adolescent sleep: Implications for behavior. *Annals of the New York Academy of Sciences*, *1021*, 276–291. https://doi.org/10.1196/annals.1308.032

Carskadon, M. A., & Tarokh, L. (2014). Developmental changes in sleep biology and potential effects on adolescent behavior and caffeine use. *Nutrition Reviews*, *72*(suppl 1), 60–64. https://doi.org/10.1111/nure.12147

Carter, R. (2015). Anxiety symptoms in African American youth. *The Journal of Early Adolescence*, *35*(3), 281–307. https://doi.org/10.1177/0272431614530809

Carter, R., Halawah, A., & Trinh, S. L. (2018). Peer exclusion during the pubertal transition: The role of social competence. *Journal of Youth and Adolescence*, *47*(1), 121–134. https://doi.org/10.1007/s10964-017-0682-8

Carter, R., Mustafaa, F. N., & Leath, S. (2018). Teachers' expectations of girls' classroom performance and behavior. *The Journal of Early Adolescence*, *38*(7), 885–907. https://doi.org/10.1177/0272431617699947

Centers for Disease Control and Prevention. (2017). *Fatal injury reports, national, regional and state, 1981–2016*. Retrieved from https://webappa.cdc.gov/sasweb/ncipc/mortrate.html

Chandra-Mouli, V., & Patel, S. V. (2017). Mapping the knowledge and understanding of menarche, menstrual hygiene and menstrual health among adolescent girls in low- and middle-income countries. *Reproductive Health*, *14*(1), 30. https://doi.org/10.1186/s12978-017-0293-6

Chen, F. R., Rothman, E. F., & Jaffee, S. R. (2017). Early puberty, friendship group characteristics, and dating abuse in US girls. *Pediatrics*, *139*(6), e20162847. https://doi.org/10.1542/peds.2016-2847

Chung, A., Backholer, K., Wong, E., Palermo, C., Keating, C., & Peeters, A. (2016). Trends in child and adolescent obesity prevalence in economically advanced countries according to socioeconomic position: A systematic review. *Obesity Reviews*, *17*(3), 276–295. https://doi.org/10.1111/obr.12360

Colrain, I. M., & Baker, F. C. (2011). Changes in sleep as a function of adolescent development. *Neuropsychology Review*, *21*(1), 5–21. https://doi.org/10.1007/s11065-010-9155-5

Costos, D., Ackerman, R., & Paradis, L. (2002). Recollections of menarche: Communication between mothers and daughters regarding menstruation. *Sex Roles*, *46*(1–2), 49–59. https://doi.org/10.1023/A:1016037618567

Cousminer, D. L., Stergiakouli, E., Berry, D. J., Ang, W., Groen-Blokhuis, M. M., Körner, A., . . . Early Growth Genetics Consortium. (2014). Genome-wide association study of sexual maturation in males and females highlights a role for body mass and menarche loci in male puberty. *Human Molecular Genetics*, *23*(16), 4452–4464. https://doi.org/10.1093/hmg/ddu150

Crockett, L. J., Carlo, G., Wolff, J. M., & Hope, M. O. (2013). The role of pubertal timing and temperamental vulnerability in adolescents' internalizing symptoms. *Development and Psychopathology*, *25*(2), 377–389. https://doi.org/10.1017/S0954579412001125

Crowley, S. J., Acebo, C., & Carskadon, M. A. (2007). Sleep, circadian rhythms, and delayed phase in adolescence. *Sleep Medicine*, *8*(6), 602–612. https://doi.org/10.1016/j.sleep.2006.12.002

Crowley, S. J., Cain, S. W., Burns, A. C., Acebo, C., & Carskadon, M. A. (2015). Increased sensitivity of the circadian system to light in early/mid-puberty. *The Journal of Clinical Endocrinology & Metabolism*, *100*(11), 4067–4073. https://doi.org/10.1210/jc.2015-2775

Currie, C., Ahluwalia, N., Godeau, E., Nic Gabhainn, S., Due, P., & Currie, D. B. (2012). Is obesity at individual and national level associated with lower age at menarche? Evidence from 34 countries in the Health Behaviour in School-aged Children Study. *The Journal of Adolescent Health*, *50*(6), 621–626. https://doi.org/10.1016/j.jadohealth.2011.10.254

Curtin, S. C., Heron, M., Miniño, A. M., & Warner, M. (2018). Recent increases in injury mortality among children and adolescents aged 10-19 years in the United States: 1999-2016. *National Vital Statistics Reports*, *67*(4), 1–16. Retrieved from http://www.ncbi.nlm.nih.gov/pubmed/29874162

Darchia, N., & Cervena, K. (2014). The journey through the world of adolescent sleep. *Reviews in the Neurosciences*, *25*(4), 585–604. https://doi.org/10.1515/revneuro-2013-0065

Das, J. K., Salam, R. A., Thornburg, K. L., Prentice, A. M., Campisi, S., Lassi, Z. S., . . . Bhutta, Z. A. (2017). Nutrition in adolescents: Physiology, metabolism, and nutritional needs. *Annals of the New York Academy of Sciences*, *1393*(1), 21–33. https://doi.org/10.1111/nyas.13330

Day, F. R., Thompson, D. J., Helgason, H., Chasman, D. I., Finucane, H., Sulem, P., . . . Perry, J. R. B. (2017). Genomic analyses identify hundreds of variants associated with age at menarche and support a role for puberty timing in cancer risk. *Nature Genetics*, *49*(6), 834–841. https://doi.org/10.1038/ng.3841

de Onis, M., Blössner, M., & Borghi, E. (2010). Global prevalence and trends of overweight and obesity among preschool children. *The American Journal of Clinical Nutrition*, *92*(5), 1257–1264. https://doi.org/10.3945/ajcn.2010.29786

de Wit, J. B. F., Stok, F. M., Smolenski, D. J., de Ridder, D. D. T., de Vet, E., Gaspar, T., . . . Luszczynska, A. (2015). Food culture in the home environment: Family meal practices and values can support healthy eating and self-regulation in young people in four European countries. *Applied Psychology. Health and Well-Being*, *7*(1), 22–40. https://doi.org/10.1111/aphw.12034

Deardorff, J., Abrams, B., Ekwaru, J. P., & Rehkopf, D. H. (2014). Socioeconomic status and age at menarche: An examination of multiple indicators in an ethnically diverse cohort. *Annals of Epidemiology*, *24*(10), 727–733. https://doi.org/10.1016/j.annepidem.2014.07.002

Deardorff, J., Ekwaru, J. P., Kushi, L. H., Ellis, B. J., Greenspan, L. C., Mirabedi, A., . . . Hiatt, R. A. (2011). Father absence, body mass index, and pubertal timing in girls: Differential effects by family income and ethnicity. *The Journal of Adolescent Health*, *48*(5), 441–447. https://doi.org/10.1016/j.jadohealth.2010.07.032

Del Giudice, M. (2018). Middle childhood: An evolutionary-developmental synthesis. In N. Halfon, C. B. Forrest, R. M. Lerner, & E. M. Faustman (Eds.), *Handbook of life course health development* (pp. 95–107). Cham, Switzerland: Springer. https://doi.org/10.1007/978-3-319-47143-3_5

Del Giudice, M., Ellis, B. J., & Shirtcliff, E. A. (2011). The adaptive calibration model of stress responsivity. *Neuroscience and Biobehavioral Reviews*, *35*(7), 1562–1592. https://doi.org/10.1016/j.neubiorev.2010.11.007

Demissie, Z., Eaton, D. K., Lowry, R., Nihiser, A. J., & Foltz, J. L. (2018). Prevalence and correlates of missing meals among high school students—United States, 2010. *American Journal of Health Promotion*, *32*(1), 89–95. https://doi.org/10.1177/0890117116667348

DeRose, L. M., & Brooks-Gunn, J. (2006). Transition into adolescence: The role of pubertal processes. In L. Balter & C. S. Tamis-LeMonda (Eds.), *Child psychology: A handbook of contemporary issues* (2nd ed., pp. 385–414). New York, NY: Psychology Press.

Diamond, L. M., Bonner, S. B., & Dickenson, J. (2015). The development of sexuality. In *Handbook of child psychology and developmental science* (pp. 1–44). Hoboken, NJ: John Wiley & Sons. https://doi.org/10.1002/9781118963418.childpsy321

Dorn, L. D., & Biro, F. M. (2011). Puberty and its measurement: A decade in review. *Journal of Research on Adolescence*, *21*(1), 180–195. https://doi.org/10.1111/j.1532-7795.2010.00722.x

Dorn, L. D., Dahl, R. E., Woodward, H. R., & Biro, F. (2006). Defining the boundaries of early adolescence: A user's guide to assessing pubertal status and pubertal timing in research with adolescents. *Applied Developmental Science*, *10*(1), 30–56.

Downs, A. C., & Fuller, M. J. (1991). Recollections of spermarche: An exploratory investigation. *Current Psychology*, *10*(1/2), 93–102. https://doi.org/10.1007/BF02686783

Dumith, S. C., Gigante, D. P., Domingues, M. R., & Kohl, H. W. (2011). Physical activity change during adolescence: A systematic review and a pooled analysis. *International Journal of Epidemiology*, *40*(3), 685–698. https://doi.org/10.1093/ije/dyq272

Ellis, B. J., Shirtcliff, E. A., Boyce, W. T., Deardorff, J., & Essex, M. J. (2011). Quality of early family relationships and the timing and tempo of puberty: Effects depend on biological sensitivity to context. *Development and Psychopathology*, *23*(1), 85–99. https://doi.org/10.1017/S0954579410000660

Emmanuel, M., & Bokor, B. R. (2017). Tanner stages. *StatPearls*. Retrieved from http://www.ncbi.nlm.nih.gov/pubmed/29262142

Esteban-Cornejo, I., Tejero-Gonzalez, C. M., Sallis, J. F., & Veiga, O. L. (2015). Physical activity and cognition in adolescents: A systematic review. *Journal of Science and Medicine in Sport*, *18*(5), 534–539. https://doi.org/10.1016/J.JSAMS.2014.07.007

Farhat, T. (2015). Stigma, obesity and adolescent risk behaviors: Current research and future directions. *Current Opinion in Psychology*, *5*, 56–66. https://doi.org/10.1016/j.copsyc.2015.03.021

Farooq, M. A., Parkinson, K. N., Adamson, A. J., Pearce, M. S., Reilly, J. K., Hughes, A. R., . . . Reilly, J. J. (2018). Timing of the decline in physical activity in childhood and adolescence: Gateshead Millennium Cohort Study. *British Journal of Sports Medicine*, *52*, 1002–1006. https://doi.org/10.1136/bjsports-2016-096933

Forrest, L. N., Zuromski, K. L., Dodd, D. R., & Smith, A. R. (2017). Suicidality in adolescents and adults with binge-eating disorder: Results from the national comorbidity survey replication and adolescent supplement. *International Journal of Eating Disorders*, *50*(1), 40–49. https://doi.org/10.1002/eat.22582

Fradkin, C., Wallander, J. L., Elliott, M. N., Tortolero, S., Cuccaro, P., & Schuster, M. A. (2015). Associations between socioeconomic status and obesity in diverse, young adolescents: Variation across race/ethnicity and gender. *Health Psychology*, *34*(1), 1–9. https://doi.org/10.1037/hea0000099

Frankel, L. L. (2002). "I've never thought about it": Contradictions and taboos surrounding American males' experiences of first ejaculation (semenarche). *Journal of Men's Studies*, *11*(1), 37–54.

Frazier-Wood, A. C., Banfield, E. C., Liu, Y., Davis, J. S., & Chang, S. (2015). Poor adherence to US dietary guidelines for children and adolescents in the National Health and Nutrition Examination Survey (NHANES) 2005-2010 population. *Circulation*, *131*(Suppl 1), abstract 27. Retrieved from http://circ.ahajournals.org/content/131/Suppl_1/A27.short

Frederick, C. B., Snellman, K., & Putnam, R. D. (2014). Increasing socioeconomic disparities in adolescent obesity. *Proceedings of the National Academy of Sciences of the United States of America*, *111*(4), 1338–1342. https://doi.org/10.1073/pnas.1321355110

Fuglset, T. S., Landr, N. I., Reas, D. L., & R, Ø. (2016). Functional brain alterations in anorexia nervosa: A scoping review. *Journal of Eating Disorders*, *4*, 32. https://doi.org/10.1186/s40337-016-0118-y

Fuligni, A. J., Arruda, E. H., Krull, J. L., & Gonzales, N. A. (2018). Adolescent sleep duration, variability, and peak levels of achievement and mental health. *Child Development*, *89*(2), e18–e28. https://doi.org/10.1111/cdev.12729

Fuzzell, L., Fedesco, H. N., Alexander, S. C., Fortenberry, J. D., & Shields, C. G. (2016). "I just think that doctors need to ask more questions": Sexual minority and majority adolescents' experiences talking about sexuality with healthcare providers. *Patient Education and Counseling*, *99*(9), 1467–1472. https://doi.org/10.1016/J.PEC.2016.06.004

Fuzzell, L., Shields, C. G., Alexander, S. C., & Fortenberry, J. D. (2017). Physicians talking about sex, sexuality, and protection with adolescents. *Journal of Adolescent Health*, *61*(1), 6–23. https://doi.org/10.1016/J.JADOHEALTH.2017.01.017

Gaddis, A., & Brooks-Gunn, J. (1985). The male experience of pubertal change. *Journal of Youth and Adolescence*, *14*(1), 61–69.

Ghaddar, S. F., Valerio, M. A., Garcia, C. M., & Hansen, L. (2012). Adolescent health literacy: The importance of credible sources for online health information. *Journal of School Health*, *82*(28–36). https://onlinelibrary.wiley.com/doi/abs/10.1111/j.1746-1561.2011.00664.x

Gibson, L. Y., Byrne, S. M., Blair, E., Davis, E. A., Jacoby, P., & Zubrick, S. R. (2008). Clustering of psychosocial symptoms in overweight children. *Australian & New Zealand Journal of Psychiatry*, *42*(2), 118–125. https://doi.org/10.1080/00048670701787560

Gila, A., Castro, J., Cesena, J., & Toro, J. (2005). Anorexia nervosa in male adolescents: Body image, eating attitudes and psychological traits. *Journal of Adolescent Health*, *36*, 221–226.

Golden, N. H., Katzman, D. K., Sawyer, S. M., Ornstein, R. M., Rome, E. S., Garber, A. K., . . . Kreipe, R. E. (2015). Update on the medical management of eating disorders in adolescents. *The Journal of Adolescent Health*, *56*(4), 370–375. https://doi.org/10.1016/j.jadohealth.2014.11.020

Goldschmidt, A. B., Wall, M. M., Zhang, J., Loth, K. A., & Neumark-Sztainer, D. (2016). Overeating and binge eating in emerging adulthood: 10-year stability and risk factors. *Developmental Psychology*, *52*(3), 475–483. https://doi.org/10.1037/dev0000086

Goodarzi, M. O. (2018). Genetics of obesity: What genetic association studies have taught us about the biology of obesity and its complications. *The Lancet Diabetes & Endocrinology*, *6*(3), 223–236. https://doi.org/10.1016/S2213-8587(17)30200-0

Gopinath, B., Flood, V. M., Burlutsky, G., Louie, J. C. Y., Baur, L. A., & Mitchell, P. (2016). Frequency of takeaway food consumption and its association with major food group consumption, anthropometric

measures and blood pressure during adolescence. *British Journal of Nutrition*, *115*(11), 2025–2030. https://doi.org/10.1017/S000711451600101X

Graber, J. A., Nichols, T. R., & Brooks-Gunn, J. (2010). Putting pubertal timing in developmental context: Implications for prevention. *Developmental Psychobiology*, *52*(3), 254–262. https://doi.org/10.1002/dev.20438

Hagman, J., Gardner, R. M., Brown, D. L., Gralla, J., Fier, J. M., & Frank, G. K. W. (2015). Body size overestimation and its association with body mass index, body dissatisfaction, and drive for thinness in anorexia nervosa. *Eating and Weight Disorders - Studies on Anorexia, Bulimia and Obesity*, *20*(4), 449–455. https://doi.org/10.1007/s40519-015-0193-0

Hardy, L. L., Mihrshahi, S., Gale, J., Drayton, B. A., Bauman, A., & Mitchell, J. (2017). 30-year trends in overweight, obesity and waist-to-height ratio by socioeconomic status in Australian children, 1985 to 2015. *International Journal of Obesity*, *41*(1), 76–82. https://doi.org/10.1038/ijo.2016.204

Harrist, A. W., Swindle, T. M., Hubbs-Tait, L., Topham, G. L., Shriver, L. H., & Page, M. C. (2016). The social and emotional lives of overweight, obese, and severely obese children. *Child Development*, *87*(5), 1564–1580. https://doi.org/10.1111/cdev.12548

Hay, P. J., & Bacaltchuk, J. (2007). Bulimia nervosa. *American Family Physician*, *75*, 1699–1702.

Herman, K. M., Hopman, W. M., & Sabiston, C. M. (2015). Physical activity, screen time and self-rated health and mental health in Canadian adolescents. *Preventive Medicine*, *73*, 112–116. https://doi.org/10.1016/J.YPMED.2015.01.030

Herman-Giddens, M. E. (2006). Recent data on pubertal milestones in United States children: The secular trend toward earlier development. *International Journal of Andrology*, *29*(1), 241–246.

Herman-Giddens, M. E., Steffes, J., Harris, D., Slora, E., Hussey, M., Dowshen, S. A., . . . Reiter, E. O. (2012). Secondary sexual characteristics in boys: Data from the Pediatric Research in Office Settings Network. *Pediatrics*, *130*(5), e1058–e1068. https://doi.org/10.1542/peds.2011-3291

Herpertz-Dahlmann, B. (2017). Treatment of eating disorders in child and adolescent psychiatry. *Current Opinion in Psychiatry*, *30*(6), 438–445. https://doi.org/10.1097/YCO.0000000000000357

Herpertz-Dahlmann, B., Dempfle, A., Konrad, K., Klasen, F., & Ravens-Sieberer; BELLA Study Group. (2015). Eating disorder symptoms do not just disappear: The implications of adolescent eating-disordered behaviour for body weight and mental health in young adulthood. *European Child & Adolescent Psychiatry*, *24*(6), 675–684. https://doi.org/10.1007/s00787-014-0610-3

Hodges-Simeon, C. R., Gurven, M., Cárdenas, R. A., & Gaulin, S. J. C. (2013). Voice change as a new measure of male pubertal timing: A study among Bolivian adolescents. *Annals of Human Biology*, *40*(3), 209–219. https://doi.org/10.3109/03014460.2012.759622

Isomaa, R., Isomaa, A.-L., Marttunen, M., Kaltiala-Heino, R., & Björkqvist, K. (2009). The prevalence, incidence and development of eating disorders in Finnish adolescents—a two-step 3-year follow-up study. *European Eating Disorders Review*, *17*(3), 199–207. https://doi.org/10.1002/erv.919

Jahns, L., Siega-Riz, A. M., & Popkin, B. M. (2001). The increasing prevalence of snacking among US children from 1977 to 1996. *Journal of Pediatrics*, *138*, 493–498.

Janssen, H. G., Davies, I. G., Richardson, L. D., & Stevenson, L. (2018). Determinants of takeaway and fast food consumption: A narrative review. *Nutrition Research Reviews*, *31*(1), 16–34. https://doi.org/10.1017/S0954422417000178

Janssen, I., Katzmarzyk, P. T., Boyce, W. F., Vereecken, C., Mulvihill, C., Roberts, C., Currie, C., & Pickett, W.; Health Behaviour in School-Aged Children Obesity Working Group. (2005). Comparison of overweight and obesity prevalence in school-aged youth from 34 countries and their relationships with physical activity and dietary patterns. *Obesity Reviews*, 6, 123–132.

Jaramillo, J., Mello, Z. R., & Worrell, F. C. (2016). Ethnic identity, stereotype threat, and perceived discrimination among Native American adolescents. *Journal of Research on Adolescence*, 26(4), 769–775. https://doi.org/10.1111/jora.12228

Joos, C. M., Wodzinski, A. M., Wadsworth, M. E., & Dorn, L. D. (2018). Neither antecedent nor consequence: Developmental integration of chronic stress, pubertal timing, and conditionally adapted stress response. *Developmental Review*, 48, 1–23. https://doi.org/10.1016/J.DR.2018.05.001

Kann, L., Kinchen, S., Shanklin, S. L., Flint, K. H., Kawkins, J., Harris, W. A., . . . Centers for Disease Control and Prevention (CDC). (2014). Youth risk behavior surveillance—United States, 2013. *Morbidity and Mortality Weekly Report*, 63(Suppl 44), 1–168. Retrieved from http://www.ncbi.nlm.nih.gov/pubmed/24918634

Katzman, D. K. (2005). Medical complications in adolescents with anorexia nervosa: A review of the literature. *International Journal of Eating Disorders*, 37, 52–59.

Kaye, W. H., Wierenga, C. E., Bailer, U. F., Simmons, A. N., & Bischoff-Grethe, A. (2013). Nothing tastes as good as skinny feels: The neurobiology of anorexia nervosa. *Trends in Neurosciences*, 36(2), 110–120. https://doi.org/10.1016/j.tins.2013.01.003

Keel, P. K. (2014). Bulimia nervosa. In R. L. Cautin & S. O. Lilienfeld (Eds.), *The encyclopedia of clinical psychology*. Hoboken, NJ: John Wiley & Sons. https://doi.org/10.1002/9781118625392.wbecp251

Kelly, Y., Zilanawala, A., Sacker, A., Hiatt, R., & Viner, R. (2017). Early puberty in 11-year-old girls: Millennium Cohort Study findings. *Archives of Disease in Childhood*, 102(3), 232–237. https://doi.org/10.1136/archdischild-2016-310475

Keski-Rahkonen, A., & Mustelin, L. (2016). Epidemiology of eating disorders in Europe. *Current Opinion in Psychiatry*, 29(6), 340–345. https://doi.org/10.1097/YCO.0000000000000278

Kessler, R. C., Berglund, P. A., Chiu, W. T., Deitz, A. C., Hudson, J. I., Shahly, V., . . . Xavier, M. (2013). The prevalence and correlates of binge eating disorder in the World Health Organization World Mental Health Surveys. *Biological Psychiatry*, 73(9), 904–914. https://doi.org/10.1016/j.biopsych.2012.11.020

Kim, S. J., Lee, Y. J., Cho, S.-J., Cho, I.-H., Lim, W., & Lim, W. (2011). Relationship between weekend catch-up sleep and poor performance on attention tasks in Korean adolescents. *Archives of Pediatrics & Adolescent Medicine*, 165(9), 806. https://doi.org/10.1001/archpediatrics.2011.128

Kleanthous, K., Dermitzaki, E., Papadimitriou, D. T., Papaevangelou, V., & Papadimitriou, A. (2017). Secular changes in the final height of Greek girls are levelling off. *Acta Paediatrica*, 106(2), 341–343. https://doi.org/10.1111/apa.13677

Kochanek, K. D., Murphy, S. L., Xu, J., & Arias, E. (2017). Mortality in the United States, 2016: Key findings data from the National Vital Statistics System. *NCHS Data Brief*, 293. Retrieved from https://www.cdc.gov/nchs/data/databriefs/db293.pdf

Kretsch, N., Mendle, J., Cance, J. D., & Harden, K. P. (2016a). Peer group similarity in perceptions of pubertal timing. *Journal of Youth and Adolescence*, 45(8), 1696–1710. https://doi.org/10.1007/s10964-015-0275-3

Kretsch, N., Mendle, J., & Harden, K. P. (2016b). A twin study of objective and subjective pubertal timing and peer influence on risk-taking. *Journal of Research on Adolescence*, 26(1), 45–59. https://doi.org/10.1111/jora.12160

Kumar, S., & Kelly, A. S. (2017). Review of childhood obesity: From epidemiology, etiology, and comorbidities to clinical assessment and treatment. *Mayo Clinic Proceedings*, 92(2), 251–265. https://doi.org/10.1016/j.mayocp.2016.09.017

Lacroix, A. E., & Whitten, R. A. (2017). Menarche. *StatPearls*. Retrieved from http://www.ncbi.nlm.nih.gov/pubmed/29261991

Lavender, J. M., Utzinger, L. M., Cao, L., Wonderlich, S. A., Engel, S. G., Mitchell, J. E., & Crosby, R. D. (2016). Reciprocal associations between negative affect, binge eating, and purging in the natural environment in women with bulimia nervosa. *Journal of Abnormal Psychology*, 125(3), 381–386. https://doi.org/10.1037/abn0000135

le Grange, D., & Schmidt, U. (2005). The treatment of adolescents with bulimia nervosa. *Journal of Mental Health*, 14(6), 587–597.

Lee, J. M., Wasserman, R., Kaciroti, N., Gebremariam, A., Steffes, J., Dowshen, S., . . . Herman-Giddens, M. E. (2016). Timing of puberty in overweight versus obese boys. *Pediatrics*, 137(2), e20150164. https://doi.org/10.1542/peds.2015-0164

Lobstein, T., Jackson-Leach, R., Moodie, M. L., Hall, K. D., Gortmaker, S. L., Swinburn, B. A., . . . McPherson, K. (2015). Child and adolescent obesity: Part of a bigger picture. *Lancet*, 385(9986), 2510–2520. https://doi.org/10.1016/S0140-6736(14)61746-3

Lock, J. (2011). Evaluation of family treatment models for eating disorders. *Current Opinion in Psychiatry*, 24(4), 274–279. https://doi.org/10.1097/YCO.0b013e328346f71e

Loessl, B., Valerius, G., Kopasz, M., Hornyak, M., Riemann, D., & Voderholzer, U. (2008). Are adolescents chronically sleep-deprived? An investigation of sleep habits of adolescents in the Southwest of Germany. *Child: Care, Health & Development*, 34(5), 549–556. https://doi.org/10.1111/j.1365-2214.2008.00845.x

Luk, J. W., Gilman, S. E., Haynie, D. L., & Simons-Morton, B. G. (2017). Sexual orientation differences in adolescent health care access and health-promoting physician advice. *Journal of Adolescent Health*, 61, 555–561. https://doi.org/10.1016/j.jadohealth.2017.05.032

Manfredi-Lozano, M., Roa, J., & Tena-Sempere, M. (2018). Connecting metabolism and gonadal function: Novel central neuropeptide pathways involved in the metabolic control of puberty and fertility. *Frontiers in Neuroendocrinology*, 48, 37–49. https://doi.org/10.1016/J.YFRNE.2017.07.008

Manganello, J. A. (2008). Health literacy and adolescents: A framework and agenda for future research. *Health Education Research*, 23(5), 840–847. https://doi.org/10.1093/her/cym069

Marceau, K., Ram, N., Houts, R. M., Grimm, K. J., & Susman, E. J. (2011). Individual differences in boys' and girls' timing and tempo of puberty: Modeling development with nonlinear growth models. *Developmental Psychology*, 47(5), 1389–1409. https://doi.org/10.1037/a0023838

Marceau, K., Ram, N., & Susman, E. (2015). Development and lability in the parent-child relationship during adolescence: Associations with pubertal timing and tempo. *Journal of Research on Adolescence*, 25(3), 474–489. https://doi.org/10.1111/jora.12139

Marques, L., Alegria, M., Becker, A. E., Chen, C., Fang, A., Chosak, A., & Diniz, J. B. (2011). Comparative prevalence, correlates of impairment, and service utilization for eating disorders across US ethnic groups: Implications for reducing ethnic disparities in health care access for eating disorders. *International Journal of Eating Disorders*, 44(5), 412–420. https://doi.org/10.1002/eat.20787

Marzilli, E., Cerniglia, L., & Cimino, S. (2018). A narrative review of binge eating disorder in adolescence: Prevalence, impact, and psychological treatment strategies. *Adolescent Health, Medicine and Therapeutics*, 9, 17–30. https://doi.org/10.2147/AHMT.S148050

McMahon, E. M., Corcoran, P., O'Regan, G., Keeley, H., Cannon, M., Carli, V., . . . Wasserman, D. (2017). Physical activity in European adolescents and associations with anxiety, depression and well-being. *European Child & Adolescent Psychiatry*, 26(1), 111–122. https://doi.org/10.1007/s00787-016-0875-9

Mendle, J. (2014). Beyond pubertal timing: New directions for studying individual differences in development. *Current Directions in Psychological Science*, 23(3), 215–219. https://doi.org/10.1177/0963721414530144

Mendle, J., & Ferrero, J. (2012). Detrimental psychological outcomes associated with pubertal timing in adolescent boys. *Developmental Review, 32*(1), 49–66. https://doi.org/10.1016/j.dr.2011.11.001

Mendle, J., & Koch, M. K. (2019). The psychology of puberty: What aren't we studying that we should? *Child Development Perspectives, 13*(3), 166–172. https://doi.org/10.1111/cdep.12333

Mendle, J., Turkheimer, E., D'Onofrio, B. M., Lynch, S. K., Emery, R. E., Slutske, W. S., & Martin, N. G. (2006). Family structure and age at menarche: A children-of-twins approach. *Developmental Psychology, 42*, 533–542.

Meng, J., Martinez, L., Holmstrom, A., Chung, M., & Cox, J. (2017). Research on social networking sites and social support from 2004 to 2015: A narrative review and directions for future research. *Cyberpsychology, Behavior, and Social Networking, 20*(1), 44–51. https://doi.org/10.1089/cyber.2016.0325

Metcalf, B. S., Hosking, J., Jeffery, A. N., Henley, W. E., & Wilkin, T. J. (2015). Exploring the adolescent fall in physical activity: A 10-yr cohort study (EarlyBird 41). *Medicine and Science in Sports and Exercise, 47*(10), 2084–2092. https://doi.org/10.1249/MSS.0000000000000644

Micali, N., Solmi, F., Horton, N. J., Crosby, R. D., Eddy, K. T., Calzo, J. P., ... Field, A. E. (2015). Adolescent eating disorders predict psychiatric, high-risk behaviors and weight outcomes in young adulthood. *Journal of the American Academy of Child & Adolescent Psychiatry, 54*(8), 652-659.e1. https://doi.org/10.1016/J.JAAC.2015.05.009

Michaelson, V., Pickett, W., Vandemeer, E., Taylor, B., & Davison, C. (2016). A mixed methods study of Canadian adolescents' perceptions of health. *International Journal of Qualitative Studies on Health and Well-Being, 11*(1), 32891. https://doi.org/10.3402/

Mielke, G. I., Brown, W. J., Nunes, B. P., Silva, I. C. M., & Hallal, P. C. (2017). Socioeconomic correlates of sedentary behavior in adolescents: Systematic review and meta-analysis. *Sports Medicine, 47*(1), 61–75. https://doi.org/10.1007/s40279-016-0555-4

Miller, M. B., Janssen, T., & Jackson, K. M. (2017). The prospective association between sleep and initiation of substance use in young adolescents. *The Journal of Adolescent Health, 60*(2), 154–160. https://doi.org/10.1016/j.jadohealth.2016.08.019

Minges, K. E., & Redeker, N. S. (2016). Delayed school start times and adolescent sleep: A systematic review of the experimental evidence. *Sleep Medicine Reviews, 28*, 86–95. https://doi.org/10.1016/j.smrv.2015.06.002

Mitchell, J. A., Rodriguez, D., Schmitz, K. H., & Audrain-McGovern, J. (2013a). Greater screen time is associated with adolescent obesity: A longitudinal study of the BMI distribution from ages 14 to 18. *Obesity (Silver Spring, Md.), 21*(3), 572–575. https://doi.org/10.1002/oby.20157

Mitchell, J. A., Rodriguez, D., Schmitz, K. H., & Audrain-McGovern, J. (2013b). Sleep duration and adolescent obesity. *Pediatrics, 131*(5), e1428–e1434. https://doi.org/10.1542/peds.2012-2368

Monteleone, A. M., Castellini, G., Volpe, U., Ricca, V., Lelli, L., Monteleone, P., & Maj, M. (2018). Neuroendocrinology and brain imaging of reward in eating disorders: A possible key to the treatment of anorexia nervosa and bulimia nervosa. *Progress in Neuro-Psychopharmacology and Biological Psychiatry, 80*, 132–142. https://doi.org/10.1016/J.PNPBP.2017.02.020

Moore, S. R., Harden, K. P., & Mendle, J. (2014). Pubertal timing and adolescent sexual behavior in girls. *Developmental Psychology, 50*(6), 1734–1745. https://doi.org/10.1037/a0036027

Mrug, S., Elliott, M. N., Davies, S., Tortolero, S. R., Cuccaro, P., & Schuster, M. A. (2014). Early puberty, negative peer influence, and problem behaviors in adolescent girls. *Pediatrics, 133*(1), 7–14. https://doi.org/10.1542/peds.2013-0628

Natsuaki, M. N., Biehl, M. C., Ge, X., & Xiaojia, G. (2009). Trajectories of depressed mood from early adolescence to young adulthood: The effects of pubertal timing and adolescent dating. *Journal of Research on Adolescence, 19*(1), 47–74. https://doi.org/10.1111/j.1532-7795.2009.00581.x

Natsuaki, M. N., Samuels, D., & Leve, L. D. (2015). Puberty, identity, and context. In K. C. McLean & M. Syed (Eds.), *The Oxford handbook of identity development* (pp. 389–405). Oxford, England: Oxford University Press. https://doi.org/10.1093/oxfordhb/9780199936564.013.005

Neberich, W., Penke, L., Lehnart, J., & Asendorpf, J. B. (2010). Family of origin, age at menarche, and reproductive strategies: A test of four evolutionary-developmental models. *European Journal of Developmental Psychology, 7*(2), 153–177. https://doi.org/10.1080/17405620801928029

Negriff, S., Blankson, A. N., & Trickett, P. K. (2015). Pubertal timing and tempo: Associations with childhood maltreatment. *Journal of Research on Adolescence, 25*(2), 201–213. https://doi.org/10.1111/jora.12128

Negriff, S., & Susman, E. J. (2011). Pubertal timing, depression, and externalizing problems: A framework, review, and examination of gender differences. *Journal of Research on Adolescence, 21*(3), 717–746. https://doi.org/10.1111/j.1532-7795.2010.00708.x

Nguyen-Louie, T. T., Brumback, T., Worley, M. J., Colrain, I. M., Matt, G. E., Squeglia, L. M., & Tapert, S. F. (2018). Effects of sleep on substance use in adolescents: A longitudinal perspective. *Addiction Biology, 23*(2), 750–760. https://doi.org/10.1111/adb.12519

Noll, J. G., Trickett, P. K., Long, J. D., Negriff, S., Susman, E. J., Shalev, I., ... Putnam, F. W. (2017). Childhood sexual abuse and early timing of puberty. *Journal of Adolescent Health, 60*(1), 65–71. https://doi.org/10.1016/j.jadohealth.2016.09.008

Nordin, S. M., Harris, G., & Cumming, J. (2003). Disturbed eating in young, competitive gymnasts: Differences between three gymnastics disciplines. *European Journal of Sport Science, 3*(5), 1–14.

Nowicka, P., & Flodmark, C.-E. (2007). Physical activity: Key issues in treatment of childhood obesity. *Acta Paediatrica, 96*, 39–45.

Obeidallah, D. A., Brennan, R. T., Brooks-Gunn, J., & Earls, F. (2004). Links between pubertal timing and neighborhood contexts: Implications for girls' violent behavior. *Journal of the American Academy of Child & Adolescent Psychiatry, 43*(12), 1460–1468.

Obeidallah, D. A., Brennan, R. T., Brooks-Gunn, J., Kindlon, D., & Earls, F. (2000). Socioeconomic status, race, and girls' pubertal maturation: Results from the project on human development in Chicago neighborhoods. *Journal of Research on Adolescence, 10*(4), 443–464.

Ogden, C. L., Carroll, M. D., Lawman, H. G., Fryar, C. D., Kruszon-Moran, D., Kit, B. K., & Flegal, K. M. (2016). Trends in obesity prevalence among children and adolescents in the United States, 1988-1994 through 2013-2014. *JAMA, 315*(21), 2292. https://doi.org/10.1001/jama.2016.6361

Omar, H., McElderry, D., & Zakharia, R. (2003). Educating adolescents about puberty: What are we missing? *International Journal of Adolescent Medicine and Health, 15*, 79–83.

Owens, J. A., Belon, K., & Moss, P. (2010). Impact of delaying school start time on adolescent sleep, mood, and behavior. *Archives of Pediatrics & Adolescent Medicine, 164*(7), 608–614. https://doi.org/10.1001/archpediatrics.2010.96

Owens, J. A., Dearth-Wesley, T., Herman, A. N., Oakes, J. M., & Whitaker, R. C. (2017). A quasi-experimental study of the impact of school start time changes on adolescent sleep. *Sleep Health, 3*(6), 437–443. https://doi.org/10.1016/j.sleh.2017.09.001

Paksarian, D., Rudolph, K. E., He, J.-P., & Merikangas, K. R. (2015). School start time and adolescent sleep patterns: Results from the U.S. National Comorbidity Survey--Adolescent Supplement. *American Journal of Public Health, 105*(7), 1351–1357. https://doi.org/10.2105/AJPH.2015.302619

Papadimitriou, A. (2016a). The evolution of the age at menarche from prehistorical to modern times. *Journal of Pediatric and*

Adolescent Gynecology, 29(6), 527–530. https://doi.org/10.1016/j.jpag.2015.12.002

Papadimitriou, A. (2016b). Timing of puberty and secular trend in human maturation. In P. Kumanov & A. Agarwal (Eds.), *Puberty* (pp. 121–136). Cham, Switzerland: Springer. https://doi.org/10.1007/978-3-319-32122-6_9

Payne, V. G., & Isaacs, L. D. (2016). *Human motor development: A lifespan approach* (9th ed.). New York, NY: Routledge.

Pbert, L., Druker, S., Barton, B., Schneider, K. L., Olendzki, B., Gapinski, M. A., . . . Osganian, S. (2016). A school-based program for overweight and obese adolescents: A randomized controlled trial. *Journal of School Health, 86*(10), 699–708. https://doi.org/10.1111/josh.12428

Pearson, N., Griffiths, P., Biddle, S. J., Johnston, J. P., McGeorge, S., & Haycraft, E. (2017). Clustering and correlates of screen-time and eating behaviours among young adolescents. *BMC Public Health, 17*(1), 533. https://doi.org/10.1186/s12889-017-4441-2

Peralta, L., Rowling, L., Samdal, O., Hipkins, R., & Dudley, D. (2017). Conceptualising a new approach to adolescent health literacy. *Health Education Journal, 76*(7), 787–801. https://doi.org/10.1177/0017896917714812

Pieters, S., Burk, W. J., Van der Vorst, H., Dahl, R. E., Wiers, R. W., & Engels, R. C. M. E. (2015). Prospective relationships between sleep problems and substance use, internalizing and externalizing problems. *Journal of Youth and Adolescence, 44*(2), 379–388. https://doi.org/10.1007/s10964-014-0213-9

Pike, K. M., Hoek, H. W., & Dunne, P. E. (2014). Cultural trends and eating disorders. *Current Opinion in Psychiatry, 27*(6), 436–442. https://doi.org/10.1097/YCO.0000000000000100

Pont, S. J., Puhl, R., Cook, S. R., & Slusser, W. (2017). Stigma experienced by children and adolescents with obesity. *Pediatrics, 140*(6), e20173034. https://doi.org/10.1542/peds.2017-3034

Puhl, R. M., Wall, M. M., Chen, C., Bryn Austin, S., Eisenberg, M. E., & Neumark-Sztainer, D. (2017). Experiences of weight teasing in adolescence and weight-related outcomes in adulthood: A 15-year longitudinal study. *Preventive Medicine, 100*, 173–179. https://doi.org/10.1016/j.ypmed.2017.04.023

Pulgarón, E. R. (2013). Childhood obesity: A review of increased risk for physical and psychological comorbidities. *Clinical Therapeutics, 35*(1), A18-32. https://doi.org/10.1016/j.clinthera.2012.12.014

Quek, Y.-H., Tam, W. W. S., Zhang, M. W. B., & Ho, R. C. M. (2017). Exploring the association between childhood and adolescent obesity and depression: A meta-analysis. *Obesity Reviews, 18*(7), 742–754. https://doi.org/10.1111/obr.12535

Raevuori, A., Keski-Rahkonen, A., & Hoek, H. W. (2014). A review of eating disorders in males. *Current Opinion in Psychiatry, 27*(6), 426–430. https://doi.org/10.1097/YCO.0000000000000113

Rasmussen, A. R., Wohlfahrt-Veje, C., Tefre de Renzy-Martin, K., Hagen, C. P., Tinggaard, J., Mouritsen, A., Mieritz, M. G., & Main, K. M. (2015). Validity of self-assessment of pubertal maturation. *Pediatrics, 135*(1), 86–93. https://doi.org/10.1542/peds.2014-0793

Reel, J. J. (2012). *Eating disorders: An encyclopedia of causes, treatment, and prevention*. Santa Barbara, CA: ABC-CLIO.

Rembeck, G., Möller, M., & Gunnarsson, R. (2006). Attitudes and feelings towards menstruation and womanhood in girls at menarche. *Acta Paediatrica, 95*(6), 707–714.

Reynolds, B. M., & Juvonen, J. (2011). The role of early maturation, perceived popularity, and rumors in the emergence of internalizing symptoms among adolescent girls. *Journal of Youth and Adolescence, 40*(11), 1407–1422. https://doi.org/10.1007/s10964-010-9619-1

Rickard, I. J., Frankenhuis, W. E., & Nettle, D. (2014). Why are childhood family factors associated with timing of maturation? A role for internal prediction. *Perspectives on Psychological Science, 9*(1), 3–15. https://doi.org/10.1177/1745691613513467

Rideout, V. J. (2010, January 20). *Generation M2: Media in the lives of 8- to 18-year-olds*. Retrieved from http://kff.org/other/event/generation-m2-media-in-the-lives-of/

Roa, J., & Tena-Sempere, M. (2014). Connecting metabolism and reproduction: Roles of central energy sensors and key molecular mediators. *Molecular and Cellular Endocrinology, 397*(1–2), 4–14. https://doi.org/10.1016/J.MCE.2014.09.027

Rodgers, R. F., Watts, A. W., Austin, S. B., Haines, J., & Neumark-Sztainer, D. (2017). Disordered eating in ethnic minority adolescents with overweight. *International Journal of Eating Disorders, 50*(6), 665–671. https://doi.org/10.1002/eat.22652

Rojas-Gaona, C. E., Hong, J. S., & Peguero, A. A. (2016). The significance of race/ethnicity in adolescent violence: A decade of review, 2005–2015. *Journal of Criminal Justice, 46*, 137–147. https://doi.org/10.1016/J.JCRIMJUS.2016.05.001

Rudolph, K. D., Troop-Gordon, W., Lambert, S. F., & Natsuaki, M. N. (2014). Long-term consequences of pubertal timing for youth depression: Identifying personal and contextual pathways of risk. *Development and Psychopathology, 26*(4 Pt 2), 1423–1444. https://doi.org/10.1017/S0954579414001126

Sadler, K. (2017). Pubertal development. In M. A. Goldstein (Ed.), *The MassGeneral Hospital for Children adolescent medicine handbook* (pp. 19–26). Cham, Switzerland: Springer. https://doi.org/10.1007/978-3-319-45778-9_3

Sagrestano, L. M., McCormick, S. H., Paikoff, R. L., & Holmbeck, G. N. (1999). Pubertal development and parent-child conflict in low-income, urban, African American adolescents. *Journal of Research on Adolescence, 9*(1), 85–107. https://doi.org/10.1207/s15327795jra0901_5

Sanders, J. O., Qiu, X., Lu, X., Duren, D. L., Liu, R. W., Dang, D., . . . Cooperman, D. R. (2017). The uniform pattern of growth and skeletal maturation during the human adolescent growth spurt. *Scientific Reports, 7*(1), 16705. https://doi.org/10.1038/s41598-017-16996-w

Schelleman-Offermans, K., Knibbe, R. A., & Kuntsche, E. (2013). Are the effects of early pubertal timing on the initiation of weekly alcohol use mediated by peers and/or parents? A longitudinal study. *Developmental Psychology, 49*(7), 1277–1285.

Schreier, H. M. C., & Chen, E. (2013). Socioeconomic status and the health of youth: A multilevel, multidomain approach to conceptualizing pathways. *Psychological Bulletin, 139*(3), 606–654. https://doi.org/10.1037/a0029416

Schulz, K. M., Molenda-Figueira, H. A., & Sisk, C. L. (2009). Back to the future: The organizational–activational hypothesis adapted to puberty and adolescence. *Hormones & Behavior, 55*(5), 597–604. https://doi.org/10.1016/j.yhbeh.2009.03.010

Scutti, S. (2015, January 26). Puberty comes earlier and earlier for girls. *Newsweek*. Retrieved from http://www.newsweek.com/2015/02/06/puberty-comes-earlier-and-earlier-girls-301920.html

Seaton, E. K., & Carter, R. (2018). Pubertal timing, racial identity, neighborhood, and school context among Black adolescent females. *Cultural Diversity and Ethnic Minority Psychology, 24*(1), 40–50. https://doi.org/10.1037/cdp0000162

Seaton, E. K., & Carter, R. (2019). Perceptions of pubertal timing and discrimination among African American and Caribbean Black girls. *Child Development, 90*(2), 480–488. https://doi.org/10.1111/cdev.13221

Seger, J. Y., & Thorstensson, A. (2000). Muscle strength and electromyogram in boys and girls followed through puberty. *European Journal of Applied Physiology, 81*(1–2), 54–61. https://doi.org/10.1007/PL00013797

Shalitin, S., & Kiess, W. (2017). Putative effects of obesity on linear growth and puberty. *Hormone Research in Paediatrics, 88*(1), 101–110. https://doi.org/10.1159/000455968

Sheehy, A., Gasser, T., Molinari, L., & Largo, R. H. (2009). An analysis of variance of the pubertal and midgrowth spurts for length and width. *Annals of Human Biology*, *26*(4), 309–331. https://doi.org/10.1080/030144699282642

Sigmund, E., Badura, P., Sigmundová, D., Voráčová, J., Zacpal, J., Kalman, M., . . . Hamrik, Z. (2018). Trends and correlates of overweight/obesity in Czech adolescents in relation to family socioeconomic status over a 12-year study period (2002–2014). *BMC Public Health*, *18*(1), 122. https://doi.org/10.1186/s12889-017-5013-1

Simmonds, M., Llewellyn, A., Owen, C. G., & Woolacott, N. (2016). Predicting adult obesity from childhood obesity: A systematic review and meta-analysis. *Obesity Reviews*, *17*, 95–107. https://doi .org/10.1111/obr.12334

Skinner, A. C., & Skelton, J. A. (2014). Prevalence and trends in obesity and severe obesity among children in the United States, 1999-2012. *JAMA Pediatrics*, *168*(6), 561. https://doi.org/10.1001/jamapediatrics.2014.21

Skinner, A. C., Ravanbakht, S. N., Skelton, J. A., Perrin, E. M., & Armstrong, S. C. (2018). Prevalence of obesity and severe obesity in US children, 1999–2016. *Pediatrics*, *141*(3), e20173459. https://doi.org/10.1542/peds.2017-3459

Skoog, T., & Özdemir, S. B. (2016). Explaining why early-maturing girls are more exposed to sexual harassment in early adolescence. *The Journal of Early Adolescence*, *36*(4), 490–509. https://doi.org/10.1177/0272431614568198

Skoog, T., Özdemir, S. B., & Stattin, H. (2016). Understanding the link between pubertal timing in girls and the development of depressive symptoms: The role of sexual harassment. *Journal of Youth and Adolescence*, *45*(2), 316–327. https://doi.org/10.1007/s10964-015-0292-2

Skoog, T., & Stattin, H. (2014). Why and under what contextual conditions do early-maturing girls develop problem behaviors? *Child Development Perspectives*, *8*(3), 158–162. https://doi.org/10.1111/cdep.12076

Smink, F. R. E., van Hoeken, D., & Hoek, H. W. (2013). Epidemiology, course, and outcome of eating disorders. *Current Opinion in Psychiatry*, *26*(6), 543–548. https://doi.org/10.1097/YCO.0b013e328365a24f

Smink, F. R. E., van Hoeken, D., Oldehinkel, A. J., & Hoek, H. W. (2014). Prevalence and severity of DSM-5 eating disorders in a community cohort of adolescents. *The International Journal of Eating Disorders*, *47*(6), 610–619. https://doi.org/10.1002/eat.22316

Sohn, K. (2016). Improvement in the biological standard of living in 20th century Korea: Evidence from age at menarche. *American Journal of Human Biology*, *29*(1). https://doi.org/10.1002/ajhb.22882

Song, Y., Ma, J., Li, L.-B., Dong, B., Wang, Z., & Agardh, A. (2016). Secular trends for age at spermarche among Chinese boys from 11 ethnic minorities, 1995-2010: A multiple cross-sectional study. *BMJ Open*, *6*(2), e010518. https://doi.org/10.1136/bmjopen-2015-010518

Spencer, D. L., McManus, M., Call, K. T., Turner, J., Harwood, C., White, P., & Alarcon, G. (2018). Health care coverage and access among children, adolescents, and young adults, 2010-2016: Implications for future health reforms. *The Journal of Adolescent Health*, *62*(6), 667–673. https://doi.org/10.1016/j.jadohealth.2017.12.012

Srensen, K., Mouritsen, A., Aksglaede, L., Hagen, C. P., Mogensen, S. S., & Juul, A. (2012). Recent secular trends in pubertal timing: Implications for evaluation and diagnosis of precocious puberty. *Hormone Research in Paediatrics*, *77*(3), 137–145. https://doi.org/10.1159/000336325

Stang, J. S., & Stotmeister, B. (2017). Nutrition in adolescence. In N. J. Temple, T. Wilson, & G. A. Bray (Eds.), *Nutrition guide for physicians and related healthcare professionals* (pp. 29–39). Cham, Switzerland: Humana. https://doi.org/10.1007/978-3-319-49929-1_4

Stansfield, R., Williams, K. R., & Parker, K. F. (2017). Economic disadvantage and homicide. *Homicide Studies*, *21*(1), 59–81. https://doi.org/10.1177/1088767916647990

Stein, J. H., & Reiser, L. W. (1994). A study of white middle-class adolescent boys' responses to "semenarche" (the first ejaculation). *Journal of Youth and Adolescence*, *23*(3), 373–384. https://doi.org/10.1007/BF01536725

Stice, E., Gau, J. M., Rohde, P., & Shaw, H. (2017). Risk factors that predict future onset of each DSM-5 eating disorder: Predictive specificity in high-risk adolescent females. *Journal of Abnormal Psychology*, *126*(1), 38–51. https://doi.org/10.1037/abn0000219

Stidham-Hall, K., Moreau, C., & Trussell, J. (2012). Patterns and correlates of parental and formal sexual and reproductive health communication for adolescent women in the United States, 2002-2008. *The Journal of Adolescent Health*, *50*(4), 410–413. https://doi.org/10.1016/j.jadohealth.2011.06.007

Stojković, I. (2013). Pubertal timing and self-esteem in adolescents: The mediating role of body-image and social relations. *European Journal of Developmental Psychology*, *10*(3), 359–377. https://doi.org/10.1080/17405629.2012.682145

Strober, M., Freeman, R., Lampert, C., Diamond, J., & Kaye, W. (2014). Controlled family study of anorexia nervosa and bulimia nervosa: Evidence of shared liability and transmission of partial syndromes. *American Journal of Psychiatry*, *157*(3), 393–401. https://psycnet.apa .org/doi/10.1176/appi.ajp.157.3.393

Stroud, C. B., & Davila, J. (2016). Pubertal timing. In R. Levesque (Ed.), *Encyclopedia of adolescence* (pp. 1–9). Cham, Switzerland: Springer. https://doi.org/10.1007/978-3-319-32132-5_14-2

Sun, Y., Mensah, F. K., Azzopardi, P., Patton, G. C., & Wake, M. (2017). Childhood social disadvantage and pubertal timing: A national birth cohort from Australia. *Pediatrics*, *139*(6), e20164099. https://doi.org/10.1542/peds.2016-4099

Tanner, J. M. (1990). *Foetus into man: Physical growth from conception to maturity*. Boston, MA: Harvard University Press.

Telzer, E. H., Fuligni, A. J., Lieberman, M. D., & Galván, A. (2013). The effects of poor quality sleep on brain function and risk taking in adolescence. *NeuroImage*, *71*, 275–283. https://doi.org/10.1016/j.neuroimage.2013.01.025

Thomas, J. J., Eddy, K. T., Ruscio, J., Ng, K. L., Casale, K. E., Becker, A. E., & Lee, S. (2015). Do recognizable lifetime eating disorder phenotypes naturally occur in a culturally Asian population? A combined latent profile and taxometric approach. *European Eating Disorders Review*, *23*(3), 199–209. https://doi.org/10.1002/erv.2357

Tinggaard, J., Mieritz, M. G., Srensen, K., Mouritsen, A., Hagen, C. P., Aksglaede, L., . . . Juul, A. (2012). The physiology and timing of male puberty. *Current Opinion in Endocrinology, Diabetes, and Obesity*, *19*(3), 197–203. https://doi.org/10.1097/MED.0b013e3283535614

Tomova, A. (2016). Body weight and puberty. In P. Kumanov & A. Agarwal (Eds.), *Puberty* (pp. 95–108). Cham, Switzerland: Springer. https://doi.org/10.1007/978-3-319-32122-6_7

Tomova, A., Lalabonova, C., Robeva, R. N., & Kumanov, P. T. (2011). Timing of pubertal maturation according to the age at first conscious ejaculation. *Andrologia*, *43*(3), 163–166. https://doi.org/10.1111/j.1439-0272.2009.01037.x

Tnnessen, E., Svendsen, I. S., Olsen, I. C., Guttormsen, A., & Haugen, T. (2015). Performance development in adolescent track and field athletes according to age, sex and sport discipline. *PLoS ONE*, *10*(6), e0129014. https://doi.org/10.1371/journal.pone.0129014

Toufexis, D., Rivarola, M. A., Lara, H., & Viau, V. (2014). Stress and the reproductive axis. *Journal of Neuroendocrinology*, *26*(9), 573–586. https://doi.org/10.1111/jne.12179

Troxel, W. M., Shih, R. A., Ewing, B., Tucker, J. S., Nugroho, A., & D'Amico, E. J. (2017). Examination of neighborhood disadvantage and sleep in a multi-ethnic cohort of adolescents. *Health & Place*, *45*, 39–45. https://doi.org/10.1016/j.healthplace.2017.03.002

Tsai, K. M., Dahl, R. E., Irwin, M. R., Bower, J. E., McCreath, H., Seeman, T. E., . . . Fuligni, A. J. (2017). The roles of parental support and family stress in adolescent sleep. *Child Development*. https://doi.org/10.1111/cdev.12917

Tunau, K., Adamu, A., Hassan, M., Ahmed, Y., & Ekele, B. (2012). Age at menarche among school girls in Sokoto, Northern Nigeria. *Annals of African Medicine*, 11, 103–107. https://doi.org/10.4103/1596-3519.93533

Tyrka, A. R., Graber, J. A., & Brooks-Gunn, J. (2000). The development of disordered eating: Correlates and predictors of eating problems in the context of adolescence. In A. J. Sameroff, M. Lewis, & S. M. Miller (Eds.), *Handbook of developmental psychopathology* (2nd ed., pp. 607–624). Dordrecht, Netherlands: Kluwer Academic Publishers.

Ullsperger, J. M., & Nikolas, M. A. (2017). A meta-analytic review of the association between pubertal timing and psychopathology in adolescence: Are there sex differences in risk? *Psychological Bulletin*, 143(9), 903–938. https://doi.org/10.1037/bul0000106

U.S. Department of Health and Human Services. (2017). United States adolescent physical health facts. Retrieved from https://www.hhs.gov/ash/oah/facts-and-stats/national-and-state-data-sheets/adolescent-physical-health-and-nutrition/united-states/index.html

Utriainen, P., Laakso, S., Liimatta, J., Jaaskelainen, J., & Voutilainen, R. (2015). Premature adrenarche - a common condition with variable presentation. *Hormone Research in Paediatrics*, 83(4), 221–231. https://doi.org/10.1159/000369458

Vernon, L., Modecki, K. L., & Barber, B. L. (2018). Mobile phones in the bedroom: Trajectories of sleep habits and subsequent adolescent psychosocial development. *Child Development*, 89(1), 66–77. https://doi.org/10.1111/cdev.12836

Vikraman, S., Fryar, C. D., & Ogden, C. L. (2015). Caloric intake from fast food among children and adolescents in the United States, 2011-2012. *NCHS Data Brief*, (213), 1–8. Retrieved from http://www.ncbi.nlm.nih.gov/pubmed/26375457

Villamor, E., & Jansen, E. C. (2016). Nutritional determinants of the timing of puberty. *Annual Review of Public Health*, 37(1), 33–46. https://doi.org/10.1146/annurev-publhealth-031914-122606

Virtanen, M., Kivimäki, H., Ervasti, J., Oksanen, T., Pentti, J., Kouvonen, A., . . . Vahtera, J. (2015). Fast-food outlets and grocery stores near school and adolescents' eating habits and overweight in Finland. *The European Journal of Public Health*, 25(4), 650–655. https://doi.org/10.1093/eurpub/ckv045

Voelker, D. K., Gould, D., & Reel, J. J. (2014). Prevalence and correlates of disordered eating in female figure skaters. *Psychology of Sport and Exercise*, 15(6), 696–704. https://doi.org/10.1016/j.psychsport.2013.12.002

Walton, G. M., & Spencer, S. J. (2009). Latent ability: Grades and test scores systematically underestimate the intellectual ability of negatively stereotyped students. *Psychological Science*, 20(9), 1132–1139. https://doi.org/10.1111/j.1467-9280.2009.02417.x

Walton, K., Kleinman, K. P., Rifas-Shiman, S. L., Horton, N. J., Gillman, M. W., Field, A. E., . . . Haines, J. (2016). Secular trends in family dinner frequency among adolescents. *BMC Research Notes*, 9(1), 35. https://doi.org/10.1186/s13104-016-1856-2

Wang, J.-L., Jackson, L. A., Zhang, D.-J., & Su, Z.-Q. (2012). The relationships among the Big Five personality factors, self-esteem, narcissism, and sensation-seeking to Chinese university students' uses of social networking sites (SNSs). *Computers in Human Behavior*, 28(6), 2313–2319. https://doi.org/10.1016/j.chb.2012.07.001

Wang, L., Kong, Q.-M., Li, K., Li, X.-N., Zeng, Y.-W., Chen, C., . . . Si, T.-M. (2017). Altered intrinsic functional brain architecture in female patients with bulimia nervosa. *Journal of Psychiatry & Neuroscience*, 42(6), 414–423. https://doi.org/10.1503/JPN.160183

Wang, Y., & Lim, H. (2012). The global childhood obesity epidemic and the association between socio-economic status and childhood obesity. *International Review of Psychiatry (Abingdon, England)*, 24(3), 176–188. https://doi.org/10.3109/09540261.2012.688195

Watson, N. F., Martin, J. L., Wise, M. S., Carden, K. A., Kirsch, D. B., Kristo, D. A., . . . Chervin, R. D.; American Academy of Sleep Medicine Board of Directors. (2017a). Delaying middle school and high school start times promotes student health and performance: An American Academy of Sleep Medicine position statement. *Journal of Clinical Sleep Medicine*, 13(4), 623–625. https://doi.org/10.5664/jcsm.6558

Watson, R. J., Adjei, J., Saewyc, E., Homma, Y., & Goodenow, C. (2017b). Trends and disparities in disordered eating among heterosexual and sexual minority adolescents. *International Journal of Eating Disorders*, 50(1), 22–31. https://doi.org/10.1002/eat.22576

Watts, A. W., Loth, K., Berge, J. M., Larson, N., & Neumark-Sztainer, D. (2017). No time for family meals? Parenting practices associated with adolescent fruit and vegetable intake when family meals are not an option. *Journal of the Academy of Nutrition and Dietetics*, 117(5), 707–714. https://doi.org/10.1016/j.jand.2016.10.026

Watts, A. W., Mason, S. M., Loth, K., Larson, N., & Neumark-Sztainer, D. (2016). Socioeconomic differences in overweight and weight-related behaviors across adolescence and young adulthood: 10-year longitudinal findings from Project EAT. *Preventive Medicine*, 87, 194–199. https://doi.org/10.1016/j.ypmed.2016.03.007

Webster, G. D., Graber, J. A., Gesselman, A. N., Crosier, B. S., & Schember, T. O. (2014). A life history theory of father absence and menarche: A meta-analysis. *Evolutionary Psychology*, 12(2), 147470491401200. https://doi.org/10.1177/147470491401200202

Wilson, G. T., Grilo, C. M., & Vitousek, K. M. (2007). Psychological treatment of eating disorders. *American Psychologist*, 62(3), 199–216.

Witchel, S. F., & Topaloglu, A. K. (2019). Puberty: Gonadarche and adrenarche. In J. F. Strauss, R. L. Barbieri, & A. R. Gargiulo (Eds.), *Yen and Jaffe's reproductive endocrinology* (pp. 394–446). Philadelphia, PA: Elsevier. https://doi.org/10.1016/B978-0-323-47912-7.00017-2

Wohlfahrt-Veje, C., Mouritsen, A., Hagen, C. P., Tinggaard, J., Mieritz, M. G., Boas, M., . . . Main, K. M. (2016). Pubertal onset in boys and girls is influenced by pubertal timing of both parents. *Journal of Clinical Endocrinology & Metabolism*, 101(7), 2667–2674. https://doi.org/10.1210/jc.2016-1073

Wong, M. M., & Brower, K. J. (2012). The prospective relationship between sleep problems and suicidal behavior in the National Longitudinal Study of Adolescent Health. *Journal of Psychiatric Research*, 46(7), 953–959. https://doi.org/10.1016/j.jpsychires.2012.04.008

Wong, M. M., Robertson, G. C., & Dyson, R. B. (2015). Prospective relationship between poor sleep and substance-related problems in a national sample of adolescents. *Alcoholism, Clinical and Experimental Research*, 39, 355–362. https://doi.org/10.1111/acer.12618

World Health Organization. (2009). BMI classification. Retrieved from http://apps.who.int/bmi/index.jsp?introPage=intro_3.html

Worthman, C. M., Dockray, S., & Marceau, K. (2019). Puberty and the evolution of developmental science. *Journal of Research on Adolescence*, 29(1), 9–31. https://doi.org/10.1111/jora.12411

Wyatt, L. C., Ung, T., Park, R., Kwon, S. C., & Trinh-Shevrin, C. (2015). Risk factors of suicide and depression among Asian American, Native Hawaiian, and Pacific Islander youth: A systematic literature review. *Journal of Health Care for the Poor and Underserved*, 26(2 Suppl), 191–237. https://doi.org/10.1353/hpu.2015.0059

Yoshikawa, H., Aber, J. L., & Beardslee, W. R. (2012). The effects of poverty on the mental, emotional, and behavioral health of children and youth: Implications for prevention. *American Psychologist*, 67(4), 272–284. https://doi.org/10.1037/a0028015

Yousefi, M., Karmaus, W., Zhang, H., Roberts, G., Matthews, S., Clayton, B., & Arshad, S. H. (2013). Relationships between age of puberty onset and height at age 18 years in girls and boys. *World Journal of Pediatrics*, 9(3), 230–238. https://doi.org/10.1007/s12519-013-0399-z

Zhu, J., Kusa, T. O., & Chan, Y.-M. (2018). Genetics of pubertal timing. *Current Opinion in Pediatrics*, *30*(4), 532–540. https://doi.org/10.1097/MOP.0000000000000642

Zimmer-Gembeck, M. J., Webb, H. J., Farrell, L. J., & Waters, A. M. (2018). Girls' and boys' trajectories of appearance anxiety from age 10 to 15 years are associated with earlier maturation and appearance-related teasing. *Development and Psychopathology*, *30*(1), 337–350. https://doi.org/10.1017/S0954579417000657

CHAPTER 3

Aïte, A., Cassotti, M., Linzarini, A., Osmont, A., Houdé, O., & Borst, G. (2018). Adolescents' inhibitory control: Keep it cool or lose control. *Developmental Science*, *21*(1), e12491. https://doi.org/10.1111/desc.12491

Albert, D., Chein, J., & Steinberg, L. (2013). The teenage brain: Peer influences on adolescent decision making. *Current Directions in Psychological Science*, *22*(2), 114–120. https://doi.org/10.1177/0963721412471347

Alberts, A., Elkind, D., & Ginsberg, S. (2007). The personal fable and risk-taking in early adolescence. *Journal of Youth & Adolescence*, *36*(1), 71–76.

Andersson, U. (2008). Working memory as a predictor of written arithmetical skills in children: The importance of central executive functions. *British Journal of Educational Psychology*, *78*(2), 181–203. https://doi.org/10.1348/000709907X209854

Ardila, A. (2013). Development of metacognitive and emotional executive functions in children. *Applied Neuropsychology: Child*, *2*(2), 82–87. https://doi.org/10.1080/21622965.2013.748388

Asato, M. R., Terwilliger, R., Woo, J., & Luna, B. (2010). White matter development in adolescence: A DTI study. *Cerebral Cortex*, *20*(9), 2122–2131. https://doi.org/10.1093/cercor/bhp282

Baddeley, A. (2012). Working memory: theories, models, and controversies. *Annual Review of Psychology*, *63*, 1–29. https://doi.org/10.1146/annurev-psych-120710-100422

Baddeley, A. (2016). Working memory. In R. J. Sternberg, S. T. Fiske, & D. J. Foss (Eds.), *Scientists making a difference: One hundred eminent behavioral and brain scientists talk about their most important contributions* (pp. 119–122). Cambridge, England: Cambridge University Press. https://doi.org/10.1017/CBO9781316422250.026

Barnett, S. M., Ceci, S. J., & Williams, W. M. (2006). Is the ability to make a bacon sandwich a mark of intelligence?, and other issues: Some reflections on Gardner's theory of multiple intelligences. In J. A. Schaler (Ed.), *Howard Gardner under fire: The rebel psychologist faces his critics* (pp. 95–114). Chicago, IL: Open Court.

Barrouillet, P., Gavens, N., Vergauwe, E., Gaillard, V., & Camos, V. (2009). Working memory span development: A time-based resource-sharing model account. *Developmental Psychology*, *45*(2), 477–490. https://doi.org/10.1037/a0014615

Basten, U., Hilger, K., & Fiebach, C. J. (2015). Where smart brains are different: A quantitative meta-analysis of functional and structural brain imaging studies on intelligence. *Intelligence*, *51*, 10–27. https://doi.org/10.1016/j.intell.2015.04.009

Battistella, G., Fornari, E., Annoni, J.-M., Chtioui, H., Dao, K., Fabrius, M., . . . Giroud, C. (2014). Long-term effects of cannabis on brain structure. *Neuropsychopharmacology*, *39*(9), 2041–2048. https://doi.org/10.1038/npp.2014.67

Bava, S., & Tapert, S. F. (2010). Adolescent brain development and the risk for alcohol and other drug problems. *Neuropsychology Review*, *20*(4), 398–413. https://doi.org/10.1007/s11065-010-9146-6

Birney, D. P., & Sternberg, R. J. (2011). The development of cognitive abilities. In M. H. Bornstein & M. E. Lamb (Eds.), *Developmental science: An advanced textbook* (6th ed., pp. 353–388). New York, NY: Psychology Press.

Bjorklund, D. F., & Myers, A. (2015). The development of cognitive abilities. In M. H. Bornstein & M. E. Lamb (Eds.), *Developmental science: An advanced textbook* (pp. 391–441). New York, NY: Psychology Press.

Blakemore, S.-J., & Mills, K. L. (2014). Is adolescence a sensitive period for sociocultural processing? *Annual Review of Psychology*, *65*, 187–207. https://doi.org/10.1146/annurev-psych-010213-115202

Brain Development Cooperative Group. (2012). Total and regional brain volumes in a population-based normative sample from 4 to 18 years: The NIH MRI Study of Normal Brain Development. *Cerebral Cortex*, *22*(1), 1–12. https://doi.org/10.1093/cercor/bhr018

Brainerd, C. J. (1978). The stage question in cognitive-developmental theory. *Behavioral and Brain Sciences*, *1*(2), 173. https://doi.org/10.1017/S0140525X00073842

Breiner, K., Li A., Cohen, A. O., Steinberg, L., Bonnie, R. J., Scott, E. S., . . . Galván, A. (2018). Combined effects of peer presence, social cues, and rewards on cognitive control in adolescents. *Developmental Psychobiology*, *60*(3), 292–302. https://doi.org/10.1002/dev.21599

Brooks-Gunn, J., Klebanov, P. K., & Duncan, G. J. (1996). Ethnic differences in children's intelligence test scores: Role of economic deprivation, home environment, and maternal characteristics. *Child Development*, *67*, 396–408.

Camos, V., Barrouillet, P., & Barrouillet, P. (2018). *Working memory in development*. London, England: Routledge. https://doi.org/10.4324/9781315660851

Carlson, N. R., & Birkett, M. A. (2014). *Foundations of behavioral neuroscience* (9th ed.). London, England: Pearson.

Carlson, S. M., Zelazo, P. D., & Faja, S. (2013). Executive function. In P. D. Zelazo (Ed.), *The Oxford handbook of developmental psychology, Vol. 1: Body and mind* (pp. 706–743). Oxford, England: Oxford University Press. https://doi.org/10.1093/oxfordhb/9780199958450.013.0025

Carpendale, J. I. M., & Lewis, C. (2015). The development of social understanding. In R. M. Lerner (Ed.), *Handbook of child psychology and developmental science* (7th ed., pp. 1–44). Hoboken, NJ: John Wiley & Sons. https://doi.org/10.1002/9781118963418.childpsy210

Casey, B. J. (2015). Beyond simple models of self-control to circuit-based accounts of adolescent behavior. *Annual Review of Psychology*, *66*, 295–319. https://doi.org/10.1146/annurev-psych-010814-015156

Cauffman, E., Shulman, E. P., Steinberg, L., Claus, E., Banich, M. T., Graham, S., & Woolard, J. (2010). Age differences in affective decision making as indexed by performance on the Iowa Gambling Task. *Developmental Psychology*, *46*(1), 193–207. https://doi.org/10.1037/a0016128

Ceci, S. J. (1991). How much does schooling influence general intelligence and its cognitive components? A reassessment of the evidence. *Developmental Psychology*, *27*, 703–722.

Ceci, S. J. (1999). Schooling and intelligence. In S. J. Ceci & W. M. Williams (Eds.), *The nature-nurture debate: The essential readings* (pp. 168–175). Oxford, England: Blackwell.

Chevalier, N., Kurth, S., Doucette, M. R., Wiseheart, M., Deoni, S. C. L. S., Dean, D. C. D., . . . Greenstein, D. (2015). Myelination is associated with processing speed in early childhood: Preliminary insights. *PLoS ONE*, *10*(10), e0139897. https://doi.org/10.1371/journal.pone.0139897

Cliffordson, C., & Gustafsson, J.-E. (2008). Effects of age and schooling on intellectual performance: Estimates obtained from analysis of continuous variation in age and length of schooling. *Intelligence*, *36*(2), 143–152. https://doi.org/10.1016/j.intell.2007.03.006

Cohen, A. O., & Casey, B. J. (2017). The neurobiology of adolescent self-control. In T. Egner (Ed.), *The Wiley handbook of cognitive control* (pp. 455–475). Chichester, England: Wiley-Blackwell. https://doi.org/10.1002/9781118920497.ch26

Cohen Kadosh, K., Johnson, M. H., Dick, F., Cohen Kadosh, R., & Blakemore, S.-J. (2013). Effects of age, task performance, and structural brain development on face processing. *Cerebral Cortex*, *23*(7), 1630–1642. https://doi.org/10.1093/cercor/bhs150

Commons, M. L., & Richards, F. A. (2002). Four postformal stages. In J. Demick & C. Andreoletti (Eds.), *Handbook of adult development* (pp. 199–219). Boston, MA: Springer. https://doi.org/10.1007/978-1-4615-0617-1_11

Cowan, N., Hismjatullina, A., AuBuchon, A. M., Saults, J. S., Horton, N., Leadbitter, K., & Towse, J. (2010). With development, list recall includes more chunks, not just larger ones. *Developmental Psychology*, *46*(5), 1119–1131. https://doi.org/10.1037/a0020618

Coyle, T. R., Pillow, D. R., Snyder, A. C., & Kochunov, P. (2011). Processing speed mediates the development of general intelligence (*g*) in adolescence. *Psychological Science*, *22*(10), 1265–1269. https://doi.org/10.1177/0956797611418243

Crone, E. A., Peters, S., & Steinbeis, N. (2018). Executive function: Development in adolescence. In S. A. Wiebe & J. Karbach (Eds.), *Executive function: Development across the life span* (pp. 58–72). Boca Raton, FL: CRC Press.

Cservenka, A., & Brumback, T. (2017). The burden of binge and heavy drinking on the brain: Effects on adolescent and young adult neural structure and function. *Frontiers in Psychology*, *8*, 1111. https://doi.org/10.3389/fpsyg.2017.01111

Cuevas, K., & Bell, M. A. (2013). Infant attention and early childhood executive function. *Child Development*, *85*(2), 397–404. https://doi.org/10.1111/cdev.12126

Deary, I. J., Penke, L., & Johnson, W. (2010). The neuroscience of human intelligence differences. *Nature Reviews Neuroscience*, *11*(3), 201. https://doi.org/10.1038/nrn2793

Deoni, S. C. L., Mercure, E., Blasi, A., Gasston, D., Thomson, A., Johnson, M., . . . Murphy, D. G. M. (2011). Mapping infant brain myelination with magnetic resonance imaging. *The Journal of Neuroscience*, *31*(2), 784–791. https://doi.org/10.1523/JNEUROSCI.2106-10.2011

Dosenbach, N. U. F., Nardos, B., Cohen, A. L., Fair, D. A., Power, J. D., Church, J. A., . . . Schlaggar, B. L. (2010). Prediction of individual brain maturity using fMRI. *Science*, *329*(5997), 1358–1361. https://doi.org/10.1126/science.1194144

Duboc, V., Dufourcq, P., Blader, P., & Roussigné, M. (2015). Asymmetry of the brain: Development and implications. *Annual Review of Genetics*, *49*(1), 647–672. https://doi.org/10.1146/annurev-genet-112414-055322

Duell, N., Steinberg, L., Icenogle, G., Chein, J., Chaudhary, N., Di Giunta, L., . . . Chang, L. (2018). Age patterns in risk taking across the world. *Journal of Youth and Adolescence*, *47*(5), 1052–1072. https://doi.org/10.1007/s10964-017-0752-y

Dumontheil, I. (2016). Adolescent brain development. *Current Opinion in Behavioral Sciences*, *10*, 39–44. https://doi.org/10.1016/j.cobeha.2016.04.012

Duyme, M., Dumaret, A. C., & Tomkiewicz, S. (1999). How can we boost IQs of "dull children"? A late adoption study. *Proceedings of the National Academy of Sciences of the United States of America*, *96*(15), 8790–8794. https://doi.org/10.1073/PNAS.96.15.8790

Elkind, D., & Bowen, R. (1979). Imaginary audience behavior in children and adolescents. *Developmental Psychology*, *15*(1), 38–44.

Figner, B., Mackinlay, R. J., Wilkening, F., & Weber, E. U. (2009). Affective and deliberative processes in risky choice: Age differences in risk taking in the Columbia Card Task. *Journal of Experimental Psychology: Learning, Memory, and Cognition*, *35*(3), 709–730. https://doi.org/10.1037/a0014983

Finn, A. S., Minas, J. E., Leonard, J. A., Mackey, A. P., Salvatore, J., Goetz, C., . . . Gabrieli, J. D. E. (2017). Functional brain organization of working memory in adolescents varies in relation to family income and academic achievement. *Developmental Science*, *20*(5), e12450. https://doi.org/10.1111/desc.12450

Flannery, K. M., & Smith, R. L. (2017). The effects of age, gender, and gender role ideology on adolescents' social perspective-taking ability and tendency in friendships. *Journal of Social and Personal Relationships*, *34*(5), 617–635. https://doi.org/10.1177/0265407516650942

Flieller, A. (1999). Comparison of the development of formal thought in adolescent cohorts aged 10 to 15 (1967-1996). *Developmental Psychology*, *35*(4), 1048.

Flynn, J. R. (2008). Still a question of black vs white? *New Scientist*, *199*, 48–50.

Ford, D. Y. (2008). Intelligence testing and cultural diversity: The need for alternative instruments, policies, and procedures. In J. L. VanTassel-Baska (Ed.), *Alternative assessments with gifted and talented students* (pp. 107–128). Waco, TX: Prufrock Press.

Fuhrmann, D., Knoll, L. J., & Blakemore, S.-J. (2015). Adolescence as a sensitive period of brain development. *Trends in Cognitive Sciences*, *19*(10), 558–566. https://doi.org/10.1016/j.tics.2015.07.008

Furby, L., & Beyth-Marom, R. (1992). Risk taking in adolescence: A decision-making perspective. *Developmental Review*, *12*(1), 1–44.

Gaillard, V., Barrouillet, P., Jarrold, C., & Camos, V. (2011). Developmental differences in working memory: Where do they come from? *Journal of Experimental Child Psychology*, *110*(3), 469–479. https://doi.org/10.1016/j.jecp.2011.05.004

Gardner, H. (2013). *The unschooled mind: How children think and how schools should teach* (Vol. 25). New York, NY: Basic Books.

Gardner, H. (2016). Multiple intelligences: Prelude, theory, and aftermath. In R. J. Sternberg, S. T. Fiske, & D. J. Foss (Eds.), *Scientists making a difference: One hundred eminent behavioral and brain scientists talk about their most important contributions* (pp. 167–170). Cambridge, England: Cambridge University Press. https://doi.org/10.1017/CBO9781316422250.037

Gardner, H. (2017). Taking a multiple intelligences (MI) perspective. *Behavioral and Brain Sciences*, *40*, e203. https://doi.org/10.1017/S0140525X16001631

Gasser, U. E., & Hatten, M. E. (1990). Central nervous system neurons migrate on astroglial fibers from heterotypic brain regions in vitro. *Proceedings of the National Academy of Sciences of the United States of America*, *87*(12), 4543-4547. https://doi.org/10.1073/pnas.87.12.4543

Gathercole, S. E. (1998). The development of memory. *Journal of Child Psychology and Psychiatry and Allied Disciplines*, *39*, 3–27.

Geier, C. F. (2013). Adolescent cognitive control and reward processing: Implications for risk taking and substance use. *Hormones and Behavior*, *64*(2), 333–342. https://doi.org/10.1016/j.yhbeh.2013.02.008

Gibb, R., & Kovalchuk, A. (2018). Brain development. In R. Gibb & B. Kolb (Eds.), *The neurobiology of brain and behavioral development* (pp. 3–27). London, England: Academic Press. https://doi.org/10.1016/B978-0-12-804036-2.00001-7

Giedd, J. N. (2018). A ripe time for adolescent research. *Journal of Research on Adolescence*, *28*(1), 157–159. https://doi.org/10.1111/jora.12378

Giedd, J. N., Lalonde, F. M., Celano, M. J., White, S. L., Wallace, G. L., Lee, N. R., & Lenroot, R. K. (2009). Anatomical brain magnetic resonance imaging of typically developing children and adolescents. *Journal of the American Academy of Child & Adolescent Psychiatry*, *48*(5), 465–470. https://doi.org/10.1097/CHI.0b013e31819f215

Giofrè, D., Mammarella, I. C., & Cornoldi, C. (2013). The structure of working memory and how it relates to intelligence in children. *Intelligence*, *41*(5), 396–406. https://doi.org/10.1016/j.intell.2013.06.006

Goddings, A.-L. (2015). The role of puberty in human adolescent brain development. In J.-P. Bourguignon, J.-C. Carel, & Y. Christen (Eds.), *Brain crosstalk in puberty and adolescence* (pp. 75–83). Cham, Switzerland: Springer. https://doi.org/10.1007/978-3-319-09168-6

Goddings, A.-L., Mills, K. L., Clasen, L. S., Giedd, J. N., Viner, R. M., & Blakemore, S.-J. (2014). The influence of puberty on subcortical brain development. *NeuroImage, 88*, 242–251. https://doi.org/10.1016/j.neuroimage.2013.09.073

Halford, G. S. (1989). Reflections on 25 years of Piagetian cognitive developmental psychology, 1963–1988. *Human Development, 32*(6), 325–357. https://doi.org/10.1159/000276484

Halpern-Felsher, B. L., & Cauffman, E. (2001). Costs and benefits of a decision. Decision-making competence in adolescents and adults. *Journal of Applied Developmental Psychology, 22*(3), 257–273.

Hamer, R., & van Rossum, E. J. (2017). Six languages in education—Looking for postformal thinking. *Behavioral Development Bulletin, 22*(2), 377–393. https://doi.org/10.1037/bdb0000030

Hanania, R., & Smith, L. B. (2010). Selective attention and attention switching: Towards a unified developmental approach. *Developmental Science, 13*(4), 622–635. https://doi.org/10.1111/j.1467-7687.2009.00921.x

Hueston, C. M., Cryan, J. F., & Nolan, Y. M. (2017). Stress and adolescent hippocampal neurogenesis: Diet and exercise as cognitive modulators. *Translational Psychiatry, 7*(4), e1081. https://doi.org/10.1038/tp.2017.48

Huttenlocher, J., Levine, S., & Vevea, J. (1998). Environmental input and cognitive growth: A study using time-period comparisons. *Child Development, 69*, 1012–1029.

Inhelder, B., & Piaget, J. (1958). *The growth of logical thinking: From childhood to adolescence.* New York, NY: Basic Books.

Isbell, E., Fukuda, K., Neville, H. J., & Vogel, E. K. (2015). Visual working memory continues to develop through adolescence. *Frontiers in Psychology, 6*, 696. https://doi.org/10.3389/fpsyg.2015.00696

Jacobus, J., Squeglia, L. M., Infante, M. A., Castro, N., Brumback, T., Meruelo, A. D., & Tapert, S. F. (2015). Neuropsychological performance in adolescent marijuana users with co-occurring alcohol use: A three-year longitudinal study. *Neuropsychology, 29*(6), 829–843. https://doi.org/10.1037/neu0000203

Javadi, A. H., Schmidt, D. H. K., & Smolka, M. N. (2014). Differential representation of feedback and decision in adolescents and adults. *Neuropsychologia, 56*, 280–288. https://doi.org/10.1016/j.neuropsychologia.2014.01.021

Jessen, K. R. (2004). Glial cells. *International Journal of Biochemistry & Cell Biology, 36*(10), 1861–1867.

Jolles, D. D., van Buchem, M. A., Crone, E. A., & Rombouts, S. A. R. B. (2011). A comprehensive study of whole-brain functional connectivity in children and young adults. *Cerebral Cortex, 21*(2), 385–391. https://doi.org/10.1093/cercor/bhq104

Kail, R. (2000). Speed of information processing: Developmental change and links to intelligence. *Journal of School Psychology, 38*, 51–61.

Kail, R. V. (2008). Speed of processing in childhood and adolescence: Nature, consequences, and implications for understanding atypical development. In J. DeLuca & J. H. Kalmar (Eds.), *Information processing speed in clinical populations* (pp. 101–123). New York, NY: Psychology Press.

Kaufman, J. C., Kaufman, S. B., & Plucker, J. A. (2013). Contemporary theories of intelligence. In D. Reisberg (Ed.), *The Oxford handbook of cognitive psychology* (pp. 811–822). Oxford, England: Oxford University Press. https://doi.org/10.1093/oxfordhb/9780195376746.013.0051

Keating, D. P. (2012). Cognitive and brain development in adolescence. *Enfance, 2012*(3), 267–279. https://doi.org/10.4074/S0013754512003035

Kilford, E. J., Garrett, E., & Blakemore, S.-J. (2016). The development of social cognition in adolescence: An integrated perspective. *Neuroscience & Biobehavioral Reviews, 70*, 106–120. https://doi.org/10.1016/J.NEUBIOREV.2016.08.016

King, P. M., & Kitchener, K. S. (2004). Reflective judgment: Theory and research on the development of epistemic assumptions through adulthood. Educational Psychologist, 39, 5–15.

King, P. M., & Kitchener, K. S. (2015). Cognitive development in the emerging adult. In J. J. Arnett (Ed.), *The Oxford handbook of emerging adulthood* (pp. 105–125). Oxford, England: Oxford University Press. https://doi.org/10.1093/oxfordhb/9780199795574.013.14

Koenis, M. M. G., Brouwer, R. M., Swagerman, S. C., van Soelen, I. L. C., Boomsma, D. I., & Hulshoff Pol, H. E. (2018). Association between structural brain network efficiency and intelligence increases during adolescence. *Human Brain Mapping, 39*(2), 822–836. https://doi.org/10.1002/hbm.23885

Kolb, B. (2015). *Fundamentals of human neuropsychology.* New York, NY: Worth.

Kuhn, D. (2012). The development of causal reasoning. *Wiley Interdisciplinary Reviews: Cognitive Science, 3*(3), 327–335. https://doi.org/10.1002/wcs.1160

Kuhn, D. (2013). Reasoning. In P. D. Zelazo (Ed.), *The Oxford handbook of developmental psychology, Vol. 1: Body and mind* (pp. 744–764). Oxford, England: Oxford University Press. https://doi.org/10.1093/oxfordhb/9780199958450.013.0026

Kundu, P., Benson, B. E., Rosen, D., Frangou, S., Leibenluft, E., Luh, W.-M., . . . Ernst, M. (2018). The integration of functional brain activity from adolescence to adulthood. *The Journal of Neuroscience, 38*(14), 3559–3570. https://doi.org/10.1523/JNEUROSCI.1864-17.2018

Labouvie-Vief, G. (2015). *Integrating emotions and cognition throughout the lifespan.* Cham, Switzerland: Springer. https://doi.org/10.1007/978-3-319-09822-7

Last, B. S., Lawson, G. M., Breiner, K., Steinberg, L., & Farah, M. J. (2018). Childhood socioeconomic status and executive function in childhood and beyond. *PLoS ONE, 13*(8), e0202964. https://doi.org/10.1371/journal.pone.0202964

Lawrence, K., Campbell, R., & Skuse, D. (2015). Age, gender, and puberty influence the development of facial emotion recognition. *Frontiers in Psychology, 6*, 761. https://doi.org/10.3389/fpsyg.2015.00761

Lawson, G. M., Hook, C. J., & Farah, M. J. (2018). A meta-analysis of the relationship between socioeconomic status and executive function performance among children. *Developmental Science, 21*(2), e12529. https://doi.org/10.1111/desc.12529

Lebel, C., & Deoni, S. (2018). The development of brain white matter microstructure. *NeuroImage, 182*, 207–218. https://doi.org/10.1016/J.NEUROIMAGE.2017.12.097

Lehman, D. R., & Nisbett, R. E. (1990). A longitudinal study of the effects of undergraduate training on reasoning. *Developmental Psychology, 26*, 952–960.

Locurto, C. (1990). The malleability of IQ as judged from adoption studies. *Intelligence, 14*(3), 275–292. https://doi.org/10.1016/S0160-2896(10)80001-7

Luna, B., Marek, S., Larsen, B., Tervo-Clemmens, B., & Chahal, R. (2015). An integrative model of the maturation of cognitive control. *Annual Review of Neuroscience, 38*(1), 151–170. https://doi.org/10.1146/annurev-neuro-071714-034054

Luna, B., Paulsen, D. J., Padmanabhan, A., & Geier, C. (2013). The teenage brain: Cognitive control and motivation. *Current Directions in Psychological Science, 22*(2), 94–100. https://doi.org/10.1177/0963721413478416

Luttikhuizen dos Santos, E. S., de Kieviet, J. F., Königs, M., van Elburg, R. M., & Oosterlaan, J. (2013). Predictive value of the Bayley scales of infant development on development of very preterm/very low birth weight children: A meta-analysis. *Early Human Development, 89*(7), 487–496. https://doi.org/10.1016/j.earlhumdev.2013.03.008

Mackintosh, J. N. (2011). *IQ and human intelligence* (2nd ed.). Oxford, England: Oxford University Press.

Margolis, A., Bansal, R., Hao, X., Algermissen, M., Erickson, C., Klahr, K. W., . . . Peterson, B. S. (2013). Using IQ discrepancy scores to examine the neural correlates of specific cognitive abilities. *Journal of Neuroscience, 33*(35), 14135–14145. https://doi.org/10.1523/JNEUROSCI.0775-13.2013

Markant, J. C., & Thomas, K. M. (2013). Postnatal brain development. In P. D. Zelazo (Ed.), *The Oxford handbook of developmental psychology, Vol. 1: Body and mind* (pp. 129–163). Oxford, England: Oxford University Press. https://doi.org/10.1093/oxfordhb/9780199958450.013.0006

Marra, R. & Palmer, B. (2004) Encouraging intellectual growth: Senior college student profiles. *Journal of Adult Development, 11*(2), 111–122. https://doi.org/10.1023/B:JADE.0000024544.50818.1f

Marti, E., & Rodriguez, C. (Eds.). (2012). *After Piaget.* New Brunswick, NJ: Transaction Publishers.

Meier, M. H., Caspi, A., Ambler, A., Harrington, H., Houts, R., Keefe, R. S. E., . . . Moffitt, T. E. (2012). Persistent cannabis users show neuropsychological decline from childhood to midlife. *Proceedings of the National Academy of Sciences of the United States of America, 109*(40), E2657–E2664. https://doi.org/10.1073/pnas.1206820109

Memmert, D. (2014). Inattentional blindness to unexpected events in 8–15-year-olds. *Cognitive Development, 32*, 103–109. https://doi.org/10.1016/J.COGDEV.2014.09.002

Mills, K. L., Dumontheil, I., Speekenbrink, M., & Blakemore, S.-J. (2015). Multitasking during social interactions in adolescence and early adulthood. *Royal Society Open Science, 2*(11), 150117. https://doi.org/10.1098/rsos.150117

Mills, K. L., Goddings, A.-L., Clasen, L. S., Giedd, J. N., & Blakemore, S.-J. (2014). The developmental mismatch in structural brain maturation during adolescence. *Developmental Neuroscience, 36*(3–4), 147–160. https://doi.org/10.1159/000362328

Mills, K. L., Goddings, A.-L., Herting, M. M., Meuwese, R., Blakemore, S.-J., Crone, E. A., . . . Tamnes, C. K. (2016). Structural brain development between childhood and adulthood: Convergence across four longitudinal samples. *NeuroImage, 141*, 273–281. https://doi.org/10.1016/J.NEUROIMAGE.2016.07.044

Mills, K., & Tamnes, C. K. (2018, September 6). Longitudinal structural and functional brain development in childhood and adolescence. *PsyArXiv.* https://doi.org/10.31234/OSF.IO/87KFT

Morris, A. S., Criss, M. M., Silk, J. S., & Houltberg, B. J. (2017). The impact of parenting on emotion regulation during childhood and adolescence. *Child Development Perspectives, 11*(4), 233–238. https://doi.org/10.1111/cdep.12238

Morris, A. S., Squeglia, L. M., Jacobus, J., & Silk, J. S. (2018). Adolescent brain development: Implications for understanding risk and resilience processes through neuroimaging research. *Journal of Research on Adolescence, 28*(1), 4–9. https://doi.org/10.1111/jora.12379

Moshman, D. (2011). *Adolescent rationality and development: Cognition, morality, and identity* (3rd ed.). New York, NY: Psychology Press.

Motta-Mena, N. V., & Scherf, K. S. (2017). Pubertal development shapes perception of complex facial expressions. *Developmental Science, 20*(4), e12451. https://doi.org/10.1111/desc.12451

Mueller, S. C., Maheu, F. S., Dozier, M., Peloso, E., Mandell, D., Leibenluft, E., . . . Ernst, M. (2010). Early-life stress is associated with impairment in cognitive control in adolescence: An fMRI study. *Neuropsychologia, 48*(10), 3037–3044. https://doi.org/10.1016/j.neuropsychologia.2010.06.013

Müller, U., & Kerns, K. (2015). The development of executive function. In R. M. Lerner (Ed.), *Handbook of child psychology and developmental science* (7th ed., pp. 1–53). Hoboken, NJ: John Wiley & Sons. https://doi.org/10.1002/9781118963418.childpsy214

Murty, V. P., Calabro, F., & Luna, B. (2016). The role of experience in adolescent cognitive development: Integration of executive, memory, and mesolimbic systems. *Neuroscience & Biobehavioral Reviews, 70*, 46–58. https://doi.org/10.1016/j.neubiorev.2016.07.034

Neisser, U., Boodoo, G., Bouchard Jr., T. J., Boykin, A. W., Brody, N., Ceci, S. J., . . . Urbina, S. (1996). Intelligence: Knowns and unknowns. *American Psychologist, 51*(2), 77–101.

Nelson, C. A. (2011). Neural development and lifelong plasticity. In D. P. Keating (Ed.), *Nature and nurture in early child development* (pp. 45–69). Cambridge, England: Cambridge University Press.

Nilsen, E. S., & Bacso, S. A. (2017). Cognitive and behavioural predictors of adolescents' communicative perspective-taking and social relationships. *Journal of Adolescence, 56*, 52–63. https://doi.org/10.1016/J.ADOLESCENCE.2017.01.004

Nisbett, R. E., Aronson, J., Blair, C., Dickens, W., Flynn, J., Halpern, D. F., & Turkheimer, E. (2013). Intelligence: New findings and theoretical developments. *American Psychologist, 67*(2), 130–159. https://doi.org/10.1037/a0026699

Noble, K. G., Houston, S. M., Brito, N. H., Bartsch, H., Kan, E., Kuperman, J. M., . . . Sowell, E. R. (2015). Family income, parental education and brain structure in children and adolescents. *Nature Neuroscience, 18*(5), 773–778. https://doi.org/10.1038/nn.3983

Noble, K. G., Houston, S. M., Kan, E., & Sowell, E. R. (2012). Neural correlates of socioeconomic status in the developing human brain. *Developmental Science, 15*(4), 516–527. https://doi.org/10.1111/j.1467-7687.2012.01147.x

Nussbaumer, D., Grabner, R. H., & Stern, E. (2015). Neural efficiency in working memory tasks: The impact of task demand. *Intelligence, 50*, 196–208. https://doi.org/10.1016/j.intell.2015.04.004

Paulsen, D. J., Hallquist, M. N., Geier, C. F., & Luna, B. (2014). Effects of incentives, age, and behavior on brain activation during inhibitory control: A longitudinal fMRI study. *Developmental Cognitive Neuroscience, 11*, 105–115. https://doi.org/10.1016/j.dcn.2014.09.003

Peeters, M., Janssen, T., Monshouwer, K., Boendermaker, W., Pronk, T., Wiers, R., & Vollebergh, W. (2015). Weaknesses in executive functioning predict the initiating of adolescents' alcohol use. *Developmental Cognitive Neuroscience, 16*, 139–146. https://doi.org/10.1016/j.dcn.2015.04.003

Penke, L., Maniega, S. M., Bastin, M. E., Valdés Hernández, M. C., Murray, C., Royle, N. A., . . . Deary, I. J. (2012). Brain white matter tract integrity as a neural foundation for general intelligence. *Molecular Psychiatry, 17*(10), 1026–1030. https://doi.org/10.1038/mp.2012.66

Perry, W. G. (1970). *Forms of intellectual and ethical development in the college years: A scheme.* San Francisco, CA: Jossey-Bass.

Phillips, M., Crouse, J., & Ralph, J. (1998). *Does the Black–White test score gap widen after children enter school?* (M. Jencks & C. Phillips, Eds.). Washington, DC: Brookings Institution Press.

Piaget, J. (1972). Intellectual evolution from adolescence to adulthood. *Human Development, 51*(1), 40–47. https://doi.org/10.1159/000112531

Picci, G., & Scherf, K. S. (2016). From caregivers to peers: Puberty shapes human face perception. *Psychological Science, 27*(11), 1461–1473. https://doi.org/10.1177/0956797616663142

Piccolo, L. R., Merz, E. C., & Noble, K. G. (2018). School climate is associated with cortical thickness and executive function in children and adolescents. *Developmental Science, 22*(1), e12719. https://doi.org/10.1111/desc.12719

Pietschnig, J., Penke, L., Wicherts, J. M., Zeiler, M., & Voracek, M. (2015). Meta-analysis of associations between human brain volume and intelligence differences: How strong are they and what do they mean? *Neuroscience & Biobehavioral Reviews, 57*, 411–432. https://doi.org/10.1016/j.neubiorev.2015.09.017

Plomin, R., & Deary, I. J. (2015). Genetics and intelligence differences: Five special findings. *Molecular Psychiatry, 20*(1), 98–108. https://doi.org/10.1038/mp.2014.105

Price, D., Jarman, A. P., Mason, J. O., & Kind, P. C. (2011). *Building brains: An introduction to neural development*. Chichester, England: Wiley-Blackwell.

Privado, J., de Urturi, C. S., Dávila, J., López, C., Burgaleta, M., Román, F. J., . . . Colom, R. (2014). White matter integrity predicts individual differences in (fluid) intelligence through working memory. *Personality and Individual Differences, 60*(Suppl), S77. https://doi.org/10.1016/j.paid.2013.07.347

Qiu, A., Mori, S., & Miller, M. I. (2015). Diffusion tensor imaging for understanding brain development in early life. *Annual Review of Psychology, 66*(1), 853–876. https://doi.org/10.1146/annurev-psych-010814-015340

Rai, R., Mitchell, P., Kadar, T., & Mackenzie, L. (2016). Adolescent egocentrism and the illusion of transparency: Are adolescents as egocentric as we might think? *Current Psychology, 35*(3), 285–294. https://doi.org/10.1007/s12144-014-9293-7

Redick, T. S., Unsworth, N., Kelly, A. J., & Engle, R. W. (2012). Faster, smarter? Working memory capacity and perceptual speed in relation to fluid intelligence. *Journal of Cognitive Psychology, 24*(7), 844–854. https://doi.org/10.1080/20445911.2012.704359

Reyna, V. F., & Farley, F. (2006). Risk and rationality in adolescent decision making: Implications for theory, practice, and public policy. *Psychological Science in the Public Interest, 7*(1), 1–44.

Reyna, V. F., & Rivers, S. E. (2008). Current theories of risk and rational decision making. *Developmental Review, 28*(1), 1–11. https://doi.org/10.1016/j.dr.2008.01.002

Rindermann, H., & Thompson, J. (2013). Ability rise in NAEP and narrowing ethnic gaps? *Intelligence, 41*(6), 821–831. https://doi.org/10.1016/j.intell.2013.06.016

Ritchie, S. J., Booth, T., Valdés Hernández, M. del C., Corley, J., Maniega, S. M., Gow, A. J., . . . Deary, I. J. (2015). Beyond a bigger brain: Multivariable structural brain imaging and intelligence. *Intelligence, 51*, 47–56. https://doi.org/10.1016/j.intell.2015.05.001

Romeo, R. D. (2017). The impact of stress on the structure of the adolescent brain: Implications for adolescent mental health. *Brain Research, 1654*, 185–191. https://doi.org/10.1016/J.BRAINRES.2016.03.021

Rose, S. A., Feldman, J. F., Jankowski, J. J., & Van Rossem, R. (2012). Information processing from infancy to 11 years: Continuities and prediction of IQ. *Intelligence, 40*(5), 445–457. https://doi.org/10.1016/j.intell.2012.05.007

Sandoval, W. A., Greene, J. A., & Bråten, I. (2016). Understanding and promoting thinking about knowledge. *Review of Research in Education, 40*(1), 457–496. https://doi.org/10.3102/0091732X16669319

Sattler, J. M. (2014). *Foundations of behavioral, social and clinical assessment of children*. La Mesa, CA: Jerome M. Sattler Publisher, Inc.

Schwartz, P. D., Maynard, A. M., & Uzelac, S. M. (2008). Adolescent egocentrism: A contemporary view. *Adolescence, 43*(171), 441–448.

Scott, E. S., Duell, N., & Steinberg, L. (2018, January 8). Brain development, social context and justice policy. *SSRN*. Retrieved from https://papers.ssrn.com/sol3/papers.cfm?abstract_id=3118366

Selman, R. L. (1980). *The growth of interpersonal understanding*. New York, NY: Academic Press.

Servant, M., Cassey, P., Woodman, G. F., & Logan, G. D. (2018). Neural bases of automaticity. *Journal of Experimental Psychology: Learning, Memory, and Cognition, 44*(3), 440–464. https://doi.org/10.1037/xlm0000454

Shearer, C. B., & Karanian, J. M. (2017). The neuroscience of intelligence: Empirical support for the theory of multiple intelligences? *Trends in Neuroscience and Education, 6*, 211–223. https://doi.org/10.1016/J.TINE.2017.02.002

Sheppard, L. D. (2008). Intelligence and speed of information-processing: A review of 50 years of research. *Personality & Individual Differences, 44*(3), 533–549.

Sherman, L. E., Rudie, J. D., Pfeifer, J. H., Masten, C. L., McNealy, K., & Dapretto, M. (2014). Development of the default mode and central executive networks across early adolescence: A longitudinal study. *Developmental Cognitive Neuroscience, 10*, 148–159. https://doi.org/10.1016/J.DCN.2014.08.002

Shulman, E. P., & Cauffman, E. (2013). Reward-biased risk appraisal and its relation to juvenile versus adult crime. *Law and Human Behavior, 37*(6), 412–423. https://doi.org/10.1037/lhb0000033

Shulman, E. P., Smith, A. R., Silva, K., Icenogle, G., Duell, N., Chein, J., & Steinberg, L. (2016). The dual systems model: Review, reappraisal, and reaffirmation. *Developmental Cognitive Neuroscience, 17*, 103–117. https://doi.org/10.1016/j.dcn.2015.12.010

Silveri, M. M., Tzilos, G. K., & Yurgelun-Todd, D. A. (2008). Relationship between white matter volume and cognitive performance during adolescence: Effects of age, sex and risk for drug use. *Addiction, 103*(9), 1509–1520. https://doi.org/10.1111/j.1360-0443.2008.02272.x

Simmonds, D., & Luna, B. (2015). *Protracted development of brain systems underlying working memory in adolescence: A longitudinal study* (Doctoral dissertation). Pittsburgh, PA: University of Pittsburgh.

Sinnott, J. D. (1998). *The development of logic in adulthood: Postformal thought and its applications*. New York, NY: Plenum.

Sinnott, J. D. (2003). Postformal thought and adult development: Living in balance. In J. Demick & C. Andreoletti (Eds.), *Handbook of adult development* (pp. 221–238). New York, NY: Kluwer.

Sisk, C. L. (2017). Development: Pubertal hormones meet the adolescent brain. *Current Biology, 27*(14), R706–R708. https://doi.org/10.1016/J.CUB.2017.05.092

Smith, A. R., Chein, J., & Steinberg, L. (2013). Impact of socio-emotional context, brain development, and pubertal maturation on adolescent risk-taking. *Hormones and Behavior, 64*(2), 323–332. https://doi.org/10.1016/j.yhbeh.2013.03.006

Smith, A. R., Steinberg, L., Strang, N., & Chein, J. (2015). Age differences in the impact of peers on adolescents' and adults' neural response to reward. *Developmental Cognitive Neuroscience, 11*, 75–82. https://doi.org/10.1016/j.dcn.2014.08.010

Sowell, E. R., Peterson, B. S., Thompson, P. M., Welcome, S. E., Henkenius, A. L., & Toga, A. W. (2003). Mapping cortical change across the human life span. *Nature Neuroscience, 6*(3), 309–315. https://doi.org/10.1038/nn1008

Spalding, K. L., Bergmann, O., Alkass, K., Bernard, S., Salehpour, M., Huttner, H. B., . . . Frisén, J. (2013). Dynamics of hippocampal neurogenesis in adult humans. *Cell, 153*(6), 1219–1227. https://doi.org/10.1016/j.cell.2013.05.002

Spear, L. P. (2018). Effects of adolescent alcohol consumption on the brain and behaviour. *Nature Reviews Neuroscience, 19*(4), 197–214. https://doi.org/10.1038/nrn.2018.10

Spielberg, J. M., Olino, T. M., Forbes, E. E., & Dahl, R. E. (2014). Exciting fear in adolescence: Does pubertal development alter threat processing? *Developmental Cognitive Neuroscience, 8*, 86–95. https://doi.org/10.1016/j.dcn.2014.01.004

Squeglia, L. M., & Gray, K. M. (2016). Alcohol and drug use and the developing brain. *Current Psychiatry Reports, 18*(5), 46. https://doi.org/10.1007/s11920-016-0689-y

Squeglia, L. M., Tapert, S. F., Sullivan, E. V., Jacobus, J., Meloy, M. J., Rohlfing, T., & Pfefferbaum, A. (2015). Brain development in heavy-drinking adolescents. *American Journal of Psychiatry*, *172*(6), 531–542. https://doi.org/10.1176/appi.ajp.2015.14101249

Stahl, E., Ferguson, L., & Kienhues, D. (2016). Diverging information and epistemic change. In J. A. Greene, W. A. Sandoval, & I. Bråten (Eds.), *Handbook of epistemic cognition* (pp. 330–342). New York, NY: Routledge. https://doi.org/10.4324/9781315795225-30

Steinberg, L. (2008). A social neuroscience perspective on adolescent risk-taking. *Developmental Review*, *28*(1), 78–106. https://doi.org/10.1016/j.dr.2007.08.002

Steinberg, L. (2013). Does recent research on adolescent brain development inform the mature minor doctrine? *Journal of Medicine and Philosophy*, *38*, 256–267. https://doi.org/10.1093/jmp/jht017

Steinberg, L., Icenogle, G., Shulman, E. P., Breiner, K., Chein, J., Bacchini, D., ... Takash, H. M. S. (2018). Around the world, adolescence is a time of heightened sensation seeking and immature self-regulation. *Developmental Science*, *21*(2), e12532. https://doi.org/10.1111/desc.12532

Sternberg, R. J. (1985). *Beyond IQ: A triarchic theory of human intelligence*. Cambridge, England: Cambridge University Press.

Sternberg, R. J. (2011). The theory of successful intelligence. In R. J. Sternberg & S. B. Kaufman (Eds.), *The Cambridge handbook of intelligence* (pp. 504–527). Cambridge, England: Cambridge University Press.

Sternberg, R. J. (2014). Teaching about the nature of intelligence. *Intelligence*, *42*, 176–179. https://doi.org/10.1016/j.intell.2013.08.010

Sternberg, R. J., Grigorenko, E. L., & Bundy, D. A. (2001). The predictive value of IQ. *Merrill-Palmer Quarterly*, *47*, 1–41.

Stiles, J., Brown, T. T., Haist, F., Jernigan, T. L., Stiles, J., Brown, T. T., ... Jernigan, T. L. (2015). Brain and cognitive development. In R. M. Lerner (Ed.), *Handbook of child psychology and developmental science* (7th ed., pp. 1–54). Hoboken, NJ: John Wiley & Sons. https://doi.org/10.1002/9781118963418.childpsy202

Symeonidou, I., Dumontheil, I., Chow, W.-Y., & Breheny, R. (2016). Development of online use of theory of mind during adolescence: An eye-tracking study. *Journal of Experimental Child Psychology*, *149*, 81–97. https://doi.org/10.1016/J.JECP.2015.11.007

Takagi, M., Youssef, G., & Lorenzetti, V. (2016). Neuroimaging of the human brain in adolescent substance users. In D. De Micheli, A. L. M. Andrade, E. A. da Silva, & M. L. Oliveira de Souza Formigoni (Eds.), *Drug abuse in adolescence* (pp. 69–99). Cham, Switzerland: Springer. https://doi.org/10.1007/978-3-319-17795-3_6

Tamnes, C. K., Herting, M. M., Goddings, A.-L., Meuwese, R., Blakemore, S.-J., Dahl, R. E., ... Mills, K. L. (2017). Development of the cerebral cortex across adolescence: A multisample study of inter-related longitudinal changes in cortical volume, surface area, and thickness. *The Journal of Neuroscience*, *37*(12), 3402–3412. https://doi.org/10.1523/JNEUROSCI.3302-16.2017

Tottenham, N., & Galván, A. (2016). Stress and the adolescent brain: Amygdala-prefrontal cortex circuitry and ventral striatum as developmental targets. *Neuroscience & Biobehavioral Reviews*, *70*, 217–227. https://doi.org/10.1016/J.NEUBIOREV.2016.07.030

Turkheimer, E., Haley, A., Waldron, M., D'Onofrio, B., & Gottesman, I. I. (2003). Socioeconomic status modifies heritability of IQ in young children. *Psychological Science*, *14*(6), 623–628.

van der Stel, M., & Veenman, M. V. J. (2014). Metacognitive skills and intellectual ability of young adolescents: A longitudinal study from a developmental perspective. *European Journal of Psychology of Education*, *29*(1), 117–137. https://doi.org/10.1007/s10212-013-0190-5

van Duijvenvoorde, A. C. K., Peters, S., Braams, B. R., & Crone, E. A. (2016). What motivates adolescents? Neural responses to rewards and their influence on adolescents' risk taking, learning, and cognitive control. *Neuroscience & Biobehavioral Reviews*, *70*, 135–147. https://doi.org/10.1016/J.NEUBIOREV.2016.06.037

Vijayakumar, N., Allen, N. B., Youssef, G., Dennison, M., Yücel, M., Simmons, J. G., & Whittle, S. (2016). Brain development during adolescence: A mixed-longitudinal investigation of cortical thickness, surface area, and volume. *Human Brain Mapping*, *37*(6), 2027–2038. https://doi.org/10.1002/hbm.23154

von Stumm, S., & Plomin, R. (2015). Socioeconomic status and the growth of intelligence from infancy through adolescence. *Intelligence*, *48*, 30–36. https://doi.org/10.1016/J.INTELL.2014.10.002

Waterhouse, L. (2006). Multiple intelligences, the Mozart effect, and emotional intelligence: A critical review. *Educational Psychologist*, *41*(4), 207–225. https://doi.org/10.1207/s15326985ep4104_1

Wechsler, D. (1944). *The measurement of adult intelligence* (3rd ed.). Baltimore, MD: Williams & Wilkins.

Wechsler, D. (2014). *Wechsler Intelligence Scale for Children* (5th ed.). San Antonio, TX: NCS Pearson.

Weil, L. G., Fleming, S. M., Dumontheil, I., Kilford, E. J., Weil, R. S., Rees, G., ... Blakemore, S.-J. (2013). The development of metacognitive ability in adolescence. *Consciousness and Cognition*, *22*(1), 264–271. https://doi.org/10.1016/J.CONCOG.2013.01.004

Whittle, S., Vijayakumar, N., Simmons, J. G., Dennison, M., Schwartz, O., Pantelis, C., ... Allen, N. B. (2017). Role of positive parenting in the association between neighborhood social disadvantage and brain development across adolescence. *JAMA Psychiatry*, *74*(8), 824. https://doi.org/10.1001/jamapsychiatry.2017.1558

Yau, J. C., & Reich, S. M. (2018). "It's just a lot of work": Adolescents' self-presentation norms and practices on Facebook and Instagram. *Journal of Research on Adolescence*. https://doi.org/10.1111/jora.12376

Yurgelun-Todd, D. (2007). Emotional and cognitive changes during adolescence. *Current Opinion in Neurobiology*, *17*(2), 251–257.

Zeidler, D. L., Sadler, T. D., Applebaum, S., & Callahan, B. E. (2009). Advancing reflective judgment through socioscientific issues. *Journal of Research in Science Teaching*, *46*(1), 74–101. https://doi.org/10.1002/tea.20281

Zhai, Z. W., Pajtek, S., Luna, B., Geier, C. F., Ridenour, T. a., & Clark, D. B. (2015). Reward-modulated response inhibition, cognitive shifting, and the orbital frontal cortex in early adolescence. *Journal of Research on Adolescence*, *25*(4), 753–764. https://doi.org/10.1111/jora.12168

Zhang, L. (1999). A comparison of U.S. and Chinese university students' cognitive development: The cross-cultural applicability of Perry's theory. *Journal of Psychology*, *133*(4), 425–440.

Zhang, L. (2004). The Perry scheme: Across cultures, across approaches to the study of human psychology. *Journal of Adult Development*, *11*(2), 123–138.

Zhang, Y., Niu, B., Yu, D., Cheng, X., Liu, B., & Deng, J. (2010). Radial glial cells and the lamination of the cerebellar cortex. *Brain Structure & Function*, *215*(2), 115–122. https://doi.org/10.1007/s00429-010-0278-5

Zhou, D., Lebel, C., Treit, S., Evans, A., & Beaulieu, C. (2015). Accelerated longitudinal cortical thinning in adolescence. *NeuroImage*, *104*, 138–145. https://doi.org/10.1016/j.neuroimage.2014.10.005

CHAPTER 4

Adelabu, D. H. (2008). Future time perspective, hope, and ethnic identity among African American adolescents. *Urban Education*, *43*(3), 347–360.

Al-Owidha, A., Green, K. E., & Kroger, J. (2009). On the question of an identity status category order: Rasch model step and scale statistics used to identify category order. *International Journal of Behavioral Development*, *33*(1), 88–96. https://doi.org/10.1177/0165025408100110

Andrew, R., Tiggemann, M., & Clark, L. (2016). Predictors and health-related outcomes of positive body image in adolescent girls: A prospective study. *Developmental Psychology*, *52*(3), 463–474. https://doi.org/10.1037/dev0000095

Babore, A., Carlucci, L., Cataldi, F., Phares, V., & Trumello, C. (2017). Aggressive behaviour in adolescence: Links with self-esteem and parental emotional availability. *Social Development*, *26*(4), 740–752. https://doi.org/10.1111/sode.12236

Bachman, J. G., O'Malley, P. M., Freedman-Doan, P., Trzesniewski, K. H., & Donnellan, M. B. (2011). Adolescent self-esteem: Differences by race/ethnicity, gender, and age. *Self and Identity*, *10*(4), 445–473. https://doi.org/10.1080/15298861003794538

Barry, C. T., Loflin, D. C., & Doucette, H. (2015). Adolescent self-compassion: Associations with narcissism, self-esteem, aggression, and internalizing symptoms in at-risk males. *Personality and Individual Differences*, *77*, 118–123. https://doi.org/10.1016/J.PAID.2014.12.036

Baumeister, R. F., & Vohs, K. D. (2018). Revisiting our reappraisal of the (surprisingly few) benefits of high self-esteem. *Perspectives on Psychological Science*, *13*(2), 137–140. https://doi.org/10.1177/1745691617701185

Becht, A. I., Nelemans, S. A., Branje, S. J. T., Vollebergh, W. A. M., Koot, H. M., Denissen, J. J. A., & Meeus, W. H. J. (2016). The quest for identity in adolescence: Heterogeneity in daily identity formation and psychosocial adjustment across 5 years. *Developmental Psychology*, *52*(12), 2010–2021. https://doi.org/10.1037/dev0000245

Becht, A. I., Nelemans, S. A., Branje, S. J. T., Vollebergh, W. A. M., Koot, H. M., & Meeus, W. H. J. (2017). Identity uncertainty and commitment making across adolescence: Five-year within-person associations using daily identity reports. *Developmental Psychology*, *53*(11), 2103–2112. https://doi.org/10.1037/dev0000374

Berzonsky, M. D., & Kuk, L. S. (2000). Identity status, identity processing style, and the transition to university. *Journal of Adolescent Research*, *15*, 81–99.

Bigler, M., Neimeyer, G. J., & Brown, E. (2001). The divided self revisited: Effects of self-concept clarity and self-concept differentiation on psychological adjustment. *Journal of Social and Clinical Psychology*, *20*(3), 396–415. https://doi.org/10.1521/jscp.20.3.396.22302

Birkeland, M. S., Breivik, K., & Wold, B. (2014). Peer acceptance protects global self-esteem from negative effects of low closeness to parents during adolescence and early adulthood. *Journal of Youth and Adolescence*, *43*(1), 70–80. https://doi.org/10.1007/s10964-013-9929-1

Blakemore, S.-J. (2012). Imaging brain development: The adolescent brain. *NeuroImage*, *61*(2), 397–406. https://doi.org/10.1016/j.neuroimage.2011.11.080

Bleidorn, W., Arslan, R. C., Denissen, J. J. A., Rentfrow, P. J., Gebauer, J. E., Potter, J., & Gosling, S. D. (2016). Age and gender differences in self-esteem—A cross-cultural window. *Journal of Personality and Social Psychology*, *111*(3), 396–410. https://doi.org/10.1037/pspp0000078

Bleidorn, W., & Ködding, C. (2013). The divided self and psychological (mal) adjustment – A meta-analytic review. *Journal of Research in Personality*, *47*(5), 547–552. https://doi.org/10.1016/J.JRP.2013.04.009

Borghuis, J., Denissen, J. J. A., Oberski, D., Sijtsma, K., Meeus, W. H. J., Branje, S., … Bleidorn, W. (2017). Big Five personality stability, change, and codevelopment across adolescence and early adulthood. *Journal of Personality and Social Psychology*, *113*(4), 641–657. https://doi.org/10.1037/pspp0000138

Bosma, H. A., & Kunnen, E. S. (2001). Determinants and mechanisms in ego identity development: A review and synthesis. *Developmental Review*, *21*(1), 39–66. https://doi.org/10.1006/drev.2000.0514

Boutakidis, I. P., Chao, R. K., & Rodriguez, J. L. (2011). The role of adolescents' native language fluency on quality of communication and respect for parents in Chinese and Korean immigrant families. *Asian American Journal of Psychology*, *2*(2), 128–139. https://doi.org/10.1037/a0023606

Bowman Heads, A. M., Glover, A. M., Castillo, L. G., Blozis, S., & Kim, S. Y. (2018). Dimensions of ethnic identity as protective factors for substance use and sexual risk behaviors in African American college students. *Journal of American College Health*, *66*(3), 178–186. https://doi.org/10.1080/07448481.2017.1400975

Brittian, A. S., Kim, S. Y., Armenta, B. E., Lee, R. M., Umaña-Taylor, A. J., Schwartz, S. J., … Hudson, M. L. (2015). Do dimensions of ethnic identity mediate the association between perceived ethnic group discrimination and depressive symptoms? *Cultural Diversity and Ethnic Minority Psychology*, *21*(1), 41–53. https://doi.org/10.1037/a0037531

Burrow, A. L., & Ong, A. D. (2010). Racial identity as a moderator of daily exposure and reactivity to racial discrimination. *Self and Identity*, *9*(4), 383–402. https://doi.org/10.1080/15298860903192496

Campbell, J. D., Trapnell, P. D., Heine, S. J., Katz, I. M., Lavallee, L. F., & Lehman, D. R. (1996). Self-concept clarity: Measurement, personality correlates, and cultural boundaries. *Journal of Personality and Social Psychology*, *70*(1), 141–156. Retrieved from https://doi.org/10.1037/0022-3514.70.1.141

Carlsson, J., Wängqvist, M., & Frisén, A. (2015). Identity development in the late twenties: A never ending story. *Developmental Psychology*, *51*(3), 334–345. https://doi.org/10.1037/a0038745

Carlsson, J., Wängqvist, M., & Frisén, A. (2016). Life on hold: Staying in identity diffusion in the late twenties. *Journal of Adolescence*, *47*, 220–229. https://doi.org/10.1016/j.adolescence.2015.10.023

Caspi, A., & Shiner, R. (2008). Temperament and personality. In M. Rutter, D. V. M. Bishop, D. S. Pine, S. Scott, J. Stevenson, E. Taylor, & A. Thapar (Eds.), *Rutter's child and adolescent psychiatry* (5th ed., pp. 182–198). Malden, MA: Blackwell Publishing. https://doi.org/10.1002/9781444300895.ch14

Chen, X., Schmidt, L. A., Chen, X., & Schmidt, L. A. (2015). Temperament and personality. In R. M. Lerner (Ed.), *Handbook of child psychology and developmental science* (7th ed., pp. 1–49). Hoboken, NJ: John Wiley & Sons. https://doi.org/10.1002/9781118963418.childpsy305

Choi, S., Lewis, J. A., Harwood, S., Mendenhall, R., & Huntt, M. B. (2017). Is ethnic identity a buffer? Exploring the relations between racial microaggressions and depressive symptoms among Asian-American individuals. *Journal of Ethnic & Cultural Diversity in Social Work*, *26*(1–2), 18–29. https://doi.org/10.1080/15313204.2016.1263815

Chung, J. M., Robins, R. W., Trzesniewski, K. H., Noftle, E. E., Roberts, B. W., & Widaman, K. F. (2014). Continuity and change in self-esteem during emerging adulthood. *Journal of Personality and Social Psychology*, *106*(3), 469–483. https://doi.org/10.1037/a0035135

Clark, D. A., Durbin, C. E., Hicks, B. M., Iacono, W. G., & McGue, M. (2016). Personality in the age of industry: Structure, heritability, and correlates of personality in middle childhood from the perspective of parents, teachers, and children. *Journal of Research in Personality*, *67*, 132–143 https://doi.org/10.1016/j.jrp.2016.06.013

Costa, P. T., McCrae, R. R., & Löckenhoff, C. E. (2019). Personality across the life span. *Annual Review of Psychology*, *70*(1), 423–448. https://doi.org/10.1146/annurev-psych-010418-103244

Crocetti, E., Branje, S., Rubini, M., Koot, H. M., & Meeus, W. (2017). Identity processes and parent-child and sibling relationships in adolescence: A five-wave multi-informant longitudinal study. *Child Development*, *88*(1), 210–228. https://doi.org/10.1111/cdev.12547

Crocetti, E., Klimstra, T., Keijsers, L., Hale, W. W., & Meeus, W. H. J. (2009). Anxiety trajectories and identity development in adolescence: A five-wave longitudinal study. *Journal of Youth & Adolescence*, *38*(6), 839–849. https://doi.org/10.1007/s10964-008-9302-y

Crocetti, E., Klimstra, T. A., Hale, W. W., Koot, H. M., & Meeus, W. H. J. (2013). Impact of early adolescent externalizing problem behaviors on identity development in middle to late adolescence: A prospective 7-year longitudinal study. *Journal of Youth and Adolescence*, *42*(11), 1745–1758. https://doi.org/10.1007/s10964-013-9924-6

Crocetti, E., Moscatelli, S., Van der Graaff, J., Rubini, M., Meeus, W., & Branje, S. (2016). The interplay of self-certainty and prosocial development in the transition from late adolescence to emerging adulthood. *European Journal of Personality*, *30*(6), 594–607. https://doi.org/10.1002/per.2084

Crocetti, E., Rubini, M., Branje, S., Koot, H. M., & Meeus, W. (2016). Self-concept clarity in adolescents and parents: A six-wave longitudinal and multi-informant study on development and intergenerational transmission. *Journal of Personality*, *84*(5), 580–593. https://doi.org/10.1111/jopy.12181

Deary, I. J., Pattie, A., & Starr, J. M. (2013). The stability of intelligence from age 11 to age 90 years: The Lothian Birth Cohort of 1921. *Psychological Science*, *24*, 2361–2368. https://doi.org/10.1177/0956797613486487

Douglass, S., & Umaña-Taylor, A. J. (2016). Time-varying effects of family ethnic socialization on ethnic-racial identity development among Latino adolescents. *Developmental Psychology*, *52*(11), 1904–1912. https://doi.org/10.1037/dev0000141

Douglass, S., & Umaña-Taylor, A. J. (2017). Examining discrimination, ethnic-racial identity status, and youth public regard among Black, Latino, and White adolescents. *Journal of Research on Adolescence*, *27*(1), 155–172. https://doi.org/10.1111/jora.12262

Dudovitz, R. N., Chung, P. J., & Wong, M. D. (2017). Teachers and coaches in adolescent social networks are associated with healthier self-concept and decreased substance use. *Journal of School Health*, *87*(1), 12–20. https://doi.org/10.1111/josh.12462

Edmonds, G. W., Goldberg, L. R., Hampson, S. E., & Barckley, M. (2013). Personality stability from childhood to midlife: Relating teachers' assessments in elementary school to observer- and self-ratings 40 years later. *Journal of Research in Personality*, *47*(5), 505–513. https://doi.org/10.1016/j.jrp.2013.05.003

Else-Quest, N. M., & Morse, E. (2015). Ethnic variations in parental ethnic socialization and adolescent ethnic identity: A longitudinal study. *Cultural Diversity and Ethnic Minority Psychology*, *21*(1), 54–64. https://doi.org/10.1037/a0037820

Erikson, E. H. (1950). *Childhood and society* (2nd ed.). New York, NY: Norton.

Erol, R. Y., & Orth, U. (2011). Self-esteem development from age 14 to 30 years: A longitudinal study. *Journal of Personality and Social Psychology*, *101*(3), 607–619. https://doi.org/10.1037/a0024299

Fadjukoff, P., Pulkkinen, L., & Kokko, K. (2016). Identity formation in adulthood: A longitudinal study from age 27 to 50. *Identity*, *16*(1), 8–23. https://doi.org/10.1080/15283488.2015.1121820

Ferguson, G. M., Hafen, C. A., & Laursen, B. (2010). Adolescent psychological and academic adjustment as a function of discrepancies between actual and ideal self-perceptions. *Journal of Youth and Adolescence*, *39*(12), 1485–1497. https://doi.org/10.1007/s10964-009-9461-5

Frijns, T., & Finkenauer, C. (2009). Longitudinal associations between keeping a secret and psychosocial adjustment in adolescence. *International Journal of Behavioral Development*, *33*(2), 145–154. https://doi.org/10.1177/0165025408098020

Fuligni, A. J., Witkow, M., & Garcia, C. (2005). Ethnic identity and the academic adjustment of adolescents from Mexican, Chinese, and European backgrounds. *Developmental Psychology*, *41*(5), 799–811. https://doi.org/10.1037/0012-1649.41.5.799

Galliher, R. V, Jones, M. D., & Dahl, A. (2011). Concurrent and longitudinal effects of ethnic identity and experiences of discrimination on psychosocial adjustment of Navajo adolescents. *Developmental Psychology*, *47*(2), 509–526. https://doi.org/10.1037/a0021061

Galliher, R. V., McLean, K. C., & Syed, M. (2017). An integrated developmental model for studying identity content in context. *Developmental Psychology*, *53*(11), 2011–2022. https://doi.org/10.1037/dev0000299

Gonzales-Backen, M. A., Bámaca-Colbert, M. Y., & Allen, K. (2016). Ethnic identity trajectories among Mexican-origin girls during early and middle adolescence: Predicting future psychosocial adjustment. *Developmental Psychology*, *52*(5), 790–797. https://doi.org/10.1037/a0040193

Gonzales-Backen, M. A., Meca, A., Lorenzo-Blanco, E. I., Des Rosiers, S. E., Córdova, D., Soto, D. W., . . . Unger, J. B. (2018). Examining the temporal order of ethnic identity and perceived discrimination among Hispanic immigrant adolescents. *Developmental Psychology*, *54*(5), 929–937. https://doi.org/10.1037/dev0000465

Goossens, L. (2001). Global versus domain-specific statuses in identity research: A comparison of two self-report measures. *Journal of Adolescence*, *24*(6), 681–699. https://doi.org/10.1006/jado.2001.0438

Graham, E. K., & Lachman, M. E. (2012). Personality stability is associated with better cognitive performance in adulthood: Are the stable more able? *The Journals of Gerontology, Series B: Psychological Sciences and Social Sciences*, *67*(5), 545–554. https://doi.org/10.1093/geronb/gbr149

Gruenenfelder-Steiger, A. E., Harris, M. A., & Fend, H. A. (2016). Subjective and objective peer approval evaluations and self-esteem development: A test of reciprocal, prospective, and long-term effects. *Developmental Psychology*, *52*(10), 1563–1577. https://doi.org/10.1037/dev0000147

Hall, S. P., & Brassard, M. R. (2008). Relational support as a predictor of identity status in an ethnically diverse early adolescent sample. *Journal of Early Adolescence*, *28*(1), 92–114. https://doi.org/10.1177/0272431607308668

Hampson, S. E., & Goldberg, L. R. (2006). A first large cohort study of personality trait stability over the 40 years between elementary school and midlife. *Journal of Personality and Social Psychology*, *91*(4), 763–779.

Harding, J. F., Hughes, D. L., & Way, N. (2017). Racial/ethnic differences in mothers' socialization goals for their adolescents. *Cultural Diversity and Ethnic Minority Psychology*, *23*(2), 281–290. https://doi.org/10.1037/cdp0000116

Harris, M. A., Gruenenfelder-Steiger, A. E., Ferrer, E., Donnellan, M. B., Allemand, M., Fend, H., . . . Trzesniewski, K. H. (2015). Do parents foster self-esteem? Testing the prospective impact of parent closeness on adolescent self-esteem. *Child Development*, *86*(4), 995–1013. https://doi.org/10.1111/cdev.12356

Harter, S. (2006). The Development of Self-Esteem. In M. H. Kernis (Ed.), *Self-esteem issues and answers: A sourcebook of current perspectives*. (pp. 144–150). New York, NY: Psychology Press.

Harter, S. (2012a). Emerging self-processes during childhood and adolescence. In M. R. Leary & J. P. Tangney (Eds.), *Handbook of self and identity* (pp. 680–715). New York, NY: Guilford Press.

Harter, S. (2012b). *The construction of the self: Developmental and sociocultural foundations* (2nd ed.). New York, NY: Guilford Press.

Heine, S. J., & Hamamura, T. (2007). In search of East Asian self-enhancement. *Personality and Social Psychology Review*, *11*(1), 4–27. https://doi.org/10.1177/1088868306294587

Hernández, M. M., Conger, R. D., Robins, R. W., Bacher, K. B., & Widaman, K. F. (2014). Cultural socialization and ethnic pride among Mexican-origin adolescents during the transition to middle school. *Child Development*, *85*(2), 695–708. https://doi.org/10.1111/cdev.12167

Hofstede, G. H. (2001). *Culture's consequences: Comparing values, behaviors, institutions, and organizations across nations*. Thousand Oaks, CA: Sage.

Hood, W., Bradley, G. L., & Ferguson, S. (2017). Mediated effects of perceived discrimination on adolescent academic achievement: A test of four models. *Journal of Adolescence*, *54*, 82–93. https://doi.org/10.1016/J.ADOLESCENCE.2016.11.011

Hughes, D., & Chen, L. (1997). When and what parents tell children about race: An examination of race-related socialization among African American families. *Applied Developmental Science*, *1*(4), 200–214. https://doi.org/10.1207/s1532480xads0104_4

Hughes, D., Del Toro, J., Harding, J. F., Way, N., & Rarick, J. R. D. (2016). Trajectories of discrimination across adolescence: Associations with academic, psychological, and behavioral outcomes. *Child Development*, *87*(5), 1337–1351. https://doi.org/10.1111/cdev.12591

Hughes, D., Hagelskamp, C., Way, N., & Foust, M. D. (2009a). The role of mothers' and adolescents' perceptions of ethnic-racial socialization in shaping ethnic-racial identity among early adolescent boys and girls. *Journal of Youth & Adolescence*, *38*(5), 605–626. https://doi.org/10.1007/s10964-009-9399-7

Hughes, D., Witherspoon, D., Rivas-Drake, D., & West-Bey, N. (2009b). Received ethnic–racial socialization messages and youths' academic and behavioral outcomes: Examining the mediating role of ethnic identity and self-esteem. *Cultural Diversity and Ethnic Minority Psychology*, *15*(2), 112–124. https://doi.org/10.1037/a0015509

Hughes, D. L., Del Toro, J., & Way, N. (2017). Interrelations among dimensions of ethnic-racial identity during adolescence. *Developmental Psychology*, *53*(11), 2139–2153. https://doi.org/10.1037/dev0000401

Jackman, D. M., & MacPhee, D. (2017). Self-esteem and future orientation predict adolescents' risk engagement. *The Journal of Early Adolescence*, *37*(3), 339–366. https://doi.org/10.1177/0272431615602756

Jespersen, K., Kroger, J., & Martinussen, M. (2013). Identity status and moral reasoning: A meta-analysis. *Identity*, *13*(3), 266–280. https://doi.org/10.1080/15283488.2013.799472

Kerpelman, J. L., Eryigit, S., & Stephens, C. J. (2008). African American adolescents' future education orientation: Associations with self-efficacy, ethnic identity, and perceived parental support. *Journal of Youth & Adolescence*, *37*(8), 997–1008. https://doi.org/10.1007/s10964-007-9201-7

Kiang, L., & Fuligni, A. J. (2009). Ethnic identity in context: Variations in ethnic exploration and belonging within parent, same-ethnic peer, and different-ethnic peer relationships. *Journal of Youth and Adolescence*, *38*(5), 732–743. https://doi.org/10.1007/s10964-008-9278-7

Klimstra, T. A., Kuppens, P., Luyckx, K., Branje, S., Hale, W. W., Oosterwegel, A., . . . Meeus, W. H. J. (2016). Daily dynamics of adolescent mood and identity. *Journal of Research on Adolescence*, *26*(3), 459–473. https://doi.org/10.1111/jora.12205

Kroger, J. (2015). Identity development through adulthood: The move toward "wholeness." In K. C. McLean & M. Syed (Eds.), *The Oxford handbook of identity development* (pp. 65–80). Oxford, England: Oxford University Press. https://doi.org/10.1093/oxfordhb/9780199936564.013.004

Kroger, J., & Marcia, J. E. (2011). The identity statuses: Origins, meanings, and interpretations. In S. J. Schwartz, K. Luyckx, & V. L. Vignoles (Eds.), *Handbook of identity theory and research* (pp. 31–53). New York, NY: Springer. https://doi.org/10.1007/978-1-4419-7988-9_2

Kroger, J., Martinussen, M., & Marcia, J. E. (2010). Identity status change during adolescence and young adulthood: A meta-analysis. *Journal of Adolescence*, *33*(5), 683–698. https://doi.org/10.1016/j.adolescence.2009.11.002

Kulig, T. C., Cullen, F. T., Wilcox, P., & Chouhy, C. (2018). Personality and adolescent school-based victimization: Do the Big Five matter? *Journal of School Violence*, 1–24. https://doi.org/10.1080/15388220.2018.1444495

Laghi, F., Baiocco, R., Lonigro, A., & Baumgartner, E. (2013). Exploring the relationship between identity status development and alcohol consumption among Italian adolescents. *The Journal of Psychology*, *147*(3), 277–292. https://doi.org/10.1080/00223980.2012.688075

Lee, C. G., Seo, D.-C., Torabi, M. R., Lohrmann, D. K., & Song, T. M. (2018). Longitudinal trajectory of the relationship between self-esteem and substance use from adolescence to young adulthood. *Journal of School Health*, *88*(1), 9–14. https://doi.org/10.1111/josh.12574

Light, A. E., & Visser, P. S. (2013). The ins and outs of the self: Contrasting role exits and role entries as predictors of self-concept clarity. *Self and Identity*, *12*(3), 291–306. https://doi.org/10.1080/15298868.2012.667914

Lillevoll, K. R., Kroger, J., & Martinussen, M. (2013). Identity status and anxiety: A meta-analysis. *Identity*, *13*(3), 214–227. https://doi.org/10.1080/15283488.2013.799432

Liu, D., Ksinan, A. J., & Vazsonyi, A. T. (2018). Maternal support and deviance among rural adolescents: The mediating role of self-esteem. *Journal of Adolescence*, *69*, 62–71. https://doi.org/10.1016/J.ADOLESCENCE.2018.09.003

Lodi-Smith, J., Spain, S. M., Cologgi, K., & Roberts, B. W. (2017). Development of identity clarity and content in adulthood. *Journal of Personality and Social Psychology*, *112*(5), 755–768. https://doi.org/10.1037/pspp0000091

Luciano, E. C., & Orth, U. (2017). Transitions in romantic relationships and development of self-esteem. *Journal of Personality and Social Psychology*, *112*(2), 307–328. https://doi.org/10.1037/pspp0000109

Luyckx, K., Teppers, E., Klimstra, T. A., & Rassart, J. (2014). Identity processes and personality traits and types in adolescence: Directionality of effects and developmental trajectories. *Developmental Psychology*, *50*(8), 2144–2153. https://doi.org/10.1037/a0037256

Marcia, J. E. (1966). Development and validation of ego-identity status. *Journal of Personality and Social Psychology*, *3*(5), 551–558.

Markus, H. R., & Kitayama, S. (2010). Cultures and selves: A cycle of mutual constitution. *Perspectives on Psychological Science*, *5*(4), 420–430. https://doi.org/10.1177/1745691610375557

Marsh, H. W., Trautwein, U., Lüdtke, O., Köller, O., & Baumert, J. (2006). Integration of multidimensional self-concept and core personality constructs: Construct validation and relations to well-being and achievement. *Journal of Personality*, *74*, 403–456.

Marshall, S. L., Parker, P. D., Ciarrochi, J., & Heaven, P. C. L. (2014). Is self-esteem a cause or consequence of social support? A 4-year longitudinal study. *Child Development*, *85*(3), 1275–1291. https://doi.org/10.1111/cdev.12176

McAdams, D. P., & Olson, B. D. (2010). Personality development: Continuity and change over the life course. *Annual Review of Psychology*, *61*(1), 517–542. https://doi.org/10.1146/annurev.psych.093008.100507

McAdams, D. P., & Zapata-Gietl, C. (2015). Three strands of identity development across the human life course. In K. C. McLean & M. Syed (Eds.), *The Oxford handbook of identity development* (pp. 81–96). Oxford, England: Oxford University Press. https://doi.org/10.1093/oxfordhb/9780199936564.013.006

McCrae, R. R., & Costa Jr., P. T. (2008). The five-factor theory of personality. In O. P. John, R. W. Robins, & L. A. Pervin (Eds.), *Handbook of personality psychology: Theory and research* (3rd ed., pp. 159–181). New York, NY: Guilford Press

McLean, K. C., Syed, M., & Shucard, H. (2016). Bringing identity content to the fore. *Emerging Adulthood*, *4*(5), 356–364. https://doi.org/10.1177/2167696815626820

McLean, K. C., Syed, M., Way, N., & Rogers, O. (2015). "[T]hey say Black men won't make it, but I know I'm gonna make it." In K. C. McLean & M. Syed (Eds.), *The Oxford handbook of identity development* (pp. 269–287). Oxford, England: Oxford University Press. https://doi.org/10.1093/oxfordhb/9780199936564.013.032

McWhirter, E. H., Garcia, E. A., & Bines, D. (2018). Discrimination and other education barriers, school connectedness, and thoughts of dropping out among Latina/o students. *Journal of Career Development*, 45(4), 330–344. https://doi.org/10.1177/0894845317696807

Meeus, W. H. J. (2011). The Study of Adolescent Identity Formation 2000-2010: A review of longitudinal research. *Journal of Research on Adolescence*, 21(1), 75–94. https://doi.org/10.1111/j.1532-7795.2010.00716.x

Meeus, W. H. J., & de Wied, M. (2007). Relationships with parents and identity in adolescence: A review of 25 years of research. In M. Watzlawik & A. Born (Eds.), *Capturing identity: Quantitative and qualitative methods* (pp. 131–147). Hoboken, NJ: John Wiley & Sons.

Mercer, N., Crocetti, E., Branje, S., van Lier, P., & Meeus, W. (2017). Linking delinquency and personal identity formation across adolescence: Examining between- and within-person associations. *Developmental Psychology*, 53(11), 2182–2194. https://doi.org/10.1037/dev0000351

Miconi, D., Moscardino, U., Ronconi, L., & Altoè, G. (2017). Perceived parenting, self-esteem, and depressive symptoms in immigrant and non-immigrant adolescents in Italy: A multigroup path analysis. *Journal of Child and Family Studies*, 26(2), 345–356. https://doi.org/10.1007/s10826-016-0562-y

Milevsky, A., Schlechter, M., Netter, S., & Keehn, D. (2007). Maternal and paternal parenting styles in adolescents: Associations with self-esteem, depression and life-satisfaction. *Journal of Child & Family Studies*, 16(1), 39–47. https://doi.org/10.1007/s10826-006-9066-5

Miller-Cotto, D., & Byrnes, J. P. (2016). Ethnic/racial identity and academic achievement: A meta-analytic review. *Developmental Review*, 41, 51–70. https://doi.org/10.1016/j.dr.2016.06.003

Mills, K. L., Goddings, A.-L., Clasen, L. S., Giedd, J. N., & Blakemore, S.-J. (2014). The developmental mismatch in structural brain maturation during adolescence. *Developmental Neuroscience*, 36(3–4), 147–160. https://doi.org/10.1159/000362328

Mills, K. L., Lalonde, F., Clasen, L. S., Giedd, J. N., & Blakemore, S.-J. (2014). Developmental changes in the structure of the social brain in late childhood and adolescence. *Social Cognitive and Affective Neuroscience*, 9(1), 123–131. https://doi.org/10.1093/scan/nss113

Morizot, J., & Le Blanc, M. (2003). Continuity and change in personality traits from adolescence to midlife: A 25-year longitudinal study comparing representative and adjudicated men. *Journal of Personality*, 71(5), 705.

Mrick, S. E., & Mrtorell, G. A. (2011). Sticks and stones may break my bones: Protective factors for the effects of perceived discrimination on social competence in adolescence. *Personal Relationships*, 18(3), 487–501. https://doi.org/10.1111/j.1475-6811.2010.01320.x

Nelson, S. C., Syed, M., Tran, A. G. T. T., Hu, A. W., & Lee, R. M. (2018). Pathways to ethnic-racial identity development and psychological adjustment: The differential associations of cultural socialization by parents and peers. *Developmental Psychology*, 54(11), 2166–2180. https://doi.org/10.1037/dev0000597

Northoff, G., & Hayes, D. J. (2011). Is our self nothing but reward? *Biological Psychiatry*, 69(11), 1019–1025. https://doi.org/10.1016/j.biopsych.2010.12.014

Oh, J. S., & Fuligni, A. J. (2010). The role of heritage language development in the ethnic identity and family relationships of adolescents from immigrant backgrounds. *Social Development*, 19(1), 202–220. https://doi.org/10.1111/j.1467-9507.2008.00530.x

Orth, U. (2017). The lifespan development of self-esteem. In J. Specht (Ed.), *Personality development across the lifespan* (pp. 181–195). London, England: Academic Press. https://doi.org/10.1016/B978-0-12-804674-6.00012-0

Orth, U., & Robins, R. W. (2014). The development of self-esteem. *Current Directions in Psychological Science*, 23(5), 381–387. https://doi.org/10.1177/0963721414547414

Oshri, A., Carlson, M. W., Kwon, J. A., Zeichner, A., & Wickrama, K. K. A. S. (2017). Developmental growth trajectories of self-esteem in adolescence: Associations with child neglect and drug use and abuse in young adulthood. *Journal of Youth and Adolescence*, 46(1), 151–164. https://doi.org/10.1007/s10964-016-0483-5

Pahl, K., & Way, N. (2006). Longitudinal trajectories of ethnic identity among urban Black and Latino adolescents. *Child Development*, 77(5), 1403–1415.

Penke, L., Denissen, J. J. A., & Miller, G. F. (2007). The evolutionary genetics of personality. *European Journal of Personality*, 21(5), 549–587. https://doi.org/10.1016/j.copsyc.2015.08.021

Pfeifer, J. H., Kahn, L. E., Merchant, J. S., Peake, S. J., Veroude, K., Masten, C. L., . . . Dapretto, M. (2013). Longitudinal change in the neural bases of adolescent social self-evaluations: Effects of age and pubertal development. *The Journal of Neuroscience*, 33(17), 7415–7419. https://doi.org/10.1523/JNEUROSCI.4074-12.2013

Pfeifer, J. H., Lieberman, M. D., & Dapretto, M. (2007). "I know you are but what am I?!": Neural bases of self- and social knowledge retrieval in children and adults. *Journal of Cognitive Neuroscience*, 19(8), 1323–1337. https://doi.org/10.1162/jocn.2007.19.8.1323

Pfeifer, J. H., & Peake, S. J. (2012). Self-development: Integrating cognitive, socioemotional, and neuroimaging perspectives. *Developmental Cognitive Neuroscience*, 2(1), 55–69. https://doi.org/10.1016/j.dcn.2011.07.012

Phinney, J. S. (1989). Stages of ethnic identity development in minority group adolescents. *The Journal of Early Adolescence*, 9(1–2), 34–49. https://doi.org/10.1177/0272431689091004

Phinney, J. S., & Chavira, V. (1992). Ethnic identity and self-esteem: An exploratory longitudinal study. *Journal of Adolescence*, 15(3), 271–281. https://doi.org/10.1016/0140-1971(92)90030-9

Phinney, J. S., & Ong, A. D. (2007). Conceptualization and measurement of ethnic identity: Current status and future directions. *Journal of Counseling Psychology*, 54(3), 271–281. https://doi.org/10.1037/0022-067.54.3.271

Pittman, J. F., Keiley, M. K., Kerpelman, J. L., & Vaughn, B. E. (2011). Attachment, identity, and intimacy: Parallels between Bowlby's and Erikson's paradigms. *Journal of Family Theory & Review*, 3(1), 32–46. https://doi.org/10.1111/j.1756-2589.2010.00079.x

Power, R., & Pluess, M. (2015). Heritability estimates of the Big Five personality traits based on common genetic variants. *Translational Psychiatry*, 5, e604. https://doi.org/10.1038/tp.2015.96

Preckel, F., Niepel, C., Schneider, M., & Brunner, M. (2013). Self-concept in adolescence: A longitudinal study on reciprocal effects of self-perceptions in academic and social domains. *Journal of Adolescence*, 36(6), 1165–1175. https://doi.org/10.1016/j.adolescence.2013.09.001

Quane, J. M., & Rankin, B. H. (2006). Does it pay to participate? Neighborhood-based organizations and the social development of urban adolescents. *Children & Youth Services Review*, 28, 1229–1250.

Ragelienė, T. (2016). Links of adolescents identity development and relationship with peers: A systematic literature review. *Journal of the Canadian Academy of Child and Adolescent Psychiatry*, 25(2), 97–105. Retrieved from http://www.ncbi.nlm.nih.gov/pubmed/27274745

Rangel, A., Camerer, C., & Montague, P. R. (2008). A framework for studying the neurobiology of value-based decision making. *Nature Reviews Neuroscience*, 9(7), 545–556. https://doi.org/10.1038/nrn2357

Reis, O., & Youniss, J. (2004). Patterns in identity change and development in relationships with mothers and friends. *Journal of Adolescent Research*, 19(1), 31–44.

Rivas-Drake, D., Hughes, D., & Way, N. (2009). A preliminary analysis of associations among ethnic-racial socialization, ethnic discrimination, and ethnic identity among urban sixth graders. *Journal of Research on Adolescence, 19*(3), 558–584. https://doi.org/10.1111/j.1532-7795.2009.00607.x

Rivas-Drake, D., Seaton, E. K., Markstrom, C., Quintana, S., Syed, M., Lee, R. M., . . . Yip, T. (2014). Ethnic and racial identity in adolescence: Implications for psychosocial, academic, and health outcomes. *Child Development, 85*(1), 40–57. https://doi.org/10.1111/cdev.12200

Rivas-Drake, D., Umaña-Taylor, A. J., Schaefer, D. R., & Medina, M. (2017). Ethnic-racial identity and friendships in early adolescence. *Child Development, 88*(3), 710–724. https://doi.org/10.1111/cdev.12790

Roberts, B. W., & Mroczek, D. (2008). Personality trait change in adulthood. *Current Directions in Psychological Science, 17*(1), 31–35. https://doi.org/10.1111/j.1467-8721.2008.00543.x

Rock, P. F., Cole, D. J., Houshyar, S., Lythcott, M., & Prinstein, M. J. (2011). Peer status in an ethnic context: Associations with African American adolescents' ethnic identity. *Journal of Applied Developmental Psychology, 32*(4), 163–169. https://doi.org/10.1016/j.appdev.2011.03.002

Romero, A. J., Edwards, L. M., Fryberg, S. A., & Orduña, M. (2014). Resilience to discrimination stress across ethnic identity stages of development. *Journal of Applied Social Psychology, 44*(1), 1–11. https://doi.org/10.1111/jasp.12192

Romero, A. J., & Roberts, R. E. (2003). The impact of multiple dimensions of ethnic identity on discrimination and adolescents' self-esteem. *Journal of Applied Social Psychology, 33*(11), 2288–2305.

Sanchez, D., Whittaker, T. A., Hamilton, E., & Arango, S. (2017). Familial ethnic socialization, gender role attitudes, and ethnic identity development in Mexican-origin early adolescents. *Cultural Diversity and Ethnic Minority Psychology, 23*(3), 335–347. https://doi.org/10.1037/cdp0000142

Sánchez-Queija, I., Oliva, A., & Parra, Á. (2017). Stability, change, and determinants of self-esteem during adolescence and emerging adulthood. *Journal of Social and Personal Relationships, 34*(8), 1277–1294. https://doi.org/10.1177/0265407516674831

Schaffhuser, K., Allemand, M., & Schwarz, B. (2017). The development of self-representations during the transition to early adolescence: The role of gender, puberty, and school transition. *The Journal of Early Adolescence, 37*(6), 774–804. https://doi.org/10.1177/0272431615624841

Schwartz, S. J. (2001). The evolution of Eriksonian and neo-Eriksonian identity theory and research: A review and integration. *Identity, 1*(1), 7–58.

Schwartz, S. J., Klimstra, T. A., Luyckx, K., Hale, W. W., Frijns, T., Oosterwegel, A., . . . Meeus, W. H. J. (2011). Daily dynamics of personal identity and self-concept clarity. *European Journal of Personality, 25*(5), 373–385. https://doi.org/10.1002/per.798

Schwartz, S. J., Klimstra, T. A., Luyckx, K., Hale, W. W., & Meeus, W. H. J. (2012). Characterizing the self-system over time in adolescence: Internal structure and associations with internalizing symptoms. *Journal of Youth and Adolescence, 41*(9), 1208–1225. https://doi.org/10.1007/s10964-012-9751-1

Schwartz, S. J., Luyckx, K., & Crocetti, E. (2015). What have we learned since Schwartz (2001)? In K. C. McLean & M. Syed (Eds.), *The Oxford handbook of identity development* (pp. 539–561). Oxford, England: Oxford University Press. https://doi.org/10.1093/oxfordhb/9780199936564.013.028

Schwartz, S. J., Zamboanga, B. L., Luyckx, K., Meca, A., & Ritchie, R. A. (2013). Identity in emerging adulthood: Reviewing the field and looking forward. *Emerging Adulthood, 1*(2), 96–113. https://doi.org/10.1177/2167696813479781

Seaton, E. K., Yip, T., Morgan-Lopez, A., & Sellers, R. M. (2012). Racial discrimination and racial socialization as predictors of African American adolescents' racial identity development using latent transition analysis. *Developmental Psychology, 48*(2), 448–458. https://doi.org/10.1037/a0025328

Seaton, E. K., Yip, T., & Sellers, R. M. (2009). A longitudinal examination of racial identity and racial discrimination among African American adolescents. *Child Development, 80*(2), 406–417. https://doi.org/10.1111/j.1467-8624.2009.01268.x

Shiner, R. L., & DeYoung, C. G. (2013). The structure of temperament and personality traits. In P. D. Zelazo (Ed.), *The Oxford handbook of developmental psychology, Vol. 2: Self and other* (p. 113–141). Oxford, England: Oxford University Press. https://doi.org/10.1093/oxfordhb/9780199958474.013.0006

Sippola, L. K., Buchanan, C. M., & Kehoe, S. (2007). Correlates of false self in adolescent romantic relationships. *Journal of Clinical Child & Adolescent Psychology, 36*(4), 515–521. https://doi.org/10.1080/15374410701653740

Soto, C. J., John, O. P., Gosling, S. D., & Potter, J. (2011). Age differences in personality traits from 10 to 65: Big Five domains and facets in a large cross-sectional sample. *Journal of Personality and Social Psychology, 100*(2), 330–348. https://doi.org/10.1037/a0021717

Spencer, M. B., & Markstrom-Adams, C. (1990). Identity processes among racial and ethnic minority children in America. *Child Development, 61*(2), 290–310. https://doi.org/10.1111/j.1467-8624.1990.tb02780.x

Spencer, M. B., Swanson, D. P., & Harpalani, V. (2015). Development of the self. In M. E. Lamb (Ed.), *Handbook of child psychology and developmental science* (pp. 1–44). Hoboken, NJ: John Wiley & Sons. https://doi.org/10.1002/9781118963418.childpsy318

Steiger, A. E., Allemand, M., Robins, R. W., & Fend, H. A. (2014). Low and decreasing self-esteem during adolescence predict adult depression two decades later. *Journal of Personality and Social Psychology, 106*(2), 325–338. https://doi.org/10.1037/a0035133

Steinberg, L. (2001). We know some things: Parent-adolescent relationships in retrospect and prospect. *Journal of Research on Adolescence, 11*(1), 1–19.

Stevens, E. N., Lovejoy, M. C., & Pittman, L. D. (2014). Understanding the relationship between actual:ideal discrepancies and depressive symptoms: A developmental examination. *Journal of Adolescence, 37*(5), 612–621. https://doi.org/10.1016/j.adolescence.2014.04.013

Syed, M., Azmitia, M., & Phinney, J. S. (2007). Stability and change in ethnic identity among Latino emerging adults in two contexts. *Identity, 7*(2), 155–178. https://doi.org/10.1080/15283480701326117

Syed, M., & Juan, M. J. D. (2012). Birds of an ethnic feather? Ethnic identity homophily among college-age friends. *Journal of Adolescence, 35*(6), 1505–1514. https://doi.org/10.1016/J.ADOLESCENCE.2011.10.012

Syed, M., Walker, L. H. M., Lee, R. M., Umana-Taylor, A. J., Zamboanga, B. L., Schwartz, S. J., . . . Huynh, Q.-L. (2013). A two-factor model of ethnic identity exploration: Implications for identity coherence and well-being. *Cultural Diversity and Ethnic Minority Psychology, 19*(2), 143–154. https://doi.org/10.1037/a0030564

Tackett, J. L. (2006). Evaluating models of the personality–psychopathology relationship in children and adolescents. *Clinical Psychology Review, 26*(5), 584–599. https://doi.org/10.1016/j.cpr.2006.04.003

Thomaes, S., Poorthuis, A., & Nelemans, S. (2011). Self-Esteem. In B. B. Brown & M. J. Prinstein (Eds.), *Encyclopedia of adolescence* (pp. 316–324). San Diego, CA: Academic Press. https://doi.org/10.1016/B978-0-12-373951-3.00037-5

Thomaes, S., Reijntjes, A., Orobio de Castro, B., Bushman, B. J., Poorthuis, A., & Telch, M. J. (2010). I like me if you like me: On the interpersonal modulation and regulation of preadolescents' state self-esteem. *Child Development, 81*(3), 811–825. https://doi.org/10.1111/j.1467-8624.2010.01435.x

Umaña-Taylor, A. J. (2016a). A post-racial society in which ethnic-racial discrimination still exists and has significant consequences for youths' adjustment. *Current Directions in Psychological Science*, 25(2), 111–118. https://doi.org/10.1177/0963721415627858

Umaña-Taylor, A. J. (2016b). Ethnic-racial identity conceptualization, development, and youth adjustment. In L. Balter & C. S. Tamis-LeMonda (Eds.), *Child psychology: A handbook of contemporary issues* (p. 505). New York, NY: Routledge.

Umaña-Taylor, A. J., Alfaro, E. C., Bámaca, M. Y., & Guimond, A. B. (2009). The central role of familial ethnic socialization in Latino adolescents' cultural orientation. *Journal of Marriage & Family*, 71(1), 46–60. https://doi.org/10.1111/j.1741-3737.2008.00579.x

Umaña-Taylor, A. J., Quintana, S. M., Lee, R. M., Cross, W. E., Rivas-Drake, D., Schwartz, S. J., . . . Seaton, E. (2014). Ethnic and racial identity during adolescence and into young adulthood: An integrated conceptualization. *Child Development*, 85(1), 21–39. https://doi.org/10.1111/cdev.12196

Valkenburg, P. M., Koutamanis, M., & Vossen, H. G. M. (2017). The concurrent and longitudinal relationships between adolescents' use of social network sites and their social self-esteem. *Computers in Human Behavior*, 76, 35–41. https://doi.org/10.1016/J.CHB.2017.07.008

Van den Akker, A. L., Deković, M., Asscher, J., & Prinzie, P. (2014). Mean-level personality development across childhood and adolescence: A temporary defiance of the maturity principle and bidirectional associations with parenting. *Journal of Personality and Social Psychology*, 107(4), 736–750. https://doi.org/10.1037/a0037248

Van Dijk, M. P. A., Branje, S., Keijsers, L., Hawk, S. T., Hale, W. W., & Meeus, W. H. J. (2014). Self-concept clarity across adolescence: Longitudinal associations with open communication with parents and internalizing symptoms. *Journal of Youth and Adolescence*, 43(11), 1861–1876. https://doi.org/10.1007/s10964-013-0055-x

Vanhalst, J., Luyckx, K., Scholte, R. H. J., Engels, R. C. M. E., & Goossens, L. (2013). Low self-esteem as a risk factor for loneliness in adolescence: Perceived - but not actual - social acceptance as an underlying mechanism. *Journal of Abnormal Child Psychology*, 41(7), 1067–1081. https://doi.org/10.1007/s10802-013-9751-y

Van Petegem, S., Brenning, K., Baudat, S., Beyers, W., & Zimmer-Gembeck, M. J. (2018). Intimacy development in late adolescence: Longitudinal associations with perceived parental autonomy support and adolescents' self-worth. *Journal of Adolescence*, 65, 111–122. https://doi.org/10.1016/J.ADOLESCENCE.2018.03.008

Vo-Jutabha, E. D., Dinh, K. T., McHale, J. P., & Valsiner, J. (2009). A qualitative analysis of Vietnamese adolescent identity exploration within and outside an ethnic enclave. *Journal of Youth and Adolescence*, 38(5), 672–690. https://doi.org/10.1007/s10964-008-9365-9

von Soest, T., Wichstrøm, L., & Kvalem, I. L. (2016). The development of global and domain-specific self-esteem from age 13 to 31. *Journal of Personality and Social Psychology*, 110(4), 592–608. https://doi.org/10.1037/pspp0000060

Vosylis, R., Erentaitė, R., & Crocetti, E. (2018). Global versus domain-specific identity processes. *Emerging Adulthood*, 6(1), 32–41. https://doi.org/10.1177/2167696817694698

Wagnsson, S., Lindwall, M., & Gustafsson, H. (2014). Participation in organized sport and self-esteem across adolescence: The mediating role of perceived sport competence. *Journal of Sport & Exercise Psychology*, 36(6), 584–594. https://doi.org/10.1123/jsep.2013-0137

Wakefield, W. D., & Hudley, C. (2007). Ethnic and racial identity and adolescent well-being. *Theory Into Practice*, 46(2), 147–154. https://doi.org/10.1080/00405840701233099

Wang, C., Xia, Y., Li, W., Wilson, S. M., Bush, K., & Peterson, G. (2016). Parenting behaviors, adolescent depressive symptoms, and problem behavior: The role of self-esteem and school adjustment difficulties among Chinese adolescents. *Journal of Family Issues*, 37, 520–542. https://doi.org/10.1177/0192513X14542433

Wang, M.-T., & Sheikh-Khalil, S. (2014). Does parental involvement matter for student achievement and mental health in high school? *Child Development*, 85(2), 610–625. https://doi.org/10.1111/cdev.12153

Wängqvist, M., Carlsson, J., van der Lee, M., & Frisén, A. (2016). Identity development and romantic relationships in the late twenties. *Identity*, 16(1), 24–44. https://doi.org/10.1080/15283488.2015.1121819

Wängqvist, M., Lamb, M. E., Frisén, A., & Hwang, C. P. (2015). Child and adolescent predictors of personality in early adulthood. *Child Development*, 86(4), 1253–1261. https://doi.org/10.1111/cdev.12362

White, R. M. B., Knight, G. P., Jensen, M., & Gonzales, N. A. (2018). Ethnic socialization in neighborhood contexts: Implications for ethnic attitude and identity development among Mexican-origin adolescents. *Child Development*, 89(3), 1004–1021. https://doi.org/10.1111/cdev.12772

Williams, J. L., Aiyer, S. M., Durkee, M. I., & Tolan, P. H. (2014). The protective role of ethnic identity for urban adolescent males facing multiple stressors. *Journal of Youth and Adolescence*, 43(10), 1728–1741. https://doi.org/10.1007/s10964-013-0071-x

Wilson, S., Schalet, B. D., Hicks, B. M., & Zucker, R. A. (2013). Identifying early childhood personality dimensions using the California Child Q-Set and prospective associations with behavioral and psychosocial development. *Journal of Research in Personality*, 47(4), 339–350. https://doi.org/10.1016/j.jrp.2013.02.010

Wouters, S., Doumen, S., Germeijs, V., Colpin, H., & Verschueren, K. (2013). Contingencies of self-worth in early adolescence: The antecedent role of perceived parenting. *Social Development*, 22(2), 242–258. https://doi.org/10.1111/sode.12010

Yip, T. (2014). Ethnic identity in everyday life: The influence of identity development status. *Child Development*, 85(1), 205–219. https://doi.org/10.1111/cdev.12107

Yip, T. (2018). Ethnic/racial identity—a double-edged sword? Associations with discrimination and psychological outcomes. *Current Directions in Psychological Science*, 27(3), 170–175. https://doi.org/10.1177/0963721417739348

Yoon, E., Adams, K., Clawson, A., Chang, H., Surya, S., & Jérémie-Brink, G. (2017). East Asian adolescents' ethnic identity development and cultural integration: A qualitative investigation. *Journal of Counseling Psychology*, 64(1), 65–79. https://doi.org/10.1037/cou0000181

Zapolski, T. C. B., Fisher, S., Banks, D. E., Hensel, D. J., & Barnes-Najor, J. (2017). Examining the protective effect of ethnic identity on drug attitudes and use among a diverse youth population. *Journal of Youth and Adolescence*, 46(8), 1702–1715. https://doi.org/10.1007/s10964-016-0605-0

CHAPTER 5

Ahlqvist, S., Halim, M. L., Greulich, F. K., Lurye, L. E., & Ruble, D. (2013). The potential benefits and risks of identifying as a tomboy: A social identity perspective. *Self and Identity*, 12(5), 563–581. https://doi.org/10.1080/15298868.2012.717709

Alexander, G. M., & Wilcox, T. (2012). Sex differences in early infancy. *Child Development Perspectives*, 6(4), 400–406. https://doi.org/10.1111/j.1750-8606.2012.00247.x

Alexander, G. M., Wilcox, T., & Woods, R. (2009). Sex differences in infants' visual interest in toys. *Archives of Sexual Behavior*, 38(3), 427–433. https://doi.org/10.1007/s10508-008-9430-1

Alfieri, T., Ruble, D. N., & Higgins, E. T. (1996). Gender stereotypes during adolescence: Developmental changes and the transition to junior high school. *Developmental Psychology*, 32(6), 1129–1137. https://doi.org/10.1037/0012-1649.32.6.1129

Allen, L. R., Watson, L. B., & VanMattson, S. B. (2020). Trans young adults' reflections on adolescent sources of extra-familial support. *Journal of LGBT Youth*, *17*(1), 1–23. https://doi.org/10.1080/19361653 .2019.1591323

Ardila, A., Rosselli, M., Matute, E., & Inozemtseva, O. (2011). Gender differences in cognitive development. *Developmental Psychology*, *47*(4), 984–990. https://doi.org/10.1037/a0023819

Auyeung, B., Baron-Cohen, S., Ashwin, E., Knickmeyer, R., Taylor, K., Hackett, G., & Hines, M. (2009). Fetal testosterone predicts sexually differentiated childhood behavior in girls and in boys. *Psychological Science*, *20*(2), 144–148. https://doi.org/10.1111/j.1467-9280.2009.02279.x

Baker, E. R., Tisak, M. S., & Tisak, J. (2016). What can boys and girls do? Preschoolers' perspectives regarding gender roles across domains of behavior. *Social Psychology of Education*, *19*(1), 23–39. https://doi.org/10.1007/s11218-015-9320-z

Banse, R., Gawronski, B., Rebetez, C., Gutt, H., & Morton, J. B. (2010). The development of spontaneous gender stereotyping in childhood: Relations to stereotype knowledge and stereotype flexibility. *Developmental Science*, *13*(2), 298–306. https:// doi.org/10.1111/j.1467-7687.2009.00880.x

Basow, S. (2008). Gender socialization, or how long a way has baby come? In J. C. Chrisler, C. Golden, & P. D. Rozee (Eds.), *Lectures on the psychology of women* (4th ed., pp. 81–95). Long Grove, IL: Waveland Press.

Beal, C. R. (1994). *Boys and girls: The development of gender roles*. New York. NY: McGraw-Hill.

Beatty, W. W. (1992). Gonadal hormones and sex differences in nonreproductive behaviors. In A. A. Gerall, H. Moltz, & I. L. Ward (Eds.), *Handbook of behavioral neurobiology: Vol. 11. Sexual differentiation* (pp. 85–128). New York, NY: Plenum.

Becerra-Culqui, T. A., Liu, Y., Nash, R., Cromwell, L., Flanders, W. D., Getahun, D., . . . Goodman, M. (2018). Mental health of transgender and gender nonconforming youth compared with their peers. *Pediatrics*, *141*(5), e20173845. https://doi.org/10.1542/PEDS.2017-3845

Belcher, B. R., Berrigan, D., Dodd, K. W., Emken, B. A., Chou, C.-P., & Spruijt-Metz, D. (2010). Physical activity in US youth: Effect of race/ ethnicity, age, gender, and weight status. *Medicine and Science in Sports and Exercise*, *42*(12), 2211–2221. https://doi.org/10.1249/ MSS.0b013e3181e1fbag9

Bem, S. L. (1974). The measurement of psychological androgyny. *Journal of Consulting and Clinical Psychology*, *42*(2), 155–162. https:// doi.org/10.1037/h0036215

Berenbaum, S. A., Blakemore, J. E. O., & Beltz, A. M. (2011). A role for biology in gender-related behavior. *Sex Roles*, *64*(11–12), 804–825. https://doi.org/10.1007/s11199-011-9990-8

Best, D. L., & Williams, J. E. (2001). Gender and culture. In D. Matsumoto (Ed.), *The handbook of culture and psychology* (pp. 195–219). Oxford, England: Oxford University Press.

Bian, L., Leslie, S.-J., & Cimpian, A. (2017). Gender stereotypes about intellectual ability emerge early and influence children's interests. *Science*, *355*(6323), 389–391. https://doi.org/10.1126/science. aah6524

Birkett, M., Newcomb, M. E., & Mustanski, B. (2015). Does it get better? A longitudinal analysis of psychological distress and victimization in lesbian, gay, bisexual, transgender, and questioning youth. *Journal of Adolescent Health*, *56*(3), 280–285. https:// doi.org/10.1016/j.jadohealth.2014.10.275

Blakemore, J. E. O. (2003). Children's beliefs about violating gender norms: Boys shouldn't look like girls, and girls shouldn't act like boys. *Sex Roles*, *48*(9/10), 411–419. https://doi.org/10.1023 /A:1023574427720

Blakemore, J. E. O., Berenbaum, S. A., & Liben, L. S. (2009). *Gender development*. New York, NY: Psychology Press.

Bonifacio, J. H., Maser, C., Stadelman, K., & Palmert, M. (2019). Management of gender dysphoria in adolescents in primary care. *Canadian Medical Association Journal*, *191*(3), E69–E75. https://doi. org/10.1503/cmaj.180672

Bornstein, M. H., Cote, L. R., Maital, S., Painter, K., Park, S.-Y., Pascual, L., . . . Vyt, A. (2004). Cross-linguistic analysis of vocabulary in young children: Spanish, Dutch, French, Hebrew, Italian, Korean, and American English. *Child Development*, *75*(4), 1115–1139.

Braams, B. R., van Duijvenvoorde, A. C. K., Peper, J. S., & Crone, E. A. (2015). Longitudinal changes in adolescent risk-taking: A comprehensive study of neural responses to rewards, pubertal development, and risk-taking behavior. *Journal of Neuroscience*, *35*(18), 7226–7238. https://doi.org/10.1523/ JNEUROSCI.4764-14.2015

Brown, C. S., & Stone, E. A. (2016). Gender stereotypes and discrimination. *In Advances in child development and behavior* (Vol. *50*, pp. 105–133). Philadelphia, PA: Elsevier. https://doi.org/10.1016/ bs.acdb.2015.11.001

Buckley, T. R. (2018). Black adolescent males: Intersections among their gender role identity and racial identity and associations with self-concept (global and school). *Child Development*, *89*(4), e311–e322. https://doi.org/10.1111/cdev.12950

Bukowski, W. M., Panarello, B., & Santo, J. B. (2017). Androgyny in liking and in being liked are antecedent to well-being in pre-adolescent boys and girls. *Sex Roles*, *76*(11–12), 719–730. https:// doi.org/10.1007/s11199-016-0638-6

Bussey, K. (2013). Gender development. In M. K. Ryan & N. R. Branscombe (Eds.), *The SAGE handbook of gender and psychology* (pp. 81–100). Thousand Oaks, CA: Sage.

Byrnes, J. P., & Takahira, S. (1993). Explaining gender differences on SAT-math items. *Developmental Psychology*, *29*(5), 805–810. https:// doi.org/10.1037/0012-1649.29.5.805

Campbell, A., Shirley, L., & Candy, J. (2004). A longitudinal study of gender-related cognition and behaviour. *Developmental Science*, *7*(1), 1–9. https://doi.org/10.1111/j.1467-7687.2004.00316.x

Card, N. A., Stucky, B. D., Sawalani, G. M., & Little, T. D. (2008). Direct and indirect aggression during childhood and adolescence: A meta-analytic review of gender differences, intercorrelations, and relations to maladjustment. *Child Development*, *79*(5), 1185–1229. https://doi.org/10.1111/j.1467-8624.2008.01184.x

Cauce, A., & Domenech-Rodriguez, M. (2002). Latino families: Myths and realities. In J. M., J. M. Contreras, K. A. Kerns, & A. M. Neal-Barnett (Eds.), *Latino children and families in the United States* (pp. 2–25). Westport, CT: Praeger.

Ceci, S. J., Ginther, D. K., Kahn, S., & Williams, W. M. (2014). Women in academic science. *Psychological Science in the Public Interest*, *15*(3), 75–141. https://doi.org/10.1177/1529100614541236

Chaplin, T. M., & Aldao, A. (2013). Gender differences in emotion expression in children: A meta-analytic review. *Psychological Bulletin*, *139*(4), 735–765. https://doi.org/10.1037/a0030737

Clark, T. C., Lucassen, M. F. G., Bullen, P., Denny, S. J., Fleming, T. M., Robinson, E. M., & Rossen, F. V. (2014). The health and well-being of transgender high school students: Results from the New Zealand Adolescent Health Survey (Youth'12). *Journal of Adolescent Health*, *55*(1), 93–99. https://doi.org/10.1016/j.jadohealth.2013.11.008

College Board. (2018). *2018 total group SAT suite of assessments annual report*. Retrieved from https://reports.collegeboard.org/ pdf/2018-total-group-sat-suite-assessments-annual-report.pdf

Colley, R. C., Garriguet, D., Janssen, I., Craig, C. L., Clarke, J., & Tremblay, M. S. (2011). Physical activity of Canadian adults: Accelerometer results from the 2007 to 2009 Canadian Health Measures Survey. *Statistics Canada*, *22*(1). Retrieved from https://www150.statcan.gc.ca/n1/en/pub/82-003-x/2011001/ article/11396-eng.pdf?st=xgAD9Eg0

Connolly, M. D., Zervos, M. J., Barone, C. J., Johnson, C. C., & Joseph, C. L. M. (2016). The mental health of transgender youth: Advances in understanding. *Journal of Adolescent Health*, *59*(5), 489–495. https://doi.org/10.1016/j.jadohealth.2016.06.012

Côté, S. M. (2009). A developmental perspective on sex differences in aggressive behaviours. In R. E. Tremblay, M. A. G. van Aken, & W. Koops (Eds.), *Development and prevention of behaviour problems: From genes to social policy* (pp. 143–163). New York, NY: Psychology Press.

Crissman, H. P., Berger, M. B., Graham, L. F., & Dalton, V. K. (2017). Transgender demographics: A household probability sample of US adults, 2014. *American Journal of Public Health*, *107*(2), 213–215. https://doi.org/10.2105/AJPH.2016.303571

Cunningham, M., Swanson, D. P., & Hayes, D. M. (2013). School- and community-based associations to hypermasculine attitudes in African American adolescent males. *The American Journal of Orthopsychiatry*, *83*(2–3), 244–251. https://doi.org/10.1111/ajop.12029

Cvencek, D., Meltzoff, A. N., & Greenwald, A. G. (2011). Math-gender stereotypes in elementary school children. *Child Development*, *82*(3), 766–779. https://doi.org/10.1111/j.1467-8624.2010.01529.x

Dasgupta, N., & Stout, J. G. (2014). Girls and women in science, technology, engineering, and mathematics. *Policy Insights from the Behavioral and Brain Sciences*, *1*(1), 21–29. https://doi.org/10.1177/2372732214549471

de Waal, F. B. M. (1993). Sex differences in chimpanzee (and human) behavior: A matter of social values? In M. Hechter, L. Nadel, & R. E. Michod (Eds.), *The origin of values* (pp. 285–303). New York, NY: Aldine de Gruyter.

Deardorff, J., Hoyt, L. T., Carter, R., & Shirtcliff, E. A. (2019). Next steps in puberty research: Broadening the lens toward understudied populations. *Journal of Research on Adolescence*, *29*(1), 133–154. https://doi.org/10.1111/jora.12402

Dickey, L. M., Hendricks, M. L., & Bockting, W. O. (2016). Innovations in research with transgender and gender nonconforming people and their communities. *Psychology of Sexual Orientation and Gender Diversity*, *3*(2), 187–194. https://doi.org/10.1037/sgd0000158

Diekman, A. B., Brown, E. R., Johnston, A. M., & Clark, E. K. (2010). Seeking congruity between goals and roles. *Psychological Science*, *21*(8), 1051–1057. https://doi.org/10.1177/0956797610377342

Donovan, R. A., & West, L. M. (2015). Stress and mental health. *Journal of Black Psychology*, *41*(4), 384–396. https://doi.org/10.1177/0095798414543014

Durwood, L., McLaughlin, K. A., & Olson, K. R. (2017). Mental health and self-worth in socially transitioned transgender youth. *Journal of the American Academy of Child and Adolescent Psychiatry*, *56*(2), 116-123.e2. https://doi.org/10.1016/j.jaac.2016.10.016

Egan, S. K., & Perry, D. G. (2001). Gender identity: A multidimensional analysis with implications for psychosocial adjustment. *Developmental Psychology*, *37*(4), 451–463. https://doi.org/10.1037/0012-1649.37.4.451

Else-Quest, N. M., Higgins, A., Allison, C., & Morton, L. C. (2012). Gender differences in self-conscious emotional experience: A meta-analysis. *Psychological Bulletin*, *138*(5), 947–981. https://doi.org/10.1037/a0027930

Else-Quest, N. M., & Hyde, J. S. (2018). *The psychology of women and gender*. Thousand Oaks, CA: Sage.

Endendijk, J. J., Groeneveld, M. G., Bakermans-Kranenburg, M. J., & Mesman, J. (2016). Gender-differentiated parenting revisited: Meta-analysis reveals very few differences in parental control of boys and girls. *PLoS ONE*, *11*(7), e0159193. https://doi.org/10.1371/journal.pone.0159193

England, D. E., Descartes, L., & Collier-Meek, M. A. (2011). Gender role portrayal and the Disney princesses. *Sex Roles*, *64*(7–8), 555–567. https://doi.org/10.1007/s11199-011-9930-7

Fast, A. A., & Olson, K. R. (2018). Gender development in transgender preschool children. *Child Development*, *89*(2), 620–637. https://doi.org/10.1111/cdev.12758

Fitzpatrick, M., & McPherson, B. (2010). Coloring within the lines: Gender stereotypes in contemporary coloring books. *Sex Roles*, *62*(1/2), 127–137. https://doi.org/10.1007/s11199-009-9703-8

Galambos, N. L., Almeida, D. M., & Petersen, A. C. (1990). Masculinity, femininity, and sex role attitudes in early adolescence: Exploring gender intensification. *Child Development*, *61*(6), 1905–1914. https://doi.org/10.1111/j.1467-8624.1990.tb03574.x

Galambos, N. L., Berenbaum, S. A., & McHale, S. M. (2009). Gender development in adolescence. In R. M. Lerner & L. Steinberg (Eds.), *Handbook of adolescent psychology* (Vol. 1, pp. 305–357). Hoboken, NJ: John Wiley & Sons. https://doi.org/10.1002/9780470479193.adlpsy001011

Gates, G. J. (2011). How many people are lesbian, gay, bisexual and transgender? *UCLA: The Williams Institute*. Retrieved from https://escholarship.org/uc/item/09h684x2

Ghavami, N., & Peplau, L. A. (2013). An Intersectional analysis of gender and ethnic stereotypes. *Psychology of Women Quarterly*, *37*(1), 113–127. https://doi.org/10.1177/0361684312464203

Ghavami, N., & Peplau, L. A. (2018). Urban middle school students' stereotypes at the intersection of sexual orientation, ethnicity, and gender. *Child Development*, *89*(3), 881–896. https://doi.org/10.1111/cdev.12763

Goddings, A.-L., Beltz, A., Peper, J. S., Crone, E. A., & Braams, B. R. (2019). Understanding the role of puberty in structural and functional development of the adolescent brain. *Journal of Research on Adolescence*, *29*(1), 32–53. https://doi.org/10.1111/jora.12408

Gottschalk, L. (2003). Same-sex sexuality and childhood gender non-conformity: A spurious connection. *Journal of Gender Studies*, *12*(1), 35–50. https://doi.org/10.1080/0958923032000067808

Gridley, S. J., Crouch, J. M., Evans, Y., Eng, W., Antoon, E., Lyapustina, M., … Breland, D. J. (2016). Youth and caregiver perspectives on barriers to gender-affirming health care for transgender youth. *Journal of Adolescent Health*, *59*(3), 254–261. https://doi.org/10.1016/J.JADOHEALTH.2016.03.017

Guimond, S., Chatard, A., & Lorenzi-Cioldi, F. (2013). The social psychology of gender across cultures. In M. K. Ryan (Ed.), *The SAGE handbook of gender and psychology* (pp. 216–233). Thousand Oaks, CA: Sage. https://doi.org/10.4135/9781446269930.n14

Haines, E. L., Deaux, K., & Lofaro, N. (2016). The times they are a-changing . . . or are they not? A comparison of gender stereotypes, 1983–2014. *Psychology of Women Quarterly*, *40*(3), 353–363. https://doi.org/10.1177/0361684316634081

Halim, M. L. D., Ruble, D. N., Tamis-LeMonda, C. S., Shrout, P. E., & Amodio, D. M. (2017). Gender attitudes in early childhood: Behavioral consequences and cognitive antecedents. *Child Development*, *88*(3), 882–899. https://doi.org/10.1111/cdev.12642

Halim, M. L., Ruble, D. N., Tamis-LeMonda, C. S., Zosuls, K. M., Lurye, L. E., & Greulich, F. K. (2014). Pink frilly dresses and the avoidance of all things "girly": Children's appearance rigidity and cognitive theories of gender development. *Developmental Psychology*, *50*(4), 1091–1101. https://doi.org/10.1037/a0034906

Halim, M. L., Ruble, D., Tamis-LeMonda, C., & Shrout, P. E. (2013). Rigidity in gender-typed behaviors in early childhood: A longitudinal study of ethnic minority children. *Child Development*, *84*(4), 1269–1284. https://doi.org/10.1111/cdev.12057

Halpern, H. P., & Perry-Jenkins, M. (2016). Parents' gender ideology and gendered behavior as predictors of children's gender-role attitudes: A longitudinal exploration. *Sex Roles*, *74*(11–12), 527–542. https://doi.org/10.1007/s11199-015-0539-0

Hanish, L. D., Fabes, R. A., Leaper, C., Bigler, R., Hayes, A. R., Hamilton, V., & Beltz, A. M. (2013). Gender: Early socialization.

In E. T. Gershoff, R. S. Mistry, & D. A. Crosby (Eds.), *Societal contexts of child development: Pathways of influence and implications for practice and policy*. Oxford, England: Oxford University Press.

Harter, S. (2006). Developmental and individual difference perspectives on self-esteem. In D. K. Mroczek & T. D. Little (Eds.), *Handbook of personality development* (pp. 311–334). New York, NY: Psychology Press.

Hatchel, T., Valido, A., De Pedro, K. T., Huang, Y., & Espelage, D. L. (2019). Minority stress among transgender adolescents: The role of peer victimization, school belonging, and ethnicity. *Journal of Child and Family Studies, 28*(9), 2467–2476. https://doi.org/10.1007/s10826-018-1168-3

Hazel, C. E., Walls, N. E., & Pomerantz, L. (2018). Gender and sexual minority students' engagement with school: The impacts of grades, feeling unsafe, and gay/straight alliances. *Contemporary School Psychology*, 1–12. https://doi.org/10.1007/s40688-018-0199-5

Herting, M. M., & Sowell, E. R. (2017). Puberty and structural brain development in humans. *Frontiers in Neuroendocrinology, 44*, 122–137. https://doi.org/10.1016/j.yfrne.2016.12.003

Hines, M. (2011). Gender development and the human brain. *Annual Review of Neuroscience, 34*(1), 69–88. https://doi.org/10.1146/annurev-neuro-061010-113654

Hines, M. (2015). Gendered development. In R. M. Lerner (Ed.), *Handbook of child psychology and developmental science* (7th ed., pp. 1–46). Hoboken, NJ: John Wiley & Sons. https://doi.org/10.1002/9781118963418.childpsy320

Hines, M., Pasterski, V., Spencer, D., Neufeld, S., Patalay, P., Hindmarsh, P. C., . . . Acerini, C. L. (2016). Prenatal androgen exposure alters girls' responses to information indicating gender-appropriate behaviour. *Philosophical Transactions of the Royal Society of London B: Biological Sciences, 371*(1688). https://doi.org/10.1098/rstb.2015.0125

Hyde, J. S. (2014). Gender similarities and differences. *Annual Review of Psychology, 65*, 373–398. https://doi.org/10.1146/annurev-psych-010213-115057

Hyde, J. S. (2016). Sex and cognition: Gender and cognitive functions. *Current Opinion in Neurobiology, 38*, 53–56. https://doi.org/10.1016/j.conb.2016.02.007

Hyde, J. S., Bigler, R. S., Joel, D., Tate, C. C., & van Anders, S. M. (2019). The future of sex and gender in psychology: Five challenges to the gender binary. *American Psychologist, 74*(2), 171–193. https://doi.org/10.1037/amp0000307

Ioverno, S., Belser, A. B., Baiocco, R., Grossman, A. H., & Russell, S. T. (2016). The protective role of gay-straight alliances for lesbian, gay, bisexual, and questioning students: A prospective analysis. *Psychology of Sexual Orientation and Gender Diversity, 3*(4), 397–406. https://doi.org/10.1037/sgd0000193

Jadva, V., Hines, M., & Golombok, S. (2010). Infants' preferences for toys, colors, and shapes: Sex differences and similarities. *Archives of Sexual Behavior, 39*(6), 1261–1273. https://doi.org/10.1007/s10508-010-9618-z

Jewell, J. A., & Brown, C. S. (2014). Relations among gender typicality, peer relations, and mental health during early adolescence. *Social Development, 23*(1), 137–156. https://doi.org/10.1111/sode.12042

Johns, M. M., Beltran, O., Armstrong, H. L., Jayne, P. E., & Barrios, L. C. (2018). Protective factors among transgender and gender variant youth: A systematic review by socioecological level. *The Journal of Primary Prevention, 39*(3), 263–301. https://doi.org/10.1007/s10935-018-0508-9

Kågesten, A., Gibbs, S., Blum, R. W., Moreau, C., Chandra-Mouli, V., Herbert, A., & Amin, A. (2016). Understanding factors that shape gender attitudes in early adolescence globally: A mixed-methods systematic review. *PLoS ONE, 11*(6), e0157805. https://doi.org/10.1371/journal.pone.0157805

Kahn, N. F., & Halpern, C. T. (2019). Is developmental change in gender-typed behavior associated with adult sexual orientation? *Developmental Psychology, 55*(4), 855–865. https://doi.org/10.1037/dev0000662

Kanka, M. H., Wagner, P., Buchmann, M., & Spiel, C. (2019). Gender-stereotyped preferences in childhood and early adolescence: A comparison of cross-sectional and longitudinal data. *European Journal of Developmental Psychology, 16*(2), 198–214. https://doi.org/10.1080/17405629.2017.1365703

Kohlberg, L. (1966). A cognitive-developmental analysis of children's sex-role concepts and attitudes. In E. E. Maccoby (Ed.), *The development of sex differences* (pp. 82–173). Stanford, CA: Stanford University Press.

Koletić, G. (2017). Longitudinal associations between the use of sexually explicit material and adolescents' attitudes and behaviors: A narrative review of studies. *Journal of Adolescence, 57*, 119–133. https://doi.org/10.1016/J.ADOLESCENCE.2017.04.006

Kornienko, O., Santos, C. E., Martin, C. L., & Granger, K. L. (2016). Peer influence on gender identity development in adolescence. *Developmental Psychology, 52*(10), 1578–1592. https://doi.org/10.1037/dev0000200

Kosciw, J. G., Greytak, E. A., Zongrone, A. D., Caitlin Clark, M. M., & Truong, N. L. (2018). *The 2017 National School Climate Survey*. Retrieved from https://files.eric.ed.gov/fulltext/ED590243.pdf

Kurtz-Costes, B., Copping, K. E., Rowley, S. J., & Kinlaw, C. R. (2014). Gender and age differences in awareness and endorsement of gender stereotypes about academic abilities. *European Journal of Psychology of Education, 29*(4), 603–618. https://doi.org/10.1007/s10212-014-0216-7

Lam, C. B., Stanik, C., & McHale, S. M. (2017). The development and correlates of gender role attitudes in African American youth. *British Journal of Developmental Psychology, 35*, 406–419. https://doi.org/10.1111/bjdp.12182

Leahey, E., & Guo, G. (2001). Gender differences in mathematical trajectories. *Social Forces, 80*(2), 713–732. https://doi.org/10.1353/sof.2001.0102

Leaper, C. (2013). Gender development during childhood. In P. D. Zelaz (Ed.), *The Oxford handbook of developmental psychology, Vol. 2: Self and other* (pp. 326–376). Oxford, England: Oxford University Press.

Leaper, C., & Brown, C. S. (2018). Sexism in childhood and adolescence: Recent trends and advances in research. *Child Development Perspectives, 12*(1), 10–15. https://doi.org/10.1111/cdep.12247

Leaper, C., Tenenbaum, H. R., & Shaffer, T. G. (1999). Communication patterns of African-American girls and boys from low-income, urban backgrounds. *Child Development, 70*, 1489–1503.

Lefkowitz, E. S., & Zeldow, P. B. (2006). Masculinity and femininity predict optimal mental health: A belated test of the androgyny hypothesis. *Journal of Personality Assessment, 87*(1), 95–101.

Levy, G. D., & Carter, D. B. (1989). Gender schema, gender constancy, and gender-role knowledge: The roles of cognitive factors in preschoolers' gender-role stereotype attributions. *Developmental Psychology, 25*, 444–449.

Li, G., Kung, K. T. F., & Hines, M. (2017). Childhood gender-typed behavior and adolescent sexual orientation: A longitudinal population-based study. *Developmental Psychology, 53*(4), 764–777. https://doi.org/10.1037/dev0000281

Liben, L. S., Bigler, R. S., & Hilliard, L. J. (2013). Gender development. In E. T. Gershoff, R. S. Mistry, & D. A. Crosby (Eds.), *Societal contexts of child development: Pathways of influence and implications for practice and policy* (pp. 3–18). Oxford, England: Oxford University Press.

Lindberg, S. M., Hyde, J. S., Petersen, J. L., & Linn, M. C. (2010). New trends in gender and mathematics performance: A meta-analysis.

Psychological Bulletin, 136(6), 1123–1135. https://doi.org/10.1037/a0021276

Lockenhoff, C. E., Chan, W., McCrae, R. R., De Fruyt, F., Jussim, L., De Bolle, M., . . . Terracciano, A. (2014). Gender stereotypes of personality: Universal and accurate? *Journal of Cross-Cultural Psychology, 45*(5), 675–694. https://doi.org/10.1177/0022022113520075

Lopez, C. M., Solomon, D., Boulware, S. D., & Christison-Lagay, E. R. (2018). Trends in the use of puberty blockers among transgender children in the United States. *Journal of Pediatric Endocrinology and Metabolism, 31*(6), 665–670. https://doi.org/10.1515/jpem-2018-0048

Mahfouda, S., Moore, J. K., Siafarikas, A., Zepf, F. D., & Lin, A. (2017). Puberty suppression in transgender children and adolescents. *The Lancet Diabetes & Endocrinology, 5*(10), 816–826. https://doi.org/10.1016/S2213-8587(17)30099-2

Malina, R. M., Bouchard, C., & Bar-Or, O. (2004). *Growth, maturation, and physical activity* (2nd ed.). Champaign, IL: Human Kinetics.

Markstrom-Adams, C. (1989). Androgyny and its relation to adolescent psychosocial well-being: A review of the literature. *Sex Roles, 21*(5–6), 325–340. https://doi.org/10.1007/BF00289595

Martin-Storey, A. (2016). Gender, sexuality, and gender nonconformity: Understanding variation in functioning. *Child Development Perspectives, 10*(4), 257–262. https://doi.org/10.1111/cdep.12194

Martin, C., Fabes, R., Hanish, L., Leonard, S., & Dinella, L. (2011). Experienced and expected similarity to same-gender peers: Moving toward a comprehensive model of gender segregation. *Sex Roles, 65*(5/6), 421–434. https://doi.org/10.1007/s11199-011-0029-y

Martin, C. L., Kornienko, O., Schaefer, D. R., Hanish, L. D., Fabes, R. A., & Goble, P. (2013). The role of sex of peers and gender-typed activities in young children's peer affiliative networks: A longitudinal analysis of selection and influence. *Child Development, 84*(3), 921–937. https://doi.org/10.1111/cdev.12032

Martin, C. L., & Ruble, D. N. (2010). Patterns of gender development. *Annual Review of Psychology, 61*, 353–381. https://doi.org/10.1146/annurev.psych.093008.100511

Martin, C. L., Ruble, D. N., & Szkrybalo, J. (2002). Cognitive theories of early gender development. *Psychological Bulletin, 128*, 903–933.

Marx, R. A., & Kettrey, H. H. (2016). Gay-straight alliances are associated with lower levels of school-based victimization of LGBTQ+ youth: A systematic review and meta-analysis. *Journal of Youth and Adolescence, 45*(7), 1269–1282. https://doi.org/10.1007/s10964-016-0501-7

McGuire, J. K., Anderson, C. R., Toomey, R. B., & Russell, S. T. (2010). School climate for transgender youth: A mixed method investigation of student experiences and school responses. *Journal of Youth and Adolescence, 39*(10), 1175–1188. https://doi.org/10.1007/s10964-010-9540-7

McHale, S. M., Crouter, A. C., & Whiteman, S. D. (2003). The family contexts of gender development in childhood and adolescence. *Social Development, 12*(1), 125–148. https://doi.org/10.1111/1467-9507.00225

Menon, M. (2011). Does felt gender compatibility mediate influences of self-perceived gender nonconformity on early adolescents' psychosocial adjustment? *Child Development, 82*(4), 1152–1162. https://doi.org/10.1111/j.1467-8624.2011.01601.x

Miller, C. F., Trautner, H. M., & Ruble, D. N. (2006). The role of gender stereotypes in children's preferences and behavior. In L. Balter & C. S. Tamis-LeMonda (Eds.), *Child psychology: A handbook of contemporary issues* (2nd ed., pp. 293–323). New York, NY: Psychology Press.

Miller, D. I., & Halpern, D. F. (2014). The new science of cognitive sex differences. *Trends in Cognitive Sciences, 18*(1), 37–45. https://doi.org/10.1016/j.tics.2013.10.011

Mustanski, B., Andrews, R., & Puckett, J. A. (2016). The effects of cumulative victimization on mental health among lesbian, gay, bisexual, and transgender adolescents and young adults. *American Journal of Public Health, 106*(3), 527–533. https://doi.org/10.2105/AJPH.2015.302976

Mustanski, B., & Liu, R. T. (2013). A longitudinal study of predictors of suicide attempts among lesbian, gay, bisexual, and transgender youth. *Archives of Sexual Behavior, 42*(3), 437–448. https://doi.org/10.1007/s10508-012-0013-9

National Assessment of Educational Progress. (2019). NAEP mathematics: National achievement-level results. *Nation's Report Card.* Retrieved from https://www.nationsreportcard.gov/math_2017/nation/achievement?grade=8

National Center for Education Statistics. (2019). *Digest of education statistics, 2018.* Washington DC: Author.

National Coalition for Women and Girls in Education. (2017). *Title IX and athletics leveling the playing field leads to long-term success.* Retrieved from http://www.ncwge.org/TitleIX45/TitleIX and Athletics.pdf

Nguyen, T.-V., McCracken, J. T., Albaugh, M. D., Botteron, K. N., Hudziak, J. J., & Ducharme, S. (2016). A testosterone-related structural brain phenotype predicts aggressive behavior from childhood to adulthood. *Psychoneuroendocrinology, 63*, 109–118. https://doi.org/10.1016/j.psyneuen.2015.09.021

Olson, K. R. (2016). Prepubescent transgender children: What we do and do not know. *Journal of the American Academy of Child & Adolescent Psychiatry, 55*(3), 155–156. https://doi.org/10.1016/j.jaac.2015.11.015

Olson, K. R., Durwood, L., DeMeules, M., & McLaughlin, K. A. (2016). Mental health of transgender children who are supported in their identities. *Pediatrics, 137*(3), e20153223. https://doi.org/10.1542/peds.2015-3223

Olson, K. R., & Enright, E. A. (2018). Do transgender children (gender) stereotype less than their peers and siblings? *Developmental Science, 21*(4), e12606. https://doi.org/10.1111/desc.12606

Olson, K. R., & Gülgöz, S. (2018). Early findings from the TransYouth Project: Gender development in transgender children. *Child Development Perspectives, 12*(2), 93–97. https://doi.org/10.1111/cdep.12268

Olson, K. R., Key, A. C., & Eaton, N. R. (2015). Gender cognition in transgender children. *Psychological Science, 26*(4), 467–474. https://doi.org/10.1177/0956797614568156

Ostrov, J. M., & Godleski, S. A. (2010). Toward an integrated gender-linked model of aggression subtypes in early and middle childhood. *Psychological Review, 117*(1), 233–242. https://doi.org/10.1037/a0018070

Panagiotakopoulos, L. (2018). Transgender medicine - puberty suppression. *Reviews in Endocrine and Metabolic Disorders, 19*(3), 221–225. https://doi.org/10.1007/s11154-018-9457-0

Passolunghi, M. C., Rueda Ferreira, T. I., & Tomasetto, C. (2014). Math-gender stereotypes and math-related beliefs in childhood and early adolescence. *Learning and Individual Differences, 34*, 70–76. https://doi.org/10.1016/j.lindif.2014.05.005

Patterson, M. L., & Werker, J. F. (2002). Infants' ability to match dynamic phonetic and gender information in the face and voice. *Journal of Experimental Child Psychology, 81*(1), 93–115. https://doi.org/10.1006/jecp.2001.2644

Pauletti, R. E., Menon, M., Cooper, P. J., Aults, C. D., & Perry, D. G. (2017). Psychological androgyny and children's mental health: A new look with new measures. *Sex Roles, 76*(11–12), 705–718. https://doi.org/10.1007/s11199-016-0627-9

Perry, D. G., & Pauletti, R. E. (2011). Gender and adolescent development. *Journal of Research on Adolescence, 21*(1), 61–74. https://doi.org/10.1111/j.1532-7795.2010.00715.x

Peter, J., & Valkenburg, P. M. (2009). Adolescents' exposure to sexually explicit internet material and notions of women as sex objects: Assessing causality and underlying processes. *Journal of Communication*, 59(3), 407–433. https://doi.org/10.1111/j.1460-2466.2009.01422.x

Peters, S., Jolles, D. J., Duijvenvoorde, A. C. K. Van, Crone, E. A., & Peper, J. S. (2015). The link between testosterone and amygdala–orbitofrontal cortex connectivity in adolescent alcohol use. *Psychoneuroendocrinology*, 53, 117–126. https://doi.org/10.1016/J.PSYNEUEN.2015.01.004

Pilar Matud, M., Bethencourt, J. M., & Ibáñez, I. (2014). Relevance of gender roles in life satisfaction in adult people. *Personality and Individual Differences*, 70, 206–211. https://doi.org/10.1016/j.paid.2014.06.046

Prentice, D. A., & Carranza, E. (2002). What women and men should be, shouldn't be, are allowed to be, and don't have to be: The contents of prescriptive gender stereotypes. *Psychology of Women Quarterly*, 26(4), 269–281. https://doi.org/10.1111/1471-6402.t01-1-00066

Price, M., Olezeski, C., McMahon, T. J., & Hill, N. E. (2019). A developmental perspective on victimization faced by gender nonconforming youth. In H. E. Fitzgerald, D. J. Johnson, D. B. Qin, F. A. Villarruel, & J. Norder (Eds.), *Handbook of children and prejudice* (pp. 447–461). Cham, Switzerland: Springer. https://doi.org/10.1007/978-3-030-12228-7_25

Priess, H. A., & Lindberg, S. M. (2018). Gender intensification. In R. J. R. Levesque (Ed.), *Encyclopedia of adolescence* (pp. 1135–1142). New York, NY: Springer. https://doi.org/10.1007/978-1-4419-1695-2_391

Priess, H. A., Lindberg, S. M., & Hyde, J. S. (2009). Adolescent gender-role identity and mental health: Gender intensification revisited. *Child Development*, 80(5), 1531–1544. https://doi.org/10.1111/j.1467-8624.2009.01349.x

Puckett, J. A., Cleary, P., Rossman, K., Mustanski, B., & Newcomb, M. E. (2018). Barriers to gender-affirming care for transgender and gender nonconforming individuals. *Sexuality Research and Social Policy*, 15(1), 48–59. https://doi.org/10.1007/s13178-017-0295-8

Quinn, P. C., & Liben, L. S. (2014). A sex difference in mental rotation in infants: Convergent evidence. *Infancy*, 19(1), 103–116. https://doi.org/10.1111/infa.12033

Quinn, P. C., Yahr, J., Kuhn, A., Slater, A. M., & Pascalis, O. (2002). Representation of the gender of human faces by infants: A preference for female. *Perception*, 31(9), 1109–1121. https://doi.org/10.1068/p3331

Raffaelli, M., & Ontai, L. L. (2004). Gender socialization in Latino/a families: Results from two retrospective studies. *Sex Roles*, 50(5/6), 287–299. https://doi.org/10.1023/B:SERS.0000018886.58945.06

Rider, G. N., McMorris, B. J., Gower, A. L., Coleman, E., & Eisenberg, M. E. (2018). Health and care utilization of transgender and gender nonconforming youth: A population-based study. *Pediatrics*, 141(3), e20171683. https://doi.org/10.1542/peds.2017-1683

Ristori, J., & Steensma, T. D. (2016). Gender dysphoria in childhood. *International Review of Psychiatry*, 28(1), 13–20. https://doi.org/10.3109/09540261.2015.1115754

Roberts, A. L., Rosario, M., Slopen, N., Calzo, J. P., & Austin, S. B. (2013). Childhood gender nonconformity, bullying victimization, and depressive symptoms across adolescence and early adulthood: An 11-year longitudinal study. *Journal of the American Academy of Child and Adolescent Psychiatry*, 52(2), 143–152. https://doi.org/10.1016/j.jaac.2012.11.006

Rogers, A. A., DeLay, D., & Martin, C. L. (2017). Traditional masculinity during the middle school transition: Associations with depressive symptoms and academic engagement. *Journal of Youth and Adolescence*, 46(4), 709–724. https://doi.org/10.1007/s10964-016-0545-8

Rogers, L. O., Scott, M. A., & Way, N. (2015). Racial and gender identity among Black adolescent males: An intersectionality perspective. *Child Development*, 86(2), 407–424. https://doi.org/10.1111/cdev.12303

Rogers, L. O., Yang, R., Way, N., Weinberg, S. L., & Bennet, A. (2019). "We're supposed to look like girls, but act like boys": Adolescent girls' adherence to masculinity norms. *Journal of Research on Adolescence*. https://doi.org/10.1111/jora.12475

Ruble, D. N., Taylor, L. J., Cyphers, L., Greulich, F. K., Lurye, L. E., & Shrout, P. E. (2007). The role of gender constancy in early gender development. *Child Development*, 78(4), 1121–1136. https://doi.org/10.1111/j.1467-8624.2007.01056.x

Rudman, L. A., & Glick, P. (2001). Prescriptive gender stereotypes and backlash toward agentic women. *Journal of Social Issues*, 57(4), 743–762. https://doi.org/10.1111/0022-4537.00239

Russell, S. T., & Fish, J. N. (2016). Mental health in lesbian, gay, bisexual, and transgender (LGBT) youth. *Annual Review of Clinical Psychology*, 12(1), 465–487. https://doi.org/10.1146/annurev-clinpsy-021815-093153

Russell, S. T., Pollitt, A. M., Li, G., & Grossman, A. H. (2018). Chosen name use is linked to reduced depressive symptoms, suicidal ideation, and suicidal behavior among transgender youth. *The Journal of Adolescent Health*, 63(4), 503–505. https://doi.org/10.1016/j.jadohealth.2018.02.003

Ryan, C., Russell, S. T., Huebner, D., Diaz, R., & Sanchez, J. (2010). Family acceptance in adolescence and the health of LGBT young adults. *Journal of Child and Adolescent Psychiatric Nursing*, 23(4), 205–213. https://doi.org/10.1111/j.1744-6171.2010.00246.x

Safer, J. D., & Chan, K. J. (2019). Review of medical, socioeconomic, and systemic barriers to transgender care. In L. Poretsky & W. C. Hembree (Eds.), *Transgender medicine*. Cham, Switzerland: Humana Press. https://doi.org/10.1007/978-3-030-05683-4_2

Santos, C. E., Galligan, K., Pahlke, E., & Fabes, R. A. (2013). Gender-typed behaviors, achievement, and adjustment among racially and ethnically diverse boys during early adolescence. *American Journal of Orthopsychiatry*, 83(2–3), 252–264. https://doi.org/10.1111/ajop.12036

Schagen, S. E. E., Cohen-Kettenis, P. T., Delemarre-van de Waal, H. A., & Hannema, S. E. (2016). Efficacy and safety of gonadotropin-releasing hormone agonist treatment to suppress puberty in gender dysphoric adolescents. *The Journal of Sexual Medicine*, 13(7), 1125–1132. https://doi.org/10.1016/j.jsxm.2016.05.004

Scott, E., & Panksepp, J. (2003). Rough-and-tumble play in human children. *Aggressive Behavior*, 29(6), 539–551. https://doi.org/10.1002/ab.10062

Seaton, G. (2007). Toward a theoretical understanding of hypermasculine coping among urban Black adolescent males. *Journal of Human Behavior in the Social Environment*, 15(2–3), 367–390. https://doi.org/10.1300/J137v15n02_21

Seelman, K. L., Forge, N., Walls, N. E., & Bridges, N. (2015). School engagement among LGBTQ high school students: The roles of safe adults and gay–straight alliance characteristics. *Children and Youth Services Review*, 57, 19–29. https://doi.org/10.1016/J.CHILDYOUTH.2015.07.021

Serbin, L. A., Powlishta, K. K., & Gulko, J. (1993). The development of sex typing in middle childhood. *Monographs of the Society for Research in Child Development*, 58(2), 1–99. https://doi.org/10.1111/j.1540-5834.1993.tb00379.x

Shields, S. A. (2008). Gender: An intersectionality perspective. *Sex Roles*, 59(5–6), 301–311. https://doi.org/10.1007/s11199-008-9501-8

Shiffman, M., VanderLaan, D. P., Wood, H., Hughes, S. K., Owen-Anderson, A., Lumley, M. M., . . . Zucker, K. J. (2016). Behavioral and emotional problems as a function of peer relationships in adolescents with gender dysphoria: A comparison with clinical and nonclinical controls. *Psychology of Sexual Orientation and Gender Diversity*, *3*(1), 27–36. https://doi.org/10.1037/sgd0000152

Shumer, D. E., & Spack, N. P. (2013). Current management of gender identity disorder in childhood and adolescence: Guidelines, barriers and areas of controversy. *Current Opinion in Endocrinology, Diabetes, and Obesity*, *20*(1), 69–73. https://doi.org/10.1097/MED.0b013e32835c711e

Sigelman, C. K., Carr, M. B., & Begley, N. L. (1986). Developmental changes in the influence of sex-role stereotypes on person perception. *Child Study Journal*, *16*(3), 191–120. Retrieved from http://psycnet.apa.org/psycinfo/1987-10006-001

Simons, L., Schrager, S. M., Clark, L. F., Belzer, M., & Olson, J. (2013). Parental support and mental health among transgender adolescents. *Journal of Adolescent Health*, *53*(6), 791–793. https://doi.org/10.1016/j.jadohealth.2013.07.019

Smith, D. S., & Juvonen, J. (2017). Do I fit in? Psychosocial ramifications of low gender typicality in early adolescence. *Journal of Adolescence*, *60*, 161–170. https://doi.org/10.1016/j.adolescence.2017.07.014

Smith, D. S., Schacter, H. L., Enders, C., & Juvonen, J. (2018). Gender norm salience across middle schools: Contextual variations in associations between gender typicality and socioemotional distress. *Journal of Youth and Adolescence*, *47*(5), 947–960. https://doi.org/10.1007/s10964-017-0732-2

Smith, S., Pieper, K., Granados, A., & Choueiti, M. (2010). Assessing gender-related portrayals in top-grossing G-rated films. *Sex Roles*, *62*(11/12), 774–786. https://doi.org/10.1007/s11199-009-9736-z

Smith, T. E., & Leaper, C. (2006). Self-perceived gender typicality and the peer context during adolescence. *Journal of Research on Adolescence*, *16*(1), 91–104. https://doi.org/10.1111/j.1532-7795.2006.00123.x

Spencer, M. B., Fegley, S., Harpalani, V., & Seaton, G. (2004). Understanding hypermasculinity in context: A theory-driven analysis of urban adolescent males' coping responses. *Research in Human Development*, *1*(4), 229–257. https://doi.org/10.1207/s15427617rhd0104_2

Spielberg, J. M., Forbes, E. E., Ladouceur, C. D., Worthman, C. M., Olino, T. M., Ryan, N. D., & Dahl, R. E. (2015). Pubertal testosterone influences threat-related amygdala–orbitofrontal cortex coupling. *Social Cognitive and Affective Neuroscience*, *10*(3), 408–415. https://doi.org/10.1093/scan/nsu062

Steensma, T. D., & Cohen-Kettenis, P. T. (2011). Gender transitioning before puberty? *Archives of Sexual Behavior*, *40*(4), 649–650. https://doi.org/10.1007/s10508-011-9752-2

Steensma, T. D., Kreukels, B. P. C., de Vries, A. L. C., & Cohen-Kettenis, P. T. (2013). Gender identity development in adolescence. *Hormones and Behavior*, *64*(2), 288–297. https://doi.org/10.1016/j.yhbeh.2013.02.020

Steensma, T. D., McGuire, J. K., Kreukels, B. P. C., Beekman, A. J., & Cohen-Kettenis, P. T. (2013). Factors associated with desistence and persistence of childhood gender dysphoria: A quantitative follow-up study. *Journal of the American Academy of Child & Adolescent Psychiatry*, *52*(6), 582–590. https://doi.org/10.1016/J.JAAC.2013.03.016

Stevens, J., Gomez-Lobo, V., & Pine-Twaddell, E. (2015). Insurance coverage of puberty blocker therapies for transgender youth. *Pediatrics*, *136*(6), 1029–1031. https://doi.org/10.1542/peds.2015-2849

Tenenbaum, H. R., & Leaper, C. (2003). Parent-child conversations about science: The socialization of gender inequities? *Developmental Psychology*, *39*(1), 34–47. https://doi.org/10.1037/0012-1649.39.1.34

ter Bogt, T. F. M., Engels, R. C. M. E., Bogers, S., & Kloosterman, M. (2010). "Shake it baby, shake it": Media preferences, sexual attitudes

and gender stereotypes among adolescents. *Sex Roles*, *63*(11–12), 844–859. https://doi.org/10.1007/s11199-010-9815-1

Thomas, A. J., Witherspoon, K. M., & Speight, S. L. (2004). Toward the development of the Stereotypic Roles for Black Women Scale. *Journal of Black Psychology*, *30*(3), 426–442. https://doi.org/10.1177/0095798404266061

Thompson, A. E., & Voyer, D. (2014). Sex differences in the ability to recognise non-verbal displays of emotion: A meta-analysis. *Cognition and Emotion*, *28*(7), 1164–1195. https://doi.org/10.1080/02699931.2013.875889

Tisak, M. S., Holub, S. C., & Tisak, J. (2007). What nice things do boys and girls do? Preschoolers' perspectives of peers' behaviors at school and at home. *Early Education and Development*, *18*(2), 183–199.

Toomey, R. B., Card, N. A., & Casper, D. M. (2014). Peers' perceptions of gender nonconformity: Associations with overt and relational peer victimization and aggression in early adolescence. *The Journal of Early Adolescence*, *34*(4), 463–485. https://doi.org/10.1177/0272431613495446

Toomey, R. B., Syvertsen, A. K., & Shramko, M. (2018). Transgender adolescent suicide behavior. *Pediatrics*, *142*(4), e20174218. https://doi.org/10.1542/peds.2017-4218

Trautner, H. M., Ruble, D. N., Cyphers, L., Kirsten, B., Behrendt, R., & Hartmann, P. (2005). Rigidity and flexibility of gender stereotypes in childhood: Developmental or differential? *Infant and Child Development*, *14*(4), 365–381. https://doi.org/10.1002/icd.399

Turner, P. J., & Gervai, J. (1995). A multidimensional study of gender typing in preschool children and their parents: Personality, attitudes, preferences, behavior, and cultural differences. *British Journal of Developmental Psychology*, *11*, 323–342.

U.S. Bureau of Labor Statistics. (2019). *Employed persons by detailed occupation, sex, race, and Hispanic or Latino ethnicity - 2018*. Retrieved from https://www.bls.gov/cps/cpsaat11.htm

Updegraff, K. A., McHale, S. M., Zeiders, K. H., Umaña-Taylor, A. J., Perez-Brena, N. J., Wheeler, L. A., & Rodriguez De Jesús, S. A. (2014). Mexican-American adolescents' gender role attitude development: The role of adolescents' gender and nativity and parents' gender role attitudes. *Journal of Youth and Adolescence*, *43*(12), 2041–2053. https://doi.org/10.1007/s10964-014-0128-5

van Beusekom, G., Baams, L., Bos, H. M. W., Overbeek, G., & Sandfort, T. G. M. (2016). Gender nonconformity, homophobic peer victimization, and mental health: How same-sex attraction and biological sex matter. *Journal of Sex Research*, *53*(1), 98–108. https://doi.org/10.1080/00224499.2014.993462

Vance, S. R., Ehrensaft, D., & Rosenthal, S. M. (2014). Psychological and medical care of gender nonconforming youth. *Pediatrics*, *134*(6), 1184–1192. https://doi.org/10.1542/peds.2014-0772

Way, N., Cressen, J., Bodian, S., Preston, J., Nelson, J., & Hughes, D. (2014). "It might be nice to be a girl . . . Then you wouldn't have to be emotionless": Boys' resistance to norms of masculinity during adolescence. *Psychology of Men & Masculinity*, *15*(3), 241–252. https://doi.org/10.1037/a0037262

Wei, W., Lu, H., Zhao, H., Chen, C., Dong, Q., & Zhou, X. (2012). Gender differences in children's arithmetic performance are accounted for by gender differences in language abilities. *Psychological Science*, *23*(3), 320–330. https://doi.org/10.1177/0956797611427168

Weinberg, M. K., Tronick, E. Z., Cohn, J. F., & Olson, K. L. (1999). Gender differences in emotional expressivity and self-regulation during early infancy. *Developmental Psychology*, *35*(1), 175–188. https://doi.org/10.1037/0012-1649.35.1.175

Weisgram, E. S. (2016). The cognitive construction of gender stereotypes: Evidence for the dual pathways model of gender differentiation. *Sex Roles*, *75*(7–8), 301–313. https://doi.org/10.1007/s11199-016-0624-z

Wierenga, L. M., Bos, M. G. N., Schreuders, E., vd Kamp, F., Peper, J. S., Tamnes, C. K., & Crone, E. A. (2018). Unraveling age, puberty and testosterone effects on subcortical brain development across adolescence. *Psychoneuroendocrinology, 91*, 105–114. https://doi.org/10.1016/J.PSYNEUEN.2018.02.034

Ybarra, M. L., Mitchell, K. J., Palmer, N. A., & Reisner, S. L. (2015). Online social support as a buffer against online and offline peer and sexual victimization among U.S. LGBT and non-LGBT youth. *Child Abuse & Neglect, 39*, 123–136. https://doi.org/10.1016/J.CHIABU.2014.08.006

Yunger, J. L., Carver, P. R., & Perry, D. G. (2004). Does gender identity influence children's psychological well-being? *Developmental Psychology, 40*(4), 572–582. https://doi.org/10.1037/0012-1649.40.4.572

Zosuls, K. M., Andrews, N. C. Z., Martin, C. L., England, D. E., & Field, R. D. (2016). Developmental changes in the link between gender typicality and peer victimization and exclusion. *Sex Roles, 75*(5–6), 243–256. https://doi.org/10.1007/s11199-016-0608-z

Zosuls, K. M., Ruble, D. N., Tamis-LeMonda, C. S., Shrout, P. E., Bornstein, M. H., & Greulich, F. K. (2009). The acquisition of gender labels in infancy: Implications for gender-typed play. *Developmental Psychology, 45*(3), 688–701. https://doi.org/10.1037/a0014053

Zucker, K. J. (2017). Epidemiology of gender dysphoria and transgender identity. *Sexual Health, 14*(5), 404–411. https://doi.org/10.1071/SH17067

Zucker, K. J., Wood, H., Singh, D., & Bradley, S. J. (2012). A developmental, biopsychosocial model for the treatment of children with gender identity disorder. *Journal of Homosexuality, 59*(3), 369–397. https://doi.org/10.1080/00918369.2012.653309

CHAPTER 6

Akers, A. Y., Holland, C. L., & Bost, J. (2011). Interventions to improve parental communication about sex: A systematic review. *Pediatrics, 127*(3), 494–510. https://doi.org/10.1542/peds.2010-2194

Akers, A. Y., Schwarz, E. B., Borrero, S., & Corbie-Smith, G. (2010). Family discussions about contraception and family planning: A qualitative exploration of Black parent and adolescent perspectives. *Perspectives on Sexual and Reproductive Health, 42*(3), 160–167. https://doi.org/10.1363/4216010

Almy, B., Long, K., Lobato, D., Plante, W., Kao, B., & Houck, C. (2016). Perceptions of siblings' sexual activity predict sexual attitudes among at-risk adolescents. *Journal of Developmental and Behavioral Pediatrics, 36*(4), 258–266.

American College of Obstetricians and Gynecologists. (2016). *ACOG Committee Opinion number 678: Comprehensive sexuality education.* Retrieved from https://www.acog.org/Clinical-Guidance-and-Publications/Committee-Opinions/Committee-on-Adolescent-Health-Care/Comprehensive-Sexuality-Education

American Public Health Association. (2006, November 8). *Abstinence and US abstinence-only education policies: Ethical and human rights concerns. Policy Statement 200610.* Retrieved from https://www.apha.org/policies-and-advocacy/public-health-policy-statements/policy-database/2014/07/18/14/05/abstinence-and-us-abstinence-only-education-policies-ethical-and-human-rights-concerns

American Public Health Association. (2014, November 18). *Sexuality education as part of a comprehensive health education program in K to 12 schools. Policy Statement 20143.* Retrieved from https://www.apha.org/policies-and-advocacy/public-health-policy-statements/policy-database/2015/01/23/09/37/sexuality-education-as-part-of-a-comprehensive-health-education-program-in-k-to-12-schools

Angley, M., Divney, A., Magriples, U., & Kershaw, T. (2015). Social support, family functioning and parenting competence in adolescent parents. *Maternal and Child Health Journal, 19*(1), 67–73. https://doi.org/10.1007/s10995-014-1496-x

APA Council of Representatives. (1996). *Resolution on sexuality education.* Retrieved from https://www.apa.org/about/policy/sexuality-education

Aronowitz, T., & Agbeshie, E. (2012). Nature of communication: Voices of 11–14 year old African-American girls and their mothers in regard to talking about sex. *Issues in Comprehensive Pediatric Nursing, 35*(2), 75–89. https://doi.org/10.3109/01460862.2012.678260

Baams, L., Pollitt, A. M., Laub, C., & Russell, S. T. (2018). Characteristics of schools with and without gay-straight alliances. *Applied Developmental Science*, 1–6. https://doi.org/10.1080/10888691.2018.1510778

Bailey, J. M., Vasey, P. L., Diamond, L. M., Breedlove, S. M., Vilain, E., & Epprecht, M. (2016). Sexual orientation, controversy, and science. *Psychological Science in the Public Interest, 17*(2), 45–101. https://doi.org/10.1177/1529100616637616

Barnett, A. P., Molock, S. D., Nieves-Lugo, K., & Zea, M. C. (2019). Anti-LGBT victimization, fear of violence at school, and suicide risk among adolescents. *Psychology of Sexual Orientation and Gender Diversity, 6*(1), 88–95. https://doi.org/10.1037/sgd0000309

Basile, K. C., DeGue, S., Jones, K., Freire, K., Dills, J., Smith, S. G., & Raiford, J. L. (2016). *STOP SV: A technical package to prevent sexual violence.* Retrieved from https://www.cdc.gov/violenceprevention/pdf/SV-Prevention-Technical-Package.pdf

Baudry, C., Tarabulsy, G. M., Atkinson, L., Pearson, J., & St-Pierre, A. (2017). Intervention with adolescent mother–child dyads and cognitive development in early childhood: A meta-analysis. *Prevention Science, 18*(1), 116–130. https://doi.org/10.1007/s11121-016-0731-7

Bersamin, M., Todd, M., Fisher, D. A., Hill, D. L., Grube, J. W., & Walker, S. (2008). Parenting practices and adolescent sexual behavior: A longitudinal study. *Journal of Marriage & Family, 70*(1), 97–112. https://doi.org/10.1111/j.1741-3737.2007.00464.x

Birkett, M., Newcomb, M. E., & Mustanski, B. (2015). Does it get better? A longitudinal analysis of psychological distress and victimization in lesbian, gay, bisexual, transgender, and questioning youth. *Journal of Adolescent Health, 56*(3), 280–285. https://doi.org/10.1016/j.jadohealth.2014.10.275

Bosse, J. D., & Chiodo, L. (2016). It is complicated: Gender and sexual orientation identity in LGBTQ youth. *Journal of Clinical Nursing, 25*(23–24), 3665–3675. https://doi.org/10.1111/jocn.13419

Brawner, B. M., & Sutton, M. Y. (2018). Sexual health research among youth representing minority populations: To waive or not to waive parental consent. *Ethics & Behavior, 28*(7), 544–559. https://doi.org/10.1080/10508422.2017.1365303

Breiding, M. J., Chen, J., & Black, M. C. (2014). *Intimate partner violence in the United States - 2010.* Retrieved from https://www.ncjrs.gov/App/Publications/abstract.aspx?ID=267363

Breiding, M. J., Smith, S. G., Basile, K. C., Walters, M. L., Chen, J., & Merrick, M. T. (2014). Prevalence and characteristics of sexual violence, stalking, and intimate partner violence victimization — National Intimate Partner and Sexual Violence Survey, United States, 2011. *Morbidity and Mortality Weekly Report, 63*(SS08), 1–18. Retrieved from https://www.cdc.gov/mmwr/preview/mmwrhtml/ss6308a1.htm

Breuner, C. C., Mattson, G., & Committee on Psychosocial Aspects of Child and Family Health. (2016). Sexuality education for children and adolescents. *Pediatrics, 138*(2), e20161348. https://doi.org/10.1542/peds.2016-1348

Brewster, K. L. (1994). Neighborhood context and the transition to sexual activity among young Black women. *Demography, 31*(4), 603. https://doi.org/10.2307/2061794

Burrus, B. B. (2018). Decline in adolescent pregnancy in the United States: A success not shared by all. *American Journal of Public Health*, *108*(Suppl 1), S5–S6. https://doi.org/10.2105/AJPH.2017.304273

Calzo, J. P., Antonucci, T. C., Mays, V. M., & Cochran, S. D. (2011). Retrospective recall of sexual orientation identity development among gay, lesbian, and bisexual adults. *Developmental Psychology*, *47*(6), 1658–1673. https://doi.org/10.1037/a0025508

Calzo, J. P., Masyn, K. E., Austin, S. B., Jun, H.-J., & Corliss, H. L. (2017). Developmental latent patterns of identification as mostly heterosexual versus lesbian, gay, or bisexual. *Journal of Research on Adolescence*, *27*(1), 246–253. https://doi.org/10.1111/jora.12266

Carey, K. B., Norris, A. L., Durney, S. E., Shepardson, R. L., & Carey, M. P. (2018). Mental health consequences of sexual assault among first-year college women. *Journal of American College Health*, 00–00. https://doi.org/10.1080/07448481.2018.1431915

Carlson, D. L., McNulty, T. L., Bellair, P. E., & Watts, S. (2014). Neighborhoods and racial/ethnic disparities in adolescent sexual risk behavior. *Journal of Youth and Adolescence*, *43*(9), 1536–1549. https://doi.org/10.1007/s10964-013-0052-0

Casares, W. N., Lahiff, M., Eskenazi, B., & Halpern-Felsher, B. L. (2010). Unpredicted trajectories: The relationship between race/ethnicity, pregnancy during adolescence, and young women's outcomes. *Journal of Adolescent Health*, *47*(2), 143–150. https://doi.org/10.1016/j.jadohealth.2010.01.013

Cass, V. C. (1979). Homosexual identity formation. *Journal of Homosexuality*, *4*(3), 219–235. https://doi.org/10.1300/J082v04n03_01

Centers for Disease Control and Prevention. (2018a). *HIV Surveillance Report*, 2017; vol. *29*. Retrieved from https://www.cdc.gov/hiv/pdf/library/reports/surveillance/cdc-hiv-surveillance-report-2017-vol-29.pdf

Centers for Disease Control and Prevention. (2018b). *New CDC analysis shows steep and sustained increases in STDs in recent years*. Retrieved from https://www.cdc.gov/nchhstp/newsroom/2018/press-release-2018-std-prevention-conference.html

Child Trends. (2017). *Sexually active teens*. Retrieved from https://www.childtrends.org/indicators/sexually-active-teens/

Child Trends. (2019). *Key facts about teen births*. Retrieved from https://www.childtrends.org/indicators/teen-births

Cohen, K. M., & Savin-Williams, R. C. (1996). Developmental perspectives on coming out to self and others. In R. C. Savin-Williams & K. M. Cohen, *The lives of lesbians, gays, and bisexuals: Children to adults* (pp. 113–151). San Diego, CA: Harcourt Brace College Publishers. Retrieved from http://psycnet.apa.org/psycinfo/1996-97027-005

Coley, R. L., Kull, M. A., & Carrano, J. (2014). Parental endorsement of spanking and children's internalizing and externalizing problems in African American and Hispanic families. *Journal of Family Psychology*, *28*(1), 22–31. https://doi.org/10.1037/a0035272

Coley, R. L., Lombardi, C. M., Lynch, A. D., Mahalik, J. R., & Sims, J. (2013). Sexual partner accumulation from adolescence through early adulthood: The role of family, peer, and school social norms. *The Journal of Adolescent Health*, *53*(1), 91–97.e2. https://doi.org/10.1016/j.jadohealth.2013.01.005

Collibee, C., Rizzo, C., Bleiweiss, K., & Orchowski, L. M. (2019). The influence of peer support for violence and peer acceptance of rape myths on multiple forms of interpersonal violence among youth. *Journal of Interpersonal Violence*, 088626051983292. https://doi.org/10.1177/0886260519832925

Collier, K. L., van Beusekom, G., Bos, H. M. W., & Sandfort, T. G. M. (2013). Sexual orientation and gender identity/expression related peer victimization in adolescence: A systematic review of associated psychosocial and health outcomes. *Journal of Sex Research*, *50*(3–4), 299–317. https://doi.org/10.1080/00224499.2012.750639

Copen, C. E., Chandra, A., & Martinez, G. (2012, August 16). Prevalence and timing of oral sex with opposite-sex partners among females and males aged 15–24 years: United States, 2007–2010. *National Health Statistics Reports*, *56*. Retrieved from https://www.cdc.gov/nchs/data/nhsr/nhsr056.pdf

Coyle, K. K., Guinosso, S. A., Glassman, J. R., Anderson, P. M., & Wilson, H. W. (2017). Exposure to violence and sexual risk among early adolescents in urban middle schools. *The Journal of Early Adolescence*, *37*(7), 889–909. https://doi.org/10.1177/0272431616642324

Cubbin, C., Brindis, C. D., Jain, S., Santelli, J., & Braveman, P. (2010). Neighborhood poverty, aspirations and expectations, and initiation of sex. *Journal of Adolescent Health*, *47*(4), 399–406. https://doi.org/10.1016/J.JADOHEALTH.2010.02.010

Cuellar, J., Jones, D. J., & Sterrett, E. (2013). Examining parenting in the neighborhood context: A review. *Journal of Child and Family Studies*, *24*(1), 195–219. https://doi.org/10.1007/s10826-013-9826-y

Davis, B., Royne Stafford, M. B., & Pullig, C. (2014). How gay-straight alliance groups mitigate the relationship between gay-bias victimization and adolescent suicide attempts. *Journal of the American Academy of Child and Adolescent Psychiatry*, *53*(12), 1271–1278.e1. https://doi.org/10.1016/j.jaac.2014.09.010

Day, J. K., Ioverno, S., & Russell, S. T. (2019). Safe and supportive schools for LGBT youth: Addressing educational inequities through inclusive policies and practices. *Journal of School Psychology*, *74*, 29–43. https://doi.org/10.1016/J.JSP.2019.05.007

De Genna, N., Larkby, C., & Cornelius, M. (2011). Pubertal timing and early sexual intercourse in the offspring of teenage mothers. *Journal of Youth & Adolescence*, *40*(10), 1315–1328. https://doi.org/10.1007/s10964-010-9609-3

de Graaf, H., Vanwesenbeeck, I., Meijer, S., Woertman, L., & Meeus, W. (2009). Sexual trajectories during adolescence: Relation to demographic characteristics and sexual risk. *Archives of Sexual Behavior*, *38*(2), 276–282. https://doi.org/10.1007/s10508-007-9281-1

Decker, M. J., Isquick, S., Tilley, L., Zhi, Q., Gutman, A., Luong, W., & Brindis, C. D. (2018). Neighborhoods matter. A systematic review of neighborhood characteristics and adolescent reproductive health outcomes. *Health & Place*, *54*, 178–190. https://doi.org/10.1016/J.HEALTHPLACE.2018.09.001

Demissie, Z., Clayton, H. B., & Dunville, R. L. (2019). Association between receipt of school-based HIV education and contraceptive use among sexually active high school students — United States, 2011–2013. *Sex Education*, *19*(2), 237–246. https://doi.org/10.1080/14681811.2018.1501358

Denford, S., Abraham, C., Campbell, R., & Busse, H. (2017). A comprehensive review of reviews of school-based interventions to improve sexual-health. *Health Psychology Review*, *11*(1), 33–52. https://doi.org/10.1080/17437199.2016.1240625

Diamond, L. M., Bonner, S. B., & Dickenson, J. (2015). The development of sexuality. In R. M. Lerner (Ed.), *Handbook of child psychology and developmental science* (7th ed., pp. 1–44). Hoboken, NJ: John Wiley & Sons. https://doi.org/10.1002/9781118963418.childpsy321

Diamond, L. M., & Savin-Williams, R. C. (2009). Adolescent sexuality. In R. M. Lerner & L. Steinberg (Eds.), *Handbook of adolescent psychology* (p. 479). Hoboken, NJ: John Wiley & Sons.

Dittus, P. J., Michael, S. L., Becasen, J. S., Gloppen, K. M., McCarthy, K., & Guilamo-Ramos, V. (2015). Parental monitoring and its associations with adolescent sexual risk behavior: A meta-analysis. *Pediatrics*, *136*(6), e1587–e1599. https://doi.org/10.1542/peds.2015-0305

Drasin, H., Beals, K. P., Elliott, M. N., Lever, J., Klein, D. J., & Schuster, M. A. (2008). Age cohort differences in the developmental milestones of gay men. *Journal of Homosexuality*, *54*(4), 381–399. https://doi.org/10.1080/00918360801991372

Dupéré, V., Lacourse, É., Willms, J. D., Tremblay, R. E., & Leventhal, T. (2008). Neighborhood poverty and early transition to sexual activity in young adolescents: A developmental ecological approach. *Child Development*, *79*(5), 1463–1476. https://doi.org/10.1111/j.1467-8624.2008.01199.x

East, P. L., Khoo, S. T., Reyes, B. T., & Coughlin, L. (2006). AAP report on pregnancy in adolescents. *Perspectives on Sexual & Reproductive Health*, *10*, 12 pp.

Easterbrooks, M. A., Chaudhuri, J. H., Bartlett, J. D., & Copeman, A. (2011). Resilience in parenting among young mothers: Family and ecological risks and opportunities. *Children and Youth Services Review*, *33*(1), 42–50. https://doi.org/10.1016/j.childyouth.2010.08.010

Epstein, M., Furlong, M., Kosterman, R., Bailey, J. A., King, K. M., Vasilenko, S. A., . . . Hill, K. G. (2018). Adolescent age of sexual initiation and subsequent adult health outcomes. *American Journal of Public Health*, *108*(6), 822–828. https://doi.org/10.2105/AJPH.2018.304372

Ernst, M., Romeo, R. D., & Andersen, S. L. (2009). Neurobiology of the development of motivated behaviors in adolescence: A window into a neural systems model. *Pharmacology Biochemistry and Behavior*, *93*(3), 199–211. https://doi.org/10.1016/J.PBB.2008.12.013

Ethier, K. A., Kann, L., & McManus, T. (2018). Sexual intercourse among high school students — 29 states and United States overall, 2005–2015. *Morbidity and Mortality Weekly Report*, *66*(5152), 1393–1397. https://doi.org/10.15585/mmwr.mm665152a1

Federal Bureau of Investigation. (2015). *Crime in the United States, 2015*. Washington, DC: Author.

Fedina, L., Holmes, J. L., & Backes, B. L. (2018). Campus sexual assault: A systematic review of prevalence research from 2000 to 2015. *Trauma, Violence, & Abuse*, *19*(1), 76–93. https://doi.org/10.1177/1524838016631129

Finer, L. B., & Philbin, J. M. (2013). Sexual initiation, contraceptive use, and pregnancy among young adolescents. *Pediatrics*, *131*(5), 886–891. https://doi.org/10.1542/peds.2012-3495

Fitzharris, J. L., & Werner-Wilson, R. J. (2004). Multiple perspectives of parent-adolescent sexuality communication: Phenomenological description of a *Rashoman* effect. *The American Journal of Family Therapy*, *32*(4), 273–288. https://doi.org/10.1080/01926180490437367

Flores, D., & Barroso, J. (2017). 21st century parent-child sex communication in the United States: A process review. *Journal of Sex Research*, *54*(4–5), 532–548. https://doi.org/10.1080/00224499.2016.1267693

Flores, D., Docherty, S. L., Relf, M. V., McKinney, R. E., & Barroso, J. V. (2019). "It's almost like gay sex doesn't exist": Parent-child sex communication according to gay, bisexual, and queer male adolescents. *Journal of Adolescent Research*, *34*(5), 528–562. https://doi.org/10.1177/0743558418757464

Flores, D., McKinney, J. R., Arscott, J., & Barroso, J. (2018). Obtaining waivers of parental consent: A strategy endorsed by gay, bisexual, and queer adolescent males for health prevention research. *Nursing Outlook*, *66*(2), 138–148. https://doi.org/10.1016/J.OUTLOOK.2017.09.001

Floyd, F. J., & Bakeman, R. (2006). Coming-out across the life course: Implications of age and historical context. *Archives of Sexual Behavior*, *35*(3), 287–296. https://doi.org/10.1007/s10508-006-9022-x

Fortenberry, J. D. (2013). Puberty and adolescent sexuality. *Hormones and Behavior*, *64*(2), 280–287. https://doi.org/10.1016/j.yhbeh.2013.03.007

Fox, A. M., Himmelstein, G., Khalid, H., & Howell, E. A. (2019). Funding for abstinence-only education and adolescent pregnancy prevention: Does state ideology affect outcomes? *American Journal of Public Health*, *109*(3), 497–504. https://doi.org/10.2105/AJPH.2018.304896

Future of Sex Education Initiative. (2012). *National sexuality education standards: Core content and skills, K-12*. Retrieved from https://siecus.org/wp-content/uploads/2018/07/National-Sexuality-Education-Standards.pdf

Galupo, M. P., Davis, K. S., Grynkiewicz, A. L., & Mitchell, R. C. (2014). Conceptualization of sexual orientation identity among sexual minorities: Patterns across sexual and gender identity. *Journal of Bisexuality*, *14*(3–4), 433–456. https://doi.org/10.1080/15299716.2014.933466

Goodson, P., Buhi, E. R., & Dunsmore, S. C. (2006). Self-esteem and adolescent sexual behaviors, attitudes, and intentions: A systematic review. *Journal of Adolescent Health*, *38*(3), 310–319. https://doi.org/10.1016/J.JADOHEALTH.2005.05.026

Gower, A. L., Forster, M., Gloppen, K., Johnson, A. Z., Eisenberg, M. E., Connett, J. E., & Borowsky, I. W. (2018). School practices to foster LGBT-supportive climate: Associations with adolescent bullying involvement. *Prevention Science*, *19*(6), 813–821. https://doi.org/10.1007/s11121-017-0847-4

Greaves, L. M., Barlow, F. K., Lee, C. H. J., Matika, C. M., Wang, W., Lindsay, C.-J., . . . Sibley, C. G. (2017). The diversity and prevalence of sexual orientation self-labels in a New Zealand national sample. *Archives of Sexual Behavior*, *46*(5), 1325–1336. https://doi.org/10.1007/s10508-016-0857-5

Greenberg, J. S. (2017). *Exploring the dimensions of human sexuality*. Burlington, MA: Jones & Bartlett.

Guttmacher Institute. (2014). *American teens' sexual and reproductive health*. Retrieved from http://www.guttmacher.org/pubs/fb_ATSRH.html

Guttmacher Institute. (2017). *Adolescent sexual and reproductive health in the United States*. Retrieved from https://www.guttmacher.org/fact-sheet/american-teens-sexual-and-reproductive-health

Guttmacher Institute. (2019). *Sex and HIV education. State laws and policies as of September 1, 2019*. Retrieved from https://www.guttmacher.org/state-policy/explore/sex-and-hiv-education

Haas, A. P., Eliason, M., Mays, V. M., Mathy, R. M., Cochran, S. D., D'Augelli, A. R., . . . Clayton, P. J. (2011). Suicide and suicide risk in lesbian, gay, bisexual, and transgender populations: Review and recommendations. *Journal of Homosexuality*, *58*(1), 10–51. https://doi.org/10.1080/00918369.2011.534038

Hagan, J., Coleman, W., Foy, J., Rhoades, H., Plant, A., Montoya, J., & Kordic, T.; American Academy of Pediatrics Committee on Psychosocial Aspects of Child and Family Health and Committee on Adolescence. (2001). Sexuality education for children and adolescents. *Pediatrics*, *108*(2), 498–502. https://doi.org/10.1542/peds.108.2.498

Halpern, C. T., Udry, J. R., & Suchindran, C. (1997). Testosterone predicts initiation of coitus in adolescent females. *Psychosomatic Medicine*, *59*, 161–171.

Halpern, C. T., Udry, R., & Suchindran, C. (1998). Monthly measures of salivary testosterone predict sexual activity in adolescent males. *Archives of Sexual Behavior*, *27*(5), 445–465. https://doi.org/10.1023/A:1018700529128

Harper, G. W., Serrano, P. A., Bruce, D., & Bauermeister, J. A. (2016). The Internet's multiple roles in facilitating the sexual orientation identity development of gay and bisexual male adolescents. *American Journal of Men's Health*, *10*, 359–376. https://doi.org/10.1177/1557988314566227

Harries, M. D., Paglia, H. A., Redden, S. A., & Grant, J. E.-M. (2018). Age at first sexual activity: Clinical and cognitive associations. *Annals of Clinical Psychiatry*, *30*(2), 102–112. Retrieved from http://www.ncbi.nlm.nih.gov/pubmed/29697711

Haydon, A. A., Herring, A. H., Prinstein, M. J., & Halpern, C. T. (2012). Beyond age at first sex: Patterns of emerging sexual behavior in adolescence and young adulthood. *The Journal of Adolescent Health*, *50*(5), 456–463. https://doi.org/10.1016/j.jadohealth.2011.09.006

Heller, J. R., & Johnson, H. L. (2010). What are parents *really* saying when they talk with their children about sexuality? *American Journal of Sexuality Education*, *5*(2), 144–170. https://doi.org/10.1080/15546128.2010.491061

Hendrix, C. L., Stowe, Z. N., Newport, D. J., & Brennan, P. A. (2018). Physiological attunement in mother–infant dyads at clinical high risk: The influence of maternal depression and positive parenting. *Development and Psychopathology*, *30*(2), 623–634. https://doi.org/10.1017/S0954579417001158

Hock, R. (2015). *Human sexuality* (4th ed.). Boston, MA: Pearson.

Holman, D. M., Benard, V., Roland, K. B., Watson, M., Liddon, N., & Stokley, S. (2014). Barriers to human papillomavirus vaccination among US adolescents. *JAMA Pediatrics*, *168*(1), 76. https://doi.org/10.1001/jamapediatrics.2013.2752

Huang, D. Y. C., Murphy, D. A., & Hser, Y.-I. (2011). Parental monitoring during early adolescence deters adolescent sexual initiation: Discrete-time survival mixture analysis. *Journal of Child and Family Studies*, *20*(4), 511–520. https://doi.org/10.1007/s10826-010-9418-z

Jaccard, J., Blanton, H., & Dodge, T. (2005). Peer influences on risk behavior: An analysis of the effects of a close friend. *Developmental Psychology*, *41*(1), 135–147. https://doi.org/10.1037/0012-1649.41.1.135

Jaramillo, N., Buhi, E. R., Elder, J. P., & Corliss, H. L. (2017). Associations between sex education and contraceptive use among heterosexually active, adolescent males in the United States. *The Journal of Adolescent Health*, *60*(5), 534–540. https://doi.org/10.1016/j.jadohealth.2016.11.025

Jeha, D., Usta, I., Ghulmiyyah, L., & Nassar, A. (2015). A review of the risks and consequences of adolescent pregnancy. *Journal of Neonatal-Perinatal Medicine*, *8*(1), 1–8. https://doi.org/10.3233/NPM-15814038

Jerman, P., & Constantine, N. A. (2010). Demographic and psychological predictors of parent-adolescent communication about sex: A representative statewide analysis. *Journal of Youth and Adolescence*, *39*(10), 1164–1174. https://doi.org/10.1007/s10964-010-9546-1

Johnson, A. Z., Sieving, R. E., Pettingell, S. L., & McRee, A.-L. (2015). The roles of partner communication and relationship status in adolescent contraceptive use. *Journal of Pediatric Health Care*, *29*(1), 61–69. https://doi.org/10.1016/j.pedhc.2014.06.008

Juster, R.-P., Smith, N. G., Ouellet, É., Sindi, S., & Lupien, S. J. (2013). Sexual orientation and disclosure in relation to psychiatric symptoms, diurnal cortisol, and allostatic load. *Psychosomatic Medicine*, *75*(2), 103–116. https://doi.org/10.1097/PSY.0b013e3182826881

Kaestle, C. E. (2019). Sexual orientation trajectories based on sexual attractions, partners, and identity: A longitudinal investigation from adolescence through young adulthood using a U.S. representative sample. *The Journal of Sex Research*, *56*(7), 811–826. https://doi.org/10.1080/00224499.2019.1577351

Kaiser Family Foundation. (2014). *Sexual health of adolescents and young adults in the United States*. Retrieved from http://kff.org/womens-health-policy/fact-sheet/sexual-health-of-adolescents-and-young-adults-in-the-united-states/

Kann, L., Kinchen, S., Shanklin, S. L., Flint, K. H., Kawkins, J., Harris, W. A., ... Centers for Disease Control and Prevention (CDC). (2014). Youth risk behavior surveillance--United States, 2013. *Morbidity and Mortality Weekly Report: Surveillance Summaries*, *63*(Suppl 4), 1–168. Retrieved from http://www.ncbi.nlm.nih.gov/pubmed/24918634

Kann, L., McManus, T., Harris, W. A., Shanklin, S. L., Flint, K. H., Queen, B., ... Ethier, K. A. (2018). Youth Risk Behavior Surveillance—United States, 2017. *MMWR Surveillance Summaries*, *67*(8), 1. https://doi.org/10.15585/MMWR.SS6708A1

Kann, L., Olsen, E. O. M., McManus, T., Harris, W. A., Shanklin, S. L., Flint, K. H., ... & Thornton, J. (2016). Sexual identity, sex of sexual contacts, and health-related behaviors among students in grades 9-12--united states and selected sites, 2015. *Morbidity and Mortality Weekly Report. Surveillance Summaries*, *65*(SS-9):1–202. https://doi.org/10.15585/mmwr.ss6509a1

Kantor, L., & Levitz, N. (2017). Parents' views on sex education in schools: How much do Democrats and Republicans agree? *PLoS ONE*, *12*(7), e0180250. https://doi.org/10.1371/journal.pone.0180250

Kelly, Y., Zilanawala, A., Tanton, C., Lewis, R., & Mercer, C. H. (2019). Partnered Intimate activities in early adolescence—Findings from the UK Millennium Cohort Study. *Journal of Adolescent Health*, *65*(3), 397–404. https://doi.org/10.1016/J.JADOHEALTH.2019.04.028

Kerpelman, J. L., McElwain, A. D., Pittman, J. F., & Adler-Baeder, F. M. (2016). Engagement in risky sexual behavior. *Youth & Society*, *48*(1), 101–125. https://doi.org/10.1177/0044118X13479614

Kirkner, A., Relyea, M., & Ullman, S. E. (2018). PTSD and problem drinking in relation to seeking mental health and substance use treatment among sexual assault survivors. *Traumatology*, *24*(1), 1–7. https://doi.org/10.1037/trm0000126

Kiselica, M. S., & Kiselica, A. M. (2014). The complicated worlds of adolescent fathers: Implications for clinical practice, public policy, and research. *Psychology of Men & Masculinity*, *15*(3), 260–274. https://doi.org/10.1037/a0037043

Kosciw, J. G., Palmer, N. A., & Kull, R. M. (2015). Reflecting resiliency: Openness about sexual orientation and/or gender identity and its relationship to well-being and educational outcomes for LGBT students. *American Journal of Community Psychology*, *55*(1–2), 167–178. https://doi.org/10.1007/s10464-014-9642-6

Krebs, C. P., Lindquist, C. H., Warner, T. D., Fisher, B. S., & Martin, S. L. (2009). College women's experiences with physically forced, alcohol- or other drug-enabled, and drug-facilitated sexual assault before and since entering college. *Journal of American College Health*, *57*(6), 639–649. https://doi.org/10.3200/JACH.57.6.639-649

Lambert, A. J., & Raichle, K. (2000). The role of political ideology in mediating judgments of blame in rape victims and their assailants: A test of the just world, personal responsibility, and legitimization hypotheses. *Personality and Social Psychology Bulletin*, *26*(7), 853–863. https://doi.org/10.1177/0146167200269010

Lara, L. A. S., & Abdo, C. H. N. (2016). Age at time of initial sexual intercourse and health of adolescent girls. *Journal of Pediatric and Adolescent Gynecology*, *29*(5), 417–423. https://doi.org/10.1016/J.JPAG.2015.11.012

Lefkowitz, E. S., & Stoppa, T. M. (2006). Positive sexual communication and socialization in the parent-adolescent context. *New Directions for Child & Adolescent Development*, *2006*(112), 39–55.

Lefkowitz, E. S., Vasilenko, S. A., & Leavitt, C. E. (2016). Oral vs. vaginal sex experiences and consequences among first-year college students. *Archives of Sexual Behavior*, *45*(2), 329–337. https://doi.org/10.1007/s10508-015-0654-6

Legate, N., Ryan, R. M., & Weinstein, N. (2012). Is coming out always a "good thing"? Exploring the relations of autonomy support, outness, and wellness for lesbian, gay, and bisexual individuals. *Social Psychological and Personality Science*, *3*(2), 145–152. https://doi.org/10.1177/1948550611411929

Levine, J. A., Emery, C. R., & Pollack, H. (2007). The well-being of children born to teen mothers. *Journal of Marriage and Family*, *69*(1), 105–122. https://doi.org/10.1111/j.1741-3737.2006.00348.x

Lichty, L. F., & Gowen, L. K. (2018). Youth response to rape: Rape myths and social support. *Journal of Interpersonal Violence*, 088626051880577. https://doi.org/10.1177/0886260518805777

Lindberg, L. D., & Orr, M. (2011). Neighborhood-level influences on young men's sexual and reproductive health behaviors. *American*

Journal of Public Health, 101(2), 271–274. https://doi.org/10.2105/AJPH.2009.185769

Lindberg, L., Santelli, J., & Desai, S. (2016). Understanding the decline in adolescent fertility in the United States, 2007–2012. *Journal of Adolescent Health, 59*(5), 577–583. https://doi.org/10.1016/j.jadohealth.2016.06.024

Lohman, B. J., & Billings, A. (2008). Protective and risk factors associated with adolescent boys' early sexual debut and risky sexual behaviors. *Journal of Youth & Adolescence, 37*(6), 723–735. https://doi.org/10.1007/s10964-008-9283-x

Longmore, M. A., Eng, A. L., Giordano, P. C., & Manning, W. D. (2009). Parenting and adolescents' sexual initiation. *Journal of Marriage and Family, 71*(4), 969–982. https://doi.org/10.1111/j.1741-3737.2009.00647.x

Lucassen, M. F., Clark, T. C., Denny, S. J., Fleming, T. M., Rossen, F. V, Sheridan, J., . . . Robinson, E. M. (2015). What has changed from 2001 to 2012 for sexual minority youth in New Zealand? *Journal of Paediatrics and Child Health, 51*(4), 410–418. https://doi.org/10.1111/jpc.12727

Macapagal, K., Coventry, R., Arbeit, M. R., Fisher, C. B., & Mustanski, B. (2017). "I won't out myself just to do a survey": Sexual and gender minority adolescents' perspectives on the risks and benefits of sex research. *Archives of Sexual Behavior, 46*(5), 1393–1409. https://doi.org/10.1007/s10508-016-0784-5

Malamuth, N. M., Addison, T., & Koss, M. (2000). Pornography and sexual aggression: Are there reliable effects and can we understand them? *Annual Review of Sex Research, 11*, 26–91. Retrieved from http://psycnet.apa.org/psycinfo/2001-17368-002

Martin, J., Hamilton, B., & Osterman, M. (2018). Births in the United States, 2017. *NCHS Data Briefs, 318*. Retrieved from https://www.cdc.gov/nchs/data/databriefs/db318.pdf

Maxwell, L., & Scott, G. (2014). A review of the role of radical feminist theories in the understanding of rape myth acceptance. *Journal of Sexual Aggression, 20*(1), 40–54. https://doi.org/10.1080/13552600.2013.773384

Maziarz, L. N., Dake, J. A., & Glassman, T. (2019). Sex education, condom access, and contraceptive referral in U.S. high schools. *The Journal of School Nursing*, 1059840519872785. https://doi.org/10.1177/1059840519872785

McClelland, S. I., & Tolman, D. L. (2014). Adolescent sexuality. In T. Tio (Ed.), *Encyclopedia of critical psychology* (pp. 40–47). New York, NY: Springer.

McConnell, E. A., Birkett, M., & Mustanski, B. (2016). Families matter: Social support and mental health trajectories among lesbian, gay, bisexual, and transgender youth. *Journal of Adolescent Health, 59*(6), 674–680. https://doi.org/10.1016/J.JADOHEALTH.2016.07.026

McElwain, A. D., & Bub, K. L. (2018). Changes in parent–child relationship quality across early adolescence: Implications for engagement in sexual behavior. *Youth & Society, 50*(2), 204–228. https://doi.org/10.1177/0044118X15626843

McElwain, N. L., & Booth-LaForce, C. (2006). Maternal sensitivity to infant distress and nondistress as predictors of infant-mother attachment security. *Journal of Family Psychology, 20*(2), 247–255. https://doi.org/10.1037/0893-3200.20.2.247

McLeod, J. D., & Knight, S. (2010). The association of socioemotional problems with early sexual initiation. *Perspectives on Sexual and Reproductive Health, 42*(2), 93–101. https://doi.org/10.1363/4209310

McQuillan, G., Kruszon-Moran, D., Markowitz, L. E., Unger, E. R., & Paulose-Ram, R. (2017). Prevalence of HPV in adults aged 18–69: United States, 2011–2014. *NCHS Data Briefs, 280*. Retrieved from https://www.cdc.gov/nchs/data/databriefs/db280.pdf

Mellins, C. A., Walsh, K., Sarvet, A. L., Wall, M., Gilbert, L., Santelli, J. S., . . . Hirsch, J. S. (2017). Sexual assault incidents among college undergraduates: Prevalence and factors associated with risk. *PLoS ONE, 12*(11), e0186471. https://doi.org/10.1371/journal.pone.0186471

Moore, S. R., Harden, K. P., & Mendle, J. (2014). Pubertal timing and adolescent sexual behavior in girls. *Developmental Psychology, 50*(6), 1734–1745. https://doi.org/10.1037/a0036027

Negriff, S., Susman, E. J., & Trickett, P. K. (2011). The developmental pathway from pubertal timing to delinquency and sexual activity from early to late adolescence. *Journal of Youth and Adolescence, 40*(10), 1343–1356. https://doi.org/10.1007/s10964-010-9621-7

Nelson, K. M., Carey, M. P., & Fisher, C. B. (2019). Is guardian permission a barrier to online sexual health research among adolescent males interested in sex with males? *The Journal of Sex Research, 56*(4–5), 593–603. https://doi.org/10.1080/00224499.2018.1481920

Newcomb, M. E., Feinstein, B. A., Matson, M., Macapagal, K., & Mustanski, B. (2018). "I have no idea what's going on out there:" Parents' perspectives on promoting sexual health in lesbian, gay, bisexual, and transgender adolescents. *Sexuality Research and Social Policy, 15*(2), 111–122. https://doi.org/10.1007/s13178-018-0326-0

Nogueira Avelar e Silva, R., van de Bongardt, D., van de Looij-Jansen, P., Wijtzes, A., & Raat, H. (2016). Mother- and father-adolescent relationships and early sexual intercourse. *Pediatrics, 138*(6). https://doi.org/10.1542/peds.2016-0782

Oberlander, S. E., Black, M. M., & Starr, J. R. H. (2007). African American adolescent mothers and grandmothers: A multigenerational approach to parenting. *American Journal of Community Psychology, 39*(1/2), 37–46. https://doi.org/10.1007/s10464-007-9087-2

Orchowski, L. M., Untied, A. S., & Gidycz, C. A. (2013). Social reactions to disclosure of sexual victimization and adjustment among survivors of sexual assault. *Journal of Interpersonal Violence, 28*(10), 2005–2023. https://doi.org/10.1177/0886260512471085

Oxford, M. L., Gilchrist, L. D., Lohr, M. J., Gillmore, M. R., Morrison, D. M., & Spieker, S. J. (2005). Life course heterogeneity in the transition from adolescence to adulthood among adolescent mothers. *Journal of Research on Adolescence, 15*(4), 479–504.

Paik, A., Sanchagrin, K. J., & Heimer, K. (2016). Broken promises: Abstinence pledging and sexual and reproductive health. *Journal of Marriage and Family, 78*(2), 546–561. https://doi.org/10.1111/jomf.12279

Panchaud, C., & Anderson, R. (2014). A definition of comprehensive sexuality education. *Demystifying data: A guide to using evidence to improve young people's sexual health and rights*. Retrieved from https://www.guttmacher.org/sites/default/files/report_downloads/demystifying-data-handouts_0.pdf

Pazol, K., Whiteman, M. K., Folger, S. G., Kourtis, A. P., Marchbanks, P. A., & Jamieson, D. J. (2015). Sporadic contraceptive use and nonuse: Age-specific prevalence and associated factors. *American Journal of Obstetrics and Gynecology, 212*(3), 324.e1–324.e8. https://doi.org/10.1016/j.ajog.2014.10.004

Perilloux, C., Easton, J. A., & Buss, D. M. (2012). The misperception of sexual interest. *Psychological Science, 23*(2), 146–151. https://doi.org/10.1177/0956797611424162

Pinquart, M. (2017). Associations of parenting dimensions and styles with externalizing problems of children and adolescents: An updated meta-analysis. *Developmental Psychology, 53*(5), 873–932. https://doi.org/10.1037/dev0000295

Plöderl, M., Wagenmakers, E.-J., Tremblay, P., Ramsay, R., Kralovec, K., Fartacek, C., & Fartacek, R. (2013). Suicide risk and sexual orientation: A critical review. *Archives of Sexual Behavior, 42*(5), 715–727. https://doi.org/10.1007/s10508-012-0056-y

Poteat, V. P., Sinclair, K. O., DiGiovanni, C. D., Koenig, B. W., & Russell, S. T. (2013). Gay-straight alliances are associated with student health: A multischool comparison of LGBTQ and heterosexual youth. *Journal of Research on Adolescence, 23*(2), 319–330. https://doi.org/10.1111/j.1532-7795.2012.00832.x

Poteat, V. P., Yoshikawa, H., Calzo, J. P., Gray, M. L., DiGiovanni, C. D., Lipkin, A., . . . Shaw, M. P. (2015). Contextualizing gay-straight alliances: Student, advisor, and structural factors related to positive youth development among members. *Child Development*, *86*(1), 176–193. https://doi.org/10.1111/cdev.12289

Pringle, J., Mills, K. L., McAteer, J., Jepson, R., Hogg, E., Anand, N., & Blakemore, S.-J. (2017). The physiology of adolescent sexual behaviour: A systematic review. *Cogent Social Sciences*, *3*(1), 1368858. https://doi.org/10.1080/23311886.2017.1368858

Rafferty, Y., Griffin, K. W., & Lodise, M. (2011). Adolescent motherhood and developmental outcomes of children in early Head Start: The influence of maternal parenting behaviors, well-being, and risk factors within the family setting. *American Journal of Orthopsychiatry*, *81*(2), 228–245. https://doi.org/10.1111/j.1939-0025.2011.01092.x

Robinson, J. P., & Espelage, D. L. (2013). Peer victimization and sexual risk differences between lesbian, gay, bisexual, transgender, or questioning and nontransgender heterosexual youths in Grades 7-12. *American Journal of Public Health*, *103*(10), 1810–1819. https://doi.org/10.2105/AJPH.2013.301387

Rosario, M., Schrimshaw, E. W., & Hunter, J. (2009). Disclosure of sexual orientation and subsequent substance use and abuse among lesbian, gay, and bisexual youths: Critical role of disclosure reactions. *Psychology of Addictive Behaviors*, *23*(1), 175–184. https://doi.org/10.1037/a0014284

Saewyc, E. M. (2011). Research on adolescent sexual orientation: Development, health disparities, stigma, and resilience. *Journal of Research on Adolescence*, *21*(1), 256–272. https://doi.org/10.1111/j.1532-7795.2010.00727.x

Samarova, V., Shilo, G., & Diamond, G. M. (2014). Changes in youths' perceived parental acceptance of their sexual minority status over time. *Journal of Research on Adolescence*, *24*(4), 681–688. https://doi.org/10.1111/jora.12071

Sampson, R. J. (1997). Collective regulation of adolescent misbehavior. *Journal of Adolescent Research*, *12*(2), 227–244. https://doi.org/10.1177/0743554897122005

Santelli, J., Kantor, L. M., Grilo, S. A., Speizer, I. S., Lindberg, L. D., Heitel, J., . . . Ott, M. A. (2017). Abstinence-only-until-marriage: An updated review of U.S. policies and programs and their impact. *Journal of Adolescent Health*, *61*(3), 273–280. https://doi.org/10.1016/J.JADOHEALTH.2017.05.031

Santelli, J., Ott, M. A., Lyon, M., Rogers, J., & Summers, D. (2006). Abstinence-only education policies and programs: A position paper of the Society for Adolescent Medicine. *The Journal of Adolescent Health*, *38*(1), 83–87. https://doi.org/10.1016/j.jadohealth.2005.06.002

Savin-Williams, R. C. (2001). *Mom, dad. I'm gay. How families negotiate coming out*. Washington, DC: American Psychological Association. https://doi.org/10.1037/10437-000

Savin-Williams, R. C. (2016). Sexual orientation: Categories or continuum? Commentary on Bailey et al. (2016). *Psychological Science in the Public Interest*, *17*(2), 37–44. https://doi.org/10.1177/1529100616637618

Savin-Williams, R. C., & Cohen, K. M. (2015). Developmental trajectories and milestones of lesbian, gay, and bisexual young people. *International Review of Psychiatry*, *27*(5), 357–366. https://doi.org/10.3109/09540261.2015.1093465

Savin-Williams, R. C., Dubé, E. M., & Dube, E. M. (1998). Parental reactions to their child's disclosure of a gay/lesbian identity. *Family Relations*, *47*(1), 7–13. https://doi.org/10.2307/584845

Savin-Williams, R. C., Joyner, K., & Rieger, G. (2012). Prevalence and stability of self-reported sexual orientation identity during young adulthood. *Archives of Sexual Behavior*, *41*(1), 103–110. https://doi.org/10.1007/s10508-012-9913-y

Savin-Williams, R. C., & Ream, G. L. (2003). Sex variations in the disclosure to parents of same-sex attractions. *Journal of Family Psychology*, *17*(3), 429–438. https://doi.org/10.1037/0893-3200.17.3.429

Sedgh, G., Finer, L. B., Bankole, A., Eilers, M. A., & Singh, S. (2015). Adolescent pregnancy, birth, and abortion rates across countries: Levels and recent trends. *The Journal of Adolescent Health*, *56*(2), 223–230. https://doi.org/10.1016/j.jadohealth.2014.09.007

Senn, C. Y., Eliasziw, M., Barata, P. C., Thurston, W. E., Newby-Clark, I. R., Radtke, H. L., & Hobden, K. L. (2015). Efficacy of a sexual assault resistance program for university women. *New England Journal of Medicine*, *372*(24), 2326–2335. https://doi.org/10.1056/NEJMsa1411131

Shulman, E. P., Smith, A. R., Silva, K., Icenogle, G., Duell, N., Chein, J., & Steinberg, L. (2016). The dual systems model: Review, reappraisal, and reaffirmation. *Developmental Cognitive Neuroscience*, *17*, 103–117. https://doi.org/10.1016/j.dcn.2015.12.010

Sieving, R. E., Eisenberg, M. E., Pettingell, S., & Skay, C. (2006). Friends' influence on adolescents' first sexual intercourse. *Perspectives on Sexual and Reproductive Health*, *38*(1), 13–19. https://doi.org/10.1363/3801306

Sigurvinsdottir, R., & Ullman, S. E. (2015). Social reactions, self-blame, and problem drinking in adult sexual assault survivors. *Psychology of Violence*, *5*(2), 192–198. https://doi.org/10.1037/a0036316

Singh, J. A., Siddiqi, M., Parameshwar, P., & Chandra-Mouli, V. (2019). World Health Organization guidance on ethical considerations in planning and reviewing research studies on sexual and reproductive health in adolescents. *The Journal of Adolescent Health*, *64*(4), 427–429. https://doi.org/10.1016/j.jadohealth.2019.01.008

Sinozich, S., & Langton, L. (2014). *Rape and sexual assault victimization among college-age females, 1995–2013*. Retrieved from https://jpp.whs.mil/Public/docs/03_Topic-Areas/07-CM_Trends_Analysis/20150918/05_BJS_SpecialReport_SexAsslt_CollegeAge_Females.pdf

Smith, S. G., Basile, K. C., Gilbert, L. K., Merrick, M. T., Patel, N., Walling, M., & Jain, A. (2017). *National Intimate Partner and Sexual Violence Survey (NISVS): 2010-2012 state report*. Retrieved from https://stacks.cdc.gov/view/cdc/46305

Social Security Administration. (1996). *Separate program for abstinence education*. Retrieved from https://www.ssa.gov/OP_Home/ssact/title05/0510.htm

Spielberg, J. M., Olino, T. M., Forbes, E. E., & Dahl, R. E. (2014). Exciting fear in adolescence: Does pubertal development alter threat processing? *Developmental Cognitive Neuroscience*, *8*, 86–95. https://doi.org/10.1016/j.dcn.2014.01.004

Stewart, A. L. (2014). The Men's Project: A sexual assault prevention program targeting college men. *Psychology of Men & Masculinity*, *15*(4), 481–485. https://doi.org/10.1037/a0033947

Suleiman, A. B., Galván, A., Harden, K. P., & Dahl, R. E. (2017). Becoming a sexual being: The 'elephant in the room' of adolescent brain development. *Developmental Cognitive Neuroscience*, *25*, 209–220. https://doi.org/10.1016/J.DCN.2016.09.004

Tang, S., Davis-Kean, P. E., Chen, M., & Sexton, H. R. (2016). Adolescent pregnancy's intergenerational effects: Does an adolescent mother's education have consequences for her children's achievement? *Journal of Research on Adolescence*, *26*, 180–193. https://doi.org/10.1111/jora.12182

Taylor, J. L. (2009). Midlife impacts of adolescent parenthood. *Journal of Family Issues*, *30*(4), 484–510.

Trejos-Castillo, E., & Vazsonyi, A. T. (2009). Risky sexual behaviors in first and second generation Hispanic immigrant youth. *Journal of Youth & Adolescence*, *38*(5), 719–731. https://doi.org/10.1007/s10964-008-9369-5

Ueno, K. (2005). Sexual orientation and psychological distress in adolescence: Examining interpersonal stressors and social support processes. *Social Psychology Quarterly*, *68*(3), 258–277.

Umaña-Taylor, A. J., Guimond, A. B., Updegraff, K. A., & Jahromi, L. (2013). A longitudinal examination of support, self-esteem, and Mexican-origin adolescent mothers' parenting efficacy. *Journal of Marriage and the Family*, *75*(3), 746–759. https://doi.org/10.1111/jomf.12019

van de Bongardt, D., de Graaf, H., Reitz, E., & Deković, M. (2014). Parents as moderators of longitudinal associations between sexual peer norms and Dutch adolescents' sexual initiation and intention. *Journal of Adolescent Health*, *55*(3), 388–393. https://doi.org/10.1016/J.JADOHEALTH.2014.02.017

van de Bongardt, D., Reitz, E., Sandfort, T., & Deković, M. (2015). A meta-analysis of the relations between three types of peer norms and adolescent sexual behavior. *Personality and Social Psychology Review*, *19*(3), 203–234. https://doi.org/10.1177/1088868314544223

Van Houdenhove, E., Gijs, L., T'Sjoen, G., & Enzlin, P. (2015). Asexuality: A multidimensional approach. *The Journal of Sex Research*, *52*(6), 669–678. https://doi.org/10.1080/00224499.2014.898015

Vasilenko, S. A., Kugler, K. C., & Rice, C. E. (2016). Timing of first sexual intercourse and young adult health outcomes. *The Journal of Adolescent Health*, *59*(3), 291–297. https://doi.org/10.1016/j.jadohealth.2016.04.019

Vickerman, K. A., & Margolin, G. (2009). Rape treatment outcome research: Empirical findings and state of the literature. *Clinical Psychology Review*, *29*(5), 431–448. https://doi.org/10.1016/j.cpr.2009.04.004

Vincke, J., & van Heeringen, K. (2002). Confidant support and the mental wellbeing of lesbian and gay young adults: A longitudinal analysis. *Journal of Community & Applied Social Psychology*, *12*(3), 181–193. https://doi.org/10.1002/casp.671

Vrangalova, Z., & Savin-Williams, R. C. (2011). Adolescent sexuality and positive well-being: A group-norms approach. *Journal of Youth and Adolescence*, *40*(8), 931–944. https://doi.org/10.1007/s10964-011-9629-7

Walker, T. Y., Elam-Evans, L. D., Yankey, D., Markowitz, L. E., Williams, C. L., Fredua, B., . . . Stokley, S. (2019). National, regional, state, and selected local area vaccination coverage among adolescents aged 13–17 years — United States, 2018. *Morbidity and Mortality Weekly Report*, *68*(33), 718–723. https://doi.org/10.15585/mmwr.mm6833a2

Wall-Wieler, E., Roos, L. L., & Nickel, N. C. (2016). Teenage pregnancy: The impact of maternal adolescent childbearing and older sister's teenage pregnancy on a younger sister. *BMC Pregnancy and Childbirth*, *16*(1), 120. https://doi.org/10.1186/s12884-016-0911-2

Warner, T. D. (2018). Adolescent sexual risk taking: The distribution of youth behaviors and perceived peer attitudes across neighborhood contexts. *Journal of Adolescent Health*, *62*(2), 226–233. https://doi.org/10.1016/J.JADOHEALTH.2017.09.007

Warner, T. D., Giordano, P. C., Manning, W. D., & Longmore, M. A. (2011). Everybody's doin' it (right?): Neighborhood norms and sexual activity in adolescence. *Social Science Research*, *40*(6), 1676–1690. https://doi.org/10.1016/j.ssresearch.2011.06.009

Watson, R. J., Grossman, A. H., & Russell, S. T. (2019). Sources of social support and mental health among LGB youth. *Youth & Society*, *51*(1), 30–48. https://doi.org/10.1177/0044118X16660110

Wesche, R., Kreager, D. A., Lefkowitz, E. S., & Siennick, S. E. (2017). Early sexual initiation and mental health: A fleeting association or enduring change? *Journal of Research on Adolescence*, *27*(3), 611–627. https://doi.org/10.1111/jora.12303

White, C. N., & Warner, L. A. (2015). Influence of family and school-level factors on age of sexual initiation. *The Journal of Adolescent Health*, *56*(2), 231–237. https://doi.org/10.1016/j.jadohealth.2014.09.017

Widman, L., Choukas-Bradley, S., Helms, S. W., Golin, C. E., & Prinstein, M. J. (2014). Sexual communication between early adolescents and their dating partners, parents, and best friends. *Journal of Sex Research*, *51*(7), 731–741. https://doi.org/10.1080/00224499.2013.843148

Widman, L., Choukas-Bradley, S., Helms, S. W., & Prinstein, M. J. (2016a). Adolescent susceptibility to peer influence in sexual situations. *The Journal of Adolescent Health*, *58*(3), 323–329. https://doi.org/10.1016/j.jadohealth.2015.10.253

Widman, L., Choukas-Bradley, S., Noar, S. M., Nesi, J., & Garrett, K. (2016b). Parent-adolescent sexual communication and adolescent safer sex behavior: A meta-analysis. *JAMA Pediatrics*, *170*(1), 52–61. https://doi.org/10.1001/jamapediatrics.2015.2731

Wilson, E. K., Dalberth, B. T., Koo, H. P., & Gard, J. C. (2010). Parents' perspectives on talking to preteenage children about sex. *Perspectives on Sexual and Reproductive Health*, *42*(1), 56–63. https://doi.org/10.1363/4205610

Wilson, L. C., & Miller, K. E. (2016). Meta-analysis of the prevalence of unacknowledged rape. *Trauma, Violence, & Abuse*, *17*(2), 149–159. https://doi.org/10.1177/1524838015576391

Witwer, E., Jones, R., & Lindberg, L. (2018). *Sexual behavior and contraceptive and condom use among U.S. high school students, 20132017*. https://doi.org/10.1363/2018.29941

CHAPTER 7

Andolina, M. W., Jenkins, K., Zukin, C., & Keeter, S. (2003). Habits from home, lessons from school: Influences on youth civic engagement. *PS - Political Science and Politics*, *36*(2), 275–280. https://doi.org/10.1017/S104909650300221X

Ballard, P. J., Hoyt, L. T., & Pachucki, M. C. (2019). Impacts of adolescent and young adult civic engagement on health and socioeconomic status in adulthood. *Child Development*, *90*(4), 1138–1154. https://doi.org/10.1111/cdev.12998

Ballard, P. J., & Syme, S. L. (2016). Engaging youth in communities: A framework for promoting adolescent and community health. *Journal of Epidemiology and Community Health*, *70*(2), 202–206. https://doi.org/10.1136/jech-2015-206110

Barry, C. M., Nelson, L. J., & Abo-Zena, M. M. (2018). Religiousness in adolescence and emerging adulthood. In R. Levesque (Ed.), *Encyclopedia of adolescence* (pp. 3101–3126). Cham, Switzerland: Springer. https://doi.org/10.1007/978-3-319-33228-4_265

Barry, C. T., Lui, J. H. L., & Anderson, A. C. (2017). Adolescent narcissism, aggression, and prosocial behavior: The relevance of socially desirable responding. *Journal of Personality Assessment*, *99*(1), 46–55. https://doi.org/10.1080/00223891.2016.1193812

Beckert, T. E. (2007). Cognitive autonomy and self evaluation in adolescence: A conceptual investigation and instrument development. *North American Journal of Psychology*, *9*(3), 579–594.

Benson, P. L., Scales, P. C., Syvertsen, A. K., & Roehlkepartain, E. C. (2012). Is youth spiritual development a universal developmental process? An international exploration. *Journal of Positive Psychology*, *7*(6), 453–470. https://doi.org/10.1080/17439760.2012.732102

Berkowitz, M. W., & Begun, A. L. (1994). Assessing how adolescents think about the morality of substance use. *Drugs & Society*, *8*(3/4), 111.

Birkinshaw, S. (2015). Spiritual friends: An investigation of childrens spirituality in the context of British urban secondary education. *British Journal of Religious Education*, *37*(1), 83–102. https://doi.org/10.1080/01416200.2014.902806

Boom, J. J., Wouters, H., & Keller, M. (2007). A cross-cultural validation of stage development: A Rasch re-analysis of longitudinal socio-moral reasoning data. *Cognitive Development*, *22*(2), 213–229.

Brugman, D. (2010). Moral reasoning competence and the moral judgment-action discrepancy in young adolescents. In W. Koops, D.

Brugman, T. J. Ferguson, & A. F. Sanders (Eds.), *The development and structure of conscience* (pp. 119–133.). New York, NY: Psychology Press.

Caprara, G. V, Barbaranelli, C., Pastorelli, C., Bandura, A., & Zimbardo, P. G. (2000). Prosocial foundations of children's academic achievement. *Psychological Science*, *11*(4), 302–306. https://doi.org/10.1111/1467-9280.00260

Carlo, G., Crockett, L. J., Wilkinson, J. L., & Beal, S. J. (2011a). The longitudinal relationships between rural adolescents' prosocial behaviors and young adult substance use. *Journal of Youth and Adolescence*, *40*(9), 1192–1202. https://doi.org/10.1007/s10964-010-9588-4

Carlo, G., Mestre, M. V., McGinley, M. M., Tur-Porcar, A., Samper, P., & Opal, D. (2014). The protective role of prosocial behaviors on antisocial behaviors: The mediating effects of deviant peer affiliation. *Journal of Adolescence*, *37*(4), 359–366. https://doi.org/10.1016/j.adolescence.2014.02.009

Carlo, G., Mestre, M. V., Samper, P., Tur, A., & Armenta, B. E. (2011b). The longitudinal relations among dimensions of parenting styles, sympathy, prosocial moral reasoning, and prosocial behaviors. *International Journal of Behavioral Development*, *35*(2), 116–124. https://doi.org/10.1177/0165025410375921

Carlo, G., Padilla-Walker, L. M., & Nielson, M. G. (2015). Longitudinal bidirectional relations between adolescents' sympathy and prosocial behavior. *Developmental Psychology*, *51*(12), 1771–1777. https://doi.org/10.1037/dev0000056

Carlo, G., White, R. M. B., Streit, C., Knight, G. P., & Zeiders, K. H. (2018). Longitudinal relations among parenting styles, prosocial behaviors, and academic outcomes in U.S. Mexican adolescents. *Child Development*, *89*(2), 577–592. https://doi.org/10.1111/cdev.12761

Chan, M., Tsai, K. M., & Fuligni, A. J. (2015). Changes in religiosity across the transition to young adulthood. *Journal of Youth and Adolescence*, *44*(8), 1555–1566. https://doi.org/10.1007/s10964-014-0157-0

Colby, A., & Damon, W. (1992). *Some do care: Contemporary lives of moral commitment*. New York, NY: Free Press.

Comunian, A. L., & Gielen, U. P. (2000). Sociomoral reflection and prosocial and antisocial behavior: Two Italian studies. *Psychological Reports*, *87*(1), 161–176.

Dawson, T. L. (2002). New tools, new insights: Kohlberg's moral judgement stages revisited. *International Journal of Behavioral Development*, *26*(2), 154–166.

Day, R. D., Jones-Sanpei, H., Smith Price, J. L., Orthner, D. K., Hair, E. C., Moore, K. A., & Kaye, K. (2009). Family processes and adolescent religiosity and religious practice: View from the NLSY97. *Marriage and Family Review*, *45*(2–3), 289–309. https://doi.org/10.1080/01494920902735109

Dollahite, D. C., & Thatcher, J. Y. (2008). Talking about religion. *Journal of Adolescent Research*, *23*(5), 611–641. https://doi.org/10.1177/0743558408322141

Duriez, B., Smits, I., & Goossens, L. (2008). The relation between identity styles and religiosity in adolescence: Evidence from a longitudinal perspective. *Personality and Individual Differences*, *44*(4), 1022–1031. https://doi.org/10.1016/j.paid.2007.10.028

Eberly-Lewis, M. B., & Coetzee, T. M. (2015). Dimensionality in adolescent prosocial tendencies: Individual differences in serving others versus serving the self. *Personality and Individual Differences*, *82*, 1–6. https://doi.org/10.1016/j.paid.2015.02.032

Eisenberg, N., Cumberland, A., Guthrie, I. K., Murphy, B. C., & Shepard, S. A. (2005). Age changes in prosocial responding and moral reasoning in adolescence and early adulthood. *Journal of Research on Adolescence*, *15*(3), 235–260. https://doi.org/10.1111/j.1532-7795.2005.00095.x

Eisenberg, N., Spinrad, T. L., & Knafo-Noam, A. (2015). Prosocial development. In R. M. Lerner (Ed.), *Handbook of child psychology and developmental science* (pp. 1–47). Hoboken, NJ: John Wiley & Sons. https://doi.org/10.1002/9781118963418.childpsy315

Erikson, E. H. (1959). *Identity and the life cycle* (Vol. 1). New York, NY: W. W. Norton.

Espinosa, M. P., & Kovářík, J. (2015). Prosocial behavior and gender. *Frontiers in Behavioral Neuroscience*, *9*, 88. https://doi.org/10.3389/fnbeh.2015.00088

Farrell, A. D., Thompson, E. L., & Mehari, K. R. (2017). Dimensions of peer influences and their relationship to adolescents aggression, other problem behaviors and prosocial behavior. *Journal of Youth and Adolescence*, *46*, 1351–1369. https://doi.org/10.1007/s10964-016-0601-4

Ferreira, P. D., Azevedo, C. N., & Menezes, I. (2012). The developmental quality of participation experiences: Beyond the rhetoric that "participation is always good!" *Journal of Adolescence*, *35*(3), 599–610. https://doi.org/10.1016/j.adolescence.2011.09.004

Finlay, A. K., Flanagan, C., & Wray-Lake, L. (2011). Civic engagement patterns and transitions over 8 years: The AmeriCorps national study. *Developmental Psychology*, *47*(6), 1728–1743. https://doi.org/10.1037/a0025360

Flanagan, C. A., Cumsille, P., Gill, S., & Gallay, L. S. (2007). School and community climates and civic commitments: Patterns for ethnic minority and majority students. *Journal of Educational Psychology*, *99*(2), 421–431. https://doi.org/10.1037/0022-0663.99.2.421

Flanagan, C. A., Kim, T., Collura, J., & Kopish, M. A. (2015). Community service and adolescents' social capital. *Journal of Research on Adolescence*, *25*(2), 295–309. https://doi.org/10.1111/jora.12137

French, D. C., Purwono, U., & Rodkin, P. C. (2012). Religiosity of adolescents and their friends and network associates: Homophily and associations with antisocial behavior. *Journal of Research on Adolescence*, *22*(2), 326–332. https://doi.org/10.1111/j.1532-7795.2012.00778.x

Gibbs, J. C., Basinger, K. S., Grime, R. L., & Snarey, J. R. (2007). Moral judgment development across cultures: Revisiting Kohlberg's universality claims. *Developmental Review*, *27*(4), 443–500. https://doi.org/10.1016/j.dr.2007.04.001

Gilligan, C. (1982). *In a different voice: Psychological theory and women's development*. Cambridge, MA: Harvard University Press.

Gilligan, C., & Attanucci, J. (1988). Two moral orientations: Gender differences and similarities. *Merrill-Palmer Quarterly*, *34*(3), 223–237.

Godfrey, E. B., & Cherng, H. Y. S. (2016). The kids are all right? Income inequality and civic engagement among our nation's youth. *Journal of Youth and Adolescence*, *45*(11), 2218–2232. https://doi.org/10.1007/s10964-016-0557-4

Goeke-Morey, M. C., & Cummings, E. M. (2017). Religiosity and parenting: Recent directions in process-oriented research. *Current Opinion in Psychology*, *15*, 7–12. https://doi.org/10.1016/j.copsyc.2017.02.006

Granqvist, P. (2002). Attachment and religiosity in adolescence: Cross-sectional and longitudinal evaluations. *Personality and Social Psychology Bulletin*, *28*, 260–270. https://doi.org/10.1177/0146167202282011

Guillaume, C., Jagers, R., & Rivas-Drake, D. (2015). Middle school as a developmental niche for civic engagement. *American Journal of Community Psychology*, *56*(3–4), 321–331. https://doi.org/10.1007/s10464-015-9759-2

Gunnoe, M. L., & Moore, K. A. (2002). Predictors of religiosity among youth aged 17-22: A longitudinal study of the National Survey of Children. *Journal for the Scientific Study of Religion*, *41*(4), 613–622. https://doi.org/10.1111/1468-5906.00141

Güroglu, B., van den Bos, W., & Crone, E. A. (2014). Sharing and giving across adolescence: An experimental study examining the development of prosocial behavior. *Frontiers in Psychology*, 5, 291. https://doi.org/10.3389/fpsyg.2014.00291

Hardie, J. H., Pearce, L. D., & Denton, M. L. (2016). The dynamics and correlates of religious service attendance in adolescence. *Youth and Society*, *48*(2), 151–175. https://doi.org/10.1177/004411 8X13483777

Hardy, S. A., & Carlo, G. (2005, June). Religiosity and prosocial behaviours in adolescence: The mediating role of prosocial values. *Journal of Moral Education*, *34*, 231–249. https://doi.org/10.1080/03057240500127210

Hardy, S. A., & King, P. E. (2019). Processes of religious and spiritual influence in adolescence: Introduction to a special section. *Journal of Research on Adolescence*, *29*(2), 244–253. https://doi.org/10.1111/jora.12509

Hart, D., Donnelly, T. M., Youniss, J., & Atkins, R. (2007). High school community service as a predictor of adult voting and volunteering. *American Educational Research Journal*, *44*(1), 197–219. https://doi.org/10.3102/0002831206298173

Helms, S. W., Gallagher, M., Calhoun, C. D., Choukas-Bradley, S., Dawson, G. C., & Prinstein, M. J. (2015). Intrinsic religiosity buffers the longitudinal effects of peer victimization on adolescent depressive symptoms. *Journal of Clinical Child and Adolescent Psychology*, *44*(3), 471–479. https://doi.org/10.1080/15374416.2013.865195

Helwig, C. C., Arnold, M. L., Tan, D., & Boyd, D. (2007). Mainland Chinese and Canadian adolescents' judgments and reasoning about the fairness of democratic and other forms of government. *Cognitive Development*, *22*(1), 96–109.

Hoffman, M. L. (2000). *Empathy and moral development: Implications for caring and justice*. Cambridge, England: Cambridge University Press.

Holder, D. W., Durant, R. H., Harris, T. L., Daniel, J. H., Obeidallah, D., & Goodman, E. (2000). The association between adolescent spirituality and voluntary sexual activity. *Journal of Adolescent Health*, *26*(4), 295–302. https://doi.org/10.1016/S1054-139X(99)00092-0

Holmes, C., Brieant, A., King-Casas, B., & Kim-Spoon, J. (2019). How is religiousness associated with adolescent risk-taking? The roles of emotion regulation and executive function. *Journal of Research on Adolescence*, *29*(2), 334–344. https://doi.org/10.1111/jora.12438

Holmes, C. J., Kim-Spoon, J., & Deater-Deckard, K. (2016). Linking executive function and peer problems from early childhood through middle adolescence. *Journal of Abnormal Child Psychology*, *44*(1), 31–42. https://doi.org/10.1007/s10802-015-0044-5

Jaffee, S., & Hyde, J. S. (2000). Gender differences in moral orientation: A meta-analysis. *Psychological Bulletin*, *126*(5), 703.

Jennings, M. K., & Stoker, L. (2004). Social trust and civic engagement across time and generations. *Acta Politica*, *39*(4), 342–379. https://doi.org/10.1057/palgrave.ap.5500077

Jennings, M. K., Stoker, L., & Bowers, J. (2009). Politics across generations: Family transmission reexamined. *Journal of Politics*, *71*(3), 782–799. https://doi.org/10.1017/S0022381609090719

Karafantis, D. M., & Levy, S. R. (2004). The role of children's lay theories about the malleability of human attributes in beliefs about and volunteering for disadvantaged groups. *Child Development*, *75*(1), 236–250. https://doi.org/10.1111/j.1467-8624.2004.00666.x

Kim-Spoon, J., McCullough, M. E., Bickel, W. K., Farley, J. P., & Longo, G. S. (2015). Longitudinal associations among religiousness, delay discounting, and substance use initiation in early adolescence. *Journal of Research on Adolescence*, *25*(1), 36–43. https://doi.org/10.1111/jora.12104

King, P. E., & Boyatzis, C. J. (2015). Religious and spiritual development. In R. M. Lerner (Ed.)., *Handbook of child psychology and developmental science* (pp. 1–48). Hoboken, NJ: John Wiley & Sons. https://doi.org/10.1002/9781118963418.childpsy323

King, P. E., & Roeser, R. W. (2009). Religion and spirituality in adolescent development. In R.M. Lerner and L. Steinberg (Eds.), *Handbook of adolescent psychology*. Hoboken, NJ: John Wiley & Sons. https://doi.org/10.1002/9780470479193.adlpsy001014

Kirshner, B. (2007). Introduction: Youth activism as a context for learning and development. *American Behavioral Scientist*, *51*(3), 367–379. https://doi.org/10.1177/0002764207306065

Knox, P. L., Fagley, N. S., & Miller, P. M. (2004). Care and justice moral orientation among African American college students. *Journal of Adult Development*, *11*(1), 41–45.

Kohlberg, L. (1969). Stage and sequence: The cognitive-developmental approach to socialization. In D. A. Goslin (Ed.), *Handbook of socialization* (pp. 347–480). Chicago, IL: Rand McNally.

Kohlberg, L. (1976). Moral stages and moralization: The cognitive developmental approach. In T. Lickona (Ed.), *Moral development and moral behavior: Theory, research, and social issues* (pp. 31–53). New York, NY: Holt, Rinehart & Winston.

Kohlberg, L., Levine, C., & Hewer, A. (1983). Moral stages: A current formulation and a response to critics. *Contributions to Human Development*, *10*, 174.

Kohlberg, L., & Ryncarz, R. A. (1990). Beyond justice reasoning: Moral development and consideration of a seventh stage. In C. N. Alexander & E. J. Langer (Eds.), *Higher stages of human development: Perspectives on adult growth* (pp. 191–207). New York, NY: Oxford University Press.

Kuther, T. L., & Higgins-D'Alessandro, A. (2000). Bridging the gap between moral reasoning and adolescent engagement in risky behavior. *Journal of Adolescence*, *23*(4), 409–423.

Labouvie-Vief, G. (2006). Emerging structures of adult thought. In J. J. Arnett & J. L. Tanner (Eds.), *Emerging adults in America: Coming of age in the 21st century* (pp. 59–84). Washington, DC: American Psychological Association.

Laible, D., McGinley, M., Carlo, G., Augustine, M., & Murphy, T. (2014). Does engaging in prosocial behavior make children see the world through rose-colored glasses? *Developmental Psychology*, *50*(3), 872–880.

Landor, A., Simons, L. G., Simons, R. L., Brody, G. H., & Gibbons, F. X. (2011). The role of religiosity in the relationship between parents, peers, and adolescent risky sexual behavior. *Journal of Youth and Adolescence*, *40*(3), 296–309. https://doi.org/10.1007/s10964-010-9598-2

Layton, E., Dollahite, D. C., & Hardy, S. A. (2011). Anchors of religious commitment in adolescents. *Journal of Adolescent Research*, *26*(3), 381–413. https://doi.org/10.1177/0743558410391260

Lee, D. B., & Neblett, E. W. (2019). Religious development in African American adolescents: Growth patterns that offer protection. *Child Development*, *90*(1), 245–259. https://doi.org/10.1111/cdev.12896

Leenders, I., & Brugman, D. D. (2005). Moral/non-moral domain shift in young adolescents in relation to delinquent behaviour. *British Journal of Developmental Psychology*, *23*(1), 65–79.

Lenzi, M., Vieno, A., Santinello, M., Nation, M., & Voight, A. (2014a). The role played by the family in shaping early and middle adolescent civic responsibility. *The Journal of Early Adolescence*, *34*(2), 251–278. https://doi.org/10.1177/0272431613485822

Lenzi, M., Vieno, A., Sharkey, J., Mayworm, A., Scacchi, L., Pastore, M., & Santinello, M. (2014b). How school can teach civic engagement besides civic education: The role of democratic school climate. *American Journal of Community Psychology*, *54*(3–4), 251–261. https://doi.org/10.1007/s10464-014-9669-8

Lerner, R. M., Wang, J., Champine, R. B., Warren, D. J. A., & Erickson, K. (2014). Development of civic engagement: Theoretical and methodological issues1. *International Journal of Developmental Sciences*, *8*(3–4), 69–79. https://doi.org/10.3233/DEV-14130

Lopez, A. B., Huynh, V. W., & Fuligni, A. J. (2011). A longitudinal study of religious identity and participation during adolescence. *Child Development, 82*(4), 1297–1309. https://doi.org/10.1111/j.1467-8624.2011.01609.x

Ludwig, K. B., & Pittman, J. F. (1999). Adolescent prosocial values and self-efficacy in relation to delinquency, risky sexual behavior, and drug use. *Youth & Society, 30*(4), 461–482. https://doi.org/10.1177/0044118X99030004004

Luengo Kanacri, B. P., Pastorelli, C., Eisenberg, N., Zuffianò, A., & Caprara, G. V. (2013). The development of prosociality from adolescence to early adulthood: The role of effortful control. *Journal of Personality, 81*(3), 302–312. https://doi.org/10.1111/jopy.12001

Mahatmya, D., Owen, J., & Carter, R. (2018). Civic involvement. In R. Levesque (Ed.), *Encyclopedia of adolescence* (pp. 1–7). Cham, Switzerland: Springer. https://doi.org/10.1007/978-3-319-32132-5_804-1

Malin, H., Ballard, P. J., & Damon, W. (2015). Civic purpose: An integrated construct for understanding civic development in adolescence. *Human Development, 58*(2), 103–130. https://doi.org/10.1159/000381655

Malin, H., Han, H., & Liauw, I. (2017). Civic purpose in late adolescence: Factors that prevent decline in civic engagement after high school. *Developmental Psychology, 53*(7), 1384–1397. https://doi.org/10.1037/dev0000322

Malti, T., Keller, M., & Buchmann, M. (2013). Do moral choices make us feel good? The development of adolescents' emotions following moral decision making. *Journal of Research on Adolescence, 23*(2), 389–397. https://doi.org/10.1111/jora.12005

Malti, T., & Latzko, B. (2010). Children's moral emotions and moral cognition: Towards an integrative perspective. *New Directions for Child & Adolescent Development, 2010*(129), 1–10. https://doi.org/10.1002/cd.272

McCullough, M. E., & Willoughby, B. L. B. (2009). Religion, self-regulation, and self-control: Associations, explanations, and implications. *Psychological Bulletin, 135*(1), 69–93. https://doi.org/10.1037/a0014213

McFarland, D. A., & Thomas, R. J. (2006). Bowling young: How youth voluntary associations influence adult political participation. *American Sociological Review, 71*(3), 401–425. https://doi.org/10.1177/000312240607100303

McGinley, M., Lipperman-Kreda, S., Byrnes, H. F., & Carlo, G. (2010). Parental, social and dispositional pathways to Israeli adolescents' volunteering. *Journal of Applied Developmental Psychology, 31*(5), 386–394. https://doi.org/10.1016/j.appdev.2010.06.001

McIntosh, H., & Youniss, J. (2010). Toward a political theory of political socialization of youth. In L. R. Sherrod, J. Torney-Purta, & C. A. Flanagan (Eds.), *Handbook of research on civic engagement in youth* (pp. 23–41). Hoboken, NJ: John Wiley & Sons. https://doi.org/10.1002/9780470767603.ch1

Meeus, W. H. J., Iedema, J., Helsen, M., & Vollebergh, W. (1999). Patterns of adolescent identity development: Review of literature and longitudinal analysis. *Developmental Review, 19*(4), 419–461.

Metz, E., McLellan, J., & Youniss, J. (2003). Types of voluntary service and adolescents' civic development. *Journal of Adolescent Research, 18*(2), 188–203. https://doi.org/10.1177/0743558402250350

Metzger, A., Alvis, L. M., Oosterhoff, B., Babskie, E., Syvertsen, A., & Wray-Lake, L. (2018). The intersection of emotional and sociocognitive competencies with civic engagement in middle childhood and adolescence. *Journal of Youth and Adolescence, 47*(8), 1663–1683. https://doi.org/10.1007/s10964-018-0842-5

Miller, J. G. (2018). Physiological mechanisms of prosociality. *Current Opinion in Psychology, 20*, 50–54. https://doi.org/10.1016/J.COPSYC.2017.08.018

Oosterhoff, B., & Wray-Lake, L. (2019). Risky politics? Associations between adolescent risk preference and political engagement. *Child Development*, cdev.13313. https://doi.org/10.1111/cdev.13313

Ottoni-Wilhelm, M., Estell, D. B., & Perdue, N. H. (2014). Role-modeling and conversations about giving in the socialization of adolescent charitable giving and volunteering. *Journal of Adolescence, 37*(1), 53–66. https://doi.org/10.1016/j.adolescence.2013.10.010

Padilla-Walker, L. M., Carlo, G., & Memmott-Elison, M. K. (2018). Longitudinal change in adolescents' prosocial behavior toward strangers, friends, and family. *Journal of Research on Adolescence, 28*(3), 698–710. https://doi.org/10.1111/jora.12362

Padilla-Walker, L. M., Carlo, G., & Nielson, M. G. (2015a). Does helping keep teens protected? Longitudinal bidirectional relations between prosocial behavior and problem behavior. *Child Development, 86*(6), 1759–1772. https://doi.org/10.1111/cdev.12411

Padilla-Walker, L. M., & Christensen, K. J. (2011). Empathy and self-regulation as mediators between parenting and adolescents' prosocial behavior toward strangers, friends, and family. *Journal of Research on Adolescence, 21*(3), 545–551. https://doi.org/10.1111/j.1532-7795.2010.00695.x

Padilla-Walker, L. M., Dyer, W. J., Yorgason, J. B., Fraser, A. M., & Coyne, S. M. (2015b). Adolescents' prosocial behavior toward family, friends, and strangers: A person-centered approach. *Journal of Research on Adolescence, 25*(1), 135–150. https://doi.org/10.1111/jora.12102

Pancer, S. M., Pratt, M., Hunsberger, B., & Alisat, S. (2007). Community and political involvement in adolescence: What distinguishes the activists from the uninvolved? *Journal of Community Psychology, 35*(6), 741–759. https://doi.org/10.1002/jcop.20176

Park, N. S., Klemmack, D. L., Roff, L. L., Parker, M. W., Koenig, H. G., Sawyer, P., & Allman, R. M. (2008). Religiousness and longitudinal trajectories in elders' functional status. *Research on Aging, 30*(3), 279–298. https://doi.org/10.1177/0164027507313001

Penner, L. A., Dovidio, J. F., Piliavin, J. A., & Schroeder, D. A. (2005). Prosocial behavior: Multilevel perspectives. *Annual Review of Psychology, 56*(1), 365–392. https://doi.org/10.1146/annurev.psych.56.091103.070141

Peviani, K. M., Brieant, A., Holmes, C. J., King-Casas, B., & Kim-Spoon, J. (2019). Religious social support protects against social risks for adolescent substance use. *Journal of Research on Adolescence*, jora.12529. https://doi.org/10.1111/jora.12529

Poppen, P. (1974). Sex differences in moral judgment. *Personality and Social Psychology Bulletin, 1*(1), 313–315. https://doi.org/10.1177/014616727400100106

Power, F. C., Higgins, A., & Kohlberg, L. (1989). *Lawrence Kohlberg's approach to moral education*. New York, NY: Columbia University Press.

Power, L., & McKinney, C. (2013). Emerging adult perceptions of parental religiosity and parenting practices: Relationships with emerging adult religiosity and psychological adjustment. *Psychology of Religion and Spirituality, 5*(2), 99–109. https://doi.org/10.1037/a0030046

Putnick, D. L., Bornstein, M. H., Lansford, J. E., Chang, L., Deater-Deckard, K., Di Giunta, L., . . . Bombi, A. S. (2018). Parental acceptance-rejection and child prosocial behavior: Developmental transactions across the transition to adolescence in nine countries, mothers and fathers, and girls and boys. *Developmental Psychology, 54*(10), 1881–1890. https://doi.org/10.1037/dev0000565

Ream, G. L., & Savin-Williams, R. C. (2006). Religious development in adolescence. In G. R. Adams & M. D. Berzonsky (Eds), *Blackwell handbook of adolescence* (pp. 50–59). Malden, MA: Blackwell Publishing. https://doi.org/10.1002/9780470756607.ch3

Rubin, B. C. (2007). "There's still not justice": Youth civic identity development amid distinct school and community contexts. *Teachers College Record, 109*(2), 449–481.

Sánchez-Jankowski, M. (2002). Minority youth and civic engagement: The impact of group relations. *Applied Developmental Science*, 6(4), 237–245. https://doi.org/10.1207/S1532480XADS0604_11

Scales, P. C., Benson, P. L., Roehlkepartain, E. C., Sesma, A., & van Dulmen, M. (2006). The role of developmental assets in predicting academic achievement: A longitudinal study. *Journal of Adolescence*, 29(5), 691–708. https://doi.org/10.1016/j.adolescence.2005.09.001

Schonert-Reichl, K. A. (1999). Relations of peer acceptance, friendship adjustment, and social behavior to moral reasoning during early adolescence. *Journal of Early Adolescence*, 19(2), 249–279.

Silke, C., Brady, B., Boylan, C., & Dolan, P. (2018). Factors influencing the development of empathy and pro-social behaviour among adolescents: A systematic review. *Children and Youth Services Review*, 94, 421–436. https://doi.org/10.1016/j.childyouth.2018.07.027

Sinha, J. W., Cnaan, R. A., & Gelles, R. J. (2007). Adolescent risk behaviors and religion: Findings from a national study. *Journal of Adolescence*, 30(2), 231–249. https://doi.org/10.1016/j.adolescence.2006.02.005

Skitka, L. J., Bauman, C. W., & Mullen, E. (2016). Morality and justice. In C. Sabbagh & M. Schmitt (Eds.), *Handbook of social justice theory and research* (pp. 407–423). New York, NY: Springer. https://doi.org/10.1007/978-1-4939-3216-0_22

Smetana, J. G., Jambon, M., & Ball, C. (2013). The social domain approach to children's moral and social judgments. In M. Killen & J. G. Smetana (Eds.), *Handbook of moral development* (pp. 23–44). New York, NY: Psychology Press. https://doi.org/10.4324/9780203581957

Smith, C., & Snell, P. (2009). *Souls in transition: The religious and spiritual lives of emerging adults*. Oxford, England: Oxford University Press.

Snider, J. B., Clements, A., & Vazsonyi, A. T. (2004). Late adolescent perceptions of parent religiosity and parenting processes. *Family Process*, 43(4), 489–502. https://doi.org/10.1111/j.1545-5300.2004.00036.x

Tarry, H., & Emler, N. (2007). Attitude, values and moral reasoning as predictors of delinquency. *British Journal of Developmental Psychology*, 25(2), 169–183. https://doi.org/10.1348/026151006x113671

Van der Graaff, J., Carlo, G., Crocetti, E., Koot, H. M., & Branje, S. (2018). Prosocial behavior in adolescence: Gender differences in development and links with empathy. *Journal of Youth and Adolescence*, 47(5), 1086–1099. https://doi.org/10.1007/s10964-017-0786-1

van Goethem, A. A. J., van Hoof, A., van Aken, M. A. G., Orobio de Castro, B., & Raaijmakers, Q. A. W. (2014). Socialising adolescent volunteering: How important are parents and friends? Age dependent effects of parents and friends on adolescents' volunteering behaviours. *Journal of Applied Developmental Psychology*, 35(2), 94–101. https://doi.org/10.1016/j.appdev.2013.12.003

van Hoorn, J., van Dijk, E., Meuwese, R., Rieffe, C., & Crone, E. A. (2016). Peer influence on prosocial behavior in adolescence. *Journal of Research on Adolescence*, 26(1), 90–100. https://doi.org/10.1111/jora.12173

Vishkin, A., Bigman, Y., & Tamir, M. (2014). Religion, emotion regulation, and well-being. In: C. Kim-Prieto (Ed.), *Religion and spirituality across cultures* (pp. 247–269). Dordrecht, Netherlands: Springer. https://doi.org/10.1007/978-94-017-8950-9_13

Walker, L. J. (2004). Progress and prospects in the psychology of moral development. *Merrill-Palmer Quarterly*, 50(4), 546–557.

Watts, R. J., & Flanagan, C. (2007). Pushing the envelope on youth civic engagement: A developmental and liberation psychology perspective. *Journal of Community Psychology*, 35(6), 779–792. https://doi.org/10.1002/jcop.20178

Weisz, A. N., & Black, B. M. (2002). Gender and moral reasoning: African American youth respond to dating dilemmas. *Journal of Human Behavior in the Social Environment*, 5(1), 35–52.

Wentzel, K. R. (2014). Prosocial behavior and peer relations in adolescence. In L. M. Padilla-Walker & G. Carlo (Eds.), *Prosocial development: A multidimensional approach* (pp. 178–200.). Oxford, England: Oxford University Press. https://doi.org/10.1093/acprof:oso/9780199964772.001.0001

White, E. S., & Mistry, R. S. (2016). Parent civic beliefs, civic participation, socialization practices, and child civic engagement. *Applied Developmental Science*, 20(1), 44–60. https://doi.org/10.1080/10888691.2015.1049346

Wilkenfeld, B. (2009). *Does context matter? How the family, peer, school, and neighborhood contexts relate to adolescents' civic engagement*. CIRCLE Working Paper 64. Retrieved from https://civicyouth.org/PopUps/WorkingPapers/WP64Wilkenfeld.pdf

Wray-Lake, L., Metzger, A., & Syvertsen, A. K. (2017). Testing multidimensional models of youth civic engagement: Model comparisons, measurement invariance, and age differences. *Applied Developmental Science*, 21(4), 266–284. https://doi.org/10.1080/10888691.2016.1205495

Wray-Lake, L., & Syvertsen, A. K. (2011). The developmental roots of social responsibility in childhood and adolescence. *New Directions for Child and Adolescent Development*, 2011(134), 11–25. https://doi.org/10.1002/cd.308

Xiao, S. X., Hashi, E. C., Korous, K. M., & Eisenberg, N. (2019). Gender differences across multiple types of prosocial behavior in adolescence: A meta-analysis of the prosocial tendency measure-revised (PTM-R). *Journal of Adolescence*, 77, 41–58. https://doi.org/10.1016/j.adolescence.2019.09.003

Yates, M., & Youniss, J. (1996). Community service and political-moral identity in adolescents. *Journal of Research on Adolescence*, 6, 271–284.

Yonker, J. E., Schnabelrauch, C. A., & DeHaan, L. G. (2012). The relationship between spirituality and religiosity on psychological outcomes in adolescents and emerging adults: A meta-analytic review. *Journal of Adolescence*, 35(2), 299–314. https://doi.org/10.1016/j.adolescence.2011.08.010

Youniss, J., McLellan, J. A., & Yates, M. (1997). What we know about engendering civic identity. *American Behavioral Scientist*, 40(5), 620–631. https://doi.org/10.1177/0002764297040005008

Zimmer-Gembeck, M. J., & Collins, W. A. (2003). Autonomy development during adolescence. In G. R. Adams & M. Berzonsky (Eds.), *Blackwell handbook of adolescence* (pp. 175–204). Oxford, England: Blackwell.

Zimmer-Gembeck, Melanie J., Geiger, T. C., & Crick, N. R. (2005). Relational and physical aggression, prosocial behavior, and peer relations. *The Journal of Early Adolescence*, 25(4), 421–452. https://doi.org/10.1177/0272431605279841

CHAPTER 8

Abar, C. C., Jackson, K. M., Colby, S. M., & Barnett, N. P. (2015). Parent–child discrepancies in reports of parental monitoring and their relationship to adolescent alcohol-related behaviors. *Journal of Youth and Adolescence*, 44(9), 1688–1701. https://doi.org/10.1007/s10964-014-0143-6

Abrego, L. J., & Gonzales, R. G. (2010). Blocked paths, uncertain futures: The postsecondary education and labor market prospects of undocumented Latino youth. *Journal of Education for Students Placed at Risk*, 15(1–2), 144–157. https://doi.org/10.1080/10824661003635168

Adams, R. E., & Laursen, B. (2007). The correlates of conflict: Disagreement is not necessarily detrimental. *Journal of Family Psychology*, 21(3), 445–458.

Administration for Children and Families. (2019). *AFCARS Report #26*. Retrieved from https://www.acf.hhs.gov/cb/resource/afcars-report-26

Ahrons, C. R. (2007). Family ties after divorce: Long-term implications for children. *Family Process, 46*(1), 53–65. https://doi.org/10.1111/j.1545-5300.2006.00191.x

Ainsworth, M. D. S., Blehar, M. C., Waters, E., & Wall, S. (1978). *Patterns of attachment*. Hillsdale, NJ: Erlbaum.

Allen, J. P., & Loeb, E. L. (2015). The autonomy-connection challenge in adolescent peer relationships. *Child Development Perspectives, 9*(2), 101–105. https://doi.org/10.1111/cdep.12111

Allen, J. P., & Miga, E. M. (2010). Attachment in adolescence: A move to the level of emotion regulation. *Journal of Social and Personal Relationships, 27*(2), 181–190. https://doi.org/10.1177/0265407509360898

Amato, P. R. (2010). Research on divorce: Continuing trends and new developments. *Journal of Marriage & Family, 72*(3), 650–666. https://doi.org/10.1111/j.1741-3737.2010.00723.x

Amato, P. R., & Anthony, C. J. (2014). Estimating the effects of parental divorce and death with fixed effects models. *Journal of Marriage and Family, 76*(2), 370–386. https://doi.org/10.1111/jomf.12100

Amato, P. R., Kane, J. B., & James, S. (2011). Reconsidering the "good divorce." *Family Relations, 60*(5), 511–524. https://doi.org/10.1111/j.1741-3729.2011.00666.x

Amato, P. R., & Sobolewski, J. M. (2001). The effects of divorce and marital discord on adult children's psychological well-being. *American Sociological Review, 66*, 900–921.

Ammaniti, M., Van Ijzendoorn, M. H., Speranza, A. M., & Tambelli, R. (2000). Internal working models of attachment during late childhood and early adolescence: An exploration of stability and change. *Attachment and Human Development, 2*(3), 328–346. https://doi.org/10.1080/14616730010001587

Arnett, J. J. (1999). Adolescent storm and stress, reconsidered. *The American Psychologist, 54*(5), 317–326. https://doi.org/10.1037/0003-066X.54.5.317

Assadi, S. M., Zokaei, N., Kaviani, H., Mohammadi, M. R., Ghaeli, P., Gohari, M. R., & van de Vijver, F. J. R. (2007). Effect of sociocultural context and parenting style on scholastic achievement among Iranian adolescents. *Social Development, 16*, 169–180.

Barone, L., Lionetti, F., & Green, J. (2017). A matter of attachment? How adoptive parents foster post-institutionalized children's social and emotional adjustment. *Attachment & Human Development, 19*(4), 323–339. https://doi.org/10.1080/14616734.2017.1306714

Baumrind, D. (1971). Current patterns of parental authority. *Developmental Psychology, 4*(Monograph 1), 1–103.

Baumrind, D. (2013). Authoritative parenting revisited: History and current status. In R. E. Larzelere, A. S. Morris, & A. W. Harrist (Eds.), *Authoritative parenting: Synthesizing nurturance and discipline for optimal child development* (pp. 11–34). Washington, DC: American Psychological Association.

Belsky, J., & Cassidy, J. (1994). Attachment and close relationships: An individual-difference perspective. *Psychological Inquiry, 5*(1), 27–30. https://doi.org/10.1207/s15327965pli0501_3

Bender, K., Yang, J., Ferguson, K., & Thompson, S. (2015). Experiences and needs of homeless youth with a history of foster care. *Children and Youth Services Review, 55*, 222–231. https://doi.org/10.1016/j.childyouth.2015.06.007

Bendezú, J. J., Pinderhughes, E. E., Hurley, S. M., McMahon, R. J., & Racz, S. J. (2018). Longitudinal relations among parental monitoring strategies, knowledge, and adolescent delinquency in a racially diverse at-risk sample. *Journal of Clinical Child and Adolescent Psychology, 47*(Suppl 1), S21–S34. https://doi.org/10.1080/15374416.2016.1141358

Beyers, W., & Goossens, L. (1999). Emotional autonomy, psychosocial adjustment and parenting: Interactions, moderating and mediating effects. *Journal of Adolescence, 22*(6), 753–769. https://doi.org/10.1006/jado.1999.0268

Bing, N. M., Nelson, W. M., & Wesolowski, K. L. (2009). Comparing the effects of amount of conflict on children's adjustment following parental divorce. *Journal of Divorce & Remarriage, 50*(3), 159–171. https://doi.org/10.1080/10502550902717699

Blos, P. (1967). The second individuation process of adolescence. *The Psychoanalytic Study of the Child, 22*, 162–186. https://doi.org/10.1080/00797308.1967.11822595

Bornstein, M. H. (2015). Children's parents. In R. M. Lerner (Ed.), *Handbook of child psychology and developmental science* (pp. 1–78). Hoboken, NJ: John Wiley & Sons. https://doi.org/10.1002/9781118963418.childpsy403

Bornstein, M. H., & Putnick, D. L. (2018). Parent–adolescent relationships in global perspective. In J. E. Lansford & P. Banati (Eds.), *Handbook of adolescent development research and its impact on global policy* (pp. 107–129). New York, NY: Oxford University Press.

Bos, H. M. W., Knox, J. R., van Rijn-van Gelderen, L., & Gartrell, N. K. (2016). Same-sex and different-sex parent households and child health outcomes. *Journal of Developmental & Behavioral Pediatrics, 37*(3), 179–187. https://doi.org/10.1097/DBP.0000000000000288

Bowlby, J. (1969). *Attachment and loss, Vol. 1: Attachment*. New York, NY: Basic Books.

Bowlby, J. (1973). *Attachment and loss, Vol. 2: Separation: Anxiety and anger*. New York, NY: Basic Books.

Bowlby, J. (1988). *A secure base: Clinical applications of attachment theory*. London, England: Routledge.

Branje, S. (2018). Development of parent-adolescent relationships: Conflict interactions as a mechanism of change. *Child Development Perspectives, 12*(3), 171–176. https://doi.org/10.1111/cdep.12278

Branje, S., Laursen, B., & Collins, W. A. (2013). Parent-child communication during adolescence. In A. L. Vangelisti (Ed.), *Routledge handbook of family communication* (2nd ed., p. 601). New York, NY: Routledge. Retrieved from https://www.routledge.com/The-Routledge-Handbook-of-Family-Communication-2nd-Edition/Vangelisti/p/book/9780415881975

Bratberg, E., & Tjøtta, S. (2008). Income effects of divorce in families with dependent children. *Journal of Population Economics, 21*(2), 439–461. https://doi.org/10.1007/s00148-005-0029-8

Bretherton, I., & Munholland, K. (2016). The internal working model construct in light of contemporary neuroimaging research. In *Handbook of attachment: Theory, research, and clinical applications* (pp. 63–88). New York, NY: Guilford Press.

Brody, G. H., & Flor, D. L. (1998). Maternal resources, parenting practices, and child competence in rural, single-parent African American families. *Child Development, 69*, 803–816.

Brooker, R. J., Berenbaum, S. A., Bricker, J., Corley, R. P., & Wadsworth, S. A. (2012). Pubertal timing as a potential mediator of adoption effects on problem behaviors. *Journal of Research on Adolescence, 22*(4), 739–745. https://doi.org/10.1111/j.1532-7795.2012.00820.x

Brown, A., Waters, C. S., & Shelton, K. H. (2017). A systematic review of the school performance and behavioural and emotional adjustments of children adopted from care. *Adoption & Fostering, 41*(4), 346–368. https://doi.org/10.1177/0308575917731064

Buchanan, C. M., & Holmbeck, G. N. (1998). Measuring beliefs about adolescent personality and behavior. *Journal of Youth and Adolescence, 27*(5), 607–627. https://doi.org/10.1023/A:1022835107795

Buist, K. L. (2018). Attachment during adolescence. In R. J. R. Levesque (Ed.), *Encyclopedia of adolescence* (pp. 1–6). Cham, Switzerland: Springer. https://doi.org/10.1007/978-3-319-32132-5_4-2

Burton, L. M., & Jarrett, R. L. (2000). In the mix, yet on the margins: The place of families in urban neighborhood and child development research. *Journal of Marriage and Family, 62*(4), 1114–1135. https://doi.org/10.1111/j.1741-3737.2000.01114.x

Campione-Barr, N. (2017). The changing nature of power, control, and influence in sibling relationships. *New Directions for Child and Adolescent Development, 2017*(156), 7–14. https://doi.org/10.1002/cad.20202

Cauce, A. M. (2008). Parenting, culture, and context: Reflections on excavating culture. *Applied Developmental Science, 12*(4), 227–229. https://doi.org/10.1080/10888690802388177

Chung, G. H., Flook, L., & Fuligni, A. J. (2009). Daily family conflict and emotional distress among adolescents from Latin American, Asian, and European backgrounds. *Developmental Psychology, 45*(5), 1406–1415. https://doi.org/10.1037/a0014163

Collins, W. A., & Steinberg, L. (2006). Adolescent development in interpersonal context. In N. Eisenberg, W. Damon, & R. M. Lerner (Eds.), *Handbook of child psychology, Vol. 3: Social, emotional, and personality development* (6th ed., pp. 1003–1067). Hoboken, NJ: John Wiley & Sons.

Cooke, J. E., Kochendorfer, L. B., Stuart-Parrigon, K. L., Koehn, A. J., & Kerns, K. A. (2018, September 20). Parent-child attachment and children's experience and regulation of emotion: A meta-analytic review. *Emotion, 19*(6), 1103–1126. https://doi.org/10.1037/emo0000504

Cuellar, J., Jones, D. J., & Sterrett, E. (2013). Examining parenting in the neighborhood context: A review. *Journal of Child and Family Studies, 24*(1), 195–219. https://doi.org/10.1007/s10826-013-9826-y

Davidson, R. D., O'Hara, K. L., & Beck, C. J. A. (2014). Psychological and biological processes in children associated with high conflict parental divorce. *Juvenile and Family Court Journal, 65*(1), 29–44. https://doi.org/10.1111/jfcj.12015

Davies, P., & Martin, M. (2014). Children's coping and adjustment in high-conflict homes: The reformulation of emotional security theory. *Child Development Perspectives, 8*(4), 242–249. https://doi.org/10.1111/cdep.12094

Davis, N. C., & Friedrich, D. (2010). Age stereotypes in middle-aged through old-old adults. *International Journal of Aging & Human Development, 70*(3), 199–212. https://doi.org/10.2190/AG.70.3.b

de Vries, S. L. A., Hoeve, M., Stams, G. J. J. M., & Asscher, J. J. (2016). Adolescent-parent attachment and externalizing behavior: The mediating role of individual and social factors. *Journal of Abnormal Child Psychology, 44*(2), 283–294. https://doi.org/10.1007/s10802-015-9999-5

DeLongis, A., & Zwicker, A. (2017). Marital satisfaction and divorce in couples in stepfamilies. *Current Opinion in Psychology, 13*, 158–161. https://doi.org/10.1016/j.copsyc.2016.11.003

Dimler, L. M., Natsuaki, M. N., Hastings, P. D., Zahn-Waxler, C., & Klimes-Dougan, B. (2017). Parenting effects are in the eye of the beholder: Parent-adolescent differences in perceptions affects adolescent problem behaviors. *Journal of Youth and Adolescence, 46*(5), 1076–1088. https://doi.org/10.1007/s10964-016-0612-1

Doodson, L., & Morley, D. (2006). Understanding the roles of non-residential stepmothers. *Journal of Divorce & Remarriage, 45*(3/4), 109–130. https://doi.org/10.1300/J087v45n03_06

Doughty, S. E., McHale, S. M., & Feinberg, M. E. (2015). Sibling experiences as predictors of romantic relationship qualities in adolescence. *Journal of Family Issues, 36*(5), 589–608. https://doi.org/10.1177/0192513X13495397

Dupuis, S. (2010). Examining the blended family: The application of systems theory toward an understanding of the blended family system. *Journal of Couple & Relationship Therapy, 9*(3), 239–251. https://doi.org/10.1080/15332691.2010.491784

East, P. L. (2009). Adolescents' relationships with siblings. In R. M. Lerner and L. Steinberg (Eds.), *Handbook of adolescent psychology* (Vol. 2, pp. 43–73). Hoboken, NJ: John Wiley & Sons. https://doi.org/10.1002/9780470479193.adlpsy002003

Ethier, K. A., Harper, C. R., Hoo, E., & Dittus, P. J. (2016). The longitudinal impact of perceptions of parental monitoring on adolescent initiation of sexual activity. *Journal of Adolescent Health, 59*(5), 570–576. https://doi.org/10.1016/j.jadohealth.2016.06.011

Farr, R. H. (2017). Does parental sexual orientation matter? A longitudinal follow-up of adoptive families with school-age children. *Developmental Psychology, 53*(2), 252–264. https://doi.org/10.1037/dev0000228

Farruggia, S. P., Germo, G. R., & Solomon, B. J. (2018). Foster care. In R. J. R. Levesque (Ed.), *Encyclopedia of adolescence* (pp. 1469–1486). Cham, Switzerland: Springer. https://doi.org/10.1007/978-3-319-33228-4_299

Fay-Stammbach, T., Hawes, D. J., & Meredith, P. (2014). Parenting influences on executive function in early childhood: A review. *Child Development Perspectives, 8*(4), 258–264. https://doi.org/10.1111/cdep.12095

Fedewa, A. L., Black, W. W., & Ahn, S. (2014). Children and adolescents with same-gender parents: A meta-analytic approach in assessing outcomes. *Journal of GLBT Family Studies, 11*(1), 1–34. https://doi.org/10.1080/1550428X.2013.869486

Freud, A. (1958). Psychological study of the child. *Adolescence, 13*, 255–278.

Fuligni, A. J., & Tsai, K. M. (2015). Developmental flexibility in the age of globalization: Autonomy and identity development among immigrant adolescents. *Annual Review of Psychology, 66*(1), 411–431. https://doi.org/10.1146/annurev-psych-010814-015111

Gallagher, A. M., Updegraff, K. A., Padilla, J., & McHale, S. M. (2018). Longitudinal associations between sibling relational aggression and adolescent adjustment. *Journal of Youth and Adolescence, 47*(10), 2100–2113. https://doi.org/10.1007/s10964-018-0871-0

Gavazzi, S. (2013). Theory and research pertaining to families with adolescents. In *Handbook of marriage and the family* (3rd ed., pp. 303–327). https://doi.org/10.1007/978-1-4614-3987-5_14

Givertz, M. (2015). Parenting styles/discipline. In C. R. Berger, M. E. Roloff, S. R. Wilson, J. P. Dillard, J. Caughlin, & D. Solomon (Eds.), *The International encyclopedia of interpersonal communication* (pp. 1–9). Hoboken, NJ: John Wiley & Sons. https://doi.org/10.1002/9781118540190.wbeic037

Glatz, T., & Buchanan, C. M. (2015). Change and predictors of change in parental self-efficacy from early to middle adolescence. *Developmental Psychology, 51*(10), 1367–1379. https://doi.org/10.1037/dev0000035

Goforth, A. N., Pham, A. V., & Oka, E. R. (2015). Parent–child conflict, acculturation gap, acculturative stress, and behavior problems in Arab American adolescents. *Journal of Cross-Cultural Psychology, 46*(6), 821–836. https://doi.org/10.1177/0022022115585140

Golombok, S., Blake, L., Slutsky, J., Raffanello, E., Roman, G. D., & Ehrhardt, A. (2018). Parenting and the adjustment of children born to gay fathers through surrogacy. *Child Development, 89*, 1223–1233. https://doi.org/10.1111/cdev.12728

Golombok, S., Mellish, L., Jennings, S., Casey, P., Tasker, F., & Lamb, M. E. (2014). Adoptive gay father families: Parent-child relationships and children's psychological adjustment. *Child Development, 85*(2), 456–468. https://doi.org/10.1111/cdev.12155

Greeff, A. P., & Du Toit, C. (2009). Resilience in remarried families. *American Journal of Family Therapy, 37*(2), 114–126. https://doi.org/10.1080/01926180802151919

Griffith, S. F., & Grolnick, W. S. (2013). Parenting in Caribbean families: A look at parental control, structure, and autonomy support. *Journal of Black Psychology, 40*(2), 166–190. https://doi.org/10.1177/0095798412475085

Grotevant, H. D., Lo, A. Y. H., Fiorenzo, L., & Dunbar, N. D. (2017). Adoptive identity and adjustment from adolescence to emerging adulthood: A person-centered approach. *Developmental Psychology, 53*(11), 2195–2204. https://doi.org/10.1037/dev0000352

Grotevant, H. D., & McDermott, J. M. (2014). Adoption: Biological and social processes linked to adaptation. *Annual Review of Psychology, 65*(1), 235–265. https://doi.org/10.1146/annurev-psych-010213-115020

Gutman, L. M., & Eccles, J. S. (2007). Stage-environment fit during adolescence: Trajectories of family relations and adolescent outcomes. *Developmental Psychology, 43*(2), 522–537. https://doi.org/10.1037/0012-1649.43.2.522

Hadiwijaya, H., Klimstra, T. A., Vermunt, J. K., Branje, S. J. T., & Meeus, W. H. J. (2017). On the development of harmony, turbulence, and independence in parent–adolescent relationships: A five-wave longitudinal study. *Journal of Youth and Adolescence, 46*, 1772–1788. https://doi.org/10.1007/s10964-016-0627-7

Hall, G. S. (1904). *Adolescence*. New York, NY: Appleton.

Harold, G. T., Aitken, J. J., & Shelton, K. H. (2007). Inter-parental conflict and children's academic attainment: A longitudinal analysis. *Journal of Child Psychology & Psychiatry & Allied Disciplines, 48*, 1223–1232.

Hart, J. R., Coates, E. E., & Smith-Bynum, M. A. (2019). Parenting style and parent-adolescent relationship quality in African American mother-adolescent dyads. *Parenting, 19*(4), 318–340. https://doi.org/10.1080/15295192.2019.1642085

Havlicek, J. R., Garcia, A. R., & Smith, D. C. (2013). Mental health and substance use disorders among foster youth transitioning to adulthood: Past research and future directions. *Children and Youth Services Review, 35*(1), 194–203. https://doi.org/10.1016/j.childyouth.2012.10.003

Heintzelman, S. J., & King, L. A. (2014). Life is pretty meaningful. *The American Psychologist, 69*(6), 561–574. https://doi.org/10.1037/a0035049

Hennon, C. B., Hildenbrand, B., & Schedle, A. (2008). Stepfamilies and children. In T. P. Gullotta & G. M. Blau (Eds.), *Family influences on childhood behavior and development: Evidence-based prevention and treatment approaches* (pp. 161–185). New York, NY: Routledge.

Hoeve, M., Dubas, J. S., Gerris, J. R. M., van der Laan, P. H., & Smeenk, W. (2011). Maternal and paternal parenting styles: Unique and combined links to adolescent and early adult delinquency. *Journal of Adolescence, 34*(5), 813–827. https://doi.org/10.1016/j.adolescence.2011.02.004

Hofer, C., Eisenberg, N., Spinrad, T. L., Morris, A. S., Gershoff, E., Valiente, C., ... Eggum, N. D. (2013). Mother-adolescent conflict: Stability, change, and relations with externalizing and internalizing behavior problems. *Social Development (Oxford, England), 22*(2), 259–279. https://doi.org/10.1111/sode.12012

Holmbeck, G. N., & Hill, J. P. (1988). Storm and stress beliefs about adolescence: Prevalence, self-reported antecedents, and effects of an undergraduate course. *Journal of Youth and Adolescence, 17*(4), 285–306. https://doi.org/10.1007/BF01537671

Hrapczynski, K. M., & Leslie, L. A. (2018). Engagement in racial socialization among transracial adoptive families with White parents. *Family Relations, 67*(3), 354–367. https://doi.org/10.1111/fare.12316

Huey, M., Hiatt, C., Laursen, B., Burk, W. J., & Rubin, K. (2017). Mother–adolescent conflict types and adolescent adjustment: A person-oriented analysis. *Journal of Family Psychology, 31*(4), 504–512. https://doi.org/10.1037/fam0000294

Huijsmans, T., Eichelsheim, V. I., Weerman, F., Branje, S. J. T., & Meeus, W. (2019). The role of siblings in adolescent delinquency next to parents, school, and peers: Do gender and age matter? *Journal of Developmental and Life-Course Criminology, 5*(2), 220–242. https://doi.org/10.1007/s40865-018-0094-9

Jensen, T. M., & Howard, M. O. (2015). Perceived stepparent–child relationship quality: A systematic review of stepchildren's perspectives. *Marriage & Family Review, 51*(2), 99–153. https://doi.org/10.1080/01494929.2015.1006717

Jones, J. D., Fraley, R. C., Ehrlich, K. B., Stern, J. A., Lejuez, C. W., Shaver, P. R., & Cassidy, J. (2018). Stability of attachment style in adolescence: An empirical test of alternative developmental processes. *Child Development, 89*(3), 871–880. https://doi.org/10.1111/cdev.12775

Juffer, F., & van IJzendoorn, M. H. (2007). Adoptees do not lack self-esteem: A meta-analysis of studies on self-esteem of transracial, international, and domestic adoptees. *Psychological Bulletin, 133*(6), 1067–1083. https://doi.org/10.1037/0033-2909.133.6.1067

Kam, J. A., Gasiorek, J., Pines, R., & Fazio, K. S. (2018). Latina/o adolescents' family undocumented-status disclosures directed at school counselors: A latent transition analysis. *Journal of Counseling Psychology, 65*(3), 267–279. https://doi.org/10.1037/cou0000259

Keijsers, L. (2016). Parental monitoring and adolescent problem behaviors: How much do we really know? *International Journal of Behavioral Development, 40*(3), 271–281. https://doi.org/10.1177/0165025415592515

Keizer, R., Helmerhorst, K. O. W., & van Rijn-van Gelderen, L. (2019). Perceived quality of the mother–adolescent and father–adolescent attachment relationship and adolescents' self-esteem. *Journal of Youth and Adolescence.* https://doi.org/10.1007/s10964-019-01007-0

Kerr, M., Stattin, H., & Burk, W. J. (2010). A reinterpretation of parental monitoring in longitudinal perspective. *Journal of Research on Adolescence, 20*(1), 39–64. https://doi.org/10.1111/j.1532-7795.2009.00623.x

Ko, H.-J., Hooker, K., Geldhof, G. J., & McAdams, D. P. (2016). Longitudinal purpose in life trajectories: Examining predictors in late midlife. *Psychology and Aging, 31*(7), 693–698. https://doi.org/10.1037/pag0000093

Kobak, R., Abbott, C., Zisk, A., & Bounoua, N. (2017). Adapting to the changing needs of adolescents: Parenting practices and challenges to sensitive attunement. *Current Opinion in Psychology, 15*, 137–142. https://doi.org/10.1016/j.copsyc.2017.02.018

Kornadt, A. E., & Rothermund, K. (2015). Views on aging: Domain-specific approaches and implications for developmental regulation. *Annual Review of Gerontology and Geriatrics, 35*(1), 121–144. https://doi.org/10.1891/0198-8794.35.121

Kuther, T. L., & Burnell, K. (2019). A life span developmental perspective on psychosocial development in midlife. *Adultspan Journal, 18*(1), 27–39. https://doi.org/10.1002/adsp.12067

Lamb, M. E. (2012). Mothers, fathers, families, and circumstances: Factors affecting children's adjustment. *Applied Developmental Science, 16*(2), 98–111. https://doi.org/10.1080/10888691.2012.667344

Lamb, M. E., & Lewis, C. (2015). The role of parent-child relationships in child development. In M. H. Bornstein & M. E. Lamb (Eds.), *Developmental science: An advanced textbook* (7th ed., pp. 469–517). New York, NY: Psychology Press.

Lansford, J. E. (2018). Divorce. In R. J. R. Levesque (Ed.), *Encyclopedia of adolescence* (pp. 1051–1056). Cham, Switzerland: Springer. https://doi.org/10.1007/978-3-319-33228-4_35

Lansford, J. E., Deater-Deckard, K., Dodge, K. A., Bates, J. E., & Pettit, G. S. (2004). Ethnic differences in the link between physical discipline and later adolescent externalizing behaviors. *Journal of Child Psychology & Psychiatry, 45*(4), 801–812. https://doi.org/10.1111/j.1469-7610.2004.00273.x

Lansford, J. E., Laird, R. D., Pettit, G. S., Bates, J. E., & Dodge, K. A. (2014). Mothers' and fathers' autonomy-relevant parenting: Longitudinal links with adolescents' externalizing and internalizing behavior. *Journal of Youth and Adolescence, 43*(11), 1877–1889. https://doi.org/10.1007/s10964-013-0079-2

Lansford, J. E., Staples, A. D., Bates, J. E., Pettit, G. S., & Dodge, K. A. (2013). Trajectories of mothers' discipline strategies and interparental conflict: Interrelated change during middle childhood. *Journal of Family Communication*, 13(3), 178–195. https://doi.org/10.1080/15267431.2013.796947

Lee, Y.-E., Brophy-Herb, H. E., Vallotton, C. D., Griffore, R. J., Carlson, J. S., & Robinson, J. L. (2016). Do young children's representations of discipline and empathy moderate the effects of punishment on emotion regulation? *Social Development*, 25(1), 120–138. https://doi.org/10.1111/sode.12141

Leloux-Opmeer, H., Kuiper, C., Swaab, H., & Scholte, E. (2016). Characteristics of children in foster care, family-style group care, and residential care: A scoping review. *Journal of Child and Family Studies*, 25(8), 2357–2371. https://doi.org/10.1007/s10826-016-0418-5

Levesque, R. J. R. (2018). Adoption. In R. J. R. Levesque (Ed.), *Encyclopedia of adolescence* (pp. 113–117). Cham, Switzerland: Springer. https://doi.org/10.1007/978-3-319-33228-4_754

Levpušček, M. P. (2006). Adolescent individuation in relation to parents and friends: Age and gender differences. *European Journal of Developmental Psychology*, 3(3), 238–264. https://doi.org/10.1080/17405620500463864

Lindell, A. K., & Campione-Barr, N. (2017). Relative power in sibling relationships across adolescence. *New Directions for Child and Adolescent Development*, 2017(156), 49–66. https://doi.org/10.1002/cad.20201

Lionetti, F., Palladino, B. E., Moses Passini, C., Casonato, M., Hamzallari, O., Ranta, M., . . . Keijsers, L. (2019). The development of parental monitoring during adolescence: A meta-analysis. *European Journal of Developmental Psychology*, 16(5), 552–580. https://doi.org/10.1080/17405629.2018.1476233

Lippold, M. A., Greenberg, M. T., & Feinberg, M. E. (2011). A dyadic approach to understanding the relationship of maternal knowledge of youths' activities to youths' problem behavior among rural adolescents. *Journal of Youth and Adolescence*, 40(9), 1178–1191. https://doi.org/10.1007/s10964-010-9595-5

Llorca, A., Richaud, M. C., & Malonda, E. (2017). Parenting, peer relationships, academic self-efficacy, and academic achievement: Direct and mediating effects. *Frontiers in Psychology*, 8. https://doi.org/10.3389/fpsyg.2017.02120

Löckenhoff, C. E., De Fruyt, F., Terracciano, A., McCrae, R. R., De Bolle, M., Costa, P. T., . . . Yik, M. (2009). Perceptions of aging across 26 cultures and their culture-level associates. *Psychology and Aging*, 24(4), 941–954. https://doi.org/10.1037/a0016901

Lopez-Tamayo, R., LaVome Robinson, W., Lambert, S. F., Jason, L. A., & Ialongo, N. S. (2016). Parental monitoring, association with externalized behavior, and academic outcomes in urban African-American youth: A moderated mediation analysis. *American Journal of Community Psychology*, 57(3–4), 366–379. https://doi.org/10.1002/ajcp.12056

Lucas-Thompson, R. G., Lunkenheimer, E. S., & Dumitrache, A. (2017). Associations between marital conflict and adolescent conflict appraisals, stress physiology, and mental health. *Journal of Clinical Child and Adolescent Psychology*, 46(3), 379–393. https://doi.org/10.1080/15374416.2015.1046179

Maccoby, E. E., & Martin, J. A. (1983). Socialization in the context of the family: Parent-child interaction. In E. M. Hetherington (Ed.), *Handbook of child psychology: Vol. 4. Socialization, personality, and social development* (4th ed., pp. 1–101). New York, NY: Wiley.

Malczyk, B. R., & Lawson, H. A. (2017). Parental monitoring, the parent-child relationship and children's academic engagement in mother-headed single-parent families. *Children and Youth Services Review*, 73, 274–282. https://doi.org/10.1016/j.childyouth.2016.12.019

Malone, P. S., Lansford, J. E., Castellino, D. R., Berlin, L. J., Dodge, K. A., Bates, J. E., & Pettit, G. S. (2004). Divorce and child behavior problems: Applying latent change score models to life event data.

Structural Equation Modeling, 11(3), 401–423. https://doi.org/10.1207/s15328007sem1103_6

Marceau, K., Ram, N., & Susman, E. J. (2015). Development and lability in the parent-child relationship during adolescence: Associations with pubertal timing and tempo. *Journal of Research on Adolescence*, 25(3), 474–489. https://doi.org/10.1111/jora.12139

Marr, E. (2017). U.S. transracial adoption trends in the 21st century. *Adoption Quarterly*, 20(3), 222–251. https://doi.org/10.1080/10926755.2017.1291458

Masche, J. G. (2010). Explanation of normative declines in parents' knowledge about their adolescent children. *Journal of Adolescence*, 33(2), 271–284. https://doi.org/10.1016/j.adolescence.2009.08.002

Matthews, T. J., & Hamilton, B. E. (2002). Mean age of mother, 1970–2000. *National Vital and Statistics Reports*, 51(1). Retrieved from https://www.cdc.gov/nchs/data/nvsr/nvsr51/nvsr51_01.pdf

Matthews, T. J., & Hamilton, B. E. (2016). Mean age of mothers is on the rise: United States, 2000–2014. *NCHS Data Brief*, 232. Retrieved from https://www.cdc.gov/nchs/products/databriefs/db232.htm

McBride, R. G., & Hays, D. G. (2012). Counselor demographics, ageist attitudes, and multicultural counseling competence among counselors and counselor trainees. *Adultspan Journal*, 11(2), 77–88. https://doi.org/10.1002/j.2161-0029.2012.00007.x

McHale, S. M., Updegraff, K. A., & Whiteman, S. D. (2012). Sibling relationships and influences in childhood and adolescence. *Journal of Marriage and the Family*, 74(5), 913–930. https://doi.org/10.1111/j.1741-3737.2012.01011.x

McKinney, C., & Renk, K. (2011). A multivariate model of parent-adolescent relationship variables in early adolescence. *Child Psychiatry and Human Development*, 42(4), 442–462. https://doi.org/10.1007/s10578-011-0228-3

McLoyd, V. C., & Smith, J. (2002). Physical discipline and behavior problems in African American, European American, and Hispanic children: Emotional support as a moderator. *Journal of Marriage and Family*, 64, 40–53.

McMillen, J. C., Zima, B. T., Scott, L. D., Auslander, W. F., Munson, M. R., Ollie, M. T., & Spitznagel, E. L. (2005). Prevalence of psychiatric disorders among older youths in the foster care system. *Journal of the American Academy of Child and Adolescent Psychiatry*, 44(1), 88–95. https://doi.org/10.1097/01.chi.0000145806.24274.d2

Milevsky, A. (2016). Parenting styles. In R. J. R. Levesque (Ed.), *Encyclopedia of adolescence* (pp. 1–6). Cham, Switzerland: Springer. https://doi.org/10.1007/978-3-319-32132-5_38-2

Miller, B. G., Kors, S., & Macfie, J. (2017). No differences? Meta-analytic comparisons of psychological adjustment in children of gay fathers and heterosexual parents. *Psychology of Sexual Orientation and Gender Diversity*, 4(1), 14–22. https://doi.org/10.1037/sgd0000203

Misca, G. (2014). The "quiet migration": Is intercountry adoption a successful intervention in the lives of vulnerable children? *Family Court Review*, 52(1), 60–68. https://doi.org/10.1111/fcre.12070

Moen, P., & Wethington, E. (1999). Midlife development in a life course context. In S. L. Willis & J. D. Reid (Eds.), *Life in the middle: Psychological and social development in middle age* (pp. 3–23). San Diego, CA: Academic Press.

Mohanty, J. (2015). Ethnic identity and psychological well-being of international transracial adoptees: A curvilinear relationship. *New Directions for Child and Adolescent Development*, 2015(150), 33–45. https://doi.org/10.1002/cad.20117

Moilanen, K. L., & Manuel, M. L. (2017). Parenting, self-regulation and social competence with peers and romantic partners. *Journal of Applied Developmental Psychology*, 49, 46–54. https://doi.org/10.1016/j.appdev.2017.02.003

Moilanen, K. L., Rasmussen, K. E., & Padilla-Walker, L. M. (2015). Bidirectional associations between self-regulation and parenting styles in early adolescence. *Journal of Research on Adolescence*, *25*(2), 246–262. https://doi.org/10.1111/jora.12125

Montgomery, J. E., & Jordan, N. A. (2018). Racial–ethnic socialization and transracial adoptee outcomes: A systematic research synthesis. *Child and Adolescent Social Work Journal*, *35*(5), 439–458. https://doi.org/10.1007/s10560-018-0541-9

Moreno, O., Janssen, T., Cox, M. J., Colby, S., & Jackson, K. M. (2017). Parent-adolescent relationships in Hispanic versus Caucasian families: Associations with alcohol and marijuana use onset. *Addictive Behaviors*, *74*, 74–81. https://doi.org/10.1016/J.ADDBEH.2017.05.029

Murry, V. M., Brody, G. H., Simons, R. L., Cutrona, C. E., & Gibbons, F. X. (2008). Disentangling ethnicity and context as predictors of parenting within rural African American families. *Applied Developmental Science*, *12*(4), 202–210. https://doi.org/10.1080/10888690802388144

Murry, V. M., & Lippold, M. A. (2018). Parenting practices in diverse family structures: Examination of adolescents' development and adjustment. *Journal of Research on Adolescence*, *28*(3), 650–664. https://doi.org/10.1111/jora.12390

Oldehinkel, A. J., Ormel, J., Veenstra, R., De Winter, A. F., Verholst, F. C., & Lansford, J. E. (2009). Parental divorce and children's adjustment. *Perspectives on Psychological Science*, *4*(2), 140–152. https://doi.org/10.1111/j.1745-6924.2009.01114.x

Palacios, J., & Brodzinsky, D. (2010). Review: Adoption research: Trends, topics, outcomes. *International Journal of Behavioral Development*, *34*(3), 270–284. https://doi.org/10.1177/0165025410362837

Palacios, J., Román, M., Moreno, C., León, E., & Peñarrubia, M.-G. (2014). Differential plasticity in the recovery of adopted children after early adversity. *Child Development Perspectives*, *8*(3), 169–174. https://doi.org/10.1111/cdep.12083

Patterson, C. J. (2017). Parents' sexual orientation and children's development. *Child Development Perspectives*, *11*(1), 45–49. https://doi.org/10.1111/cdep.12207

Perrin, E. C., & Siegel, B. S. (2013). Promoting the well-being of children whose parents are gay or lesbian. *Pediatrics*, *131*(4), e1374-83. https://doi.org/10.1542/peds.2013-0377

Pew Research Center. (2015, December 17). *Parenting in America: The American family today*. Retrieved from http://www.pewsocialtrends.org/2015/12/17/1-the-american-family-today/

Pinderhughes, E. E., Zhang, X., & Agerbak, S. (2015). "American" or "Multiethnic"? Family ethnic identity among transracial adoptive families, ethnic-racial socialization, and children's self-perception. *New Directions for Child and Adolescent Development*, *2015*(150), 5–18. https://doi.org/10.1002/cad.20118

Pinquart, M. (2017). Associations of parenting dimensions and styles with externalizing problems of children and adolescents: An updated meta-analysis. *Developmental Psychology*, *53*(5), 873–932. https://doi.org/10.1037/dev0000295

Pinquart, M., & Gerke, D. C. (2019). Associations of parenting styles with self-esteem in children and adolescents: A meta-analysis. *Journal of Child and Family Studies*, *28*, 2017–2035. https://doi.org/10.1007/s10826-019-01417-5

Potter, D. (2010). Psychosocial well-being and the relationship between divorce and children's academic achievement. *Journal of Marriage & Family*, *72*(4), 933–946. https://doi.org/10.1111/j.1741-3737.2010.00740.x

Ram, B., & Hou, F. (2003). Changes in family structure and child outcomes: Roles of economic and familial resources. *Policy Studies Journal*, *31*(3), 309–330.

Renk, K., Liljequist, L., Simpson, J. E., & Phares, V. (2005). Gender and age differences in the topics of parent-adolescent conflict. *Family Journal*, *13*(2), 139–149. https://doi.org/10.1177/1066480704271190

Reynolds, E. K., MacPherson, L., Matusiewicz, A. K., Schreiber, W. M., & Lejuez, C. W. (2011). Discrepancy between mother and child reports of parental knowledge and the relation to risk behavior engagement. *Journal of Clinical Child and Adolescent Psychology*, *40*(1), 67–79. https://doi.org/10.1080/15374416.2011.533406

Rivas-Drake, D., Seaton, E. K., Markstrom, C., Quintana, S., Syed, M., Lee, R. M., . . . Yip, T. (2014). Ethnic and racial identity in adolescence: Implications for psychosocial, academic, and health outcomes. *Child Development*, *85*(1), 40–57. https://doi.org/10.1111/cdev.12200

Robinson, O. C., & Wright, G. R. T. (2013). The prevalence, types and perceived outcomes of crisis episodes in early adulthood and midlife: A structured retrospective-autobiographical study. *International Journal of Behavioral Development*, *37*(5), 407–416. https://doi.org/10.1177/0165025413492464

Rodriguez, S. (2017). "People hide, but I'm here. I count:" Examining undocumented youth identity formation in an urban community-school. *Educational Studies*, *53*(5), 468–491. https://doi.org/10.1080/00131946.2017.1322970

Rosnati, R., Pinderhughes, E. E., Baden, A. L., Grotevant, H. D., Lee, R. M., & Mohanty, J. (2015). New trends and directions in ethnic identity among internationally transracially adopted persons: Summary of special issue. *New Directions for Child and Adolescent Development*, *2015*(150), 91–95. https://doi.org/10.1002/cad.20121

Rote, W. M., & Smetana, J. G. (2016). Beliefs about parents' right to know: Domain differences and associations with change in concealment. *Journal of Research on Adolescence*, *26*, 334–344. https://doi.org/10.1111/jora.12194

Ruff, S. C., Durtschi, J. A., & Day, R. D. (2018). Family subsystems predicting adolescents' perceptions of sibling relationship quality over time. *Journal of Marital and Family Therapy*, *44*(3), 527–542. https://doi.org/10.1111/jmft.12265

Samek, D. R., Rueter, M. A., Keyes, M. A., McGue, M., & Iacono, W. G. (2015). Parent involvement, sibling companionship, and adolescent substance use: A longitudinal, genetically informed design. *Journal of Family Psychology*, *29*(4), 614–623. https://doi.org/10.1037/fam0000097

Scharf, M., & Mayseless, O. (2007). Putting eggs in more than one basket: A new look at developmental processes of attachment in adolescence. *New Directions for Child and Adolescent Development*, pp. 1–22. https://doi.org/10.1002/cd.191

Scharf, M., Mayseless, O., & Kivenson-Baron, I. (2004). Adolescents' attachment representations and developmental tasks in emerging adulthood. *Developmental Psychology*, *40*(3), 430–444. https://doi.org/10.1037/0012-1649.40.3.430

Shapiro, D. N. (2014). Stepparents and parenting stress: The roles of gender, marital quality, and views about gender roles. *Family Process*, *53*(1), 97–108. https://doi.org/10.1111/famp.12062

Shapiro, D. N., & Stewart, A. J. (2011). Parenting stress, perceived child regard, and depressive symptoms among stepmothers and biological mothers. *Family Relations*, *60*(5), 533–544. https://doi.org/10.1111/j.1741-3729.2011.00665.x

Skinner, O. D., & McHale, S. M. (2016). Parent–adolescent conflict in African American families. *Journal of Youth and Adolescence*, *45*(10), 2080–2093. https://doi.org/10.1007/s10964-016-0514-2

Solmeyer, A. R., McHale, S. M., & Crouter, A. C. (2014). Longitudinal associations between sibling relationship qualities and risky behavior across adolescence. *Developmental Psychology*, *50*(2), 600–610. https://doi.org/10.1037/a0033207

Sorkhabi, N. (2005). Applicability of Baumrind's parent typology to collective cultures: Analysis of cultural explanations of parent socialization effects. *International Journal of Behavioral Development*, *29*(6), 552–563.

Sosic-Vasic, Z., Kröner, J., Schneider, S., Vasic, N., Spitzer, M., & Streb, J. (2017). The association between parenting behavior and executive functioning in children and young adolescents. *Frontiers in Psychology*, *8*, 472. https://doi.org/10.3389/fpsyg.2017.00472

Sroufe, L. A. (2016). The place of attachment in development. In J. Cassidy & P. R. Shaver (Eds.), *Handbook of attachment: Theory, research, and clinical applications* (pp. 997–1010). New York, NY: Guilford Press.

Stacks, A. M., Oshio, T., Gerard, J., & Roe, J. (2009). The moderating effect of parental warmth on the association between spanking and child aggression: A longitudinal approach. *Infant & Child Development*, 18(2), 178–194. https://doi.org/10.1002/icd.596

Steinberg, L., & Silverberg, S. B. (1986). The vicissitudes of autonomy in early adolescence. *Child Development*, 57(4), 841.

Stern, J. A., & Cassidy, J. (2018). Empathy from infancy to adolescence: An attachment perspective on the development of individual differences. *Developmental Review*, 47, 1–22. https://doi.org/10.1016/J.DR.2017.09.002

Størksen, I., Røysamb, E., Moum, T., & Tambs, K. (2005). Adolescents with a childhood experience of parental divorce: A longitudinal study of mental health and adjustment. *Journal of Adolescence*, 28(6), 725–739. https://doi.org/10.1016/j.adolescence.2005.01.001

Suárez-Orozco, C. (2017). Conferring disadvantage. *Journal of Developmental & Behavioral Pediatrics*, 38(6), 424–428. https://doi.org/10.1097/DBP.0000000000000462

Talleyrand, R. M., & Vojtech, J. T.-G. (2018). Potential stressors of undocumented Latinx youth: Implications and recommendations for school counselors. *Professional School Counseling*, 22(1), 2156759X1984716. https://doi.org/10.1177/2156759x19847168

Tamis-LeMonda, C. S., Briggs, R. D., McClowry, S. G., & Snow, D. L. (2009). Maternal control and sensitivity, child gender, and maternal education in relation to children's behavioral outcomes in African American families. *Journal of Applied Developmental Psychology*, 30(3), 321–331. https://doi.org/10.1016/j.appdev.2008.12.018

Tasker, F., & Patterson, C. J. (2007). Research on gay and lesbian parenting: Retrospect and prospect. *Journal of GLBT Family Studies*, 3(2/3), 9–34.

Teachman, J. (2008). Complex life course patterns and the risk of divorce in second marriages. *Journal of Marriage & Family*, 70(2), 294–305. https://doi.org/10.1111/j.1741-3737.2008.00482.x

Tucker, C. J., Updegraff, K., & Baril, M. E. (2010). Who's the boss? Patterns of control in adolescents' sibling relationships. *Family Relations*, 59(5), 520–532. https://doi.org/10.1111/j.1741-3729.2010.00620.x

Uji, M., Sakamoto, A., Adachi, K., & Kitamura, T. (2013). The impact of authoritative, authoritarian, and permissive parenting styles on children's later mental health in Japan: Focusing on parent and child gender. *Journal of Child and Family Studies*, 23(2), 293–302. https://doi.org/10.1007/s10826-013-9740-3

van der Wal, R. C., Finkenauer, C., & Visser, M. M. (2019). Reconciling mixed findings on children's adjustment following high-conflict divorce. *Journal of Child and Family Studies*, 28(2), 468–478. https://doi.org/10.1007/s10826-018-1277-z

Van Doorn, M. D., Branje, S. J. T., & Meeus, W. H. J. (2011). Developmental changes in conflict resolution styles in parent-adolescent relationships: A four-wave longitudinal study. *Journal of Youth and Adolescence*, 40(1), 97–107. https://doi.org/10.1007/s10964-010-9516-7

Wallerstein, J. S., & Lewis, J. M. (2004). The unexpected legacy of divorce: Report of a 25-year study. *Psychoanalytic Psychology*, 21(3), 353–370.

Wang, M.-T., Dishion, T. J., Stormshak, E. A., & Willett, J. B. (2011). Trajectories of family management practices and early adolescent behavioral outcomes. *Developmental Psychology*, 47(5), 1324–1341. https://doi.org/10.1037/a0024026

Wang, M. T., Degol, J. L., & Amemiya, J. L. (2019). Older siblings as academic socialization agents for younger siblings: Developmental pathways across adolescence. *Journal of Youth and Adolescence*. https://doi.org/10.1007/s10964-019-01005-2

Weaver, J. M., & Schofield, T. J. (2015). Mediation and moderation of divorce effects on children's behavior problems. *Journal of Family Psychology*, 29(1), 39–48. https://doi.org/10.1037/fam0000043

Weis, R., & Toolis, E. E. (2010). Parenting across cultural contexts in the USA: Assessing parenting behaviour in an ethnically and socioeconomically diverse sample. *Early Child Development & Care*, 180(7), 849–867. https://doi.org/10.1080/03004430802472083

Weymouth, B. B., Buehler, C., Zhou, N., & Henson, R. A. (2016). A meta-analysis of parent-adolescent conflict: Disagreement, hostility, and youth maladjustment. *Journal of Family Theory & Review*, 8(1), 95–112. https://doi.org/10.1111/jftr.12126

Wheeler, L. A., Killoren, S. E., Whiteman, S. D., Updegraff, K. A., McHale, S. M., & Umaña-Taylor, A. J. (2016). Romantic relationship experiences from late adolescence to young adulthood: the role of older siblings in Mexican-origin families. *Journal of Youth and Adolescence*, 45(5), 900–915. https://doi.org/10.1007/s10964-015-0392-z

White, L., & Rogers, S. J. (2000). Economic circumstances and family outcomes: A review of the 1990s. *Journal of Marriage and the Family*, 62, 1035–1051.

Whiteman, S. D., Jensen, A. C., & McHale, S. M. (2017). Sibling influences on risky behaviors from adolescence to young adulthood: Vertical socialization or bidirectional effects? *New Directions for Child and Adolescent Development*, 2017(156), 67–85. https://doi.org/10.1002/cad.20197

Whiteside, M. F., & Becker, B. J. (2000). Parental factors and the young child's postdivorce adjustment: A meta-analysis with implications for parenting arrangements. *Journal of Family Psychology*, 14, 5–26.

Wiley, M. O. (2017). Adoption research, practice, and societal trends: Ten years of progress. *American Psychologist*, 72(9), 985–995. https://doi.org/10.1037/amp0000218

Willoughby, T., & Hamza, C. A. (2011). A longitudinal examination of the bidirectional associations among perceived parenting behaviors, adolescent disclosure and problem behavior across the high school years. *Journal of Youth and Adolescence*, 40(4), 463–478. https://doi.org/10.1007/s10964-010-9567-9

Wilson, S. L., & Weaver, T. L. (2009). Follow-up of developmental attainment and behavioral adjustment for toddlers adopted internationally into the USA. *International Social Work*, 52(5), 679–684. https://doi.org/10.1177/0020872809337684

Yoshikawa, H., Kholoptseva, J., & Suárez-Orozco, C. (2013). The role of public policies and community-based organizations in the developmental consequences of parent undocumented status. *Social Policy Report*, 27(3), 1–24. https://doi.org/10.1002/j.2379-3988.2013.tb00076.x

Zill, N. (2015). The paradox of adoption. *Institute for Family Studies*. Retrieved from https://ifstudies.org/blog/the-paradox-of-adoption/

CHAPTER 9

Albert, D., Chein, J., & Steinberg, L. (2013). The teenage brain: Peer influences on adolescent decision making. *Current Directions in Psychological Science*, 22(2), 114–120. https://doi.org/10.1177/0963721412471347

Allen, J. P., Porter, M. R., McFarland, F. C., Marsh, P., & McElhaney, K. B. (2005). The two faces of adolescents' success with peers: Adolescent popularity, social adaptation, and deviant behavior. *Child Development*, 76(3), 747–760. https://doi.org/10.1111/j.1467-8624.2005.00875.x

Andrews, N. C. Z., Hanish, L. D., & Santos, C. E. (2017). Reciprocal associations between delinquent behavior and social network position during middle school. *Journal of Youth and Adolescence*, 46(9), 1918–1932. https://doi.org/10.1007/s10964-017-0643-2

Arseneault, L. (2018). Annual research review: The persistent and pervasive impact of being bullied in childhood and adolescence: Implications for policy and practice. *Journal of Child Psychology and Psychiatry, 59*(4), 405–421. https://doi.org/10.1111/jcpp.12841

Bagci, S. C., Rutland, A., Kumashiro, M., Smith, P. K., & Blumberg, H. (2014). Are minority status children's cross-ethnic friendships beneficial in a multiethnic context? *The British Journal of Developmental Psychology, 32*(1), 107–115. https://doi.org/10.1111/bjdp.12028

Bauminger, N., Finzi-Dottan, R., Chason, S., & Har-Even, D. (2008). Intimacy in adolescent friendship: The roles of attachment, coherence, and self-disclosure. *Journal of Social and Personal Relationships, 25*(3), 409–428. https://doi.org/10.1177/0265407508090866

Benner, A. D., & Wang, Y. (2017). Racial/ethnic discrimination and adolescents' well-being: The role of cross-ethnic friendships and friends' experiences of discrimination. *Child Development, 88*(2), 493–504. https://doi.org/10.1111/cdev.12606

Bierman, K. L., Kalvin, C. B., & Heinrichs, B. S. (2014). Early childhood precursors and adolescent sequelae of grade school peer rejection and victimization. *Journal of Clinical Child and Adolescent Psychology, 44*(3), 367–379. https://doi.org/10.1080/15374416.2013.873983

Blakemore, S.-J. (2018). Avoiding social risk in adolescence. *Current Directions in Psychological Science, 27*(2), 116–122. https://doi.org/10.1177/0963721417738144

Booth-Laforce, C., Oh, W., Kim, A. H., Rubin, K. H., Rose-Krasnor, L., & Burgess, K. (2006). Attachment, self-worth, and peer-group functioning in middle childhood. *Attachment and Human Development, 8*(4), 309–325. https://doi.org/10.1080/14616730601048209

Bowker, A. (2004). Predicting friendship stability during early adolescence. *The Journal of Early Adolescence, 24*(2), 85–112. https://doi.org/10.1177/0272431603262666

Bowker, A., & Ramsay, K. (2018). Friendship characteristics. In R. J. R. Levesque (Ed.), *Encyclopedia of adolescence* (pp. 1–8). Cham, Switzerland: Springer. https://doi.org/10.1007/978-3-319-32132-5_49-2

Bowker, J. C., Fredstrom, B. K., Rubin, K. H., Rose-Krasnor, L., Booth-LaForce, C., & Laursen, B. (2010). Distinguishing children who form new best-friendships from those who do not. *Journal of Social and Personal Relationships, 27*(6), 707–725. https://doi.org/10.1177/0265407510373259

Brechwald, W. A., & Prinstein, M. J. (2011). Beyond homophily: A decade of advances in understanding peer influence processes. *Journal of Research on Adolescence, 21*(1), 166–179. https://doi.org/10.1111/j.1532-7795.2010.00721.x

Brown, B., Bank, H., & Steinberg, L. (2008). Smoke in the looking glass: Effects of discordance between self- and peer rated crowd affiliation on adolescent anxiety, depression and self-feelings. *Journal of Youth & Adolescence, 37*(10), 1163–1177. https://doi.org/10.1007/s10964-007-9198-y

Brown, B. B., & Larson, J. (2009). Peer relationships in adolescence. In R. M. Lerner & L. Steinberg (Eds.), *Handbook of adolescent psychology* (pp. 74–103). Hoboken, NJ: John Wiley & Sons. shttps://doi.org/10.1002/9780470479193.adlpsy002004

Buhrmester, D., & Furman, W. (1987). The development of companionship and intimacy. *Child Development, 58*(4), 1101–1113. https://doi.org/10.2307/1130550

Chein, J., Albert, D., O'Brien, L., Uckert, K., & Steinberg, L. (2011). Peers increase adolescent risk taking by enhancing activity in the brain's reward circuitry. *Developmental Science, 14*(2), F1–F10. https://doi.org/10.1111/J.1467-7687.2010.01035.X

Child Trends. (2019). *Dating among teens.* Retrieved from https://www.childtrends.org/indicators/dating

Choukas-Bradley, S., Giletta, M., Cohen, G. L., & Prinstein, M. J. (2015). Peer influence, peer status, and prosocial behavior: An experimental investigation of peer socialization of adolescents' intentions to volunteer. *Journal of Youth and Adolescence, 44*(12), 2197–2210. https://doi.org/10.1007/s10964-015-0373-2

Choukas-Bradley, S., Giletta, M., Widman, L., Cohen, G. L., & Prinstein, M. J. (2014). Experimentally measured susceptibility to peer influence and adolescent sexual behavior trajectories: A preliminary study. *Developmental Psychology, 50*(9), 2221–2227. https://doi.org/10.1037/a0037300

Cillessen, A. H. N., & van den Berg, Y. H. M. (2012). Popularity and school adjustment. In A. Ryan & G. W. Ladd (Eds.), *Peer relationships and adjustment at school* (pp. 135–164). Charlotte, NC: Information Age Publishing.

Collibee, C., Furman, W., & Shoop, J. (2019). Risky interactions: Relational and developmental moderators of substance use and dating aggression. *Journal of Youth and Adolescence, 48*(1), 102–113. https://doi.org/10.1007/s10964-018-0950-2

Collins, W. A., Welsh, D. P., & Furman, W. (2009). Adolescent romantic relationships. *Annual Review of Psychology, 60*, 631–652. https://doi.org/10.1146/annurev.psych.60.110707.163459

Connolly, J., Craig, W., Goldberg, A., & Pepler, D. (1999). Conceptions of cross-sex friendships and romantic relationships in early adolescence. *Journal of Youth and Adolescence, 28*(4), 481–494.

Connolly, J., Craig, W., Goldberg, A., & Pepler, D. (2004). Mixed-gender groups, dating, and romantic relationships in early adolescence. *Journal of Research on Adolescence, 14*, 185–207.

Connolly, J., & McIsaac, C. (2011). Romantic relationships in adolescence. In M. K. Underwood & L. H. Rosen (Eds.), *Social development: Relationships in infancy, childhood, and adolescence* (pp. 180–203). New York, NY: Guilford Press.

Connolly, J., Nguyen, H. N. T., Pepler, D., Craig, W., & Jiang, D. (2013). Developmental trajectories of romantic stages and associations with problem behaviours during adolescence. *Journal of Adolescence, 36*(6), 1013–1024. https://doi.org/10.1016/j.adolescence.2013.08.006

Cooley, J. L., & Fite, P. J. (2016). Peer victimization and forms of aggression during middle childhood: The role of emotion regulation. *Journal of Abnormal Child Psychology, 44*(3), 535–546. https://doi.org/10.1007/s10802-015-0051-6

Coplan, R. J., Rose-Krasnor, L., Weeks, M., Kingsbury, A., Kingsbury, M., & Bullock, A. (2013). Alone is a crowd: Social motivations, social withdrawal, and socioemotional functioning in later childhood. *Developmental Psychology, 49*(5), 861-875.

Cornell, D., Shukla, K., & Konold, T. (2015). Peer victimization and authoritative school climate: A multilevel approach. *Journal of Educational Psychology, 107*(4), 1186–1201. https://doi.org/10.1037/edu0000038

Cross, J. R. (2018). Crowds. In *Encyclopedia of adolescence* (pp. 573–580). Cham, Switzerland: Springer. https://doi.org/10.1007/978-1-4419-1695-2_44

Cross, J. R., & Fletcher, K. L. (2009). The challenge of adolescent crowd research: Defining the crowd. *Journal of Youth & Adolescence, 38*(6), 747–764. https://doi.org/10.1007/s10964-008-9307-6

Daspe, M., Arbel, R., Ramos, M. C., Shapiro, L. A. S., & Margolin, G. (2019). Deviant peers and adolescent risky behaviors: The protective effect of nonverbal display of parental warmth. *Journal of Research on Adolescence, 29*(4), 863–878. https://doi.org/10.1111/jora.12418

De La Rue, L., Polanin, J. R., Espelage, D. L., & Pigott, T. D. (2017). A meta-analysis of school-based interventions aimed to prevent or reduce violence in teen dating relationships. *Review of Educational Research, 87*(1), 7–34. https://doi.org/10.3102/0034654316632061

de Water, E., Burk, W. J., Cillessen, A. H. N., & Scheres, A. (2017). Substance use and decision-making in adolescent best friendship dyads: The role of popularity. *Social Development*, 26(4), 860–875. https://doi.org/10.1111/sode.12227

DeLay, D., Laursen, B., Bukowski, W. M., Kerr, M., & Stattin, H. (2016). Adolescent friend similarity on alcohol abuse as a function of participation in romantic relationships: Sometimes a new love comes between old friends. *Developmental Psychology*, 52(1), 117–129. https://doi.org/10.1037/a0039882

Delsing, M. J. M. H., ter Bogt, T. F. M., Engels, R. C. M. E., & Meeus, W. H. J. (2007). Adolescents' peer crowd identification in the Netherlands: Structure and associations with problem behaviors. *Journal of Research on Adolescence*, 17(2), 467–480. https://doi.org/10.1111/j.1532-7795.2007.00530.x

Dijkstra, J. K., Berger, C., & Lindenberg, S. (2011). Do physical and relational aggression explain adolescents' friendship selection? The competing roles of network characteristics, gender, and social status. *Aggressive Behavior*, 37(5), 417–429. https://doi.org/10.1002/ab.20402

Duan, L., Chou, C.-P., Andreeva, V., & Pentz, M. (2009). Trajectories of peer social influences as long-term predictors of drug use from early through late adolescence. *Journal of Youth & Adolescence*, 38(3), 454–465. https://doi.org/10.1007/s10964-008-9310-y

Dumas, T. M., Davis, J. P., & Ellis, W. E. (2019). Is it good to be bad? A longitudinal analysis of adolescent popularity motivations as a predictor of engagement in relational aggression and risk behaviors. *Youth & Society*, 51(5), 659–679. https://doi.org/10.1177/0044118X17700319

Ellis, W. E., & Zarbatany, L. (2017). Understanding processes of peer clique influence in late childhood and early adolescence. *Child Development Perspectives*, 11(4), 227–232. https://doi.org/10.1111/cdep.12248

Erdley, C. A., & Day, H. J. (2017). Friendship in childhood and adolescence. In M. Hojjat & A. Moyer (Eds.), *The psychology of friendship* (pp. 3–19). New York, NY: Oxford University Press. https://doi.org/10.1093/acprof:oso/9780190222024.003.0001

Erikson, E. H. (1959). *Identity and the life cycle* (Vol. 64). New York, NY: W. W. Norton and Company.

Espelage, D. L., Low, S. K., & Jimerson, S. R. (2014). Understanding school climate, aggression, peer victimization, and bully perpetration: Contemporary science, practice, and policy. *School Psychology Quarterly*, 29(3), 233–237.

Ethier, K. A., Harper, C. R., Hoo, E., & Dittus, P. J. (2016). The longitudinal impact of perceptions of parental monitoring on adolescent initiation of sexual activity. *Journal of Adolescent Health*, 59(5), 570–576. https://doi.org/10.1016/j.jadohealth.2016.06.011

Ettekal, I., & Ladd, G. W. (2015). Developmental pathways from childhood aggression-disruptiveness, chronic peer rejection, and deviant friendships to early-adolescent rule breaking. *Child Development*, 86(2), 614–631. https://doi.org/10.1111/cdev.12321

Exner-Cortens, D., Eckenrode, J., & Rothman, E. (2013). Longitudinal associations between teen dating violence victimization and adverse health outcomes. *Pediatrics*, 131(1), 71–78. https://doi.org/10.1542/peds.2012-1029

Farrell, A. D., Thompson, E. L., & Mehari, K. R. (2017). Dimensions of peer influences and their relationship to adolescents' aggression, other problem behaviors and prosocial behavior. *Journal of Youth and Adolescence*, 46, 1351–1369. https://doi.org/10.1007/s10964-016-0601-4

Fellmeth, G. L., Heffernan, C., Nurse, J., Habibula, S., & Sethi, D. (2013). Educational and skills-based interventions for preventing relationship and dating violence in adolescents and young adults. *Cochrane Database of Systematic Reviews*, 6, CD004534. https://doi.org/10.1002/14651858.CD004534.pub3

Ferguson, S. M., & Ryan, A. M. (2019). It's lonely at the top: Adolescent students' peer-perceived popularity and self-perceived social contentment. *Journal of Youth and Adolescence*, 48(2), 341–358. https://doi.org/10.1007/s10964-018-0970-y

Fite, P. J., Hendrickson, M., Rubens, S. L., Gabrielli, J., & Evans, S. (2013). The role of peer rejection in the link between reactive aggression and academic performance. *Child & Youth Care Forum*, 42(3), 193–205. https://doi.org/10.1007/s10566-013-9199-9

Foshee, V. A., McNaughton Reyes, H. L., Vivolo-Kantor, A. M., Basile, K. C., Chang, L.-Y., Faris, R., & Ennett, S. T. (2014). Bullying as a longitudinal predictor of adolescent dating violence. *The Journal of Adolescent Health*, 55(3), 439–444. https://doi.org/10.1016/j.jadohealth.2014.03.004

Foshee, V. A., McNaughton Reyes, L., Tharp, A. T., Chang, L.-Y., Ennett, S. T., Simon, T. R., . . . Suchindran, C. (2015). Shared longitudinal predictors of physical peer and dating violence. *The Journal of Adolescent Health*, 56(1), 106–112. https://doi.org/10.1016/j.jadohealth.2014.08.003

French, D. C., & Cheung, H. S. (2018). Peer relationships. In J. E. Lansford & P. Banati (Eds.), *Handbook of adolescent development research and its impact on global policy* (pp. 130–149). New York, NY: Oxford University Press. https://doi.org/10.1093/oso/9780190847128.003.0007

Fujimoto, K., & Valente, T. W. (2015). Multiplex congruity: Friendship networks and perceived popularity as correlates of adolescent alcohol use. *Social Science and Medicine*, 125, 173–181. https://doi.org/10.1016/j.socscimed.2014.05.023

Furman, W. (2018). The romantic relationships of youth. In W. M. Bukowski, B. Laursen, & K. H. Rubin (Eds.), *Handbook of peer interactions, relationships, and groups* (pp. 410–428). New York, NY: Guilford Press.

Furman, W., & Collibee, C. (2014). A matter of timing: Developmental theories of romantic involvement and psychosocial adjustment. *Development and Psychopathology*, 26(4 Pt 1), 1149–1160. https://doi.org/10.1017/S0954579414000182

Furman, W., Collibee, C., Lantagne, A., & Golden, R. L. (2019). Making movies instead of taking snapshots: Studying change in youth's romantic relationships. *Child Development Perspectives*, 13(3), 135–140. https://doi.org/10.1111/cdep.12325

Furman, W., & Rose, A. J. (2015). Friendships, romantic relationships, and peer relationships. In R. M. Lerner (Ed.), *Handbook of child psychology and developmental science* (pp. 1–43). Hoboken, NJ: John Wiley & Sons. https://doi.org/10.1002/9781118963418.childpsy322

Furman, W., & Shomaker, L. B. (2008). Patterns of interaction in adolescent romantic relationships: Distinct features and links to other close relationships. *Journal of Adolescence*, 31(6), 771–788. https://doi.org/10.1016/j.adolescence.2007.10.007

Gangel, M. J., Keane, S. P., Calkins, S. D., Shanahan, L., & O'Brien, M. (2017). The association between relational aggression and perceived popularity in early adolescence: A test of competing hypotheses. *The Journal of Early Adolescence*, 37(8), 1078–1092. https://doi.org/10.1177/0272431616642327

Gest, S. D., Davidson, A. J., Rulison, K. L., Moody, J., & Welsh, J. A. (2007). Features of groups and status hierarchies in girls' and boys' early adolescent peer networks. *New Directions for Child & Adolescent Development*, 2007(118), 43–60.

Giordano, P. C., Soto, D. A., Manning, W. D., & Longmore, M. A. (2010). The characteristics of romantic relationships associated with teen dating violence. *Social Science Research*, 39(6), 863–874. https://doi.org/10.1016/j.ssresearch.2010.03.009

Gomez, H. L., Iyer, P., Batto, L. L., & Jensen-Campbell, L. A. (2011). Friendships and adjustment. In R. J. R. Levesque, *Encyclopedia of adolescence* (pp. 1086–1094). New York, NY: Springer. https://doi.org/10.1007/978-1-4419-1695-2_48

Graham, S., Munniksma, A., & Juvonen, J. (2014). Psychosocial benefits of cross-ethnic friendships in urban middle schools. *Child Development*, 85(2), 469–483. https://doi.org/10.1111/cdev.12159

Gremmen, M. C., Dijkstra, J. K., Steglich, C., & Veenstra, R. (2017). First selection, then influence: Developmental differences in friendship dynamics regarding academic achievement. *Developmental Psychology*, *53*(7), 1356–1370. https://doi.org/10.1037/dev0000314

Guimond, F., Laursen, B., Hartl, A. C., & Cillessen, A. H. N. (2019). Differences in internalizing symptoms anticipate adolescent friendship dissolution. *Journal of Research on Adolescence*, *29*(4), 924–937. https://doi.org/10.1111/jora.12432

Ha, T., Dishion, T. J., Overbeek, G., Burk, W. J., & Engels, R. C. M. E. (2014). The blues of adolescent romance: Observed affective interactions in adolescent romantic relationships associated with depressive symptoms. *Journal of Abnormal Child Psychology*, *42*(4), 551–562. https://doi.org/10.1007/s10802-013-9808-y

Ha, T., Overbeek, G., & Engels, R. C. M. E. (2010). Effects of attractiveness and social status on dating desire in heterosexual adolescents: An experimental study. *Archives of Sexual Behavior*, *39*(5), 1063–1071. https://doi.org/10.1007/s10508-009-9561-z

Hartl, A. C., Laursen, B., & Cillessen, A. H. N. (2015). A survival analysis of adolescent friendships. *Psychological Science*, *26*(8), 1304–1315. https://doi.org/10.1177/0956797615588751

Helms, S. W., Choukas-Bradley, S., Widman, L., Giletta, M., Cohen, G. L., & Prinstein, M. J. (2014). Adolescents misperceive and are influenced by high-status peers' health risk, deviant, and adaptive behavior. *Developmental Psychology*, *50*(12), 2697–2714. https://doi.org/10.1037/a0038178

Herrman, J. W. (2009). There's a fine line...Adolescent dating violence and prevention. *Pediatric Nursing*, *35*(3), 164–170.

Hiatt, C., Laursen, B., Mooney, K. S., & Rubin, K. H. (2015). Forms of friendship: A person-centered assessment of the quality, stability, and outcomes of different types of adolescent friends. *Personality and Individual Differences*, *77*, 149–155. https://doi.org/10.1016/j.paid.2014.12.051

Hiatt, C., Laursen, B., Stattin, H., & Kerr, M. (2017). Best friend influence over adolescent problem behaviors: Socialized by the satisfied. *Journal of Clinical Child & Adolescent Psychology*, *46*(5), 695–708. https://doi.org/10.1080/15374416.2015.1050723

Hofmann, V., & Müller, C. M. (2018). Avoiding antisocial behavior among adolescents: The positive influence of classmates' prosocial behavior. *Journal of Adolescence*, *68*, 136–145. https://doi.org/10.1016/j.adolescence.2018.07.013

Hopmeyer, A., & Medovoy, T. (2017). Emerging adults' self-identified peer crowd affiliations, risk behavior, and social–emotional adjustment in college. *Emerging Adulthood*, *5*(2), 143–148. https://doi.org/10.1177/2167696816665055

Hutson, E., Kelly, S., & Militello, L. K. (2018). Systematic review of cyberbullying interventions for youth and parents with implications for evidence-based practice. *Worldviews on Evidence-Based Nursing*, *15*(1), 72–79. https://doi.org/10.1111/wvn.12257

Hymel, S., & Swearer, S. M. (2015). Four decades of research on school bullying: An introduction. *American Psychologist*, *70*(4), 293–299. https://doi.org/10.1037/a0038928

Hysing, M., Askeland, K. G., La Greca, A. M., Solberg, M. E., Breivik, K., & Sivertsen, B. (2019). Bullying involvement in adolescence: Implications for sleep, mental health, and academic outcomes. *Journal of Interpersonal Violence*, 088626051985340. https://doi.org/10.1177/0886260519853409

Jones, J. D., Fraley, R. C., Ehrlich, K. B., Stern, J. A., Lejuez, C. W., Shaver, P. R., & Cassidy, J. (2018). Stability of attachment style in adolescence: An empirical test of alternative developmental processes. *Child Development*, *89*(3), 871–880. https://doi.org/10.1111/cdev.12775

Jordan, J. W., Stalgaitis, C. A., Charles, J., Madden, P. A., Radhakrishnan, A. G., & Saggese, D. (2018). Peer crowd identification and adolescent health behaviors: Results from a statewide representative study. *Health Education & Behavior*, 109019811875914. https://doi.org/10.1177/1090198118759148

Juvonen, J., & Graham, S. (2014). Bullying in schools: The power of bullies and the plight of victims. *Annual Review of Psychology*, *65*, 159–185. https://doi.org/10.1146/annurev-psych-010213-115030

Juvonen, J., Wang, Y., & Espinoza, G. (2013). Physical aggression, spreading of rumors, and social prominence in early adolescence: Reciprocal effects supporting gender similarities? *Journal of Youth and Adolescence*, *42*(12), 1801–1810. https://doi.org/10.1007/s10964-012-9894-0

Kansky, J., & Allen, J. P. (2018). Long-term risks and possible benefits associated with late adolescent romantic relationship quality. *Journal of Youth and Adolescence*, *47*(7), 1531–1544. https://doi.org/10.1007/s10964-018-0813-x

Kawabata, Y., & Crick, N. R. (2011). The significance of cross-racial/ethnic friendships: Associations with peer victimization, peer support, sociometric status, and classroom diversity. *Developmental Psychology*, *47*(6), 1763–1775. https://doi.org/10.1037/a0025399

Klima, T., & Repetti, R. L. (2008). Children's peer relations and their psychological adjustment: Differences between close friendships and the larger peer group. *Merrill-Palmer Quarterly*, *54*(2), 151–178. https://doi.org/10.1353/mpq.2008.0016

Kochendorfer, L. B., & Kerns, K. A. (2017). Perceptions of parent-child attachment relationships and friendship qualities: Predictors of romantic relationship involvement and quality in adolescence. *Journal of Youth and Adolescence*, *46*(5), 1009–1021. https://doi.org/10.1007/s10964-017-0645-0

Kochendorfer, L. B., & Kerns, K. A. (2019). A meta-analysis of friendship qualities and romantic relationship outcomes in adolescence. *Journal of Research on Adolescence*, jora.12505. https://doi.org/10.1111/jora.12505

Kornbluh, M., & Neal, J. W. (2016). Examining the many dimensions of children's popularity. *Journal of Social and Personal Relationships*, *33*(1), 62–80. https://doi.org/10.1177/0265407514562562

Kreager, D. A., Molloy, L. E., Moody, J., & Feinberg, M. E. (2016). Friends first? The peer network origins of adolescent dating. *Journal of Research on Adolescence*, *26*(2), 257–269. https://doi.org/10.1111/jora.12189

Kretschmer, T., Veenstra, R., Deković, M., & Oldehinkel, A. J. (2017). Bullying development across adolescence, its antecedents, outcomes, and gender-specific patterns. *Development and Psychopathology*, *29*(3), 941–955. https://doi.org/10.1017/S0954579416000596

Kuppens, S., Laurent, L., Heyvaert, M., & Onghena, P. (2013). Associations between parental psychological control and relational aggression in children and adolescents: A multilevel and sequential meta-analysis. *Developmental Psychology*, *49*(9), 1697–1712. https://doi.org/10.1037/a0030740

Ladd, G. W. (2006). Peer rejection, aggressive or withdrawn behavior, and psychological maladjustment from ages 5 to 12: An examination of four predictive models. *Child Development*, *77*(4), 822–846.

Ladd, G. W., & Kochenderfer-Ladd, B. (2016). Research in educational psychology: Social exclusion in school. In P. Riva & J. Eck (Eds.), *Social exclusion* (pp. 109–132). Cham, Switzerland: Springer. https://doi.org/10.1007/978-3-319-33033-4_6

Lam, C. B., McHale, S. M., & Crouter, A. C. (2014). Time with peers from middle childhood to late adolescence: Developmental course and adjustment correlates. *Child Development*, *85*(4), 1677–1693. https://doi.org/10.1111/cdev.12235

Lansford, J. E., Costanzo, P. R., Grimes, C., Putallaz, M., Miller, S., & Malone, P. S. (2009). Social network centrality and leadership status: Links with problem behaviors and tests of gender differences. *Merrill-Palmer Quarterly*, *55*(1), 1–25.

Lansford, J. E., Laird, R. D., Pettit, G. S., Bates, J. E., & Dodge, K. A. (2014). Mothers' and fathers' autonomy-relevant parenting: Longitudinal links with adolescents' externalizing and internalizing behavior. *Journal of Youth and Adolescence*, *43*(11), 1877–1889. https://doi.org/10.1007/s10964-013-0079-2

Lansford, J. E., Malone, P. S., Dodge, K. A., Pettit, G. S., & Bates, J. E. (2010). Developmental cascades of peer rejection, social information processing biases, and aggression during middle childhood. *Development & Psychopathology*, *22*(3), 593–602. https://doi.org/10.1017/S0954579410000301

Larson, R. W., Clore, G. L., & Wood, G. A. (1999). The emotions of romantic relationships: Do they wreak havoc on adolescents? In W. Furman, B. Brown, & C. Feiring (Eds.), *The development of romantic relationships in adolescence* (pp. 19–49). Cambridge, England: Cambridge University Press. https://doi.org/10.1017/CBO9781316182185.003

Laursen, B. (2017). Making and keeping friends: The importance of being similar. *Child Development Perspectives*, *11*(4), 282–289. https://doi.org/10.1111/cdep.12246

Leadbeater, B., Banister, E., Ellis, W., & Yeung, R. (2008). Victimization and relational aggression in adolescent romantic relationships: The influence of parental and peer behaviors, and individual adjustment. *Journal of Youth & Adolescence*, *37*(3), 359–372. https://doi.org/10.1007/s10964-007-9269-0

Lenhart, A. (2015, August 6). Social media and teen friendships. *Pew Research Center*. Retrieved from https://www.pewinternet.org/2015/08/06/chapter-4-social-media-and-friendships/

Little, K., & Welsh, D. (2018). Romantic experiences. In R. J. R. Levesque (Ed.), *Encyclopedia of adolescence* (pp. 3186–3194). Cham, Switzerland: Springer. https://doi.org/10.1007/978-3-319-33228-4_53

Lodder, G. M. A., Scholte, R. H. J., Goossens, L., & Verhagen, M. (2017). Loneliness in early adolescence: Friendship quantity, friendship quality, and dyadic processes. *Journal of Clinical Child and Adolescent Psychology*, *46*(5), 709–720. https://doi.org/10.1080/15374416.2015.1070352

Logue, S., Chein, J., Gould, T., Holliday, E., & Steinberg, L. (2014). Adolescent mice, unlike adults, consume more alcohol in the presence of peers than alone. *Developmental Science*, *17*(1), 79–85. https://doi.org/10.1111/desc.12101

Low, S., & Shortt, J. W. (2017). Family, peer, and pubertal determinants of dating involvement among adolescents. *Journal of Research on Adolescence*, *27*(1), 78–87. https://doi.org/10.1111/jora.12257

Luciano, E. C., & Orth, U. (2017). Transitions in romantic relationships and development of self-esteem. *Journal of Personality and Social Psychology*, *112*(2), 307–328. https://doi.org/10.1037/pspp0000109

Madsen, S. D., & Collins, W. A. (2011). The salience of adolescent romantic experiences for romantic relationship qualities in young adulthood. *Journal of Research on Adolescence*, *21*(4), 789–801. https://doi.org/10.1111/j.1532-7795.2011.00737.x

Maes, M., Nelemans, S. A., Danneel, S., Fernández-Castilla, B., Van den Noortgate, W., Goossens, L., & Vanhalst, J. (2019). Loneliness and social anxiety across childhood and adolescence: Multilevel meta-analyses of cross-sectional and longitudinal associations. *Developmental Psychology*, *55*(7), 1548–1565. https://doi.org/10.1037/dev0000719

Markiewicz, D., & Doyle, A. B. (2016). Best friends. In R. Levesque (Ed.), *Encyclopedia of adolescence* (pp. 1–8). Cham, Switzerland: Springer. https://doi.org/10.1007/978-3-319-32132-5_314-2

Markovic, A., & Bowker, J. C. (2017). Friends also matter: Examining friendship adjustment indices as moderators of anxious-withdrawal and trajectories of change in psychological maladjustment. *Developmental Psychology*, *53*(8), 1462–1473. https://doi.org/10.1037/dev0000343

Menting, B., Koot, H., & van Lier, P. (2014). Peer acceptance and the development of emotional and behavioural problems: Results from a preventive intervention study. *International Journal of Behavioral Development*, *39*(6), 530–540. https://doi.org/10.1177/0165025414558853

Monahan, K. C., Dmitrieva, J., & Cauffman, E. (2014). Bad romance: Sex differences in the longitudinal association between romantic relationships and deviant behavior. *Journal of Research on Adolescence*, *24*(1), 12–26. https://doi.org/10.1111/jora.12019

Moore, S. E., Norman, R. E., Suetani, S., Thomas, H. J., Sly, P. D., & Scott, J. G. (2017). Consequences of bullying victimization in childhood and adolescence: A systematic review and meta-analysis. *World Journal of Psychiatry*, *7*(1), 60–76. https://doi.org/10.5498/wjp.v7.i1.60

Moore, S. R., Harden, K. P., & Mendle, J. (2014). Pubertal timing and adolescent sexual behavior in girls. *Developmental Psychology*, *50*(6), 1734–1745. https://doi.org/10.1037/a0036027

Mrug, S., Borch, C., & Cillessen, A. H. N. (2011). Other-sex friendships in late adolescence: Risky associations for substance use and sexual debut? *Journal of Youth and Adolescence*, *40*(7), 875–888. https://doi.org/10.1007/s10964-010-9605-7

Nese, R. N. T., Horner, R. H., Dickey, C. R., Stiller, B., & Tomlanovich, A. (2014). Decreasing bullying behaviors in middle school: Expect respect. *School Psychology Quarterly*, *29*(3)(3), 272–286.

Nesi, J., Widman, L., Choukas-Bradley, S., & Prinstein, M. J. (2017). Technology-based communication and the development of interpersonal competencies within adolescent romantic relationships: A preliminary investigation. *Journal of Research on Adolescence*, *27*(2), 471–477. https://doi.org/10.1111/jora.12274

Nickerson, A. B., & Nagle, R. J. (2005). Parent and peer attachment in late childhood and early adolescence. *The Journal of Early Adolescence*, *25*(2), 223–249. https://doi.org/10.1177/0272431604274174

Niolon, P. H., Vivolo-Kantor, A. M., Latzman, N. E., Valle, L. A., Kuoh, H., Burton, T., . . . Tharp, A. T. (2015). Prevalence of teen dating violence and co-occurring risk factors among middle school youth in high-risk urban communities. *Journal of Adolescent Health*, *56*(2), S5–S13. https://doi.org/10.1016/j.jadohealth.2014.07.019

Olweus, D. (2013). School bullying: Development and some important challenges. *Annual Review of Clinical Psychology*, *9*(1), 751–780. https://doi.org/10.1146/annurev-clinpsy-050212-185516

Olweus, D., & Limber, S. P. (2010). Bullying in school: Evaluation and dissemination of the Olweus Bullying Prevention Program. *American Journal of Orthopsychiatry*, *80*(1), 124–134. https://doi.org/10.1111/j.1939-0025.2010.01015.x

Parkhurst, J. T., & Hopmeyer, A. (1998). Sociometric popularity and peer-perceived popularity: Two distinct dimensions of peer status. *The Journal of Early Adolescence*, *18*(2), 125–144. https://doi.org/10.1177/0272431698018002001

Perren, S., Ettekal, I., & Ladd, G. (2013). The impact of peer victimization on later maladjustment: Mediating and moderating effects of hostile and self-blaming attributions. *Journal of Child Psychology and Psychiatry, and Allied Disciplines*, *54*(1), 46–55. https://doi.org/10.1111/j.1469-7610.2012.02618.x

Pope, A. W., & Bierman, K. L. (1999). Predicting adolescent peer problems and antisocial activities: The relative roles of aggression and dysregulation. *Developmental Psychology*, *35*(2), 335–346. https://doi.org/10.1037/0012-1649.35.2.335

Poulin, F., & Chan, A. (2010). Friendship stability and change in childhood and adolescence. *Developmental Review*, *30*(3), 257–272. https://doi.org/10.1016/j.dr.2009.01.001

Pozzoli, T., Gini, G., & Vieno, A. (2012). The role of individual correlates and class norms in defending and passive bystanding behavior in bullying: A multilevel analysis. *Child Development*, *83*(6), 1917–1931. https://doi.org/10.1111/j.1467-8624.2012.01831.x

Prinstein, M. J., & La Greca, A. M. (2004). Childhood peer rejection and aggression as predictors of adolescent girls' externalizing and health risk behaviors: A 6-year longitudinal study. *Journal of Consulting & Clinical Psychology*, 72, 103–112.

Rizzo, C. J., Joppa, M., Barker, D., Collibee, C., Zlotnick, C., & Brown, L. K. (2018). Project Date SMART: A dating violence (DV) and sexual risk prevention program for adolescent girls with prior DV exposure. *Prevention Science*, 19, 416–442. https://doi.org/10.1007/s11121-018-0871-z

Roach, A. (2018). Supportive peer relationships and mental health in adolescence: An integrative review. *Issues in Mental Health Nursing*, 39(9), 723–737. https://doi.org/10.1080/01612840.2018.1496498

Rodkin, P. C., & Roisman, G. I. (2010). Antecedents and correlates of the popular-aggressive phenomenon in elementary school. *Child Development*, 81(3), 837–850. https://doi.org/10.1111/j.1467-8624.2010.01437.x

Rogers, A. A., Ha, T., Updegraff, K. A., & Iida, M. (2018). Adolescents' daily romantic experiences and negative mood: A dyadic, intensive longitudinal study. *Journal of Youth and Adolescence*, 47(7), 1517–1530. https://doi.org/10.1007/s10964-017-0797-y

Rose, A. J., & Asher, S. R. (2017). The social tasks of friendship: Do boys and girls excel in different tasks? *Child Development Perspectives*, 11(1), 3–8. https://doi.org/10.1111/cdep.12214

Rose, A. J., Schwartz-Mette, R. A., Glick, G. C., Smith, R. L., & Luebbe, A. M. (2014). An observational study of co-rumination in adolescent friendships. *Developmental Psychology*, 50(9), 2199–2209. https://doi.org/10.1037/a0037465

Rubin, K., Fredstrom, B., & Bowker, J. (2008). Future directions in friendship in childhood and early adolescence. *Social Development*, 17(4), 1085–1096. https://doi.org/10.1111/j.1467-9507.2007.00445.x

Rubin, K. H., Bukowski, W. M., & Bowker, J. C. (2015). Children in peer groups. In M. H. Bornstein & T. Leventhal (Eds.), *Handbook of child psychology and developmental science* (pp. 1–48). Hoboken, NJ: John Wiley & Sons. https://doi.org/10.1002/9781118963418.childpsy405

Rubin, K. H., Coplan, R. J., & Bowker, J. C. (2009). Social withdrawal in childhood. *Annual Review of Psychology*, 60(1), 141–171. https://doi.org/10.1146/annurev.psych.60.110707.163642

Rubin, K. H., Wojslawowicz, J. C., Rose-Krasnor, L., Booth-LaForce, C., & Burgess, K. B. (2006). The best friendships of shy/withdrawn children: Prevalence, stability, and relationship quality. *Journal of Abnormal Child Psychology*, 34(2), 143–157. https://doi.org/10.1007/s10802-005-9017-4

Ryan, A. M., & Shin, H. (2018). Peers, academics, and teachers. In W. M. Bukowski, B. Laursen, & K. H. Rubin (Eds.), *Handbook of peer interactions, relationships, and groups* (pp. 637–656). New York, NY: Guilford Press.

Savin-Williams, R. C. (2019). Developmental trajectories and milestones of sexual-minority youth. In S. Lamb & J. Gilbert (Eds.), *The Cambridge handbook of sexual development* (pp. 156–179). Cambridge, England: Cambridge University Press. https://doi.org/10.1017/9781108116121.009

Scalco, M. D., Meisel, S. N., & Colder, C. R. (2016). Misperception and accurate perception of close friend substance use in early adolescence: Developmental and intervention implications. *Psychology of Addictive Behaviors*, 30(3), 300–311. https://doi.org/10.1037/adb0000175

Scalco, M. D., Trucco, E. M., Coffman, D. L., & Colder, C. R. (2015). Selection and socialization effects in early adolescent alcohol use: A propensity score analysis. *Journal of Abnormal Child Psychology*, 43(6), 1131–1143. https://doi.org/10.1007/s10802-014-9969-3

Scharf, M., Mayseless, O., & Kivenson-Baron, I. (2004). Adolescents' attachment representations and developmental tasks in emerging adulthood. *Developmental Psychology*, 40(3), 430–444. https://doi.org/10.1037/0012-1649.40.3.430

Sears, H. A., Byers, E. S., & Price, E. L. (2007). The co-occurrence of adolescent boys' and girls' use of psychologically, physically, and sexually abusive behaviours in their dating relationships. *Journal of Adolescence*, 30(3), 487–504. https://doi.org/10.1016/j.adolescence.2006.05.002

Shetgiri, R., Lin, H., & Flores, G. (2013). Trends in risk and protective factors for child bullying perpetration in the United States. *Child Psychiatry and Human Development*, 44(1), 89–104. https://doi.org/10.1007/s10578-012-0312-3

Shin, H., & Ryan, A. M. (2014). Early adolescent friendships and academic adjustment: Examining selection and influence processes with longitudinal social network analysis. *Developmental Psychology*, 50(11), 2462–2472. https://doi.org/10.1037/a0037922

Shulman, S., Tuval-Mashiach, R., Levran, E., & Anbar, S. (2006). Conflict resolution patterns and longevity of adolescent romantic couples: A 2-year follow-up study. *Journal of Adolescence*, 29(4), 575–588. https://doi.org/10.1016/j.adolescence.2005.08.018

Simon, V. A., Aikins, J. W., & Prinstein, M. J. (2008). Romantic partner selection and socialization during early adolescence. *Child Development*, 79(6), 1676–1692. https://doi.org/10.1111/j.1467-8624.2008.01218.x

Smith-Darden, J. P., Kernsmith, P. D., Reidy, D. E., & Cortina, K. S. (2017). In search of modifiable risk and protective factors for teen dating violence. *Journal of Research on Adolescence*, 27(2), 423–435. https://doi.org/10.1111/jora.12280

Sroufe, L. A. (2016). The place of attachment in development. In J. Cassidy & P. R. Shaver (Eds.), *Handbook of attachment: Theory, research, and clinical applications* (pp. 997–1010). New York, NY: Guilford Press.

Steinberg, L., & Monahan, K. C. (2007). Age differences in resistance to peer influence. *Developmental Psychology*, 43(6), 1531–1543. https://doi.org/10.1037/0012-1649.43.6.1531

Sullivan, H. S. (1953). *The interpersonal theory of psychiatry*. New York, NY: W. W. Norton & Company.

Sumter, S. R., Bokhorst, C. L., & Westenberg, P. M. (2018). Resistance and conformity. In R. J. R. Levesque (Ed.), *Encyclopedia of adolescence* (pp. 3149–3160). Cham, Switzerland: Springer. https://doi.org/10.1007/978-3-319-33228-4_327

Sussman, S., Pokhrel, P., Ashmore, R. D., & Brown, B. B. (2007). Adolescent peer group identification and characteristics: A review of the literature. *Addictive Behaviors*, 32, 1602–1627.

Swearer, S. M., & Hymel, S. (2015). Understanding the psychology of bullying: Moving toward a social-ecological diathesis-stress model. *The American Psychologist*, 70(4), 344–353. https://doi.org/10.1037/a0038929

Titzmann, P. F., Brenick, A., & Silbereisen, R. K. (2015). Friendships fighting prejudice: A longitudinal perspective on adolescents' cross-group friendships with immigrants. *Journal of Youth and Adolescence*, 44(6), 1318–1431. https://doi.org/10.1007/s10964-015-0256-6

Troop-Gordon, W. (2017, February 1). Peer victimization in adolescence: The nature, progression, and consequences of being bullied within a developmental context. *Journal of Adolescence*, 55, 116–128. https://doi.org/10.1016/j.adolescence.2016.12.012

Twenge, J. M., & Park, H. (2019). The decline in adult activities among U.S. adolescents, 1976–2016. *Child Development*, 90(2), 638–654. https://doi.org/10.1111/cdev.12930

Vagi, K. J., Rothman, E. F., Latzman, N. E., Tharp, A. T., Hall, D. M., & Breiding, M. J. (2013). Beyond correlates: A review of risk and protective factors for adolescent dating violence perpetration. *Journal of Youth and Adolescence*, 42(4), 633–649. https://doi.org/10.1007/s10964-013-9907-7

van de Bongardt, D., Reitz, E., Sandfort, T., & Deković, M. (2014). A meta-analysis of the relations between three types of peer norms and adolescent sexual behavior. *Personality and Social Psychology Review*, *19*, 203–234. https://doi.org/10.1177/1088868314544223

van de Bongardt, D., Yu, R., Deković, M., & Meeus, W. H. J. (2015). Romantic relationships and sexuality in adolescence and young adulthood: The role of parents, peers, and partners. *European Journal of Developmental Psychology*, *12*(5), 497–515. https://doi.org/10.1080/17405629.2015.1068689

van Dijk, A., Poorthuis, A. M. G., & Malti, T. (2017). Psychological processes in young bullies versus bully-victims. *Aggressive Behavior*, *43*(5), 430–439. https://doi.org/10.1002/ab.21701

Van Hoorn, J., Crone, E. A., & Van Leijenhorst, L. (2017). Hanging out with the right crowd: Peer influence on risk-taking behavior in adolescence. *Journal of Research on Adolescence*, *27*(1), 189–200. https://doi.org/10.1111/jora.12265

van Hoorn, J., van Dijk, E., Meuwese, R., Rieffe, C., & Crone, E. A. (2016). Peer influence on prosocial behavior in adolescence. *Journal of Research on Adolescence*, *26*(1), 90–100. https://doi.org/10.1111/jora.12173

Van Petegem, S., Brenning, K., Baudat, S., Beyers, W., & Zimmer-Gembeck, M. J. (2018). Intimacy development in late adolescence: Longitudinal associations with perceived parental autonomy support and adolescents' self-worth. *Journal of Adolescence*, *65*, 111–122. https://doi.org/10.1016/J.ADOLESCENCE.2018.03.008

Verkooijen, K. T., de Vries, N. K., & Nielsen, G. A. (2007). Youth crowds and substance use: The impact of perceived group norm and multiple group identification. *Psychology of Addictive Behaviors*, *21*(1), 55–61. https://doi.org/10.1037/0893-164x.21.1.55

Waasdorp, T. E., & Bradshaw, C. P. (2011). Examining student responses to frequent bullying: A latent class approach. *Journal of Educational Psychology*, *103*(2), 336–352. https://doi.org/10.1037/a0022747

Weigard, A., Chein, J., Albert, D., Smith, A., & Steinberg, L. (2014). Effects of anonymous peer observation on adolescents' preference for immediate rewards. *Developmental Science*, *17*(1), 71–78. https://doi.org/10.1111/desc.12099

Weisz, A. N., & Black, B. M. (2008). Peer intervention in dating violence: Beliefs of African-American middle school adolescents. *Journal of Ethnic & Cultural Diversity in Social Work*, *17*(2), 177–196. https://doi.org/10.1080/15313200801947223

Wentzel, K. R. (2014). Prosocial behavior and peer relations in adolescence. In G. C. Laura M. Padilla-Walker (Ed.), *Prosocial development: A multidimensional approach* (pp. 178-200). Oxford, England: Oxford University Press.

Will, G.-J., van Lier, P. A. C., Crone, E. A., & Güroğlu, B. (2016). Chronic childhood peer rejection is associated with heightened neural responses to social exclusion during adolescence. *Journal of Abnormal Child Psychology*, *44*(1), 43–55. https://doi.org/10.1007/s10802-015-9983-0

Williams, T. S., Connolly, J., Pepler, D., Laporte, L., & Craig, W. (2008). Risk models of dating aggression across different adolescent relationships: A developmental psychopathology approach. *Journal of Consulting and Clinical Psychology*, *76*(4), 622–632. https://doi.org/10.1037/0022-006x.76.4.622

Wincentak, K., Connolly, J., & Card, N. (2017). Teen dating violence: A meta-analytic review of prevalence rates. *Psychology of Violence*, *7*(2), 224–241. https://doi.org/10.1037/a0040194

Wojslawowicz Bowker, J. C., Rubin, K. H., Burgess, K. B., Booth-Laforce, C., & Rose-Krasnor, L. (2006). Behavioral characteristics associated with stable and fluid best friendship patterns in middle childhood. *Merrill-Palmer Quarterly*, *52*(4), 671–693.

Wolke, D., & Lereya, S. T. (2015, September 1). Long-term effects of bullying. *Archives of Disease in Childhood*, *100*, 879–885. https://doi.org/10.1136/archdischild-2014-306667

Ybarra, M. L., Price-Feeney, M., & Mitchell, K. J. (2019). A cross-sectional study examining the (in)congruency of sexual identity,

sexual behavior, and romantic attraction among adolescents in the US. *Journal of Pediatrics*, *214*, 201–208. https://doi.org/10.1016/j.jpeds.2019.06.046

Yeager, D. S., Dahl, R. E., & Dweck, C. S. (2018). Why interventions to influence adolescent behavior often fail but could succeed. *Perspectives on Psychological Science*, *13*(1), 101–122. https://doi.org/10.1177/1745691617722620

Yeager, D. S., Fong, C. J., Lee, H. Y., & Espelage, D. L. (2015). Declines in efficacy of anti-bullying programs among older adolescents: Theory and a three-level meta-analysis. *Journal of Applied Developmental Psychology*, *37*, 36–51. https://doi.org/10.1016/j.appdev.2014.11.005

CHAPTER 10

Aguiar, A., Eubig, P. A., & Schantz, S. L. (2010). Attention deficit/hyperactivity disorder: A focused overview for children's environmental health researchers. *Environmental Health Perspectives*, *118*(12), 1646–1653. https://doi.org/10.1289/ehp.1002326

Akos, P., Rose, R. A., & Orthner, D. (2014). Sociodemographic moderators of middle school transition effects on academic achievement. *The Journal of Early Adolescence*, *35*(2), 170–198. https://doi.org/10.1177/0272431614529367

Alivernini, F., & Lucidi, F. (2011). Relationship between social context, self-efficacy, motivation, academic achievement, and intention to drop out of high school: A longitudinal study. *The Journal of Educational Research*, *104*(4), 241–252. https://doi.org/10.1080/00220671003728062

Alley, K. M. (2019). Fostering middle school students' autonomy to support motivation and engagement. *Middle School Journal*, *50*(3), 5–14. https://doi.org/10.1080/00940771.2019.1603801

American Association on Intellectual and Developmental Disabilities. (2010). *Intellectual disability: Definition, classification, and systems of supports*. Washington, DC: Author.

American Psychiatric Association. (2013). *Diagnostic and statistical manual of mental disorders DSM-5* (5th ed.). Washington, DC: Author.

Anderson, M., & Jiang, J. (2018,May 31). Teens, social media & technology 2018. *Pew Research Center*. Retrieved from https://www.pewresearch.org/internet/2018/05/31/teens-social-media-technology-2018/

Archer, L., DeWitt, J., Osborne, J., Dillon, J., Willis, B., & Wong, B. (2012). Science aspirations, capital, and family habitus: How families shape children's engagement and identification with science. *American Educational Research Journal*, *49*(5), 881–908. https://doi.org/10.3102/0002831211433290

Aronson, P. (2008). Breaking barriers or locked out? Class-based perceptions and experiences of postsecondary education. *New Directions for Child & Adolescent Development*, *2008*(119), 41–54. https://doi.org/10.1002/cd.208

Assadi, S. M., Zokaei, N., Kaviani, H., Mohammadi, M. R., Ghaeli, P., Gohari, M. R., & van de Vijver, F. J. R. (2007). Effect of sociocultural context and parenting style on scholastic achievement among Iranian adolescents. *Social Development*, *16*, 169–180.

Aunola, K., & Stattin, H. (2000). Parenting styles and adolescents' achievement strategies. *Journal of Adolescence*, *23*(2), 205–223.

Bachman, J. G., Johnston, L. D., & O'Malley, P. M. (2014). *Monitoring the Future: Questionnaire responses from the nation's high school seniors, 2012*. Retrieved from http://monitoringthefuture.org/datavolumes/2012/2012dv.pdf

Bachman, J. G, Staff, J., O'Malley, P. M., & Freedman-Doan, P. (2013). Adolescent work intensity, school performance, and substance use: Links vary by race/ethnicity and socioeconomic status. *Developmental Psychology*, *49*(11), 2125–2134. https://doi.org/10.1037/a0031464

Barber, B. K., & Olsen, J. A. (2004). Assessing the transitions to middle and high school. *Journal of Adolescent Research*, *19*(1), 3–30.

Battin-Pearson, S., & Newcomb, M. D. (2000). Predictors of early high school dropout: A test of five theories. *Journal of Educational Psychology*, *92*(3), 568–582.

Benner, A. D. (2011). The transition to high school: Current knowledge, future directions. *Educational Psychology Review*, *23*(3), 299–328. https://doi.org/10.1007/s10648-011-9152-0

Benner, A. D., Boyle, A. E., & Bakhtiari, F. (2017). Understanding students' transition to high school: Demographic variation and the role of supportive relationships. *Journal of Youth and Adolescence*, *46*(10), 2129–2142. https://doi.org/10.1007/s10964-017-0716-2

Benner, A. D., Boyle, A. E., & Sadler, S. (2016). Parental involvement and adolescents' educational success: The roles of prior achievement and socioeconomic status. *Journal of Youth and Adolescence*, *45*(6), 1053–1064. https://doi.org/10.1007/s10964-016-0431-4

Benner, A. D., & Graham, S. (2009). The transition to high school as a developmental process among multiethnic urban youth. *Child Development*, *80*(2), 356–376. https://doi.org/10.1111/j.1467-8624.2009.01265.x

Berninger, V. W., & Wolf, B. J. (2009). *Teaching students with dyslexia and dysgraphia: Lessons from teaching and science*. Baltimore, MD: Paul H. Brookes Publishing.

Bexkens, A., Huizenga, H. M., Neville, D. A., Collot d'Escury-Koenigs, A. L., Bredman, J. C., Wagemaker, E., & Van der Molen, M. W. (2019). Peer-influence on risk-taking in male adolescents with mild to borderline intellectual disabilities and/or behavior disorders. *Journal of Abnormal Child Psychology*, *47*(3), 543–555. https://doi.org/10.1007/s10802-018-0448-0

Bexkens, A., Jansen, B. R. J., Van der Molen, M. W., & Huizenga, H. M. (2016). Cool decision-making in adolescents with behavior disorder and/or mild-to-borderline intellectual disability. *Journal of Abnormal Child Psychology*, *44*(2), 357–367. https://doi.org/10.1007/s10802-015-9996-8

Boonk, L., Gijselaers, H. J. M., Ritzen, H., & Brand-Gruwel, S. (2018). A review of the relationship between parental involvement indicators and academic achievement. *Educational Research Review*, *24*, 10–30. https://doi.org/10.1016/j.edurev.2018.02.001

Booth, M. Z., & Gerard, J. M. (2014). Adolescents' stage-environment fit in middle and high school: The relationship between students' perceptions of their schools and themselves. *Youth & Society*, *46*(6), 735–755. https://doi.org/10.1177/0044118X12451276

Borich, G. D. (2017). *Effective teaching methods: Research-based practice* (9th ed.). New York, NY: Pearson.

Bourgeron, T. (2015). From the genetic architecture to synaptic plasticity in autism spectrum disorder. *Nature Reviews Neuroscience*, *16*(9), 551–563. https://doi.org/10.1038/nrn3992

Bowers, A. J., & Sprott, R. (2012). Examining the multiple trajectories associated with dropping out of high school: A growth mixture model analysis. *The Journal of Educational Research*, *105*(3), 176–195. https://doi.org/10.1080/00220671.2011.552075

Bozick, R., & DeLuca, S. (2011). Not making the transition to college: School, work, and opportunities in the lives of American youth. *Social Science Research*, *40*(4), 1249–1262. https://doi.org/10.1016/j.ssresearch.2011.02.003

Bronkema, R., & Bowman, N. A. (2017). A residential paradox? Residence hall attributes and college student outcomes. *Journal of College Student Development*, *58*(4), 624–630. https://doi.org/10.1353/csd.2017.0047

Burchinal, M., Roberts, J. E., Zeisel, S. A., Hennon, E. A., & Hooper, S. (2006). Social risk and protective child, parenting, and child care factors in early elementary school years. *Parenting: Science & Practice*, *6*(1), 79–113.

Burden, P. R., & Byrd, D. M. (2019). *Methods for effective teaching: Meeting the needs of all students* (8th ed.). New York, NY: Pearson.

Byrnes, V., & Ruby, A. (2007). Comparing achievement between K–8 and middle schools: A large-scale empirical study. *American Journal of Education*, *114*(1), 101–135.

Cappadocia, M. C., Weiss, J. A., & Pepler, D. (2012). Bullying experiences among children and youth with autism spectrum disorders. *Journal of Autism and Developmental Disorders*, *42*(2), 266–277. https://doi.org/10.1007/s10803-011-1241-x

Carrion-Castillo, A., Franke, B., & Fisher, S. E. (2013). Molecular genetics of dyslexia: An overview. *Dyslexia (Chichester, England)*, *19*(4), 214–240. https://doi.org/10.1002/dys.1464

Carter, E. W. (2018). Supporting the social lives of secondary students with severe disabilities: Considerations for effective intervention. *Journal of Emotional and Behavioral Disorders*, *26*(1), 52–61. https://doi.org/10.1177/1063426617739253

Castro, M., Expósito-Casas, E., López-Martín, E., Lizasoain, L., Navarro-Asencio, E., & Gaviria, J. L. (2015). Parental involvement on student academic achievement: A meta-analysis. *Educational Research Review*, *14*, 33–46. https://doi.org/10.1016/j.edurev.2015.01.002

Chan, L. K. S., & Moore, P. J. (2006). Development of attributional beliefs and strategic knowledge in years 5–9: A longitudinal analysis. *Educational Psychology*, *26*(2), 161–185. https://doi.org/10.1080/01443410500344209

Chen, Y.-C., Sudre, G., Sharp, W., Donovan, F., Chandrasekharappa, S. C., Hansen, N., . . . Shaw, P. (2018). Neuroanatomic, epigenetic and genetic differences in monozygotic twins discordant for attention deficit hyperactivity disorder. *Molecular Psychiatry*, *23*(3), 683–690. https://doi.org/10.1038/mp.2017.45

Cheng, W., Rolls, E. T., Gu, H., Zhang, J., & Feng, J. (2015). Autism: Reduced connectivity between cortical areas involved in face expression, theory of mind, and the sense of self. *Brain*, *138*(Pt 5), 1382–1393. https://doi.org/10.1093/brain/awv051

Christenson, S. L., & Thurlow, M. L. (2004). School dropouts: Prevention considerations, interventions, and challenges. *Current Directions in Psychological Science*, *13*(1), 36–39. https://doi.org/10.1111/j.0963-7214.2004.01301010.x

Ciarrochi, J., Heaven, P. C. L., & Davies, F. (2007). The impact of hope, self-esteem, and attributional style on adolescents' school grades and emotional well-being: A longitudinal study. *Journal of Research in Personality*, *41*(6), 1161–1178. https://doi.org/10.1016/j.jrp.2007.02.001

Clark, K. A., Helland, T., Specht, K., Narr, K. L., Manis, F. R., Toga, A. W., & Hugdahl, K. (2014). Neuroanatomical precursors of dyslexia identified from pre-reading through to age 11. *Brain*, *137*, 3136–3141. https://doi.org/10.1093/brain/awu229

Cleary, M., Walter, G., & Jackson, D. (2011). "'Not always smooth sailing'": Mental health issues associated with the transition from high school to college. *Issues in Mental Health Nursing*, *32*(4), 250–254. https://doi.org/10.3109/01612840.2010.548906

Coelho, V. A., Marchante, M., & Jimerson, S. R. (2017). Promoting a positive middle school transition: A randomized-controlled treatment study examining self-concept and self-esteem. *Journal of Youth and Adolescence*, *46*(3), 558–569. https://doi.org/10.1007/s10964-016-0510-6

Collier, P., & Morgan, D. (2008). "Is that paper really due today?": Differences in first-generation and traditional college students' understandings of faculty expectations. *Higher Education*, *55*(4), 425–446. https://doi.org/10.1007/s10734-007-9065-5

Cooper, S. M., Kurtz-Costes, B., & Rowley, S. J. (2010). The schooling of African American children. In J. L. Meece & J. S. Eccles (Eds.), *Handbook of research on schools, schooling and human development* (pp. 275–292). New York, NY: Routledge.

Cornell, D., Gregory, A., Huang, F., & Fan, X. (2013). Perceived prevalence of teasing and bullying predicts high school dropout rates. *Journal of Educational Psychology*, *105*(1), 138–149.

Covarrubias, R., & Fryberg, S. A. (2015). Movin' on up (to college): First-generation college students' experiences with family achievement guilt. *Cultural Diversity and Ethnic Minority Psychology*, *21*(3), 420–429. https://doi.org/10.1037/a0037844

Crockett, L. J., Petersen, A. C., Graber, J. A., Schulenberg, J. E., & Ebata, A. (1989). School transitions and adjustment during early adolescence. *The Journal of Early Adolescence*, *9*(3), 181–210. https://doi.org/10.1177/0272431689093002

Croninger, R. G., & Lee, V. E. (2001). Social capital and dropping out of high school: Benefits to at-risk students of teachers' support and guidance. *Teachers College Record*, *103*(4), 548–582.

Crosnoe, R., & Benner, A. D. (2015). Children at school. In M. H. Bornstein & T. Leventhal (Eds.), *Handbook of child psychology and developmental science* (pp. 1–37). Hoboken, NJ: John Wiley & Sons. https://doi.org/10.1002/9781118963418.childpsy407

Dajani, D. R., & Uddin, L. Q. (2016). Local brain connectivity across development in autism spectrum disorder: A cross-sectional investigation. *Autism Research*, *9*(1), 43–54. https://doi.org/10.1002/aur.1494

Demanet, J., & van Houtte, M. (2012). School belonging and school misconduct: The differing role of teacher and peer attachment. *Journal of Youth and Adolescence*, *41*(4), 499–514. https://doi.org/10.1007/s10964-011-9674-2

Desilver, D. (2019, June 27). In the U.S., teen summer jobs aren't what they used to be. *Pew Research Center*. Retrieved from https://www.pewresearch.org/fact-tank/2019/06/27/teen-summer-jobs-in-us/

Devenish, B., Hooley, M., & Mellor, D. (2017, March 1). The pathways between socioeconomic status and adolescent outcomes: A systematic review. *American Journal of Community Psychology*, *59*, 219–238. https://doi.org/10.1002/ajcp.12115

Devine, A., Hill, F., Carey, E., & Szucs, D. (2018). Cognitive and emotional math problems largely dissociate: Prevalence of developmental dyscalculia and mathematics anxiety. *Journal of Educational Psychology*, *110*(3), 431–444. https://doi.org/10.1037/edu0000222

Döhla, D., & Heim, S. (2016). Developmental dyslexia and dysgraphia: What can we learn from the one about the other? *Frontiers in Psychology*, *6*, 2045. https://doi.org/10.3389/fpsyg.2015.02045

Dornbusch, S. M., Ritter, P. L., Mont-Reynaud, R., & Chen, Z. (1990). Family decision making and academic performance in a diverse high school population. *Journal of Adolescent Research*, *5*(2), 143–160.

Dotterer, A. M., Lowe, K., & McHale, S. M. (2014). Academic growth trajectories and family relationships among African American youth. *Journal of Research on Adolescence*, *24*(4), 734–747. https://doi.org/10.1111/jora.12080

Douglass, S., Yip, T., & Shelton, J. N. (2014). Intragroup contact and anxiety among ethnic minority adolescents: Considering ethnic identity and school diversity transitions. *Journal of Youth and Adolescence*, *43*(10), 1628–1641. https://doi.org/10.1007/s10964-014-0144-5

Doyle-Thomas, K. A. R., Lee, W., Foster, N. E. V., Tryfon, A., Ouimet, T., Hyde, K. L., . . . Anagnostou, E. (2015). Atypical functional brain connectivity during rest in autism spectrum disorders. *Annals of Neurology*, *77*(5), 866–876. https://doi.org/10.1002/ana.24391

Duchesne, S., Larose, S., & Feng, B. (2019). Achievement goals and engagement with academic work in early high school: Does seeking help from teachers matter? *Journal of Early Adolescence*, *39*(2), 222–252. https://doi.org/10.1177/0272431617737626

Dupéré, V., Dion, E., Leventhal, T., Archambault, I., Crosnoe, R., & Janosz, M. (2018). High school dropout in proximal context: The triggering role of stressful life events. *Child Development*, *89*(2), e107–e122. https://doi.org/10.1111/cdev.12792

Dupere, V., Leventhal, T., Dion, E., Crosnoe, R., Archambault, I., & Janosz, M. (2015). Stressors and turning points in high school and dropout: A stress process, life course framework. *Review of Educational Research*, *85*(4), 591–629. https://doi.org/10.3102/0034654314559845

Dweck, C. S. (2017). The journey to children's mindsets —and beyond. *Child Development Perspectives*, *11*(2), 139–144. https://doi.org/10.1111/cdep.12225

Dweck, C. S., & Yeager, D. S. (2019). Mindsets: A view from two eras. *Perspectives on Psychological Science*, *14*(3), 481–496. https://doi.org/10.1177/1745691618804166

Eccles, J. S., & Roeser, R. W. (2011). Schools as developmental contexts during adolescence. *Journal of Research on Adolescence*, *21*(1), 225–241. https://doi.org/10.1111/j.1532-7795.2010.00725.x

Eccles, J. S., & Roeser, R. W. (2015). School and community influences on human development. In M. H. Bornstein & M. E. Lamb (Eds.), *Developmental science: An advanced textbook* (7th ed., pp. 645–727). New York, NY: Psychology Press.

Eshraghi, A. A., Liu, G., Kay, S.-I. S., Eshraghi, R. S., Mittal, J., Moshiree, B., & Mittal, R. (2018). Epigenetics and autism spectrum disorder: Is there a correlation? *Frontiers in Cellular Neuroscience*, *12*, 78. https://doi.org/10.3389/fncel.2018.00078

Espinoza, G., & Juvonen, J. (2011). Perceptions of the school social context across the transition to middle school: Heightened sensitivity among Latino students? *Journal of Educational Psychology*, *103*(3), 749–758. https://doi.org/10.1037/a0023811

Evans, S. W., Owens, J. S., Wymbs, B. T., & Ray, A. R. (2018). Evidence-based psychosocial treatments for children and adolescents with attention deficit/hyperactivity disorder. *Journal of Clinical Child & Adolescent Psychology*, *47*(2), 157–198. https://doi.org/10.1080/15374416.2017.1390757

Feldman, R. S. (2017). *The first year of college: Research, theory, and practice on improving the student experience and increasing retention.* Cambridge, England: Cambridge University Press.

Felmlee, D., McMillan, C., Inara Rodis, P., & Osgood, D. W. (2018). Falling behind: Lingering costs of the high school transition for youth friendships and grades. *Sociology of Education*, *91*(2), 159–182. https://doi.org/10.1177/0038040718762136

Ferguson, R. F., & Lamback, S. (2014). *Creating pathways to prosperity: A blueprint for action.* Report issued by the Pathways to Prosperity Project at the Harvard Graduate School of Education and the Achievement Gap Initiative at Harvard University. Retrieved from http://www.agi.harvard.edu/pathways/CreatingPathwaystoProsperityReport2014.pdf

Fischer, M. J. (2007). Settling into campus life: Differences by race/ethnicity in college involvement and outcomes. *Journal of Higher Education*, *78*, 125–161.

Freeman, J., & Simonsen, B. (2015). Examining the impact of policy and practice interventions on high school dropout and school completion rates: A systematic review of the literature. *Review of Educational Research*, *85*(2), 205–248. https://doi.org/10.3102/0034654314554431

Frostad, P., Pijl, S. J., & Mjaavatn, P. E. (2014). Losing all interest in school: Social participation as a predictor of the intention to leave upper secondary school early. *Scandinavian Journal of Educational Research*, *59*(1), 110–122. https://doi.org/10.1080/00313831.2014.904420

Fuchs, L. S., Malone, A. S., Schumacher, R. F., Namkung, J., & Wang, A. (2017). Fraction intervention for students with mathematics difficulties: Lessons learned from five randomized controlled trials. *Journal of Learning Disabilities*, *50*(6), 631–639. https://doi.org/10.1177/0022219416677249

Garcia, P. R. J. M., Restubog, S. L. D., Bordia, P., Bordia, S., & Roxas, R. E. O. (2015). Career optimism: The roles of contextual support and career decision-making self-efficacy. *Journal of Vocational Behavior*, *88*, 10–18. https://doi.org/10.1016/j.jvb.2015.02.004

Gentle-Genitty, C. (2009). Best practice program for low-income African American students transitioning from middle to high school. *Children & Schools*, *31*(2), 109–117.

Golden, A. R., Griffin, C. B., Metzger, I. W., & Cooper, S. M. (2018). School racial climate and academic outcomes in African American adolescents: The protective role of peers. *Journal of Black Psychology*, *44*(1), 47–73. https://doi.org/10.1177/0095798417736685

Goldstein, S. E., Boxer, P., & Rudolph, E. (2015). Middle school transition stress: Links with academic performance, motivation, and school experiences. *Contemporary School Psychology*, *19*(1), 21–29. https://doi.org/10.1007/s40688-014-0044-4

Gonzalez, A.-L., & Wolters, C. A. (2006). The relation between perceived parenting practices and achievement motivation in mathematics. *Journal of Research in Childhood Education*, *21*(2), 203–217.

Gordon, M. S. (2016). Community disadvantage and adolescent's academic achievement: The mediating role of father influence. *Journal of Child and Family Studies*, *25*(7), 2069–2078. https://doi.org/10.1007/s10826-016-0380-2

Gordon, M. S., & Cui, M. (2018). The intersection of race and community poverty and its effects on adolescents' academic achievement. *Youth and Society*, *50*(7), 947–965. https://doi.org/10.1177/0044118X16646590

Graves, J. M., Mackelprang, J. L., Barbosa-Leiker, C., Miller, M. E., & Li, A. Y. (2017). Quality of life among working and non-working adolescents. *Quality of Life Research*, *26*(1), 107–120. https://doi.org/10.1007/s11136-016-1376-5

Graves, J. M., Whitehill, J. M., Miller, M. E., Brooks-Russell, A., Richardson, S. M., & Dilley, J. A. (2019). Employment and marijuana use among Washington state adolescents before and after legalization of retail marijuana. *Journal of Adolescent Health*, *65*(1), 39–45. https://doi.org/10.1016/j.jadohealth.2018.12.027

Greenberger, E., & Steinberg, L. (1986). *When teenagers work: The psychological and social costs of adolescent employment*. New York, NY: Basic Books.

Greene, K. M., & Staff, J. (2012). Teenage employment and career readiness. *New Directions for Youth Development*, *2012*(134), 7–8, 23–31. https://doi.org/10.1002/yd.20012

Gremmen, M. C., Dijkstra, J. K., Steglich, C., & Veenstra, R. (2017). First selection, then influence: Developmental differences in friendship dynamics regarding academic achievement. *Developmental Psychology*, *53*(7), 1356–1370. https://doi.org/10.1037/dev0000314

Hahamy, A., Behrmann, M., & Malach, R. (2015). The idiosyncratic brain: Distortion of spontaneous connectivity patterns in autism spectrum disorder. *Nature Neuroscience*, *18*(2), 302–309. https://doi.org/10.1038/nn.3919

Haimovitz, K., & Dweck, C. S. (2017). The origins of children's growth and fixed mindsets: New research and a new proposal. *Child Development*, *88*(6), 1849–1859. https://doi.org/10.1111/cdev.12955

Hall, L. J. (2018). *Autism spectrum disorders: From theory to practice*. New York, NY: Pearson.

Hassan, K. El. (2008). Identifying indicators of student development in college. *College Student Journal*, *42*(2), 517–530.

Hawk, L. W., Fosco, W. D., Colder, C. R., Waxmonsky, J. G., Pelham, W. E., & Rosch, K. S. (2018). How do stimulant treatments for ADHD work? Evidence for mediation by improved cognition. *Journal of Child Psychology and Psychiatry*. https://doi.org/10.1111/jcpp.12917

Heaven, P. C. L., & Ciarrochi, J. (2008). Parental styles, conscientiousness, and academic performance in high school: A three-wave longitudinal study. *Personality and Social Psychology Bulletin*, *34*(4), 451–461. https://doi.org/10.1177/0146167207311909

Heikura, U., Taanila, A., Hartikainen, A.-L., Olsen, P., Linna, S.-L., von Wendt, L., & Järvelin, M.-R. (2008). Variations in prenatal sociodemographic factors associated with intellectual disability: A study of the 20-year interval between two birth cohorts in northern Finland. *American Journal of Epidemiology*, *167*(2), 169–177. https://doi.org/10.1093/aje/kwm291

Henry, K. L., Knight, K. E., & Thornberry, T. P. (2012). School disengagement as a predictor of dropout, delinquency, and problem substance use during adolescence and early adulthood. *Journal of Youth and Adolescence*, *41*(2), 156–166. https://doi.org/10.1007/s10964-011-9665-3

Heward, W. L. (2018). *Exceptional children: An introduction to special education* (11th ed.). New York, NY: Pearson.

Hinshaw, S. P. (2018). Attention deficit hyperactivity disorder (ADHD): Controversy, developmental mechanisms, and multiple levels of analysis. *Annual Review of Clinical Psychology*, *14*(1), 291–316. https://doi.org/10.1146/annurev-clinpsy-050817-084917

Holas, I., & Huston, A. C. (2012). Are middle schools harmful? The role of transition timing, classroom quality and school characteristics. *Journal of Youth and Adolescence*, *41*(3), 333–345. https://doi.org/10.1007/s10964-011-9732-9

Hopson, L. M., & Lee, E. (2011). Mitigating the effect of family poverty on academic and behavioral outcomes: The role of school climate in middle and high school. *Children and Youth Services Review*, *33*(11), 2221–2229. https://doi.org/10.1016/j.childyouth.2011.07.006

Horowitz, S. H., Rawe, J., & Whittaker, M. C. (2017). *The state of learning disabilities: Understanding the 1 in 5*. New York, NY: National Center for Learning Disabilities.

Hsieh, P.-H. P., & Schallert, D. L. (2008). Implications from self-efficacy and attribution theories for an understanding of undergraduates' motivation in a foreign language course. *Contemporary Educational Psychology*, *33*(4), 513–532. https://doi.org/10.1016/j.cedpsych.2008.01.003

Hull, J. V., Dokovna, L. B., Jacokes, Z. J., Torgerson, C. M., Irimia, A., & Van Horn, J. D. (2017). Resting-state functional connectivity in autism spectrum disorders: A review. *Frontiers in Psychiatry*, *7*, 205. https://doi.org/10.3389/fpsyt.2016.00205

Hwang, N. Y., & Domina, T. (2017). The links between youth employment and educational attainment across racial groups. *Journal of Research on Adolescence*, *27*(2), 312–327. https://doi.org/10.1111/jora.12277

Hwang, N. Y., Reyes, M., & Eccles, J. S. (2019). Who holds a fixed mindset and whom does it harm in mathematics? *Youth and Society*, *51*(2), 247–267. https://doi.org/10.1177/0044118X16670058

Im, M. H., Hughes, J. N., Cao, Q., & Kwok, O. M. (2016). Effects of extracurricular participation during middle school on academic motivation and achievement at Grade 9. *American Educational Research Journal*, *53*(5), 1343–1375. https://doi.org/10.3102/0002831216667479

Jacobson, L. A., Crocetti, D., Dirlikov, B., Slifer, K., Denckla, M. B., Mostofsky, S. H., & Mahone, E. M. (2018). Anomalous brain development is evident in preschoolers with attention-deficit/hyperactivity disorder. *Journal of the International Neuropsychological Society*, *24*(6), 531–539. https://doi.org/10.1017/S1355617718000103

Jain, S., & Cohen, A. K. (2013). Behavioral adaptation among youth exposed to community violence: A longitudinal multidisciplinary study of family, peer and neighborhood-level protective factors. *Prevention Science*, *14*(6), 606–617. https://doi.org/10.1007/s11121-012-0344-8

Janosz, M., Archambault, I., Morizot, J., & Pagani, L. S. (2008). School engagement trajectories and their differential predictive relations to dropout. *Journal of Social Issues*, *64*(1), 21–40. https://doi.org/10.1111/j.1540-4560.2008.00546.x

Jia, Y., Konold, T. R., & Cornell, D. (2016). Authoritative school climate and high school dropout rates. *School Psychology Quarterly, 31*(2), 289–303. https://doi.org/10.1037/spq0000139

Jury, M., Smeding, A., Stephens, N. M., Nelson, J. E., Aelenei, C., & Darnon, C. (2017). The experience of low-SES students in higher education: Psychological barriers to success and interventions to reduce social-class inequality. *Journal of Social Issues, 73*(1), 23–41. https://doi.org/10.1111/josi.12202

Juvonen, J., Kogachi, K., & Graham, S. (2018). When and how do students benefit from ethnic diversity in middle school? *Child Development, 89*(4), 1268–1282. https://doi.org/10.1111/cdev.12834

Kalogrides, D., Loeb, S., & Béteille, T. (2013). Systematic sorting: Teacher characteristics and class assignments. *Sociology of Education, 86*(2), 103–123. https://doi.org/10.1177/0038040712456555

Kana, R. K., Maximo, J. O., Williams, D. L., Keller, T. A., Schipul, S. E., Cherkassky, V. L., . . . Müller, R. (2015). Aberrant functioning of the theory-of-mind network in children and adolescents with autism. *Molecular Autism, 6*(1), 59. https://doi.org/10.1186/s13229-015-0052-x

Kantamneni, N., McCain, M. R. C., Shada, N., Hellwege, M. A., & Tate, J. (2018). Contextual factors in the career development of prospective first-generation college students. *Journal of Career Assessment, 26*(1), 183–196. https://doi.org/10.1177/1069072716680048

Karbach, J., Gottschling, J., Spengler, M., Hegewald, K., & Spinath, F. M. (2013). Parental involvement and general cognitive ability as predictors of domain-specific academic achievement in early adolescence. *Learning and Instruction, 23*, 43–51. https://doi.org/10.1016/j.learninstruc.2012.09.004

Karlson, K. B. (2015). Expectations on track? High school tracking and adolescent educational expectations. *Social Forces, 94*(1), 115–141. https://doi.org/10.1093/sf/sov006

Kaufmann, L., Mazzocco, M. M., Dowker, A., von Aster, M., Göbel, S. M., Grabner, R. H., . . . Nuerk, H.-C. (2013). Dyscalculia from a developmental and differential perspective. *Frontiers in Psychology, 4*, 516. https://doi.org/10.3389/fpsyg.2013.00516

Kennedy, T. M., & Ceballo, R. (2014). Who, what, when, and where? Toward a dimensional conceptualization of community violence exposure. *Review of General Psychology, 18*(2), 69–81. https://doi.org/10.1037/gpr0000005

Khan, A. J., Nair, A., Keown, C. L., Datko, M. C., Lincoln, A. J., & Müller, R.-A. (2015). Cerebro-cerebellar resting state functional connectivity in children and adolescents with autism spectrum disorder. *Biological Psychiatry, 78*(9), 625. https://doi.org/10.1016/J.BIOPSYCH.2015.03.024

Kidger, J., Araya, R., Donovan, J., & Gunnell, D. (2012). The effect of the school environment on the emotional health of adolescents: A systematic review. *Pediatrics, 129*(5), 925–949. https://doi.org/10.1542/peds.2011-2248

King, P. M., & Kitchener, K. S. (2015). Cognitive development in the emerging adult. In J. J. Arnett (Ed.), *The Oxford handbook of emerging adulthood* (pp. 105–125). Oxford, England: Oxford University Press. https://doi.org/10.1093/oxfordhb/9780199795574.013.14

King, V. L., & Mrug, S. (2018). The relationship between violence exposure and academic achievement in African American Adolescents is moderated by emotion regulation. *Journal of Early Adolescence, 38*(4), 497–512. https://doi.org/10.1177/0272431616675973

Kingery, J. N., Erdley, C. A., & Marshall, K. C. (2011). Peer acceptance and friendship as predictors of early adolescents' adjustment across the middle school transition. *Merrill-Palmer Quarterly, 57*(3), 215–243. https://doi.org/10.1353/mpq.2011.0012

Kingston, S., & Rose, A. (2015). Do the effects of adolescent employment differ by employment intensity and neighborhood context? *American Journal of Community Psychology, 55*(1–2), 37–47. https://doi.org/10.1007/s10464-014-9690-y

Krei, M. S., & Rosenbaum, J. E. (2000). Career and college advice to the forgotten half: What do counselors and vocational teachers advise? *Teachers College Record, 103*(5), 823–842. Retrieved from http://eric.ed.gov/?id=EJ638357

Kucian, K., & von Aster, M. (2015). Developmental dyscalculia. *European Journal of Pediatrics, 174*(1), 1–13. https://doi.org/10.1007/s00431-014-2455-7

Kuo, M. H., Orsmond, G. I., Cohn, E. S., & Coster, W. J. (2013). Friendship characteristics and activity patterns of adolescents with an autism spectrum disorder. *Autism, 17*(4), 481–500. https://doi.org/10.1177/1362361311416380

Kuusikko, S., Pollock-Wurman, R., Jussila, K., Carter, A. S., Mattila, M.-L., Ebeling, H., . . . Moilanen, I. (2008). Social anxiety in high-functioning children and adolescents with Autism and Asperger syndrome. *Journal of Autism and Developmental Disorders, 38*(9), 1697–1709. https://doi.org/10.1007/s10803-008-0555-9

Lapsley, D., & Hardy, S. A. (2017). Identity formation and moral development in emerging adulthood. In L. M. Padilla-Walker and L. J. Nelson (Eds.), *Flourishing in emerging adulthood: Positive development during the third decade of life* (pp. 14–39). New York, NY: Oxford University Press. https://doi.org/10.1093/acprof:oso/9780190260637.003.0002

Legette, K. (2018). School tracking and youth self-perceptions: Implications for academic and racial identity. *Child Development, 89*(4), 1311–1327. https://doi.org/10.1111/cdev.12748

Lewis, R. B., Wheeler, J. J., & Carter, S. L. (2017). *Teaching students with special needs in general education classrooms.* Boston, MA: Pearson.

Li, J. J. (2019). Assessing phenotypic and polygenic models of ADHD to identify mechanisms of risk for longitudinal trajectories of externalizing behaviors. *Journal of Child Psychology and Psychiatry and Allied Disciplines.* https://doi.org/10.1111/jcpp.13071

Lonigan, C. J. (2015). Literacy Development. In L. S. Liben & U. Muller (Eds.), *Handbook of child psychology and developmental science* (pp. 763–804). Hoboken, NJ: John Wiley & Sons. https://doi.org/10.1002/9781118963418.childpsy218

Madjar, N., & Cohen-Malayev, M. (2016). Perceived school climate across the transition from elementary to middle school. *School Psychology Quarterly, 31*(2), 270–288. https://doi.org/10.1037/spq0000129

Mahoney, J. L. (2014). School extracurricular activity participation and early school dropout: A mixed-method study of the role of peer social networks. *Journal of Educational and Developmental Psychology, 4*(1), p143. https://doi.org/10.5539/jedp.v4n1p143

Maier, K. S. (2005). Transmitting educational values: Parent occupation and adolescent development. In B. Schneider & L. J. Waite (Eds.), *Being together, working apart: Dual-career families and the work-life balance* (pp. 396–418). Cambridge, England: Cambridge University Press.

Markus, H. R., & Kitayama, S. (1991). Culture and the self: Implications for cognition, emotion, and motivation. *Psychological Review, 98*(2), 224–253. https://doi.org/10.1037/0033-295X.98.2.224

Masi, A., DeMayo, M. M., Glozier, N., & Guastella, A. J. (2017). An overview of autism spectrum disorder, heterogeneity and treatment options. *Neuroscience Bulletin, 33*(2), 183–193. https://doi.org/10.1007/s12264-017-0100-y

Mastropieri, M. A., & Scruggs, T. E. (2017). *The inclusive classroom: Strategies for effective differentiated instruction.* New York, NY: Pearson Education.

Mayes, S. D., Breaux, R. P., Calhoun, S. L., & Frye, S. S. (2019). High prevalence of dysgraphia in elementary through high school students with ADHD and autism. *Journal of Attention Disorders, 23*(8), 787–796. https://doi.org/10.1177/1087054717720721

Mayes, S. D., Frye, S. S., Breaux, R. P., & Calhoun, S. L. (2018). Diagnostic, demographic, and neurocognitive correlates of dysgraphia in students with ADHD, autism, learning disabilities, and neurotypical development. *Journal of Developmental and Physical Disabilities*, *30*(4), 489–507. https://doi.org/10.1007/s10882-018-9598-9

Mayhew, M. J., Rockenbach, A. N., Bowman, N. A., Seifert, T. A., Wolniak, G. C., Pascarella, E. T., & Terenzini, P. Y. (2016). *How college affects students (Vol. 3): 21st century evidence that higher education works*. Hoboken, NJ: John Wiley & Sons.

McClure, J., Meyer, L. H., Garisch, J., Fischer, R., Weir, K. F., & Walkey, F. H. (2011). Students' attributions for their best and worst marks: Do they relate to achievement? *Contemporary Educational Psychology*, *36*(2), 71–81. https://doi.org/10.1016/j.cedpsych.2010.11.001

McKenzie, K., Milton, M., Smith, G., & Ouellette-Kuntz, H. (2016). Systematic review of the prevalence and incidence of intellectual disabilities: Current trends and issues. *Current Developmental Disorders Reports*, *3*(2), 104–115. https://doi.org/10.1007/s40474-016-0085-7

McLoyd, V. C., & Hallman, S. K. (2018). Antecedents and correlates of adolescent employment: Race as a moderator of psychological predictors. *Youth & Society*, 0044118X1878163. https://doi.org/10.1177/0044118X18781637

McPheeters, M. L., Davis, A., Navarre, J. R., & Scott, T. A. (2011). Family report of ASD concomitant with depression or anxiety among US children. *Journal of Autism and Developmental Disorders*, *41*(5), 646–653. https://doi.org/10.1007/s10803-010-1085-9

Meece, J. L., Anderman, E. M., & Anderman, L. H. (2006). Classroom goal structure, student motivation, and academic achievement. *Annual Review of Psychology*, *57*(1), 487–503. https://doi.org/10.1146/annurev.psych.56.091103.070258

Menon, V. (2016). Working memory in children's math learning and its disruption in dyscalculia. *Current Opinion in Behavioral Sciences*, *10*, 125–132. https://doi.org/10.1016/j.cobeha.2016.05.014

Midgley, C., Anderman, E., & Hicks, L. (1995). Differences between elementary and middle school teachers and students: A goal theory approach. *The Journal of Early Adolescence*, *15*(1), 90–113. https://doi.org/10.1177/0272431695015001006

Moilanen, K. L., Rasmussen, K. E., & Padilla-Walker, L. M. (2015). Bidirectional associations between self-regulation and parenting styles in early adolescence. *Journal of Research on Adolescence*, *25*(2), 246–262. https://doi.org/10.1111/jora.12125

Monaghan, D. B., & Attewell, P. (2015). The community college route to the bachelor's degree. *Educational Evaluation and Policy Analysis*, *37*(1), 70–91. https://doi.org/10.3102/0162373714521865

Monahan, K. C., Lee, J. M., & Steinberg, L. (2011). Revisiting the impact of part-time work on adolescent adjustment: Distinguishing between selection and socialization using propensity score matching. *Child Development*, *82*(1), 96–112. https://doi.org/10.1111/j.1467-8624.2010.01543.x

Morris, D. S. (2016). Extracurricular activity participation in high school: Mechanisms linking participation to math achievement and 4-year college attendance. *American Educational Research Journal*, *53*(5), 1376–1410. https://doi.org/10.3102/0002831216667579

Mortimer, J. T., & Johnson, M. K. (1998). New perspectives on adolescent work and the transition to adulthood. In R. Jessor (Ed.), *New perspectives on adolescent risk behavior*. (pp. 425–496). New York, NY: Cambridge University Press.

Mueller, C. E., & Anderman, E. M. (2010). Middle school transitions and adolescent development. In J. L. Meece and J. S. Eccles (Eds.), *Handbook of research on schools, schooling and human development* (pp. 216–233). New York, NY: Routledge. https://doi.org/10.4324/9780203874844

Muenks, K., Wigfield, A., & Eccles, J. S. (2018). I can do this! The development and calibration of children's expectations for success and competence beliefs. *Developmental Review*, *48*, 24–39. https://doi.org/10.1016/J.DR.2018.04.001

National Center for Education Statistics. (2017a). *Digest of Education Statistics, 2017*. Retrieved from https://nces.ed.gov/pubs2018/2018070.pdf

National Center for Education Statistics. (2017b). Dropout rates. *The Condition of Education*. Retrieved from https://nces.ed.gov/programs/coe/indicator_coj.asp

National Center for Education Statistics. (2017c). Immediate college enrollment rate. *The Condition of Education*. Retrieved from https://nces.ed.gov/programs/coe/indicator_cpa.asp

National Center for Education Statistics. (2017d). *Status and trends in the education of racial and ethnic groups*. Retrieved from https://nces.ed.gov/programs/raceindicators/index.asp

National Center for Education Statistics. (2017e). Undergraduate retention and graduation rates - indicator April (2017). *The Condition of Education*. Retrieved from https://nces.ed.gov/programs/coe/indicator_ctr.asp

National Middle School Association. (2003). *This we believe: Successful schools for young adolescents*. Westerville, OH: Author.

Neel, C. G. O., & Fuligni, A. (2013). A longitudinal study of school belonging and academic motivation across high school. *Child Development*, *84*(2), 678–692. https://doi.org/10.1111/j.1467-8624.2012.01862.x

Nelson, R. M., & DeBacker, T. K. (2008). Achievement motivation in adolescents: The role of peer climate and best friends. *The Journal of Experimental Education*, *76*(2), 170–189. https://doi.org/10.3200/JEXE.76.2.170-190

Ng, F. F.-Y., Pomerantz, E. M., & Lam, S. (2007). European American and Chinese parents' responses to children's success and failure: Implications for children's responses. *Developmental Psychology*, *43*(5), 1239–1255. https://doi.org/10.1037/0012-1649.43.5.1239

Ojeda, L., Navarro, R. L., & Morales, A. (2011). The role of la familia on Mexican American men's college persistence intentions. *Psychology of Men & Masculinity*, *12*(3), 216–229. https://doi.org/10.1037/a0020091

Orbe, M. P. (2008). Theorizing multidimensional identity negotiation: Reflections on the lived experiences of first-generation college students. *New Directions for Child & Adolescent Development*, *2008*(120), 81–95.

Orkin, M., May, S., & Wolf, M. (2017). How parental support during homework contributes to helpless behaviors among struggling readers. *Reading Psychology*, *38*(5), 506–541. https://doi.org/10.1080/02702711.2017.1299822

Orsmond, G. I., Krauss, M. W., & Seltzer, M. M. (2004, June). Peer relationships and social and recreational activities among adolescents and adults with autism. *Journal of Autism and Developmental Disorders*, *34*, 245–256. https://doi.org/10.1023/B:JADD.0000029547.96610.df

Parra-Cardona, J. R., Cordova, D., Holtrop, K., Villarruel, F. A., & Wieling, E. (2008). Shared ancestry, evolving stories: Similar and contrasting life experiences described by foreign born and U.S. born Latino parents. *Family Process*, *47*(2), 157–172. https://doi.org/10.1111/j.1545-5300.2008.00246.x

Patros, C. H. G., Alderson, R. M., Kasper, L. J., Tarle, S. J., Lea, S. E., & Hudec, K. L. (2016). Choice-impulsivity in children and adolescents with attention-deficit/hyperactivity disorder (ADHD): A meta-analytic review. *Clinical Psychology Review*, *43*, 162–174. https://doi.org/10.1016/j.cpr.2015.11.001

Patton, L. D., Renn, K. A., Guido-DiBrito, F., & Quaye, S. J. (2016). *Student development in college: Theory, research, and practice*. Hoboken, NJ: John Wiley & Sons.

Perry, R. P., Stupnisky, R. H., Daniels, L. M., & Haynes, T. L. (2008). Attributional (explanatory) thinking about failure in new achievement settings. *European Journal of Psychology of Education*, *23*(4), 459–475. https://doi.org/10.1007/BF03172753

Peterson, R. L., & Pennington, B. F. (2012). Developmental dyslexia. *Lancet, 379*(9830), 1997–2007. https://doi.org/10.1016/S0140-6736(12)60198-6

Phillips, L. T., Stephens, N. M., & Townsend, S. S. M. (2016). *Access is not enough: Cultural mismatch persists to limit first-generation students' opportunities for achievement throughout college*. Retrieved from https://www.scholars.northwestern.edu/en/publications/access-is-not-enough-cultural-mismatch-persists-to-limit-first-ge

Picci, G., & Scherf, K. S. (2015, May 1). A two-hit model of autism: Adolescence as the second hit. *Clinical Psychological Science, 3*, 349–371. https://doi.org/10.1177/2167702614540646

Pinquart, M. (2017). Associations of parenting dimensions and styles with externalizing problems of children and adolescents: An updated meta-analysis. *Developmental Psychology, 53*(5), 873–932. https://doi.org/10.1037/dev0000295

Pomerantz, E. M., & Dong, W. (2006). Effects of mothers' perceptions of children's competence: The moderating role of mothers' theories of competence. *Developmental Psychology, 42*(5), 950–961. https://doi.org/10.1037/0012-1649.42.5.950

Pomerantz, E. M., Ng, F. F.-Y., Cheung, C. S.-S., & Qu, Y. (2014). Raising happy children who succeed in school: Lessons from China and the United States. *Child Development Perspectives, 8*(2), 71–76. https://doi.org/10.1111/cdep.12063

Preston, C., Goldring, E., Guthrie, J. E., Ramsey, R., & Huff, J. (2017). Conceptualizing Essential components of effective high schools. *Leadership and Policy in Schools, 16*, 525–562. https://doi.org/10.1080/15700763.2016.1205198

Próspero, M., Russell, A. C., & Vohra-Gupta, S. (2012). Effects of motivation on educational attainment. *Journal of Hispanic Higher Education, 11*(1), 100–119. https://doi.org/10.1177/1538192711435556

Raftery, J. N., Grolnick, W. S., & Flamm, E. S. (2012). Families as facilitators of student engagement: Toward a home-school partnership model. In S. L. Christenson, A. L. Reschly, & C. Wylie (Eds.), *Handbook of research on student engagement* (pp. 343–364). Boston, MA: Springer. https://doi.org/10.1007/978-1-4614-2018-7_16

Rambaran, J. A., Hopmeyer, A., Schwartz, D., Steglich, C., Badaly, D., & Veenstra, R. (2017). Academic functioning and peer influences: A short-term longitudinal study of network-behavior dynamics in middle adolescence. *Child Development, 88*(2), 523–543. https://doi.org/10.1111/cdev.12611

Ramus, F. (2014). Neuroimaging sheds new light on the phonological deficit in dyslexia. *Trends in Cognitive Sciences, 18*(6), 274–275. https://doi.org/10.1016/j.tics.2014.01.009

Rapin, I. (2016). Dyscalculia and the calculating brain. *Pediatric Neurology, 61*, 11–20. https://doi.org/10.1016/j.pediatrneurol.2016.02.007

Rattan, A., Savani, K., Chugh, D., & Dweck, C. S. (2015). Leveraging mindsets to promote academic achievement: Policy recommendations. *Perspectives on Psychological Science, 10*(6), 721–726. https://doi.org/10.1177/1745691615599383

Rauscher, K. J., Wegman, D. H., Wooding, J., Davis, L., & Junkin, R. (2013). Adolescent work quality: A view from today's youth. *Journal of Adolescent Research, 28*(5), 557–590. https://doi.org/10.1177/0743558412467676

Reyna, C. (2008). Ian is intelligent but Leshaun is lazy: Antecedents and consequences of attributional stereotypes in the classroom. *European Journal of Psychology of Education, 23*(4), 439–458. https://doi.org/10.1007/BF03172752

Richards, T. L., Grabowski, T. J., Boord, P., Yagle, K., Askren, M., Mestre, Z., ... Berninger, V. (2015). Contrasting brain patterns of writing-related DTI parameters, fMRI connectivity, and DTI–fMRI connectivity correlations in children with and without dysgraphia or dyslexia. *NeuroImage: Clinical, 8*, 408–421. https://doi.org/10.1016/J.NICL.2015.03.018

Robbins, S. B., Allen, J., Casillas, A., Peterson, C. H., & Le, H. (2006). Unraveling the differential effects of motivational and skills, social, and self-management measures from traditional predictors of college outcomes. *Journal of Educational Psychology, 98*(3), 598–616.

Rocheleau, G. C. (2018). Long-term relationships between adolescent intense work and deviance: Are there differences by social class? *Advances in Life Course Research, 37*, 69–78. https://doi.org/10.1016/j.alcr.2018.08.002

Roeser, R. W., Eccles, J. S., & Sameroff, A. J. (2000). School as a context of early adolescents' academic and social-emotional development: A summary of research findings. *Elementary School Journal, 100*(5), 443–471. https://doi.org/10.1086/499650

Rosenbaum, J. E., & Person, A. E. (2003). Beyond college for all: Policies and practices to improve transitions into college and jobs. *Professional School Counseling, 6*(4), 252.

Rudolph, K. D., Lambert, S. F., Clark, A. G., & Kurlakowsky, K. D. (2001). Negotiating the transition to middle school: The role of self-regulatory processes. *Child Development, 72*(3), 929–947.

Rueger, S. Y., Chen, P., Jenkins, L. N., & Choe, H. J. (2014). Effects of perceived support from mothers, fathers, and teachers on depressive symptoms during the transition to middle school. *Journal of Youth and Adolescence, 43*(4), 655–670. https://doi.org/10.1007/s10964-013-0039-x

Rutledge, S. A., Cohen-Vogel, L., Osborne-Lampkin, L., & Roberts, R. L. (2015). Understanding effective high schools: Evidence for personalization for academic and social emotional learning. *American Educational Research Journal, 52*(6), 1060–1092. https://doi.org/10.3102/0002831215602328

Ryan, A. M., & Patrick, H. (2001). The classroom social environment and changes in adolescents' motivation and engagement during middle school. *American Educational Research Journal, 38*(2), 437–460.

Salend, S. J. (2015). *Creating inclusive classrooms: Effective, differentiated and reflective practices*. Boston, MA: Pearson College Division.

Sandin, S., Lichtenstein, P., Kuja-Halkola, R., Hultman, C., Larsson, H., & Reichenberg, A. (2017). The heritability of autism spectrum disorder. *JAMA, 318*(12), 1182–1184. https://doi.org/10.1001/jama.2017.12141

Schachar, R. (2014). Genetics of attention deficit hyperactivity disorder (ADHD): Recent updates and future prospects. *Current Developmental Disorders Reports, 1*(1), 41–49. https://doi.org/10.1007/s40474-013-0004-0

Schalock, R. L. (2015). Intellectual disability. In R. L. Cautin & S. O. Lilienfeld (Eds.), *The Encyclopedia of clinical psychology* (pp. 1–7). Hoboken, NJ: John Wiley and Sons. https://doi.org/10.1002/9781118625392.wbecp062

Schurz, M., Wimmer, H., Richlan, F., Ludersdorfer, P., Klackl, J., & Kronbichler, M. (2015). Resting-state and task-based functional brain connectivity in developmental dyslexia. *Cerebral Cortex, 25*, 3502–3514. https://doi.org/10.1093/cercor/bhu184

Schwartz, D., Lansford, J. E., Dodge, K. A., Pettit, G. S., & Bates, J. E. (2014). Peer victimization during middle childhood as a lead indicator of internalizing problems and diagnostic outcomes in late adolescence. *Journal of Clinical Child and Adolescent Psychology*. https://doi.org/10.1080/15374416.2014.881293

Seidman, E., Aber, J. L., & French, S. E. (2004). The organization of schooling and adolescent development. In K. I. Maton, C. J. Schellenbach, B. J. Leadbeater, & A. L. Solarz (Eds.), *Investing in children, youth, families, and communities: Strengths-based research and policy*. (pp. 233–250). Washington, DC: American Psychological Association.

Seidman, E., Lambert, L. E., Allen, L., & Aber, J. L. (2003). Urban adolescents' transition to junior high school and protective family transactions. *Journal of Early Adolescence, 23*(2), 166–194.

Senju, A. (2012). Spontaneous theory of mind and its absence in autism spectrum disorders. *The Neuroscientist, 18*(2), 108–113. https://doi.org/10.1177/1073858410397208

Shea, S. E. (2012). Intellectual disability (mental retardation). *Pediatrics in Review, 33*(3), 110-121; https://doi.org/10.1542/pir.33-3-110

Sigstad, H. M. H. (2016). Significance of friendship for quality of life in adolescents with mild intellectual disability: A parental perspective†. *Journal of Intellectual and Developmental Disability, 41*(4), 289–298. https://doi.org/10.3109/13668250.2016.1200018

Simpkins, S. D., Delgado, M. Y., Price, C. D., Quach, A., & Starbuck, E. (2013). Socioeconomic status, ethnicity, culture, and immigration: Examining the potential mechanisms underlying Mexican-origin adolescents' organized activity participation. *Developmental Psychology, 49*(4), 706–721. https://doi.org/10.1037/a0028399

Skomsvold, P. (2014, October 2). *Profile of undergraduate students: 2011-12* (web tables). Retrieved from https://nces.ed.gov/pubsearch/pubsinfo.asp?pubid=2015167

Snowling, M. J. (2013). Early identification and interventions for dyslexia: A contemporary view. *Journal of Research in Special Educational Needs, 13*(1), 7–14. https://doi.org/10.1111/j.1471-3802.2012.01262.x

Song, J., Bong, M., Lee, K., & Kim, S. Il. (2015). Longitudinal investigation into the role of perceived social support in adolescents' academic motivation and achievement. *Journal of Educational Psychology, 107*(3), 821–841. https://doi.org/10.1037/edu0000016

Spera, C. (2005). A review of the relationship among parenting practices, parenting styles, and adolescent school achievement. *Educational Psychology Review, 17*(2), 125–146.

Srour, M., & Shevell, M. (2014). Genetics and the investigation of developmental delay/intellectual disability. *Archives of Disease in Childhood, 99*(4), 386–389. https://doi.org/10.1136/archdischild-2013-304063

Staff, J., & Uggen, C. (2003). The fruits of good work: Early work experiences and adolescent deviance. *Journal of Research in Crime & Delinquency, 40*(3), 263–290.

Staff, J., Vaneseltine, M., Woolnough, A., Silver, E., & Burrington, L. (2012). Adolescent work experiences and family formation behavior. *Journal of Research on Adolescence, 22*(1), 150–164. https://doi.org/10.1111/j.1532-7795.2011.00755.x

Staff, J., Yetter, A. M., Cundiff, K., Ramirez, N., Vuolo, M., & Mortimer, J. T. (2019). Is adolescent employment still a risk factor for high school dropout? *Journal of Research on Adolescence.* https://doi.org/10.1111/jora.12533

Steinberg, L., Fegley, S., & Dornbusch, S. M. (1993). Negative impact of part-time work on adolescent adjustment: Evidence from a longitudinal study. *Developmental Psychology, 29*(2), 171–180.

Steinmayr, R., Weidinger, A. F., Schwinger, M., & Spinath, B. (2019). The importance of students' motivation for their academic achievement – replicating and extending previous findings. *Frontiers in Psychology, 10,* 1730. https://doi.org/10.3389/fpsyg.2019.01730

Stephens, N. M., Fryberg, S. A., Markus, H. R., Johnson, C. S., & Covarrubias, R. (2012). Unseen disadvantage: How American universities' focus on independence undermines the academic performance of first-generation college students. *Journal of Personality and Social Psychology, 102*(6), 1178–1197. https://doi.org/10.1037/a0027143

Sterzing, P. R., Shattuck, P. T., Narendorf, S. C., Wagner, M., & Cooper, B. P. (2012). Bullying involvement and autism spectrum disorders: Prevalence and correlates of bullying involvement among adolescents with an autism spectrum disorder. *Archives of Pediatrics and Adolescent Medicine, 166*(11), 1058–1064. https://doi.org/10.1001/archpediatrics.2012.790

Sutton, A., Langenkamp, A. G., Muller, C., & Schiller, K. S. (2018). Who gets ahead and who falls behind during the transition to high school? Academic performance at the intersection of race/ethnicity and gender. *Social Problems, 65*(2), 154–173. https://doi.org/10.1093/socpro/spx044

Swinton, A. D., Kurtz-Costes, B., Rowley, S. J., & Okeke-Adeyanju, N. (2011). A longitudinal examination of African American adolescents' attributions about achievement outcomes. *Child Development, 82*(5), 1486–1500. https://doi.org/10.1111/j.1467-8624.2011.01623.x

Symonds, W. C., Schwartz, R., & Ferguson, R. F. (2011). *Pathways to prosperity: Meeting the challenge of preparing young Americans.* Retrieved from https://www.gse.harvard.edu/sites/default/files/documents/Pathways_to_Prosperity_Feb2011-1.pdf

Tarver, J., Daley, D., & Sayal, K. (2014). Attention-deficit hyperactivity disorder (ADHD): An updated review of the essential facts. *Child: Care, Health and Development, 40*(6), 762–774. https://doi.org/10.1111/cch.12139

Thapar, A., Cooper, M., Eyre, O., & Langley, K. (2013). What have we learnt about the causes of ADHD? *Journal of Child Psychology and Psychiatry, and Allied Disciplines, 54*(1), 3–16. https://doi.org/10.1111/j.1469-7610.2012.02611.x

Tipton-Fisler, L. A., Rodriguez, G., Zeedyk, S. M., & Blacher, J. (2018). Stability of bullying and internalizing problems among adolescents with ASD, ID, or typical development. *Research in Developmental Disabilities, 80,* 131–141. https://doi.org/10.1016/j.ridd.2018.06.004

Torpey, E. (2019). Education pays. *U.S. Bureau of Labor Statistics Career Outlook.* Retrieved from https://www.bls.gov/careeroutlook/2019/data-on-display/education_pays.htm

Tyler, J. H., & Lofstrom, M. (2009). Finishing high school: Alternative pathways and dropout recovery. *The Future of Children, 19*(1), 77–103. http://doi.org/10.1353/foc.0.0019

U.S. Bureau of Labor Statistics. (2015). *Labor force statistics from the current population survey: Employment status of the civilian noninstitutional population by age, sex, and race.* Retrieved from http://www.bls.gov/cps/cpsaat03.htm

U.S. Department of Labor. (2015). *Registered apprenticeship national results: Fiscal year 2014.* Retrieved from http://doleta.gov/oa/data_statistics.cfm

Vasquez-Salgado, Y., Greenfield, P. M., & Burgos-Cienfuegos, R. (2015). Exploring home-school value conflicts. *Journal of Adolescent Research, 30*(3), 271–305. https://doi.org/10.1177/0743558414561297

Vaughn, S., & Klingner, J. K. (1998). Students' perceptions of inclusion and resource room settings. *Journal of Special Education, 32,* 79–88.

Véronneau, M. H., Vitaro, F., Brendgen, M., Dishion, T. J., & Tremblay, R. E. (2010). Transactional analysis of the reciprocal links between peer experiences and academic achievement from middle childhood to early adolescence. *Developmental Psychology, 46*(4), 773–790. https://doi.org/10.1037/a0019816

Voisin, D. R., Kim, D. H., & Hong, J. S. (2018). A closer look at school bonding among African American adolescents in low-income communities: A latent class analysis. *Journal of Health Psychology, 23*(11), 1424–1437. https://doi.org/10.1177/1359105316658970

Voorhies, W., Dajani, D. R., Vij, S. G., Shankar, S., Turan, T. O., & Uddin, L. Q. (2018). Aberrant functional connectivity of inhibitory control networks in children with autism spectrum disorder. *Autism Research, 11*(11), 1468–1478. https://doi.org/10.1002/aur.2014

Walpole, M. (2008). Emerging from the pipeline: African American students, socioeconomic status, and college experiences and outcomes. *Research in Higher Education, 49*(3), 237–255. https://doi.org/10.1007/s11162-007-9079-y

Wang, M.-T., & Fredricks, J. A. (2014). The reciprocal links between school engagement, youth problem behaviors, and school dropout during adolescence. *Child Development*, 85(2), 722–737. https://doi.org/10.1111/cdev.12138

Wang, M.-T., Hill, N. E., & Hofkens, T. (2014). Parental involvement and African American and European American adolescents' academic, behavioral, and emotional development in secondary school. *Child Development*, 85(6), 2151–2168. https://doi.org/10.1111/cdev.12284

Wang, M.-T., & Hofkens, T. L. (2019). Beyond classroom academics: A school-wide and multi-contextual perspective on student engagement in school. *Adolescent Research Review*. https://doi.org/10.1007/s40894-019-00115-z

Wang, Y., Zhang, Y., Liu, L., Cui, J., Wang, J., Shum, D. H. K., . . . Chan, R. C. K. (2017). A meta-analysis of working memory impairments in autism spectrum disorders. *Neuropsychology Review*, 27(1), 46–61. https://doi.org/10.1007/s11065-016-9336-y

Ward, L., Siegel, M. J., & Davenport, Z. (2012). *First generation college students: Understanding and improving the experience from recruitment to commencement*. San Francisco, CA: Jossey-Bass.

Waters, S. K., Lester, L., & Cross, D. (2014). Transition to secondary school: Expectation versus experience. *Australian Journal of Education*, 58(2), 153–166. https://doi.org/10.1177/0004944114523371

Watson, S. M. R., & Gable, R. A. (2013). Unraveling the complex nature of mathematics learning disability: Implications for research and practice. *Learning Disability Quarterly*, 36(3), 178–187. https://doi.org/10.1177/0731948712461489

Way, N., Reddy, R., & Rhodes, J. (2007). Students' perceptions of school climate during the middle school years: Associations with trajectories of psychological and behavioral adjustment. *American Journal of Community Psychology*, 40(3–4), 194–213. https://doi.org/10.1007/s10464-007-9143-y

Weiss, C. C., & Bearman, P. S. (2007). Fresh starts: Reinvestigating the effects of the transition to high school on student outcomes. *American Journal of Education*, 113(3), 395–421.

Wentzel, K. R. (2002). Are effective teachers like good parents? Teaching styles and student adjustment in early adolescence. *Child Development*, 73(1), 287–301. https://doi.org/10.1111/1467-8624.00406

Wigfield, A., & Eccles, J. S. (1994). Children's competence beliefs, achievement values, and general self-esteem. *Journal of Early Adolescence*, 14(2), 107–139.

Wigfield, A., Eccles, J. S., Fredricks, J. A., Simpkins, S., Roeser, R. W., & Schiefele, U. (2015a). Development of achievement motivation and engagement. In M. Lamb (Ed.), *Handbook of child psychology and developmental science* (pp. 1–44). Hoboken, NJ: John Wiley & Sons. https://doi.org/10.1002/9781118963418.childpsy316

Wigfield, A., Muenks, K., & Rosenzweig, E. Q. (2015b). *Children's achievement motivation in school*. In C. M. Rubie-Davies, J. M. Stephens, & P. Watson (Eds.), *Routledge international handbook of social psychology of the classroom* (pp. 1–12). New York, NY: Routledge. https://doi.org/10.4324/9781315716923

Wright, A. W., Austin, M., Booth, C., & Kliewer, W. (2016). Exposure to community violence and physical health outcomes in youth: A systematic review. *Journal of Pediatric Psychology*, jsw088. https://doi.org/10.1093/jpepsy/jsw088

Yager, Z., Diedrichs, P. C., Ricciardelli, L. A., & Halliwell, E. (2013). What works in secondary schools? A systematic review of classroom-based body image programs. *Body Image*, 10(3), 271–281. https://doi.org/10.1016/j.bodyim.2013.04.001

Yeager, D. S., & Dweck, C. S. (2012). Mindsets that promote resilience: When students believe that personal characteristics can be developed. *Educational Psychologist*, 47(4), 302–314. https://doi.org/10.1080/00461520.2012.722805

Yeager, D. S., Hanselman, P., Walton, G. M., Murray, J. S., Crosnoe, R., Muller, C., . . . Dweck, C. S. (2019). A national experiment reveals where a growth mindset improves achievement. *Nature*, 573(7774), 364–369. https://doi.org/10.1038/s41586-019-1466-y

Yu, C., Li, X., Wang, S., & Zhang, W. (2016). Teacher autonomy support reduces adolescent anxiety and depression: An 18-month longitudinal study. *Journal of Adolescence*, 49, 115–123. https://doi.org/10.1016/j.adolescence.2016.03.001

CHAPTER 11

Adachi, P. J. C., & Willoughby, T. (2016). The longitudinal association between competitive video game play and aggression among adolescents and young adults. *Child Development*, 87(6), 1877–1892. https://doi.org/10.1111/cdev.12556

Albert, D., Chein, J., & Steinberg, L. (2013). The teenage brain: Peer influences on adolescent decision making. *Current Directions in Psychological Science*, 22(2), 114–120. https://doi.org/10.1177/0963721412471347

Allara, E., Ferri, M., Bo, A., Gasparrini, A., & Faggiano, F. (2015). Are mass-media campaigns effective in preventing drug use? A Cochrane systematic review and meta-analysis. *BMJ Open*, 5(9), e007449. https://doi.org/10.1136/bmjopen-2014-007449

American Academy of Pediatrics. (n.d.). AAP Media Plan: Family Media Plan. *Healthychildren.org*. Retrieved from https://www.healthychildren.org/English/media/Pages/default.aspx

Anderson, C. A., Berkowitz, L., Donnerstein, E., Huesmann, L. R., Johnson, J. D., Linz, D., . . . Wartella, E. (2003). The influence of media violence on youth. *Psychological Science in the Public Interest*, 4(3), 81–110. https://doi.org/10.1111/j.1529-1006.2003.pspi_1433.x

Anderson, C. A., Bushman, B. J., Bartholow, B. D., Cantor, J., Christakis, D., Coyne, S. M., . . . Ybarra, M. (2017). Screen violence and youth behavior. *Pediatrics*, 140(Suppl 2), S142–S147. https://doi.org/10.1542/peds.2016-1758T

Anderson, M., & Jiang, J. (2018a, May 31). Teens, social media & technology 2018. *Pew Research Center*. Retrieved from https://www.pewresearch.org/internet/2018/05/31/teens-social-media-technology-2018/

Anderson, M., & Jiang, J. (2018b, November 28). Teens and their experiences on social media. *Pew Research Center*. Retrieved from https://www.pewinternet.org/2018/11/28/teens-and-their-experiences-on-social-media/

Anderson, P., de Bruijn, A., Angus, K., Gordon, R., & Hastings, G. (2009). Impact of alcohol advertising and media exposure on adolescent alcohol use: A systematic review of longitudinal studies. *Alcohol and Alcoholism*, 44(3), 229–243. https://doi.org/10.1093/alcalc/agn115

Antheunis, M. L., Schouten, A. P., & Krahmer, E. (2016). The role of social networking sites in early adolescents' social lives. *The Journal of Early Adolescence*, 36(3), 348–371. https://doi.org/10.1177/0272431614564060

Austin, E. W., & Pinkleton, B. E. (2016). The viability of media literacy in reducing the influence of misleading media messages on young people's decision-making concerning alcohol, tobacco, and other substances. *Current Addiction Reports*, 3(2), 175–181. https://doi.org/10.1007/s40429-016-0100-4

Bányai, F., Zsila, Á., Király, O., Maraz, A., Elekes, Z., Griffiths, M. D., . . . Demetrovics, Z. (2017). Problematic social media use: Results from a large-scale nationally representative adolescent sample. *PLoS ONE*, 12(1), e0169839. https://doi.org/10.1371/journal.pone.0169839

Barrense-Dias, Y., Berchtold, A., Surís, J.-C., & Akre, C. (2017). Sexting and the definition issue. *The Journal of Adolescent Health*, 61(5), 544–554. https://doi.org/10.1016/j.jadohealth.2017.05.009

Bavelier, D., & Davidson, R. J. (2013). Games to do you good. *Nature*, 494(7438), 425–426. https://doi.org/10.1038/494425a

Benowitz-Fredericks, C. A., Garcia, K., Massey, M., Vasagar, B., & Borzekowski, D. L. G. (2012). Body image, eating disorders, and the relationship to adolescent media use. *Pediatric Clinics of North America*, *59*(3), 693–704, ix. https://doi.org/10.1016/j.pcl.2012.03.017

Best, P., Manktelow, R., & Taylor, B. (2014). Online communication, social media and adolescent wellbeing: A systematic narrative review. *Children and Youth Services Review*, *41*, 27–36. https://doi.org/10.1016/J.CHILDYOUTH.2014.03.001

Boot, W. R., Blakely, D. P., & Simons, D. J. (2011). Do action video games improve perception and cognition? *Frontiers in Psychology*, *2*, 226. https://doi.org/10.3389/fpsyg.2011.00226

Breuer, J., Vogelgesang, J., Quandt, T., & Festl, R. (2015). Violent video games and physical aggression: Evidence for a selection effect among adolescents. *Psychology of Popular Media Culture*, *4*(4), 305–328. https://doi.org/10.1037/ppm0000035

Browne, K. D., & Hamilton-Giachritsis, C. (2005). The influence of violent media on children and adolescents: A public-health approach. *The Lancet*, *365*(9460), 702–710. https://doi.org/10.1016/S0140-6736(05)17952-5

Calvert, S. L. (2015). Children and digital media. In R. M. Lerner (Ed.), *Handbook of child psychology and developmental science* (7th ed., pp. 1–41). Hoboken, NJ: John Wiley & Sons. https://doi.org/10.1002/9781118963418.childpsy410

Calvert, S. L., Appelbaum, M., Dodge, K. A., Graham, S., Nagayama Hall, G. C., Hamby, S., . . . Hedges, L. V. (2017). The American Psychological Association Task Force assessment of violent video games: Science in the service of public interest. *American Psychologist*, *72*(2), 126–143. https://doi.org/10.1037/a0040413

Choi, H., Van Ouytsel, J., & Temple, J. R. (2016). Association between sexting and sexual coercion among female adolescents. *Journal of Adolescence*, *53*, 164–168. https://doi.org/10.1016/J.ADOLESCENCE.2016.10.005

Collins, R. L., Elliott, M. N., Berry, S. H., Kanouse, D. E., Kunkel, D., Hunter, S. B., & Miu, A. (2004). Watching sex on television predicts adolescent initiation of sexual behavior. *Pediatrics*, *114*(3), e280–e289. https://doi.org/10.1542/peds.2003-1065-L

Collins, R. L, Martino, S. C., Elliott, M. N., & Miu, A. (2011). Relationships between adolescent sexual outcomes and exposure to sex in media: Robustness to propensity-based analysis. *Developmental Psychology*, *47*(2), 585–591. https://doi.org/10.1037/a0022563

Collins, R. L, Martino, S. C., Kovalchik, S. A., Becker, K. M., Shadel, W. G., & D'Amico, E. J. (2016). Alcohol advertising exposure among middle school-age youth: An assessment across all media and venues. *Journal of Studies on Alcohol and Drugs*, *77*(3), 384–392. https://doi.org/10.15288/jsad.2016.77.384

Collins, R. L, Martino, S. C., Kovalchik, S. A., D'Amico, E. J., Shadel, W. G., Becker, K. M., & Tolpadi, A. (2017). Exposure to alcohol advertising and adolescents' drinking beliefs: Role of message interpretation. *Health Psychology*, *36*(9), 890–897. https://doi.org/10.1037/hea0000521

Comic Book Legal Defense Fund. (2019). History of comics censorship, part 1. Retrieved from http://cbldf.org/resources/history-of-comics-censorship/history-of-comics-censorship-part-1/

Common Sense Media. (2019). *What is media literacy, and why is it important?* Retrieved from https://www.commonsensemedia.org/news-and-media-literacy/what-is-media-literacy-and-why-is-it-important

Cranwell, J., Britton, J., & Bains, M. (2017). "F*ck it! let's get to drinking—poison our livers!": A thematic analysis of alcohol content in contemporary YouTube music videos. *International Journal of Behavioral Medicine*, *24*(1), 66–76. https://doi.org/10.1007/s12529-016-9578-3

Cranwell, J., Murray, R., Lewis, S., Leonardi-Bee, J., Dockrell, M., & Britton, J. (2015). Adolescents' exposure to tobacco and alcohol content in YouTube music videos. *Addiction*, *110*(4), 703–711. https://doi.org/10.1111/add.12835

Creamer, M. R., Delk, J., Case, K., Perry, C. L., & Harrell, M. B. (2018). Positive outcome expectations and tobacco product use behaviors in youth. *Substance Use & Misuse*, *53*(8), 1399–1402. https://doi.org/10.1080/10826084.2017.1404104

Dake, J. A., Price, J. H., Maziarz, L., & Ward, B. (2012). Prevalence and correlates of sexting behavior in adolescents. *American Journal of Sexuality Education*, *7*(1), 1–15. https://doi.org/10.1080/15546128.2012.650959

de Vries, D. A., Peter, J., de Graaf, H., & Nikken, P. (2016). Adolescents' social network site use, peer appearance-related feedback, and body dissatisfaction: Testing a mediation model. *Journal of Youth and Adolescence*, *45*(1), 211–224. https://doi.org/10.1007/s10964-015-0266-4

DeCamp, W., & Ferguson, C. J. (2017). The impact of degree of exposure to violent video games, family background, and other factors on youth violence. *Journal of Youth and Adolescence*, *46*(2), 388–400. https://doi.org/10.1007/s10964-016-0561-8

Dooley, J. J., Pyżalski, J., & Cross, D. (2009). Cyberbullying versus face-to-face bullying. *Zeitschrift Für Psychologie / Journal of Psychology*, *217*(4), 182–188. https://doi.org/10.1027/0044-3409.217.4.182

Eisner, M. P., & Malti, T. (2015). Aggressive and violent behavior. In R. M. Lerner (Ed.), *Handbook of child psychology and developmental science* (7th ed., pp. 1–48). Hoboken, NJ: John Wiley & Sons. https://doi.org/10.1002/9781118963418.childpsy319

Elmore, K. C., Scull, T. M., & Kupersmidt, J. B. (2017). Media as a "super peer": How adolescents interpret media messages predicts their perception of alcohol and tobacco use norms. *Journal of Youth and Adolescence*, *46*(2), 376–387. https://doi.org/10.1007/s10964-016-0609-9

Erikson, E. H. (1959). *Identity and the life cycle* (Vol. 64). New York, NY: W. W. Norton.

Fahy, A. E., Stansfeld, S. A., Smuk, M., Smith, N. R., Cummins, S., & Clark, C. (2016). Longitudinal associations between cyberbullying involvement and adolescent mental health. *Journal of Adolescent Health*, *59*(5), 502–509. https://doi.org/10.1016/J.JADOHEALTH.2016.06.006

Fardouly, J., & Vartanian, L. R. (2016). Social media and body image concerns: Current research and future directions. *Current Opinion in Psychology*, *9*, 1–5. https://doi.org/10.1016/J.COPSYC.2015.09.005

Ferguson, C. J. (2013). Violent video games and the Supreme Court: Lessons for the scientific community in the wake of *Brown v. Entertainment Merchants Association*. *American Psychologist*, *68*(2), 57–74. https://doi.org/10.1037/a0030597

Ferguson, C. J. (2015). Do angry birds make for angry children? a meta-analysis of video game influences on children's and adolescents' aggression, mental health, prosocial behavior, and academic performance. *Perspectives on Psychological Science*, *10*(5), 646–666. https://doi.org/10.1177/1745691615592234

Ferguson, C. J., Nielsen, R. K. L., & Markey, P. M. (2016). Does sexy media promote teen sex? A meta-analytic and methodological review. *Psychiatric Quarterly*, 1–10. https://doi.org/10.1007/s11126-016-9442-2

Gabrielli, J., Traore, A., Stoolmiller, M., Bergamini, E., & Sargent, J. D. (2016). Industry television ratings for violence, sex, and substance use. *Pediatrics*, *138*(3), e20160487. https://doi.org/10.1542/peds.2016-0487

Gerbner, G., Gross, L., Morgan, M., Signorielli, N., Shanahan, J., Gross, L., . . . Shanahan, J. (2002). Growing up with television: Cultivation processes. In J. Bryant & D. Zillmann (Eds.), *Media effects advances in theory and research* (pp. 53–78). New York, NY: Routledge. https://doi.org/10.4324/9781410602428-7

Gottfried, J. A., Vaala, S. E., Bleakley, A., Hennessy, M., & Jordan, A. (2013). Does the effect of exposure to TV sex on adolescent sexual behavior vary by genre? *Communication Research*, *40*(1), 73–95. https://doi.org/10.1177/0093650211415399

Grenard, J. L., Dent, C. W., & Stacy, A. W. (2013). Exposure to alcohol advertisements and teenage alcohol-related problems. *Pediatrics*, *131*(2), e369–e379. https://doi.org/10.1542/peds.2012-1480

Grogan, S. (2016). *Body image* (3rd ed.). London, England: Routledge. https://doi.org/10.4324/9781315681528

Hamm, M. P., Newton, A. S., Chisholm, A., Shulhan, J., Milne, A., Sundar, P., . . . Hartling, L. (2015). Prevalence and effect of cyberbullying on children and young people. *JAMA Pediatrics*, *169*(8), 770. https://doi.org/10.1001/jamapediatrics.2015.0944

Handschuh, C., La Cross, A., & Smaldone, A. (2019). Is sexting associated with sexual behaviors during adolescence? A systematic literature review and meta-analysis. *Journal of Midwifery & Women's Health*, *64*(1), 88–97. https://doi.org/10.1111/jmwh.12923

Heffer, T., Good, M., Daly, O., MacDonell, E., & Willoughby, T. (2019). The longitudinal association between social-media use and depressive symptoms among adolescents and young adults: An empirical reply to Twenge et al. (2018). *Clinical Psychological Science*, *7*(3), 462–470. https://doi.org/10.1177/2167702618812727

Hilgard, J., Engelhardt, C. R., & Rouder, J. N. (2017). Overstated evidence for short-term effects of violent games on affect and behavior: A reanalysis of Anderson et al. (2010). *Psychological Bulletin*, *143*(7), 757–774. https://doi.org/10.1037/bul0000074

Houck, C. D., Barker, D., Rizzo, C., Hancock, E., Norton, A., & Brown, L. K. (2014). Sexting and sexual behavior in at-risk adolescents. *Pediatrics*, *133*(2), e276-82. https://doi.org/10.1542/peds.2013-1157

Houghton, S., Lawrence, D., Hunter, S. C., Rosenberg, M., Zadow, C., Wood, L., & Shilton, T. (2018). Reciprocal relationships between trajectories of depressive symptoms and screen media use during adolescence. *Journal of Youth and Adolescence*, *47*(11), 2453–2467. https://doi.org/10.1007/s10964-018-0901-y

Huesmann, L. R. (2007). The impact of electronic media violence: Scientific theory and research. *The Journal of Adolescent Health*, *41*(6 Suppl 1), S6–S13. https://doi.org/10.1016/j.jadohealth.2007.09.005

Huesmann, L. R., & Eron, L. D. (Eds.) (1986). *Television and the aggressive child: A cross national comparison*. London, England: Routledge.

Huesmann, L. R., Lagerspetz, K., & Eron, L. D. (1984). Intervening variables in the TV violence-aggression relation: Evidence from two countries. *Developmental Psychology*, *20*(5), 746–775. https://doi.org/10.1037/0012-1649.20.5.746

Huesmann, L. R., Moise-Titus, J., Podolski, C.-L., & Eron, L. D. (2003). Longitudinal relations between children's exposure to TV violence and their aggressive and violent behavior in young adulthood: 1977-1992. *Developmental Psychology*, *39*(2), 201–221. https://doi.org/10.1037/0012-1649.39.2.201

Jackson, K. M., Janssen, T., & Gabrielli, J. (2018). Media/marketing influences on adolescent and young adult substance abuse. *Current Addiction Reports*, *5*(2), 146–157. https://doi.org/10.1007/s40429-018-0199-6

Jeong, S.-H., Cho, H., & Hwang, Y. (2012). Media literacy interventions: A meta-analytic review. *The Journal of Communication*, *62*(3), 454–472. https://doi.org/10.1111/j.1460-2466.2012.01643.x

Jernigan, D., Noel, J., Landon, J., Thornton, N., & Lobstein, T. (2017). Alcohol marketing and youth alcohol consumption: A systematic review of longitudinal studies published since 2008. *Addiction (Abingdon, England)*, *112*(Suppl 1), 7–20. https://doi.org/10.1111/add.13591

Katz, E., Blumler, J. G., & Gurevitch, M. (1973). Uses and gratifications research. *Public Opinion Quarterly*, *37*(4), 509. https://doi.org/10.1086/268109

Kim, S., Colwell, S. R., Kata, A., Boyle, M. H., & Georgiades, K. (2018). Cyberbullying victimization and adolescent mental health: Evidence of differential effects by sex and mental health problem type. *Journal of Youth and Adolescence*, *47*(3), 661–672. https://doi.org/10.1007/s10964-017-0678-4

Kleemans, M., Daalmans, S., Carbaat, I., & Anschütz, D. (2018). Picture perfect: The direct effect of manipulated Instagram photos on body image in adolescent girls. *Media Psychology*, *21*(1), 93–110. https://doi.org/10.1080/15213269.2016.1257392

Kosenko, K., Luurs, G., & Binder, A. R. (2017). Sexting and sexual behavior, 2011-2015: A critical review and meta-analysis of a growing literature. *Journal of Computer-Mediated Communication*, *22*(3), 141–160. https://doi.org/10.1111/jcc4.12187

Krahé, B. (2012). Report of the Media Violence Commission. *Aggressive Behavior*, *38*(5), 335–341. https://doi.org/10.1002/ab.21443

Labella, M. H., & Masten, A. S. (2018). Family influences on the development of aggression and violence. *Current Opinion in Psychology*, *19*, 11–16. https://doi.org/10.1016/J.COPSYC.2017.03.028

Lenhart, A. (2009, December 15). Teens and sexting. *Pew Research Center*. Retrieved from https://www.pewinternet.org/2009/12/15/teens-and-sexting/

Lenhart, A. (2015, August 6). Social media and teen friendships. *Pew Research Center*. Retrieved from https://www.pewinternet.org/2015/08/06/chapter-4-social-media-and-friendships/

Lobel, A., Engels, R. C. M. E., Stone, L. L., Burk, W. J., & Granic, I. (2017). Video gaming and children's psychosocial wellbeing: A longitudinal study. *Journal of Youth and Adolescence*, *46*(4), 884–897. https://doi.org/10.1007/s10964-017-0646-z

Madigan, S., Ly, A., Rash, C. L., Van Ouytsel, J., & Temple, J. R. (2018). Prevalence of multiple forms of sexting behavior among youth. *JAMA Pediatrics*, *172*(4), 327. https://doi.org/10.1001/jamapediatrics.2017.5314

Mantey, D. S., Cooper, M. R., Clendennen, S. L., Pasch, K. E., & Perry, C. L. (2016). e-Cigarette marketing exposure is associated with e-cigarette use among US youth. *The Journal of Adolescent Health*, *58*(6), 686–690. https://doi.org/10.1016/j.jadohealth.2016.03.003

McAnally, H. M., Robertson, L. A., Strasburger, V. C., & Hancox, R. J. (2013). Bond, James Bond: A review of 46 years of violence in films. *JAMA Pediatrics*, *167*(2), 195. https://doi.org/10.1001/jamapediatrics.2013.437

McCrae, N., Gettings, S., & Purssell, E. (2017). Social media and depressive symptoms in childhood and adolescence: A systematic review. *Adolescent Research Review*, *2*(4), 315–330. https://doi.org/10.1007/s40894-017-0053-4

McLean, S. A., Paxton, S. J., & Wertheim, E. H. (2016). Does media literacy mitigate risk for reduced body satisfaction following exposure to thin-ideal media? *Journal of Youth and Adolescence*, *45*(8), 1678–1695. https://doi.org/10.1007/s10964-016-0440-3

McLean, S. A., Paxton, S. J., Wertheim, E. H., & Masters, J. (2015). Photoshopping the selfie: Self photo editing and photo investment are associated with body dissatisfaction in adolescent girls. *International Journal of Eating Disorders*, *48*(8), 1132–1140. https://doi.org/10.1002/eat.22449

Meier, E. P., & Gray, J. (2014). Facebook photo activity associated with body image disturbance in adolescent girls. *Cyberpsychology, Behavior, and Social Networking*, *17*(4), 199–206. https://doi.org/10.1089/cyber.2013.0305

Michikyan, M., & Suárez-Orozco, C. (2016). Adolescent media and social media use. *Journal of Adolescent Research*, *31*(4), 411–414. https://doi.org/10.1177/0743558416643801

Modecki, K. L., Minchin, J., Harbaugh, A. G., Guerra, N. G., & Runions, K. C. (2014). Bullying prevalence across contexts: A meta-analysis measuring cyber and traditional bullying. *Journal of Adolescent Health*, *55*(5), 602–611. https://doi.org/10.1016/J.JADOHEALTH.2014.06.007

Morgenstern, M., Sargent, J. D., Sweeting, H., Faggiano, F., Mathis, F., & Hanewinkel, R. (2014). Favourite alcohol advertisements and binge drinking among adolescents: A cross-cultural cohort study. *Addiction*, *109*(12), 2005–2015. https://doi.org/10.1111/add.12667

Mori, C., Temple, J. R., Browne, D., & Madigan, S. (2019). Association of sexting with sexual behaviors and mental health among adolescents. *JAMA Pediatrics*, *173*(8), 770. https://doi.org/10.1001/jamapediatrics.2019.1658

National Association for Media Literacy Education. (2019). *Media literacy defined*. Retrieved from https://namle.net/publications/media-literacy-definitions/

Nesi, J., Choukas-Bradley, S., & Prinstein, M. J. (2018a). Transformation of adolescent peer relations in the social media context: Part 1—A theoretical framework and application to dyadic peer relationships. *Clinical Child and Family Psychology Review*, *21*(3), 267–294. https://doi.org/10.1007/s10567-018-0261-x

Nesi, J., Choukas-Bradley, S., & Prinstein, M. J. (2018b). Transformation of adolescent peer relations in the social media context: Part 2—Application to peer group processes and future directions for research. *Clinical Child and Family Psychology Review*, *21*(3), 295–319. https://doi.org/10.1007/s10567-018-0262-9

O'Hara, R. E., Gibbons, F. X., Gerrard, M., Li, Z., & Sargent, J. D. (2012). Greater exposure to sexual content in popular movies predicts earlier sexual debut and increased sexual risk taking. *Psychological Science*, *23*(9), 984–993. https://doi.org/10.1177/0956797611435529

Olweus, D. (2012). Cyberbullying: An overrated phenomenon? *European Journal of Developmental Psychology*, *9*(5), 520–538. https://doi.org/10.1080/17405629.2012.682358

Orben, A., & Przybylski, A. K. (2019). Screens, teens, and psychological well-being: Evidence from three time-use-diary studies. *Psychological Science*, *30*(5), 682–696. https://doi.org/10.1177/0956797619830329

Plaisier, X. S., & Konijn, E. A. (2013). Rejected by peers—Attracted to antisocial media content: Rejection-based anger impairs moral judgment among adolescents. *Developmental Psychology*, *49*(6), 1165–1173. https://doi.org/10.1037/a0029399

Portnoy, D. B., Wu, C. C., Tworek, C., Chen, J., & Borek, N. (2014). Youth curiosity about cigarettes, smokeless tobacco, and cigars: Prevalence and associations with advertising. *American Journal of Preventive Medicine*, *47*(2 Suppl 1), S76–S86. https://doi.org/10.1016/j.amepre.2014.04.012

Przybylski, A. K. (2014). Electronic gaming and psychosocial adjustment. *Pediatrics*, *134*(3), e716–e722. https://doi.org/10.1542/peds.2013-4021

Przybylski, A. K., & Weinstein, N. (2017). A large-scale test of the Goldilocks hypothesis. *Psychological Science*, *28*(2), 204–215. https://doi.org/10.1177/0956797616678438

Rice, E., Gibbs, J., Winetrobe, H., Rhoades, H., Plant, A., Montoya, J., & Kordic, T. (2014). Sexting and sexual behavior among middle school students. *Pediatrics*, *134*(1), e21–e28. https://doi.org/10.1542/peds.2013-2991

Rice, E., Rhoades, H., Winetrobe, H., Sanchez, M., Montoya, J., Plant, A., & Kordic, T. (2012). Sexually explicit cell phone messaging associated with sexual risk among adolescents. *Pediatrics*, *130*(4), 667–673. https://doi.org/10.1542/peds.2012-0021

Rideout, V. (2015). *The Common Sense census: Media use by tweens and teens*. Retrieved from https://static1.squarespace.com/static/5ba15befec4eb7899898240d/t/5ba261f24fa51a7fb2c19904/1537368577261/CSM_TeenTween_MediaCensus_FinalWebVersion_1%281%29.pdf

Rideout, V., & Robb, M. B. (2018). Social media, social life: Teens reveal their experiences. *Common Sense Media*. Retrieved from https://www.commonsensemedia.org/research/social-media-social-life-2018

Roberts, D. F., Henriksen, L., & Foehr, U. G. (2009). Adolescence, adolescents, and media. In R. M. Lerner & L. Steinberg (Eds.), *Handbook of adolescent psychology: Contextual influences on adolescent development* (pp. 314–344). Hoboken, NJ: John Wiley & Sons. Retrieved from https://psycnet.apa.org/record/2009-05795-009

Rubin, A. M. (2002). The uses-and-gratifications perspective of media effects. In J. Bryant & D. Zillmann (Eds.), *Media effects advances in theory and research* (pp. 535–558). New York, NY: Routledge. https://doi.org/10.4324/9781410602428

Runions, K. C. (2013). Toward a conceptual model of motive and self-control in cyber-aggression: Rage, revenge, reward, and recreation. *Journal of Youth and Adolescence*, *42*(5), 751–771. https://doi.org/10.1007/s10964-013-9936-2

Rydell, A.-M. (2016). Violent media exposure, aggression and CU traits in adolescence: Testing the selection and socialization hypotheses. *Journal of Adolescence*, *52*, 95–102. https://doi.org/10.1016/J.ADOLESCENCE.2016.07.009

Saleem, M., Anderson, C. A., & Gentile, D. A. (2012). Effects of prosocial, neutral, and violent video games on children's helpful and hurtful behaviors. *Aggressive Behavior*, *38*(4), 281–287. https://doi.org/10.1002/ab.21428

Scull, T. M., Malik, C. V., & Kupersmidt, J. B. (2014). A media literacy education approach to teaching adolescents comprehensive sexual health education. *The Journal of Media Literacy Education*, *6*(1), 1–14. Retrieved from http://www.ncbi.nlm.nih.gov/pubmed/27081579

Ševčíková, A. (2016). Girls' and boys' experience with teen sexting in early and late adolescence. *Journal of Adolescence*, *51*, 156–162. https://doi.org/10.1016/j.adolescence.2016.06.007

Shulman, E. P., Smith, A. R., Silva, K., Icenogle, G., Duell, N., Chein, J., & Steinberg, L. (2016). The dual systems model: Review, reappraisal, and reaffirmation. *Developmental Cognitive Neuroscience*, *17*, 103–117. https://doi.org/10.1016/j.dcn.2015.12.010

Slater, M. D., Henry, K. L., Swaim, R. C., & Anderson, L. L. (2003). Violent media content and aggressiveness in adolescents. *Communication Research*, *30*(6), 713–736. https://doi.org/10.1177/0093650203258281

Slonje, R., & Smith, P. K. (2008). Cyberbullying: Another main type of bullying? *Scandinavian Journal of Psychology*, *49*(2), 147–154. https://doi.org/10.1111/j.1467-9450.2007.00611.x

Smith, S., Ferguson, C., & Beaver, K. (2018). A longitudinal analysis of shooter games and their relationship with conduct disorder and self-reported delinquency. *International Journal of Law and Psychiatry*, *58*, 48–53. https://doi.org/10.1016/J.IJLP.2018.02.008

Steele, J. R., & Brown, J. D. (1995). Adolescent room culture: Studying media in the context of everyday life. *Journal of Youth and Adolescence*, *24*(5), 551–576. https://doi.org/10.1007/BF01537056

Steinberg, L. (2010). A dual systems model of adolescent risk-taking. *Developmental Psychobiology*, *52*(3), 216–224. https://doi.org/10.1002/dev.20445

Steinberg, L., & Monahan, K. C. (2011). Adolescents' exposure to sexy media does not hasten the initiation of sexual intercourse. *Developmental Psychology*, *47*(2), 562–576. https://doi.org/10.1037/a0020613

Sung Hong, J., Lee, J., Espelage, D. L., Hunter, S. C., Upton Patton, D., & Rivers, T. (2016). Understanding the correlates of face-to-face and cyberbullying victimization among U.S. adolescents: A social-ecological analysis. *Violence and Victims*, *31*(4), 638–663. https://doi.org/10.1891/0886-6708.VV-D-15-00014

Temple, J. R., & Choi, H. (2014). Longitudinal association between teen sexting and sexual behavior. *Pediatrics*, *134*(5), e1287–e1292. https://doi.org/10.1542/peds.2014-1974

Temple, J. R., Le, V. D., van den Berg, P., Ling, Y., Paul, J. A., & Temple, B. W. (2014). Brief report: Teen sexting and psychosocial health. *Journal of Adolescence*, *37*(1), 33–36. https://doi.org/10.1016/j.adolescence.2013.10.008

Temple, J. R., Paul, J. A., van den Berg, P., Le, V. D., McElhany, A., & Temple, B. W. (2012). Teen sexting and its association with sexual behaviors. *Archives of Pediatrics & Adolescent Medicine*, *166*(9), 828–833. https://doi.org/10.1001/archpediatrics.2012.835

Tiggemann, M., & Slater, A. (2013). NetGirls: The Internet, Facebook, and body image concern in adolescent girls. *International Journal of Eating Disorders*, *46*(6), 630–633. https://doi.org/10.1002/eat.22141

Tiggemann, M., & Slater, A. (2014). NetTweens. *The Journal of Early Adolescence*, *34*(5), 606–620. https://doi.org/10.1177/0272431613501083

Turner, K. H., Jolls, T., Hagerman, M. S., O'Byrne, W., Hicks, T., Eisenstock, B., & Pytash, K. E. (2017). Developing digital and media literacies in children and adolescents. *Pediatrics*, *140*(Suppl 2), S122–S126. https://doi.org/10.1542/peds.2016-1758P

Uhls, Y. T., Ellison, N. B., & Subrahmanyam, K. (2017). Benefits and costs of social media in adolescence. *Pediatrics*, *140*(Suppl 2), S67–S70. https://doi.org/10.1542/peds.2016-1758E

Vahedi, Z., Sibalis, A., & Sutherland, J. E. (2018). Are media literacy interventions effective at changing attitudes and intentions towards risky health behaviors in adolescents? A meta-analytic review. *Journal of Adolescence*, *67*, 140–152. https://doi.org/10.1016/J.ADOLESCENCE.2018.06.007

Van Ouytsel, J., Madigan, S., Ponnet, K., Walrave, M., & Temple, J. R. (2019). Adolescent sexting: Myths, facts, and advice. *NASN School Nurse*, 1942602X1984311. https://doi.org/10.1177/1942602X19843113

Van Ouytsel, J., Ponnet, K., Walrave, M., & d'Haenens, L. (2017). Adolescent sexting from a social learning perspective. *Telematics and Informatics*, *34*(1), 287–298. https://doi.org/10.1016/J.TELE.2016.05.009

Van Ouytsel, J., Walrave, M., Ponnet, K., & Heirman, W. (2015). The association between adolescent sexting, psychosocial difficulties, and risk behavior. *The Journal of School Nursing*, *31*(1), 54–69. https://doi.org/10.1177/1059840514541964

Van Ouytsel, J., Walrave, M., Ponnet, K., & Temple, J. R. (2018). Sexting. In R. Hobbs & P. Mihailidis (Eds.), *The international encyclopedia of media literacy* (pp. 1–6). Hoboken, NJ: John Wiley & Sons. https://doi.org/10.1002/9781118978238.ieml0219

Walrave, M., Heirman, W., & Hallam, L. (2014). Under pressure to sext? Applying the theory of planned behaviour to adolescent sexting. *Behaviour & Information Technology*, *33*(1), 86–98. https://doi.org/10.1080/0144929X.2013.837099

Ward, L. M., & Friedman, K. (2006). Using TV as a guide: Associations between television viewing and adolescents' sexual attitudes and behavior. *Journal of Research on Adolescence*, *16*, 133–156.

Wiedeman, A. M., Black, J. A., Dolle, A. L., Finney, E. J., & Coker, K. L. (2015). Factors influencing the impact of aggressive and violent media on children and adolescents. *Aggression and Violent Behavior*, *25*, 191–198. https://doi.org/10.1016/J.AVB.2015.04.008

Wood, M. A., Bukowski, W. M., & Lis, E. (2016). The digital self: How social media serves as a setting that shapes youth's emotional experiences. *Adolescent Research Review*, *1*(2), 163–173. https://doi.org/10.1007/s40894-015-0014-8

Ybarra, M. L., & Mitchell, K. J. (2014). "Sexting" and its relation to sexual activity and sexual risk behavior in a national survey of adolescents. *The Journal of Adolescent Health*, *55*(6), 757–764. https://doi.org/10.1016/j.jadohealth.2014.07.012

Young, B., Lewis, S., Katikireddi, S. V., Bauld, L., Stead, M., Angus, K., … Langley, T. (2018). Effectiveness of mass media campaigns to reduce alcohol consumption and harm: A systematic review. *Alcohol and Alcoholism*, *53*(3), 302–316. https://doi.org/10.1093/alcalc/agx094

Zycha, I., Ortega-Ruiza, R., & Del Rey, R. (2015). Systematic review of theoretical studies on bullying and cyberbullying: Facts, knowledge, prevention, and intervention. *Aggression and Violent Behavior*, *23*, 1–21. https://doi.org/10.1016/J.AVB.2015.10.001

CHAPTER 12

Afifi, T. O., & MacMillan, H. L. (2011). Resilience following child maltreatment: A review of protective factors. *La Résilience Aprés La Maltraitance Clans l'enfance: Une Revue Des Facteurs Protecteurs*, *56*(5), 266–272.

Alati, R., Baker, P., Betts, K. S., Connor, J. P., Little, K., Sanson, A., & Olsson, C. A. (2014). The role of parental alcohol use, parental discipline and antisocial behaviour on adolescent drinking trajectories. *Drug and Alcohol Dependence*, *134*(1), 178–184. https://doi.org/10.1016/j.drugalcdep.2013.09.030

American Academy of Child and Adolescent Psychiatry. (2018). *Teen suicide. Facts for families*. Retrieved from https://www.aacap.org/AACAP/Families_and_Youth/Facts_for_Families/FFF-Guide/Teen-Suicide-010.aspx

American Psychiatric Association. (2013). *Diagnostic and statistical manual of mental disorders* (5th ed.). Washington, DC: Author.

Andersen, T. S. (2015). Race, ethnicity, and structural variations in youth risk of arrest: Evidence from a national longitudinal sample. *Criminal Justice and Behavior*, *42*, 900–916. https://doi.org/10.1177/0093854815570963

Australian Institute of Health and Welfare. (2016). *Leading causes of death*. Retrieved from http://www.aihw.gov.au/deaths/leading-causes-of-death/

Bachman, J. G., O'Malley, P. M., Freedman-Doan, P., Trzesniewski, K. H., & Donnellan, M. B. (2011). Adolescent self-esteem: Differences by race/ethnicity, gender, and age. *Self and Identity*, *10*(4), 445–473. https://doi.org/10.1080/15298861003794538

Baglivio, M. T., Jackowski, K., Greenwald, M. A., & Howell, J. C. (2014). Serious, violent, and chronic juvenile offenders. *Criminology & Public Policy*, *13*(1), 83–116. https://doi.org/10.1111/1745-9133.12064

Bauman, S., Toomey, R. B., & Walker, J. L. (2013). Associations among bullying, cyberbullying, and suicide in high school students. *Journal of Adolescence*, *36*(2), 341–350. https://doi.org/10.1016/j.adolescence.2012.12.001

Beesdo, K., Knappe, S., & Pine, D. S. (2009). Anxiety and anxiety disorders in children and adolescents: Developmental issues and implications for DSM-V. *Psychiatric Clinics of North America*, *32*, 483–524. https://doi.org/10.1016/j.psc.2009.06.002

Bendezú, J. J., Pinderhughes, E. E., Hurley, S. M., McMahon, R. J., & Racz, S. J. (2018). Longitudinal relations among parental monitoring strategies, knowledge, and adolescent delinquency in a racially diverse at-risk sample. *Journal of Clinical Child and Adolescent Psychology*, *47*(Suppl 1), S21–S34. https://doi.org/10.1080/15374416.2016.1141358

Benson, M. A., Compas, B. E., Layne, C. M., Vandergrift, N., Pašalić, H., Katalinksi, R., & Pynoos, R. S. (2011). Measurement of post-war coping and stress responses: A study of Bosnian adolescents. *Journal of Applied Developmental Psychology*, *32*(6), 323–335. https://doi.org/10.1016/j.appdev.2011.07.001

Bentley, K. H., Nock, M. K., & Barlow, D. H. (2014). The four-function model of nonsuicidal self-injury: Key directions for future research. *Clinical Psychological Science*, *2*(5), 638–656. https://doi.org/10.1177/2167702613514563

Berkel, T. D. M., & Pandey, S. C. (2017). Emerging role of epigenetic mechanisms in alcohol addiction. *Alcoholism: Clinical and Experimental Research*, *41*(4), 666–680. https://doi.org/10.1111/acer.13338

Bjärehed, J., Wångby-Lundh, M., & Lundh, L.-G. (2012). Nonsuicidal self-injury in a community sample of adolescents: Subgroups, stability, and associations with psychological difficulties. *Journal of Research on Adolescence*, 22(4), 678–693. https://doi.org/10.1111/j.1532-7795.2012.00817.x

Bowman, M. A., Prelow, H. M., & Weaver, S. R. (2007). Parenting behaviors, association with deviant peers, and delinquency in African American adolescents: A mediated-moderation model. *Journal of Youth & Adolescence*, 36, 517–527.

Boyer, T. W., & Byrnes, J. P. (2016). Risk-taking. In R. Levesque (Ed.), *Encyclopedia of adolescence* (pp. 1–5). Cham, Switzerland: Springer. https://doi.org/10.1007/978-3-319-32132-5_15-2

Brent, D. A. (2009). Youth depression and suicide: Selective serotonin reuptake inhibitors treat the former and prevent the latter. *Canadian Journal of Psychiatry*, 54(2), 76–77.

Brooks-Russell, A., Simons-Morton, B., Haynie, D., Farhat, T., & Wang, J. (2014). Longitudinal relationship between drinking with peers, descriptive norms, and adolescent alcohol use. *Prevention Science*, 15(4), 497–505. https://doi.org/10.1007/s11121-013-0391-9

Brumariu, L. E. (2015). Parent-child attachment and emotion regulation. *New Directions for Child and Adolescent Development*, 2015(148), 31–45. https://doi.org/10.1002/cad.20098

Brumback, T., Worley, M., Nguyen-Louie, T. T., Squeglia, L. M., Jacobus, J., & Tapert, S. F. (2016). Neural predictors of alcohol use and psychopathology symptoms in adolescents. *Development and Psychopathology*, 28(4 Pt 1), 1209–1216. https://doi.org/10.1017/S0954579416000766

Buchanan, C. M., & Bruton, J. H. (2016). Storm and stress. In R. Levesque (Ed.), *Encyclopedia of adolescence* (pp. 1–12). Cham, Switzerland: Springer. https://doi.org/10.1007/978-3-319-32132-5_111-2

Byrne, M. L., Whittle, S., Vijayakumar, N., Dennison, M., Simmons, J. G., & Allen, N. B. (2017). A systematic review of adrenarche as a sensitive period in neurobiological development and mental health. *Developmental Cognitive Neuroscience*, 25, 12–28. https://doi.org/10.1016/J.DCN.2016.12.004

Canetto, S. S., & Sakinofsky, I. (1998). The gender paradox in suicide. *Suicide and Life-Threatening Behavior*, 28, 1–23.

Carbia, C., Cadaveira, F., López-Caneda, E., Caamaño-Isorna, F., Rodriguez Holguin, S., & Corral, M. (2017). Working memory over a six-year period in young binge drinkers. *Alcohol*, 61, 17–23. https://doi.org/10.1016/j.alcohol.2017.01.013

Carver, H., Elliott, L., Kennedy, C., & Hanley, J. (2017). Parent–child connectedness and communication in relation to alcohol, tobacco and drug use in adolescence: An integrative review of the literature. *Drugs: Education, Prevention and Policy*, 24(2), 119–133. https://doi.org/10.1080/09687637.2016.1221060

Cash, S. J., Bridge, J. A., & McNamara, P. (2018). Suicide. In R. J. R. Levesque (Ed.), *Encyclopedia of adolescence* (pp. 3881–3889). Cham, Switzerland: Springer. https://doi.org/10.1007/978-3-319-33228-4_87

Centers for Disease Control and Prevention. (2017). *10 leading causes of death, by age group, United States - 2015*. Retrieved from https://www.cdc.gov/injury/images/lc-charts/leading_causes_of_death_age_group_2015_1050w740h.gif

Chaplin, T. M., Sinha, R., Simmons, J. A., Healy, S. M., Mayes, L. C., Hommer, R. E., & Crowley, M. J. (2012). Parent-adolescent conflict interactions and adolescent alcohol use. *Addictive Behaviors*, 37(5), 605–612. https://doi.org/10.1016/j.addbeh.2012.01.004

Chen, P., Voisin, D. R., & Jacobson, K. C. (2013). Community violence exposure and adolescent delinquency: Examining a spectrum of promotive factors. *Youth & Society*, 48, 33–57. https://doi.org/10.1177/0044118X13475827

Child Trends Databank. (2019). *Teen suicide*. Retrieved from https://www.childtrends.org/indicators/suicidal-teens

Choukas-Bradley, S., Giletta, M., Widman, L., Cohen, G. L., & Prinstein, M. J. (2014). Experimentally measured susceptibility to peer influence and adolescent sexual behavior trajectories: A preliminary study. *Developmental Psychology*, 50(9), 2221–2227. https://doi.org/10.1037/a0037300

Cicchetti, D. (2016). Socioemotional, personality, and biological development: Illustrations from a multilevel developmental psychopathology perspective on child maltreatment. *Annual Review of Psychology*, 67(1), 187–211. https://doi.org/10.1146/annurev-psych-122414-033259

Ciocanel, O., Power, K., Eriksen, A., & Gillings, K. (2017). Effectiveness of positive youth development interventions: A meta-analysis of randomized controlled trials. *Journal of Youth and Adolescence*, 46(3), 483–504. https://doi.org/10.1007/s10964-016-0555-6

Claes, L., Luyckx, K., Baetens, I., Van de Ven, M., & Witteman, C. (2015). Bullying and victimization, depressive mood, and non-suicidal self-injury in adolescents: The moderating role of parental support. *Journal of Child and Family Studies*, 24(11), 3363–3371. https://doi.org/10.1007/s10826-015-0138-2

Claus, R. E., Vidal, S., & Harmon, M. (2017). Racial and ethnic disparities in the police handling of juvenile arrests. *National Criminal Justice Reference Service*. Retrieved from https://www.ncjrs.gov/App/Publications/abstract.aspx?ID=272982

Coffey, C., & Patton, G. C. (2016). Cannabis use in adolescence and young adulthood. *The Canadian Journal of Psychiatry*, 61(6), 318–327. https://doi.org/10.1177/0706743716645289

Cohen, J. R., So, F. K., Hankin, B. L., & Young, J. F. (2019). Translating cognitive vulnerability theory into improved adolescent depression screening: A receiver operating characteristic approach. *Journal of Clinical Child and Adolescent Psychology*, 48(4), 582–595. https://doi.org/10.1080/15374416.2017.1416617

Corrieri, S., Heider, D., Conrad, I., Blume, A., König, H.-H., & Riedel-Heller, S. G. (2014). School-based prevention programs for depression and anxiety in adolescence: A systematic review. *Health Promotion International*, 29(3), 427–441. https://doi.org/10.1093/heapro/dat001

Cox, M. J., Janssen, T., Lopez-Vergara, H., Barnett, N. P., & Jackson, K. M. (2018). Parental drinking as context for parental socialization of adolescent alcohol use. *Journal of Adolescence*, 69, 22–32. https://doi.org/10.1016/j.adolescence.2018.08.009

Cservenka, A. (2016). Neurobiological phenotypes associated with a family history of alcoholism. *Drug and Alcohol Dependence*, 158, 8–21. https://doi.org/10.1016/j.drugalcdep.2015.10.021

Cservenka, A., & Brumback, T. (2017). The burden of binge and heavy drinking on the brain: Effects on adolescent and young adult neural structure and function. *Frontiers in Psychology*, 8, 1111. https://doi.org/10.3389/fpsyg.2017.01111

Curtin, S. C., & Heron, M. (2019). Death rates due to suicide and homicide among persons aged 10-24: United States, 2000-2017. *NCHS Data Brief*, (352), 1–8. Retrieved from http://www.ncbi.nlm.nih.gov/pubmed/31751202

Cusimano, M. D., & Sameem, M. (2011). The effectiveness of middle and high school-based suicide prevention programmes for adolescents: A systematic review. *Injury Prevention*, 17(1), 43–49. https://doi.org/10.1136/ip.2009.025502

Cutuli, J. J., Ahumada, S. M., Herbers, J. E., Lafavor, T. L., Masten, A. S., & Oberg, C. N. (2017). Adversity and children experiencing family homelessness: Implications for health. *Journal of Children and Poverty*, 23(1), 41–55. https://doi.org/10.1080/10796126.2016.1198753

Delisi, M. (2015). Age–crime curve and criminal career patterns. In J. Morizot & L. Kazemian (Eds.), *The development of criminal and antisocial behavior: Theory, research and practical applications* (pp. 51–63). Cham, Switzerland: Springer. https://doi.org/10.1007/978-3-319-08720-7_4

Department of Health and Human Services. (2019). *United States adolescent mental health facts*. Retrieved from https://www.hhs.gov/ash/oah/facts-and-stats/national-and-state-data-sheets/adolescent-mental-health-fact-sheets/united-states/index.html

Dishion, T. J., & Patterson, G. R. (2016). The development and ecology of antisocial behavior: Linking etiology, prevention, and treatment. In D. Cicchetti (Ed.), *Developmental psychopathology* (pp. 1–32). Hoboken, NJ: John Wiley & Sons. https://doi.org/10.1002/9781119125556.devpsy315

Domhardt, M., Münzer, A., Fegert, J. M., & Goldbeck, L. (2015). Resilience in survivors of child sexual abuse: A systematic review of the literature. *Trauma, Violence & Abuse, 16*(4), 476–493. https://doi.org/10.1177/1524838014557288

Domitrovich, C. E., Durlak, J. A., Staley, K. C., & Weissberg, R. P. (2017). Social-emotional competence: An essential factor for promoting positive adjustment and reducing risk in school children. *Child Development, 88*(2), 408–416. https://doi.org/10.1111/cdev.12739

Dopp, A. R., Borduin, C. M., White, M. H., & Kuppens, S. (2017). Family-based treatments for serious juvenile offenders: A multilevel meta-analysis. *Journal of Consulting and Clinical Psychology, 85*(4), 335–354. https://doi.org/10.1037/ccp0000183

Dube, S. R., Miller, J. W., Brown, D. W., Giles, W. H., Felitti, V. J., Dong, M., & Anda, R. F. (2006). Adverse childhood experiences and the association with ever using alcohol and initiating alcohol use during adolescence. *Journal of Adolescent Health, 38*(4), 444.e1–444.e10. https://doi.org/10.1016/j.jadohealth.2005.06.006

Duncan, S. C., Duncan, T. E., & Strycker, L. A. (2006). Alcohol use from ages 9 to 16: A cohort-sequential latent growth model. *Drug and Alcohol Dependence, 81*(1), 71–81. https://doi.org/10.1016/j.drugalcdep.2005.06.001

Durlak, J. A., Weissberg, R. P., Dymnicki, A. B., Taylor, R. D., & Schellinger, K. B. (2011). The impact of enhancing students' social and emotional learning: A meta-analysis of school-based universal interventions. *Child Development, 82*(1), 405–432. https://doi.org/10.1111/j.1467-8624.2010.01564.x

Eichas, K., Ferrer-Wreder, L., & Olsson, T. M. (2019). Contributions of positive youth development to intervention science. *Child & Youth Care Forum, 48*(2), 279–287. https://doi.org/10.1007/s10566-018-09486-1

Eisenberg, N., Haugen, R., Spinrad, T. L., Hofer, C., Chassin, L., Qing, Z., . . . Liew, J. (2010). Relations of temperament to maladjustment and ego resiliency in at-risk children. *Social Development, 19*(3), 577–600. https://doi.org/10.1111/j.1467-9507.2009.00550.x

Ellis, B. J., Bianchi, J., Griskevicius, V., & Frankenhuis, W. E. (2017). Beyond risk and protective factors: An adaptation-based approach to resilience. *Perspectives on Psychological Science, 12*(4), 561–587. https://doi.org/10.1177/1745691617693054

Englund, M. M., Siebenbruner, J., Oliva, E. M., Egeland, B., Chung, C.-T., & Long, J. D. (2013). The developmental significance of late adolescent substance use for early adult functioning. *Developmental Psychology, 49*(8), 1554–1564. https://doi.org/10.1037/a0030229

Evans, S. Z., Simons, L. G., & Simons, R. L. (2014). Factors that influence trajectories of delinquency throughout adolescence. *Journal of Youth and Adolescence, 45*, 156–171. https://doi.org/10.1007/s10964-014-0197-5

Fairchild, G., Hawes, D. J., Frick, P. J., Copeland, W. E., Odgers, C. L., Franke, B., . . . & De Brito, S. A. (2019). Conduct disorder. *Nature Reviews Disease Primers, 5*(1), 1–25. https://doi.org/10.1038/s41572-019-0095-y

Farrell, A. D., Thompson, E. L., & Mehari, K. R. (2017). Dimensions of peer influences and their relationship to adolescents' aggression, other problem behaviors and prosocial behavior. *Journal of Youth and Adolescence, 46*, 1351–1369. https://doi.org/10.1007/s10964-016-0601-4

Federal Bureau of Investigation. (2019). Table 38: Arrests by age, 2018. *2018 Crime in the United States*. Retrieved from https://ucr.fbi.gov/crime-in-the-u.s/2018/crime-in-the-u.s.-2018/topic-pages/tables/table-38

Feldstein Ewing, S. W., Sakhardande, A., & Blakemore, S.-J. (2014). The effect of alcohol consumption on the adolescent brain: A systematic review of MRI and fMRI studies of alcohol-using youth. *NeuroImage: Clinical, 5*, 420–437. https://doi.org/10.1016/j.nicl.2014.06.011

Fergusson, D. M., & Horwood, L. J. (2002). Male and female offending trajectories. *Development and Psychopathology, 14*(1), 159–177.

Fergusson, D. M., Woodward, L. J., & Horwood, L. J. (2000). Risk factors and life processes associated with the onset of suicidal behaviour during adolescence and early adulthood. *Psychological Medicine, 30*, 23–39.

Fisher, H. L., Moffitt, T. E., Houts, R. M., Belsky, D. W., Arseneault, L., & Caspi, A. (2012). Bullying victimisation and risk of self harm in early adolescence: Longitudinal cohort study. *BMJ (Clinical Research Ed.), 344*, e2683. https://doi.org/10.1136/bmj.e2683

Flannery, D. J., Hussey, D., & Jefferis, E. (2005). Adolescent delinquency and violent behavior. In T. P. Gullotta & G. R. Adams (Eds.), *Handbook of adolescent behavioral problems: Evidence-based approaches to prevention and treatment* (pp. 415–438). Boston, MA: Springer. https://doi.org/10.1007/0-387-23846-8_19

Frost, A., Hoyt, L. T., Chung, A. L., & Adam, E. K. (2015). Daily life with depressive symptoms: Gender differences in adolescents' everyday emotional experiences. *Journal of Adolescence, 43*, 132–141. https://doi.org/10.1016/j.adolescence.2015.06.001

Ge, X., Natsuaki, M. N., Neiderhiser, J. M., & Reiss, D. (2009). The longitudinal effects of stressful life events on adolescent depression are buffered by parent-child closeness. *Development & Psychopathology, 21*(2), 621–635. https://doi.org/10.1017/s0954579409000339

Geier, C. F. (2013). Adolescent cognitive control and reward processing: Implications for risk taking and substance use. *Hormones and Behavior, 64*(2), 333–342. https://doi.org/10.1016/j.yhbeh.2013.02.008

Giletta, M., Burk, W. J., Scholte, R. H. J., Engels, R. C. M. E., & Prinstein, M. J. (2013). Direct and indirect peer socialization of adolescent nonsuicidal self-injury. *Journal of Research on Adolescence, 23*(3), 450–463. https://doi.org/10.1111/jora.12036

Gould, M., Jamieson, P., & Romer, D. (2003). Media contagion and suicide among the young. *American Behavioral Scientist, 46*(9), 1269.

Gould, M. S., Kleinman, M. H., Lake, A. M., Forman, J., & Midle, J. B. (2014). Newspaper coverage of suicide and initiation of suicide clusters in teenagers in the USA, 1988-96: A retrospective, population-based, case-control study. *The Lancet Psychiatry, 1*(1), 34–43. https://doi.org/10.1016/S2215-0366(14)70225-1

Gray, K. M., & Squeglia, L. M. (2018). Research review: What have we learned about adolescent substance use? *Journal of Child Psychology and Psychiatry and Allied Disciplines, 59*, 618–627. https://doi.org/10.1111/jcpp.12783

Grossman, A. H., Park, J. Y., & Russell, S. T. (2016). Transgender youth and suicidal behaviors: Applying the interpersonal psychological theory of suicide. *Journal of Gay & Lesbian Mental Health, 20*(4), 329–349. https://doi.org/10.1080/19359705.2016.1207581

Hall, B., & Place, M. (2010). Cutting to cope – a modern adolescent phenomenon. *Child: Care, Health & Development, 36*(5), 623–629. https://doi.org/10.1111/j.1365-2214.2010.01095.x

Hanson, K. L., Thayer, R. E., & Tapert, S. F. (2014). Adolescent marijuana users have elevated risk-taking on the balloon analog risk task. *Journal of Psychopharmacology, 28*(11), 1080–1087. https://doi.org/10.1177/0269881114550352

Hanson, K. L., Winward, J. L., Schweinsburg, A. D., Medina, K. L., Brown, S. A., & Tapert, S. F. (2010). Longitudinal study of cognition among adolescent marijuana users over three weeks of abstinence. *Addictive Behaviors, 35*(11), 970–976. https://doi.org/10.1016/j.addbeh.2010.06.012

Harris-McKoy, D., & Cui, M. (2012). Parental control, adolescent delinquency, and young adult criminal behavior. *Journal of Child and Family Studies, 22*(6), 836–843. https://doi.org/10.1007/s10826-012-9641-x

Hart, A. B., & Kranzler, H. R. (2015). Alcohol dependence genetics: Lessons learned from genome-wide association studies (GWAS) and post-GWAS analyses. *Alcoholism: Clinical and Experimental Research, 39*(8), 1312–1327. https://doi.org/10.1111/acer.12792

Haw, C., Hawton, K., Niedzwiedz, C., & Platt, S. (2013). Suicide clusters: A review of risk factors and mechanisms. *Suicide & Life-Threatening Behavior, 43*(1), 97–108. https://doi.org/10.1111/j.1943-278X.2012.00130.x

Hawton, K., Hill, N. T. M., Gould, M., John, A., Lascelles, K., & Robinson, J. (2020). Clustering of suicides in children and adolescents. *The Lancet Child & Adolescent Health, 4*(1), 58–67. https://doi.org/10.1016/s2352-4642(19)30335-9

Henggeler, S. W., & Schaeffer, C. M. (2018). Multisystemic Therapy®: Clinical procedures, outcomes, and implementation research. In *APA handbook of contemporary family psychology: Family therapy and training* (Vol. 3, pp. 205–220). Washington, DC: American Psychological Association. https://doi.org/10.1037/0000101-013

Hepper, P. G., Dornan, J. C., & Lynch, C. (2012). Sex differences in fetal habituation. *Developmental Science, 15*(3), 373–383. https://doi.org/10.1111/j.1467-7687.2011.01132.x

Hoeben, E. M., Meldrum, R. C., Walker, D., & Young, J. T. N. (2016). The role of peer delinquency and unstructured socializing in explaining delinquency and substance use: A state-of-the-art review. *Journal of Criminal Justice, 47*, 108–122. https://doi.org/10.1016/j.jcrimjus.2016.08.001

Hopkins, K. D., Taylor, C. L., D'Antoine, H., & Zubrick, S. R. (2012). Predictors of resilient psychosocial functioning in Western Australian Aboriginal young people exposed to high family-level risk. In M. Ungar (Ed.), *The social ecology of resilience* (pp. 425–440). New York, NY: Springer. https://doi.org/10.1007/978-1-4614-0586-3_33

Howell, B. R., McMurray, M. S., Guzman, D. B., Nair, G., Shi, Y., McCormack, K. M., . . . Sanchez, M. M. (2017). Maternal buffering beyond glucocorticoids: Impact of early life stress on corticolimbic circuits that control infant responses to novelty. *Social Neuroscience, 12*(1), 50–64. https://doi.org/10.1080/17470919.2016.1200481

Jain, S., & Cohen, A. K. (2013). Behavioral adaptation among youth exposed to community violence: A longitudinal multidisciplinary study of family, peer and neighborhood-level protective factors. *Prevention Science, 14*(6), 606–617. https://doi.org/10.1007/s11121-012-0344-8

Johnston, L. D., Miech, R. A., O'Malley, P. M., Bachman, J. G., Schulenberg, J. E., & Patrick, M. E. (2019). *Monitoring the Future national survey results on drug use 1975–2018: Overview, key findings on adolescent drug use.* Retrieved from http://monitoringthefuture.org//pubs/monographs/mtf-overview2018.pdf

Kandel, D., & Kandel, E. (2015). The Gateway Hypothesis of substance abuse: Developmental, biological and societal perspectives. *Acta Paediatrica, 104*(2), 130–137. https://doi.org/10.1111/apa.12851

Kann, L., Kinchen, S., Shanklin, S. L., Flint, K. H., Kawkins, J., Harris, W. A., . . . Centers for Disease Control and Prevention (CDC). (2014). Youth risk behavior surveillance--United States, 2013. *Morbidity and Mortality Weekly Report. Surveillance Summaries, 63*(4 Suppl 4), 1–168. Retrieved from http://www.ncbi.nlm.nih.gov/pubmed/24918634

Kim, S. Y., Chen, Q., Wang, Y., Shen, Y., & Orozco-Lapray, D. (2013). Longitudinal linkages among parent-child acculturation discrepancy, parenting, parent-child sense of alienation, and adolescent adjustment in Chinese immigrant families. *Developmental Psychology, 49*(5), 900–912. https://doi.org/10.1037/a0029169

Kim, S. Y., Qi, C., Jing, L., Xuan, H., & Ui Jeong, M. (2009). Parent-child acculturation, parenting, and adolescent depressive symptoms in Chinese immigrant families. *Journal of Family Psychology, 23*(3), 426–437. https://doi.org/10.1037/a0016019

Klemera, E., Brooks, F. M., Chester, K. L., Magnusson, J., & Spencer, N. (2017). Self-harm in adolescence: Protective health assets in the family, school and community. *International Journal of Public Health, 62*(6), 631–638. https://doi.org/10.1007/s00038-016-0900-2

Kuhlman, K. R., Olson, S. L., & Lopez-Duran, N. L. (2014). Predicting developmental changes in internalizing symptoms: Examining the interplay between parenting and neuroendocrine stress reactivity. *Developmental Psychobiology, 56*(5), 908–923. https://doi.org/10.1002/dev.21166

Labella, M. H., Narayan, A. J., McCormick, C. M., Desjardins, C. D., & Masten, A. S. (2019). Risk and adversity, parenting quality, and children's social-emotional adjustment in families experiencing homelessness. *Child Development, 90*(1), 227–244. https://doi.org/10.1111/cdev.12894

Lee, K. T. H., Lewis, R. W., Kataoka, S., Schenke, K., & Vandell, D. L. (2018). Out-of-school time and behaviors during adolescence. *Journal of Research on Adolescence, 28*(2), 284–293. https://doi.org/10.1111/jora.12389

Lerner, R. M., Buckingham, M. H., Champine, R. B., Greenman, K. N., Warren, D. J. A., Weiner, M. B., . . . Weiner, M. B. (2015). Positive development among diverse youth. In R. A. Scott, S. M. Kosslyn, & M. Buchmann (Eds.), *Emerging trends in the social and behavioral sciences* (pp. 1–14). John Wiley & Sons: Hoboken, NJ. https://doi.org/10.1002/9781118900772.etrds0260

Lerner, R. M., Tirrell, J. M., Dowling, E. M., Geldhof, G. J., Gestsdóttir, S., Lerner, J. V., . . . Sim, A. T. R. (2019). The end of the beginning: Evidence and absences studying positive youth development in a global context. *Adolescent Research Review, 4*(1), 1–14. https://doi.org/10.1007/s40894-018-0093-4

Leung, R. K., Toumbourou, J. W., & Hemphill, S. A. (2014). The effect of peer influence and selection processes on adolescent alcohol use: A systematic review of longitudinal studies. *Health Psychology Review, 8*(4), 426–457. https://doi.org/10.1080/17437199.2011.587961

Li, J. J., Berk, M. S., & Lee, S. S. (2013). Differential susceptibility in longitudinal models of gene-environment interaction for adolescent depression. *Development and Psychopathology, 25*(4 Pt 1), 991–1003. https://doi.org/10.1017/S0954579413000321

Lisdahl, K. M., Gilbart, E. R., Wright, N. E., & Shollenbarger, S. (2013). Dare to delay? The impacts of adolescent alcohol and marijuana use onset on cognition, brain structure, and function. *Frontiers in Psychiatry, 4*, 53. https://doi.org/10.3389/fpsyt.2013.00053

Liu, R. T., & Mustanski, B. (2012). Suicidal ideation and self-harm in lesbian, gay, bisexual, and transgender youth. *American Journal of Preventive Medicine, 42*(3), 221–228. https://doi.org/10.1016/j.amepre.2011.10.023

Lockwood, J., Daley, D., Townsend, E., & Sayal, K. (2017). Impulsivity and self-harm in adolescence: A systematic review. *European Child & Adolescent Psychiatry, 26*(4), 387–402. https://doi.org/10.1007/s00787-016-0915-5

Lopez-Larson, M. P., Rogowska, J., Bogorodzki, P., Bueler, C. E., McGlade, E. C., & Yurgelun-Todd, D. A. (2012). Cortico-cerebellar abnormalities in adolescents with heavy marijuana use. *Psychiatry Research: Neuroimaging, 202*(3), 224–232. https://doi.org/10.1016/j.pscychresns.2011.11.005

Lopez-Tamayo, R., LaVome Robinson, W., Lambert, S. F., Jason, L. A., & Ialongo, N. S. (2016). Parental monitoring, association with externalized behavior, and academic outcomes in urban African-American youth: A moderated mediation analysis. *American Journal of Community Psychology, 57*(3–4), 366–379. https://doi.org/10.1002/ajcp.12056

Lubman, D. I., Cheetham, A., & Yücel, M. (2015). Cannabis and adolescent brain development. *Pharmacology & Therapeutics*, *148*, 1–16. https://doi.org/10.1016/j.pharmthera.2014.11.009

Luthar, S. S., Crossman, E. J., Small, P. J., Luthar, S. S., Crossman, E. J., & Small, P. J. (2015). Resilience and adversity. In M. E. Lamb (Ed.), *Handbook of child psychology and developmental science* (pp. 1–40). Hoboken, NJ: John Wiley & Sons. https://doi.org/10.1002/9781118963418.childpsy307

Lynskey, M. T., & Agrawal, A. (2018). Denise Kandel's classic work on the gateway sequence of drug acquisition. *Addiction*, *113*(10), 1927–1932. https://doi.org/10.1111/add.14190

Madge, N., Hewitt, A., Hawton, K., De Wilde, E. J., Corcoran, P., Fekete, S., . . . Ystgaard, M. (2008). Deliberate self-harm within an international community sample of young people: Comparative findings from the Child & Adolescent Self-harm in Europe (CASE) Study. *Journal of Child Psychology & Psychiatry*, *49*(6), 667–677. https://doi.org/10.1111/j.1469-7610.2008.01879.x

Mahatmya, D., & Lohman, B. (2011). Predictors of late adolescent delinquency: The protective role of after-school activities in low-income families. *Children and Youth Services Review*, *33*(7), 1309–1317. https://doi.org/10.1016/j.childyouth.2011.03.005

Mann, F. D., Patterson, M. W., Grotzinger, A. D., Kretsch, N., Tackett, J. L., Tucker-Drob, E. M., & Harden, K. P. (2016). Sensation seeking, peer deviance, and genetic influences on adolescent delinquency: Evidence for person-environment correlation and interaction. *Journal of Abnormal Psychology*, *125*(5), 679–691. https://doi.org/10.1037/abn0000160

Manuck, S. B., & McCaffery, J. M. (2014). Gene-environment interaction. *Annual Review of Psychology*, (65), 41–70.

Marriott, C., Hamilton-Giachritsis, C., & Harrop, C. (2014). Factors promoting resilience following childhood sexual abuse: A structured, narrative review of the literature. *Child Abuse Review*, *23*(1), 17–34. https://doi.org/10.1002/car.2258

Marshall, E. J. (2014). Adolescent alcohol use: Risks and consequences. *Alcohol and Alcoholism (Oxford, Oxfordshire)*, *49*(2), 160–164. https://doi.org/10.1093/alcalc/agt180

Marshall, S. K., Tilton-Weaver, L. C., & Stattin, H. (2013). Non-suicidal self-injury and depressive symptoms during middle adolescence: A longitudinal analysis. *Journal of Youth and Adolescence*, *42*(8), 1234–1242. https://doi.org/10.1007/s10964-013-9919-3

Mason, W. A., & Spoth, R. L. (2011). Longitudinal associations of alcohol involvement with subjective well-being in adolescence and prediction to alcohol problems in early adulthood. *Journal of Youth and Adolescence*, *40*(9), 1215–1224. https://doi.org/10.1007/s10964-011-9632-z

Masten, A. S. (2016). Resilience in developing systems: The promise of integrated approaches. *European Journal of Developmental Psychology*, *13*(3), 297–312. https://doi.org/10.1080/17405629.2016.1147344

Masten, A. S., & Cicchetti, D. (2016). Resilience in development: Progress and transformation. In D. Cicchetti (Ed.), *Developmental psychopathology* (pp. 1–63). Hoboken, NJ: John Wiley & Sons. https://doi.org/10.1002/9781119125556.devpsy406

Masten, A. S., & Monn, A. R. (2015). Child and family resilience: A call for integrated science, practice, and professional training. *Family Relations*, *64*(1), 5–21. https://doi.org/10.1111/fare.12103

Maughan, B., Collishaw, S., & Stringaris, A. (2013). Depression in childhood and adolescence. *Journal of the Canadian Academy of Child and Adolescent Psychiatry*, *22*(1), 35–40. Retrieved from https://www.ncbi.nlm.nih.gov/pmc/articles/PMC3565713/

Mazerolle, P., Patterson, G. R., DeBaryshe, B. D., & Ramsey, E. (2015). A developmental perspective on antisocial behavior. In P. Mazerolle (Ed.), *Developmental and life-course criminological theories* (pp. 29–35). New York, NY: Taylor & Francis. https://doi.org/10.4324/9781315094908-2

Meruelo, A. D., Castro, N., Cota, C. I., & Tapert, S. F. (2017). Cannabis and alcohol use, and the developing brain. *Behavioural Brain Research*, *325*(Part A), 44–50. https://doi.org/10.1016/j.bbr.2017.02.025

Miech, R. a., Johnston, L. D., O'Malley, P. M., Bachman, J. G., Schulenberg, J. E., & Patrick, M. E. (2017). *Monitoring the Future national survey results on drug use, 1975–2016: Volume I, Secondary school students*. Retrieved from http://www.monitoringthefuture.org/pubs/monographs/mtf-vol1_2016.pdf

Miranda-Mendizábal, A., Castellvi, P., Parés-Badell, O., Almenara, J., Alonso, I., Blasco, M. J., . . . Alonso, J. (2017). Sexual orientation and suicidal behaviour in adolescents and young adults: Systematic review and meta-analysis. *The British Journal of Psychiatry*, *211*(2), 77–87. https://doi.org/10.1192/bjp.bp.116.196345

Miyake, A., & Friedman, N. P. (2012). The nature and organization of individual differences in executive functions. *Current Directions in Psychological Science*, *21*(1), 8–14. https://doi.org/10.1177/0963721411429458

Moffitt, T. E. (2017). Adolescence-limited and life-course-persistent antisocial behavior: A developmental taxonomy. In K. M. Beaver (Ed.), *The termination of criminal careers* (pp. 405–432). New York, NY: Taylor & Francis. https://doi.org/10.4324/9781315096278-3

Moffitt, T. E. (2018). Male antisocial behaviour in adolescence and beyond. *Nature Human Behaviour*, *2*, 177–186. https://doi.org/10.1038/s41562-018-0309-4

Moffitt, T. E., Arseneault, L., Belsky, D., Dickson, N., Hancox, R. J., Harrington, H., . . . Caspi, A. (2011). A gradient of childhood self-control predicts health, wealth, and public safety. *Proceedings of the National Academy of Sciences*, *108*(7), 2693–2698. https://doi.org/10.1073/pnas.1010076108

Monahan, K. C., Steinberg, L., Cauffman, E., & Mulvey, E. P. (2013). Psychosocial (im)maturity from adolescence to early adulthood: Distinguishing between adolescence-limited and persisting antisocial behavior. *Development and Psychopathology*, *25*(4 Pt 1), 1093–1105. https://doi.org/10.1017/S0954579413000394

Muehlenkamp, J. J., Claes, L., Havertape, L., & Plener, P. L. (2012). International prevalence of adolescent non-suicidal self-injury and deliberate self-harm. *Child and Adolescent Psychiatry and Mental Health*, *6*, 10. https://doi.org/10.1186/1753-2000-6-10

Müller-Oehring, E. M., Kwon, D., Nagel, B. J., Sullivan, E. V, Chu, W., Rohlfing, T., . . . Pohl, K. M. (2018). Influences of age, sex, and moderate alcohol drinking on the intrinsic functional architecture of adolescent brains. *Cerebral Cortex*, *28*(3), 1049–1063. https://doi.org/10.1093/cercor/bhx014

Mustanski, B., & Liu, R. T. (2013). A longitudinal study of predictors of suicide attempts among lesbian, gay, bisexual, and transgender youth. *Archives of Sexual Behavior*, *42*(3), 437–448. https://doi.org/10.1007/s10508-012-0013-9

Nagin, D. S. (2016). Group-based trajectory modeling and criminal career research. *Journal of Research in Crime and Delinquency*, *53*(3), 356–371. https://doi.org/10.1177/0022427815611710

Nair, R. L., Roche, K. M., & White, R. M. B. (2018). Acculturation gap distress among Latino Youth: Prospective links to family processes and youth depressive symptoms, alcohol use, and academic performance. *Journal of Youth and Adolescence*, *47*(1), 105–120. https://doi.org/10.1007/s10964-017-0753-x

Nanayakkara, S., Misch, D., Chang, L., & Henry, D. (2013). Depression and exposure to suicide predict suicide attempt. *Depression and Anxiety*, *30*(10), 991–996. https://doi.org/10.1002/da.22143

National Institute of Mental Health. (2019). *Major depression*. Retrieved from https://www.nimh.nih.gov/health/statistics/major-depression.shtml

National Institute on Drug Abuse. (2017). National survey on drug use and health: Trends in prevalence of various drugs for ages 12 or older, ages 12 to 17, ages 18 to 25, and ages 26 or older; 2015-2016 (in percent). *National Survey of Drug Use and Health*. Retrieved from https://www.drugabuse.gov/national-survey-drug-use-health

Natsuaki, M. N., Shaw, D. S., Neiderhiser, J. M., Ganiban, J. M., Harold, G. T., Reiss, D., & Leve, L. D. (2014). Raised by depressed parents: Is it an environmental risk? *Clinical Child and Family Psychology Review*, *17*(4), 357–367. https://doi.org/10.1007/s10567-014-0169-z

Nguyen, D. J., Kim, J. J., Weiss, B., Ngo, V., & Lau, A. S. (2018). Prospective relations between parent–adolescent acculturation conflict and mental health symptoms among Vietnamese American adolescents. *Cultural Diversity and Ethnic Minority Psychology*, *24*, 151–161. https://doi.org/10.1037/cdp0000157

Nock, M. K. (2009). Why do people hurt themselves? New insights into the nature and functions of self-injury. *Current Directions in Psychological Science*, *18*(2), 78–83. https://doi.org/10.1111/j.1467-8721.2009.01613.x

Nock, M. K., Prinstein, M. J., & Sterba, S. K. (2009). Revealing the form and function of self-injurious thoughts and behaviors: A real-time ecological assessment study among adolescents and young adults. *Journal of Abnormal Psychology*, *118*(4), 816–827. https://doi.org/10.1037/a0016948

Office for National Statistics. (2015,February 27). *What are the top causes of death by age and gender?* Retrieved from http://visual.ons.gov.uk/what-are-the-top-causes-of-death-by-age-and-gender/

Office of Juvenile Justice and Delinquency Prevention. (2019, October 31). Juvenile arrest rate trends. *OJJDP Statistical Briefing Book*. Retrieved from https://www.ojjdp.gov/ojstatbb/crime/JAR_Display.asp?ID=qa05261

Osher, D., Kidron, Y., Brackett, M., Dymnicki, A., Jones, S., & Weissberg, R. P. (2016). Advancing the science and practice of social and emotional learning. *Review of Research in Education*, *40*(1), 644–681. https://doi.org/10.3102/0091732X16673595

Palmer, R. H. C., Young, S. E., Hopfer, C. J., Corley, R. P., Stallings, M. C., Crowley, T. J., & Hewitt, J. K. (2009). Developmental epidemiology of drug use and abuse in adolescence and young adulthood: Evidence of generalized risk. *Drug & Alcohol Dependence*, *102*(1–3), 78–87. https://doi.org/10.1016/j.drugalcdep.2009.01.012

Pedersen, E. R., Osilla, K. C., Miles, J. N. V., Tucker, J. S., Ewing, B. A., Shih, R. A., & D'Amico, E. J. (2017). The role of perceived injunctive alcohol norms in adolescent drinking behavior. *Addictive Behaviors*, *67*, 1–7. https://doi.org/10.1016/j.addbeh.2016.11.022

Pérez-González, A., Guilera, G., Pereda, N., & Jarne, A. (2017). Protective factors promoting resilience in the relation between child sexual victimization and internalizing and externalizing symptoms. *Child Abuse & Neglect*, *72*, 393–403. https://doi.org/10.1016/J.CHIABU.2017.09.006

Petersen, I. T., Lindhiem, O., LeBeau, B., Bates, J. E., Pettit, G. S., Lansford, J. E., & Dodge, K. A. (2018). Development of internalizing problems from adolescence to emerging adulthood: Accounting for heterotypic continuity with vertical scaling. *Developmental Psychology*, *54*(3), 586–599. https://doi.org/10.1037/dev0000449

Piquero, A. R., Jennings, W. G., Diamond, B., Farrington, D. P., Tremblay, R. E., Welsh, B. C., & Gonzalez, J. M. R. (2016). A meta-analysis update on the effects of early family/parent training programs on antisocial behavior and delinquency. *Journal of Experimental Criminology*, *12*(2), 229–248. https://doi.org/10.1007/s11292-016-9256-0

Piquero, A. R., & Moffitt, T. E. (2013). Moffitt's developmental taxonomy of antisocial behavior. In G. Bruinsma & D. Weisburd (Eds.), *Encyclopedia of criminology and criminal justice* (pp. 3121–3127). New York, NY: Springer.

Pompili, M., Lester, D., Forte, A., Seretti, M. E., Erbuto, D., Lamis, D. A., . . . Girardi, P. (2014). Bisexuality and suicide: A systematic review of the current literature. *The Journal of Sexual Medicine*, *11*(8), 1903–1913. https://doi.org/10.1111/jsm.12581

Rose, A. J., Schwartz-Mette, R. A., Glick, G. C., Smith, R. L., & Luebbe, A. M. (2014). An observational study of co-rumination in adolescent friendships. *Developmental Psychology*, *50*(9), 2199–2209. https://doi.org/10.1037/a0037465

Ross, S., Heath, N. L., & Toste, J. R. (2009). Non-suicidal self-injury and eating pathology in high school students. *American Journal of Orthopsychiatry*, *79*(1), 83–92. https://doi.org/10.1037/a0014826

Rueger, S. Y., Chen, P., Jenkins, L. N., & Choe, H. J. (2014). Effects of perceived support from mothers, fathers, and teachers on depressive symptoms during the transition to middle school. *Journal of Youth and Adolescence*, *43*(4), 655–670. https://doi.org/10.1007/s10964-013-0039-x

Rueger, S. Y., Malecki, C. K., Pyun, Y., Aycock, C., & Coyle, S. (2016). A meta-analytic review of the association between perceived social support and depression in childhood and adolescence. *Psychological Bulletin*, *142*(10), 1017–1067. https://doi.org/10.1037/bul0000058

Rulison, K., Patrick, M. E., & Maggs, J. (2015). Linking peer relationships to substance use across adolescence. In R. A. Zucker & S. A. Brown (Eds.), *The Oxford handbook of adolescent substance abuse* (Vol. 1, pp. 389–420). New York, NY: Oxford University Press. https://doi.org/10.1093/oxfordhb/9780199735662.013.019

Russell, S. T., & Fish, J. N. (2016). Mental health in lesbian, gay, bisexual, and transgender (LGBT) youth. *Annual Review of Clinical Psychology*, *12*(1), 465–487. https://doi.org/10.1146/annurev-clinpsy-021815-093153

Samek, D. R., Hicks, B. M., Keyes, M. A., Iacono, W. G., & McGue, M. (2017). Antisocial peer affiliation and externalizing disorders: Evidence for Gene × Environment × Development interaction. *Development and Psychopathology*, *29*(1), 155–172. https://doi.org/10.1017/S0954579416000109

Schwartz-Mette, R. A., & Smith, R. L. (2018). When does co-rumination facilitate depression contagion in adolescent friendships? Investigating intrapersonal and interpersonal factors. *Journal of Clinical Child and Adolescent Psychology*, *47*(6), 912–924. https://doi.org/10.1080/15374416.2016.1197837

Scoliers, G., Portzky, G., Madge, N., Hewitt, A., Hawton, K., de Wilde, E. J., . . . Van Heeringen, K. (2009). Reasons for adolescent deliberate self-harm: A cry of pain and/or a cry for help? *Social Psychiatry & Psychiatric Epidemiology*, *44*(8), 601–607. https://doi.org/10.1007/s00127-008-0469-z

Search Institute. (2017). *The asset approach: 40 elements of healthy development, 2017 update*. Retrieved from https://www.search-institute.org/product/the-asset-approach-40-elements-of-healthy-development-2017-update/

Selby, E. A., Nock, M. K., & Kranzler, A. (2014). How does self-injury feel? Examining automatic positive reinforcement in adolescent self-injurers with experience sampling. *Psychiatry Research*, *215*(2), 417–423. https://doi.org/10.1016/j.psychres.2013.12.005

Shirk, S. R., Gudmundsen, G., Kaplinski, H. C., & McMakin, D. L. (2008). Alliance and outcome in cognitive-behavioral therapy for adolescent depression. *Journal of Clinical Child & Adolescent Psychology*, *37*(3), 631–639. https://doi.org/10.1080/15374410802148061

Shore, L., Toumbourou, J. W., Lewis, A. J., & Kremer, P. (2018). Review: Longitudinal trajectories of child and adolescent depressive symptoms and their predictors—A systematic review and meta-analysis. *Child and Adolescent Mental Health*, *23*(2), 107–120. https://doi.org/10.1111/camh.12220

Silveri, M. M., Dager, A. D., Cohen-Gilbert, J. E., & Sneider, J. T. (2016). Neurobiological signatures associated with alcohol and drug use in the human adolescent brain. *Neuroscience & Biobehavioral Reviews*, *70*, 244–259. https://doi.org/10.1016/j.neubiorev.2016.06.042

Simons, J. S., Wills, T. A., & Neal, D. J. (2014). The many faces of affect: A multilevel model of drinking frequency/quantity and alcohol dependence symptoms among young adults. *Journal of Abnormal Psychology, 123*(3), 676–694. https://doi.org/10.1037/a0036926

Spear, L. P. (2018). Effects of adolescent alcohol consumption on the brain and behaviour. *Nature Reviews Neuroscience, 19*(4), 197–214. https://doi.org/10.1038/nrn.2018.10

Squeglia, L. M., & Gray, K. M. (2016). Alcohol and drug use and the developing brain. *Current Psychiatry Reports, 18*(5), 46. https://doi.org/10.1007/s11920-016-0689-y

Squeglia, L. M., Tapert, S. F., Sullivan, E. V., Jacobus, J., Meloy, M. J., Rohlfing, T., & Pfefferbaum, A. (2015). Brain development in heavy-drinking adolescents. *American Journal of Psychiatry, 172*(6), 531–542. https://doi.org/10.1176/appi.ajp.2015.14101249

Stanford, S., Jones, M. P., & Hudson, J. L. (2017). Rethinking pathology in adolescent self-harm: Towards a more complex understanding of risk factors. *Journal of Adolescence, 54*, 32–41. https://doi.org/10.1016/j.adolescence.2016.11.004

Statistics Canada. (2015). *The 10 leading causes of death, 2011.* Retrieved from http://www.statcan.gc.ca/pub/82-625-x/2014001/article/11896-eng.htm

Steinberg, L., & Monahan, K. C. (2007). Age differences in resistance to peer influence. *Developmental Psychology, 43*(6), 1531–1543. https://doi.org/10.1037/0012-1649.43.6.1531

Stewart, J. G., Valeri, L., Esposito, E. C., & Auerbach, R. P. (2018). Peer victimization and suicidal thoughts and behaviors in depressed adolescents. *Journal of Abnormal Child Psychology, 46*(3), 581–596. https://doi.org/10.1007/s10802-017-0304-7

Strang, N. M., Chein, J. M., & Steinberg, L. (2013). The value of the dual systems model of adolescent risk-taking. *Frontiers in Human Neuroscience, 7*, 223. https://doi.org/10.3389/fnhum.2013.00223

Substance Abuse and Mental Health Services Administration. (2013). *Results from the 2012 National Survey on Drug Use and Health: Mental health findings.* Rockville, MD: Author.

Takagi, M., Youssef, G., & Lorenzetti, V. (2016). Neuroimaging of the human brain in adolescent substance users. In D. De Micheli, A. L. M. Andrade, E. A. da Silva, & M. L. O. de Souza Formigoni (Eds.), *Drug abuse in adolescence* (pp. 69–99). Cham, Switzerland: Springer. https://doi.org/10.1007/978-3-319-17795-3_6

Tapia-Rojas, C., Carvajal, F. J., Mira, R. G., Arce, C., Lerma-Cabrera, J. M., Orellana, J. A., . . . Quintanilla, R. A. (2017). Adolescent binge alcohol exposure affects the brain function through mitochondrial impairment. *Molecular Neurobiology, 55*(5), 4473–4491. https://doi.org/10.1007/s12035-017-0613-4

Taubner, S., Gablonski, T. C., & Fonagy, P. (2019). Conduct disorder. In A. Bateman & P. Fonagy (Eds.), *Handbook of mentalizing in mental health practice* (2nd ed.). Washington, DC: American Psychiatric Association Publishing.

Tawa, E. A., Hall, S. D., & Lohoff, F. W. (2016). Overview of the genetics of alcohol use disorder. *Alcohol and Alcoholism, 51*, 507–514. https://doi.org/10.1093/alcalc/agw046

Taylor, R. D., Oberle, E., Durlak, J. A., & Weissberg, R. P. (2017). Promoting positive youth development through school-based social and emotional learning interventions: A meta-analysis of follow-up effects. *Child Development, 88*(4), 1156–1171. https://doi.org/10.1111/cdev.12864

Thapar, A., Collishaw, S., Pine, D. S., & Thapar, A. K. (2012). Depression in adolescence. *Lancet, 379*(9820), 1056–1067. https://doi.org/10.1016/S0140-6736(11)60871-4

Toomey, R. B., Syvertsen, A. K., & Shramko, M. (2018). Transgender adolescent suicide behavior. *Pediatrics, 142*(4), e20174218. https://doi.org/10.1542/peds.2017-4218

Traub, F., & Boynton-Jarrett, R. (2017). Modifiable resilience factors to childhood adversity for clinical pediatric practice. *Pediatrics, 139*(5), e20162569. https://doi.org/10.1542/peds.2016-2569

Trucco, E. M., Colder, C. R., Wieczorek, W. F., Lengua, L. J., & Hawk, L. W. (2014). Early adolescent alcohol use in context: How neighborhoods, parents, and peers impact youth. *Development and Psychopathology, 26*(2), 425–436. https://doi.org/10.1017/S0954579414000042

Uddin, M., Jansen, S., & Telzer, E. H. (2017). Adolescent depression linked to socioeconomic status? Molecular approaches for revealing premorbid risk factors. *BioEssays, 39*(3), 1600194. https://doi.org/10.1002/bies.201600194

Ungar, M. (2015). Practitioner review: Diagnosing childhood resilience—a systemic approach to the diagnosis of adaptation in adverse social and physical ecologies. *Journal of Child Psychology and Psychiatry, 56*(1), 4–17. https://doi.org/10.1111/jcpp.12306

van der Vorst, H., Vermulst, A. A., Meeus, W. H. J., Deković, M., & Engels, R. C. M. E. (2009). Identification and prediction of drinking trajectories in early and mid-adolescence. *Journal of Clinical Child and Adolescent Psychology, 38*(3), 329–341. https://doi.org/10.1080/15374410902851648

van Duijvenvoorde, A. C. K., Peters, S., Braams, B. R., & Crone, E. A. (2016). What motivates adolescents? Neural responses to rewards and their influence on adolescents' risk taking, learning, and cognitive control. *Neuroscience & Biobehavioral Reviews, 70*, 135–147. https://doi.org/10.1016/J.NEUBIOREV.2016.06.037

Verhulst, B., Neale, M. C., & Kendler, K. S. (2015). The heritability of alcohol use disorders: A meta-analysis of twin and adoption studies. *Psychological Medicine, 45*(5), 1061–1072. https://doi.org/10.1017/S0033291714002165

Vermeulen-Smit, E., Koning, I. M., Verdurmen, J. E. E., Van der Vorst, H., Engels, R. C. M. E., & Vollebergh, W. A. M. (2012). The influence of paternal and maternal drinking patterns within two-partner families on the initiation and development of adolescent drinking. *Addictive Behaviors, 37*(11), 1248–1256. https://doi.org/10.1016/j.addbeh.2012.06.005

Veroude, K., Zhang-James, Y., Fernàndez-Castillo, N., Bakker, M. J., Cormand, B., & Faraone, S. V. (2016). Genetics of aggressive behavior: An overview. *American Journal of Medical Genetics Part B: Neuropsychiatric Genetics, 171*(1), 3–43. https://doi.org/10.1002/ajmg.b.32364

Vidal, S., Steeger, C. M., Caron, C., Lasher, L., & Connell, C. M. (2017). Placement and delinquency outcomes among system-involved youth referred to multisystemic therapy: A propensity score matching analysis. *Administration and Policy in Mental Health and Mental Health Services Research, 44*(6), 853–866. https://doi.org/10.1007/s10488-017-0797-y

Waid, J., & Uhrich, M. (2019). A scoping review of the theory and practice of positive youth development. *The British Journal of Social Work*, bcy130. https://doi.org/10.1093/bjsw/bcy130

Weissberg, R. P. (2019). Promoting the social and emotional learning of millions of school children. *Perspectives on Psychological Science, 14*(1), 65–69. https://doi.org/10.1177/1745691618817756

Wicki, M., Mallett, K. A., Jordan, M. D., Reavy, R., Turrisi, R., Archimi, A., & Kuntsche, E. (2018). Adolescents who experienced negative alcohol-related consequences are willing to experience these consequences again in the future. *Experimental and Clinical Psychopharmacology, 26*(2), 132–137. https://doi.org/10.1037/pha0000184

Windle, M., & Zucker, R. A. (2010). Reducing underage and young adult drinking: How to address critical drinking problems during this developmental period. *Alcohol Research & Health, 33*(1/2), 29–44.

Winward, J. L., Hanson, K. L., Tapert, S. F., & Brown, S. A. (2014). Heavy alcohol use, marijuana use, and concomitant use by adolescents are associated with unique and shared cognitive decrements. *Journal of the International Neuropsychological Society, 20*(8), 784–795. https://doi.org/10.1017/S1355617714000666

Woolard, J., & Scott, E. (2009). The legal regulation of adolescence. In R. Lerner & L. Steinberg (Eds.), *Handbook of adolescent psychology* (3rd ed., pp. 345–371). New York, NY: John Wiley & Sons.

Xu, J., Kochanek, K. D., Murphy, S. L., & Arias, E. (2014). Mortality in the United States, 2012. *NCHS Data Brief, (168)*, 1–8. Retrieved from http://europepmc.org/abstract/med/25296181

Zajac, K., Randall, J., & Swenson, C. C. (2015, July 1). Multisystemic therapy for externalizing youth. *Child and Adolescent Psychiatric Clinics of North America, 24*, 601–616. https://doi.org/10.1016/j.chc.2015.02.007

AUTHOR INDEX

Baker, E. R., 116
Baker, F. C., 36
Bakermans-Kranenburg, M. J., 115
Bakhtiari, F., 207
Ball, C., 150
Ballard, P. J., 157, 158, 159
Ballesteros, M. F., 49
Baltes, P. B., 10
Bámaca, M. Y., 100
Bámaca-Colbert, M. Y., 102
Bandettini, P. A., 21
Bandura, A., 14, 15, 154
Banfield, E. C., 43
Banister, E., 198
Bank, H., 188
Bankole, A., 139
Banks, D. E., 102
Banse, R., 108, 117
Bányai, F., 235
Barbaranelli, C., 154
Barber, B. K., 36, 207
Barber, B. L., 36, 207
Barbosa-Leiker, C., 217
Barckley, M., 88
Bargh, J. A., 13
Baril, M. E., 167
Barlow, D. H., 254
Barnes- Najor, J., 102
Barnett, A. P., 133
Barnett, N. P., 169
Barnett, S. M., 77
Barone, C. J., 178
Barone, L., 178
Bar-Or, O., 109
Barrense-Dias, Y., 237
Barrios, L. C., 122
Barroso, J., 127, 135
Barroso, J. V., 138
Barrouillet, P., 71, 72
Barry, C. M., 154, 155, 156
Barry, C. T., 92, 151
Bartel, K. A., 36
Bartlett, J. D., 140
Basile, K. C., 141
Basinger, K. S., 150
Basow, S., 114
Bass, R. W., 21
Basten, U., 75
Bates, J. E., 169, 172, 174, 190, 212
Battistella, G., 63
Batto, L. L., 183
Baudat, S., 93, 186
Baudry, C., 140
Bauermeister, J. A., 133
Bauman, C. W., 147
Bauman, S., 253
Baumeister, R. F., 92
Baumert, J., 86
Baumgartner, E., 97
Bauminger, N., 186
Baumrind, D., 172, 173
Bauserman, R., 25
Bava, S., 65
Bavelier, D., 228
Baxter, K., 4
Beal, C. R., 115
Beal, S. J., 153
Beardslee, W. R., 51
Bearman, P. S., 206
Beatty, W. W., 112
Beaulieu, C., 59

Beaver, K., 231
Becerra-Culqui, T. A., 121
Becht, A. I., 95, 96
Beck, C. J. A., 175
Becker, B. J., 176
Beckert, T. E., 147
Beekman, A. J., 121
Beesdo, K., 250
Begley, N. L., 118
Begun, A. L., 151
Behera, D., 36
Behera, M. R., 36
Behrmann, M., 212
Belcher, B. R., 109
Bell, M. A., 74
Bellair, P. E., 128
Belon, K., 37
Belser, A. B., 122
Belsky, J., 171
Beltran, O., 122
Beltz, A., 113
Beltz, A. M., 32, 113
Belzer, M., 122
Bem, S. L., 110
Bender, K., 178
Bender, P. K., 21
Bendezú, J. J., 169, 175, 258
Benner, A. D., 184, 205, 206, 207, 208, 209
Bennet, A., 119
Benoit, A., 38, 39
Benowitz-Fredericks, C. A., 47, 235
Benson, M. A., 260
Benson, P. L., 154, 158
Bentley, K. H., 254
Berchtold, A., 237
Berenbaum, S. A., 32, 109, 110, 113, 177
Bergamini, E., 229
Berge, J. M., 44
Berger, C., 189
Berger, M. B., 120
Berk, M. S., 251
Berkel, T. D. M., 249
Berkman, N. D., 47, 48, 49
Berkowitz, M. W., 151
Berninger, V. W., 214
Bersamin, M., 138
Berzonsky, M. D., 95
Best, D. L., 108
Best, P., 234
Béteille, T., 209
Bethencourt, J. M., 111
Bexkens, A., 211
Beyers, W., 93, 171, 186
Beyth-Marom, R., 65
Bian, L., 117
Bianchi, J., 262
Bickel, W. K., 156
Biehl, M., 39
Biehl, M. C., 38
Bierman, K. L., 189, 190
Bigler, M., 86
Bigler, R. S., 120
Bigman, Y., 156
Billings, A., 135
Binder, A. R., 237
Bines, D., 101
Bing, N. M., 176
Birkeland, M. S., 92
Birkett, M., 121, 122, 132, 133
Birkett, M. A., 58
Birkinshaw, S., 155

Birney, D. P., 16, 68
Biro, F., 38
Biro, F. M., 35, 39
Bischoff- Grethe, A., 48
Bjärehed, J., 254
Bjorklund, D. F., 74
Björkqvist, K., 48
Blacher, J., 211
Black, B. M., 150
Black, M. C., 141, 177
Black, M. M., 140
Black, W. W., 177
Blader, P., 60
Blakely, D. P., 228
Blakemore, J. E. O., 109, 113, 116, 117
Blakemore, S.-J., 33, 59, 60, 64, 79, 87, 88, 193, 248
Blankson, A. N., 41
Blanton, H., 136
Bleakley, A., 232
Blehar, M. C., 170
Bleich, S. N., 47
Bleidorn, W., 86, 89, 91
Bleiweiss, K., 141
Blos, P., 171
Blössner, M., 45
Blozis, S., 102
Blumberg, H., 184
Blumenthal, H., 39
Blumler, J. G., 228
Bo, A., 233
Bockting, W. O., 120
Bode, L., 20
Bogers, S., 115
Bogin, B., 32
Bokhorst, C. L., 92
Bokor, B. R., 34
Bong, M., 203
Bonifacio, J. H., 122
Bonner, S. B., 33, 131
Boom, J. J., 149
Boonk, L., 209
Boot, W. R., 228
Booth, C., 210
Booth, M. Z., 205
Booth-LaForce, C., 135, 186, 190
Borch, C., 184
Bordia, P., 220
Bordia, S., 220
Borduin, C. M., 259
Borek, N., 233
Borghi, E., 45
Borghuis, J., 88
Borich, G. D., 209
Bornstein, M. H., 109, 166, 172, 173, 174
Borrero, S., 135
Borzekowski, D. L. G., 47, 235
Bos, H. M. W., 111, 133, 177
Bosch, A. M., 36
Bosma, H. A., 95
Bosse, J. D., 131
Bost, J., 135
Bouchard, C., 109
Boulware, S. D., 122
Bounoua, N., 168
Bourgeron, T., 212
Boutakidis, I. P., 100
Bowen, R., 79
Bowers, A. J., 218
Bowers, J., 158
Bowker, A., 183, 184, 186

D'Amico, E. J., 283
Damon, W., 150, 157
Daniels, L. M., 202
D'Antoine, H., 260
Dapretto, M., 87
Darchia, N., 37
Das, J. K., 41
Dasgupta, N., 109
Daspe, M., 192
Davenport, Z., 220
Davidson, A. J., 187
Davidson, R. D., 175
Davidson, R. J., 228
Davies, F., 202
Davies, I. G., 44
Davies, P., 175
Davila, J., 38, 39
Davis, A., 213
Davis, B., 133
Davis, J. P., 189
Davis, J. S., 43
Davis, K. S., 131
Davis, L., 216
Davis, N. C., 166
Davis-Kean, P. E., 140
Davison, C., 52
Dawson, T. L., 149
Day, F. R., 41
Day, H. J., 184
Day, J. K., 133
Day, R. D., 155, 167
De Pedro, K. T., 121
Deardorff, J., 35, 37, 41, 42, 121
Dearth-Wesley, T., 37
Deary, I. J., 75, 76, 88
Deater-Deckard, K., 156, 174
Deaux, K., 108
DeBacker, T. K., 204
DeBaryshe, B. D., 259
de Bruijn, A., 232–233
DeCamp, W., 231
Decker, M. J., 137
De Genna, N., 139, 140
Degol, J. L., 167
de Graaf, H., 128, 134, 236
DeHaan, L. G., 156
de Kieviet, J. F., 74
Deković, M., 88, 134, 136, 190, 192, 196
De La Rue, L., 198
DeLay, D., 118, 197
Delemarre-van de Waal, H. A., 122
Delgado, M. Y., 203
Del Giudice, M., 33
Delisi, M., 257
Delk, J., 233
DeLongis, A., 177
Del Rey, R., 236
Delsing, M. J. M. H., 188
Del Toro, J., 99, 101
DeLuca, S., 221
Demanet, J., 208
DeMayo, M. M., 212
DeMeules, M., 122
Demissie, Z., 43, 138
Denford, S., 143
Denissen, J. J. A., 88
Dent, C. W., 233
Denton, M. L., 154
Deoni, S., 59
Deoni, S. C. L., 59
de Onis, M., 45

Department of Health and Human Services, 50, 250
Dermitzaki, E., 43
DeRose, L. M., 33
Desai, S., 139
Descartes, L., 115
Desilver, D., 216
Desjardins, C. D., 262
Devenish, B., 210
Devine, A., 214
de Vries, A. L. C., 118
de Vries, D. A., 236
de Vries, N. K., 188
de Vries, S. L. A., 170
de Waal, F. B. M., 112
de Water, E., 184
de Weerth, C., 20
de Wied, M., 97
de Wit, J. B. F., 44
Dexter, A. L., 16
DeYoung, C. G., 88
d'Haenens, L., 238
Diamond, G. M., 132
Diamond, J., 47
Diamond, L. M., 131
Diaz, R., 122
Dick, F., 64
Dickenson, J., 33, 131
Dickey, C. R., 191
Dickey, L. M., 120
Diedrichs, P. C., 209
Diekman, A. B., 110
DiGiovanni, C. D., 133
Dijkstra, J. K., 189, 192, 203
Dimler, L. M., 172
Dinella, L., 115
Dinh, K. T., 100
Dion, J., 327
Dishion, T. J., 169, 197, 209, 258
Dittus, P. J., 130, 135, 169, 197
Divney, A., 140
Dmitrieva, J., 197
Docherty, S. L., 138
Dockray, S., 41
Dodd, D. R., 49
Dodge, K. A., 169, 172, 174, 190, 212
Dodge, T., 136
Döhla, D., 214
Dolan, P., 152
Dollahite, D. C., 155
Dolle, A. L., 230
Domenech-Rodriguez, M., 116
Domhardt, M., 261, 262
Domina, T., 216, 217
Domingues, M. R., 44
Domitrovich, C. E., 263
Dong, W., 203
Donnellan, M. B., 10, 89, 250
Donnelly, T. M., 157
D'Onofrio, B., 76
Donovan, J., 208
Donovan, R. A., 119
Doodson, L., 176
Dooley, J. J., 236
Dopp, A. R., 259
Dorn, L. D., 38, 39, 41
Dornan, J. C., 253
Dornbusch, S. M., 208, 217
Dosenbach, N. U. F., 61, 62
Dotterer, A. M., 208
Doucette, H., 92

Doughty, S. E., 168
Douglass, S., 100, 102, 207
Doumen, S., 92
Dovidio, J. F., 158
Downs, A. C., 36
Doyle, A. B., 184
Doyle-Thomas, K. A. R., 212
Drasin, H., 132
Dreher, E., 10
Duan, L., 193
Dubas, J. S., 40, 173
Dube, E. M., 132
Dubé, E. M., 132
Dube, S. R., 249
Duboc, V., 60
du Bois-Reymond, M., 9, 10
Duchesne, S., 202, 206
Dudley, D., 52
Dudovitz, R. N., 86
Duell, N., 65
Dufourcq, P., 60
Dumaret, A. C., 76
Dumas, T. M., 189, 193
Dumith, S. C., 44
Dumitrache, A., 175
Dumontheil, I., 64, 65, 79
Dunbar, N. D., 178
Duncan, G. J., 76
Duncan, S. C., 249
Duncan, T. E., 249
Dunne, P. E., 48
Dunsmore, S. C., 130
Dunville, R. L., 138
Dupere, V., 218
Dupéré, V., 137, 218
Dupuis, S., 176
Durbin, C. E., 88
Duriez, B., 155
Durkee, M. I., 102
Durlak, J. A., 251, 262
Durney, S. E., 141
Durtschi, J. A., 167
Durwood, L., 122
Du Toit, C., 176
Duyme, M., 76
Dweck, C. S., 191, 202
Dyer, W. J., 151
Dymnicki, A. B., 251
Dyson, R. B., 37

Earls, F., 42
East, P. L., 140, 167
Easterbrooks, M. A., 140
Easton, J. A., 141
Eaton, D. K., 43
Eaton, N. R., 120
Ebata, A., 206
Ebbeling, C. B., 43
Eberly-Lewis, M. B., 152
Eccles, J. S., 171, 202, 206, 208
Eckenrode, J., 198
Edmonds, G. W., 88
Edwards, L. M., 99
Egan, S. K., 117
Ehrensaft, D., 121
Eichas, K., 263
Eichelsheim, V. I., 167
Eilers, M. A., 139
Eisenberg, M. E., 46, 123, 136
Eisenberg, N., 9, 151, 152, 153, 262
Eisner, M. P., 229

Ekele, B., 41
Ekwaru, J. P., 35
Elder, J. P., 138
Elkind, D., 79
Elliott, L., 249
Elliott, M. N., 232
Ellis, B. J., 33, 37, 262
Ellis, W., 98, 198
Ellis, W. E., 187, 189, 193
Ellison, N. B., 234
Elmore, K. C., 233
Else-Quest, N. M., 100, 110
Emery, C. R., 140
Emler, N., 151
Emmanuel, M., 34
Endendijk, J. J., 115
Enders, C., 115
Eng, A. L., 134
Engelhardt, C. R., 231
Engels, R. C. M. E., 92, 115, 188, 194, 197, 231,
     249, 254
England, D. E., 115
Engle, R. W., 74
Englund, M. M., 247
Enns, J. T., 16
Enright, E. A., 121
Enright, R. D., 5
Enzlin, P., 131
Epstein, M., 130
Erdley, C. A., 184, 186, 192, 208
Erentaitė, R., 97
Erickson, K., 157
Eriksen, A., 262
Erikson, E., 13
Erikson, E. H., 13, 94, 155, 185, 235
Ernst, M., 134
Erol, R. Y., 91
Eron, L. D., 230
Eryigit, S., 102
Eshraghi, A. A., 212
Eshraghi, R. S., 212
Eskenazi, B., 140
Espelage, D. L., 121, 133, 191, 198
Espinosa, M. P., 152
Espinoza, G., 189, 207
Esposito, E. C., 253
Essex, M. J., 37
Esteban-Cornejo, I., 44
Estell, D. B., 158
Ethier, K. A., 128, 129, 169, 197
Ettekal, I., 189, 190
Eubig, P. A., 213
Evans, A., 59
Evans, S., 190
Evans, S. W., 213
Evans, S. Z., 258, 259
Exner-Cortens, D., 198
Eyre, O., 213

Fabes, R., 115
Fabes, R. A., 118
Fadjukoff, P., 96
Faggiano, F., 233
Fagley, N. S., 150
Fahy, A. E., 236
Fairchild, G., 256
Faja, S., 72
Farah, M. J., 72
Fardouly, J., 235
Farhat, T., 47, 249
Farley, F., 65

Farley, J. P., 156
Farooq, M. A., 44
Farr, R. H., 177
Farrell, A. D., 153, 193, 258
Farrell, L. J., 39
Farruggia, S. P., 178
Fast, A. A., 120, 121
Fay-Stammbach, T., 173
Fazio, K. S., 178
Federal Bureau of Investigation, 141, 256
Fedesco, H. N., 51
Fedewa, A. L., 177
Fedina, L., 141
Fegert, J. M., 261
Fegley, S., 118, 217
Feinberg, M. E., 168, 169, 195
Feinstein, B. A., 138
Feldman, J. F., 74–75
Feldman, R. S., 220
Feldstein Ewing, S. W., 248
Felix, E. D., 27
Fellmeth, G. L., 198
Felmlee, D., 205
Fend, H. A., 91, 92
Feng, B., 202
Feng, J., 212
Ferguson, C., 231
Ferguson, C. J., 231, 232
Ferguson, G. M., 87
Ferguson, K., 178, 231
Ferguson, L., 68
Ferguson, R. F., 221
Ferguson, S., 101, 231
Ferguson, S. M., 189
Fergusson, D. M., 253, 256
Ferreira, P. D., 158
Ferrero, J., 38, 39
Ferrer-Wreder, L., 263
Ferri, M., 233
Festl, R., 230
Feurer, C., 20
Fiebach, C. J., 75
Field, R. D., 115
Figner, B., 65
Finer, L. B., 130, 139
Finkenauer, C., 86, 175
Finlay, A. K., 158
Finn, A. S., 72
Finney, E. J., 230
Finzi-Dottan, R., 186
Fiorenzo, L., 178
Fischer, M. J., 220
Fish, J. N., 121, 253
Fisher, B. S., 141
Fisher, C. B., 26, 27, 102, 128
Fisher, H. L., 254
Fisher, S., 102
Fisher, S. E., 214
Fite, P. J., 190
Fitzharris, J. L., 135
Fitzpatrick, M., 115
Flamm, E. S., 203
Flanagan, C., 158
Flanagan, C. A., 158, 159
Flannery, D. J., 256, 259
Flannery, K. M., 79
Fletcher, K. L., 187, 188
Flieller, A., 67
Flodmark, C.-E., 47
Flook, L., 169
Flor, D. L., 174

Flores, D., 127, 135, 138
Flores, G., 190
Floyd, F. J., 132
Flynn, J. R., 75, 76
Foehr, U. G., 232
Foltz, J. L., 43
Fonagy, P., 256
Fong, C. J., 191
Forbes, E. E., 65, 134
Ford, D. Y., 76
Forge, N., 122
Forman, J., 253
Forrest, L. N., 49
Fortenberry, J. D., 34, 51, 52, 127, 139
Foshee, V. A., 198
Foust, M. D., 100
Fox, A. M., 143
Fradkin, C., 45, 46
Franke, B., 214
Frankel, L. L., 36
Frankenhuis, W. E., 41, 262
Fraser, A. M., 151
Frazier-Wood, A. C., 43
Frederick, C. B., 44, 45
Fredricks, J. A., 218
Fredstrom, B., 184
Freedman-Doan, P., 89, 216, 250
Freeman, J., 218
Freeman, R., 47
French, D. C., 155, 183, 186
French, S. E., 206
Freud, A., 171
Freud, S., 13
Friedman, K., 232
Friedman, N. P., 258
Friedrich, D., 166
Frijns, T., 86
Frisén, A., 88, 96, 97
Frost, A., 251
Frostad, P., 218
Fryar, C. D., 43
Fryberg, S. A., 99, 220
Frye, S. S., 214
Fuchs, L. S., 214
Fuglset, T. S., 48
Fuhrmann, D., 59
Fujimoto, K., 189, 193
Fukuda, K., 71
Fuligni, A., 208, 209
Fuligni, A. J., 36, 37, 99, 100, 102, 154, 155,
     169
Fulkerson, J. A., 48
Fuller, M. J., 36
Furby, L., 65
Furman, W., 194, 195, 196, 197, 198
Future of Sex Education Initiative (2012),
     143, 144
Fuzzell, L., 51, 52

Gable, R. A., 214
Gablonski, T. C., 256
Gabrielli, J., 190, 229, 232
Gaddis, A., 35
Gaillard, V., 71, 72, 73
Galambos, N. L., 110, 115, 117, 118
Gallagher, A. M., 168
Gallay, L. S., 158
Galligan, K., 118
Galliher, R. V., 95, 101
Galupo, M. P., 131
Galván, A., 37, 61, 65, 134

Haines, E. L., 108
Haines, J., 48
Halawah, A., 38
Hale, W. W., 86, 97
Haley, A., 76
Halford, G. S., 16, 69–70
Halim, M. L., 113, 119
Halim, M. L. D., 113
Hall, B., 254
Hall, G. S., 5, 7, 27, 167, 245
Hall, L. J., 212
Hall, S. D., 249
Hall, S. P., 97
Hallal, P. C., 44
Hallam, L., 238
Halliwell, E., 209
Hallman, S. K., 216, 217
Hallquist, M. N., 65
Halpern, C. T., 111, 128, 134
Halpern, D. F., 109
Halpern, H. P., 121
Halpern-Felsher, B. L., 65, 140
Hamamura, T., 92
Hamer, R., 68, 69
Hamilton, B., 139
Hamilton, B. E., 166
Hamilton, E., 100
Hamilton-Giachritsis, C., 230, 261
Hamm, M. P., 236
Hampson, S. E., 88
Hamza, C. A., 169
Han, H., 158
Hanania, R., 71
Hancox, R. J., 229
Handschuh, C., 237
Hanish, L., 115
Hanish, L. D., 114, 189
Hankin, B. L., 252
Hanley, J., 249
Hannema, S. E., 122
Hansen, L., 52
Hansen, N., 52
Hanson, K. L., 248
Harbaugh, A. G., 236
Harden, K. P., 39, 128, 134, 197
Hardie, J. H., 154
Harding, J. F., 100, 101
Hardy, L. L., 45
Hardy, S. A., 152, 155, 156, 219
Har-Even, D., 186
Harmon, M., 256
Harold, G. T., 174
Harpalani, V., 97, 118
Harper, C. R., 169, 197
Harper, G. W., 133
Harrell, M. B., 233
Harries, M. D., 130
Harrington, H., 288
Harris, G., 48
Harris, M. A., 92
Harris-McKoy, D., 258
Harrist, A. W., 46
Harrop, C., 261
Hart, A. B., 249
Hart, D., 157
Hart, J. R., 173
Harter, S., 85, 86, 87, 90, 110
Hartl, A. C., 185
Harwood, S., 102
Hashi, E. C., 151
Hassan, K. EL, 219

Hassan, M., 41
Hastings, G., 233
Hastings, P. D., 172
Hatchel, T., 121, 122
Haugen, T., 34
Haun, D., 25
Havertape, L., 254
Havighurst, R. J., 10
Havlicek, J. R., 178
Haw, C., 253, 254
Hawes, D. J., 173
Hawk, L. W., 213
Hawk, S. T., 249
Hawton, K., 253
Hay, P. J., 48
Haydon, A. A., 128
Hayes, D. J., 87
Hayes, D. M., 18
Haynes, T. L., 202
Haynie, D., 249
Haynie, D. L., 51
Hays, D. G., 166
Hazel, C. E., 122
He, J.-P., 37
Heath, N. L., 254
Heaven, P. C. L., 92, 202, 208
Heffer, T., 235
Heffernan, C., 198
Hegewald, K., 209
Heikura, U., 212
Heim, S., 214
Heimer, K., 143
Heine, S. J., 10, 92
Heinrichs, B. S., 190
Heintzelman, S. J., 166
Heirman, W., 237, 238
Heller, J. R., 135
Hellwege, M. A., 220
Helmerhorst, K. O. W., 170
Helms, S. W., 135, 136, 156, 188
Helsen, M., 155
Helwig, C. C., 150
Hemphill, S. A., 249
Hendricks, M. L., 120
Hendrickson, M., 190
Hendrix, C. L., 140
Hendry, L. B., 9
Henggeler, S. W., 260
Henley, W. E., 44
Hennessy, M., 232
Hennon, C. B., 176
Hennon, E. A., 207
Henrich, J., 10
Henriksen, L., 232
Henry, D., 253
Henry, K. L., 218, 230
Hensel, D. J., 102
Henson, R. A., 169
Hepper, P. G., 253
Herman, A. N., 37
Herman, K. M., 46
Herman-Giddens, M. E., 36, 43
Hernández, M. M., 100
Heron, M., 49, 252, 253
Herpertz-Dahlmann, B., 48
Herring, A. H., 128
Herman, J. W., 197, 198
Herting, M. M., 113
Heward, W. L., 215
Hewer, A., 149
Heyvaert, M., 190

Hiatt, C., 169, 184, 193
Hiatt, R., 42
Hicks, B. M., 88
Hicks, L., 206
Hicks, T., 258
Higgins, A., 110, 149
Higgins, E. T., 118
Higgins-D'Alessandro, A., 151
Hildenbrand, B., 176
Hilgard, J., 231
Hilger, K., 75
Hill, F., 214
Hill, J. P., 167
Hill, N. E., 210
Himmelstein, G., 143
Hines, A. R., 6
Hines, M., 109, 111, 112, 113, 114, 116
Hinshaw, S. P., 213
Hipkins, R., 52
Hiriscau, I. E., 27
Hirsh-Pasek, K., 24
Ho, R. C. M., 46
Hock, R., 141
Hodges-Simeon, C. R., 34
Hoeben, E. M., 258
Hoek, H. W., 47, 48
Hoeve, M., 170, 173
Hofer, C., 169
Hoffman, M. L., 157
Hofkens, T., 210
Hofkens, T. L., 210
Hofmann, V., 193
Hofstede, G. H., 99
Holas, I., 208
Holder, D. W., 156
Holland, C. L., 135
Hollenstein, T., 6
Holliday, E., 193
Holman, D. M., 138
Holmbeck, G. N., 37, 167
Holmes, C., 156
Holmes, C. J., 156
Holmes, J. L., 141
Holmstrom, A., 43
Holtrop, K., 203
Holub, S. C., 116–117
Homma, Y., 48
Hong, J. S., 50, 210
Hoo, E., 169, 197
Hood, W., 101
Hook, C. J., 72
Hooker, K., 166
Hooley, M., 210
Hooper, S., 207
Hope, M. O., 39
Hopkins, K. D., 260
Hopman, W. M., 46
Hopmeyer, A., 188
Hopson, L. M., 210
Horner, R. H., 191
Horowitz, S. H., 213, 214
Horwood, L. J., 253, 256
Hosking, J., 44
Hou, F., 176
Houck, C. D., 237
Houghton, S., 235
Houltberg, B. J., 65
Houshyar, S., 101
Houston, S. M., 62
Howard, K. I., 6
Howard, M. O., 177

Manktelow, R., 234
Mann, F. D., 258
Manning, W. D., 130, 134, 197
Mantey, D. S., 233
Manuck, S. B., 258
Manuel, M. L., 171
Marceau, K., 37, 39, 41, 166
Marchante, M., 206
Marcia, J. E., 95, 96
Marek, S., 16, 59
Margolin, G., 141, 192
Margolis, A., 75
Markant, J. C., 58, 59
Markey, P. M., 232
Markiewicz, D., 184
Markovic, A., 190
Markowitz, L. E., 138
Markstrom-Adams, C., 98, 111, 119
Markus, H. R., 7, 15, 92, 204, 220
Marques, L., 21
Marques, P., 48
Marr, E., 177
Marra, R., 69
Marriott, C., 261
Marsh, H. W., 86
Marsh, P., 189
Marshall, E. J., 247
Marshall, K. C., 208
Marshall, S. K., 254
Marshall, S. L., 92
Marti, E., 68
Martin, C., 115
Martin, C. L., 108, 114, 115, 116
Martin, J., 139
Martin, J. A., 173
Martin, M., 175
Martin, S. L., 141
Martinez, G., 128
Martinez, L., 43
Martino, S. C., 232
Martin-Storey, A., 111
Martinussen, M., 96, 97
Marttunen, M., 48
Marx, R. A., 122
Marzilli, E., 48
Masche, J. G., 169
Maser, C., 122
Masi, A., 212
Mason, J. O., 59
Mason, S. M., 44
Mason, W. A., 247
Massey, M., 47, 235
Masten, A. S., 230, 260, 261, 262
Mastropieri, M. A., 215
Masyn, K. E., 131
Matson, M., 138
Matthews, T. J., 166
Mattson, G., 142
Matusiewicz, A. K., 169
Matute, E., 109
Maughan, B., 251
Maxwell, L., 141
May, S., 203
Mayes, S. D., 214
Mayhew, M. J., 219, 220
Maynard, A. M., 79
Mayr, E., 10
Mays, V. M., 132
Mayseless, O., 171, 186
Mazerolle, P., 259
Maziarz, L., 237

Maziarz, L. N., 138
McAdams, D. P., 88, 96, 97, 166
McAnally, H. M., 229
McBride, R. G., 166
McCaffery, J. M., 258
McCain, M. R. C., 220
McClelland, S. I., 127, 130
McClowry, S. G., 174
McClure, J., 204
McConnell, E. A., 133
McCormick, C. M., 262
McCormick, E., 7
McCormick, S. H., 37
McCrae, N., 235
McCrae, R. R., 88, 235
McCullough, M. E., 156
McDermott, J. M., 177
McElderry, D., 36
McElhaney, K. B., 189
McElwain, A. D., 135
McElwain, N. L., 135
McFarland, D. A., 157
McFarland, F. C., 189
McGinley, M., 153
McGue, M., 88, 167, 258
McGuire, J. K., 121, 122
McHale, J. P., 100
McHale, S. M., 110, 114, 118, 167, 168, 169,
    187, 208
McIntosh, H., 158
McIsaac, C., 195, 196
McKenzie, K., 211
McKinney, C., 155, 173
McKinney, J. R., 127
McKinney, R. E., 138
McLaughlin, K. A., 122
McLean, K. C., 96, 101
McLean, S. A., 101, 236, 239
McLellan, J., 158
McLellan, J. A., 157
McLeod, J. D., 130
McLoyd, V. C., 174, 216, 217
McMahon, E. M., 44
McMahon, R. J., 169, 258
McMahon, T. J., 111
McMakin, D. L., 252
McManus, T., 128
McMillan, C., 205
McMillen, J. C., 178
McMorris, B. J., 123
McNamara, P., 253
McNulty, T. L., 128
McPheeters, M. L., 213
McPherson, B., 115
McQuillan, G., 138
McRee, A.-L., 138
McWhirter, E. H., 101
Meca, A., 9, 97
Medina, M., 101
Medovoy, T., 188
Meece, J. L., 203
Meeus, W., 128
Meeus, W. H. J., 86, 94, 95, 96, 97, 98, 128,
    155, 167, 168, 188, 196, 249
Mehari, K. R., 153, 193, 258
Mehl, M. R., 19
Meier, E. P., 236
Meier, M. H., 63
Meijer, S., 128
Meisel, S. N., 193
Meldrum, R. C., 258

Mellins, C. A., 141
Mello, Z. R., 50
Mellor, D., 210
Meltzoff, A. N., 117
Memmert, D., 71
Memmott-Elison, M. K., 152
Mendenhall, R., 102
Mendle, J., 32, 38, 39, 41, 42, 197
Menezes, I., 158
Meng, J., 43
Menon, M., 111, 117
Menon, V., 216
Mensah, F. K., 41
Menting, B., 190
Mercer, C. H., 128
Mercer, N., 97–98
Meredith, P., 173
Merikangas, K. R., 37
Merrick, M. T., 303
Meruelo, A. D., 248
Merz, E. C., 72
Mesman, J., 115
Mestre, M. V., 149
Metcalf, B. S., 44
Metz, E., 158
Metzger, A., 157
Metzger, I. W., 209
Meuwese, R., 153, 193
Micali, N., 49
Michaelson, V., 52
Michikyan, M., 235
Miconi, D., 92
Midgley, C., 206
Midle, J. B., 253
Miech, R. A., 20, 247
Mielke, G. I., 44
Miga, E. M., 171
Milevsky, A., 92, 172
Militello, L. K., 191
Miller, B. G., 177
Miller, C. F., 116–117
Miller, D. I., 109
Miller, G. F., 88
Miller, J. G., 150
Miller, J. W., 114
Miller, K. E., 13, 16, 141
Miller, M. B., 37
Miller, M. E., 217
Miller, M. I., 59
Miller, P. H., 13, 16
Miller, P. M., 150
Miller-Cotto, D., 102
Mills, K., 61
Mills, K. L., 60, 64, 65, 79, 87
Milton, M., 211
Minchin, J., 236
Minges, K. E., 37
Miniño, A. M., 49
Miranda-Mendizbbal, A., 253
Misca, G., 178
Misch, D., 253
Mistry, J., 18
Mistry, R., 18
Mistry, R. S., 158
Mitchell, J. A., 37, 46
Mitchell, K. J., 122, 196, 238
Mitchell, L. L., 9, 10
Mitchell, P., 79
Mitchell, R. C., 131
Miu, A., 232
Miyake, A., 258

Mjaavatn, P. E., 218
Modecki, K. L., 36, 236
Moen, P., 166
Moffitt, T. E., 256, 257, 258, 259
Mohanty, J., 178
Moilanen, K. L., 171, 173, 208
Moise-Titus, J., 230
Molenda-Figueira, H. A., 32
Molinari, L., 33
Möller, M., 36
Molloy, L. E., 195
Molock, S. D., 133
Monaghan, D. B., 219
Monahan, K. C., 192, 197, 216, 217, 232, 256, 258
Monn, A. R., 261, 262
Montague, P. R., 87
Monteleone, A. M., 48
Monteleone, P., 48
Montgomery, J. E., 178
Mont-Reynaud, R., 208
Moody, J., 187, 195
Mooney, K. S., 184
Moore, J. K., 122
Moore, L. C., 16
Moore, P. J., 202
Moore, S. E., 190
Moore, S. R., 197
Morales, A., 204
Moreau, C., 36
Moreno, C., 178
Moreno, O., 169
Morgan, D., 220
Morgan-Lopez, A., 100
Morgenstern, M., 233
Mori, C., 237
Mori, S., 59
Morizot, J., 218
Morley, D., 176
Morris, A. S., 60, 65
Morris, D. S., 210
Morris, P. A., 17
Morse, E., 100
Mortimer, J. T., 217
Morton, J. B., 108
Morton, L. C., 110
Moscardino, U., 92
Moshman, D., 68
Moss, P., 37
Motta-Mena, N. V., 64
Moum, T., 176
Mrick, S. E., 101, 102
Mroczek, D., 88
Mrtorell, G. A., 101, 102
Mrug, S., 38, 184, 210
Muehlenkamp, J. J., 254
Mueller, C. E., 206
Mueller, S. C., 72
Muenks, K., 202, 203
Mullen, E., 147
Muller, C., 207
Müller, C. M., 150, 193
Müller, R., 59
Müller, U., 16, 72
Müller-Oehring, E. M., 248
Mulvey, E. P., 256
Munholland, K., 170
Munniksma, A., 184
Münzer, A., 261
Murphy, B. C., 151
Murphy, D. A., 130, 135

Murphy, S. L., 49
Murphy, T., 153
Murray, C. J. L., 45
Murry, V. M., 174, 176
Murty, V. P., 71, 73
Mustafaa, F. N., 40
Mustanski, B., 26, 121, 123, 128, 132, 133, 138, 253
Mustelin, L., 48
Myers, A., 74

Nagin, D. S., 258
Nagle, R. J., 185
Nair, R. L., 252
Namkung, J., 214
Nanayakkara, S., 253
Narayan, A. J., 262
Narendorf, S. C., 212
Nassar, A., 140
Nation, M., 158
National Assessment of Educational Progress, 109
National Association for Media Literacy Education, 239
National Center for Education Statistics, 5, 108, 218, 219, 220–221
National Coalition for Women and Girls in Education, 108
National Institute of Mental Health, 250
National Institute on Drug Abuse, 249
National Middle School Association, 205
Natsuaki, M., 38, 39, 172, 251
Navarre, J. R., 213
Navarro, R. L., 204
Neal, D. J., 248
Neal, J. W., 189
Neale, M. C., 249
Neberich, W., 41
Neblett, E. W., 156
Neel, C. G. O., 208, 209
Negriff, S., 39, 41, 130
Neiderhiser, J. M., 251
Neimeyer, G. J., 86
Neisser, U., 75
Nelemans, S., 89
Nelson, C. A., 61
Nelson, K. M., 128
Nelson, L. J., 100, 101, 102, 154, 176
Nelson, R. M., 204
Nelson, W. M., 10
Nese, R. N. T., 191
Nesi, J., 135, 194, 235, 236
Netter, S., 92
Nettle, D., 41
Neumark-Sztainer, D., 44, 46, 48, 49
Neville, H. J., 71
Newcomb, M. E., 121, 123, 132, 138
Newport, D. J., 140
Ng, F. F.-Y., 204
Ngo, V., 252
Nguyen, D. J., 252
Nguyen, H. N. T., 195
Nguyen, T.-V., 113
Nguyen-Louie, T. T., 37
Nichols, T. R., 37
Nickel, N. C., 139
Nickerson, A. B., 185
Niedzwiedz, C., 253
Nielsen, G. A., 188
Nielsen, M., 25
Nielsen, R. K. L., 232

Nielson, M. G., 151, 153
Niepel, C., 86
Nieves-Lugo, K., 133
Nihiser, A. J., 43
Nikken, P., 236
Nikolas, M. A., 38, 39
Nilsen, E. S., 78, 79
Niolon, P. H., 198
Nisbett, R. E., 67, 75, 76
Noar, S. M., 135
Noble, K. G., 62, 63, 72
Nóbrega, C., 46
Nocita, G., 19
Nock, M. K., 254
Noel, J., 233
Nogueira Avelar e Silva, R., 130
Nolan, Y. M., 59
Noll, J. G., 41
Nordin, S. M., 48
Norenzayan, A., 10
Norris, A. L., 141
Northoff, G., 87
Nowicka, P., 47
Nunes, B. P., 44
Nurse, J., 198
Nussbaumer, D., 74

Oakes, J. M., 37
Obeidallah, D., 42
Oberlander, S. E., 140
Oberle, E., 262
O'Brien, L., 193
O'Brien, M., 189
Offer, D., 6
Office for National Statistics, 253
Ogden, C. L., 43, 45, 46
Oh, J. S., 99
O'Hara, K. L., 175
O'Hara, R. E., 232
Ohlsson, C., 43
Ojeda, L., 204
Oka, E. R., 169
Okeke-Adeyanju, N., 202
Okun, M. S., 21
Oldehinkel, A. J., 47, 175, 190
Olezeski, C., 111
Olino, T. M., 65, 134
Oliva, A., 92
Olsen, I. C., 34
Olsen, J. A., 207
Olson, B. D., 88
Olson, J., 122
Olson, K. L., 109
Olson, K. R., 120, 121, 122
Olson, S. L., 251
Olsson, T. M., 263
Olweus, D., 190, 191, 236
O'Malley, P. M., 89, 216, 250
Omar, H., 36
Ong, A. D., 99, 101, 102
Onghena, P., 190
Ontai, L. L., 116
Ooi, L. L., 19
Oosterhoff, B., 157
Oosterlaan, J., 74
Orbe, M. P., 220
Orben, A., 229
Orchowski, L. M., 141
Orduña, M., 99
Orkin, M., 203
Orobio de Castro, B., 158

SUBJECT INDEX